DEVON'S HOME FRONT DIARIES 1937–1945

A British poster designed to discourage the recording of information which would be useful to the enemy, c1940-45.

To Nick,

DEVON'S
HOME FRONT DIARIES
1937–1945

Best wishes,

Todd Gray

Todd Gray

THE MINT PRESS

For Charlene Cavallaro Shields,
with gratitude for six decades of friendship

First published 2025

A publication of The Mint Press
Taddyforde House South
Taddyforde Estate
New North Road, Exeter EX4 4AT

website: www.stevensbooks.co.uk
tele: 01392 459760
email: sales@themintpress.co.uk

ISBN 978 1903 356 85 2

A CIP catalogue record for this book is available from the British Library

This publication is printed on acid-free paper

Typeset, printed and bound by Short Run Press Ltd, Exeter, EX2 7LW

Supporters

Philip J. Milton & Company Charitable Foundation
Museum of Barnstaple & North Devon Development Trust
Bideford Bridge Trust

CONTENTS

PREFACE

In 2005, like many others, I watched Victoria Wood portray Nella Last in *Housewife 49*. I wondered then how useful her diary could be in teaching and research but it was not until 31 July 2007 that I read my first Mass Observation text. Dozens of accounts later I understood how instructive they could be about Devon; a hundred other texts later made me question assumptions I had made about the wartime generation.

I have one principal purpose in writing this book: these writings help us unravel Devon's relatively recent past. They may have more of a resonance in this part of the country (where perhaps life has changed to a lesser degree than in most of Britain). But each year fewer remain of the generation that lived to VJ Day and in 2022 the nation lost its most prominent wartime connection with the passing of Elizabeth II. These writings will augment, for many of us, our own memories of that generation. They not only help explain their lives but illume the present. Unfortunately, that generation's experiences have a marked relevance for modern society as the country rearms and we once again contemplate the prospect of warfare in Western Europe.

Our Mass Observation Writers lived with the phrase *Keep Calm and Carry On* and learned how to *Grin and Bear It*. I find myself asking can their writings help us to do the same when this is needed once again?

Taddyforde, Exeter
1 September 2025

1 A Ministry of Information poster, published in 1939, utilising a phrase which had been in general use since the 1920s.

INTRODUCTION

The generation that endured the Home Front of the Second World War was tested in ways no other in Britain had been before or since. During all hours of day and night millions of lives were repeatedly interrupted by the sound of air raid sirens and they felt terror when a plane flew overhead. Most had family, friends or acquaintances who were casualties of the air attacks. Many learned to cope with the prospect of their own sudden and violent death. They lived with the blackout, adapted to short rations and many volunteered for wartime service. Otherwise quiet lives were fundamentally transformed by war. They were tested.

The extraordinary Mass Observation (MO) archive is a unique means of understanding the lives of a handful of some 800,000 men and women who lived in Devon during these years.[1] It brings out their personal feelings, perspectives and values around their own lives as well as their thoughts on the society in which they lived.

Ordinarily it would be unsafe to assume that diarists write for the benefit of others. However, in the case of MO Writers we can be sure that this intention existed from the outset. They wanted their voices to be heard and hoped their observations would prove beneficial to society. These writers were often introspective and, although prone to self-disclosure, many were careful about the anonymity of third parties; other individuals were often referred to by their initials. The diarists recorded events and reflected upon the course of their own lives. Often, they ruminated upon their place in the world as it changed around them. These writings show a need to adapt to sudden restrictions and opportunities. They also provide insights into another generation's perspectives on the wider world, when the British Empire was at its height.

To some degree the lives of the diarists recorded here are unrecognisable. One diarist lived without access to electricity, few had flown in an airplane and many were unlikely to have yet watched a television. They obtained their daily news from the wireless, newspapers or from social exchange. Most communicated with other people in person or exchanged cards and letters which were delivered twice a day. Many MO writers had one single, long career. It would be decades before this generation would become familiar with personal computers, the internet and mobile telephones. In the Devon countryside the term AI was understood as the abbreviation for Artificial Insemination.

These texts can be viewed with a sense of nostalgia, a look back upon a simpler time albeit one in which society was tested by war. However, the Writers' commentaries relate to our own lives in several notable ways. In 1937, 1938 and 1939 they wrote about anticipating war on the Continent and later, during the midst of that war, they witnessed dislocation and the movement of people at a level previously unknown in British history. Also, on the Home Front many children's lives were impacted by evacuation and they were exposed to the continual threat of aerial bombardment. Adults and children experienced what must have been extraordinary levels of anxiety and, again, this was repeatedly remarked upon by the Writers.

Mass Observation

On 30 January 1937 three English researchers began Mass Observation, a project to observe and record popular attitudes and beliefs. In effect, they aimed to understand public opinion through investigating a wide range of topics by bridging class and social barriers. It was 'an anthropology of ourselves'.

Typische Heckenlandschaft in Devon. (Bei Coryton.)

2 The German documents for Operation Sea Lion (Unternehmen Seelöwe), the planned Nazi invasion of Britain, 1940, included this image captioned 'Typical Devon landscape of sheep and hedges at Coryton'.

Tom Harrisson, an anthropologist, Humphrey Jennings, a documentary film-maker, and Charles Madge, a poet and journalist, had met through the *New Statesmen* where they published an open letter which announced their project. Hundreds of volunteers were recruited to form 'a national panel' which would comment on a series of questionnaires. Their texts generated a series of books. At its height the panel comprised nearly a thousand members.

In 1940, following the outbreak of war, MO began producing reports on morale for the Ministry of Information's Home Intelligence Unit. The late thirties and 1940s were the project's most active years. In 1949 MO became a limited company and focused more closely on market research. Thereafter it began to diminish and fade. In 1970 the pre-1949 material was deposited at the University of Sussex but in the 1980s the project was reinvigorated with a new stage of diary-writing.

From the start MO appealed to a number of Devonians but some quickly discovered they were unsuitable. For instance, in 1938 Kenneth MacRae Burnett, a seventeen-year-old who lived at Swilly in Plymouth, explained that while canvassing his acquaintances he found his circle was too limited to judge public opinion: fellow apprentices were only interested in test matches and football and his father 'said he did not want anything to do with my *Communist* nonsense'.[2]

MO utilised two classes of individuals. There were Invesigators who were paid to produce commissioned work and there were also Observers, volunteers who answered directives and wrote diaries. Although Plymouth was the subject of a series of reports written by Investigators during the war, Devon features more prominently amongst the diarists and directive respondents. However, it did not have the Observers who produced reports of 'overheards' (the comments heard uttered by strangers) or who conducted surveys. They wrote mainly from London and Bolton as well as other places including Worcester and Bristol. Perhaps one of Devon's more unusual MO connections was the public canvassing which was commissioned by Richard Acland, the Liberal MP for Barnstaple.[3]

The Writers

This collection comprises sixty-five Writers who commented on Devon. They do not provide an accurate portrait of society but instead offer slices of individual lives. A

OPPOSITE:* *3-6 Four posters embracing one of the chief topics of everyday conversation often noted by the Writers: the progress of the war and the role of allied nations.

BRITAIN'S EUROPEAN ALLIES
ATTACK IN BRITISH AIRCRAFT
BELGIUM
CZECHOSLOVAKIA
FRANCE
GREECE
HOLLAND
LUXEMBOURG
NORWAY
POLAND
YUGOSLAVIA

British fighters sweep hourly
across occupied France,
cheered by French peasants

The R.A.F.'s intensive bombing of Germany's war industries continues.
VICTORY OF THE ALLIES
IS ASSURED

British guns blast a way through Axis defences in North Africa
THE DOWNFALL OF THE
DICTATORS IS ASSURED

7 *A number of the Writers, not surprisingly, referenced the contribution made by women in the war.*

breakdown of their genders, ages and interests shows they were not broadly representative. Three individuals, I. Shorland, Thomas Brody and an unidentified serviceman, did not give biographical details but, fortunately, information can be gleaned from other sources about the remaining Writers. Thus, we can begin to understand who they were and what, if anything, they shared in common.

Like their counterparts across the country, the majority of the 'Devon' volunteers were members of the middle-class. This is not surprising given they would have had more spare leisure time and sufficient education to participate. There were twenty-six women and thirty-seven men. Their ages varied from sixteen to sixty-eight; the average age was thirty-two. Twenty-seven were aged between sixteen and twenty-six years old. Five (**28**, **30**, **32**, **52**, **68**) were vegetarians as was another (**59**) except for her occasional consumption of rabbit meat. A number of Writers discussed being Socialists, two (**30**, **62**) were Communists and one (**4**) admitted to being a former member of the British Union of Fascists. Most diarists were in employment: one (**52**) was an actress, another (**33**) was a driver, one more (**59**) was a domestic worker, another was a serviceman (**60**), four (**25**, **28**, **30**, **36**) were writers, four (**9**, **13**, **44**, **57**) worked in agriculture, eight (**1**, **4**, **11**, **15**, **31**, **35**, **37**, **50**) were clerks and seventeen (**3**, **5**, **14**, **18**, **21**, **24**, **26**, **39**, **47**, **49**, **54**, **56**, **58**, **66-7**, **69-70**) were teachers. Only three (**17**, **32**, **68**) were retired. Seven (**7**, **10**, **19**, **34**, **61-2**, **64**) were students.

It is noticeable that no Writer commented upon being members of a Masonic, Buffalo, Oddfellows or Rotary Lodge. Only one woman had joined the Women's Institute (**68**) and few mentioned being members of a church group.

One set (**66-7**) were husband and wife. Two were cousins (**26**)[4] and another two (**9**, **13**) were mother and daughter; their mother/grandmother, Amy Montague, was also an MO Writer.[5] Two (**1**) Writers living near Newton Abbot appear to have known each other as did another two, or possibly three

(**34, 39, 50**), in Plymouth. Thirty-six (**1-4, 6-11, 14, 16, 18-19, 22, 24, 26, 31, 34-7, 45-6, 49-50, 53-4, 56-7, 61-4, 69, 72**) were single, twenty-five (**5, 12-13, 15, 17, 21, 23, 27-30, 32-3, 39, 47, 51-2, 55, 58-9, 65-7, 70-1**) were married and three (**17, 52, 59**) were estranged. Some Writers were most likely in unrecognised partnerships. (**17, 30, 69**) A minority were born and raised in Devon. Nearly all of the remainder had relocated to the county, some as part of the great wartime dislocation of evacuees, refugees and servicemen and servicewomen. Some men and women were short-term visitors. (**5-6, 11, 14, 17, 24-6, 29, 36, 51, 53, 56-8, 61-2, 67, 70**) Some were merely commenting on Devon. (**12, 38**)

Some panel writers explained their reasons for contributing to MO. Mary Bateson (**3**) was not only interested in the minutiae of modern life but also thought 'I like writing but have not a creative enough mind to find satisfactory themes of my own and this seemed to provide me with plenty of material'. Gwendoline Holmes (**16**) felt the project was 'the only chance I have of being able to say exactly what I think without someone contradicting me or saying I'm being silly.' Edward Glanfield (**7**) hoped his writings would be useful to future generations and that they would help society understand how other people lived.[6]

Devon's sixty-five Writers did not lead society nor were they the very poor. Many had a good education, were keen to observe and wanted to make a contribution outside of their normal lives. MO's volunteers have been described as being the young, the radical or potentially radical. They were 'anxious to engage'.[7] This accurately describes many of Devon's Writers but a number of them were also very individualistic, if not idiosyncratic, which would have made them stand out from the rest of society. A few had particularly strong or forceful characters and perhaps more were unusually distinctive. Some could be described as eccentric or at least they did not readily conform with society's norms. At the very least many pursued their lives in a singular manner. It is difficult to identify another common thread amongst them other than their readiness, if not eagerness, to examine their lives and to record society as well as their personal views and perspectives.

Eleven Devonian contributors have not been included in this volume. One is an account written by 'Miss Bere' of Copplestone which has not survived nor is it known whether she was Rosa, Ada or Kate, the three unmarried sisters who lived together in a house which was named Greystone. Other Writers wrote comparatively little such as Miss Juliet Parker, who served in the Women's Royal Naval Service and lived in Mannamead in Plymouth in 1942. She wrote an interesting passage on her new mode of transport ('It may be of interest that one of my chief wartime innovations is hitch-hiking which I do on every possible occasion').[8] In January 1939 twenty-one-year-old Charles Powell Phillips of Rockstone in Abbotskerswell answered only one directive regarding music. He preferred symphony and chamber music to jazz in contrast to his father ('The stuff is alright to dance to and some of the tunes aren't so bad. I think so many of the tunes

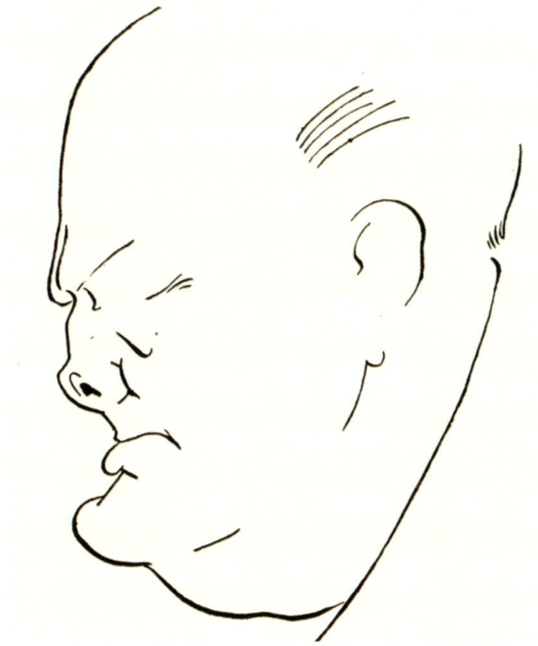

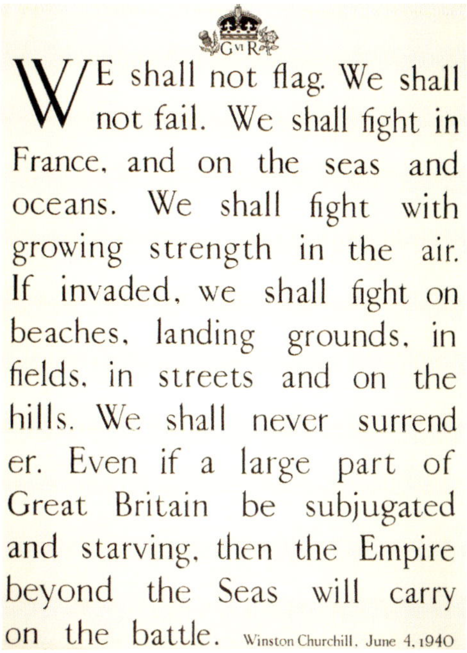

G VI R

WE shall not flag. We shall not fail. We shall fight in France, and on the seas and oceans. We shall fight with growing strength in the air. If invaded, we shall fight on beaches, landing grounds, in fields, in streets and on the hills. We shall never surrender. Even if a large part of Great Britain be subjugated and starving, then the Empire beyond the Seas will carry on the battle. Winston Churchill, June 4, 1940

FAR LEFT:
8 *Caricature of Prime Minister Winston Churchill, 1942.*

LEFT:
9 *Excerpt of Churchill's speech given in the House of Commons on 4 June 1940.*

are spoilt by the silly words.') and his sister who enjoyed dance music with the exception of 'ultra-hot swing'.[9]

Some Devonians may have written texts which have not survived. This includes Minnie Watson, a farmer's wife in Monkokehampton and organiser for the Women's Voluntary Service during the war, who answered three directives in 1943. She expressed her views on Bank Holidays ('Bank holiday in the country, where I live, is exactly the same as all other days. Cows still want to be milked and hens fed - also people!') and on her ideal vacation ('I do not want to see any development of civil aviation after the war. Can see no good reason for dashing over the world. I should not use planes at all and I do not like the idea of the air being full of aircraft. There is only one type of holiday for me - camping by car - staying about three or four days in each spot, then moving on.'). This self-professed housewife was content with life in her village ('As I own my home, it has everything I want in it. The only thing it lacks is electricity which however is not in the village. That might be an improvement.').

Likewise, F. Barker, a fifty-two-year-old evacuee from the Channel Islands, was living at 5 West Cliff Road in Dawlish in 1942 when he answered two directives. He wrote about his health ('Putting on weight myself but meet many elderly females who are getting jittery') and Winston Churchill ('The only man fit for the job - clearing up his predecessor's mistakes'). He also cited the sentiments expressed by an American acquaintance ('John Bull is going to get the biggest licking he has ever had in his life but he will have the pants off Hitler before he's done with him.').

Some MO Writers mentioned Devon in passing. This includes a twenty-nine-year-old widow from Maida Vale in 1941 ('a young soldier, returning from leave spent at his home in Devon, said that people from the towns were always coming to the village and asking for milk, but the village people hardly had enough for themselves, let alone any over to spare for outsiders: *they* were taking it all *and that's in Devon mind you*!'). A Dorset man made the acquaintance of a Devonian in 1941 ('Met a woman who has been helping in a nursery school in Devon... She told us their favourite game was air-raids which they instantly resorted to if left to themselves.')[10] Likewise, a thirty-seven-year-old housewife from Blackheath mentioned an unidentified part of Devon that same year. She had spoken to her friend Tom Robertson who had a vacation somewhere in the county. Her reference to a German raid may have been that on 7 November 1941 which involved nearly two hundred RAF bombers:

'Told all about the Devon holiday. Andy only child at hotel and was made a great fuss by all and everyone. Big aerodrome nearby, so place full of officers' wives. The hotel used rather as a club by the cadets. He was there just after the big raid on Berlin. All the aerodrome thrilled and swaggering about as if they [were] the sole perpetrators of the excursion. Everyone in the village knew all details and were equally prideful. Tom had amusing anecdotes to tell having made himself very pally with the commandant. One might be repeated. Some time back Nazis happened to find the landing ground and dropped a couple on runway. Ground closed to incoming traffic until repairs completed, all planes being warned by radio to go on or turn back. Important personage touring coastal defences happened along. Disregarded warning and his plane came down. Sentry immediately put all in plane under arrest for disobeying orders. Much spluttering from big man who demanded to see commandant. When he did see him, was told that here his authority was not as great as that of his man running the aerodrome. He had disobeyed an order and must either stay here under arrest or return by road. Man insisted that GHQ be rung, when commandant would be ticked off and big man allowed to continue in his plane. When rung, GHQ upheld commandant, said big man to stay there until sent for. Car arrived next morning and he drove off shame-faced.'.[11]

Likewise, Moretonhampstead-born Audrey Neck (1915-97), a twenty-four-year-old civil servant living in Croydon, only commented upon her accent:

'Mine is an accent on its own, a sort of Devon-London mixture. I do not care a jot what people think of it, although when I first went to school here, from Devon, the other children's laughter made me a bit self-conscious for a time. I try to speak as clearly as I can for other peoples' comfort, but stick to my pronunciation of bath and dance; trying to alter it would only start affectation, which I despise. As I am strongly individualistic by nature, it suits me to have an accent slightly different from other people!'[12]

Similar comments were made by H. Higgs, an unmarried twenty-eight-year-old laboratory assistant. At the start of the war he lived in Kent but came from Devon:

'I was more than encouraged to become sensitive to my brogue by the frequency of the jokes and taunts levied at it. This resulted in some early attempts to

10 *Lynmouth, as depicted by Robert Marris (1750-1827) in the early nineteenth century, had retained its rural charm when Mrs Medd visited in 1944.*

copy Londoners as often as I could remember to do so but this soon proved too much of an effort. I gradually reconciled myself to the circumstances and eventually ceased to worry about it. Time has also been a healing factor in that the longer one associates with a particular people, the more does one become like them. Consequently, my Westcountry accent has very largely disappeared – in fact, my *cultivated London accent* has now a tendency to raise a few smiles amongst Plymouth relatives.'[13]

A thirty-year-old social worker from Sussex described her fortnight's holiday in Devon in 1940:

'For the first time in my life I spent the Christmas holiday at Torquay. This was decided on because my family all wanted to go away from the barrage and blitz at Purley and I had a friend evacuated to Torquay who could get rooms for us. So I spent nearly a fortnight there with my mother and sister and actually spent the quietest time I have ever had and the most ascetic. We rented some very comfortable rooms in Babbacombe and theoretically did our own catering. Food was dear in Torquay and we made very little effort to get poultry for Christmas Day, so we were finally invited to share our landlady's veal and Christmas pudding and she surprisingly produced mince pies too.'[14]

Dorothy Medd, a fifty-one-year-old vegetarian who later classified herself as a 'servant in husband's house', fled from Sevenoaks to Minehead in 1944 and spent a fortnight at Westwood in Lynton. She wrote:

'Guest house quite good which I found through an ad in the *Times*, run by a Captain and Mrs H. Other inmates 3 ancient old ladies, one ditto male, 2 young females. Lots of nice vegetables for meal so can miss out meat easily. Lovely bedroom looking over hills and sea and very peaceful. Falls down on wallpapers and very shabby but a good spot to pay 4½ guineas and just what the doctor ordered for shattered nerves.'

11 Unfinished watercolour of the confluence of the West Lyn and East Lyn rivers, 1849.

She enjoyed the views, partook of local entertainment ('on to town hall to watch a local hop. Mostly girls dancing together having a lean time now the soldiers have gone'), commented on evacuees ('many mattresses laid out in town hall for evacuees who have been coming in during the week blindly hoping to find someone to take them in', 'hotel full up with Londonish people and a big proportion of the Chosen, all looking rather miserable. A trio now plays *light music* there after dinner which is rather trying'), met unexpected people ('talked to glamorous Yugo-Slav with scarlet claws and two children, who has come here from bombs and desperately wants house near London, and to ancient old lady who has been here 15 months, is miserable but has nowhere to go') and noted the lack of air raids ('perfect peace here, very rarely an aeroplane about').[15]

The texts

More than 100 MO Writers wrote texts of various lengths on Devon. Altogether more than 100,000 words were written about the county. Four texts (**25**, **28**, **30**, **36**) were by professional writers. The variety of styles and content invigorates the texts. There are some memorable passages: in Plymouth a woman wrote about her love of sharing books ('I certainly feel the urge to suckle others with my books, there is always someone lying, restlessly, at times, on my intellectual breasts'), a Newton Abbot lecturer outlined sex ('At 18 I and my friends would frequently carry love-making even with comparatively strange women to the extent of nudity and mutual masturbation.'), an Exonian feared a German invasion ('I have a friend, a refugee, who intends to poison himself the moment the Nazis come into the neighbourhood. I am very tempted to follow his example.') and a twenty-one-year-old Plymouth student was embarrassed by 'an unavoidable gastronomic indiscretion'. (**47**, **25**, **27**, **20**, **7**)

MO had five classes of material. At its inception in 1937 it asked individuals to answer questionnaires ('directives') on a variety of public and personal subjects. Responses from 39 individuals are included in the main body of this volume. Secondly, this collection includes 30 surveys written on the 12th day of various months in 1937 and 1938; these outlined the itineraries of 23 individuals. Thirdly, in 1939 MO branched out and requested the public write diaries. Some 500 men and women across the country contributed until 1967 and this volume has extracts relating to Devon written by 29 individuals. Four analyses ('file reports') on Plymouth were written by MO investigators. These have been summarised. Finally, a handful of Writers composed self-reports, biographical accounts of themselves. Four of them were connected to Devon.

There was an extraordinary range of topics. In 1938 a Plymouth man answered questions about 'The Lambeth Walk', a popular dance which originated as a song in 1937. In 1939 it was described by the Nazi party as degenerate. Mr R. J. Powell wrote:

> 'I made enquiries regarding this dance and apparently it is very popular in this part of the world. Its chief appeal is that everybody joins in and is a very good dance for a large ballroom. The tune is rather captivating and moves with a delightful rhythm. It has been very popular here as I understand that the vibration caused by the dancers has caused the dance to be cut down. Apparently, the dancers move in unison and the effect of seven or eight hundred dancers in unison can have severe vibratory effects if the floor is not on the ground floor of the building. At a dance I attended the other night in the town it was encored time and time again'.

Likewise, Mrs Ruth Pickwoad commented from Crediton:

> 'Before getting your card (and finding out about *The Lambeth Walk*) I thought it was a popular song out of some show. I first heard of it through my husband, on his return from London, telling me that a new popular tune was being played where ever he went, it was catchy and he liked it. The same night we heard it over the air and he said *That's 'The Lambeth Walk' that I was telling you about*. After that I recognised it – constantly. The only comments I have heard about it has been from my own children when they have heard it broadcast. *I like that tune, don't you*?
>
> I have not had any good opportunities of getting the opinions of friends. One had forgotten how she had first heard of it, saying rather vaguely, *It's a dance, isn't it*?'[16]

'The Lambeth Walk' was also mentioned in the Sidford texts.

Some Writers were remarkably effective in describing parts of Devon such as Dennis Frone's account of the Hobby Drive at Clovelly. Likewise, Mary Bateson's narrative of Barnstaple Fair is captivating and George Raine shines a perceptive light on the people of Beer as they celebrated the coronation of George VI on 12 May 1937. Hugh Dent uniquely described the descent of Plymouth into the chaos of war from the perspective of a Conscientious Objector while the following year Mariella Vaughan chronicled her shock, dismay and horror at the subsequent destruction of that city. Perhaps the most illuminating is Diana Murray Hill's writing which lays bare some failings and characteristics of the residents of Sidford.

Naomi Mitchison had the highest degree of fame of the Writers and her Devon writing demonstrates why she had earned for herself a national reputation. Jack Lindsay was another well-known author and his skills are apparent in his prose.

There are unexpected texts including one written by a groom on his honeymoon in North Devon in 1941. He recorded intimate moments with his bride. (**29**) There is also an account of two Welsh teenagers who went on a lark and travelled to Plymouth for a one-day adventure (**35**) and a visiting vicar reported from the margins of Dartmoor how the morals of local women had been transformed by American servicemen (**53**). Some correspondents outlined how the war had intruded into their dreams. (**7-9**) They included Mrs Pickwoad of Crediton:

> 'I was in the kitchen making vegetable soup. We had vegetable soup every day for a long time but there was nothing else in the house to eat. I put it on the table, very worried because I was unable to vary it except by leaving out some ingredient. My husband said *I'm sick of this filthy muck*.'

On another night:

> 'I was in the garden on a lovely autumn day, looking over the hills. Over Exeter I hear a dull explosion, then another, and another, coming regularly and rhythmically. I thought with horror *Exeter is being bombed*. I woke to find my husband snoring!'[17]

Some accounts are particularly literary with absorbing prose. Dennis Frone captured a moment at Bideford Railway Station with sharp clarity. Boris Ford summarised with great wit upper middle-class society in Torquay before the war: St Marychurch was, he suggested, a place the English went to die but then refused to do so. Jack Lindsay's skills as a writer

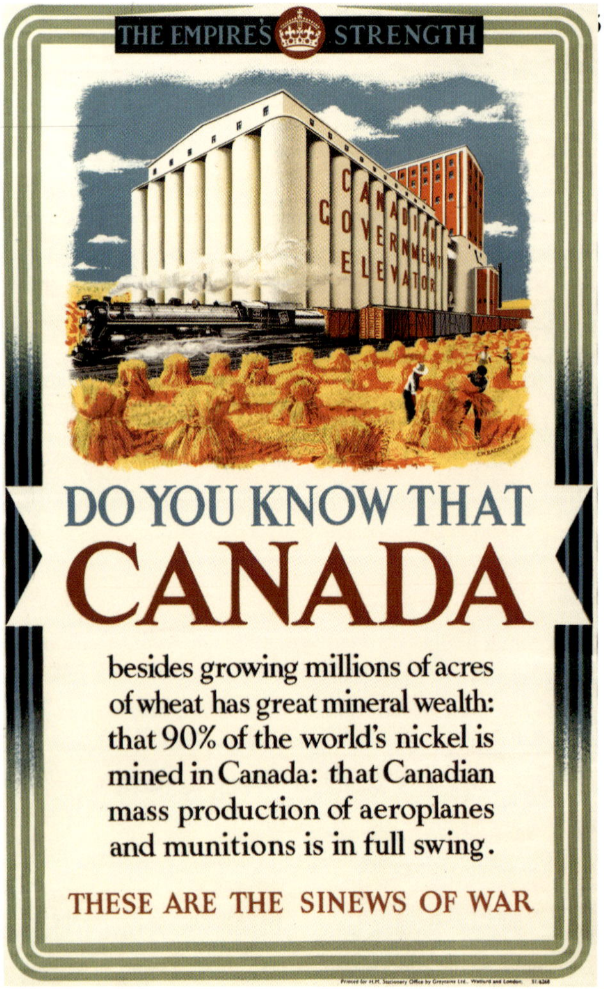
THE EMPIRE'S STRENGTH
CANADIAN GOVERNMENT ELEVATOR
DO YOU KNOW THAT
CANADA
besides growing millions of acres of wheat has great mineral wealth: that 90% of the world's nickel is mined in Canada: that Canadian mass production of aeroplanes and munitions is in full swing.
THESE ARE THE SINEWS OF WAR

THE EMPIRE'S STRENGTH
DO YOU KNOW THAT
INDIA
supplies all the jute for making sacks and sandbags: that more than half Britain's needs of livestock foods come from India as well as tea, rice, hides, skins, cotton and manganese.
THESE ARE THE SINEWS OF WAR

—TO VICTORY
CANADA

YOUR HELP WILL BRING
VICTORY

are obvious in his closely-observed summations of the lives and characters of his Paignton neighbours.

The writings of Ruth Pickwoad are extraordinary for her candour. She provided intriguing details of wartime Crediton but her thoughts on class and the role of women few can now relate to her. She took for granted her part in Britain's empire and was aware of how her social background comprehensively dominated her life and how friends, neighbours and strangers perceived her.

Mrs Pickwoad was one of the few to allude to the place of women at this time. It had been less than ten years since women were granted the same voting rights as men. She summarised a conversation she had had with two elderly spinster ladies; they stressed the importance of young women being able to support themselves financially but Mrs Pickwoad found herself unable to assert her belief that having children was the prime concern for a woman. Another Writer (**68**) noted a female relation felt it unbecoming for a woman to be drunk. As the only man present, in 1944 George Shipway chaired a public meeting of Women For Westminster, the movement which was started two years earlier to increase the number of female members of Parliament from thirteen.[18] Mariella Vaughan noted instances of domestic abuse at her pub in Ringmore.

It could appear that the MO Writers in general recorded their lives without restraint: within the texts for outside Devon can be found passages on intimate subjects otherwise seldom recorded at this time ('the result of war-talk on me nowadays is a nice mixture of flatulence and suffocation', 'I lead an idle and rather dissipated existence… General condition of health was rather poor due to over indulgence in smoking, drinking and fornicating. Catarrh and piles were about averagely inconveniencing…Went to the W. C. and defecated. Returned to sitting room and wrote a note to Fortnum & Mason explaining that they had sent me someone else's account by mistake', 'a man at lunchtime every day stands between surface shelters and makes motions imitating masturbation at the girls working in Mead & Fields Cracker Factory seen through windows and at St Ursula's Convent next door', 'a young woman, in course of discussion with me, as to whether men or women had a better time, remarked *Of course menstruation is a nuisance* but still maintained preference for the life of a woman', and 'I wonder how many of the onlookers thought, as I did, that the calf in the picture ought really to be a huge phallus.').[19]

These passages are not commonplace and, although there is a general sense of frankness and candour, all writers recorded only a portion of any day's events let alone their thoughts whether intimate or not.

Social structure

Social divisions were commonly alluded to. For instance, in 1939 a nineteen-year-old engineering student in London once mused about his family:

> 'My mother, however, often reminisces on the days down at Heavitree, Exeter, when they used to drive into church or service at the cathedral and all the good people bowed and curtsied as the *Quality* passed by. The family, Pennells, moved in the best county society.'[20]

Three female Writers had the most to say about social structure and discussed it in terms of culture, occupation and wealth. In Bideford Miss Brown considered herself upper middle class and commented upon her disappointment with the divisions which became apparent between her and her boyfriend who was only middle-class. Meanwhile, from Crediton Mrs Pickwoad was equally insistent she was a member of the gentry but wrote at length about the differences between her social associations and those of her parents. The most extensive text was written by Miss Hill at Sidford: she outlined the chasm between the villagers and the 'immigrants', wealthier and higher status individuals who had moved to the area.

For the purposes of visual identification MO itself divided society into four social groups.: A, 'rich people', B, 'the middle classes', C, 'artisans and skilled workers' and D, 'unskilled workers or economically trained of our people'. This was outlined in Plymouth's file reports. (**40-42**)

Thus, in August 1940 a conversation was recorded as between F 35 B (a female aged 35 in Group B) and F 25 B at Notting Hill Gate. The first woman said 'Plymouth & Hull have been bombed and Bournemouth. Bournemouth badly I believe'. The second woman who lived at Plymouth responded 'I always bring my gas mask up with me but no one has them here and they all stare at you'.[21]

Miss Flora Meaden, a twenty-six-year-old Londoner who was employed by the BBC, commented upon her origins in a question about class:

***OPPOSITE:* 12-15** *Four posters promoting the empire's contribution to the war, 1940s.*

> 'My family lives in patriarchal fashion, my father and his brother in houses adjoining with a common garden, and my grandparents until they died in a house with a garden also backing on the common garden. My grandmother traced her family back to the Gilberts (Sir Humphrey) and the Winters (Admiral Winter went as far as the straits of Magellan with Drake). Most of my other forebears were Devon people and were only (in my grandfather's time) one generation settled in London. I was brought up on this story, which usually ended with a melancholy thought that if our immediate forebears hadn't all been younger sons and if money hadn't been left to hospitals, we MIGHT have been living in a large house in Devon with park and farmland. We used to be taken to look at the various family houses - through the palings - during our summer holidays. Because of this, I was convinced in my childhood that our family was different and more special than everyone else in suburban Chiswick.'[22]

Race and nationality

In 1939 MO asked Writers about their views about Black people ('How do you feel about Negroes? Write down the first thing that comes into your head'). Not surprisingly, some comments jar with modern sensibilities such as those by Miss Edith Oakley, a thirty-six-year-old foreign correspondent who lived in Glasgow. Of Black people she wrote:

> 'The traffic in Negro slaves was introduced by Hawkins, a native of the town in which I was brought up. Every Plymouth child is trained on the tales of Drake, Raleigh, Hawkins and the rest, and their coats of arms are in the Guildhall there. Hawkins' is of a Negro in chains. Somehow or other I seem to have imbued the Elizabethan view of Negroes which many years' open adherence to the higher moral principles has not dissolved. While deploring the American attitude towards Blacks, I myself deep down find it hard to believe that people with black skins, woolly hair and odd faces can be human.'[23]

Other appraisals of the Black race were positive but, like those on Jewish people, diverse.

R. J. Powell, a single twenty-six-year-old chemist who moved from Lancashire to Plymouth in 1939, was asked about his views of 'Negroes' ('lack of education keeps them down. Have not rid myself of the thought of a Black skin. Happy people when left alone, their songs are simple but moving. I should think quite logical people', 'a race which needs correct White guidance in order to develop' and 'I feel they are a branch of the human race which either through environmental or through being a separate branch in evolution are not equal to the White race in mental ability.')

Mr Powell, a Quaker and Socialist, also commented upon his view of the French ('culturally sound, temperamental, excitable, good writers') and the Germans ('easily led, brave solid, fascinating language'. Later MO also asked for opinions of other nationalities and in January 1943 they were also asked about their 'present' feelings about the Australians, Belgians, Chinese, Germans, Japanese and Russians.[24] Many impressions were coloured by wartime experiences such as those in 1943 of Kathleen Daniell who wrote of the Vichy government ('A puppet government living out the worst traits inherent in the French natural character. The fruit of French indecision and the fault of the French people'), the 'fighting French' ('I don't trust them whatever their beliefs they are French'), the Italians ('Little yellow-bellies who were never meant for war'), Americans ('Rather loud-mouthed, actions not living up to the boasts they make'), the Dutch ('On the whole a brave, trustworthy nation'), the Polish ('I am very sorry for the nation as a whole but know little of the people') and the Czechs ('I know very little of the Czechs in this country. I have never met any and there are few in this area.').[25]

Many other Writers also claimed that they had yet to meet members of other races or nationalities. Typical of them was Tom Edridge of Newton Ferrers who commented 'As I make practically no contact with Jews in this village, I cannot have any basis for opinion. I imagine there may be resentment at Jews securing jobs while we have our mass of unemployed.'[26] **(3, 8, 13, 27-8, 31, 50)**

Travel

Many Writers described journeys before and during the war by car, train or on foot. When Miss Ausden visited in 1940 she remarked upon obscured signs and local people staring as she passed through the narrow lanes.

Forty-one-year-old housewife Mrs Nellie Underwood of Sheffield made a promise to herself:

> 'The day before this war began, we were all ready to set out for a quiet, beautiful spot in North Devon, a holiday we had discussed for years. We deferred it because of the state of affairs. But we did not abandon it and we reckon we are owed that holiday. So, as soon as we get

this war over, we are going to see what accommodation there is, and if we can get any, we shall go there. War or not, we like quiet holidays and prefer country to seaside, but if we can get both, as at the place in North Devon, that is champion.'[27]

Devon's isolation and beauty appealed to those in parts of the country threatened by bombing or invasion. In 1942, for instance, George Simmonds, a thirty-two-year-old laboratory chemist, wrote 'there is a tendency to get right away from the district for a holiday even as far as Devon and Cornwall. So many people have been without a real holiday since the war began that they feel they really deserve one this year.'[28] The following year Mrs G. Chalmers, a thirty-two-year-old former musician in London, expressed similar sentiments:

'I would like to go to our farm. It isn't ours of course but members of the family have spent some very happy holidays there. It is in Devonshire about 15 miles from the Bristol Channel and as far from the Atlantic coast, about ten miles north of Dartmoor. It is almost entirely dairy farming and the food produced in the form of milk, eggs, butter, vegetables, fruit, poultry and an unfailing supply of cream. The people are beautifully clean, cheerful, obliging and very competent. When we came the second time we were received like old friends. It is 1½ miles from the nearest village, but a splendid centre for motoring in Devon and Cornwall and the views from the house are very wide and beautiful.'[29]

Mrs V. E. Gray of Clapham in London likewise yearned for Devon ('Would welcome a holiday on a farm in Devon where I spent one week of restful happiness in 1942')[30] but that summer it was Eric Wood, a twenty-three-year-old employed at an aircraft factory in Southampton, who managed it:

'I was on holiday in North Devon on August Bank Holiday. We arranged a day out in a way under which no demand for public services of any kind would be required. This arrangement was decided upon in order to avoid queueing and also from a patriotic point of view. In the morning it rained, so in order to bring novelty into the holiday we went out into a field and sat in a sheep pen and read. After lunch the weather cleared. We walked four miles to the sea and bathed and lounged on the sands, had a picnic tea and walked home four miles to a cooked supper.'[31]

Other MO Writers had travelled to Devon for work or military service including eighteen-year-old Robert Mortlock of Chelmsford in 1941:

***16** A NAAFI poster, c1939.*

'Up as usual at seven, tidied my bed, swept under it, cleaned one of the stoves, shaved and washed. Breakfast then at eight. This is my usual programme down here in Devon in camp. My training then commenced at ten to nine. My day finished at five when I sat down to a well-earned tea.

A *smoking* concert was taking place that evening in the NAAFI canteen. So my friend and I completed our cleaning and after supper at seven, went along to see what talent could come from the ranks of so many rookie marines. The depot dance band was in attendance. I quenched my thirst with two pints of the very weak NAAFI beer. I stayed until about nine when I made my way back to the hut. I made my bed then entered slumberland before *Lights Out* had sounded.'[32]

In 1942 MO enquired about travel and this enlisted a

17 Wartime poster utilising the slang word Cheerio, which had become popular in the First World War.

reply from 'RF' regarding Devon and careless talk:

'On Saturday January 3 1942 investigator travelled by the 12.50 from Waterloo to Exeter. The train was full but there were seats to spare. A great many children evidently returning to their evacuation billets after the Christmas holidays were on the train. These mostly got off at Andover or Salisbury.

In investigator's compartment there were six Servicemen, 1 army and 5 RAF. It was a non-smoker but several of them smoked occasionally. Two airmen discussed Lysander aircraft in some details across the carriage, revealing the fact that they were being redesigned and mentioning speeds etc.

The train stopped at Woking, Andover, Salisbury, Templecombe, Sherborne, Yeovil Junction and arrived at Exeter about 25 minutes later (5.05 pm).'[33]

Public houses

In May 1943 MO asked about public houses and some Writers otherwise commented on them in passing, particularly one who described his pub crawls as an Exeter college student. Another Writer (**31**) worked behind the bar in a pub. Miss H. M. Butt of Pomphlett in Plymouth added in 1943:

'The public houses in this neighbourhood are rather mixed, one or two more akin to the country pub and the majority noisy and crowded. I prefer a country pub where one can think in comparative peace and frequently join in the conversation with the local residents, probably ending with a game of darts! My pet aversion is the town *hotel*, where it is not advisable for a woman to go alone and where most people's idea of having a good time seems to be to make as much noise as possible.

The idea of the pub in small towns and villages is that these are a social centre; and it is one idea that can be developed in larger places. The distinction between the public saloons or lounges might well be wiped out, leaving one or more rooms for general use, and another for any recreations likely to be required, in effect, more of a social club.'[34]

In 1945 MO conducted an investigation into juvenile drinking and interviewed two classes of twelve-year-olds in Devon. It concluded that Devonian children were more likely to be familiar with cider than beer and that it was consumed with the consent of their parents at home.[35]

Language

In June 1939 MO asked 'do you make a habit of using the following words and phrases? If not, what is your reaction when they are used by others?' These words were 'cheerio' (used during the Great War particularly in the Royal Navy), 'toodle-oo' (by 1907 also used to express a farewell), 'okey-doke' (American slang by 1934), 'old boy' (dating back to the early 1600s and in modern use as characterizing upper-class speech); 'not half' (a late medieval phrase used to indicate nothing like), 'ta' (eighteenth-century expression of thanks), 'chum' (formerly used to describe a flat-mate but in modern usage to describe an intimate friend), 'pal' (an eighteenth century confederate but now used to describe a close friend) and 'mate' (from the late medieval period indicating a close friend).[36]

Miss Oakley in Glasgow responded 'I don't know what okey-doke means nor toodle-oo though I do remember that it was common in Plymouth a quarter of a century ago.'. In Bideford Miss Brown (**8**) wrote that she used words such as cheerio and okay but became irritated when one man repeatedly called another old boy. She regarded it as 'common' and felt it slovenly 'and almost insolent manners' for a tradesman to say ta instead of thank you.[37] Other Devon Writers also outlined their thoughts on words such as chum, mate and old boy.[38] (**13**, **28**) MO writers outside the county made similar comments about language as an indicator of social class: one Londoner used cheerio, okay, not half and old boy, was amused by toodle-oo, annoyed by okey-doke and left indifferent to bye-bye, ta, chum, pal and mate. Another Londoner first heard okey-doke from a Marx Brothers' film while another thought okey-doke and toodle-oo suggested ignorance and a lack of education.[39]

In June 1942 MO asked respondents which words had been introduced by the war. A twenty-year-old Plymouth sailor listed six words and terms: 'Mundangus (rubbish, much, litter), Spam (canned meat), Pongos (Englishmen), Clippy (bus conductress), Security (morale and intelligence) and Red Caps (military police)'. He also gave 'bitz' and 'spew' as wartime words.[40]

A former Plymouth actress noted introductions such as 'blitz', 'going off like a bomb' and 'play ball'. The latter she thought meant to cooperate or help. She responded in length about other terms:

> 'I do not think that I have used a great many of the slang words which have been coined during this war but many of my friends have and I daresay I do sometimes.
>
> Tickety-boo. I use this sometimes, I caught it from a WAAF friend who uses it when she means she is getting drunk or is drunk, and I in the same capacity. Actually, I think it just means that everything is fine and if a person says *I am tickety-boo* he means *I am fine* rather than *I am drunk* – but that is what she means.
>
> Flat spin. This I do not use but several people I know do. *I am in a flat spin* meaning I am losing control and don't quite know where I am. This I have found used by civilians.
>
> Browned off. This is currently used by acquaintances of mine to describe a state of acute boredom.
>
> Wizard. This I have heard now since the commencement of the war and I have not heard it so much lately. It means *super*. One of my men friends not in the army always uses it. *I had a wizard time*, etc.'

A London MO Writer composed a 'War Dictionary' in 1941 and noted 'browned off' as meaning amongst the RAF boredom.[41]

A retiree living in Paignton commented upon obscenities:

> 'My beliefs about obscenity and swearing are very definite: an important *class distinction* – those who swear and those who do not. I judge that I am fortunate in only rarely hearing swearing. Novels give the impression that people nearly all swear, but this is far from being so. I regard it as a silly habit, either showing want of self-control or a foolish desire to appear *modern*.
>
> Swearing consists in using the name of God or Christ and I rarely hear it. Obscene words occasionally heard: *bloody* (I do not know in what way it is obscene but apparently it is legally so regarded), *bugger* used sometimes by people one would expect to avoid such, *f*ck* heard in boyhood last century but never now.'[42]

Writer **2** listed words he considered inappropriate. To modern eyes these may come across as limited and tame but it would be a mistake to assume a greater variety of words were not spoken amongst at least some of the population from 1937 to 1945. This was demonstrated when another MO writer, following a weekend in March 1941, asked fifty RAF men 'what did you go out to do?' Their most popular answers were 'pictures', 'drinking' and '*ucking'.

The men replied in detail ('*un* and beer, got both, consequently I am *ucking broke now and won't be able to go out for a *ucking long time', 'I went out *ucking broke and came back *ucking broke Monday. I went after some *un*'.)

When asked what he missed most, a thirty-five-year-old answered 'Miss most? *un*, *un*, *un*'. His reply to feelings about the Vichy government was 'I have got *uck all to think about any of the *un*s, *uck all. What I am *ucking liking for is *ucking peace. *uck 'em all'. Other replies were similar to the first question ('*ucking money, home comforts, *un*, sexual intercourse', '*ucking cigarettes and beer') and the second ('*ucking wash-out', 'smash the *uckers').

In 1942 a Plymouth Wren referred to various obscenities used in another branch of the military, the navy. Their prevalence among at least some servicemen contrasts with its scarcity recorded by MO Writers.[43]

Wartime Devon, 1939-45

Fifteen Devon MO Writers wrote during the two years preceding the war. Their daily itineraries, like ours today, were dominated by work, socialising and meal times. However, the pre-war life of Writer **1** at Abbotskerswell was already affected by gas exercises as were others. There are very different descriptions of the commemoration of the armistice in Barnstaple, Crediton and Woodbury in 1937. The first was a school assembly, the second an individual's itinerary on that day and the last was a parish observance as witnessed by the local school headmaster.

The majority of the texts were written during the war and clearly demonstrate how life on the Home Front differed according to where one lived. In Devon one of the greatest contrasts was between Plymouth and the rest of the county. Fifty-six MO Writers commented upon a multitude of aspects of life. One, Miss Audrey Neck, formerly of Moretonhampstead but then living in Croydon, wrote about the start of the war in September 1939:

> 'In the evening said goodbye to Mother who was fetched by my brother-in-law in his car: he is to take her, my sister and nephew to Devon to relations tomorrow. Felt most tearful, wonder when I should see her again. Blast Hitler! Had a sentimental time picking out old snapshots from the album to take with me in case the house is destroyed by fire. They are mostly old Devon ones with members of the family in them. Feel all nervy and upset, this breaking up of family life is much worse than I thought.'[44]

Others also shared their details of these first few days of warfare.

Devon in 1939, as now, had a diversity of communities. It was Britain's third largest county in terms of geographical size, much of which remained in mixed agricultural use, but two great tracts, Dartmoor and Exmoor, were given over to seasonal pasturage. Fishing remained an important industry with Brixham being the leading port. Devon has always had a relatively low population; in 1939 there were 781,243 residents, not quite two per cent of the national total.[45]

Its two cities had very different characters; Plymouth, with Devonport, was dominated by the Royal Navy while Exeter remained the regional capital for local government, education and religion. For nearly two hundred years both coastlines had been developed for tourism and as retirement communities. Devon was attractive to summer visitors partly because of the comparative lack of nineteenth-century industrialisation and winter tourists appreciated the milder climate. These factors shaped its wartime character.

Life then in Devon would appear isolated compared with modern life, but news was readily available. Writers alluded to listening to BBC broadcasts as well as German radio. Lord Haw Haw was mentioned several times. Some commented upon rumours (**4**, **6**, **8**, **32**, **29**, **55**) which mostly concerned unreported air raids, the activities of supposed fifth-columnists and German spies, and even an attempted invasion of Plymouth. These wartime tales differed from the everyday nature of local gossip ('These Bidefordians seem to know all the personal affairs of every other Bidefordian and have an amazing knowledge of the local genealogical trees'.).

At the start of the war, on 3 September 1939, all British men aged between 18 and 41 were required to register for military service. This was subsequently increased to men aged up to 51 while all men in their fifties had to perform some form of national service. In 1941 further legislation was passed for the conscription of unmarried women and childless widows in their twenties. Initially, men and women engaged in *reserved* occupations, meaning those working in key industries, were exempt as were those who were found medically unfit. Additional exemptions were later added.

Conscientious objectors had to justify their views before tribunals and, if successful, were given non-combatant employment. Four men (**19**, **27**, **29**, **39**) discussed being Conscientious Objectors. Each was aged between 18 and 31. One of them, Hugh Dent (**39**) commented that the only difficulties he experienced were those with fellow pacifists. There were also female Conscientious Objectors among the writers including Agnes Norman. (**23**) Seven months after writing her Devon account Mrs Norman was interviewed by a policeman to whom it had been reported that she was a pacifist and that she had made seditious remarks in public:

***OPPOSITE: 18-21** Four posters encouraging women to enlist in war work.*

ARP
WOMEN
WANTED
APPLY: LOCAL BRANCH WOMEN'S VOLUNTARY SERVICES.

SERVE IN THE WAAF
WITH THE MEN WHO FLY

NATIONAL SERVICE
WOMEN WANTED
TO HELP THE CHILDREN
FROM EVACUATED AREAS
THE CHILDREN LEAVE FOR SCHOOL
A TALK IN THE VILLAGE HALL
EFFICIENT COOKS AND HELPERS PREPARE THE MID DAY MEAL
PLAYING AFTER SCHOOL HOURS
THE AFTERNOON DARNING AND MENDING CLUB
DOMESTIC HELP TO KEEP THE CHILDREN HEALTHY AND HAPPY
THESE ARE JOBS WHICH WILL HAVE TO BE DONE. ALL WOMEN LOVE CHILDREN AND LIKE TO HELP THEM. OFFER YOUR SERVICES
APPLY TO YOUR LOCAL COUNCIL
OR LOCAL BRANCH OF THE
WOMENS VOLUNTARY SERVICES

WOMEN WANTED
AS
AMBULANCE
DRIVERS
AMBULANCE
OFFER YOUR SERVICES TO YOUR LOCAL COUNCIL
OR ANY BRANCH OF WOMEN'S VOLUNTARY SERVICES
CIVIL DEFENCE

'It had been reported that I had said *I will not do any war work because it would mean acquiescing in war.* I replied that I could not at the moment remember making any such statement but that certainly was my position. I would not knowingly do anything to release another person for activities which I believed to be wholly wrong. We have not heard anything more from the police and I do not suppose we shall, but the incident is a further indication of what is in our midst.'

In 1919 she married Clarence Norman (1886-1974) who had been imprisoned for being a Conscientious Objector during the First World War. He went on hunger strike and was on two occasions force-fed.[46]

Evacuees and refugees

The MO Writers across Devon discussed Devon's reception of, and attitudes towards, those individuals seeking sanctuary in terms which often contrasted with the cheery reports which appeared in local newspapers.

On 3 September mobilisation involving the conscription of all men aged from 18 to 42, had an immediate effect in Devon as elsewhere but two days before Operation Pied Piper had begun: that day over a million people began leaving 'target areas', mostly industrialised centres thought liable to be bombed, for 'reception' areas. Devon was exclusively a reception area with the exception of Plymouth, which until May 1941 was a 'neutral' area. A considerable number of men, women and children from the Channel Islands also relocated to Devon. In the spring of 1944 the government established a Restricted Area in order to safeguard military preparations for the invasion of France. This included a ten-mile strip along the county's two coastlines.

In addition to the evacuees, there were 'refugees' who privately arranged their relocation. It has been estimated that some 60,000 evacuees and refugees came to Devon in 1939, equal to a tenth of its pre-war population. The three boroughs thought to have experienced the greatest population increases were Totnes (14.0%), Torquay (17.5%) and Honiton (20.2%) but there were still higher increases amongst Urban District Councils at Budleigh Salterton (22.8%), Northam (23.4%), Crediton (26.2%), Dawlish (28.9%) and Sidmouth (33.6%).[47]

In 1940 a London MO Writer recorded his conversation with a man who had just returned from Dawlish where he visited his wife:

'He said it was lovely, no sirens, no gun fire. A local inhabitant [had] proudly pointed to a spot, when actually a bomb fell quite five miles away in an open field. It certainly proves the fact that no one can realise the life in London till they have actually been there.'[48]

22 A warning about the dangers of war, 1942.

While Devon's remoteness made it attractive to those seeking safety from the Luftwaffe, others thought its position made it liable to be invaded. In 1940 a family in Edgware discussed their options:

'Mother plumps for Devon but a cousin, whose husband wants her to leave London and go to Torquay when he is called up, says that she is afraid they might land parachutists en masse on the Devonshire moors.'[49]

Likewise, another Writer, living in Ilford in Essex, reported that in 1938 his landlord and his wife debated whether to send their two children to Devon where friends had agreed to take them.[50] In the first year of the war an MO writer living in Scotland speculated that Devon would be invaded first:

> 'The Bulletin had a lot to the effect that we were expecting the invasion on a part of the South Coast at which the cliffs rise steeply from the sea; inland there is a lake that German seaplanes would use and there are roads to two main towns. I said to Mother, that is just like the South Devon coast; Burrator might be the lake and Plymouth and Exeter the towns. I am beginning to wonder if the German idea is to keep our Air Force busy in the South East, while they have their eye on the South West for the invasion.'[51]

Evacuees were a common topic amongst the Writers. Perhaps No. **4** at Barnstaple should have had the most to write given he was a clerk at the town council's Evacuation Office. However, it was only occasionally that Eric Gulliver wrote at length such as on 13 February 1941:

> 'Today I was glad to witness the arrival of the *final word* forms which should have arrived months ago. A summary of the activities preceding the printing of these forms will explain the position in which the local Evacuation office finds itself at the moment.
>
> Some weeks ago the Local Authorities heard that 300 children with accompanying helpers were to be sent from Bristol to Barnstaple. Within a week the requisite number of questionnaires, a copy of which has already been sent to you, had been prepared. The following week my fellow worker and myself were busily occupied with naming and addressing the questionnaires. The third week the replies were pouring in and our time was fully occupied with the assorting and classification of these replies. Last week, and this too till today, there has been nothing to do, because the post office has held us till this morning the late *Postage Due* replies to the questionnaires.
>
> Those 300 children and accompanying adults are coming next Wednesday, and within a week, those 200 forms have got to be filled up and sent round to the householders concerned. 100 satisfactory billets have been obtained from the replies to the questionnaire. Social Helpers sent to investigate and help in the preparation of the billet – and finally the meeting and the satisfactory billeting of the evacuees concerned.
>
> A lot of work for 4½ days but the Barnstaple evacuation office can and will do it.'

Mr Gulliver repeated four observations commonly made about evacuees: their reputation for poor hygiene, difficulties in obtaining food rations, resentment at their presence among local people and, yet somewhat curiously, disliking their sudden return to their London homes without any notice. It was commonplace to describe London children as dirty: No. **5** had heard that one host discovered her evacuee children were covered with lice. Tales were repeated: No. **1** heard that a Barnstaple woman discovered her bath was filled with coal and that the children used the back of their wardrobes as a toilet. A similar horror story was told in Crediton ('Recently a woman told her that she had complained to the woman who was with her that her child had made a mess on the carpet. *There!*, replied the evacuee mother, *and I told her always to go on the linoleum*.'). No. **8** reported evacuee rumours, stories and fears. Some local people, mostly women, also discussed means of avoiding having to host either children or adults and questioned how their food rations could stretch to cover extra people.

In some cases the difficulties were caused by mixing the social classes but there was also a clash between urban and rural people. No. **10**, an evacuee student in Bideford, neatly summarised this ('They are always complaining of the evacuees in the town, natural I suppose when their very uneventful normal life is so interrupted. They can't seem to get used to the Londoners who are entirely different in temperament.'). No. **13** also saw differences and concluded evacuee women were 'very much more attractive and human' than local women.

The evacuees came in waves; many thousands arrived in Devon in the first few days of the war. More came as bombing intensified in 1941 and new bombs in 1944 produced another great exodus from London to towns such as Ashburton (350), Barnstaple (75), Dawlish (1,140), Exeter (2,600), Newton Abbot (1,700), Paignton (850), Teignmouth (1,300) and Torquay (1,100). Other mothers and children followed them.[52] Writers from Torbay (**32**) and Newton Abbot (**27**) commented on what became a strained situation. Businesses which normally rented rooms to tourists found themselves obliged to house evacuees. There was also pressure on local transport and concern about supplies of food.

One Devon Writer (**59**) related second-hand stories of Londoners living in the Underground while another (**19**) reported Exeter women resented evacuees' purchases of local supplies of clothes. From Ringmore (**52**) came tales of the 'carrying on' of evacuee women. The most extensive report was written in the East Devon village of Sidford. Diana Murray Hill (**55**) described in detail the personal situations of evacuated women and children.

In 1942 an MO Writer living in West Drayton, Middlesex, relayed an unfortunate story of evacuees:

> 'We had a visitor today who is working in a big house in Devon where evacuated London County Council have been dumped. She outlined the following state of affairs.
>
> 1, There is a staff of 20 to 73 children.
>
> 2, The staff have all the best food. They have all the butter. The children have margarine. The children eat up the vegetables, the staff leave before having any fresh. The children have no fresh tea – it is all brewed for the staff and then drained off. 50 hens are kept but the children never see any of their eggs. The matron is able to send away large packets of food to her friends.
>
> 3, No inspector has ever visited the place.'[53]

Some Devonians also became evacuees and, in some instances, received criticism for their behaviour. In 1942 Adelaide Poole, an unmarried trained nurse living in Sussex, wrote in her diary:

> 'Have just heard of one of the cruellest treatments I have heard in a long time. A young relative with three children, the youngest four months, who lives in a country house where she has to carry every drop of drinking water from a pump in the village, invited a young girl to stay for a week or two because they had raids (Teignmouth) where she lived. After two weeks Mother arrived to fetch her home but said she had come to stay because she was on the verge of a nervous breakdown. (so was the young mother) She was invited for a week and stayed a month. Then, when they were to go home, the father (blind) wrote for them to stay on and he would join them. All the cooking in the house is done by the 72-year-old grandmother, who has a broken hip in which she wears a ten-pound brace. My relative did put her foot down then and the selfish woman, who should have seen it for herself, [said] that her mother was unable to do such a lot of cooking. So, after still another week they found another place. The woman said, however, she did not like the way the young girl was treated by the grandmother (after staying six weeks). But halfway through the visit the sailor husband arrived home on leave (he is on a minesweeper and had not seen his new baby until then). The young wife writes me that his leave [was] all spoilt by these people being around in the small house all the time. Even the neighbours said they ought to have cleared out when the sailor came home. And he may not have another leave for a year as the navy people do not get the many leaves given to the soldiers (when they are at home).'[54]

The migration of several hundred thousand people into communities across the length of Devon was the greatest in the county's history. Our Writers repeatedly reported some acceptance but they more loudly recorded many Devonians' resentment of and hostility towards evacuees and refugees who, while being largely White, British and Christian, also had cultural and class differences that were impossible to ignore or tolerate.

Civil defence

Seven months before the outbreak of war the *Sunday Graphic* ran a competition for its readers to name a new type of steel air raid shelter. Two hundred and forty-seven suggestions were sent including eleven from Devon. The *Ark* was submitted by four Devonians. Two women had similar thoughts: Mrs W. A. Cummins of Peverell near Plymouth regarded it as 'an up-to-date version of Noah's Ark' while it reminded Miss Bartlett of Exeter of 'the first shelter from storm and adversity'. The remaining reasons were different: Mr G. J. Taylor of Barnstaple suggested *Air Raid Kiosk* because 'all who enter are safe' and Mrs Burnell of Bampton thought safety was suggested by *Air Raid Kover*.

From Croyde Bay Mrs M. Bassett wrote offering *Arps*, an abbreviation of *Air Raid Protection Shelters* with the reasoning that, 'better an 'arp here below, than a harp above!'. Mrs M. Chidgey's suggestion was also unusual. Her reason for *LIsaFE* was 'that their purpose was to save as many lives as possible in time of war'. Miss Graeme of Torquay submitted *Cromwells*, 'because they are protectors', Mr Stanbridge of South Devon offered *Handy-Andies* 'firstly because they are handy and secondly because they were part of St John Ambulances scheme for ARP' and Mrs G. M. Denny of Sidmouth wrote that *Gunbrella* was appropriate 'in token of the prime minister and the present period'. Mrs E. M. Jones of Exeter had a novel entry: *Stealaways*, 'by reason they are made of steel and will be an ideal place to steal away if an air raid comes'. Likewise, *Heltershelter* was the unusual suggestion of Mrs Cuthbertson of Torquay 'because we will all run for such good protection'.[55]

Just as the evacuees arrived, life changed with the

23 'Blackout', the Coast Guard mascot that joined the invasion of France, June 1944.

24 Photograph entitled 'One of the RCAF's most popular shows, the Blackouts, revamped their entire show and presented the new version to homegoing air force personnel at the RCAF's Reparation Depot in Torquay', 6 August.

introduction of the blackout on 1 September 1939. The following day a Torquay policeman said there was 'room for improvement' in the public's adherence of regulations. Over the following five years hundreds of Devonians would be fined for breaking the law and dozens would die in accidents caused by the lack of light.[56] Thirteen Writers commented on living with blackout restrictions (**8-9**, **13**, **18**, **24-5**, **32-3**, **54-5**, **61**, **64**, **66**) and one (**8**) wrote of initial resistance. She also blamed 'stupid and slow-witted elderly' pedestrians for being responsible for their own deaths. The dim-out was introduced in September 1944 although not consistently. There were some local complaints recorded by the Ministry of Information in the closing weeks of 1944 ('If Lyme Regis, why not Sidmouth? Why should Totnes be dark when Bournemouth is lit?').[57] Restrictions were finally lifted on 30 April 1945.

British civil defence plans were prompted by the anticipation in the early 1930s of war with Germany and by the destruction caused by aerial bombardment in the Spanish Civil War. The appointment of wardens, the issuing of gas masks and the introduction of identity cards were other early manifestations of the war. One Torquay diarist (**64**) commented that local people anticipated air raids during the first few days of war and on 2 August 1940 Arthur Collins, a married thirty-eight-year-old clerk in Sheffield, expected Devon would be bombed. He wrote in his diary:

> 'We have been enjoying beautiful weather this week & had times been normal I should have been visiting Devon or Cornwall. I spent my best holiday ever in Devon last year & just managed to get it in before the war started. Before I went only kept thinking that war might come. I remember saying *We'll have a look at Devon before it gets bombed to bits* and then we were coming home we said *Thank you, Hitler for not starting before we had got our holidays in*. Two weeks later he did start & the holiday was pretty-well knocked-out of us. The problem now is, when is the next holiday to be and where is the necessary brass coming?'[58]

In Bideford a Writer (**10**) thought local people were 'nervy' about air raids despite the town not having had one and another diarist in Exeter (**19**) felt Exonians were more afraid of bombing than those in areas which had already been hit quite hard. At least two Writers dreamed of air attacks (**8-9**) and another (**4**) admitted that his parents' 'nerves' about bombing caused them to flee Beckenham for the safety of Barnstaple.

Writers noted bombs falling in Plymouth, Sidmouth and Torbay (**37, 48, 32**) and one in Plymouth (**39**) commented upon the impact on his daily life. This Conscientious Objector served as a warden and had mixed attitudes towards the disruption caused while teaching and debated with his wife over whether to stay in bed during alarms. Likewise, Muriel Friend (**59**) chronicled the alarms and sounds of planes, bombs and air defences from her home near the mouth of the Dart. In contrast, a seventeen-year-old working in Plymouth (**50**) casually noted that each morning his first task at work was to retrieve his typewriter from storage in a shelter.

Sirens, mock exercises and the building of private and public shelters had preceded the first bombings in Devon during the summer of 1940. Some two thousand civilians lost their lives in Devon during the war; this was approximately 2.9% of the 70,000 or so who died across Britain in air attacks. Devon's diarists noted local air raids in the two most devastated places, Plymouth and Exeter. The description of Writer **52** seeing Plymouth for the first time since the start of war is extraordinary. The majority of Devon's towns had at least one air raid and a surprising number of villages were also attacked. Even the hotel at Burgh Island in Bigbury was bombed.[59] No Devon Writer mentioned the two most harrowing attacks, those at Aveton Giffard on 26 January 1943, in which nearly every house in the village was damaged, and at St Marychurch on 30 May 1943 in which twenty-one children died.

A characteristic of the bombing was the unevenness of the attacks. At the start of 1941 an MO Writer living in Scotland wrote 'Letters replying to our Christmas greetings are coming in now. News from Exeter (*get many alerts but not raids*), Southampton (*like hell let loose*), Isle of Wight (*terrible*), Plymouth (*some raids but quite bearable*).' She was yet to know that Plymouth would suffer most in 1941 and Exeter in 1942. The situation would remain fluid through to 1944.[60]

From 1940 to 1944 Devon suffered warfare within its boundaries for the first time since the Civil War three hundred years earlier. Moreover, the bombing was of a greater duration and higher density than at any point in its history. Our Writers recorded anxiety and depression amongst portions of the public and the effect bombing had on general morale. It is notable, in comparison with today, that there was a lack of public discussion on addressing the consequential effects on the public's mental health, in particular that on children.

Rationing

The sale of many consumer items, including petrol, was restricted. Food was rationed from 1940: bacon, butter, cheese, meat and sugar were available through coupons while biscuits, cereals, dried goods and tinned goods were given on a points system. Other food supplies, such as fruit and vegetables, were also often in short supply. However, Writers commented on the availability of sweets in Barnstaple, cakes in Lynmouth, oranges in Lynton, vegetables in Plymouth and biscuits in Stoke Fleming.

Clothes were rationed from 1941. Muriel Friend admitted to wearing one woollen vest for up to three weeks before changing it. She seems to have considered herself unconventional but was aware of social conventions:

> 'I leave off my silk knickers in the summer, wearing a long silk vest under a cotton frock, or I have done without even that. It saves wear and tear on clothes and I am always in and out of a bathing costume in the afternoons. I could not wear so little in more *civilised* conditions.'

***25** Photograph for an American audience entitled 'A British suburban housewife surrenders coupons for her supply of bacon. Consumers may purchase no more than four ounces of bacon per week and not more than twenty-three cents worth of other meats', 1944.*

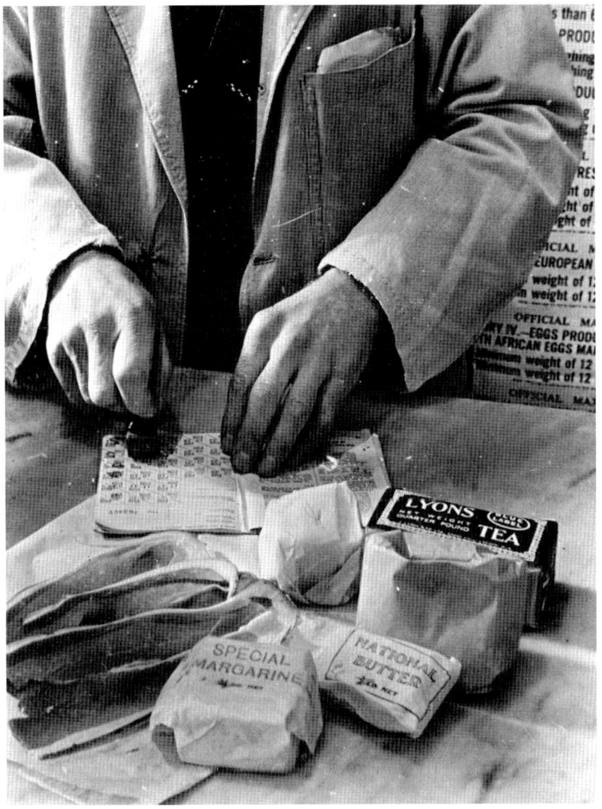

26 Photograph intended for an American audience entitled 'A shopkeeper cancels the coupons in a British housewife's ration book for the tea, sugar, cooking fats and bacon she is allowed for one week. Most foods in Britain are rationed and some brand names are given the designation National', 1943.

Another middle-aged woman (**21**), living in Exeter, acknowledged rationing had forced her to wear clothes for longer and that she was more likely to mend them. 'Even then', she added, 'they are usually not thrown away. For instance, a petticoat too worn to be wearable, provides enough stuff for a baby's dress and a much-mended coat made a skirt and jacket for a small girl. On the whole, I dress in a very similar manner and in similar colours as before and change clothes as usual. I have given up wearing hats except on formal occasions.'

In Bideford a twenty-nine-year-old (**8**) divulged she spent considerable time choosing her clothes partly because she was 'short and plump'. Miss Brown dressed for two different reasons: 'I like to look as pretty as possible in order to be appreciated by men and so as not to be thought dowdy by other women.' She believed nearly all men her age preferred women to wear make-up.

In contrast, a middle-aged and married woman had different thoughts. (**13**) She was fearful of dressing too young for her age ('I'm afraid of looking like *mutton dressed as lamb*.'). She wore stockings because it was expected of her, did not wear shorts because it was presumed she would not and wore make-up surreptitiously because her peers disapproved.

An eighteen-year-old student (**64**) outlined generational preferences:

> 'On clothes, my parents like the old-fashioned vests while I like the newer lighter kind. Also, they have a different taste in cut and colour, liking navy, blue and brown while I stick to grey. Liking me to wear a raincoat while I like a light summer coat. In shoes we like the same type but go to different shops. They use True Form while I like Russell & Bromleys.'

A thirty-eight-year-old disclosed he had different tastes from his seventy-seven-year-old father:

> 'I have never had the concern for clothes that my father had. Hats I have not worn since I lived in a village and could please myself. I imagine this disregard for appearances to be general. I wear an absolute minimum, shorts in summer and by the time I have finished with clothes, a tramp would reject them. I never remember seeing my father in a suit even slightly *shabby*. He thinks a gentleman should look smart. If I go shopping in the nearest town I generally change into a less forlorn pair of bags and a coat instead of the usual pull-over. Evening dress I hate.'

His views were more conventional than those of a near contemporary in Paignton. This thirty-seven-year-old did not own a suit and had last purchased one in 1933. Moreover:

> 'I have fads or I would have if I had any money. I should prefer to wear only cotton, no animal matter and for boots good vegetable products. However, this kind of thing needs a lot of cash. My reasons are partly emotional. I can't bear any form of parasitism and man's dependence on animals I consider loathsome (am vegetarian in diet, no animal products, again very hard for a person without much money), partly for health considerations, since I don't see how anyone can be healthy while wearing or eating animal stuff. Also, since unearthing the various womb-fantasies in myself, I dislike animal clothes further. [Gustav] Jäeger, the man who started one branch of woollens, by the way, was a paranoic with fantasies about the necessity for animal stinks to protect one. That's enough about fads.

I dislike fashions in either men's or women's clothes. Style is a matter of personal taste and non-distortion of the body is another matter. About 99% of fashion however consists of distortion and is thus lunatic in various ways and so I dislike it, as I imagine any sane person would.'

Morality and sexual behaviour

MO was interested to learn how the war influenced morals. A Sussex Writer mentioned hearing from her cousin who was 'an attractive woman of 28 working in rural Devon'. This relation had written 'that she is glad to help with entertainments and dances for troops but is very sick of the way so many expect her to wish to end the evening. She finds a good stout pair of leather gloves, with which to push them away, useful. As she is tall and, undoubtedly, [she] knows her own mind, one wonders how younger and fluffy ones get on'.[61] From Dawlish a new resident wrote about younger people:

'Down here I get the impression that they are enjoying the opportunity to earn money by jobbing and delivery which was formerly done by their elder brothers or fathers. As for their morals, I don't think they are any worse than they would have been before the war or at any time had the morals of the opposite sex been as lax as they are today. I suppose I've got old-fashioned ideas through being in *exile* for so long but I always look upon a female who sneaks a cigarette in the street in the same way that I would regard one of her sex who advertised her profession by the copious use of lipstick. The fact that they are possibly honorary members of that profession makes it the more reprehensible in my eyes!'[62]

Sex and morality were discussed, sometimes frankly, by nine other Writers. For instance, a sixteen-year-old (**6**) believed that the aim of any soldier on a night out was straightforward: they wanted alcohol and sex. Some views were very individualistic including those of a sixty-nine-year-old visitor (**68**) who gave his thoughts on the prevalence of lesbianism amongst Roman Catholic nuns; he made an unusual assessment of the viability of artificial male and female sex organs. Another elderly man (**32**) believed women had babies in order to avoid munitions work and disapproved of sexual relations outside marriage. He also wrote that 'the war seems to be responsible for a great increase in immorality and this probably is largely due to young women having been seduced while under the influence of intoxicants. Apart from the war, the relations between the sexes seemed to have improved very much, there being much more artless, simple and natural relations'.[63]

Two Writers discussed generational differences in morality. One (**15**) was unsure if his or the younger generation had achieved a better 'sense of real clean-living and thinking'. He acknowledged his generation had been ignorant about sex and that their means of obtaining information had been furtive. In contrast, another (**27**) felt standards had fallen because of the 'repressed' state to which sex had been relegated. He believed the Victorians had made sex synonymous with sin and that their myths had been exposed by two world wars. In effect, he felt the decline in sexual morality was behaviour returning to its natural state.

A couple (**66-7**) were the most open of all the Writers about their sex lives. The woman reported that hers was 'much happier and freer', was not interested in those of other people and believed such matters should remain private. Her husband wrote nearly two thousand words about sex. He regarded his views as progressive and revealed that he considered religious attitudes towards sex restrictive, believed in sex education, supported sex outside marriage and defended homosexuality. He also discussed extra-marital affairs, prostitution, wartime sexual changes, self-gratification and the prevalence of sex in most conversations. Curiously, he saw a difference between sex indulged in by his generation compared with that experienced by men only three years younger. Also of interest are his assessments of other men and their conversations about sex.

No Devon MO Writer admitted to engaging in sexual relations with a member of the same sex. It would have been imprudent for a male given men were imprisoned for homosexuality until 1967. National MO Writers occasionally referenced gay men through disparate terms such as pansy, sodomite and effeminate but in respect to women they were more likely to deploy the single term, lesbian.[64] However, their comments indicate they were more familiar with same sex relations between men than between women. An MO Writer, a married forty-year-old rubber technologist from Sutton Coldfield, highlighted general ignorance when he recounted to his friends his favourite article of 1942 which had appeared in *The New Statesman*:

'Somewhere hidden from the public eye one may find a large room full of elderly ladies, getting an obvious kick out of reading in a large variety of languages the private letters of other people. This is a branch of censorship.

> One day - this is a true story - the colonel, to whom these ladies report, asked if any one there had found anything of importance. *Well*, said one of the censors, *I have here one letter which I am afraid I don't really understand. I think it must be written by a Lesbian. Really*, said the colonel, *that is very interesting. Is there any lady among you who reads Lesbian?*'

This MO Writer's friends revealed their ignorance about lesbianism: fewer than ten per cent of them understood what the term meant.[65] They may have been more familiar with the *Lesbian*, a Liverpool steamer of that name which was interned in 1940 by the Vichy government. Lesbianism was discussed by a small number of MO Writers including most notably by a male London civil defence worker in 1942 ('If lesbianism is described as a perversion, it seems definitely on the increase in certain quarters notably Mayfair, Bloomsbury and Chelsea. Many people think it's normal.' and 'Recent rumours point to lesbian love being much on the increase not only in the women's forces and on civil defence stations but also amongst married women whose husbands have been called up. It is suggested that numbers of decent girls have been initiated into these practices by refugees especially in districts like Bloomsbury.'). He also asserted that Leslie was the 'polite term' for a lesbian.[66]

While in general there appears to have been considerable differences in familiarity between MO Writers, on the other hand one of them even disclosed a limerick:

> 'A lesbian dame of Khartoum
> Took a nancy-boy up to her room,
> As she put out the light
> She said *Let's get this right.*
> *Who does what, and with which, and to whom?*'[67]

Irrespective of this range in the public's understanding, from an examination of the life histories of the Devon Writers it can be surmised that among them was one gay man and several lesbians (or 'lesbian-like').[68]

Only one Devon Writer (**13**) mentioned paedophilia. With any sensitive subject it is a matter of conjecture as to how much diarists in general left unwritten. Nevertheless, there can be indications as to character in the texts. In 1944 a Newton Abbot serviceman outlined his ideas and hopes for post-war Britain. He revealed extreme opinions on women including banning their smoking cigarettes in the street, setting an age limit for the sale of face powders and lipstick, requiring a mandatory length for skirts and restricting work to within the home. He also believed all married men and women should be tattooed on their arms. Perhaps it is not surprising that two years later this solider served six months' imprisonment for the indecent assault of two girls and in 1968 was convicted of indecent exposure.[69]

Services

The war moved thousands of men and women in military service across Devon as in the rest of Britain. Writer **8** noticed how prevalent military uniforms were in Plymouth in 1939 and many others in this collection observed servicemen in their villages and towns. In 1943 a Devon soldier found himself reacquainted with a London teacher who had previously been evacuated to his home. This Wiltshire MO Writer recorded on 1 January that he had a soldier billeted with him:

> 'He sat near my cousin who is 28 and a schoolteacher. Suddenly my cousin (a she!) said *Haven't I seen you somewhere before? Where do you come from?* From the reply, she discovered that she had stayed at this chap's parent's farm in Devon when her school was evacuated from London, and of course was in the house with this chap! Strange to relate, my mother looked up her address book and there was this soldier's home address, to which, of course, she had written letters to my cousin.'[70]

Some MO Writers were serving in the armed forces and described their experiences of Devon such as 'GH' in 1941 who travelled by train:

> 'Reach Plymouth about eight o'clock. I looked closely for the great sign *Prepare to meet thy God* that used to stand in field [a] few miles from Plymouth and on which have commented in M-O reports and didn't see it, so presumably it's been removed at last. Unload kit bags and hammocks which have found their way onto this train (sent to London from Skegness, I suppose, and put on 1.30 at Paddington) and then crowd into R.N. lorry and reach HMS Drake (ie Royal Naval Barracks, Devonport) about 15 minutes later. My God! I can imagine nothing more like a great prison than these barracks. I'm glad I'm only staying here one night – we commission candidates are going on to HMS Raleigh tomorrow. Then we have supper. Supper! Cold salt dumplings and stewed gristle. The convicts at Dartmoor, not so far away, can't have worse food than this.'[71]

Many servicemen were foreign-born. A Kew MO Writer

reported a conversation he had on 25 August 1944:

> 'Dr F came up from Devon today – I haven't seen him for ages and we had lots to talk about. What most interested me were his stories about the American invasion of his part of the world. A niece of a great friend of his works in the Land Army on a farm some distance away from the village where they live. She'd been working late one evening and it was just getting dusk when she was walking home, feeling rather tired. A little way along a jeep caught up with her and a voice asked her if she'd like a lift. She felt a bit doubtful but her feet decided her and she got in, only to find herself at close quarters with an outsized black man. However, she crossed her fingers and hoped for the best. When they arrived at her house, the Negro asked her if her father would still be up and if he might go in and see him. Naturally she was surprised, but as he was so polite she took him in. He introduced himself to her father and said he just wanted to warn him that he mustn't let his daughter go taking lifts from White Americans – *they're no good*. Dr F tells me they've had the Negroes in their village for ages and they began by making them welcome even to the extent of having a weekly dance and providing hostesses from the local girls. These dances have been a complete success and there has never been one incident to make them regret their attitude. Far from it – the girls love dancing with the Negroes because of course they're so good at it. There were other stories of the Negroes intervening when the whites were making a nuisance of themselves with women.'[72]

Another unusual comment was made the year before by a Writer living near Bristol who had a letter from a friend in South Devon who had written '(if greeted) I should say *Good Morning* to a coloured American. After all, they are fighting for us and some are as well-educated as any of us – better'.[73]

American servicemen preparing for the invasion of France were noted by Writers on both coasts of Devon (**32**, **59**, **70**). Dennis Argent, a twenty-seven-year-old wireless operator and clerk in the Royal Corps of Signals, recorded a letter he received from a WAAF in Devon written on 15 June 1944:

> 'You wrote on D-Day, a day long waited for – a time to rejoice? I might have thought so had I never met any Yanks and Eddie in particular. As you know, circumstances prevented us getting in touch with each other after our broken date on the Saturday and I lived day-by-day in the hope that the ban would be lifted. Instead, we were confined to camp. On the Tuesday our telephone was cut off. He went out that night and his plane was one of two which failed to return. Here on camp the tension that day was terrific. To help the morale we got up an impromptu dance and it was a grand success, everyone came, and everyone let themselves go, though at the time it seemed a forced kind of gaiety – too gay. Our watch was on a 29 [29 hours off duty] which made CC [Confined to Camp] doubly hard. I remember after getting into bed quite late, hearing the planes going out – that wasn't unusual of course, but somehow something was different – it was like the lull before a storm. The hut was restless, everybody tossed and turned but when we did sleep, we woke late. It must have been 10am and then of course we knew.'[74]

***27** Poster designed to aid American servicemen in identifying English soldiers, 1942.*

Amongst the Devon Writers were women who joined the Women's Auxiliary Air Force (**8**) and the Land Army

28 Children watching D-Day preparations at Blackpool Sands near Dartmouth.

(**9, 57**). In 1941 Gladys Lasky (1922-1988), a London-born nineteen-year-old single residential nursery school probationer, filled in a questionnaire about her thoughts on war service. She was then living at Knowstone Manor near South Molton which she referred to as a Quaker hostel. She also described herself as a Jewish Quaker who had feminist leanings but disregarded a question as to whether she was high or low brow ('There is no such thing, it's a matter of education'). She recognised that the war had changed her ('I am getting less of a pacifist'). Miss Lasky had worked as a clerk at the start of the war but wanted to progress to theatre design ('it satisfies me most') when hostilities ceased. She had initially preferred either the WAAF or WRNS and was not interested in the ATS. Her 'feelings change with each new ATS girl I meet'. Miss Lasky felt the ATS advertisements were 'attractive girls' who 'usually look as though they've had good pre-ATS salaries, with their permed hair and expensively-groomed faces'. Her response on her interests ('art, music, ballet dancing, theatre') augured her subsequent career in America in the teaching of ballet.[75]

MO's Writers show how life in 1937 and 1938 became tinged with the prospect of a second world war. Subsequent wartime accounts illustrate how life was tested by the first widescale warfare being fought on British soil since the 1640s. By then, memories of the Civil War had long faded and the country was mentally unprepared for aerial bombardment. Air raids would kill two thousand Devonians, dislocate many thousands more and the misery of war would strike the most remote villages. The following accounts show how war tried a generation.

Each of these Writers discussed life discoloured by German aggression and ambitions: the daily existence of the wartime generation was dominated by the war. These Writers were keen to record their lives and thoughts and they displayed an earnestness in putting down historical markers. They share an apparent candour, honesty and frankness. The majority of their texts illuminate both the extraordinary and the everyday that defined life in Devon.

Acknowledgements

This project is ambitious and I have incurred many debts. First of all, I would like to thank the trustees of Mass Observation through Curtis Brown for permission to reproduce the texts. I am also grateful to the staffs of the Devon Heritage Centre, Plymouth Archives and the University of Sussex Special Collections at The Keep, in particular Jessica Scantlebury of Mass Observation, for their assistance. Many Writers' family members, friends and acquaintances have shared their knowledge, memories and photographs. I would like to particularly thank Jenepher Allen, Guy Barker, Peter Barr, Kate Beckett, Esther Floud, John Frone, Iain George, Janet Hall, Kath Hasler, Stella Loterijman, Tabitha Lucas, Anne Miller, Mary Mitchison, Prof. Tim Mitchison, Janine Monaghan, Steffi Philpotts, Judith Taylor, Roger Winter and Chris Wollacott. I am grateful to Elly Babbedge, Dr Helen Bradley, Sue Jackson and Dr Andrew Thrush for their help with the text. I would also like to thank Clare Anning and Laura Rowe (Badminton School), James Bellchambers, Amelia Brooks (Brambletye School), Prof. Anne Cranny-Francis, Tamerlaine Gambie (Newton & Noss Parish Council), Bill Hardiman, Robin Hogg, Richard Lee (W. H. Tildesley Ltd), Emily Morley-Fletcher (Pinewood School), Patricia Malcolmson, Prof. Robert Malcolmson, Barry Morris, Terry Potter, Andy Salmon, Sue Taylor (Stoke Fleming Library), Chris Walpole, Sasha Walton-Jackman (Yealmpton Parish Council) and Karen Wilson (Tedburn History & Information Society). Finally, I would like to acknowledge Keith Stevens for his continuing support and encouragement.

Abbreviations

ARP	Air Raid Precautions
ATC	Air Training Corps
ATS	Auxiliary Territorial Service
CO	Conscientious Objector
FANY	First Aid Nursing Yeomanry
GHQ	General Headquarters
GOM	Grand Old Man
LCT	Landing Craft Transport
LDV	Local Defence Volunteers
MO	Mass Observation
NAAFI	Navy, Army and Air Force Institutes
RAF	Royal Air Force
VAD	Voluntary Aid Detachment
WAAF	Women's Auxiliary Airforce

Note

Quotations have been transcribed in full with an ellipsis used to indicate an omission of words. Some titles given to Writers, notably Actress, Clerk, Housewife, Secretary and Typist, are taken from self-descriptions. Some others, such as Land Girl, have been supplied.

THE WRITERS

ABBOTSKERSWELL (& NEWTON ABBOT, PAIGNTON & GALMPTON)

The largely rural parish of Abbotskerswell, situated on the main road from Newton Abbot to Torquay, had a population in 1931 of some six hundred and forty-two people. The village's MO Writer (1) may have been familiar with Charles Powell Phillips, a neighbour who contributed to the project two years later. Neither mentioned any apprehensions about the impending conflict with Germany. During the war shallow trenches were dug near the village school to provide protection from air raids and some seventy Londoners were evacuated to the village.[76]

1. Max Powling, Clerk, 1937

Essex-born Maximilian Smith Powling (1915-1989) lived with his parents and sister at Aller House on the main road from Newton Abbot to Kingskerswell. He worked as a surveyor for Newton Abbot Rural District Council and his father was the owner of the Devon Hide, Skin and Manure Company which had a factory at Aller Mills, nearly adjoining the family home. Twenty-two-year-old Powling recorded three day-surveys in 1937.[77]

24 August 1937

Of his first survey, written on 24 August, Mr Powling admitted he had a 'fierce determination' to send a very full account. Part of it was written during work hours when 'I was left practically to my own devices and could do exactly what I myself wanted to do and not what a weak and peevish devil called Gray wanted me to do'. He had three overriding thoughts that day: first, a song he heard on the radio kept coming into his thoughts, second, he resented being unable to enjoy the good weather and third, he was surprised MO expected so much from 'a new observer'. In respect to the weather, he made the only reference to a girlfriend. On this day:

'I was working in the office all day long; owing to holiday time we are short-handed and, although I had very little to do in the office, there was even less doing outside, as work does, in the most peculiar fashion, fall away abruptly during August in September. Although I am not invariably in the office, I do a great deal of what is done, so that the day was, in the main, a normal one, except that I had less to do, or found less to do, than is usually the case.

My health was just normal. I was not bubbling over with *joie de vivre* but nevertheless I was feeling fit and well. The weather was glorious all day, in an office not too hot, and with hardly a cloud in the sky. Early on there had been a very heavy mist and as the day progressed this promise was amply fulfilled.

I very rarely dream and I had not done so that night.

I live in a fair-sized house in the country, two miles away from the town of Newton Abbot, which has a population of 20,000 people. A main road is 250 yards away and four miles to the south lies Torquay. Aller itself is a tiny hamlet consisting of half a dozen houses, a farm house and an old mill. There are fields on all sides and beyond the main road, a densely wooded hill rising at the rear of which is an open moorland. A mile up the valley in the direction of Torquay lies the village of Kingskerswell. It is largely residential and has a population of perhaps 2,000.

Near the house is our old mill, complete with stream and water wheel. About a dozen men are employed. The house has a large garden in front of it and a vegetable garden further up the lane. The former has a small stream running through it, with about two dozen fruit trees and two rather small pieces of lawn. The whole thing is well-protected from the road by high walls and trees but is itself very open and sunny.

I am an Assistant in the Surveyor's and Housing Inspector's office of the Newton Abbot Rural District Council. We all work in a new block of offices recently erected at a cost of £8,000 and our furniture and fittings are very modern and efficient. I share an office with another Assistant nearly 10 years older than I am and a drawing office with another age 24.

A considerable number of people are employed in clay mining and in the Great Western Railway sheds. Moreover, Newton Abbot is an important market town and a large section of its population is of the residential type.

I woke up fairly early, sixish, and as I didn't feel like going to sleep again, I lay in my tent listening to the sounds around me, all very subdued and distant; they were all so wholly familiar that if I hadn't previously determined to listen, I should have been oblivious of them and would have sworn that the morning was as silent as the dead of night.

First of all, there were the birds; a robin near me was uttering its peculiar, jagged, metallic twitter and further off, a starling was squeaking excitedly. Now and again there came the soothing coo of pigeons and the unmistakable cry of a moorhen from the stream; as a faint and distant background there was the monotonous, undistinguished, chirping of sparrows. I didn't hear a single thrush or blackbird singing but once there was the sound of a thrush energetically hammering a snail upon a stone. Far away there was the sound of ducks and geese and once the barking of a dog.

A heavy mist hung over everything, giving promise of another scorching day and as I looked in vain for the sun, I began to wonder what the time was: Father had gone away to Cornwall and so I couldn't just sleep on until he came and called me.

I had slept all the night on my right-hand side, as usual, and when I woke, I had turned over onto my left-side for ten minutes, then on my back and thence back onto my right-hand side again. This I repeated fitfully for nearly an hour and then at last I heard my mother's voice faintly from the house and I decided that it was time to get up. But still I couldn't make the necessary effort until I had recourse to a childish trick of counting slowly from one up to the year of my age, now twenty-two, and then at last, I sat up and began dressing. When I had pulled on most of my clothes, I went down to the house and found that the time was fifteen minutes to eight by the clock, but that, as usual, meant very little, as the clock might be anything from two to twenty minutes fast.

Soon I went upstairs to the bathroom and began washing. There was a whole cistern full of hot water but I didn't feel energetic enough to have a bath just then, so I contented myself with washing my face and hands. I always use Cuticura soap and while my face was still wet, I picked up a shaving brush, made a lather with the Cuticura and shaved with an Ever-Ready razor. The actual job of shaving took less than three minutes.

Next, I went downstairs for breakfast, and, wanting to know the time, switched on Radio Normandy while I started eating. The programme was far better than usual, with no advertising, and the records they played were light and tuneful jingles ideally suited for breakfast time music. *Poor Little Angeline* is the best example of this sort of thing I can think of. For the second time within a week I heard a tune new to me called *Zarena* by Ganne and it stuck in my memory throughout the rest of the day.

I am not musical but I really should like to know more about this tune. Is it new or, if old, why resurrected? If resurrected, by whom? Do the announcers choose records themselves when a programme is not sponsored by an advertiser?

Breakfast usually consists of a grapefruit without any sugar, bacon and eggs and sometimes fried tomatoes, tea, brown bread with marmalade. The only variety lies in taking this menu and changing the order of everything and rarely wading through things in their logical order.

At 8.25 I finished breakfast and switched off the wireless in the middle of a tune; we had had no time signal but I had managed to remember just how fast the clock was the night before, and anyway, the time didn't matter so very much as all that.

I walked out into the garden and found that the mist was still in possession. By chance I dipped my fingers into the small ticket pocket just inside my jacket and found there a message I had been given on the previous Saturday morning and which I had completely forgotten. It was quite unimportant but it reminded me that I have two memories: I am usually so wrapped up in my own thoughts that people tell me things and if I think that the message is unimportant, I only too often forget all about it. If, however, I come to the surface and think *I must remember this*, I concentrate on it for a moment and I remember it for months.

At 8.40 I went into the house again, put on a collar and tie, cleaned my teeth, buttered the brown bread I was taking with me as part of my dinner and finally left home at 8.45 to walk along the main road to Newton Abbot. The sun was now shining in a clear sky and as I went, I made a few notes about the morning to date.

After I had walked about a mile, and the time was just after 9am, I was picked up by Mr Rice, one of our rate collectors. Mr Rice is a special constable and is attending a course of lectures on anti-gas precautions and they had been a practical demonstration the night before when they all had worn their respirators in a room filled with poison gas, and by taking the merest whiff, they had to identify each gas. The time before a whiff of bromide, which is now apparently out of fashion, had given him a headache which lasted 36 hours. He was not therefore looking forward to tear gas, mustard gas, and Lewisite when he had given me a lift home the previous evening.

He began cheerfully: *Nothing in tear gas, my boy, nothing at all.* And he went on to tell me all about the night before. Phrases which stuck in my memory were *Mustard Gas, the king of all gases; Lewisite its first cousin; The new respirators – marvelous things, marvelous, got every confidence in 'em, every confidence. I've used the old ones in the war and I know.* Throughout this I ask occasional questions and make sympathetic noises, all of which passes as *good listening*.

We arrived at the office soon after ten minutes past nine and I open the half dozen letters for our department and find that there is nothing important or exciting in them so I sit down and begin writing up the day to date. No one of any importance comes in until 9.45am which leaves me half an hour to get started but three or four people drop in one after another and I have to talk to them and answer their questions as well as write my report. The only important caller was [Zennith] Webber, red-headed, good-natured, my own age, who is a pupil in the department.

Webber begins *Do you want to earn some money*? I never like the sound of this; it spells work and you never see the money or it isn't half enough.

I hedged. *I had the same offer yesterday, helping the farmer opposite us to thresh his wheat. I didn't accept.*

He laughed and explained that two horses were absolute certs – a friend of his had had it from a professional firm of tipsters; Ipsden today and Kept On tomorrow. He hadn't the faintest idea where or when they were running but he was definitely doing them. The idea was so novel to me (the only bet I have ever had in my life was on the Derby of four years ago), and I like the names of the horses so gave him 2 shillings with my blessing.

As he went out, I heard Beer, one of my friends, talking to a builder's son in the corridor outside.

B.S. … *Cox's outing last Saturday.*
Beer *Teetotal, I suppose?*
B.S. *Like Hell it was.*

At about 10 o'clock in walked Mr [Arthur] Gray, the head of our department. I smiled cheerfully and said *Good Morning*. No reply and no smile, it was just as if he hadn't seen me or heard me. I think disgustedly, *You miserable bastard.*

Soon he begins asking me about a parcel he had brought in just before his holiday. *Did you post it?*

If you asked me to post it, then I certainly posted it, but I don't remember anything about it. This sort of reply invariably ruffles him. He runs on about the parcel not having reached its destination, insinuating that it was all my fault and that it was causing him a world of trouble, while I gradually remember seeing it lying about for a few hours and just when I was going to ask if he wanted it posted, it disappeared and I forgot all about it.

He starts again, adopting different tactics. *I distinctly remember telling you to post it.* Of course, he had never said anything of the kind and he knows that as well as I do, but it is a difficult charge to answer for if you reply confidently *You did nothing of the sort*, it implies that you remember the whole incident and everything concerning it and only a moment before you have been saying that you know nothing at all about it. The only reply is a confident denial and a counter attack, thus *I'm quite sure you didn't Mr Gray*, and here a shot in the dark which is probably the truth, *in fact, I distinctly remember you taking it away yourself and posting it.*

As a general rule this counter is as unfair and ungrounded as his first attack, but it does most definitely take the wind out of his sails and frustrates his little attempt to put the blame for his own mistakes on me.

He then sat down and dictated a skeleton outline of four letters that he wanted me to type and promptly disappeared. These letters, callers, the phone and the blue sky kept me busy until twelve, when Gray returned, now in a more reasonable frame of mind; after pottering around in his amiable way and trying to find something to pick fault in, and failing, he finally left at 12.15pm and I didn't see him for the rest of the day.

I tidied up, washed and at 12.20pm sat down to write some more of my report. At 12.55 Reeve, another assistant, asked me to help him with some typing, but we abandoned this at 1 o'clock.

Outside it was still a glorious day and I sat in the shade and ate my dinner, the brown bread and butter, plus three bananas and two oranges. I finished these at 1.25, washed myself and at 1.30 sat down again with my report and carried on until 1.55, when Reeve returned and we worked until 3.05pm. From 3.05 until 3.20 I wrote my report, by when I had caught up with myself and then I began typing it.

I am not an expert typer, and for any work which I wish to be careful with, I fall back upon five fingers. When the work is not so important, as for specifications, I give myself practice with all the fingers, but I am not as fast or as safe with them all as with the four or five. Towards the end I began making mistakes, but by 5.40 I had finished.

At 5.45pm I left the office and did some shopping for my mother, picked up my bicycle from the cycle-shop and rode home. I found that my father had returned from Cornwall and I began asking him questions about his trip and how he had got on: the ground was almost burnt up and it was impossible to do anything with it; orders were few and far between. Cornwall, however, was simply alive with visitors and Father saw more fast and dangerous driving than anywhere else in his life.

At 6.30 I had dinner – cold mutton, lettuce, tomatoes and potatoes boiled with milk and butter, with stewed apples and custard as dessert. Unfortunately the apples were in the initial stages of *turning* and I left them severely alone.

At 7pm I finished dinner and had a final glance through the *News Chronicle;* the only things that had interested me were the reports on Yorkshire's and Middlesex's cricket matches and a column conducted by Dogberry. Not so many months ago I used to read the paper through from beginning to end, but this practice is one that has dropped right out of life. The same is true of my reading. Up to the end of 1936 I used to read as many as three or four books a week and now I read them at the rate of one a month. With what am I replacing all this? Mass Observation, I hope.

Until 7.20 I walked around the buildings to see what work had been done in the factory amongst the waste paper and reading an old copy of the *Auto Car*. I then came in and collected writing materials, found a deckchair and went up to the upper part of the garden which was catching the evening sun and began writing.

29 *Ipsden, ridden by Sam Wragg (1909-1983), won the Nunthorpe Sweepstakes at York on 24 August 1937.*

At 7.40 I went into the house to listen to the sports news and particularly to hear how Ipsden had fared. Ipsden, I had read, was one of our best sprinters but unfortunately up against nearly all the rest of our good sprinters. The race was the Nunthorpe Stakes at York and I felt rather pleased to think that for the first time in my life I wanted to know what had won the 3.35.

Middlesex won, fine. Yorkshire could only draw, better still. And miracle of miracles, Ipsden won. The announcer had only just given out the name of the third horse, when Dad said *Well, turn that rubbish off, we don't want to listen to that.*

Neither my mother or my father worry very much about

any of my activities or opinions but if they knew that I had a shilling on a horse, I believe that they would pass a sleepless night. While I was in the house only the merest gleam in my eyes betrayed my amusement but when I got outside, I found myself throwing stones around and grinning all over my face. Beginner's luck? Well hardly that. I haven't the slightest intention of even beginning.

At 8.15 I was out in the garden again answering the remainder of the questions on the day-survey and this occupied me until 8.50pm when it was too late and too dark to stay out any longer and so I packed up and went in.

As I was still feeling rather energetic, I decided to take the dog for a walk and so I wandered off down the country lanes with the terrier for perhaps three quarters of a mile and then slowly returned. Quite half a dozen cars passed me and the memory of one of them and its number stayed with me very easily - a Hillman Minx BAC 79. The BAC means to me the British Automatic Company and 79 used to be our old telephone number.

I always think that the twilight evenings of August and September are one of the best parts of our year and I believe that I could walk for hours through the night when I might stir a foot all day. It doesn't therefore need much of an excuse to get me out on an evening like this and taking a dog for a run is as good as any I know.

I returned at 9.35 and found someone talking about scrambled eggs and ten minutes later I was sitting down to the finest supper I know, brown bread and butter and a large helping of hot scrambled eggs.

At 9.55 I cleaned my teeth with Kolynos and a Halex No. 7 (I have to get a new one every few weeks) and went off up the garden to my tent and was asleep within ten minutes of leaving the house.'

12 September 1937

Mr Powling's carried out his second survey on 12 September. It was preceded by a note that 'The day was typical of a Sunday in the summer months. I was feeling just a little tired from my unaccustomed exertions of the preceding week but apart from that I was in normal health. The weather was exceptional…'

He recorded:

'I was sleeping in the house that night and awoke at roughly 5 o'clock; found it bitterly cold, while outside there was a slight mist and a cock crowing. I pulled an eiderdown over myself and went to sleep again immediately.

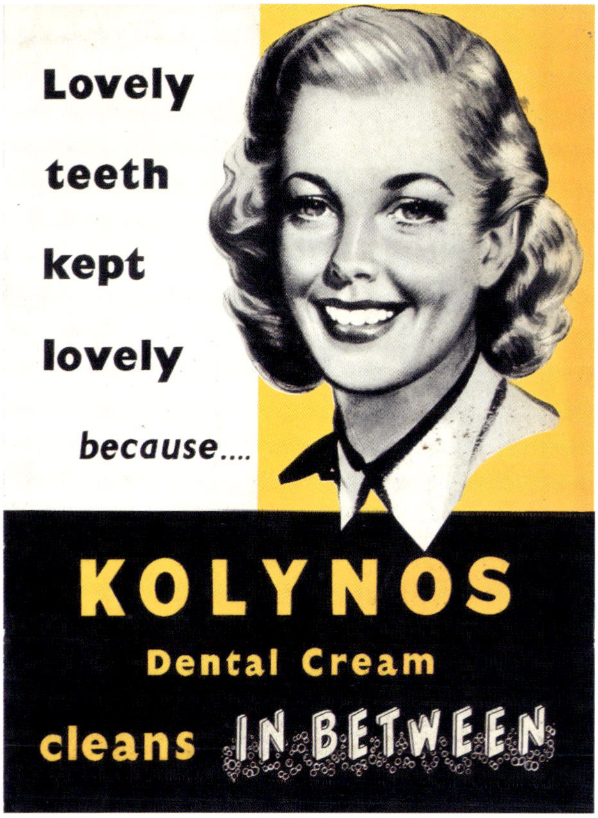

30 *Display board for Kolynos, the toothpaste created in the early 1900s. The Greek name was originally advertised as meaning Disease Preventer.*

I was awakened again by Mother bringing me a cup of tea and telling me the time was 8 o'clock. I drank the tea and then dozed for perhaps half an hour, after which I really woke up and lay thinking until Father called me at 9.45, when I got up, did some simple stretching exercises to loosen myself up and finally dressed. Next week I hope to start again on Muller. At 10.05 I went downstairs.

Father and Mother had finished their breakfasts long ago but I began mine with my sister [Viola], who had just come down. I had milk and Kellogg's All Bran, followed by brown bread, butter and Velveeta and finally marmalade.

At 10.30 I went out into the garden to find the sun shining gloriously and a light breeze blowing; the house and garden are very sheltered and to notice any breeze at all meant that in that on open ground there must have

***31** Torquay viewed from the road from Paignton, possibly by John Sanders (1768-1826), early 1800s.*

been a very stiff wind blowing. I went up to where my tent was standing, took it down (the work of a minute) and then lay on the bed and sunbathed. Before long I took off all my clothes except a pair of shorts, fetched a couple of books and newspapers and stayed there happily until 1.30pm.

I did not do very much reading however. I looked up the solution of the previous week's crossword in the *Sunday Times,* glanced at the film criticism, read Miss [Caroline] Lejeune in the *Observer* and read the football and cricket reports. I then turned to *I Would be Private* by Miss Rose Macaulay and read perhaps 50 pages and then dropped that. It is her verbal felicity that fascinates me most, but then that's almost the only thing I read a book for nowadays. I finished up with *The Lighter Side of School Life* by Ian Hay, a very old favourite. This probably lasted for an hour or so and then I was glad to lie in the sun and simply relax and although my mind may have skimmed over one or two things my mind was nearly as blank as it ever is in waking hours.

At 1.30 I began to think about dinner and picked up all the sheets, blankets, pillows, and palliasses that had formed my bed, taking them indoors. I had finished with sleeping out for another summer, and gladly too.

I then dressed properly and at 1.50 we all sat down to dinner. At 2 o'clock we turned on the wireless and listened to the Short Story but owing to constant interruptions and the fact that I had to leave before it was over, I am afraid Mr [Algernon] Blackwood didn't have a very satisfactory audience.

At 2.15 I left home and cycled to Paignton; the sky had now clouded over and I felt the full force of the wind for the first time and as it has veered and was now coming up from the South West, I was cycling into it. Consequently I did not arrive until 2.55. I was spending the rest of the day with a friend of mine named Knight and as soon as I reached his house we left to catch a Brixham bus which deposited us at Galmpton, from where we slowly walked two miles to Greenway. Conversation with Knight consists entirely of listening to him relating some mistake or misfortune or trouble and then he will proceed to view it from every angle and analyse it for your benefit, finding every now and again some other terrifying prospect that up to then had been overlooked and finally dismissing it with a confident *Everything will be all right in the end.* Ten minutes later you will realise with a start that he is still talking about it.

Upon our arrival at Greenway, which is nothing but a name and a tiny jetty, we took the small ferry across the river Dart to Dittisham and hired a rowing boat. The river is notoriously difficult, being full of mud banks and creeks and currents, due to its being a very tidal river and I was looking forward to it considerably, mainly because it would give Knight something to worry about to his heart's content.

We decided to explore Galmpton Creek, which is two miles up the river and rowed strenuously thither against the tide. We knew that the tide goes out like a mill-race and that our chances of getting stuck on a mud-bank were pretty good, but we were not prepared for the thorough-going fashion in which we got stuck before we knew anything about it and it took five minutes' desperate effort to get off with only a minute to spare.

Considerably chastened, we rowed around looking for a suitable place to pull in and eat our tea but everything

32-3 Views of Greenaway House and Dittisham, early 1900s.

was mud; the sky had by now become heavily overcast and rain was spitting so by five o'clock we decided to get back to Dittisham and have our tea there.

We quickly returned, mainly by trying to row one another round by circles, without much success, and finally tied up at the little pier and went in search of our boatman, who charged us 1 shilling 6 pence, which, in view of the reputation Dittisham boatmen have, is distinctly cheap.

It was now raining heavily and in the first lull we caught

the ferry back to Greenway and ate our tea among the trees. There came another heavy storm, and when we had watched that go over, decided to return to Paignton before rain came in for the night. A half-hearted drizzle accompanied us all the way back to the main Brixham-Paignton road, where we caught a bus to Paignton and reached Knight's home at 7 o'clock.

For half an hour we listened to Radio Luxembourg and read papers and magazines and when, when Mr Knight came in and reported it was raining steadily, we abandoned any hope of going out that evening and settled down to play cards. Double Rummy is as good a game as I know for three players, though I hadn't played it for years, so we played on and on and not until 11 o'clock did we stop. I had eaten a few sandwiches during play and left at once for home.

The rain had stopped and a few stars were out and in Paignton the air was warm but by the time I had left Torquay behind, a chill wind had crept up and I was thankful to arrive home at 11.45. Mother and Father were still up talking to friends but I was too tired to sit up and talk with them so I crept off to bed and was probably asleep by midnight.'

34 Dittisham on the Dart, c1850-80.

12 October 1937

Mr Powling's third day-survey was on 12 October. He preceded it with the comment that he was in the 'Office all the morning, surveying all the afternoon. This is perfectly normal day's work. I wasn't feeling quite as good as I usually [am] but as soon as I was doing something this was quickly forgotten. The early part of the morning was glorious; the sun shone brightly and the sky was clear but at 11 o'clock a solid bank of cloud came up from the East and we saw no more of the sun after that. It never became very cold, however, and the sky, although grey, was warm-looking. No dreams.'

He further wrote:

'I first remembered hearing Father moving about in his bedroom and guessed accordingly that the time must be soon after 7 o'clock. I knew I should probably be called in perhaps 20 minutes time, so I lay dozing but I am quite confident that this must've lasted over an hour as it was only 7.20 and, finally, he called me. This meant that I first wakened up at approximately 6.15am.

Ten minutes later I got up, did some exercises for ten minutes and then dressed. I went into the bathroom and shaved. I was using a new razor blade (an Ever-Ready) and by dint of supreme care managed not to cut myself. I then put on my collar and tie and went downstairs and cleaned my shoes. Upon coming into the kitchen, I found that the time was 7.50am.

Upon the mantlepiece was Mass Observation's Directive for October 12th and I was rather perturbed to see that the envelope was addressed by Mr Charles Madge himself [one of the founders of MO].

It then struck me that I was not sure when October 12th was. I had an idea that it was on Wednesday but upon looking at the calendar found that it was today. This was news to me.

I sat down to breakfast which consisted of milk and All Bran, fried bacon, eggs and tomatoes, tea and bread and marmalade. Whilst I was eating this, I heard the sound of the newspaper being pushed through the door and accordingly went to get it, since MO wanted my opinions of the front page, though otherwise I shouldn't have bothered.

At 8.25 I finished breakfast and strolled out into the garden.

The rest of the family

35 Aerial photograph of Dittisham taken by the Luftwaffe, 15 May 1943.

Father [Leonard]

Father's movements are shrouded in mystery. He is always the first up in the morning, perhaps 7 o'clock, though this may vary and, as I am never up, I am not sure what happens next. Almost certainly he rushes to the door and looks through the mail for writs, cheques and solicitors' letters, etc., and he then lights the fire. While this burns up, he washes at the sink in the scullery, does not shave, and then lays the table. By this time Mother is down and takes over, about 7.30am and Dad goes out into the factory where the men are starting work. For probably three quarters of an hour or an hour he supervises them and then comes in to breakfast. His meal is the same as mine except that he does not have milk and All Bran. He usually looks at the paper the whole time he is having breakfast and leaves within twenty minutes of coming in.

Mother [Edith]

Mother is called by Father when he goes down, but she never gets up right away and Dad again calls her at 7.15am, whereupon she dresses and washes in the bathroom. She is downstairs by 7.30 and begins preparing breakfast. After she has served the three breakfasts, she sits down to her own at about 8.45am, when she is alone, and she may glance at the newspaper or read a book. I believe she sits on over the breakfast table till 9.15 or so, when she begins washing up.

Sister [Viola]

After being called twice by Father and three or four times by Mother, she rises at 7.45 and spends the next 15 minutes dressing, washing, etc., as she always washes the last thing at night, she only freshens herself up with a quick splash in the morning and never lingers in the bathroom. Certainly, we rarely meet there and I may be using it for twenty minutes. She is downstairs by or soon after 8 o'clock and then begins a terrific struggle to eat her breakfast, clean her teeth and leave the house by 8.20 to catch a bus and half way up the garden path she remembers something that she had forgotten and rushes back for it, while Mother says, for perhaps the fifth time, *You'll miss that bus if you don't look out.*

36 *An English breakfast, 1930s.*

Habits of friends

Zennith Webber, [male] aged 22

Rises at 8 and usually postpones washing and shaving until after breakfast. Breakfast consists of grapefruit, then Post Toasties, cold milk, sugar and then coffee. This is followed by one of three things: poached egg or toast, or fruit with toast, or fried sausages. White bread, butter and jam. Paper read: *Daily Express*.

Mr Webber

Rises at 6.30 and washes, shaves, etc. before breakfast. Breakfast at 7.45am. This always consists of a meat or fried dish with fried bread, potatoes or eggs. Coffee. Perhaps toast. Paper: *Daily Mail*.

Mrs Webber

She has breakfast in bed at 8.45am and rises at 10am. Breakfast is usually fried bacon and egg, toasted butter [sic], marmalade and coffee.'

By 1939 Mr Powling's parents Leonard and Edith moved to 24 Willake Road in Newton Abbot. By this time Powling himself had relocated to Hope Cove and was employed by Kingsbridge Rural District Council as a sanitary inspector. During the war he served with the Royal Army Medical Corps in North Africa and Italy. Afterwards Mr Powling returned to Devon and by 1961 he was appointed Chief Devon Public Health Inspector. He died in Kingsteignton in 1989.[78]

BAMPTON

In 1939 this North Devon market town on the border with Somerset was home to some 1,400 residents.[79]

2. Christopher Medlycott, Fur farmer/ Instructor, 1942

During the war Sir James Christopher Medlycott (1904-1986) relocated to Devon from Sandford Orcas Manor in Dorset because of his poor health. He had recently endured two bouts of influenza and moved temporarily to what had been the private nursing home for gentlemen at Wonham House, a substantial Victorian country house.[80] Shortly after he arrived Sir Christopher answered an MO query about language:

> 'I do not like hearing really bestial language at all. I could quote the following words as being most undesirable to use – *bloody, buggering, fucking, whore or whorish, and bitch.*
>
> So far as I can think at present, other swear words that I have heard do not amount to very much and are usually somewhat harmless. I don't [illegible word] that once in a way, I just occasionally mind hearing one of the above but to use the above continuously, I think can be most unpleasant, lower all standards of conversation, in other words being obscene. I have used the word bloody on some occasions rarely and realise it is not at all desirable, but find it does come out to describe something very detestable in a way that nothing else does quite.'

Later that year Sir Christopher was employed as a survey instructor.[81]

BARNSTAPLE

In the 1800s the capital of North Devon had successfully reinvented itself following the collapse of its cloth industry. Barnstaple switched to producing furniture and machine-made lace in the nineteenth and early twentieth centuries, continued to make pottery and became attractive as a retirement centre.

In 1939 the town had 15,103 residents. That year it experienced an influx of 423 people, an increase of 2.2% in the population, and Barnstaple Rural District had grown by 18.5%. Evacuees continued to arrive in 1940 and 1941. The town of Barnstaple's official number of evacuees was 2,022 but this number was liable to fluctuation: in May 1941 it was calculated that the town was hosting 1,442 mothers and children. Five months later their number dropped to 1,310.[82]

37 *Barnstaple by Albert John Herbert, c1855.*

Barnstaple Fair was cancelled when war was announced. The town's mayor was then onboard SS *Laconia* returning from America. He apologised: 'I am profoundly sorry and now it is up to us, one and all, to do something to help our country through. I am more anxious than ever to be home to do all I possibly can if only in a small way'. He watched the crew prepare the ship in case of attack and, upon its safe arrival in Liverpool, was given a gas mask for his journey back to Devon.[83] The town had longstanding ties with America. In 1866 sending its condolences to the widow of President Abraham Lincoln.[84]

In 1940 the Ministry of Information recorded public sentiment and attitudes towards the war: on 29 July 'increased defence measures in Barnstaple are improving morale', on 26 August 'a noticeable improvement of morale in Barnstaple is apparent', on 2 September complaints were made of ill-fitting gas masks and on 1 October 'Barnstaple is reported to have taken its first bombs very well'. In 1941 a rumour instigated by Lord Haw Haw was current that the town was to be bombed on Christmas Day.[85]

On 24 August 1940 an MO Writer reported having read two letters from Barnstaple. A fifty-two-year-old housewife had written:

> 'I see in the *Express* this morning that Britain will have to surrender or be destroyed. I wonder what will happen… If Winston had been at the head earlier, Hitler would not have had such luck… Let's hope it will be over soon, it gets on my nerves'.

She noted that the observance of Barnstaple Fair was limited to a 'toast and ale function at the guildhall to keep the custom up until we get back to normal' and that 'iron railings round the square have been taken up and it looks much nicer without them'.

A second housewife, unmarried and ten years older, wrote that her nephew had returned from Dunkirk: 'he had a bullet through his helmet but still he came home safely'.[86]

Barnstaple, like many Devon towns and villages, had limited experience of bombing despite the air raid sirens sounding on 130 occasions. The first was heard on 11 September 1940 and the last on 16 May 1944. The longest warning occurred from 10.25pm to 3.00am on 23 April 1941. North Devon experienced incidental bombing. The first took place on 28 August 1940 when an incendiary bomb fell at Bratton Clovelly but it caused no damage. The following night more incendiaries were dropped on Knowle and Heddon Mill in Georgeham. During September that

38 An example of North Devon's traditional pottery, a harvest jug made in the early 1800s.

year a German plane crashed at Martinhoe Common, bombs were dropped on Instow and a string of explosives fell on Barnstaple but did little damage. This may have been the attack later reported as having comprised ten high explosive and incendiary bombs that fell in the town 'and district':

> 'Three children were asleep in a bedroom in Carlton Terrace. A high explosive demolished the bay window of the room underneath, brought down the front railings and hurled grass, earth and debris in all directions. Some even vaulted the roof. But the children were quite unharmed and were brought down by firemen.
>
> On the opposite side of the street a child had a remarkable escape. A huge block of tar macadam and stone, weighing over one cwt, flew through the air into the room and via a ceiling fell on to the floor 6 inches from where a two-year-old boy was sleeping. The child was not even scratched.
>
> A greenhouse in Victoria Street lost most of its glass

and some stone walling at the bottom of the garden collapsed. One of the working-class dwellings in Cyprus Terrace had a crater in the back garden. Some walls crumbled and glass was shattered and that was all apart from the usual tale of broken windows and a few tiles fracturing. As for the other bombs, most fell on open ground in building estates in Clinton Road. The incendiaries fell in fields a couple of miles away. And that is the total wreckage of the *wrecked* ancient borough of Barnstaple'.[87]

Other bombs reportedly fell on 6 July, 27 September and 7 November.[88]

More bombs fell on Braunton on 31 March 1941 and a train travelling from Ilfracombe to Barnstaple was machine-gunned. Braunton had two further attacks in April and again on 4 May when bombs shook houses as far away as Barnstaple. On 16 July Barumites watched a German plane catch fire and crash.[89] An RAF Intelligence report reveals that the following year a Junkers Ju 88 landed at Chivenor Aerodome in error.[90]

Wartime Barnstaple was relatively quiet and to some degree life carried on as before. The second Barnstaple diarist (4) commented upon the large number of evacuees in the town and on the shortages of some food items. A few years later Arthur Mee did not notice any scars left behind by the war and summarised the town as 'certainly it is very, very old and crowded with memories and symbols of its past'.[91]

3. Mary Bateson, Teacher, 1937-9

This thirty-two-year-old unmarried schoolteacher was living with her father John at No. 11 Ashleigh Road when she contributed to Mass Observation. Mary Elizabeth Bateson (1904-1990) initially heard of the project through the *News Chronicle* and later explained her reasons for writing ('I like writing but have not a creative enough mind to find satisfactory themes of my own and this seemed to provide me with plenty of material'). Also, she had 'interest in details of ordinary life'. In her leisure time she enjoyed folk dancing, raising money for Spanish refugees and visiting the Soviet Union.[92] Of particular interest are Miss Bateson's three day-surveys of 1937 and her response to a directive in 1939.[93]

12 August 1937

She described Barnstaple in a day-survey when war was a matter of general speculation:

> 'I live in the small and pleasant town of Barnstaple, the chief in North Devon and situated on the River Taw, a fine stretch of water at high tide. My father and I live in a cheerful house facing a bowling green and some hard tennis courts.
>
> I teach English and scripture at the Girls' Grammar School, pleasantly set on high ground and looking onto the river and the hills. I am the junior English Mistress. The children at the Grammar School are rather slow but very jolly and good-natured. The staff, with one exception besides myself, have been at the school for years, from ten to twenty-seven. They do not welcome innovations. The Head has been here for three years.

39 11 Ashleigh Road, Barnstaple, part of the building known as Berrydene and the home of Miss Mary Bateson from 1937 to 1939.

> Barnstaple is a fairly prosperous town and very proud of its age. It is a very conventional place, a fair proportion of its population being retired people whose chief occupation, the women's especially, seems to be playing bridge.
>
> The people of Barnstaple find work in the two potteries, a glove factory, a furniture factory and in shops and offices. The district round is agricultural and much business is done in Barnstaple on Tuesdays at the cattle market and on Fridays at the very attractive fruit and vegetable market. There is a larger and poorer slum district than you would expect in a town like Barnstaple.

***40** Miss Bateson's description of Barnstaple Fair illustrates how different it was in 1937 from this agricultural country fair depicted by Thomas Rowlandson in the early 1800s.*

University extension lectures are held each winter but are not well-attended and the Workers' Educational Authority lectures had to be dropped this year as they received so little support. An amateur operatic Society (rather exclusive) gives a show once a year but the choral society has very few members. The Barnstaple Folk Dance Centre is supported chiefly by country people who live several miles out of Barnstaple. There are two cinemas but no theatre and though local dramatic efforts are well-supported, small but good travelling companies get a very poor attendance so they don't come now.'

A month later she attended Barnstaple Fair, still the highlight of the town's year, and wrote what is perhaps its most descriptive account:

'Barnstaple Fair, 15th, 16th & 17th September 1937

It was Thursday and the second night of Barnstaple's annual fair. We set off soon enough after 8 o'clock and as we neared the centre of the town we noticed the unwonted number of people in the streets. Near the bus station dozens of cars were parked and now the people walked in two streams, one leaving the fair - many carrying enormous toy rabbits and dogs or boxes of chocolates and ornaments from the various stalls - and the other streaming towards it. Most people look cheerful and exchange greetings with the many friends whom they pass. We remarked that there can be heard no noise from the fair tonight while last night we heard the blaze of the organs and the raucous shouts in our sitting room.

Outside the fire station at the beginning of Castle Street stand a few people grouped round a van placarded with denunciating texts. These people are singing hymns but nobody takes much notice as everyone is intent on the fair.

We come now to the small stalls lighted by gas flares. A small crowd watches as one man makes some sort of emulsion. I cannot gather what, another stares at rows

***41** A travelling fortune teller visiting her customer, 1827, in contrast to Barnstaple Fair where patrons visited tents and caravans in 1937.*

of curled heads of hair on a hair-waving stall while the man who sells powders etc. for dogs is for the time being neglected. Across the road stand men selling favours and not getting much trade. We can proceed only slowly as everyone stops to look at the most interesting stalls, or at stalls where a few people have already gathered. All the time the stall holders keep up a quick patter advertising their wares.

Now Castle Street opens out into the much broader North Walk and we come up upon the largest stalls. The *Chocolate King* and the fruit merchant are both haranguing their audiences through an amplifier and, since the stalls are next one another, the effect for the passer-by is somewhat muddled. The *Chocolate King* proceeds to fill a large bag with goods from his stall. *One for Ma, Something for Dad, A little bit for Tom, One for the Baby* he roars and finally hands the bagful to someone in the crowd. The price of all this I cannot catch because of the neighbouring fruit-merchant's clamour. The stalls which we next passed look inviting - hot potatoes, hot *dogs* and farings they sell without the aid of amplifiers. Here also stand fortune-tellers' tents & caravans into which a few girls are entering.

At length we have reached the amusement fair and here the crowd is much denser and it is often difficult to make progress at all. The rifle-ranges which we first pass seem to be doing no trade at all and I see one or two of the women stallholders pluck young men by the sleeves and almost thrust a rifle into their hands to no purpose. The coconut shies are doing a little better and the stalls which offer pyramids of tin cans to be knocked down with a grand clatter by wooden balls are still busier.

I noticed the people who pass me walking in the opposite direction. Some of them laugh and joke, some push and jostle but most walk as if in a dream. I wonder what I look like.

The noise is now stunning and the lights are dazzling. From a huge tower come hoots and shrieks and I see people going in through the door, not in hand. They toil up to the top. I see their legs through the window high up and then slide gloriously helter-skelter down, screaming as they slide.

Next to this prance the horses round and round, brazen tunes blaring out the while. The horses are only

***42-4** The galloping horses, part of the Noah's Art fairground merry-go-round ride, 1930s.*

moderately popular - old-fashioned I imagine. Beyond this is a new roundabout very like a *Noah's Ark* but with motorcycles for the riders instead of an assortment of animals. This is very popular. It swoops round at bewildering speed. I feel giddy merely watching it and the riders cling on desperately. As soon as it stops, the onlookers surge onto the platform and seize each a motorcycle.

I feel my feet cold now and realise that I ought to have had more sense than to come to the fairground stockingless and wearing sandals. We have had a good deal of rain though it is fine now and the ground is covered with black, squelching mud.

We next inspect the *Dodge'ems* which seem always immensely popular. There are a few youngsters steering and looking grave and important and incidentally steering rather well, and great numbers of adults colliding with one another, going the wrong way - to the annoyance of the attendant who leaps at the offending car and wrenches the wheel around - getting stuck against the side and all the while shrieking and laughing. There is always an audience at the *Dodge'ems.* When I see the jams which nearly every driver gets at some time or other (some get nothing but jams) I conclude that the audience has the better time - though since I haven't tried the *Dodge'ems*, I am no fit judge.

The Dragon next attracts us. Here you sit two or three on a seat, eight face outwards. Near that whirls *Noah's Ark* and beyond that stands another *Dodge'em.* It is amazing to see the bystanders swarm at the roundabouts as soon as the turn is over. It is amusing to watch those coming off. Some are quite hardened and show no signs of having been bumped or whirled but others find it difficult to walk straight and many look dazed. It is mostly the youngest people who patronise the roundabouts.

A raucous voice to my left comes from a boxing booth and informs us that a bout will soon begin between two renowned (one world-renowned) champions. On the platform stand several men, one Negro, in dressing gowns and below waits a crowd of older men and women until the doors open.

Now we come to smaller stalls and shows, and among these is a hand-worked roundabout for really young children. It looks out of place and old-fashioned among all these mechanical devices. It makes no contribution to the clamour or glamour of the fair, making no noise and showing now lights. Two small children ride on it while the proprietor laboriously turns his wheel. No one looks at it tonight but it may be more popular in the afternoon when small children are brought to the fair.

The small side stalls at this part of the fair are doing moderate business especially the darts stalls which youths and boys frequent. Two of the three peep shows are kept very busy indeed. Their monstrosities are advertised through amplifiers and we are invited to see the woman with five perfect legs, the sheep with the goat's head and other portions of its anatomy belonging to other animals and a bevy of dancing girls. People flock into these shows in very merry mood. The third peep show seems for the time to be in the sole charge of a small and very attractive boy who begs us for the charge of a penny to see the largest rat. This does not appear to interest people very much. This is almost the end of the fair. There are left only a few fortune tellers' caravans and through the window of one, the curtains of which have not been drawn quite to, we see the bent head of the seer as she ponders over somebody's future.

We now begin our return journey and move fairly quickly to the more crowded part of the fair, where the roundabouts stand in a line on one hand and the brilliantly lighted penny-rolling stalls stand on the other. We intend to inspect these now but before we do so, we are attracted by a little group round *Max* who is making a quick sketch of a young country-looking man. We watch with admiration. In an amazingly short time, three or four minutes, he has produced a very good likeness. He adds his name with a flourish, exhibits his drawing and rolls it up in tissue paper and takes his one shilling. The young man looks pleased. A rather nice-looking girl, who has several times informed us that he drew her when she was five, now stands forward to be drawn again and again we watch with interest. In a few strokes there she is. I'd like to be drawn myself but I haven't the courage to stand forth. I like *Max's* face; it is elderly and long and humorous.

We pass on to the stalls where you roll pennies, drop pennies on coins, throw pennies at boxes of sweets and buy lottery tickets. All these are brightly lighted and popular though I don't think they are quite as popular, nor do they seem as many, as last year. I notice one small boy who has an arm full of boxes of sweets but I see that he leans well over the bar and almost places his penny on one of the front tins. Everyone else seems to observe the rules of the game - if you can call it such. Young and old seem to enjoy these stalls. The lottery stall is noisy. The proprietor talks all the time, exciting the bystanders and as the lights flash up and down, now on this town and now on that, a long whine is emitted which dies away as the machine slows down. Finally the light rests at such and such a town and the person with that name on his ticket takes a prize. It is from this stall that the people get enormous toy rabbits and dogs.

The throng is still as great as ever. We pause to watch the Toddles which always amuses my father but in a few minutes that we stand there only one old man toddles through the open doorway. The rifle ranges that had been so quiet an hour and a half ago are now doing brisk trade and there is much shattering of glass. The tin cans are clattering down; the dart stalls and coconut shies are all fairly busy.

Everybody has been very good-natured, whether they have had a try at everything or have been merely onlookers and I notice now a pleasant woman at a biscuit and faring stall offers a plate of biscuits and farings to the Indians with bushy beards and turbaned heads who sell carpets earlier in the day. They smile and shake their heads but she presses them and they accept her gift. The hot potato man looks tired but he speaks kindly and pleasantly to a small girl who has come for a potato. There has been no drunkenness nor brawling nor unseemly behaviour of any kind. Of course, tomorrow night the fair will be merrier. It is market day and country folk for a good many miles round will come in for the annual jollification. What a day they'll have; market in the morning and earlier afternoon, tea in a café and then the whole of the rest of the afternoon and evening at the fair.

On our way out we pass the fruit merchant who has collected quite a crowd. I catch only snatches of his patter but I gather that he is making a joke about the rising generation and a war. Nobody laughs at that, however, so he goes on to something else. We pass the smaller stalls and the favour sellers in Castle Street, the din and glare decreasing as we proceed. The evangelists have now around them a throng of people who are listening to a fiery little man who declares that the Christian is surrounded by sin and he must keep himself from it. He must avoid it and the contamination of things that are worldly.

We leave the fair and all connected with it behind us. It

45 The Royal family several years after the incident at the Cenotaph in which Stanley Storey, aged 43, disrupted the Two Minutes' Silence by rushing toward the king while shouting 'No More War. End this hypocrisy.'

is amazingly quiet. The moon is shining and when we reach Oakley Road, the greater part of which contains no house, we see the stars. Our own road is quite deserted. We feel suddenly that we are very tired.'

11 November 1937

Two months later Miss Bateson's mind focused on her school's commemoration of the Great War:

'Armistice Day, 1937

10.30am Came from the class I had been teaching into the Staff Room where I prepared to settle down to work as I had a free period. I bought a poppy (each year poppies and collecting boxes are sent up to school and each girl who wishes to and that's everyone I believe, buys a poppy and sticks it into a cross and then the whole cross of poppies is taken to the war memorial by two of the senior prefects). Miss X gave me a penny as a contribution towards Spanish Relief for which I was collecting.

About 10.35 I sat down to correct some scripture essays. Miss C came in and seeing the poppies said that foreign-made poppies were being sold in England. There had been a warning about them on the wireless. She said that people seem to draw the line at nothing. Miss X replied that human nature hasn't yet reached a very high level. Miss C. then spoke about the boycott on Japanese goods. She felt it was not much use for a private person to attempt a boycott for it was so simple for Japanese goods to bear the mark *Made in England*.

About 10.56 The school bell rang. I put away my books, took my hymn book and went into the hall. The girls were trooping in in silence and we all assembled as for morning prayers. We were to listen in to part of the Cenotaph service. The commands of the officers and the very military form of the ceremony jarred upon me. I thought of the trouble that seems brewing in Poland and the unhappy plight of Spain and China.

11 o'clock The guns and our town hooter sounded for silence and simultaneously came a disturbance at the Cenotaph - a man's voice screaming something about war. It sounded horrible. His cries were soon stifled and I wondered what they were doing to him and what he had tried to say. The children must have felt upset by the disturbance but except for a sort of tensing, which one could feel, no one showed that she had noticed it.

11.02 The end of the silence. The school joined in the hymn & *God Save the King*. I didn't. I didn't feel like singing.

11.10 We all filed out. In the staff room the disturbance was spoken about. Most of the staff thought it horrible and that such behaviour would hurt any cause. Miss G. thought it was propaganda. I said it sounded to me like someone wildly hysterical on whom the militariness of the service in the present state of affairs had worked. Miss J. thought that an ex-serviceman with no pension or work or a workless man driven frantic might have done it. Others said that that formed no excuse for such behaviour at such a time. Miss P. however said *You don't know what his state of mind was* and most of us agreed.

Conversation followed on other subjects, the wireless etc. and was much quieter than usual. We were to have playtime till 11.20 instead of from 11 to 11.15.

Miss X then asked if the report of a desired armistice in Spain was true. We replied that there was nothing in the papers about it.

Ramsay MacDonald was mentioned and his death discussed. One said he was worn out. Miss P. said that whether you agreed with him or not, he was a great man. Miss J. replied that whatever he did, he died a traitor. He betrayed his own principles in 1931 and destroyed the work of Arthur Henderson who wore out his life looking for peace. Since the Labour Government left office in 1931 International Affairs had gone from bad to infinitely worse and Ramsay Macdonald must bear some responsibility for this. Many of us agreed.

11.30 The bell rang for the resumption of lessons. We took up our books and went to our classes.'

Directives: anti-Semitism

Fifteen months later, in February 1939, she addressed another topic. She had been asked to write about *The Jewish Problem* and referenced the local presence of the Blackshirts. The first recorded fascist meeting had taken place in March 1934 and an office was opened in the town six months later. Sir Oswald Mosley's appearance at the Pannier Market occurred on 6 October. Advertisements promised the audience would hear 'how fascism will save your country and your job'. Some two thousand local men and women heard him speak for more than two hours.[94] Miss Bateson wrote:

> 'In the district in which I live, as far as I can gather, people are sympathetic towards the Jews and regard with abhorrence the treatment which certain countries are giving them. But nobody seems to have any clear idea as to where they ought to live or what should become of them. Not much is said about them except when a new wave of horrors is brought to our notice in the papers whereupon people say to one another how dreadful it is that such thing should happen. On the 7th of February I noted the following conversation at dinner at school. Miss K. mentioned Malcolm McDonald's speech the previous night on the wireless and said what a good case both Arabs and Jews seem to have. Miss A. replied *The Jews have done amazing things in Palestine and the Arabs don't like them for that*.

46 *British campaign poster of the National Council for Civil Liberties with the slogan 'It shall not happen here,' 1943.*

I, with *Comrades & Citizens* in mind, said what excellent farmers they made and how remarkable that is since they have been off the land for so long. According to Lord Addison the creation of a good farmer is a very long and difficult process and can only proceed if the right sort of men are chosen. Miss A. replied *Yes, but they don't take to the land at home* to which I said *They've had no chance, they've never been allowed to own land and become farmers.* Miss K., who had taught school at Southend and Brighton, said what excellent brains they have. They won a great many distinctions, always in WSC and many scholarships. Whereupon Miss G. added *It is the same in Leeds. There are many Jews in one part of the town and nearly all of the scholarships go to the Jew. They have brilliant results.* Miss K. said *You tell them a thing once and they know it and they don't only remember, they reason.* Miss A. then asked what sort of girls they were to teach and how they got on with Gentile girls to which Miss K replied *They were very nice girls and there was in the schools to which I taught a happy, pleasant atmosphere. There was no friction observable between English and Jewish girls.* The conversation then ended with Miss A. in saying that Jews seemed able to adapt themselves to almost any life…

There is as far as I can make out hardly any anti-Semitism in this district. Some years ago, about four, two of Mosley's young men gave a harangue on the iniquities of the Jews at Ilfracombe, so I heard, but it doesn't seem to have made much impression and Mosley himself about three years ago held a meeting in Barnstaple market hall. The hall was packed but his violent outburst against the Jews gained him no applause. He gave no facts anyhow. He merely abused the Jews.

My father says that amongst the many men he knows in Barnstaple he has not heard anti-Semitic talk. Nevertheless I have met with one slight indication of anti-Semitism though it is not from a real inhabitant of Barnstaple but from one who lives here in school term time and at home in the holidays.

Only two people have I heard in Barnstaple any anti-Semitic ideas expressed and one of those two has ceased now to express them. Indeed the ideas have been merely hinted [at] rather than expressed.

These two people were rather impressed by the Black Shirt young men at Ilfracombe and by Mosley in Barnstaple. In fact, it was rather the fluency and physique of the speakers rather than what they said that impressed them and made them willing to believe what they were told.

One of them has since expressed to me her disgust of the treatment of Jews in Germany but the other only a few weeks back, after reading the English version of *Mein Kampf* which she declared to be infinitely more reasonable and respectful to the English than she had been led to believe, hinted that he had understandable reasons for treating the Jews as he has treated and is treating them.

Secondary School teachers (women), with these it is rather only a slight indication towards Anti-Semitism because the public opinion here is against it.

47 A Nazi rally in Quedlinburg, 1936.

I haven't many hates but one of them is anti-Semitism. Of all the blind, cruel, stupid beliefs that people have let themselves be driven by, this seems to me the worst. It's utterly senseless and is destroying not only men and women who are capable of rendering to their various countries good service but is rotting the minds of those who believe in it and practise it. There seems to be no more depressing picture than that of the Jew Baiter or of the men and women who watches with enjoyment. It is even more depressing than the heart-rending picture of the Jews themselves and their unbelievable sufferings for it seems as though the light of reason is going from men.

I know the Jews do often show unpleasant traits in their character but they are only the traits of an oppressed people and since we Europeans have done the oppressing constantly for hundreds of years, I don't see how we can rightly complain. We ought now to try to make up for our past mistakes.

I know that most businessmen dislike Jews but, as far as I've been able to gather, it is because the Jews are better businessmen. It seems to me that it is the system which is wrong, not the fact that Jews do well in it. By no means all great capitalists are Jews. One finds in the Soviet Union, where nobody can be a capitalist, that the Jews are as useful and worthy citizens as any. And even if the Jews are the unscrupulous, money-loving creatures they are made out to be, it does not in the very least excuse any part of the treatment that they are undergoing in Germany or Austria, etc.

When we consider what the Jews as a race have given us, when we think of their splendid intellectual powers, their work in music, science, medicine, religion [and] philosophy, we ought to be glad to have such people. Not starve them but then rather than to deride them, mass them in those inhumane institutions, concentration camps and finally kill them. I suppose Germany at present, amongst other things, dislikes their international outlook.

I do not know any people who call themselves Jews though I work with two who obviously have Jewish blood in them. With one I am on very friendly terms. The other I do not like but I have never connected the things in her that I dislike with the Jewish strain in her. She is a very clever woman and so is my friend but the latter is moody and subject to fits of the deepest gloom.

My mother lived in her girlhood next-door to a family of Jews whom she very much liked and respected. I have been brought up from my childhood to believe that Jews as a whole are a hard-working, clever [and] just set of people who have not in the past had fair treatment and who, like Scots, are erroneously believed to have an over great liking for money. I have not found any good-enough justification for altering that belief.

I do not know any *funny stories* about Jews.'

Miss Bateson attended local meetings of the League of Nations and it may have been there that she met her future husband, Richard John Baker (1912-1990), whom she married in 1941. Barnstaple's other MO Writer also attended those meetings and it is likely that the two knew one another. Did they also realise they were both MO contributors?[95]

4. Eric Gulliver, Clerk, 1940-1

On Saturday, 14 December 1940 sixteen-year-old Eric Percy Arnold Gulliver (1924-1987), arrived with his mother, father and two other relatives. For the next four months they lodged in Pilton at 36 Pilton Street with their landlady Mrs Mary Kidwell (1870-1951). Mr Gulliver contributed a diary from 27 November 1940 to 19 December 1941 and answered two directives.[96]

48 36 Pilton Street, Pilton, the home of Mr Eric Gulliver in 1940 and 1941.

Barnstaple

The teenager was unhappy with the move ('astounded by news that my parents, for some unknown reason, are leaving St Albans. Going to Barnstaple in Devon on Saturday' and 'mental excitement, not that I am looking forward to going to Barnstaple, far from it. At the first opportunity I'll go back to Beckenham'). His first entry was not hopeful:

'Very, very unhappy. But until I get a job my destiny is not my own. Now 200 miles from home – when before was 50. A case of extremes. Modern house and furniture of 1940 to fifteenth-century house with Victorian furniture. But the faces have not changed –

there is that expression, so difficult to define, which gives one the impression of a situation which is so unfortunate that it is impossible to evade it. Well, perhaps I'll be able to settle down tomorrow, and write at length. My impression is that Barnstaple is not an interesting town and will not serve as a compromise for Beckenham or St Albans for that matter.'

He was pleasantly surprised on the following day:

'Visited the [North Devon] Athenaeum and the public library. Very interesting. The Public Library is very weak as regards non-fiction, but what it has in this line is excellent. The Atheneum is really a non-fiction library, it has a large and comprehensive selection of books, but there is little material which has been printed after 1930 in the arts selection. Cezanne is the latest. The whole series of Oxford pamphlets is on show - good work. But there is no sign of any newspaper but the *Times*. *Picture Post*, *Horizon* and *New Statesman* and *Nation* are, I noticed with disgust, not included in the list of magazines.

Am not able to listen to the radio down here, and I only get the chance to see the headlines of the newspapers – with the result that I am now not well-informed about current world affairs.'

***49** a picturesque view of Pilton Street by H. B. Wimbush, 1908. No. 36 is situated towards the top on the left-hand side.*

***50** London children amidst bomb rubble, 1940.*

It is unlikely that he realised that a former librarian, Nancy Brown, was also an MO diarist who had recently resigned from the Athenaeum.

Mr Gulliver's diaries for 1940 and 1941 comprise some 350 pages. Not surprisingly, entries reveal he missed his friends and former life. In respect to politics he expressed an interest in communism but admitted after later leaving Barnstaple:

> 'Today I have been turning out some old papers. Amongst them I found a British Union of Fascists membership card. How pathetically silly and young we all were. Then I didn't understand what it all meant. Then I knew that progress had come to the Third Reich but I didn't realise that it was progress in the wrong direction. *Britain first* indeed. *We give ourselves to Britain. We stand for peace*. Balls!'

This teenager sometimes wrote about the war in short notes ('As I write this entry some carollers are singing *Good King Wenceslaus* – Oh! What is the use? I wonder how long it will be before the day comes, that we will be able to sit down to our Christmas fare in peace?') and others were much longer:

> 'In a conversation today, the topic of evacuees happened to crop up. It appeared that the Londoners had made rather a bad impression on the town. I was told this story. A certain house was lent to the government by a lady who was, for the time being, living away from home. Some evacuees came from London. The lady returned and with horror found that the bath had been used as a coal cellar and that the children had used the back of the wardrobes for a lavatory. This emphasised the fact that the slums must be cleared and that a wider system of education must be introduced to bring into its scope the children of all classes. It also showed that the evacuee was not wholly to blame — the local authorities were also in the wrong. The ignorant should be instructed in the way of living cleanly. The services at the Food and Registration Offices are excellent, fairly good educational facilities are provided for the children – but there the matter ends. No provision is made for the *cheering--up of the evacuees*. Concerts should be held, clubs formed and welfare centres instituted.'

His subjects included food:

> 'I have a complaint to make. It seems to me that the Ministry of Food is very reluctant to side-track supplies from the depopulated towns to those whose population is now double or treble the peace time figures. We have been told time and time again, that there is enough rationed foods to go round, but only today I found that my butcher could only supply me with half my rations because, as he said, the supplies weren't enough to go round. The excuse of transport may be offered, admittedly dislocation is bound to occur, but surely there isn't permanent dislocation on the service from London to the West? To verify my case before I left Beckenham, a considerable amount of people had already moved from the district, but the amounts of foods supplied to the shops had not been cut down in proportion to the number of people who had moved. This was shown by the fact that some of the grocers were able to supply their customers with often double rations. To Lord Woolton I say *Yours is one of the most efficient ministries that exist, but in some ways your policy is not farsighted enough. Sidetrack the supplies from the towns that don't need them to the towns that do!*'

In another passage he commented on evacuees' rations:

> 'Further light on the food question. Party of evacuees down here – 6 adults, 1 child. Meat amount due for Christmas 12s. Amount allowed by butcher 2s 10d. Local householder at same shop gets her full rations. At the grocers – local housewife gets double her ration in bacon; evacuee gets barely her ration. This racket must be stopped. It is plain that the National Food Regulations need tightening up. Why should the evacuee have to put up with second choice? We're all in this war together, we should equally share its blessings and curses'.

He wrote about the shortage of sweets on 24 December:

> 'I went into three confectioners today. *Any sweets*? I enquired, *No, none* was the answer in each case. *Bad for business*? I enquired. *Yes, if we don't get some stock, we'll have to close shop*, was the answer. *Strange*, I said, *that in some towns there are enough sweets to go around and in others there is none. Transport* was the reply. *In some cases yes, but in others negligence and near-sightedness*, I said. *That was all*. I walked out.'

And again three days later:

> 'Many shops are not reopening until Monday in Barnstaple because of the shortage of supplies. Soap is almost unobtainable. Many of the sweetshops and

tobacconists have very little to sell. I have been told twice that if supplies do not arrive by January the shop will have to shut.'

He expressed firm opinions:

'I went to a cinema the other day and saw posted on a board a notice announcing a forthcoming concert in aid of the troops. Strange that the only visible signs of entertainment for the forces and evacuees have been concerts arranged at cinemas by private individuals. This curious repetition of facts which are taking place both in St Albans and Barnstaple, leads me to believe that the local authorities are not doing much in the way of entertaining their guests. There is a gloomy YMCA building down here, but it definitely looks uninviting. To my mind the soldiers off-duty can only be spent by two alternatives — women or beer.

But the answer to this state of affairs is not so simple as some people lead us to imagine. Fill up the soldiers off-duty with a comprehensive system of variety shows, concerts, lectures, and reading facilities - the result will be that the lecture halls will be half-empty because 90% of the soldiers will prefer sex and drink. I personally have heard of more than one case where an imaginative far-sighted officer has provided full recreational activities and the result his lecture hall was more than half-empty.

What then is the remedy for this present state of affairs, what is the reason for this chaotic condition? Why, the answer is, lack of education. I fully agree with Edward Hulton's motion that education should be a primary part of military training. Many of the young men who enter the army have been so poorly educated that they can't appreciate good books, lectures, and instructional films. Others, due to the sordidness of their environment, and to their inability to find relaxation and enjoyment in music and the other arts, enter the army full of pent-up energy. And dear old Nature, Horrible Old Nature, has only one channel for the release of pent-up energy.

Educate the soldier. Let him see that he's fighting for freedom against slavery, for the beauty of England, for God knows, the only citadel of reason in this patchwork world! Help him to appreciate the beauty of art, and show him that there are other pleasures which can be attained from sources other than beer and sex.'

***51** Wendell Wilkie in 1940, the year he was the Republican nominee for the American presidency.*

Occasionally he repeated rumours, as on February 6th:

'*Have you heard*? was whispered at every corner of the street. *What? Why about Wendell Wilkie. Well? As he was boarding the clipper at Lisbon on his return to the USA he said that he was proud of German parentage.*

This news swept round Barnstaple like wildfire – later in the day it was quoted in the news-bulletins. But although Wendell Wilkie, President Roosevelt's envoy to this country, had added that his heart and soul was in the fight for the preservation of democracy, yet the general public opinion was one of mistrust and apprehension in Britain today. There is a predominant *jumpiness*, not an anxiety no, but that sense of *eager looking for news* which was characteristic of the peoples of France in the days before the collapse. I feel that within three months the destiny of the British Empire and the whole world too for that matter, will be determined. Victory? Defeat? I think a 50-50 chance.'

There was also a rumour of a fifth-columnist:

'Tonight, during the air raid whilst coming home from the cinema, I went into the evacuation office and was told that one of our helpers had seen a light from a roof in Vicarage Street which flashed every time a German plane passed over. The police had been informed of the fact – I don't think it was a product of the imagination.'

His one entry regarding his father Percy, a builder, concerned rumours:

'Father comes for a short visit. Whole evening taken up with conversation on activities and topics national and social. Most interesting was the fact that an invasion has already been attempted.

The husband of the lady with whom my father is staying, is now serving in the navy - stationed at present in Plymouth. He reports that late one night a fortnight ago, the sailors and marines were ordered to action stations with fired bayonets. That night the rumble of heavy guns was heard.

In the train today, in a conversation a gentleman said that he had heard from a reliable source that several German sailors had been washed up on the shore at Weston-super-Mare.'

On February 9th Mr Gulliver was questioned about wartime service:

'*Hallo!* It was my reporter friend of the League of Nations meeting. *How does the new call-up affect you? What call-up*? I said. *Why, the nineteens*. *Oh*, I hastily explained *I am not yet seventeen. What are you going to join – RAF? Why, don't you remember - I am not keen on joining any of the services — perhaps they'll let me join the Quaker Ambulance Corps.*

I thought of him as I walked up the hill — another career ruined. He didn't want this bloody war - but neither did I. It had so turned over things, my whole life had become one of suppression, I had become dulled because of unrecognition. I was lonely — far away from my friends and what was I? Why, a small-time clerk, a junior earning £1 1s a week copying and adding up forms all day - a job which anyone could have done.

Perhaps life, the boredom of my present existence, would be relieved if I joined the air force. I was too young. I knew that — but I'd fool them somehow.

Then I thought of the Air Training Corps, I never knew about it till the days of registration in Barnstaple were passed. How could it be otherwise, than a flop with only 58 applications in a district of now over 20,000 people when it wasn't propagandised in the town, when there was only one feeble notice in an inconspicuous back-street.

Well stick it out to Easter I must, perhaps when I get back to St Albans, I will be able to find some outlet for my energy.'

52 British evacuees in Australia, 1940.

Mr Gulliver found employment at the Evacuation Office which was located within walking distance at 124 Boutport Street. On February 12th he shared some local knowledge:

'Whilst sorting out the billeting allowance receipt forms, I told the social workers about 14 Pilton Street, a house with five rooms and only one occupant. *People like that should be compelled to take in evacuees, after all she's not ill, and right now there are evacuees who, because they can't find billets, are sleeping on straw in the (covered) market place. Disgraceful*. I agreed.'

The office had been given the task of finding homes for Bristol evacuees. On 21 February he noted:

'By nightfall all the Bristol children had been found billets. This time there was no repetition of the scandalous incident of small children sleeping on straw in a cold drafty market place. But the same cannot be

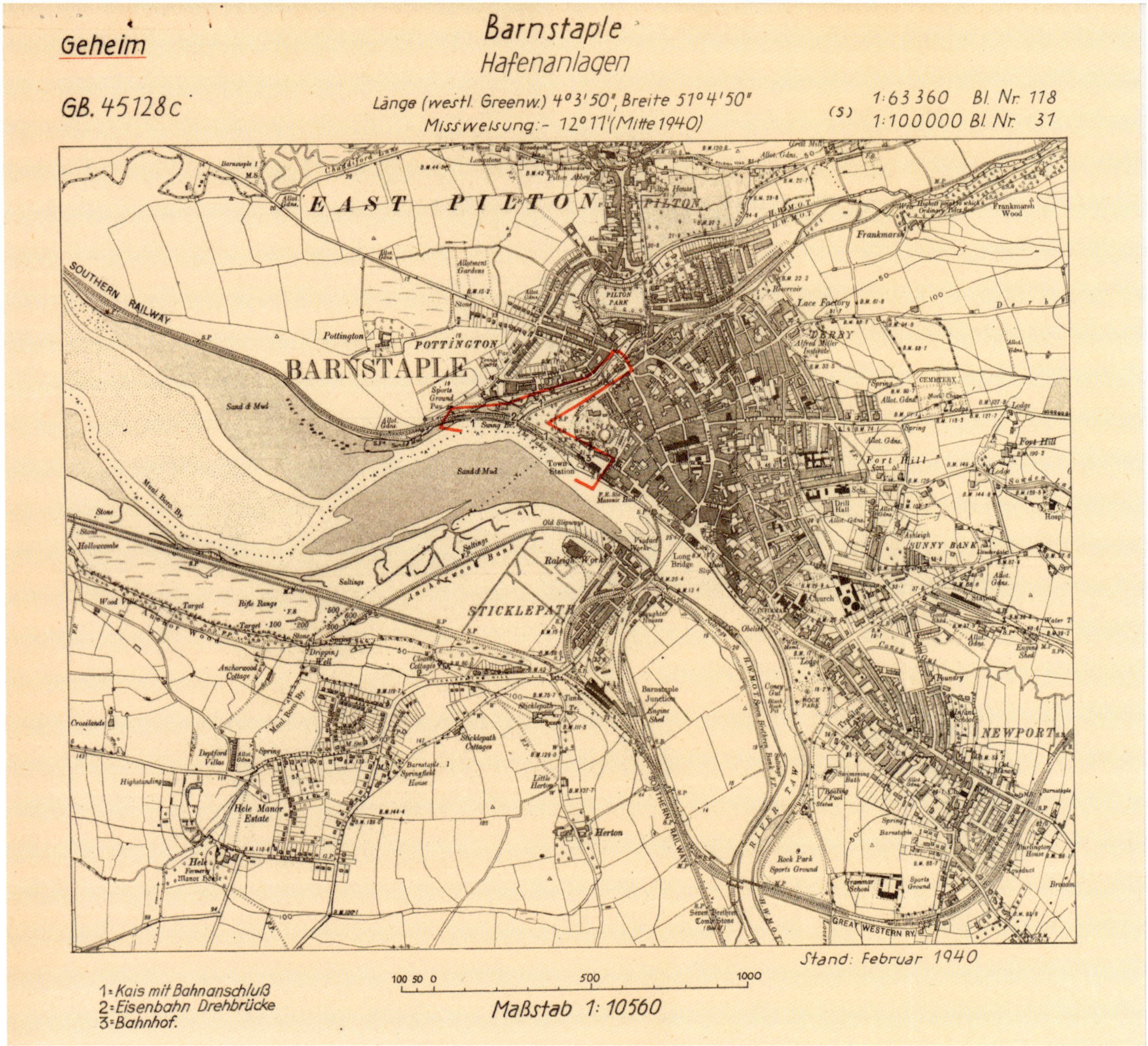

53 The Luftwaffe's target dossier for Barnstaple, February 1940, with the strategic area noted in red.

said of all the other reception towns in Devon. The disgraceful story of the chaotic conditions caused by the Ilfracombe householders locking their doors to the evacuees has even appeared in *The Daily Telegraph*.'

His work was the diary's main topic. On 10 March 1941 he wrote:

'One of the things that cause the staff of the Evacuation Offices in the Reception Area a lot of head worry is the case of evacuees who suddenly pop back to their home town without informing the local authorities. A little care and consideration would save a lot of time and needless worry. Then again there are those evacuees who delight in changing billets every few months - they are away from home, things aren't quite what they might be, we all realise that and sympathise. But if they only thought for a moment, and would try to make themselves happy, then conditions would be better for all concerned.

The horrors of war were forcibly brought upon us all when we heard that one of our fellow workers in the office downstairs had lost her husband in the night-raid on London over the weekend. Only those who are brought so near to reality can truly understand what war means.'

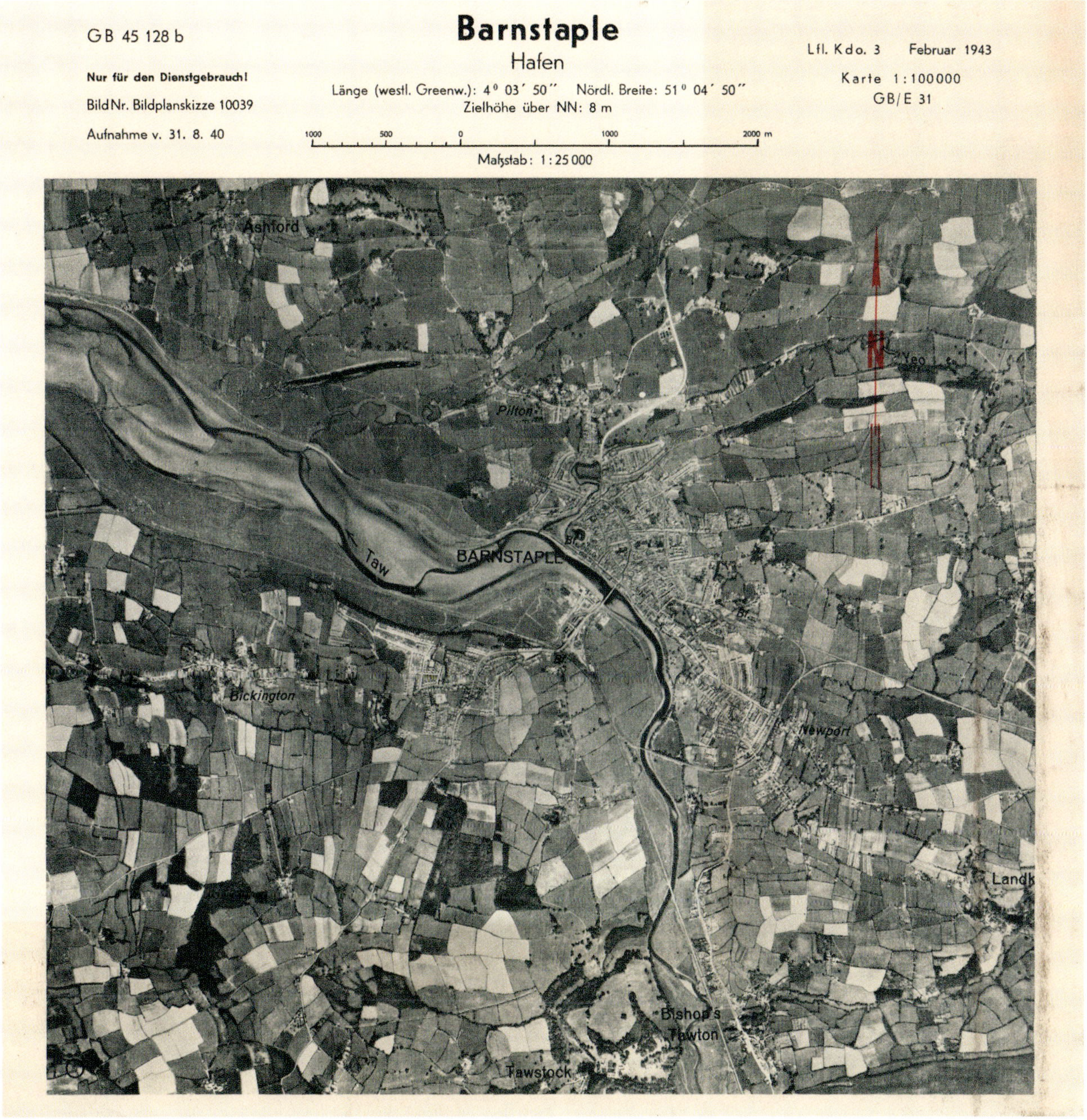

***54** German aerial map of the halen (harbour) at Barnstaple, February 1943.*

Ten days later he added:

> 'Superb weather still holds out: air raid during day. German plane glides serenely overhead. Warnings sound again tonight, last night London witnessed another heavy raid - chiefly centred on the dockside area. Evacuees still come – but evacuees still go. It is a crying shame that these children should be taken back — I know two little kids they're going back to London soon. As I write this entry, I seem to feel that tenseness, that vagueness of action, that indefinite feeling coming back. God, I wish that something would happen – quick!'

Another entry two days later added a level of complexity:

> 'Looking round at the shops today I was impressed by the number of sweets that were on show. Whereas a month or two ago one went weeks without seeing a

single sweet, now it is possible to get them practically every clay. Other foods are severely rationed, cheese is difficult to get yes. But I feel that generally this strict restriction of foodstuffs is, not proving detrimental to the national health. As far as I can see there is only one type of foodstuff which is really missed, and that by the children more than the adults, and that is fresh fruit. Oranges are impossible to get. The price of apples is too high for the average housekeeper. I fully realise that the maximum amount of shipping is required for the transport of munitions, but I do feel that if one orange was given every week to all young people, children, adolescents it would pay in the long run.

Ten-minute warning in Barnstaple today, raid centred on Plymouth last night.'

On March 26th he admitted there were difficulties at home ('Relations with parents and relatives are again today strained. I guess all this bloody suspense is getting on everybody's nerves... To return to the point, at home it is noticeable how arguments so quickly spring into being at the raising of trivial controversial points. It all seems so senseless. Here are five people, with the chance to stay in a fairly safe area for the rest of the war, and today they kick up a racket about going back to London, just because they disagree with the landlady over some trifling incident'). A week later, on April 2nd, Mr Gulliver was uprooted ('This afternoon I came home to be dramatically told we were all leaving Barnstaple on Saturday. And all because of some damned silly argument! God, it makes me sick! At least my parents might have had the decency to give me the chance to give my boss a week's notice.'). His last entry in Barnstaple was regretful:

'Today I have been clearing up my work at the Evacuation Office. Trying to leave everything up to date for my fellow worker, Mr Atwood. Seems as if he'll have to carry on alone. Maybe I'm sentimental, but this afternoon's saying goodbye to my Boutport Street friends was touching, very touching, *Very, very sorry that I was leaving, you have been kind, very kind. If you come back to Barnstaple there will always be a position for you in this office. Sorry you're leaving, very sorry.* What could I say? Nothing. Nobody could have been given a better send-off. And me, a guy who has only worked there for three months. I shall always remember that job, my fellow workers in Barnstaple. As to what I'm going to do now, I can't say. Even now I don't know where I'm going tomorrow…'

Mr Gulliver later reflected:

'Well, in November 1940 due to the effects of the air raids on my parents' nerves, they decided that we should leave Beckenham for the duration. I hotly opposed the idea but as I am at present dependent on my parents, what could I do? In due course we went down to Barnstaple with relations. After a week's hanging about I began to get bored and decided that I would look for a job. I have described how I obtained a position in Evacuation, how I became deeply interested in and absorbed by the whole business.'

Mr Gulliver married in 1948; he and his wife had two children both of whom died young. The diarist himself died in East Sussex in 1987, aged 62.

BEER

This picturesque East Devon fishing village, with a population of 1,266 in 1931, was known for producing lace for Victoria's wedding gown in 1840 and for its quarries. An RAF Chain Home Low radar station was established on Beer Head by 1941.[97] On 11 September 1939 an MO Writer, who signed himself as KJR, wrote a one-page report on evacuees at Beer:

'Five busloads of evacuees returned this week to London because the natives would not put up with slum dwellers. On the day after evacuation, Beer was in an uproar of indignation especially at receiving mothers with small children. One mother with two crippled children had failed to find lodgings at 11.30pm. Complaints specified, babies dirty the bed, no nappies used. Woman came with no proper shoes, *wearing bedroom slippers*. One woman refused to help with washing up because she was being paid for by government.'[98]

Two other MO Writers recorded their visits to Beer before the war and at the near end of it.

5. George Raine, Teacher, 1937

George Raine (1880-1971) was a schoolmaster in Ilford, Essex and a Methodist lay preacher when he went on holiday

55 Fore Street, Beer, in the early 1900s.

to Devon in 1937. Thirty-one years earlier Mr Raine had married Jessie Wilkie (1880-1973) and in 1908 they had a daughter, Kathleen, who was to later find fame as a poet. Her biographer described her father's religious standards as narrow and uncompromising and his faith as 'a daily oppression, for he lived his life according to the rule, where a clear line between saints and sinners allowed no mercy or understanding either for those who were not of his faith or for those who were, but had transgressed'.[99] Another side of Mr Raine is revealed through his day-survey of Beer.[100]

12 May 1937: the coronation

Mr Raine described the events marking the coronation of King George VI on Wednesday, 12 May, which were overshadowed by the abdication of the latter's brother, Edward VIII, five months earlier. Mr Raine and his wife visited a café while in Beer; perhaps the Brook Café or the Beer Bay Tea Rooms.[101]

> '9.12 An unemployed man (George, *of the age of* 45 to 47) called at our hut. He had said the night before that all ex-servicemen were to parade with medals and decorations at 9.45am at schoolroom to march with children to a service at church from 10 – 10.45. He appeared at our hut at 10.00 having merely reported himself at the parade. He said he had no use for that kind of thing – he had seen enough of it. (We knew he had been in the Regular Army and been in the Retreat from Mons.)
>
> 10.00 to 10.45 We proceeded into the village - much be-flagged and very similar to towns and villages we passed through on Tuesday. Met several people (mostly of the poorer working class) wearing Coronation ribbons very self-consciously. Boys with gaudy red, white & blue paper. It appeared from scraps of conversation that there was much veiled competition between streets and even individual houses. Friends passing and loudly commentating: *I've seen your house this morning, it's lovely. Have you? Doesn't the west end of (the village) look fine? Your flags are a credit to you!*
>
> One man told me (the ex-soldier George Chick) that

he had been up at 6am putting up bunting & paper festoons on his house. He had some pieces left over so he nailed them in a whip-like bunch on his door and, still having some small pieces of red, white and blue paper, he had made a frame of them for a portrait of the King (cut from the *News Chronicle*) & nailed it on his door. His comment on the whole street (Common Row) was interesting. He said *There wasn't a scrap of decoration to be seen yesterday and people said Common Row has nothing showing but we put it all up late last night & this morning*. (Common Row means the Row leading to the Common)

We called on Miss Mutter who keeps a *Miscellaneous* Shop in the Fore Street. She was keenly listening in to the broadcast from London. Her interest was far away but she gave me a rough account of what was to happen in Beer. And called in a friend – a man on the Coronation Committee - to tell us more. She was not greatly interested. He gave us a full plan of the day's doings which we followed through fairly thoroughly. (I learned afterwards that Miss Mutter listened in to London for seven consecutive hours.)

Noon. As I passed a group of fishermen in Sunday best – blue serge trousers, blue jerseys & blue close-fitting knitted caps – one of the chief talkers of the group (8 or 9 men of middle-age) was saying *It was in 1900 when I first came & in 1901 the Queen...* They were evidently recounting previous experiences & I thought he was referring to his experiences in the navy. Many of the fishermen have seen naval service.

12.30 Sat on the cliff & watched the sea & passing people – mostly villagers. One man – might be a visitor or local tradesman – came down with a dog. Dog decorated with coronation ribbons – drew much attention. Man looked pleased & basked silently in the admiration which his originality had called forth.

12.40 Went to a cafe to lunch. We were the only patrons (cold ham & salad). Noticed a portrait of Mrs Simpson & a large black & white newspaper photograph of King George V in naval uniform. No sign of present king & queen. After lunch got into conversation with proprietress of café. She was very busy making pasties for afternoon catering etc. Casually drew attention to picture of Mrs Simpson half-hidden behind some flowers. She said *Yes, I think her a remarkable woman. I know no harm of* [sic] *her. I have had that picture often turned to the wall & I had a beautiful one of her pulled down & burnt during the winter, when we had fires. I cannot talk to everybody like this for I have to be careful in business but I do think we have lost a good king – one who had sympathy with the working classes & that is largely why he had to go. They got rid of him. If he had married a princess, & lived with Mrs S., he could have been crowned today. I cried when he abdicated. I think his farewell speech was splendid.*

56 *Programme for the coronation of George VI and Elizabeth as king and queen of the United Kingdom and the Dominions of the British Commonwealth, Emperor and Empress of India, 12 May 1937.*

She turned on the *wireless* for us & we listened in from 1.20 to 2.20. This was mostly from within the abbey. While the prayer *Wherefore with Angels and Archangels & all the Company of Heaven* was proceeding there was much clamping about in the kitchen and at the *Sursam Corda* there was much bustling and banging. While the Archbishop was reciting passages in the Holy

Communion *Hear What St John sayeth* a customer came into the outer-shop and gave his order, in the same ecclesiastical tones, for tobacco (This customer was an old man between 65 – 75 who had seen service in India and gave graphic accounts of long waits in the streets – of standing still for hours, in full kit etc. etc. etc. He was slightly cynical in his reminiscences).

While the national anthem was being sung, somebody, I think it was the cafe proprietress, ran hurriedly and heavily upstairs to dress for the afternoon's doings. Part of the noisy interference with our listening (it did not annoy so much as divert our attention) was a hurried rush of some woman, on the committee of management for the Beer Coronation Fete, into the cafe to command the proprietress to provide tea for the jazz band of the town. She paid no attention to the broadcast!

Note. This jazz band is a company of youths aged 18 to 20 who have trained themselves as a band to play on piano – accompanied with drum and tambourine percussion, a somewhat limited selection of popular tunes. They paraded the village on foot & at times in a motor lorry – gaily adorned in red, white and blue ribbons. They were in evidence at various points from 10 to 1. They concentrated on the children's sports 2 to 4.30 and were at the social in the large garage to give selections and fill in the intervals of waiting. Their repertoire included *Daisy Bell*, *Two Lovely Black Eyes*, *After the Ball* - tunes all from 1887 to 1900. The only patriotic selection was *Land of Hope and Glory* but the greatest urge was to play *Daisy Daisy Give Me Your Answer True*.

2.20 We proceeded to the waterfront where a yachting race with 10 entries began at 2.30 and as there was little wind, was still in progress when we left at 4pm.

On the same beach as ourselves was a short Devonian lady much interested in the yacht boat race as her two sons were competitors. She was keen on that but remarked that Beer usually showed its loyalty far more emphatically than on this occasion. It was too near the Silver Jubilee she thought. We suggested divided loyalty to the Duke of Windsor. She warmed up then on theological grounds. If the Duke of Windsor had sinned, he must bear his punishment himself and not bring punishment upon the people as the bible tells us kings bring God's wrath upon the people, but we were

57 *Edward VIII when Prince of Wales, c.1915-1920.*

not to punish the Duke of Windsor. We were none of us as good as we ought to be and we should leave him to God. At the same time there was no evidence of personal enthusiasm for King George the Sixth and she just accepted the situation with a touch of resentment against Duke of Windsor which may have meant she preferred him.

2.45. A Mr Thorn, builder and decorator and organist in the congregational chapel, was my next victim. He had been listening into the Abbey services. It had moved him tremendously. His emotions were stirred by the ancient traditions, the setting, the music (which he was proud to think was all English except the Handel!) and the religious connections of it all. This from a Congregationalist – the most direct representatives of militant Puritanism at present in England.

3.00 - 4.15 We watched the children's races and games. Money prizes – 1s for 1st, 6d for 2nd and 3d for 3rd. The interest was purely personal and local. There was also maypole dancing and country dancing superintended by the day-school teachers of the village.

When the children's tea was arranged for 4.30 at the school at the opposite end of the village, there was a joyful stampede of children in that direction. The joy of feeding together is a great thing in the lives of these bairns. When we got to the school, there were some of the younger ones in tears, due to weariness and hysteria but they recovered at tea. Coronation mugs were given to all children, even the baby born on the previous day. The oldest man, an old sailor, and the oldest woman (from the almshouses next door) presented the mugs.

A lady of the district (not present) gave each girl a silk handkerchief, and each boy a six-penny piece in the new coinage. We then went home to tea (4.30) and when we returned to the village at 6pm the children were making the school ring with words singularly inappropriate to childhood - *Pack all your troubles in your old kit bag and smile*! They followed this by relating, *fortissimo*, how various numbers of men accompanied by a dog *went to mow a meadow*.

58 George VI florin (two shillings), 1947.

Strangely enough when [we] went out at night to view bonfires (miles away) and fireworks (within the mile radius) there were several youths in a garage singing a similar numerical song about green bottles (decreasing numbers) hanging on a wall.

6.30 – 9.30 Social

We arrived about 10 minutes late. The large garage about 120 ft square had been white-washed and cleaned and the iron girder roof filled with flags of the small triangular variety and small clusters of balloons. Flags of various types were on the walls and most prominent was the Stars and Stripes which was about 20 feet long.

The programme included musical selections (which we had heard all day) from the aforesaid jazz band, a cabaret to come on at the time of the king's speech (8pm), songs by residents, dancing & a whist drive. Dancing to continue until 2am. The songs sung were of the well-known and traditional kind. My friend, Thorn, sang quite well - a song in praise of Devon and Devon maids and *Land of Hope and Glory* (Elgar). A girl of the village aged about 16 but of enormous size, dressed in evening dress of a man, sang comic songs *You can't do that there 'ere* and *The evening went a little bit higher* in Kate Lay style! A fisherman's wife sang *The Londonderry Air*.

But the performance which was received with acclamation was the cabaret show done by eight village girls who came to the platform at 7.50. They were dressed, somewhat incongruously, in red, white and blue skirts obviously homemade. They marched about the stage doing various patterns in country dance manner for five minutes and sang *Three cheers for the Red, White and Blue*. The chief sentiment in this is *The army and the Navy forever*.

Three Cheers for the Red, White and Blue then followed the king's speech which was received respectfully enough. Mr Baldwin had proceeded him in the name of Great Britain, *Northern* Ireland the Isle of Man and the Channel Islands. Everybody seemed to be conscious of the king's difficulty in speaking, but were very attentive and considerate. The attempt at joining in the national anthem was almost a fiasco but was saved from absolute disaster by switching off and beginning again and singing the two less disreputable stanza of this same piece of vulgarity.

A lady sitting next to me said she liked the king's voice better than that of the Duke of Windsor. It had a deeper quality and was not so *cockney*.

Then followed votes of thanks in the usual include-everybody kind. The most noteworthy element in the speeches was that voiced with great sincerity by the local baker that we had gone through a unique

***59-62** The Allies and the Empire were often depicted in Britain's patriotic war posters.*

OUR EMPIRE IS
UNITED AGAINST
NAZI TYRANNY

TWO YEARS AGO
The British Empire
stood alone...
TODAY, FOUR-FIFTHS OF
THE WORLD IS UNITED
AGAINST AXIS TYRANNY

By Land, Sea and Air
THE ALLIES ARE HITTING BACK

M. HUBERT PIERLOT
QUEEN WILHELMINA
Dr. BENES
KING HAAKON
GENERAL DE GAULLE
GENERAL SIKORSKI
KING GEORGE of the HELLENES
Grand Duchess of LUXEMBOURG
KING PETER
LEADERS OF THE ALLIED NATIONS
WHOSE HEADQUARTERS
ARE IN BRITAIN
PRINTED IN ENGLAND

experience that day and it reminded us that there was no country on Earth where there was so much happiness, prosperity and freedom as in England and that we should show *the foreigner* in no one certain terms that we valued our happiness and freedom. (no prosperity this time)

There was no mention of the king and it seemed as if all mention of him was kept in the background as far as possible and when mention was made it was in the direction of implied apology e.g. his deeper voice and his sincerity.

The cabaret then continued. Members of it sang *The English Rose*, *Bonnie Banks of Loch Lomond*, *Land of my Father*, *Mother McCree*. Another cabaret turn was an elaborate reading of *A reg'lar, reg'lar Royal Queen* from Gilbert & Sullivan's *Gondoliers*. The last turn was the cabaret dressed as sailor girls and boys dancing horn pipes. For Beer, like most Devon places, has a strong naval tradition and the emphasis was continually on the sea and the navy.

The general impression I got of the whole day was that people were glad of an opportunity to let themselves go but in every case it resulted (or so it seemed to me) in competitive expression (often quite conventional) and where more original (as in the jazz band and the girls cabaret show) it was frank self-advertisement affording an opportunity to be seen and heard and in the case of older people recounting what they had done in times past.

On the whole we had a most enjoyable day in perfect warm weather - hardly a threatening cloud. The people seem quite satisfied that they had done their patriotic duty. They were greatly interested in one another and the cheering of efforts at entertainment was cordial. On the whole, even if tinged with irony, from brothers and *friends*. England and Empire seem to them to be the community - Beer. There was little evidence of any larger loyalty. If there was that larger loyalty, I missed it - yet it may be there.'

Mr Raine presumably returned to Ilford shortly afterwards for the start of the new academic year. Two years later he was evacuated with his school to Ipswich where he continued to write for Mass Observation.

6. Enid Atkinson, Researcher, 1944

Miss Enid Atkinson (1898-1978) was an economic and social researcher and a prominent supporter of the League of Nations and the National Council of Women. She resided in Newcastle-upon-Tyne and visited Devon because of family connections: her seventy-five-year-old aunt Mary Maddison (1869-1956) had recently moved into a new flat in Beer. She also referenced 'Mrs W', who may have been her aunt's sixty-two-year-old widowed companion, Mrs Marion Wilding (1882-1962), with whom in 1939 she had lived at Botter Gate in Newton Abbot. In 1944 the two women shared the flat in Beer. The nature of their relationship is undetermined. Miss Atkinson's diary was entitled 'The End of the War'.[102]

'Sept. 1st (Friday) … Arrived Seaton alone, bus late (glad we had the foresight to ask for sandwiches in the train), arrived in Beer, unpacked, had tea, then had a look at sea and went up to Mrs W's & Aunt M[ary]'s new flat. Stayed till dinner time. Had lobster for supper, first time this season, went to bed early, a terrific gale of wind and rain all night.

Saturday (Sept. 2nd), Wettish, sat in lounge knitting till driven out while fathers pay farewell visits. Aunt M[ary] called so did Mrs H, changed our rooms over, then went out for a bit. After midday meal sat on cliff above beach and knitted, then went to tea at flat & stayed till supper time. After supper lady asked me to play bridge but couldn't make up a four as people say they have come here for a rest. Several women here with children from London. One, quite young, has a young girl to

18. Steilküste in Devonshire (BB 36).

63 Germany's published invasion materials included this view of Beer entitled 'Steep cliffs in Devonshire', 1940.

look after her small boy. How's that, Mr [Aneurin] Bevin?

Sunday (Sept. 3rd) Fifth anniversary of our declaration of war on Germany. Most people in Beer went to church… Fine in morning so walked over cliffs nearly to Branscombe. Afternoon wettish so knitted and read, then went to tea at flat. Mr G from University of Cambridge there, really lives in Florence. Much upset by feared devastation. Thinks Germans may have used his villa for a battery site (he fought in Greece in last war) says they have blown up the most beautiful bridge in the world. Lights later going out after dinner so went for a walk and then to bed.

Monday (Sept. 4th), A wet day so stayed in hotel waiting room… Went up to flat before dinner and decided it was no good trying to go to Lyme Regis. Tried to phone Bovey Tracey after lunch but 1½ hours delay so knitted and read *The Forest and the Ford* till time to go to the flat for tea. After tea, attended a frock for Aunt M, then went for a walk as it had cleared up. After supper read *F&F* and finally got through to B.T. Evacuees have not arrived and M doesn't think they will now, so wants Aunt M to go through. Said *Isn't the news wonderful. I*

64-5 *Patriotic posters praised the help from the men of the Empire.*

can hardly believe it. (she and Aunt M thought the war wouldn't last 6 months in the beginning!)

Sept. 5th (Tuesday) A fine day at last! Waiters told us at breakfast that our troops were into Holland and it is rumoured that American troops are into Germany. Germans are withdrawing their troops from Finland and (it is said) Norway and Greece. Spent morning sitting on cliff top knitting and reading, got caught in a

***66** Fish was not rationed during the war but supplies were erratic and unlike those offered by pre-war fishmongers.*

violent shower. Mrs W came down to see us and make arrangements (already made) about going to Lyme Regis. Drove over to Lyme Regis in a hired car, sat on front, explored town and museum. They seem to have had a pulling-down mania round about the thirties which has removed the last vestiges of the old town. Refused tea at a GG hotel, wonder if they can do this to members. Get tea at a café & wandered about till car returned from other errands…

Sept. 6th (Wed.) Went into Seaton by doubling up with some people who had ordered a car, returned same way (Mrs W horrified and said nothing could induce her to share a car with anybody!). Spent most of morning hanging about station & town waiting for Mrs B who was coming from the next station, also for fish which cannot be had (save for dabs) in these seaside places except by train (local fish goes away by train). So late when they arrived that we got no fish and saw very little of Mrs B. Saw the wreck of an LCT on the beach said a, to have been mined, b, to have broken loose while being towed to Plymouth. Had been there a week and now unguarded and swarming with children. Quite hot for here & now, so bathed before ten, then went to flat for ten and did some sewing, listened to 6 o'clock news, dined… talked to Lord H who lives at Limpsfield [Surrey] and appears to have had a front seat for the doodlebugs (appears that after 4 days there have been some more) says he saw one attacked by a plane, collide with a balloon, balloon burst & bomb crashed & plane only just avoided both. Grand sight…

Sept. 7th (Thursday), Had a sherry party for Father B & Mrs G… Afterwards Mrs W and Aunt M stayed to lunch. Not very successful as rabbit, and Mrs W just wouldn't eat it. Later D, Aunt M & I went up to a lovely 15th century house and had tea. We would all have preferred to walk home through the lanes but Mrs W insisted on sending car. The whole fact of the matter is that people in her position haven't been made nearly uncomfortable enough by the war (instance the characters in Angela Thirkell's novels whether they are being most hardly done by because they have no butter) and in consequence I expect we shall have another one.

Sept. 8th (Friday), went to visit Mrs O whose son (RGF) has just been home on leave after 3½ years foreign service. It now transpires that he got married to a WAAF on draft leave and as Mrs O says *things failed at the church door* as you might say. However, I suppose, as she has talked about it, all is now well. Afterwards went in car to Sidmouth, stopping at Branscombe to have a look at the 15th century church. They have restored a little of the fresco - do wish the Office of Works would liaise over their job and get on with them, for while they think it quite unnecessary to clean our office windows or see that the floor is washed, they do that sort of job well.

Sidmouth still behind barbed wire, saw a few Yankee sailors about and not much else. Driver says he has seen in paper that boys of 18-19 will have to do 12 months' service after the war – a daft idea but dear to the hearts of the Tories who will use it to relieve the unemployment figures…

Sept. 9 (Saturday), said to have been white frost last night. Morning so cold that I came out without a hat, later so hot that I could hardly bear it. Walked and sat alone on cliffs, afternoon went to tea with one of Beer's *old families*. Live in a lovely house with a garden cut out of cliff-side. Told me when this house was built it cost£40 to level lawn, thought it would have cost nearer £400 now. Feel this is an awful lot of money in this village, though only industry fishing & (since war) net-making factory. Told me Red Cross fete held at next house realised £1,000 in one afternoon. Some more people have arrived from London for a well-earned rest. One elderly woman told me she was at a First Aid Rest in Victoria. Had slept there and never had her clothes off for 6 weeks. After supper, some more of them talking, one said time war was over all was done with or she didn't know what sort of life we should have to lead, probably return to living in caves like pre-historic men. Another said so far as she was concerned, she had had to live in the shelters till last Thursday and felt it was exactly like living in a cave. Said there had been a strong rumour in London last week that war was over. Germans having capitulated. It now appears that we are not yet in Holland.

Sept. 10th (Sunday) Another very hot day. Packed up parcels and took them up to flat, did some sewing. After dinner sat 2 hours on cliff in boiling sun knitting, then went to tea at flat. After tea Mrs W went to church and Miss B came in. After supper (lobster) wrote up diaries and read. Aunt M says Miss B (their landlord) a bit queer and her maid, who has *brain storms* when German planes come over, says Hitler is looking for her and gets under table. Agrees with me that many people in Beer are a bit barmy. Man in the hotel says he went to explore quarries and found them shut off by steel doors so far in, informed him that this place so hush-hush that MPs (VP) always on duty, live there in fact, says he never saw any signs of sentries or army at all. Is this the fruits of a week of victories!...

Sept. 11th (Monday), left Beer 9.30 by car, caught 10am train from Seaton, due London 2.42…'

Miss Atkinson never married and died in Newcastle in 1978 after a lifetime of campaigning for world peace and women's rights.[103]

BELSTONE

In the 1930s there were some 321 residents in this moorland parish. Its appeal to tourists is seen in these two day-surveys.

7. Edward Glanfield, Student, 1937

Edward Dalzell Glanfield (1916-1997) was an undergraduate at Exeter College, Oxford, and during the summer break lived with his parents at 4 Lockyer Road in Plymouth. In 1937 he wrote four day-surveys for MO of which two in September and another in December related to Belstone.[104]

12 September 1937

'Moorlands Hotel, Belstone, nr Okehampton, Devon, as I have not previously sent you a survey from this place, I append a description of surroundings.

Moorlands Hotel consists of a number of private sitting and bed rooms; grid electric light, hot water, good plain cooking and all *refinements* though without pretentious modernisms. This run by Mrs Perch [sic], assisted by girl-servant about 18 *living in* and man servant about 40 *living out*. Latter very brisk and has the fondness of an Oxford scout for work, tobacco and conversation. Place full up and a bit understaffed but everyone looked

67 *Moorlands House, Belstone, 2025.*

68 *The nearby village of Belstone, early 1900s.*

after well, myself in particular perhaps because [I have been] known *since so high* by Mrs Perch [Pike]. Her husband, a very cheerful little man, runs the farm attached and does the chauffering to Okehampton Station and for expeditions arranged by the guests.

Visitors mostly old and apparently unmarried ladies, with nasty little dogs and sometimes idiotic-looking big ones. An occasional elderly gentleman and, still more occasionally, families with very small children and nurse. Place open all year and extremely quiet at all times.

Village of Belstone, a fairly well-known holiday resort for north quarter of Dartmoor – agreed by Dartmoor writers to be the finest, since it contains the wildest scenery and highest tors. The native inhabitants are either Moor farmers, granite-quarriers, boarding-house or hotel-keepers and small tradesmen. Resident visitors mainly middle-class, trippers sometimes by charabanc but latter only for day and do not penetrate much beyond village. Occasional gypsies to pick whortleberries on moor. But the roads made on the other side of Belstone Tor in connection with the artillery range on Halstock Down, together with the nearness of the celebrated Cranmere Pool, attract a lot of motor traffic in summer, though this does not touch Belstone.

Cranmere Pool worthy of note; must have been quite a respectable moorland tarn long ago but bank breached and only in rainy weather does it hold more than a puddle of water. Normally just a large oval depression of no interest at all but for its associations. These are 1, difficulty of finding it, actually easy enough by Yes Tor approach and in midsummer explorers can be seen heading for it from all directions. 2, danger of drowning in surrounding fens. This only exists, if at all, near the river-heads and people visit the Pool, even in midwinter, alone. 3, the Cranmere Post Box, a tin box is kept in a cache in the bank of the pool, in which visitors leave stamped addressed cards to be collected by the next comer, who will in turn leave his and take the previous ones with him to post on his way home. This practice dates from at least 1905.

Further up the Taw Valley lies Taw Marsh, a broad heathery plain of considerable size. This is used as pasture from May – August, when the Okehampton Artillery Ranges prevent the rest of the north quarter being used for the purpose. But the Belstone farmers have several very old venville or common land rights over much of the neighbourhood and they receive compensation from the War Office for loss of pasturage elsewhere. It was recently proposed by a rather questionable private enterprise to construct a reservoir on Taw Marsh but, much to the relief of the Belstone farmers, the bill was rejected by the House of Lords.

I imagine that any Oxford undergraduate on long vacation is pretty well master of his own time and I am particularly so since I am living entirely by myself at this hotel (chiefly with the purpose of doing some work before my return to Oxford) and am bound only by meal times.

Thus, it is hard to say whether last Sunday was typical for such a person, in particularly so for myself, as I was influenced by the wishes or habits of no one else. The one way in which it was not typical for me was that I couldn't settle down to letter-writing or other scribbling of which I usually do a large amount on Sundays with either my wonted enthusiasm or success in getting something done.

To my mind, a typical Sunday contains most of the following ingredients:

1, Meals tend to be half-an-hour later.

2, People tend to be more sluggish, perhaps due to Sunday clothes and, 3, heavier meals. However much I try to avoid it, I always have the feeling that on Sundays I have been trapped into eating twice as much as I want to and four times as much as I really need. A hot Sunday lunch makes me twice as bloated as exactly the same meal on a weekday and this is quite irrespective of previous exercise.

4, A lost, sheepish, don't-quite-know-what-to-do atmosphere amongst people in the streets, like visitors from another planet at the Two Minutes' Silence.

5, Smug pompous respectability in town; riff-raffery in country.

6, Dismal clanking of church bells. I cannot understand why this doesn't make people want to put leagues between them and the churches.

Personal attributes to Sundays:

A, Impossibility of receiving letters irritates me, also plethoric lethargy I can never escape after meals.

B, A day when conscience does not demand that I should make an attempt to do official work (law) and when I can therefore do a lot of hard and really interesting work on my scribbling. It is very rarely the least effort for me to take considerable pains to make the latter as good as I can, probably because I am not obliged to do it. On this account. I much look forward to Sundays.

C, Such dull respectable people abroad that my Sunday *constitutional* is not half as interesting as my week-day ones are.

Health:

Good until about 4.30pm when I returned from a walk feeling clammy and stuffy. Indigestion began about 6 and went on all evening though not violently enough to incommode me. Either due to sudden change of temperature or to eating some foul sugary biscuits at tea - felt hungry on coming in at 4.30 and didn't realise what I was doing until too late. Often wondered whether to consult a dietician but he would probably be a crank or stop me drinking wine or want to operate on me. Later on, my nose became a bit bunged up, squirted Endrine down it on retiring. Hope I don't catch a head-cold, for it will fuddle my head, make me incapable for work and unable to smoke.

Weather:

Frost in early morning, later crisp and sunny - just as I like it. But by afternoon it clouded over and was just like a mild winter day, chilly when not moving about and stuffy when one was. Intermittent drizzling mist began about 3.45pm and slight South West wind, fatal to good weather in this part of the country. Heavy rain from 5pm to 8.30pm. So disgusted with it by then that I took no further notice of it.

Striking dreams

I did have one for once, so vivid I remembered it easily on awakening. First, my mother and I were watching flight of aircraft in formation from top window of my home at Plymouth. One machine, flying very low the whole time, crashed into roof of house opposite. Short fade out. With someone in unrecognisable part of Ledbury, Herefordshire, where a railway branch line joined main track. Gasometer nearby. Suddenly a huge express loco (apparently runaway) roared down branch-line, pitching from side to side. Horrified moment while I thought it would strike the gasometer. It joined the main track and then I realised it would charge full-tilt into an up train. Short but frightful tension ended by an appalling crash. I seem to remember that the gasometer joined in the chorus by blowing up. A goods train screamed past with brakes full on. Heard someone say *Hundreds killed.* Finally, at home in Plymouth once more talking with my mother about the accident which now seemed to have occurred in Germany. She was making me an offer to send out my father and grandfather to clear up the debris. *Finis.*

Reflection leads me to believe the whole nightmare was product of subconscious war phobia but it might equally have been caused by an unavoidable gastronomic indiscretion the previous night.'

69 - 70 *Two British posters recognising help from the West African colonies.*

12 September 1937

Mr Glanfield wrote a second day-survey in Belstone.

'7am roused by light. (I find this the least painful method and always leave my curtains undrawn). Excellent effect of sunrise light on heathery slopes of Cosden (big Dartmoor hill) but not enough to stop me going to sleep again.

8.15am Roused by maid (see description of surroundings) with cup of tea. She makes it too strong, but I always forget to tell her. She distracts me with an inevitable comment on the weather. Great effort to make any coherent or intelligible reply but she seems to expect it of me.

8.45am Got up. Slippers and shoes downstairs (cleaned shoes always left in sitting-room). Feet chilly. Went to fetch slippers in shirt and trousers, hoping I should meet none of the old *beldames* on the way in case my attire, though perfectly decent, might shock one of them.

8.50am Bedroom invaded by wasp after wasp, perhaps due to the bay rum mixture with which I am struggling not too successfully to stop my hair falling out. Downstairs again (with dressing gown as precaution against possible female prudery) this time to fetch Flit machine.

8.55am – 9.20am Shaving, dressing and slaughtering wasps - at least five. Believe Flit gives the brutes an agonising death. When brought down, they seem to try to sting themselves to a quicker death in their death throes. Yesterday I took to squashing them after they had become helpless. While, however, I am not abnormally sadistic, it gives me great satisfaction to destroy them. Their ability to sting me if I attempt to ward off their aggravating intentions without the help of Flit, and their futile existence (at least I know of no way in which they are useful) induce me to believe that is a public duty to destroy them as much as possible. Bees, too, can certainly sting but they do produce honey, on which account I wouldn't hurt a hair on their bodies.

9.20am Rather late for breakfast but I knew it would be cold ham. Read *Sketches by Boz* for first time. Good example of Mass Observation. Most of books in my room are edifying Evangelistic tripe but there is a copy of Francis Griffin Stoke's translation of *Epistolae Obscurorum Virorum* (1925 edition, Chatto & Windus). Understand Mrs Perch acquired all these books in a mass. Wonder how the devil the *Epistolae* got amongst them? Excellent historical introduction by Stokes and the dog Latin of letters well translated into dog English.

10am Finished after-breakfast cigarette and began to write long letter to an old Westminster friend now in a West African regiment on the Gold Coast. He had recently written, and begged me to reply, saying how much correspondence was appreciated in the lonely Outposts of Empire; and I started with every intention of sending him one of my best efforts.

11.45am Filled one page of typescript (single spacing), but then I began to be at a complete loss for anything further to say. What on earth had I done or seen or heard that would interest the chap? Last met him in June 1936. Don't know what his taste may be by now. Skim through diary for this period, search for news barren of inspiration or any subject likely to instruct, elevate and amuse. In a black rage. Started off in capital style and now every possible subject threatened to develop into a novel, what with the explanation necessary to introduce it.

12 noon. Gave up in despair and return to Dickens. A mother and her two small sons return from walk; elder boy tries to be funny by talking in Cockney accent.

Mother: *Roger don't talk like that*!

Her voice, which is of the plaintive nagging sort, makes me suspect that as a mother, she's a tomfool (something wrong with my genders there) but in fairness I must admit her boys look the proverbial *picture of health and happiness.*

12 noon – lunch. More Dickens and wasp-slaughtering. Numbers of latter bear out my grandfather's remark that *If you kill one, twenty will come to the funeral.* Well, in this case it was their own funeral. My grandfather always tries to shoo wasps out of the window, rather than kill them. The last time he did so, he got stung. I considered he simply asked for it.

1.15pm lunch. My Oxford style, Brown bread and cheese and a glass of red Rioja. Spanish wines seem to me to have much more flavour than the equivalent French *Vin ordinaire.* Hope this blasted Civil War won't queer the market or for Sherry either.

1.35pm More Dickens. Later sat down to letter again, but it still proved unwritable. Woman tried to get Okehampton vet on the 'phone to attend to a dog that had swallowed a bone - gluttonous brut! Give me a cat any day. But vet out and his return uncertain. More wasp-slaughtering, window sill becoming a charnel house. Must have bumped off at least 20 in course of day.

3.20pm Out for fresh air and nothing else. Grey day and unless the weather is good, and I mean to do at least 8 miles, or unless I have congenial company, my mind becomes intensely bored with exercising my body. On such occasions I only go out because I dread feeling like a boiled owl if I don't.

Up Taw Valley, since most likely place for MO on Moor. Two youths and small boy on upper track one playing *Pack up your troubles* on mouth-organ. A few cars in good condition at end of track but not a soul visible. That means the usual trippers were deterred by the weather or the end because I have noticed that the trippers here (and elsewhere) don't bother to penetrate any distance into the Moor when the roads stop. Most of them wander a few yards away from their charabanc and picnic on the village green. Others, at most, go no farther than the beginning of the Moor itself. Only hikers and true Dartmoor enthusiasts go right into the hinterland. Private cars can get a little nearer the outskirts than the charabanc by means of a rough track. Consequently, their occupants can go further up the valley before their legs give way and they settle down with their hampers.

Hence, I expected to find, and did, only one or two middle-class families on the northern (nearer) edge of Taw Marsh. First, a picnic party of two women and one man, all middle-aged. Next, a father, mother and two young sons - all with bare feet and building a dam across the stream with small boulders (stream incidentally not very full in spite of recent heavy rains) and still further up a father, mother and small son also bare-footed and gazing speculatively at another dam made by some other people the previous Sunday (I happened to see the latter doing so at the time). Couldn't decide whether this family meant to wreck the dam or reinforce it.

3.40pm Disgusted with lack of material for MO and decided to climb Belstone Tor in faint hope there might be someone there or on other side. Began to do so, when a slight drizzling mist came on. Milky look about sky to the south. Swore violently at it, to the alarm of a sheep. Slight commotion amongst families down in valley. A good half mile away from them but their voices clearly audible. They called *Coo-ee* to each other (believe this originally Australian means of attracting attention at a distance. Is it a relic of Anzacs?) but seemed uncertain whether to retreat on account of weather spoiling. I climbed further up; mist increased in thickness. Hadn't had enough fresh air but resolved to return home since this was wetting in and as heavy rain and too damn hot already to put on Macintosh. Drizzle stopped a bit the next moment, started to climb again in hope that it mightn't come to much. But, on reaching top a blustering South West wind blew clouds of the stuff at me and I stumbled down the side I had ascended back home and in none too sweet a temper.

4.15pm Reached Moorlands in a muck sweat, which was intensified by fire in my room. Clothes damp, so had to stand in front of it a few minutes, fuming within and without.

4.30pm China tea and biscuits - no more brought in at my request in case I overeat myself in a fit of absent-minded gluttony and spoil my dinner. More weather-talk with maid when she brought it in. Why do people take such a morbid delight in discussing its all too obvious defects?

4.45pm Fatal presentiment that, despite precautions, I have eaten too many biscuits. Can't imagine why I did; most of them revoltingly sweet and sandwiched with bilious cream, the kind with which a very young child might excusably make himself sick at a party, but which, had my appetite been less indiscriminate, I should never dream of touching.

5pm Heard mother of two small boys telling maid in corridor that she had overwound and broken the first watch she had bought from Marks & Spencer's and then her second similar ditto lost half an hour every day. Think this was by way of apology for her continual late returns from walks for meals. Should have thought she could have afforded a more expensive but more reliable watch. However, a woman's idea of economy is often weird and wonderful. Heard one of her sons remark *But Mummy, you said yesterday it gained half an hour*!

Her reply incoherent. Which was more erratic – her watch or her truthfulness? Children invariably seem to be far more honest than adults and consequently the formers' company is to me far preferable to the latter's, though this perhaps because I don't often have it.

Start of a most depressing evening. Causes: heavy rain, complete inability to write that damn letter or indeed anything else, gnawing pain in my midriff, stuffiness in nose and entire absence in *Sketches by Boz* of a single likeable character. Boys scampering up and down stairs and passage and chuckling. Something charming and infectious about a child's laugh. Wish I had children of my own to keep me young and cheerful. But on reflection, if I had to choose between domestic bliss and drinking sound wine the scales will come down with a crash in favour of wine.

6.45pm Blazing hot bath to try to raise my spirits. Only partially successful. Tried to whistle first movement of Mozart Flute Concerto in D, but did it very badly this evening.

7.30pm Cold supper, but glass of white Rioja gave me a fair appetite (that's a characteristic of Sundays I forgot to mention – the evening meal usually is cold, probably because of Sunday being a maid's half-day).

8.15pm Rest of night spent in depressing myself with Dicken's reprehensible characters. I like his slightly pompous style and the period he wrote of has a certain sharp if sordid fascination. But there is a sameness

71 Photograph taken at Okehampton entitled 'Members of a U.S. infantry division in England march down into natural coliseum for maneuvers in conjunction with field artillery', 1 Sept. 1943.

about all the sketches – match-making mamas, elderly buffoons, asinine young ladies and foppish young men and I cannot stand his constant moralising, however good an effect it may have had.

Finally reduced to reading some of my own stuff - the height of egotism! But its fault stood out with irritating clearness and its good points seem to have existed only in my imagination.

11pm This an early hour for me to prepare for sleep, but lights are expected to be turned off by then. Tonight, however, I felt so thoroughly fed up with myself, everybody and everything that I was quite ready for it as something definite to do. Brushed teeth, wound up watch and in bed. Know I shan't feel like work tomorrow after such a futile, unsatisfying day.'

13 December 1937

Five months later he supplied a third day-survey:

'Monday, 13 December, 1.30 to 6pm, Moorland Hotel, Belstone, near Okehampton, Devon

1.30pm Returned from lunch to my sitting room. My hearth swept up by landlady during meal. Lit a Rothman's Gold Flake No. 1 and continued reading Trollope's *Barchester Towers*.

1.45 Cigarette finished, still reading Trollope.

2.00 Made out laundry list and wrapped up washing in a very clumsy parcel.

2.10 To Belstone Village and washerwoman's house. Latter out. Pencilled note pinned on raffia shopping bag hanging from front door knob to ask baker's van man to leave two loaves. Decided to return later with my washing.

On way back to Moorlands, saw a little woman (spectacles, brown coat) waddling along in gum boots ahead of me - probably wife of local cottager. As I approached, she turned around at sounds at my footsteps, half threw up her arms and made a face of astonishment. Then she turned and went on. A fox hound was running along between us (whose I don't know, saw it yesterday afternoon in different parts of village. Seems to be lost for no one apparently in charge of it at either time) and on my overtaking the woman, she turned leftwards away from me and began to shoo the *hound* (that is sheer pedantry, not reverence for hunting) away.

Dropped washing in my car in garage. Up Taw valley. River in a tremendous flood; fine site. This due rather to heavy snow in last few days and subsequent thaw than to heavy rainfall. Flood made walk more interesting, because I know the site of that valley by heart, beautiful though it is A few bedraggled sheep; cattle and horses on side of Belstone Tor. Not a soul to be seen.

Returned by cart-track higher up. Weather now fine. Looked unsettled before. Not unpleasantly cold. Very wet underfoot.

3.30pm Inspected oil, tyres, water of my car. Engine started at once. Let it take over briskly some minutes to warm up while I made Mass Observation notes. Road from Moorlands in shocking state – puddles, potholes, wet leaves and slush - though quite harmless because too narrow and steep for more than about 10 mph. Surface improves on approaching Belstone. Tried again at washerwoman's cottage; same result. Cold air makes car (1935 Morris 8) very lively. Think the steering will be the next thing to go wrong with it.

3.45 Dropping into Okehampton. This town seems to me to be without a single redeeming architectural feature and indeed few of any sort. Notice two new Belisha crossings. In the concentration of driving (which gives me a great deal of pleasure and to which I always give as much attention as I can) I quite forget I should be Mass-Observing and don't notice half of what I might.

Park car on left of main street. On getting out, I see it is outside a white parking line. Not worth altering its position but I hurry in case some rozzer [policeman] is nearby spoiling for a summons. Inspect posters outside local Odeon cinema; nothing there this week that I want to see. I think one film was called *Camille* and the other *Together in Love*, or words to an equally nauseating effect, with the Dionne Quins as star attractions. Small children often give me pleasure, but the only use I have for the Quins is that they have given rise to two very good jokes. (details on application is unknown) Into small newsagents. Clicking noise in adjoining room makes me realise it is also a hair-dressing establishment. Man (shop very dark, so no description possible) calls *Er Shop*! and younger man emerges. I buy *Western Morning News*. Notice unobscured word of heading of another paper on rack, in huge capitals JAPAN. I think *What have those damned swine been up to now*? Then I notice the paper is the *Express* and reflect *Oh, that bloody rag*!

72 *The Dionne quintuplets, born in Canada in 1934, were the first to survive infancy. This souvenir handkerchief was produced in about 1939.*

Return to car and start back at once. Children emerging from schools; overtake two boys on bikes, swerving about up the hill but little car traffic. Stopped for petrol at wayside station. Last time I called there I was served by what I thought was a retired naval officer. This time the man is another, pleasant face, sandy moustache, cap, corduroy knee breeches and stockings. Makes no conversation. Suspect he is anxious to get back to a fire and probably a cup of tea. He offers to unwrap the Duckham's Adcoid tablet my chilly fingers are fumbling with; does so and drops it into tank in no time. Cart driver makes room for me to pass in Narrow Tongue Lane. His alacrity embarrasses me. Still late by the time I arrive – 4.15.

According to the world-time indicator in the Piccadilly Tube Station there is about a quarter hour difference in sunset between London and Plymouth, of which Belstone lies roughly north. Smoke cigarette and do crossword in paper. Usually the *Western Morning News* has some item in it, e.g. on temperance, divorce, education or militarism, that will put me into a most enjoyable fury. But today there is nothing to make my blood really boil and I feel flat in consequence. Find I have forgotten to post letters in Oakhampton. I parked outside General Post Office and at the time it nearly reminded me but not quite strongly enough. Go out and slip them into nearby box. Feet feel cold and a little damp. Wonder whether they are wet enough to necessitate change of socks and shoes.

4.30 I am still debating this point when my landlady tells me tea is ready. Go into another room and eat

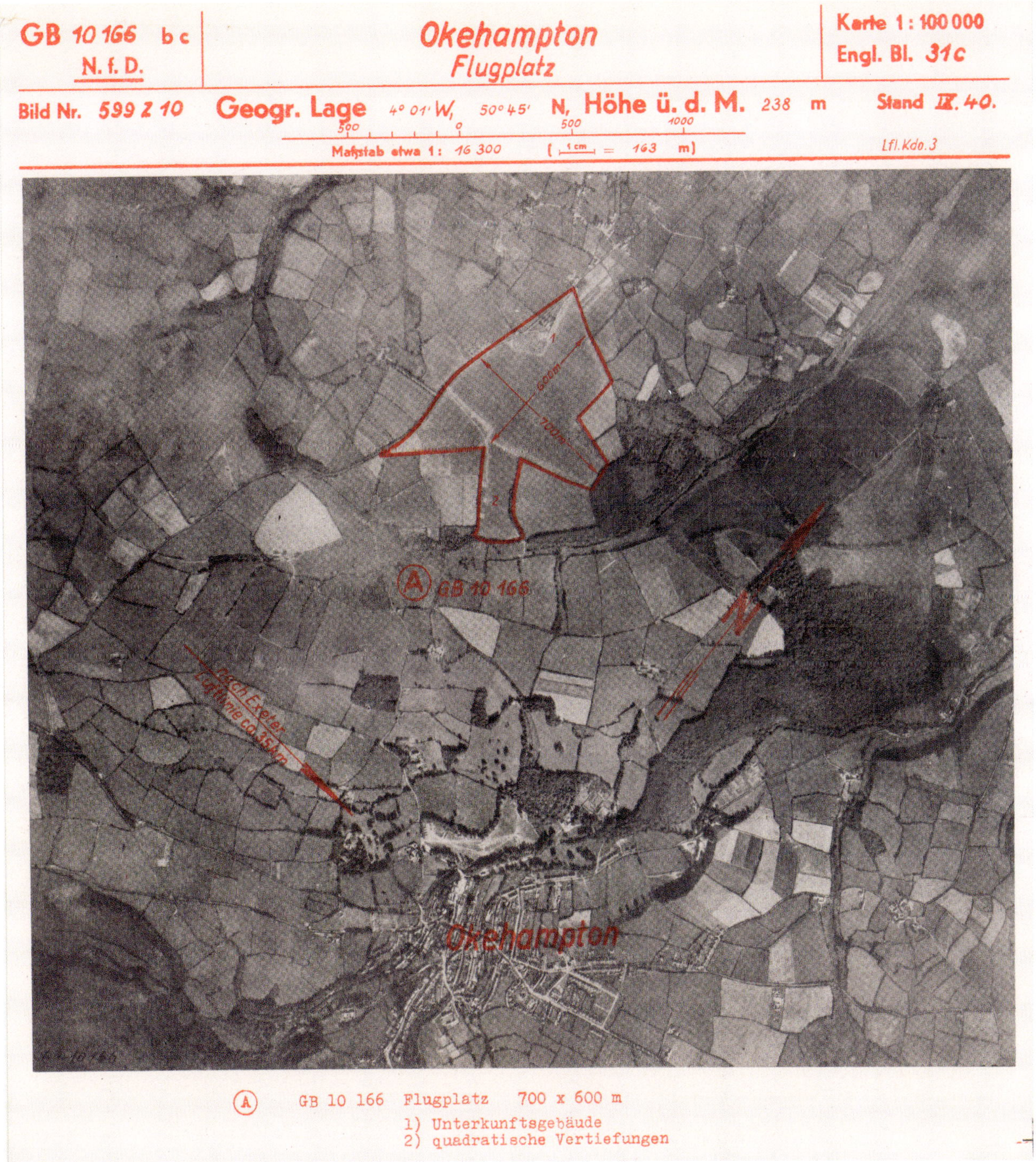

73 German aerial photograph of Okehampton, 1940.

scones, cream and a great deal of honey, though its stickiness on my hands make me swear and afterwards go upstairs to wash them. Since I have gone upstairs, I decided to change my socks and shoes.

5.45 My landlady's five-year-old daughter brings me a letter just left by the second and last delivery. The letter is nothing more interesting than an invoice from a well-known London book-seller, stating that a deposit I made some time ago is only 4 shillings and that I owe them 3 shillings 10 pence in respect of a recent purchase. This is clerical incompetence on their part; my deposit is actually 8 shillings. To make this clear to them will require a somewhat detailed letter and the sum involved is so small that I might pay up what I don't owe but for the fact that on every occasion I have dealt with them I have been much annoyed by their careless and dilatory business habits and that therefore, on the whole, the satisfaction of telling them where they get off will outweigh the trouble of doing so. I set about it, typing the letter and quoting a business reference in letters and figures about a yard long. It would interest me to know on what system these references are composed. This firm gives me a different one to quote with every letter it sends me. I try to make the position so clear that even a halfwit could understand it and this occupies me until about 6 o'clock.

I forgot to mention that on my return from Okehampton I stopped again at the washerwoman's cottage. She was still out; two sandwich loaves had been left in the raffia basket on the door knob. I left my washing on her doorstep.

Perhaps I need hardly add that few of the afternoon's incidents formed part of any routine. For instance I went into Okehampton merely because a, I wanted to give my car some exercise after nearly a week standing still, b, I like driving it, c, Okehampton might offer some scope for Mass Observation whereas Belstone would be most unlikely to do so. Nor do I usually buy any newspaper when I am out here, in spite of the fact that I am completely cut off from news of any sort. If the king were to be assassinated or London air-raided, I doubt if I should hear of it unless I went to the pub that night.'

The hotel, sometimes called the Moorland Private Hotel and listed in various directories as a private hotel, boarding house and apartments, closed in the 1950s but the Pike family continue to reside in the building which is now known as Moorlands House. Mr Glanfield also wrote a day-survey for Plymouth (**34**).

BIDEFORD

This North Devon town, located on the River Torridge three miles from the Bristol Channel, rivalled Barnstaple. Its prosperity came from the holiday trade, boat-building and glove-making.[105] The population was smaller than that of Barnstaple; in 1939 it stood at 9,969. That year the town experienced an influx of 675 people, a population increase of 7.2%. In comparison, Bideford Rural District had grown by 8.3% that year. By 1941 the borough had hosted more than 2,000 evacuees. In the months following the end of the war a town official recollected that the first contingent was the largest: some 1,500 London children had arrived between 13 and 16 June 1940. A month later Selhurst Grammar School pupils relocated to Bideford and were followed by a 'large influx' of Londoners in the autumn of 1941. Others came through official channels from Plymouth and Bristol as well as individuals and small groups who came on their own volition. The Chief Billeting Officer felt the peak was reached in February 1941 when 2,322 individuals were billeted or housed in requisitioned housing. About 250 individuals remained in Bideford in July 1945 and decided to stay rather than return to their former homes.[106]

There were some unforeseen consequences of evacuation: in 1940 Elsie Raylor, a London evacuee, wore a new mink-marmot coat in Bideford shortly after a visit from her husband William, a Metropolitan police constable who had been convicted of looting a furrier's shop in London.[107] The influx also included an unnamed woman referred to in September 1940 by Miss Adelaide Poole, a sixty-year-old MO diarist from Sussex, who wrote:

'As a contrast to my undisturbed life, my sister-in-law, a widow, very well off, with her daughter (19) left her nice flat in Hove in May and went to Bournemouth to an expensive hotel there. Wrote me how nice it was with whist-drives, dances and golf but *some of the people are going to Wales. Where is the safest place*? I suggested any

74 *Bideford in the early 1900s looking down the river Torridge.*

75 *A picturesque view of Bideford by Henry Bowser Wimbush produced for Raphael Tuck & Sons, 1908.*

quite inland village but she said she didn't want to go to *a tin-pot inland place*. Then they had a raid warning and had to go into a shelter for most of the night, so that settled Bournemouth for her. She went to Teddington, then to some place in the suburbs and the last I have heard they are both in Bideford, Devon, which she says is so lovely and quiet and helping her nerves, but she won't be able to stay long – too expensive. Her husband

76 *A view of Bideford with Long Bridge, c1850-70.*

77 German photograph of Bideford, 1940, included with Operation Sea Lion invasion plans, entitled Road Bridge in Bideford. Stone bridge with semi-circular arches over the River Torridge. Seen from Upcot Hill.

78 Luftwaffe map of Bideford, February 1940, which highlighted strategic areas in red.

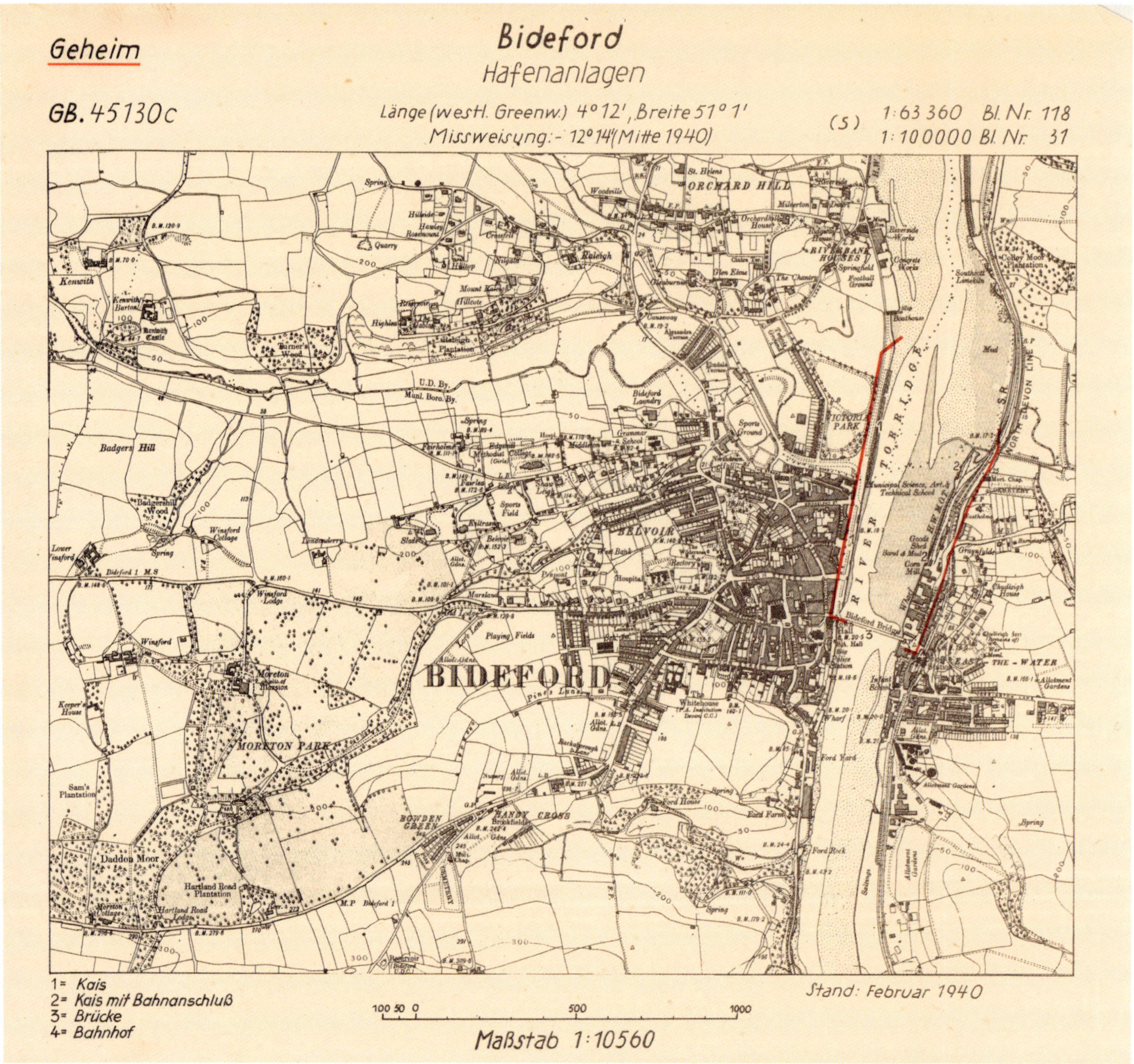

***79** German aerial photograph of the hafenanlage (harbour installation) at Bideford, February 1943.*

died three years ago and the considerable property is not yet settled.'[108]

Something of the character of the town was captured on 18 October 1940 by Olga Muller, a sixty-nine-year-old widow who also lived in Sussex. That day her niece arrived from Bideford:

> 'Niece is poultry expert for North Devon. Works under county council. Has lately taken course in fruit bottling and preserving. Also does ARP night driving, canteen work, rides when she gets a chance, and goes to soldiers' dances as she feels they better meet some *sensible* girls too. Has had numbers of Pioneer Corps in Bideford, musicians of Vienna operas, singers of renown, etc. but all disliked by Hitler because they happen to be full or part Jew.'[109]

Bideford had a much quieter war in respect to air raids than some Devon towns. Two bombs fell at Bowden Green and a Canadian plane crashed on 7 March 1945 near the gas works. Three men lost their lives.[110] There was one Bideford casualty from an air raid: in 1941 Harry Lucas of 14 North Road died in the bombing of Plymouth.

British Rola Ltd, the manufacturer of the RAF B3 vacuum pump, relocated from London after a bomb destroyed one of its factories. The entire plant was moved over the course of three days. Forty employees came to Bideford and another 450 local men and women were subsequently employed by the firm.[111] During the war Bideford also produced wooden minesweepers and small patrol boats at Blackmore & Sons, the small shipyard at Ford Yard. This eventually included HMS *Stedham*, a 106-foot inshore vessel built in 1955.[112]

Both Bideford diarists commented on the abundance of evacuees, the housing of whom was the port's main contribution to the war effort.

8. Nancy Brown, Librarian, 1939-40

80 British blackout poster by the Ministry of War Transport, by 1943.

Miss Nancy Kathleen Beresford Brown (1910-1983) was born in Pilton near Barnstaple. Her father, a solicitor who had served as County Coroner and Barnstaple's mayor, had died suddenly in 1930 and her Irish-born mother subsequently married Brigadier Walter Richard Reid of Phayre House in Northam. Miss Brown contributed diaries from 1939 to 1941 and also answered directives from 1939 to 1942.

She worked as a librarian at the North Devon Athenaeum in Barnstaple and reported to MO that there had been fewer borrowers when war broke out but, after a week, they had returned along with new borrowers including voluntary evacuees. She claimed the blackout had forced people to stay at home at night and read books.[113]

Miss Brown resigned on 8 June 1940 in order to join the war effort ('left the library today for good, with the intention of joining the WAAF soon. The attitude of the directors is that I am a fool and they wash their hands of me. My place is filled and will not be kept open… I must say I am not looking forward to leaving peaceful Devonshire and going to the WAAF in London just as the bombs begin to fall.'). She subsequently experienced bombing and wrote of her experiences one night in a shelter ('the anti-aircraft guns sounded just like a high tide on the pebble ridge at Westward Ho! and the dull thuds that one heard were like waves breaking on the rocks').[114]

Directives: blackout, personal appearance, class and dance halls

She asserted some decided opinions as in 1939 on the deaths being caused by blackout ('I know that a large number of people are being killed on the roads but that is their own fault if they will walk on the road, instead of the pavement, and wear dark colours. They are invisible to motorists and they ought to know it. It is mostly elderly people who get knocked down because they are so stupid and slow-witted.'). The following year she was unhappy with the BBC's news reports:

> 'They so annoy me that for the last 10 days I have stopped listening to them. All through the time when the war really started on the Western front and the Germans were making such an awful push to the gap left by the French, the BBC would announce their advance and then say to reassure us that it was only a few isolated motorised units far in advance of the real German columns who had entered Arras, Amiens, Abbeville, Calais, etc. These units, it added, were in a very dangerous position. What was the use of trying to allow the country to sleep even with the enemy at the gate? Secondly, there is about 20 minutes news in every bulletin about the RAF as though they were the only men fighting. I know they are very brave and marvellous. We don't need to be told that in every news. It is quite apparent. The BBC ram the RAF down our throats to such an extent that I now do not bother to listen to what they have been doing. I am quite sure the men in the RAF would be the first to deplore all this publicity. The BEF seem almost reduced to non-entities. I think there is too much talk in the BBC news and too little information at the end of it all.'

Insights into Miss Brown's character were revealed in her replies on her personal appearance:

'I take pains to have as nice clothes as I can afford and

to look as neat and well-groomed as possible and to dress with good taste because I am short and plump, so unless I choose my clothes with care, I can easily look untidy and messy. I like to look as pretty as possible in order to be appreciated by men and so as not to be thought dowdy by other women.'

She thought 'Nine young men out of ten like make-up. They hate to see a pale face. It makes a girl look smarter, up-to-date and more brilliant and noticeable'. Not surprisingly, she was careful in her choice of clothes:

'I spend quite a long time studying dress catalogues and making a list of what clothes I want each season, planning ahead and sticking to a colour scheme. I do not choose the latest fashions in hair, clothes or hats unless they suit me and the occasions for which I chiefly need them. I spend about £35 a year on clothes, hair, face creams, etc. There are no real factors which make it difficult to keep up to a desirable standard except that one would always like to buy the dress that is a little more expensive that one can afford. I don't buy it.'

Miss Brown was also certain of her position in society, she was upper middle class:

'because my father and grandfather belonged to it and because, although I am not particularly sociable, my friends are in that class and not the tradesmen class. Because I have a pedigree and my people are well-connected. Not a question of income. My mother and I lived in a labourer's cottage for 3 years but still belonged to the same class'.

She added:

'Sometimes I am a little embarrassed with servants when conversation has to be made with them. I can't think of anything to say to them. But as long as they keep the conversation going, I am quite at home. So also with smart and somewhat blasé young men. They bore me and I bore them. Thus, we are doubtless mutually embarrassed. I am at home always with my own class and with farmers or cottage folk.'.[115]

Miss Brown remained on her own but just before the war her situation temporarily changed:

'I recently made a new friend of a young man of my own age. I previously thought that class would make no difference if your ideas and likes and dislikes were the same. He belongs to the middle class. But I have discovered after a little closer acquaintanceship that the difference in class seems to produce in us contrary ideas upon everything. He likes bands and piers and girls all dressed up and masses of people – to be in a crowd. All these things are distasteful to me. His clothes, though good, don't seem quite right somehow. The expressions he uses often jar upon me. He thinks dressing for dinner smart, I have never thought much about it one way or the other. He is rather ashamed of old clothes, I have never thought of them as detrimental to a man. The more we see each other, the less pleased we are with each other and the wider grows the invisible gulf between us, the more we exchange opinions.'[116]

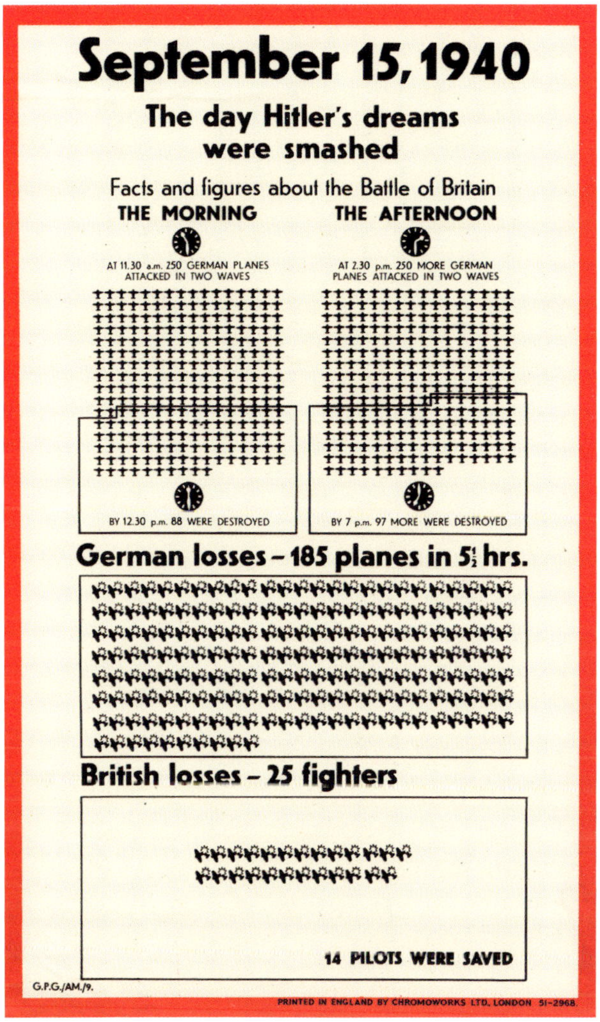

81 Poster celebrating the Battle of Britain, 1940.

Miss Brown had firm views on music including dance music ('music with a distinct and regular beat, played in ballrooms and dance halls for ballroom dancing, with or without song refrains'), jazz ('the same as above but in many cases discordant and blaring with much use of saxophones') and swing music ('an awful discordant aimless noise without rhyme or rhythm or any break in the flow of music, which is relayed once a week from America'). She recalled:

> 'The first dance I ever went to was a terminal college dance. Four of us went with our partners, had dinner beforehand [and] then we went back to college by taxi to the dance. We all danced with each other's partners but mostly with our own. My partner and I sat out all of the *Paul Jones* and *Excuse The Dances* because I dislike dancing with strangers. I do not dance *Excuse Me Dances*.'

She was more open to dance halls ('cheap popular form of entertainment. I believe one can dance on a good floor to an excellent band and see some first-class dancing') and professional dance partners ('a very good idea, they must meet a need or they wouldn't be there. Of course, I suppose in some low haunts they are simply *street girls*. But everyone has got to live somehow.').

82 Recruitment poster for the ATS and WAAF, 1942.

Plymouth

Miss Brown wrote a diary for two days in October 1939:

> 'Caught the 8am bus to Plymouth, a journey of three hours, for an interview with the Women's Auxiliary Air Force. Passengers included five sailors returning from weekend leave. An absolute roar of laughter went up as on route we passed a farmer in a car drawn by an old horse. He had fixed shafts to the car and it was ambling slowly along the road. The streets were full of people shopping. The balloon barrage was up and it seemed to be a very slender protection in itself. It was the first time I had seen a long barrage. Saw various women and girls going about with badges in their hats or on their arms, or in full uniform. All seemed very full of themselves. My interview was not a success as I said I had to give a month's notice to my employer and the interviewer said I must come at 24 hours' notice which was what I had feared. So that was that. I was interviewed by a toothless old hag in a green cardigan suit.
>
> The journey back was accomplished in the same time as by daylight except although we travelled some 60 miles along narrow twisting roads the bus drivers are indeed splendid workers. Our only incident in a tedious journey home was running over a hound, poor thing. It was killed instantly. I heard the bus conduct say *Oh, Hitler will soon commit suicide.*
>
> Spent the afternoon having my hair *permed*. Thought I had better have it done now in case my hairdresser was called up soon. He is a young man about 25 and had no enthusiasm for the war at all. He thought it was all the fault of the politicians to let Germany get so strong. *They should have jumped on her when she went into the Rhine*.'[117]

War dreams

Miss Brown also wrote a war dreams diary in the opening months of the war:

83 *Miss Nancy Brown wrote of having war dreams including one of Josef Stalin.*

'22.9.39 I was in the WAAF or some such company and put my hand up to vote for something whilst standing in the ranks. Woke up to find my hand above my head.

I am anxious to join the WAAF.

24.9.39 I was with a large congregation in church. We sang the National Anthem very falteringly as we had no organ and we did not seem to know the words.

We sang the National Anthem in church last week.

25.9.39 I was sitting in a tea garden in a place called Criccington which I was told on placard on the table was pronounced Criccus, talking to the Minister of Education who told me that there would shortly be no fish at all on the market.

Result, I expect, of reading in the paper about the failure of the Billingsgate scheme.

26.9.39 I and some other people tracked Stalin, who was organising a spy gang, to his lair in a cave under a railway line. He gave orders by wireless on a plane.

A result, I think, of a film I went to a week or so ago about gangsters who were organised by a headman who directed them by wireless.

An air raid. I sheltered in an upstairs room with some children. They would press their noses against a French window. The windows were smashed in by the children who were only slightly injured. I had to bind up their hands.

Result, I think, of going to see Wuthering Heights on Saturday and seeing Heathcliff deliberately putting his hands through the glass of his window and later having them bound up by Flora Robson.

12.11.39 Dreamt I was on sentry duty with a man friend. Between us we pumped a German sentry who told us that there was going to be an attack soon but that it was lost already as the Germans didn't want to win it.

An example of wishful dreaming.

23.11.39 Dreamt I was out in an air raid in the country and could only find inadequate cover from gas being sprayed on me. The aircraft flew so low I could see the crews. In the distance there were British warships.

Result of account of raid on Shetlands on the news that same evening? The announcer used the underlined sentence exactly.

[Dreamt] that I read in the paper that Dr Goebbels had died in bed at the age of 54. It created little sensation, however. He died of eating his own words!'

1939

Miss Brown's first diaries covered the period from 11 August to 10 September 1939 and 13 November to 15 December 1939:

'Monday, August 11 1939 Still on holiday. Walked into the town this morning (about 1 mile), do some shopping and hire a prawning net. Came home, cleaned my car. Met girl at bus whom I had asked for tennis. Played tennis on usual club day. About 15 people present. Talk at tea chiefly concerned Hitler, i.e. as to

84-5 *Miss Brown dreamed of Nazi officials and wrote that in Bideford Hitler was part of everyday conversation*

whether or not he had a double, or such like irrelevant arguments. Spent evening at home, reading, writing and listening to wireless. We dislike having to shut out the twilight by pulling the black curtain before lighting the lights.

Tuesday, August 12 1939 Went out shrimping at Westward Ho! all the morning. Played croquet in the afternoon and tennis in the evening. My stepfather went to a meeting to decide about the senseless practice of having voluntary workers having to sit by a telephone in a neighbouring village night and day waiting for an air raid warning. It was sensibly decided to let the auxiliary firemen man the telephone as they have to be on duty and are paid to do it. One gentleman at the meeting thought it senseless having air raid warnings in scattered townlets in Devon at all. He thought quite reasonably that long before the motor siren had gone its rounds the air raid would have been gone. It is generally considered that all these lighting restrictions on cars and roads are hysterical nonsense when airplanes of the enemy are 600 miles away. I think they will soon be relaxed.

August 14 1939, Wednesday Another wet day so went to the cinema in the afternoon. At 6pm drove into Barnstaple to do duty as auxiliary ambulance driver. From 9pm to 7am I had to go out in the van after dark to practice driving. Not as difficult as I anticipated. Sleep half-dressed, wrapped in rugs, prepared to go out if called. Each pair of us dress one night a week and is on call one day a week. So my obligations are not heavy. Think it very unlikely we shall be needed for an air raid here. More likely to be used to meet troop hospital trains. People have more or less given up carrying gas masks. I think bacteria raids, against which we have no protection, would be far more horrible.

Shop in Bideford in morning. Walk in to save petrol. Fill in form asking for extra petrol. Do not think I shall get it. Bathed in the afternoon. Very cold. Read, sewed and listened to the wireless in the evening.

Friday, August 16 1939 Went blackberry picking in the morning. Played tennis in the afternoon. Usual club day. About 20 people present. Had car filled up with petrol. Long queue at garage. Everyone keyed up to make do with their petrol rations. Anti-climax when we heard on 9 o'clock news petrol rations for a week reprieved.

Sunday, August 17th Cleaned car, washed and dried hair in the morning. Drove over to aunt for tea. Did not hear till 4 o'clock news that Russians had entered Poland. All thought it very ominous. Drove home, had supper afterwards. Wrote weekly letter to brother [Gerald] in Rhodesia.

Monday, August 18th 1939 Did weekly wash. Shopped in the town. Played tennis at usual club day. Heard news of loss of *Courageous*, depressing news, at 9 o'clock news.

Tuesday, August 19th 1939 Holiday ended yesterday. Started work again at library today. A good many new borrowers since I have been away. New residents mostly from London. Library quite busy with lending books but little reference work being done. Left work at 6pm and returned home.

Wednesday, August 20th 1939 On duty at library till 6pm. A lovely day. From 6pm – 9pm had 3 hours to fit in before going on night duty for auxiliary ambulance duty. Between 6pm – 9pm walk in the park, go to the cinema and have some supper at snack bar. 9pm – 10pm Practice drive of ambulance in the dark. Pretty stiff test backing up hills down black winding country lanes. 10pm returned to ambulance depot and slept there till 7pm [sic] next morning.

30th August 1939, evening, RAC scout at Cross Roads has a bet with me - ½lb of chocolate & packet of cigarettes that there will be no war. He is apparently buoyed up by *News Chronicle* who say that 2 German regiments deserted to Poland. He says *You See the Germans won't fight when the time comes*. I am unconvinced.

Thursday afternoon, August 31st Played tennis having made the date a week ago. Company cheerful in spite of 2 o'clock news that evacuation had begun. 2 men present thought that as Hitler had made a pact with Russia, he could do anything and would get out of war yet.

My cousin came in this morning. I said *Things look bleak*. She said *Well I don't know*. Several people have told me we shall get out of it like we did in the last crisis. Few people of my opinion seemed to realise that we would honour our obligations and the general opinion seems that we shall get out of it like last time.

Thursday, Aug. 31st I said to a girl of about 30 this morning, *The Mikado is at the cinema but I just don't feel like going now*. Her reply was *Yes, it is rather a pity, this nice weather*.

On hearing 7pm news, went to ask garage proprietor if I should in future be able to get parts for my car which is a fiat, Italian make. He said *Oh yes* and he thought Italy would back out and be neutral anyway.

Thursday, August 31st Heard on wireless at 9pm that Russian pact had been [illegible word], which knocked on the head many people's idea that she was going to back out of it.

August 31st Thursday evening, 10.15pm Heard English broadcast from German station of Hitler's 16 Points. Was surprised at the negotiation suddenly being blurted out when our government so quiet about it all. Hitler's points seemed to be quite a reasonable solution IF Germany would stick to them, which no one could trust her to do.

Friday, September 1st Waited up for 12 o'clock news on English German station but nothing fresh except that German said *Heavy fighting had broken out in Poland* which sounded ominous.

September 1st 1939, Friday Read papers which give Hitler's 16 points as I heard on the wireless the night before. No suggestion that war has broken out in *Times* and *Daily Express*.

11am in library A lady comes in to ask if she has left an umbrella behind. I hand her the umbrella (possibly a symbolic action!) as she tells me that the wireless has just said that war has started. Danzig had fallen and Germany was marching further into Poland. A man – reader in the reference library, remains unmoved, copying out particulars of his family tree. Discuss with Head Librarian future plans. Both agree, must live from day-to-day and no good wildly volunteering to give up jobs for whole time war work.

2pm Head Librarian comes back from lunch to say she has had a wire offering her a commandant's position in the Women's Territorial Army. She hopes to accept it and I am to carry on in her place, probably single-handed with her salary. I am pleased at the prospect of salary but fear that I shall feel imprisoned in the library and will want to rush wildly off enlisting in something.

Town seems perfectly ordinary. It is busy as it always is on Friday market day, though faces do not look very cheerful, and few if any smiling faces are to be seen.

Friday, September 2nd 1939 10am Head Librarian went in to see chairman of directors of the library regarding offer of position in the Territorials (Women). Mr Brewer very testy. Refused to give his permission without meeting of directors. Said *And how is the athenaeum to go on? I consider you are doing much more useful work here*. So that is that till directors meeting on Monday. 2.30pm Attended meeting of Auxiliary Ambulance Drivers to which I have belonged for some time. We are instructed to do one night's duty each for week and be on call one day each. 5pm Attended to lightening restriction on car. 10pm Heard news. Our doubts as to whether we are actually at war or not seem to be owing to France. Wonder if France is going to back out and leave us to go in alone.

Sunday, September 3rd 1939 10am Hear announcement on wireless of Britain's Ultimatum. Between 10am and 11am do my washing which I always do on Sunday. Turn on wireless at 5 to 11am when zero hour is approaching and hear good lady talking soothingly of apple dumplings. Mother goes on with her Sunday washing and says call me at 11.15 to hear the Prime Minister's speech. 11.15am Hear Prime Minister's speech with calm but with inner feeling of awful blackness and depression. 4pm went to tea with some relatives. They had neither stored food nor made curtains. Had laughed at mother making curtains & pooh-poohed the idea. Saying there would be no war. *Hitler would climb down and anyway they were not going to get curtains. Paper would do.*

So war came and they with great difficulty bought some paper. Tried it out and found of course it was quite inefficient and took hours to do every window. With even greater difficulty they got a few yards of black cloth. As every shop was besieged with *Foolish Virgins* who had left all them to the last.

Monday, September 5th 1939 At work in the library as usual. Library quiet, not much business done.

86 *A British poster referencing female ambulance drivers such as Miss Brown.*

Directors' meeting. They state they cannot spare Miss Drake. So Territorial scheme falls apart.

Tuesday, September 6th 1939 I start my fortnight's leave as previously arranged. I was to have gone to Kent but am staying at home now. I feel inactive and rather cut off from what is going on. I sew and read and bathe, and we all listen frequently to the news.

Wednesday, 6 Sept. 1939 Volunteer for clerical work at Women's Voluntary Services depot. Bathed [in the sea] at 11am. Bathe again at 6pm.

September 7 1939, Wednesday Bathed at 11.30am. This afternoon grappled with lighting restrictions on car. Read papers and books. Bathe again at 6pm, after supper write letters.

87 A blackout poster with artwork by Fougasse, c1939.

88 A Christmas card which may have been to Miss Brown's taste, having the message 'when we queue for our chop in the butcher's shop, we take our weekly ration!'. The original painting was the work of John Kynnersley Kirby in 1944 and depicted a Bishop's Stortford butcher.

Monday, September 8th 1939 Perfectly glorious weather. Bathed with 2 other girls this morning. Sewed and read in the afternoon. Bathed and sat on the sand after tea.

Saturday, September 9th 1939 Sat on the sand. Bathing and sunbathing most of the day. Cinema re-opened this evening. There was quite a long queue wanting to go in. Saw my favourite Rex Harrison in *The Silent Battle*.

Sunday, September 10 1939 Went to church in the morning. In the afternoon went to tea with relations to whom we always go on Sundays. Great discussion upon blackouting windows, scarcity of black paper etc. Also heard various awful tales of evacuees.

13.11.39 Heard news of raid on the Shetlands. This is a comic war so far. Millions spent on ARP and what do the Germans do but raid the Shetlands out in the back of beyond where one would imagine they would be almost completely out of touch with the world.

14.11.39 Went out on ARP practice as ambulance attendant. There seemed an enormous number of willing helpers to deal with everything. Everything went off very cheerily with plenty of torches flashing in every direction.

15.11.39 Started my Xmas shopping, was struck by the extra inanity of Xmas cards this year. Verses about peace and tranquillity and wishes for the merriest Xmas you have ever had. Had the greatest difficulty in buying a box of cards with no such extravagant hopes.

17.11.39 Listened in to *The Shadow of the Swastika*. I think it is cheap vulgar propaganda and is very boring and does the BBC no credit.

25.11.39 I always turn on the German News as the BBC news glosses over any losses we have or doesn't mention them. Sure enough last night the German news gave out the loss of the *Belfast*. The news was hastily put out in the BBC news at 12 o'clock. The news was known in America, S. Africa and Germany before we had it.

29.11.39 Twice during the last fortnight I have heard the rumour that the German wireless had said *We know what you are doing at Cleave and Morwenstow.* (RAF Camps are being built there, about 25 miles from here). No one has actually met the person who hears this announcement with his own ears. And the rumour that a small seaside town nearby the camp had been bombed.

2.11.39 I strongly dislike this new bill being brought in in which persons can be imprisoned without trial. It is nothing but Fascism and Communism. We may be fighting for the liberty of the Germans but are whittling away our own liberties at the same time. On Sunday 29th October the rector of Bideford spoke strongly in the pulpit against the new bill by which a soldier may claim pay for a woman with whom he is living who is not his wife. I agree with him and that that it sets the married woman's status at naught.

9.11.39 I overheard a worker in the street say *Hitler says he's ready for a 5 year war*, a 2nd workman *That's what 'ee says.* My reactions to the news of the attempted assassination was of sincere regret that it did not kill him. I think if he was out of the way the war would go flop.

10.11.39 Hear that news at 1pm is ominous. Germany is evidently going to invade Holland. Went this evening to *The Lion Has Wings*. I was keenly interested in all the parts about the air force but whenever Merle Oberon came into it I felt bored and irritated. There is of course a lot of slushy propaganda. England and all perfect, and Germany always wrong.

12.11.39 Schoolmaster came into the library today and said what he was afraid of was that Holland and Belgium would capitulate to Germany to save their country having to support [blank].

5.12.39 The Bus Co. are trying out a gas-engined bus. I unfortunately have to go home on it. It is painfully slow and can hardly get up the slightest incline. I trust it will soon be taken off.

8.12.39 Rumours:

German airplanes had been known to have flown over Barnstaple, North Devon.

That the German wireless news announcer had said that they knew there was an airport being constructed at Heanton [Punchardon], nearby.

That a submarine had been sunk by an airplane off Croyde nearby.

That an old man at a village nearby had been stopped by a young man and asked a number of leading questions. He then gave the old man 7s 6d which so frightened him that he rang up the police. The young man had, however, vanished.

All these rumours were told me by a farmer's daughter prefaced by *I've heard* or *Someone told me*. In the last case she knew the name of the old man.

15.12.39 Much talk in the bus of bus conductor and other men about the sea battle outside Rio de Janeiro. With debates on the situation in international law.

All these rumours heard at a sherry party given by a retired colonel:

That cars go to the edge of the cliff at Westward Ho! And lights have been seen flashing from there across to another part of the coast.

They know what was happening at Okehampton.

That a German man has taken a house opposite the council chambers, Northam.'

Miss Brown's entries for the first months of 1940 mostly concerned international news with only an occasional item of local interest such as on 23 February ('drove over to some friend at Windsor with terrible tales of billeting there – one old lady had died of the shock! And awful ones of the treatment of the VADs and the FANYs'). She was posted to Bristol that summer and returned at the end of the year ('I have been home on leave in North Devon. I found it much

***OPPOSITE: 89-92** Warnings about the danger of gossip.*

LOOSE TALK
CAN COST LIVES
DISTRIBUTED IN THE INTEREST OF NATIONAL DEFENSE, AND AS A MEANS OF OBTAINING FUNDS FOR AMBULANCES WHEREVER NEEDED. BRITISH AND AMERICAN AMBULANCE CORPS, INC., 420 LEXINGTON AVENUE, NEW YORK CITY

BITS OF CARELESS TALK
ARE PIECED TOGETHER BY THE ENEMY
England
Convoy sails for
tonight

BEWARE
Whether alone or in a crowd,
Never write or say aloud,
What you're loading, whence you hail,
Where you're bound for, when you sail.
—ABOVE ALL NEVER GIVE AWAY
THE MOVEMENTS OF H.M. SHIPS
Printed for H.M. Stationery Office by Wightman & Co., Ltd.

DON'T TALK
yourself into it

***93** Public praise for the Free French and British in Syria, 1941.*

***94** At the end of the war, in 1945, an exhumation was made of the bodies of some 250 Dutch Resistance fighters who were executed by the Germans in dunes near the Hague.*

changed; unrationed foods get more and more difficult to obtain. Cheese, biscuits, marmalade, chocolate especially. The town seems crowded with people. The streets are as they are in August in the height of the holiday season, but full of women, old women who have come to Devon to save their useless skins. Old made-up hags, drinking coffee in the cafes. Women with children I excuse, but there seemed plenty of young, married women about in trousers, with no children. I do not see why the government does not use its powers to force them to work at something instead of idling round the town eating all the residents' food supplies.')

Directives: race, nationality and anti-Semitism

In 1939 Miss Brown answered questions regarding race including *Negroes* ('fine people in their own country… all right when not interfered with English people. They only imitate our worst faults including drinking too much, eating unwholesome food, immorality and wearing too many clothes'), the French ('after a visit to Paris, not as excitable as I have always been led to suppose') and the Germans ('lacking in imagination and humour. Follow each other like sheep and like being ordered about.').

The following year she again wrote at length about nationalities:

Vichy government ('a dirty lot of weak double-crossers.')

Free French forces ('Of no practical use whatever.')

The Poles ('Badly organised in their own countries. But they are doing great work in the RAF. They are brave and daring fighters.')

The Czechs ('The same opinion as for the Poles.')

The Jews ('An unfortunate but unpleasant people.')

The Italians ('A dirty lot of back-stabbers but will not easily be swept aside and defeated.')

The Americans ('Money-grubbing, double-crossers. They are helping us because it pays them to do so.')

The Dutch ('Have brought their defeat upon themselves by not combining with us and with neighbouring states. A liability as a so-called ally.')

The Greeks ('Will only stand up against Italy for a month at the most.')

Miss Brown's views were particularly critical following the capitulation of western Europe to the Germans ('We have been betrayed on one side by the French and on the other side by the Belgians. It is no good depending upon any foreigner, they are all the same. They can't go straight it seems. If we win this war, it will be all our own effort and the Empire.'). She specifically wrote of the Belgians ('I do not see, however, why we should feed and maintain Belgian

95-7 *Ministry of Health posters enlisting support for evacuees.*

refugees here. Let them look out for themselves or starve in their own country. We have our own mouths to feed.') and she described the French as 'filthy' and a 'dirty lot of murderers'. Her fullest description was withering ('the dirty French have given in now. I hope they all rot and starve in their homes, men, women and children. I hope Hitler flays them alive… the craven, gibbering cowards'). Miss Brown concluded:

> 'We are well rid of all these dirty foreigners as allies. We can depend on ourselves. Anyway, let all Europe starve. Why should we care? I hope every French man, woman and child will be thrown out of this country *neck and crop*. And what has that psalm-singing President Roosevelt been doing during this crisis but going on a cruise, after promising to send over a few more planes every week, which of course America will charge top-price for. He thinks he has salved America's conscience thereby.'

In 1940 she replied more fully about the 'Jewish Question' and replied she did not know of a 'funny story' regarding Jewish people ('None that I can think of at the moment. I always find them rather boring, usually about a Scotchman and a Jew and money.'). Neither did she personally know a Jew ('My stepfather plays golf with a man called Tamworth who is reputed to be a Jew called Cohen who changed his name during the war. There is also a little photographer in a backstreet in Barnstaple. There is no Jewish synagogue nearer than Exeter 40 miles away.'). Miss Brown summed up her thoughts about Jewish people ('Hitler's persecution of the Jews, harmful to Germany, cruel and stupid. That he is a fanatic with a hysterical hatred of Jews. But there is no Jewish question affecting North Devon because there is no Jewish community.').

Evacuees

The strangers she wrote about at greatest length were the evacuees from London. In October 1940 she suggested that the local view was:

> 'I think the general attitude is one of dread of having unknown women and children in one's nice clean house. People fear that their maids will leave. When we heard that we were not to receive the full list of evacuees, the general feeling was that we had got a reprieve.
>
> Two or three months ago a lady came to interview Mother regarding taking evacuees. She said *You needn't take them you know. You can always say you are taking relatives*. My mother, however, felt that she must do her bit and nobly volunteered for 2 children and a mother.
>
> An aunt of mine also has volunteered to take two

children but unlike ours, her maid was bitterly disappointed when she heard that no evacuees were coming. She had arranged to have them both sleeping in her room and referred to them as Poor Little Toads.

A good many people arranged to take their relatives in rather than have strange people in the house.

I overheard a woman in the street (working-class) say *There now, them children aren't coming now, they say, just when I've bought more crockery and all.*'

In respect to the financial implications and provisioning of food for evacuees, Miss Brown thought:

'These problems have not actually arisen yet but Mother is wondering how domestic economy can be best arranged including food kept separate, separate cooking. She cannot afford to support 2 children and a mother on wartime rations and it might be difficult to deny them our own food and they would [be] sure to live on our sugar, tea, butter, vegetables even if they bought their own meat and bread.

The general attitude is Grin & Bear It, and hope that they will soon be taken off our hands and put in properly-organised camps when and if they are planted on us.

Two of the ladies responsible for evacuation accommodation in this area are not taking any themselves, though they have plenty of room. Another rich widow with a big house said she would rather give her house as a hospital than have evacuated children and have to stay and look after them. A doctor's wife said *If only she knew what her husband would be told to do in the event of war, she would know what to do herself.* She would not stay at home if he was sent away and have to look after someone else's brats. (She has two children of her own.)

Sunday, September 10th [I] went out to tea this afternoon and heard several stories of what people were enduring with evacuees in other areas.

1, That a woman was going to adopt her two children evacuees if she liked them. Her enthusiasm, however, was much dampened when the children arrived; she took off their clothes to bathe them and found them covered with lice.

2, A cousin of mine has a friend in Dorset whom she had heard from to say that in Wareham they have the most awful people from Camberwell.

3, One woman goes out and gets dead drunk every night and leaves three children behind in the house.

4, Another has 2 Jewish boys of 15 whom they have no control over at all.

5, Another household has 3 girls of about 13 to 15 from a remand home, who take a terrible amount of supervision.

An Air Raid warden in a neighbouring village said when someone asked him if evacuees were coming, *Not at present, and a good thing too from what I have heard from other districts.*

Nevertheless, in spite of misgivings and dread at to the refugees, there has been all over North Devon no lack of offers of accommodation for these evacuees. Northam with a population of 7,000 was expecting 600.

It was said that if you refused to take children, you would be forced to take in old people, and rather than do that, people volunteered for the children.'

After her wartime service Miss Brown returned to live at Phayre House and died in Bideford in 1983. She never married.

9. Margaret Pickwoad, Land Girl, 1940 & 1942

Margaret Pickwoad (1921-2008), raised in Crediton, was an unmarried eighteen-year-old, and in the Land Army, when she began writing for Mass Observation. She contributed a diary for 14 October 1940 and answered several directives in 1940 and 1942.[118] Her mother was Diarist **13**.

Bideford

In August 1940 Miss Pickwoad described attitudes in Bideford towards the war:

> 'The general attitude to the war in this area seems to be that *It'll last a year or so but we're bound to win through in the end – we always do*! No one seems unduly perturbed about what will happen next, except the inevitable few scare-mongers or the *Nervy* people. One woman refused to visit friends in a village six miles away for the day, saying that *We're asked not to travel in wartime and besides, one never knows*!
>
> The farmers, of course, bring up the food question, pointing out that not only are we producing food (e.g. grain crops and root crops) but that we can gain supplies from America, whereas the Germans with a wheat crop generally regarded as a failure, will experience great difficulty in obtaining supplies from outside and will therefore starve at the approach of winter.
>
> Others say that they can give us definite views, as they regard war as entirely wrong and therefore take very little interest in it.
>
> I'm afraid this report is a little vague but, working as I am in the country, I see few people during the week and have to observe all I can during Saturday and Sunday.'

A month later, in September, she noted that 'Air raids have not changed my life at all' and that in general:

> 'The air war hasn't touched this district at all, but the other night I dreamed I was running frantically down a long windswept road in rainy darkness with the wild jangling of church bells in my ears! Since that, I occasionally hear phantom bells, when I work alone! I read a lot, and always have, and listen to the wireless very little, exactly the same as usual'.

By October she felt that local people had altered their view of the war:

> 'During the past few weeks our district has been

98 British poster extolling the work of the Land Army, 1939-45.

99 Photograph entitled 'Food in England. The British Women's Land Army swings into action. Shown here at haymaking, these typists, clerks and salesgirls are helping during the crop season to supply England with much-needed food', 1943.

100 Photograph entitled 'Food in England. A woman in Britain's Land Army clears out a pig-house. Along with many other British women she works on a farm to supply her country with essential food', 1943.

watching the war with renewed interest probably because it has come so much nearer to us, and so much more exciting. The torpedoing of the Evacuee liner [SS *City of Benares*] was, I think, the most inhumane incident that has yet happened. Everyone round here agrees on this.

The German air losses are causing great glee! *What was last night's score*? asks someone, every morning.

Sometimes we are startled by loud and rather near explosions which are we believe caused by anti-gun practice. It never fails to cause a disturbance, and the various guesses as to its origin are extremely amusing and highly improbable.

We have all become used to hearing reports on the Battle of London. The first day's report was received with shocked amazement everywhere but our spirits were like India-rubber, as we heard of the wonderful behaviour of the homeless and bereaved mothers and children and of the gallant and self-less deeds of the ARP workers, firemen and in fact everybody connected with rescue work and caring for the homeless.

101 Photograph entitled 'Food in England. Members of the Women's Land Army in Britain help drain marshy land to provide extra arable acreage and grazing ground. With three large drag-line machines they are preparing 4,000 acres of soggy Devon land for grazing.', 1943.

Events outside Great Britain are not quite so clear to us down here, but general opinion seems to think that if the U.S. come to our aid, Japan will come in against us, but that the latter, in her weakened state, is no great menace. Russia, will, we all think, stay put. Sorry for such a short report but we're still very busy. I will try, however, to send in one as often as I can.'

That month in 1940 she also thought about the future of the British Empire ('Before the war I thought of the British Empire collectively as being all part of Britain and under her but now I feel that each dominion is gradually becoming more and more independent; more like staunch allies, who have their own private battles to fight as well as ours.') and again when she wrote 'I suppose the government advertising campaign about the Empire is calculated to stir the imagination of the people and make them even more patriotic. I've heard very little, if any, comment round here, but I do think that it is a good thing, as there seem to be many people who are dubious about the ultimate results of the war, because they are ignorant of the Empire's true strength.'

The end of the year brought further reflection:

'Until the December directive I hadn't thought much about 1941. I suppose, during the winter months, we'll have to contend mainly with boredom, but I read a lot and draw, and the long dark evenings pass very quickly. I'm not in any way pessimistic about 1940. I think the latest run of events has rather encouraged me and that if we really do take the obvious opportunity in the Mediterranean, I think 1941 should see at least a turn for the better. Anyway, I hope so! The only thing is, things happen with such startling rapidity that anything may happen! (If you can understand this rather long-winded explanation!)

I haven't made any changes in my Christmas plans this year. Last Christmas was my first away from home, but I had the weekend off and I'm doing the same this year.

The six main inconveniences of wartime in my estimation are blackout, petrol rationing, food rationing, transport difficulties, restricted use of cameras and not being allowed to roam when and where you like over now prohibited areas.'

The Land Army

In September 1940 Miss Pickwoad recalled her first year in the Land Army:

'I joined the Land Army in August last year and got my first job in October. First impressions are now vague: I seem to remember a whirl of new and extremely interesting jobs and a lot of hitherto undiscovered muscles. Everyone was very kind and anxious to help me on in various ways, until I'd get used to the new routine. I was not altogether new to the life, having lived all my life in the country and surrounded by animals and pets, so I adapted myself very soon to farming.

I then proceeded to try my hand at anything I could! Cutting cabbages on a frosty morning; driving a tractor, carting water to the poultry when all the pipes were frozen and hundreds of other experiences in addition to my main job, that of poultry-keeping. Spring came and I was shifted to my present farm where corn harvesting is now in full swing.

I've met many farmers since I've been a member and have taken an interest in their discussions. With every day that passes, I see more and more of the very unfair deal that the farmers are getting. Practically everything they produce and sell is price-controlled. Eggs, corn and potatoes are only a few of the productions which are controlled. Wages have risen and the prices of farm produce have not, to my mind, risen sufficiently to allow the farmer to pay his men easily. Most farmers round here have dispensed with a man and are consequently over-working themselves and their remaining men, in an effort to produce food for the seemingly ungrateful and mean public! Instead of bringing more to the land, the new wages have forced many off it.

Another farm grumble is against schoolboy labour during the holidays. *Pack of young varmints*, they say, *running over everything and mucking it all up*. And I'm afraid they're not very grateful for the help the public does give them!'

Two years later she outlined her work day in the Land Army:

'On Wednesday, February 25th, I got up at 7am. On going downstairs I lit the lamp and the oil stove to heat water for calf gruel, collected a bucket of warm water and the milk strainer, drank a cup of tea and went milking. We finished milking about 8.15 and then I fed the calves (ten of them) and went to breakfast (porridge, bread and margarine and tea) at about 8.45. After this I fed my poultry and ferrets and scrubbed the milk pails. This took until about 10.10am. Then I collected a horse, harnessed up and took the two churns of milk down to the cross roads. I got back about 10.45, and had a cup of tea, after un-harnessing the horse at about 11.00. From then until about 1pm I was down in the meadow spreading muck. When I saw the men going to dinner I came up, fed my chicks and went into dinner about 1.30. After dinner I collected an armful of firewood for our huge open fireplace, mixed up the calves' feed and fed them, this taking until 3.15. I then sawed logs for the fire until nearly 4 o'clock, when I fed the poultry, collected, washed and packed the eggs and prepared to go milking by 5. We (the Cow Man and I) finished at about 10 to 6 when I dipped up the milk and washed the pails.

After tea which we finished at about 6.20, I changed into a frock, shut up the poultry and went in. We settled down by the fireside, where I went on with *Invitation to the Waltz* and glanced at the papers. Supper (a cup of cocoa and some bread and butter) was at 9.30 and at 10pm I went to bed.'

In 1946 Miss Pickwoad married Robert Wortham Pickwoad Major, a distant relation. She died in 2008. Her mother Ruth, who lived at Crediton, was also a contributor (**13**) and described her daughter in 1938, when she was aged sixteen years and six months. She then stood at five feet and six and a half inches tall and weighed nine stone and three and a half pounds.

'Margaret is well-developed and well-proportioned with good carriage and abounding vitality. She is rather handsome with an unusual quantity of curly brown hair, very rosy cheeks and hazel eyes. At the age of one I left her in [the] charge of an old-fashioned nanny at the home of my parents while I spent a year in West Africa with my husband. I had breast-fed her for nine months. On my return I found her advanced for her age, talking fluently, her affections divided between the nurse and a toy dog which I had given her on my departure. (She still takes this to bed with her.)

She had attacks of Acidosis which were outgrown by the time she was seven, but unusual excitement still sometimes brings on an attack. The nurse was nervous and made a great show of fright at the approach of cattle, etc. Fortunately the baby was amused at sudden scrambles over hedges and would often give false alarms. She would also pretend to put dangerous objects in her mouth to excite the nurse. The child would let me do nothing for her without tears. I expressed the wish to take her out and overheard Nanny say *You've got to go out with Mummy, but don't cry, you'll soon be back with your old Nanny*. I sacked her at once.'[119]

10. Donald Bell, Student, 1941

Donald Bell (1923-1992) was born in York and relocated to Croydon but, after his family home was bombed in either 1940 or 1941, moved to Bideford. Weeks later Mr Bell was enrolled at King's College, London. He wrote a war diary for MO from 16 July to 30 September 1941 and answered directives in 1949 and 1951.[120]

'July 16... Being evacuated to Devon (Bideford) I find it very interesting to note the reactions of my hosts (true Devonians) to the war. I have found that a, they take no interest whatever in the campaigns etc. - their knowledge of geography is very limited, b, the only items in the news of interest to them are the major air attacks on this country and food news, c, they alternatively support the war against Hitler ('there have always been wars anyway') and condemn it as stupid saying it ought to be stopped, d, their authority on nearly all topics is the bible - they are primitive (very) Methodists.

July 17... Most Bidefordians are very nervy although they have suffered nothing from air raids etc. They are always complaining of the evacuees in the town (natural I suppose when their very uneventful normal life is so interrupted). They can't seem to get used to the Londoners who are entirely different in temperament.

July 18 It seems to me Bideford is in many respects about 100 years behind the times. I find the Bideford character sometimes unbearable but hearty, the people are kind etc. But their ideas on world events are puerile in the extreme. Bideford being a stronghold of chapel-

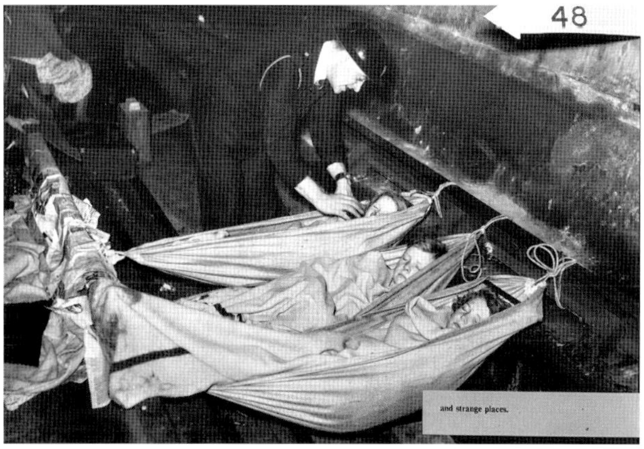

102 - 104 *Three photographs by F. R. Johnson of the London Blitz which were exhibited in 1943.*

goers, religion of the narrowest kind seems to permeate its life. Sunday is set aside (or perhaps I should call it the *Sabbath*) from all the other days in the week. My hostess refuses to do work of any kind but the most necessary nature, e.g. she prepares the Sunday dinner on a Saturday. She is also of the opinion that the war should be stopped on a Sunday and continue during the week.

July 20 As I am swotting for exams, I find it easier to work upstairs to avoid the gossip that goes on below. These Bidefordians seem to know all the personal affairs of every other Bidefordian and have an amazing knowledge of the local genealogical trees. I came across a pamphlet today which amused me (The front room is full of these pamphlets which are consumed religiously every Sunday afternoon). It told, in very crude English, and in a very elementary manner, of the conversion to Methodism of a *playboy,* a communist and a high churchman. Try as I would, I could find no atom of logical argument in it. These people feed avidly on, what is to my mind, this emotional rubbish. Incidentally, the same pamphlet described as *palliatives of the devil* smoking, radio, cinema and theatre. It sums up the viewpoint of most Bidefordians and makes the average Londoner down here very much like a fish out of water.

July 24 I am returning to London in two days and the prospect fills me with considerable elation. No more Bideford. Whoopee!!

July 25 Last day at school. This fact coupled, with the freedom of getting away from my Bideford billet, will make the future very different from the past year. I am going up to King's College, London at the end of September and for four weeks in the meantime I shall be teaching at York, my birthplace. I shall spend a week at my home in Croydon. The sense of freedom after working for scholarships for a solid year is terrific. I can now read all those tempting books which I have had regretfully to put on one side.'

Mr Bell returned to his home in Croydon, which had been damaged by bombing, and in September was evacuated to Bristol with the rest of King's College. He then recalled an aspect of his time in Bideford:

> 'When I was in Bideford I felt the tobacco shortage: I used to do the rounds of the tobacconists and if I was lucky, I managed to obtain an odd ounce of tobacco about once a fortnight. What surprised me was the difference in demand for tobacco and cigarettes – news of a shop with a few packets of cigarettes just in would bring great numbers rushing to it from all over the town, whereas the tobacco seemed to go much more steadily.'

Mr Bell married twice, in 1945 and 1977, and had three sons but few other biographical details have been found. He died in 1992.[121]

105 Clovelly by William Turner, early to mid-1800s.

CLOVELLY (& BIDEFORD)

This north Devon port remains a privately-owned village known for its picturesque character and herring fishery. In 1931 it had 528 residents in 1931.[122] It is unlikely that Writer **11** could have anticipated Clovelly's wartime events such as when in 1942 the coxswain of the lifeboat was awarded two guineas for personally rescuing ten crewmembers of a Dutch steamer which had been bombed and sunk. Likewise, the lifeboat crew members were recognised in 1944 for having rescued eight men from parts of the prefabricated port erected for the Normandy beaches. Equally surprising to Mr Fone would have been the events of 24 August 1943 when an RAF plane crashed at Higher Clovelly. All crewmembers died.

The war in Clovelly was particularly distinguished by it hosting several hundred evacuees from Deptford, Peckham, Bristol and Plymouth. It was not without its problems: in the spring of 1941 Plymouth City Council debated the billeting of three families at the Coastguard House in Clovelly. One mother alleged that the four-bedroom building was unfit for occupation. She said they:

> 'were taken to an empty coastguard house which should have been fumigated because it had been closed up for two years. When they opened the front door, the smell was terrible. We were taken inside and found all the rooms filthy dirty and full of dead flies. They gave us a camp bed and a couple of army blankets, one to sleep on and one to cover us, and when we asked for a pillow, we were told we were not entitled to one. We tried to scrub out a couple of rooms to make them fit to live in and myself and the other lady and our families were all sickening for colds by this time. The walls of the house were dripping with wet, there having been a burst pipe last winter and it had been allowed to go right down through all the walls and they were green with damp. I found I could not stand the dirt and bad conditions any longer, so have returned to Plymouth.'

The particulars were later disputed.[123] Towards the end of the war, on 29 December 1943, the main part of Clovelly Court was destroyed by fire.[124] Writer **11** had a very different experience of Clovelly.

11. Dennis Frone, Clerk, 1937

Twenty-one-year-old Dennis William Rodney Frone (1916-1973) wrote his day account on the last day of a fortnight-holiday in 1937. He had been born in Hackney and in 1937 lived with his parents near Epping Forest in Essex. He was employed by the Commonwealth Bank of Australia as a junior bank clerk. Mr Frone wrote a day-survey on 12 September and provided three responses to directives in 1939 and 1940.[125]

106 *Mr Dennis Frone in about 1970.*

12 September 1937

Mr Frone had enjoyed his two weeks' holiday:

> 'After a very sound night's sleep, I awoke feeling very fit indeed. Fourteen days of fairly strenuous walking with clean sea air to breathe had brought a very considerable change in my general health, my appearance and my mental outlook. The depressing effect which my job has upon me had worn off and I felt like continuing my holiday for months. The weather contributed to my mood of optimism. There was brilliant sunshine but a cold breeze from the north-west. Later on this brought across clouds. In the evening as I trained home to London it was raining a fine drizzle.'

His account began with his awakening:

> 'Nearly always on awakening it takes the mind some time to regain complete consciousness.
>
> This morning I was completely aware of my surroundings, almost immediately I awoke. It did not take any time to realise that I had been sleeping in a strange bedroom in a strange place. My sleep had been sound and when I opened my eyes at 7.10am, the sun was slanting across the street and in at my window. From where I lay, I could see the sea at the bottom of the street. Beneath the sloping bedroom floor, my landlady was apparently laying the breakfast and I could hear scraps of conversation above the clattering of cups and saucers. Outside was the click-clack of the donkeys which are used for carrying both passengers and goods up the cobbled Clovelly streets. I lay still and wished I could be there for ever.
>
> At 7.45 there was a knock at the bedroom door. I said *Thank you* and then made the most of another two minutes before taking the plunge for my shaving water. I wondered whether it would be advisable to draw the blind down while I washed and dressed. The houses are on top of one another in Clovelly and there is not much privacy from the street. Also, I was naked, I try and do without pyjamas on a walking tour in order to keep down the weight of kit. But to pull the blind down would have meant blotting out the view. I overcame my scruples and got on with the washing.
>
> Breakfast was at 8.30. I was well ahead with my two fried eggs and bacon when the other boarders arrived. They were a married couple and three others whose relationship I was not able to deduce. They appeared to be mother and grown-up son. The other person may have been the mother's sister. They wanted to know where the closest church was. I had just finished explaining to them how to get to the church at Clovelly Church, which I had seen the previous day, when the maid came in and told them that there was one round the corner, just behind the New Inn. I talked to the

***107** High Street, Clovelly, 1905.*

***108** View of Clovelly by Samuel Palmer, c1848-58. The Hobby Drive runs along the tops of the cliffs.*

married couple, who were on a cycling tour after that.

I had determined to walk the famous Hobby Drive on my way to Bideford and so I made my way up the hill to the entrance, after I had settled with the landlady. I had heard that it was free on a Sunday but I did not expect to find it shut. I was in consequence forced to find a secluded spot and climb the fence.

In spite of the fact that the drive was supposed to be closed, I had not gone far when I ran into a large party of girls accompanied by two elderly women. They seemed to be on their way for a swim but where I could not think. The coast is certainly not suitable just by Clovelly. This was rather galling to me. I had been carefully on the lookout for keepers or forest wardens, intending to dive into the bushes or hearing a foot step. I said *Good morning* and though they looked rather strangely at me, no comments were passed. I wondered how they would get out at the other end, as the gates were locked. Then it occurred to me that they might be guests of the owner. Perhaps the owner herself (Lady Asquith I believe) accompanied them. But I did not bother myself for long over this.

Through clearings in the trees could be seen Barnstaple Bay. It was the sort of view which one *drinks in*. Certainly the blueness of the unruffled sea and the yellowness of the distant cliffs and sand-dunes around Baggy Point were vivid enough to become fixed in my memory. I felt incensed at the thought of being told to clear off by some game-keeper or other. On reaching the other end of the drive, I found it necessary to push through some tangly undergrowth and climb a couple of barbed wire fences owing to the gates being locked. I then found myself in a field of stubble, partly ploughed up.

At about 12.30 I reached the main road and pushed open the bar-door of, I think it was, the Coach and Horses. There were a very mixed crowd refreshing and amusing themselves. The dart-board was well-patronised. A group of visitors in white flannels were, very surprisingly, playing some locals, very rustically clad, for drinks. A couple of girls in shorts lounging up against one of those bagatelle affairs, watched the play. The inn keeper was busy replenishing the glasses of two or three onlookers seated at a table in the corner. It seemed uncanny to see him fill tankard after tankard with half-pints or pints or quarts of ale or cider with scarcely a nod from his customers. So well did he know exactly what they wanted.

My half pint of cider went down very well and I thought about getting something to eat. They did not seem to do lunches at the inn and so I walked back to a cottage where I had seen them advertised. The woman who opened the door was not one of the anxious-to-feed-you-as-much-as-you-can-eat farmer's-wife-type which one is led to expect in Devon and Cornwall. (But in fairness I must say that they are to be found in out-of-the-way places.) She seemed very displeased at seeing me and immediately started to try and get rid of me by saying that she had *only got cold*. I could see into the dining room and the table was laid for her lodgers who were just coming down to dinner. She was not keen on having anyone from outside just then apparently. I said that *cold* was just what I wanted and went in.

The cold was ham and salad and biscuits and cheese. The lodgers were two couples who seemed to have an unlimited stock of private jokes. After lunch I took the bus into Bideford but apart from the river Torridge and the bridge I saw little of that town.

On the platform awaiting the 2.39 to Waterloo was a fairly large crowd of people, about seventy or eighty, and I began to fear that I should not get a seat.

I was not surprised to see, among the crush, a group of people which one always seems to see on the provincial railway station. They seem to be quite inseparable from railway stations. Quite at home with porters and railway officials, they stroll about seemingly with the object of making themselves as conspicuous as possible. Judging from the equipment, they had been on a huntin' and fishin' holiday on the moors and everyone on the station had got to know about it. The most vociferous member of the party looked like a retired Indian Army Officer. He had the typical *bronzed* countenance, the usual moustache and the know-how-to-deal-with-men look about him. He very soon had the porters on the move and even the pompous and officious station-master was sticking *Waterloo* labels on the luggage.

The luggage incidentally, consisted of 26 cases besides other equipment all stacked up on a trolley. In spite of this activity he found time, when not looking up and down the line or comparing his watch with the station clock, to talk to his small son and daughter. To them and to other members of the party he conversed in a calm and self-confident way and this together with a reassuring smile was no doubt meant to impress all about him with his great experience in the art of railway travel...

***109** The Hobby Drive in the early 1900s.*

Five minutes before the train arrived there was some discussion as to which luggage was to go into the guards' van and what should accompany them. Eventually the matter was settled and the *colonel* was left, much to the amusement of onlookers, carrying a wicker-work basket from which projected large lemonade bottles filled with milk, thermos-flasks and paper bags. From the right-hand pocket of his tailor-cut tweed sports-jacket projected a folded copy of the *Times* or it may have been the *Telegraph*.

He seemed to become conscious of the fact that he was holding a somewhat undignified-looking object but the arrival of the train allowed him to overcome any embarrassment which he may have had. The journey home was long and uneventful.'

During the war, three years later, Mr Frone admitted his life was largely uneventful and that 'the greater part of the day is spent at a more or less monotonous job and the leisure time in trying to compensate for it in some way'. The advent of war brought 'a feeling of excitement, a release from the everyday routine and a relaxation from many of the necessary restraints of civilized living in peace time'. Frone might have read *Picture Post* on 13 July 1940 when a feature writer cited Clovelly in his article 'What We Are Fighting For'. He pointed out that the lights had gone out all over Europe and that Hitler was determined to snuff out this final candle. The writer stressed it was a war for the very land of England:

> 'This is a war for everything that we can see from our own window. For the cottages at the end of the lane and the old bridge by the mill. We are fighting for the very soil and stuff of Britain. Intact for a thousand years, it is not to be tampered with now. Lambeth Walk is not to be a stamping ground for storm troopers. Stratford-on-Avon is to be no site for Goering to build a castle. Clovelly gives no admittance to the Gestapo.'

Mr Frone married in 1967, worked as a professional photographer for magazines including *Country Life* and died in 1973.[126]

***110** This photograph of Clovelly was published in the materials for the German invasion of England, 1940, with the caption 'The boat harbour dries out at low tide. The houses are built on terraces close to the densely-wooded steep slope. View from north.' Two other photographs were entitled 'Wooded cliff coast at Clovelly up to 110 metres high. One meter foreground at low tide, dry pebble beach' and 'View from the east of Clovelly (600 inhabitants), a fishing village on a steep, densely-populated cliff. A narrow pebbly beach 1 metre in foreground. Rocky outcrops and offshore cliffs.'*

111 - 112 Two views of pre-war Cockington.

COCKINGTON

This ancient parish, and small village, in Torquay appealed to the resort's burgeoning tourist population from the late nineteenth-century.

12. Iris Forrest, Housewife, 1943

Mrs Ivy Iris Forrest (1899-1977) of Warwickshire had a holiday in Torbay during 1942 and a year later wrote about her favourite pub as part of a response to an MO query about alcohol consumption. The building had been designed by Sir Edwin Lutyens and opened on 23 May 1936:

> 'I would like more gaiety in the pubs. One of the best pubs I know is at Cockington - The Drum [Inn], it's called, in the village where Cockington Forge is, near Torquay. The village is thatched, and so is the pub, although it is quite modern, only built a few years ago. But that pub is what every good pub should be. The architecture first fits in with the surroundings. It has gardens, and an outside paved place with tables for those who like fresh air. Inside, it has a bar, a cosy room with a fine big brick fireplace. There is a restaurant, and you could have even last year quite attractive meals. There is also a room licensed for music, furnished with a piano, and while those behind the bar have access to this room, no other compartment of the house does. That is, if you want to join the community singing, you go out of the door and round to the proper room. In this way, those who want to be rowdy and bawl away, do so without interfering with anybody else.

113 The Drum Inn, 2025.

> Last year during our holiday at Torquay, it was a real pleasure to go to this pub – although it was crowded and most other people had discovered it, too - in the evenings and drink cider matured in sherry casks. I would like to see more of such pubs, not exactly the same, but built to conform with the needs of the people who go there, because then they would become cheaper and more people could enjoy them. The kind of pub I like least is the old-fashioned late Victorian structure, where the seats are covered in black or maroon leather, where the slightly unpleasant smell of stale beer has penetrated the woodwork.'[127]

CREDITON

This market town, situated eight miles from Exeter on the ancient road to North Devon, had prospered from cloth-making until the early 1800s. A series of disastrous fires in the eighteenth century are responsible for the more modern appearance of the town compared with Dartmouth, Totnes or Ashburton. In 1939 Crediton had 4,366 residents. The Urban District had increased by 978 people in the previous year; this was a staggering 26.2% rise.[128] The chairman of the rural district council regarded the first wave of evacuees in 1939 as 'a complete and absolute wash-out'. He had been prepared for the arrival 990 evacuees over three days but only 157 arrived. Later that year a group of 75 evacuees arrived in the town. The town later found it difficult to accommodate evacuees in private houses and attributed this to young married women being already engaged, former billets were being occupied by the Land Army and many Kirtonians were

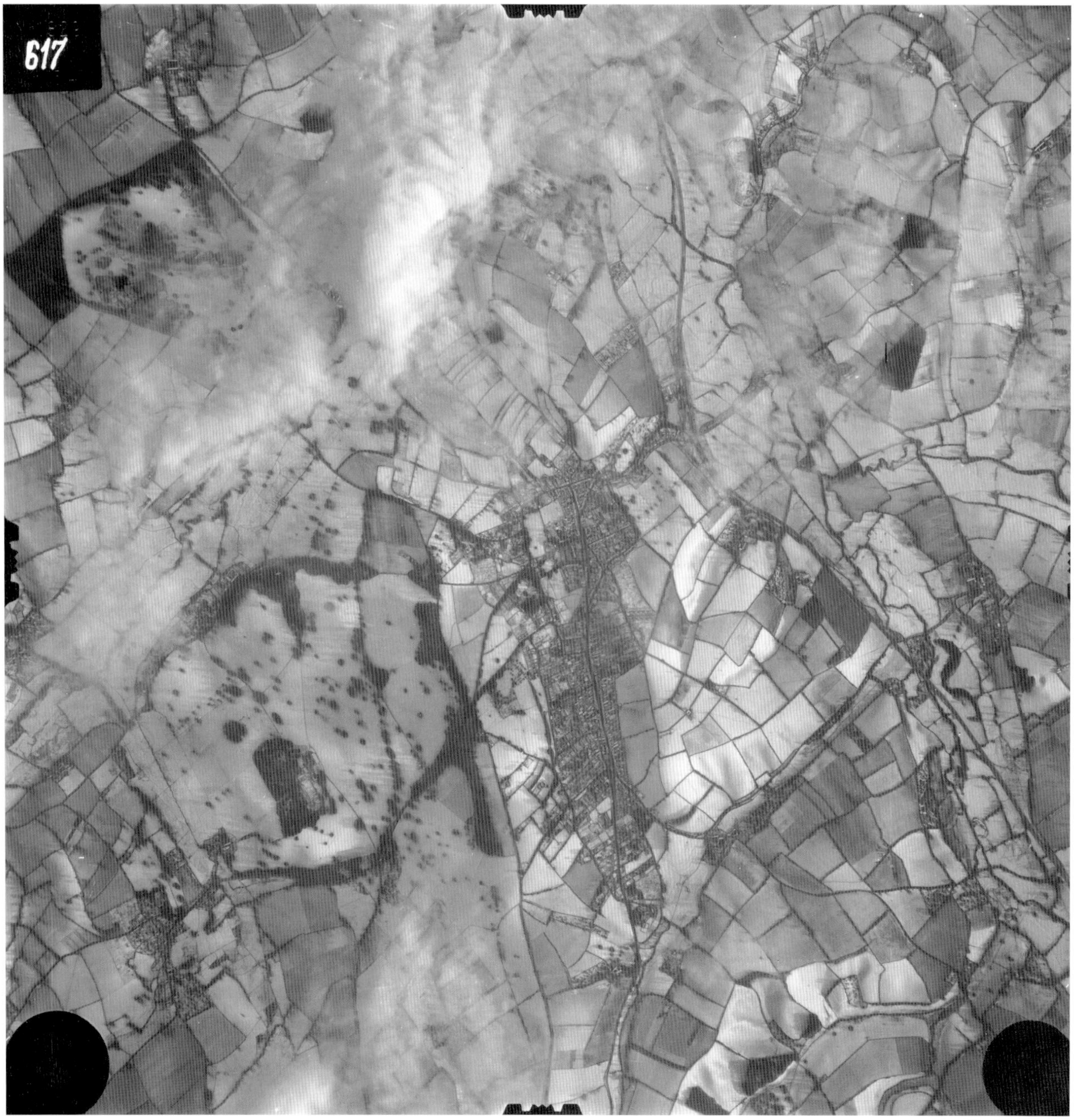

114 Aerial photograph of Crediton taken by the Luftwaffe, 4 January 1941.

too old. Evacuees were still arriving as late as 1944: at that time the town had 1,300 evacuees who came privately.[129]

The Telephone Censorship Department recorded a conversation on Thursday, 9 January 1941, between a member of staff of the Ministry of Health at Bristol with a council officer at Crediton:

> 'Crediton: *Tomorrow? It's absurd. You don't give me any time.*
>
> Bristol*: It's as much time as is ever given - but make it Sat*urday.
>
> Crediton: *Saturday. Impossible.*
>
> Bristol: *It's always done that way. The London children register, and then they must be evacuated within five days.*
>
> Crediton: *How many in this batch?*
>
> Bristol: *There are 120.*
>
> Crediton: *Well, where do you think I am going to get 120 homes in that time? And how do you think the people can get their homes ready in that time? It's ridiculous and it's unreasonable.*
>
> Bristol: *Well, that's the way it's always done and I'm afraid we must ask you to do it. We sent 1,000 in this way last week.*
>
> Crediton: *Well, I think it's most unreasonable and you can't justify it in any way. I've got a council meeting on Saturday too, which means that all the officers will be busy – you are managing the whole thing appallingly.*
>
> Bristol: *Well, you'll just have to put up with it and I'm afraid you'll have to arrange transport for them too.*
>
> (disgusted slam of receiver from Crediton)'[130]

In 1940 Queenie Burrin, a Crediton resident, testified at the coroner's inquest into the death of her mother: it was determined that seventy-three-year-old Caroline Godfrey had committed suicide following her discovery of a decapitated body of an air raid victim in her back garden in London. An air raid was recorded at Crediton on 19 August 1940[131] and shortly beforehand the Ministry of Information reported there had been 'criticism of alleged muddle of air raid warning at Crediton'.[132]

13. Ruth Pickwoad, Poultry Farmer, 1937-42

Although Ruth Frances Pickwoad (1896-1989) described herself to MO as being either a housewife or as having no occupation, she and her husband were poultry farmers at Pounds Hill which lies immediately outside the town. She had been raised nearby at Penton. Her father was a retired army officer and her mother may have been viewed as unconventional given she had been a Suffragette and member of the Chartered Society of Masseuses and Medical Gymnastics. Mrs Pickwoad had four daughters: Margaret also known as Peggy (1921-2008), June (1924-?2018), Jennifer also known as Tuppy (1931-2021) and Susan (1933-).

__115__ Pounds Hill, home of Mrs Ruth Pickwoad while she wrote diaries for Mass Observation, 2025.

On 25 August 1920, in Crediton's parish church, she married Ernest Conrad Pickwoad, a member of the Nigerian Civil Service. The couple moved to West Africa in 1922. His father had been District Commissioner of Corozal in British Honduras and the family had been established in that colony or in the West Indies since at least the early 1800s.[133] In about 1923 Ruth and Ernest Pickwoad returned to England, appear to have gone back to Africa but were living at Pounds Hill in 1937.

Mrs Pickwoad wrote three day-surveys on 11 November 1937, 12 January 1938 and 17 April 1938 and was a directive respondent in 1939, 1940 and 1942.[134]

11 November 1937

On Armistice Day she wrote:

> '10.30 Finished ironing the children's clothes. My husband leaned through the nursery window and we discussed the two-minute silence. I said that if there were such a thing as survival after death, I thought the

***116-119** Four posters featuring Potato Pete, the popular Ministry of Food character who from 1941 to 1945 promoted the growing and consumption of potatoes.*

dead would hate it. For those of us who lost our people in the war, it seems odd to set aside two minutes a year for remembrance when they are still as much in our thoughts as if they were alive but away. It seems pointless for the post-war people to take part in it when it means so little to them. I hate Armistice Day because it makes me so unhappy - and yet I have an unreasonable feeling that it is cowardly to avoid being made unhappy on behalf of those who were so much more unhappy. My husband said he thought the silence should be abolished. Then he began to mix hot mash for the fowls, cursing and saying he hated doing it. I think he wanted me to help him but I said I would if he'd finish my ironing.

10.40 Saw the mutton into the stove and scalded out the butter tub and washed my hands. Made the butter by stirring scalded cream with the flat of my hand till it granulated and separated from the buttermilk, after which I washed it, salted it and patted it away

10.56 Washed and locked myself into the bathroom in case the two babies, who had gone for a walk with the char's husband, should find me and want to talk. The factory siren hooted and the only sound seem to be the murmuring of the voices of the char and the fourteen-year-old maid. (The char started to work today as the *general* has gone home to nurse a relation.) I think this was the first occasion on which they had attempted any conversation. The siren went again and from the town came the faint notes of the Reveille.

11.05 Washed out the bath and the basin and then went down and peeled some potatoes and onions and put them in with the meat. Finished making some apricot fool.

11.30 Suddenly thought of mint sauce and went into the garden to look for some, but went instead to admire the work I did yesterday. It is a perfect day. The ground is thick with yellow elm leaves.'

***120** Cover of Potato Pete's recipe book, 1942.*

She also provided an account of the following day, November 12th, in which she indicated her social class:

> '9.15 Finished breakfast but remained at table for a little talking about the possibility of renewed friendly relations with Germany and Italy, America's changed attitude in the future (in which I still believe) of the League [of Nations].
>
> 9.25 Dressed my youngest child Susan, who had been allowed to have breakfast in bed for a long-promised treat. She had filled my bed with chips from a pencil she had been sharpening, bits of plasticine and at the very bottom

***121** Wartime hygiene poster, 1941.*

***122** The triumph of Christianity over Nazism in an undated British poster.*

was one of the cats.

9.35 Cleared up the mess, made my bed and those of the two youngest children, swept my room and dusted it and sent *Tuppy*, the other child, off to her grandmother's house for lessons.

10.15 Washed out the bath and basin. Then washed the linoleum in the two children's rooms and the bathroom floor. Took two rugs out into the garden to beat them. My spirits always rise when I get out of the house even though it is only to beat rugs. All the time I am working I am followed about by Susan and my golden retriever Amber, who both get in the way.

10.40 Notice the grates are very rusty, so fetch paint from the workshop and painted three rarely used grates.

11.00 Prepared potatoes, carrots, celery and peeled apples. Put vegetables on oil stove to start a stew.

11.30 Made tea for husband, maid and char, and drank it, sitting on the kitchen table and listening to husband talking about hens.

11.40 Made a pudding with the apples and got on with the stew. Added some roasted and pounded peanuts as an experiment. Made a chocolate cake and put it in electric oven. Washed cabbage. Put plates to heat. Susan and Tuppy both playing happily in garden. Tuppy having returned at 11.15. Put potatoes on to boil.

12.30 Put cabbage to boil and added a spot of sherry to the mutton stew, also two tomatoes as an afterthought. Made a filling for the cake, then dished up and served dinner at 1.00, when Peggy and June, the eldest daughters, returned from the high school for their dinner.

During dinner the elder children were taciturn and preoccupied, taking their cue as always from their father. Tuppy came in about five minutes late and when I asked her why she replied mysteriously *Ha Ha*. Was amused and said no more. She burst into tears when two flies dived from the ceiling to a passionate death in her stew. Her father said it was a judgement. He praised my stew as *an extremely succulent dish* and I felt a little bucked. The two smallest daughters began a fantastic conversation about staircases leading up to Heaven and down to Hell. I have never taught them anything about Heaven or Hell. My husband left the table to go out to the hens, then the elder girls left for school again, leaving me to finish shovelling apple pudding into their sisters till 1.30.'

12 January 1938

Two months later her account contains some surprises:

'6.00pm Finished washing eggs. There were nearly 200, all very muddy. I left about half for my husband to do later.

6.15 Went to drawing room to hear remainder of news, then read the story of Joseph and his brethren to the two smallest daughters, 4 and 6, from my new *Bible designed to be read as Literature*. They asked for a few points to be made clear and listened enthralled.

6.45 Got buttered biscuits and milk for children and undressed them and gave them hot bath. S[usan] (4) was jealous because she saw me give T[uppy] a hug when I put the towel round her and protested. When she was in bed she said *I am going to have a dream tonight about hell mommy. If you go to hell I shall come and let you out because I love you so much.* I said *Thank you very much.* I wonder where she learnt about hell. From servants, probably, under great provocation.

7.20 Maid told me there was no butter, so made some.

7.35 Maid brought supper into drawing room on tray. When we are alone, we like it like that in winter as the dining room is cold. Soup and macaroni cheese.

8.00 Heard T[uppy] crying upstairs. A strong wind had sprung up and her door had slammed, leaving her in the dark. Shut a window and propped the door open so that she could see by the passage light and hear people.

123 British poster extolling Bovril and the consumption of eggs, 1939.

The two elder children, both in drawing room, reading. M, the char-woman's 11-year-old child, still occupying nursery where she has been all the evening (uninvited). I had suggested that if the children melted away, she might return home without having to be sent. I do not wish to send her as the char is slightly mental, taking offense very easily. As I have just secured her niece as cook, I am anxious to keep peace at any price. The child is quite nice but, since seeing her rather often in the company of a man who has been in trouble for sexual offences, I am slightly uneasy about her. The man is a friend of her parents.

8.45 My dog started howling dismally. She is in season, secured in a shed. At the sound I was overcome again by depression. Two nights ago I went out to find she had killed J's little dog which was in the same condition. They had been together all their lives. I had to lie about the cause of her death. Went out and took her for a short run. Passed through kitchen. New cook exclaimed *Oh, what a beautiful dog* and M (now in kitchen) put arms around her and kisses her on the head. I could not bear seeing dog praised and fondled and took her out quickly. I am surprised at having taken so violently against the dog. I know it is unreasonable. All the evening I keep remembering the little corpse with its torn throat. Listened to the news and sent children off to bed. Later they returned in dressing gowns, kissed us *Good Night*. My husband talked about Italy's position in event of war.

9.20 Got sewing (a smock for Susan) and worked till 10.20. Husband reading *Wild West Magazine*. From time to time he suggested that I should go to bed as I was looking tired.

10.20 Fed dog and cut up meat for cats. Gathered them all together in my arms (five of them at present and disagreeing) and looked in to show husband who laughed and said *My God*! Put them in shed. Made sure rabbits had been fed - also mice and budgerigar. Fed parrot. Husband said *Do you realise it's nearly midnight*? Replied it was only just after 11. Had hot bath with lashings of Christmas bath salts. Husband said firmly it was too late for reading in bed.

11.45 Fell asleep immediately.'

17 April 1938

Her account of Easter 1938 outlined her family life:

'7.45 I was woken by Susan (just 5) pulling my hand into her cot and hugging it. T got out of bed and put on electric kettle for tea. S[usan] got into our bed and then Tuppy (6) came in and presented T and me with a 1d Easter egg which she had bought secretly. After a time she said *I invented something to say when I gave you the egg, but I didn't say it*. I asked what it was.

A very Happy Easter,
That's all I've got to say,
A very Happy Easter and
I laid this egg today.

She gave S. a smaller egg. S pushed it inside her pyjamas, cackled loudly and produced the egg again triumphantly.

8.00 Had morning tea and played with the children.

8.45 Dressed in the bathroom, returned and dressed S. and made her cot and own bed. Took Easter eggs down and arranged them on the breakfast table.

9.15 Breakfast. Fish cakes, coffee, toast, butter and marmalade. Bournvita for children. T gave me a large chocolate egg and P and J had bought T and self very large ones filled [with] chocolate creams with money provided by loving aunt. I gave P cardboard egg containing belt, handkerchiefs and sweets, J belt and small cactus for her collection, E toy boat and wood bracelet, and Tuppy wooden boat and jointed wood nurse with pram. S had to be stopped from eating Easter eggs instead of fish cakes and could not be got to eat much breakfast. T gave them all chocolate eggs.

9.45-10.30 Sent children to do *potty* and went out to help T with fowls. Scrubbed out water troughs and filled them with clean water. They drink between 30 – 40 gallons daily.

10.30-11.45 Prepared dinner. Made *Floating Island*, roasted beef and potatoes, prepared cauliflower and mixed Yorkshire pudding.

11.45 Went into fields with S to dig up some horse-radish for sauce. My mother looked in to ask if we were going down to supper and brought the children soap eggs. I thanked God they were not more chocolate. Children re-appeared from church where they had accompanied ex-nurse at her suggestion and without enthusiasm. They showed me more eggs (milk chocolate) collected from aunt. They gave me items of news – Sir John now singing in quire, collection for vicar so ex-nurse, who had brought 2d, took other 1d home again. Some notes in collection. Query: who had put them? etc. etc.

12.45 Left kitchen and read papers in drawing room. T very pleased that his astrological forecast promised immediate and over-due good fortune. Last week he was promised small wind-fall and next post brought Postal Order for 12s 6d. Was not encouraging. Finished cooking and served dinner. Maid out. Smaller girl going in afternoon so eager to be punctual.

1.45 Did a bit of tidying and my bedroom, which I should have done in morning.

2.30 Combed six Angora rabbits, sitting on hutch and talking to A (husband's nephew, 17). A. generally painfully shy but he talked quite freely about seal fishing and one of his masters at school who had led a life of adventure but taught scripture which struck A as very incongruous. Cut some grass and did some weeding and watered sweet peas. Clipped the wool off S's rabbit as it was too matted to comb.

3.30 D (sister-in-law) arrived and sat in garden sewing. Gave her Easter Egg filled with chocolates as she likes sweets but gets hers at Woolworth's. Gave A one also. Sat on door-step and listened to D talking about house she is going to buy. P and J got tea.

5.00 – 5.30 Tea. D ate most of the Marmite sandwiches and could see P and J getting restive as last one went before they got a chance themselves. Afterwards J voiced indignation to me – didn't see why grown-ups could be greedy and get away with it. Told her she should have seized sandwich earlier, knowing aunt. Helped them wash up and tidied kitchen. Milked cow and washed out bottle for kids. Watched children milk goats and feed kids with cow's milk. (cow's milk now not fit for humans owing to udder inflammation)

6.30-7.30 Got S and Tuppy's suppers (boiled eggs, toast and oranges) and bathed them and put them to bed. Rushed down with T to supper with my parents and sister. D left about 7.15. Miss W. (old friend of my mother) also there. She slipped into her place before the rest and snaffled a neat whiskey unobserved by anyone except self. Then she helped herself to a good stiff one with soda. Wondered if she was in pain, as years ago she was smashed up in an accident and still suffers. Cold salt beef, tongue and veal to choose from. Had beef and tongue with a lot of excellent salad and decided to drink. Chose plum pudding in preference to gooseberry tart and then found it difficult to finish. Talked about P's career with Miss W. (retired headmistress of big London school). She asked me if I had brought them up to realise they must work for their livings, as they were brought up free from responsibilities. Rather resented last remark and wondered if there was any truth in it. The elder ones are frequently left in charge of younger ones, are entirely responsible for their ponies and have to work quite hard. They have realised since the beginning that they must have jobs. They have a great deal of

124 Marmite advertisement referencing Air Raid Precautions.

freedom and I expect not enough discipline to please an ex-headmistress. Wondered about faint antagonism between Miss W. and self. She agreed agriculture a good line for P In drawing room talked about relative merits of single and married life for women. Am all for having babies at almost any price and hope all my daughters will marry, but stressed advantages of singleness in presence of two elderly spinsters as did not want to flaunt happiness. Both argued against me. Miss W. disgusted at her sister's determination to get her daughters married and doing it. I said I hated match-making but would oppose professions in which my daughters would never meet any men. Listened to news. Discussed greenhouse plants with my sister as I am buying portable greenhouse. Miss W. said of course I could never have azaleas as big as one we were looking at, as small greenhouses held so very little and it would be quite unsuitable and she has very little room in hers. Found mine was 3 foot bigger and liked her much better when she became human and said *curse you*, which was what she had been thinking all the evening.

9.45 T. and I went home. Fed rabbits, parrot, dog, three cats and hunted kittens which were eventually found under side-board. Put them to bed and read papers, idled and talked to T.

10.30 Had hot bath, took papers and *I Knew Hitler* to bed with me. At 11.30 T came to bed, very sleepy and not wanting to read, so I thought I'd better put out light. Thought vaguely for a few minutes and then fell asleep.'

Crediton and the prospect of war

In 1938 Mrs Pickwoad recorded Kirtonians' feelings about the prospect of war:

'Sept. 18th Friend, thinking war inevitable early in October, asked me to house her boy if it was dangerous for him to go to Liverpool for holidays. Retired South African farmer, about 50, said *No War*.

Sept. 24th Saturday Lady MCG told me her gardener, on 23rd, has asked her if she thought war would break out during the following week as he wished to finish mending the barn first. *Are you going to fight*? she asked. *Yes, us got to fight of course but us must mend barn first. Tisn't safe to leave.*

25th Woman, 50, no occupation, said she did not think there would be a war and never had. She did not intend to do war work if there was.

26th Sadler, aged about 45, in reply to *When is there going to be a war*? *Oh don't say such a thing*! in a tone which suggested that he did not really expect it.

Baker's assistant, aged about 25, in reply to the same question *One can't say but it looks pretty black now*. He was vague about what he would do. *I suppose we'll all have to do something. I'll drive a lorry perhaps.*

27th Woman, no occupation, aged 60, expected war in early October. Went to police station same day to ask them to let her know if at any time she could be of service driving car.

28th Gardener, aged 44 (leg lost in last war) said he expected war on October 1st and was going to be 2nd Class Nursing Orderly.

28th Retired civil servant, 49, thought war was inevitable and yet had persistent feeling that *Something sensational would happen at the last moment*. He intended to offer his services to government in any capacity they thought suitable.'

Directives: class, language and race

In June 1939 Mrs Pickwoad summarised her background:

'I think I belong to *the gentry* for want of a better word. I have never questioned this. I was brought up in a country house full of ancestral portraits of important and sometimes titled ancestors. I was addressed as *Miss* by servants, nurses and gardeners from the earliest age and was reprimanded for playing with children who belonged to a different class. My pedigree includes Edward 3, Edward 1, Henry 3, James 2 of Scotland, Robert the Bruce, Henri 1 of France and umpteen equally illustrious names which all help to deepen my conviction that I'm *gentry*.

We never had much money but my father always had enough private means to keep the place just going and to send us to *good* schools. The people I met when a child were invariably of our own class. My relations were mainly in the Army, Navy, Judicial or Civil Service.'

She also described the differences between herself and her parents regarding her social mingling in which her lack of money largely figured:

'I frequently entertain people on whom my parents would not have called and am on friendly terms with people of many different classes. For example, I have stayed with a man who worked in a West African store (an ex-carpenter), whose wife was a typist, in their little Manchester home. This man was kind and friendly in Africa, hence the continued friendship. The reason why I have made friends out of my own class is partly that I have found things in common with them and partly because I meet so few people of my own class, and those I do meet are mostly damned dull and too well off. I hesitate to ask people here when they are used to cocktails and butlers, and I can only offer them beer handed sloppily by a dirty little servant of fourteen.

I found I have more in common with women who empty their own slops and look after their own children. In short, I tend to mix with a *lower* (forgive the odious term) class because through having less money I have more in common with them. All this I think applies to mostly to country life. In London I never considered *class*. I made friends with the people whose ideas and outlook interested me. On thinking over my friends, I could not place some of them in a class at all.

I feel ill at ease when entertained by the small-business type of person because however hard I tried to be natural, they always seem ill at ease with me. They laugh too loudly at my jokes and agree too readily with everything I say and take too much trouble about my comfort. I get on well with really poor people and feel no embarrassment as a rule. With the *County* I feel faintly superior and antagonistic and inclined to throw bricks about to take the fox's side and defend Stalin and refer to the awful lot of washing up we are making. I am really at ease with my own servants, but that is because they are not at ease with me. My children tell me they even have a different voice for me. I am happiest with my own class, because on the whole I find them easier to understand, but I am only really happy when they have the same sort of mentality and not too much money. I find money a dreadful barrier.'

Her thoughts on money may not have been shared by her parents:

'I think the working classes are on the whole the most generous, the farming class the meanest (once or twice I have been round with a subscription book), the small business people the most thrifty (our retired grocers and butchers invariably retire, build a good house and often run a car) and I think the unfortunate landed gentry think and talk most about money because they need it so badly.'

Mrs Pickwoad was frank about her circumstances:

'The house we live in was the gardener's cottage on my father's estate. We took it originally because the rent was moderate, my husband was going abroad and I had to have some sort of home in which to have a baby. We have stayed here partly because we are able to rent the land we need, partly to be near my people, lately because there is a good school here and, in any case, we have never had enough money to face a move. If we got any money, we should move to any sort of place we could call our own.

125 The Green in the early 1900s.

We are less conventional, less sociable, we don't go to tennis parties or play bridge. We are more happy-go-lucky and much dirtier. Our living room contains anything from a garden rake to a litter of kittens. When visitors arrive it takes quite a time to clear a small table and a chair. When I visit our neighbours, they have beautiful clean drawing rooms. They always talk about people I have never met and read books I have never read and they seem to think with the *Times* or the *Telegraph* and never with their own heads. I don't exactly know what the difference is, but it's enough to make me loathe going out. An exception is an ex-headmistress who settled here to be near my mother and who is human.'

In 1939 she commented upon slang words:

'*Cheerio* is often used by my friends and I make the same reply.
Bye-Bye I associate with a nurse I had who always says it in a peculiar way so that it has become a joke.
Toodleoo I rarely hear. It suggests someone pretty awful.
Okay I have learned to put up with. My daughters use it.
Okidoke suggests someone worse than *Toodleoo*.
Not half I like. I associated it with friendly, working people.
Ta makes me shudder, especially from a fat draper.

Old Boy I don't like. It makes me think of too-hearty business men.
Chum is another word I react against. *Pal* also, but I can trace this back.
Mate is a good word, I like it.'

Mrs Pickwoad also noted generational differences:

'I can't think of any difference between my own outlook on health and hygiene and that of my younger relatives and friends. So far, I have never had to think about my health. I have brought up my family so far entirely without the use of purgatives or laxatives, though I regard constipation as the root of all evil. I treat them with suitable foods or with starvation, as the ailments require. I have noticed that people of my age and older take a lot of notice of medicines. A middle-aged relative was with us for a short a month some time ago and left behind her more than a dozen empty medicine bottles. I have also noticed that older people are mostly cleaner than young ones. Young visitors often don't wash in the mornings if they bathe at night. The elderly ones are most meticulous. A middle-aged man visitor changed completely every time he sweated slightly, took medicines of several kinds every day including cough mixture (to prevent colds) and iodine, and wore lengths of red flannel around his tummy. Old people talk about their health, but I don't know any young ones at present who ever think or worry about it.

I only have views about diet as regards growing children. I always plan meals with their growth and general development at the back of my mind and in a rough and ready way. See that they are well-balanced with a liberal calcium and vitamin content.

My young married friends are the same as myself in this, also my eldest daughter when she does the housekeeping. I cannot think of any differences between my own taste in food and those of the younger generation. I eat anything except *innards* and drink anything I can get, even cooking sherry.

My ideas about clothes for myself have changed as I've got older. I don't wear the same sort of things as my daughters as I'm afraid of looking like *mutton dressed as lamb* but I do not in the least disapprove or disagree with their taste.

I do, however, notice that my mother (aged about 74) is gently disapproving when she notices how few clothes my children wear and tactfully suggests that they should put on stockings etc. A few days ago my eldest daughter (just 18) was amused at Granny asking *Does your mother know that you are going out to tea in those shorts*? Most young girls I know wear practically no underclothes, sometimes only a brassiere and knickers, and in the country, bare legs and very short skirts. I don't often wear stockings myself at home but I put them on to go out because I hate to be conspicuous - middle-aged women generally wear stockings and so I fall into line. For the same reason I don't wear shorts, though my family often urges me too.

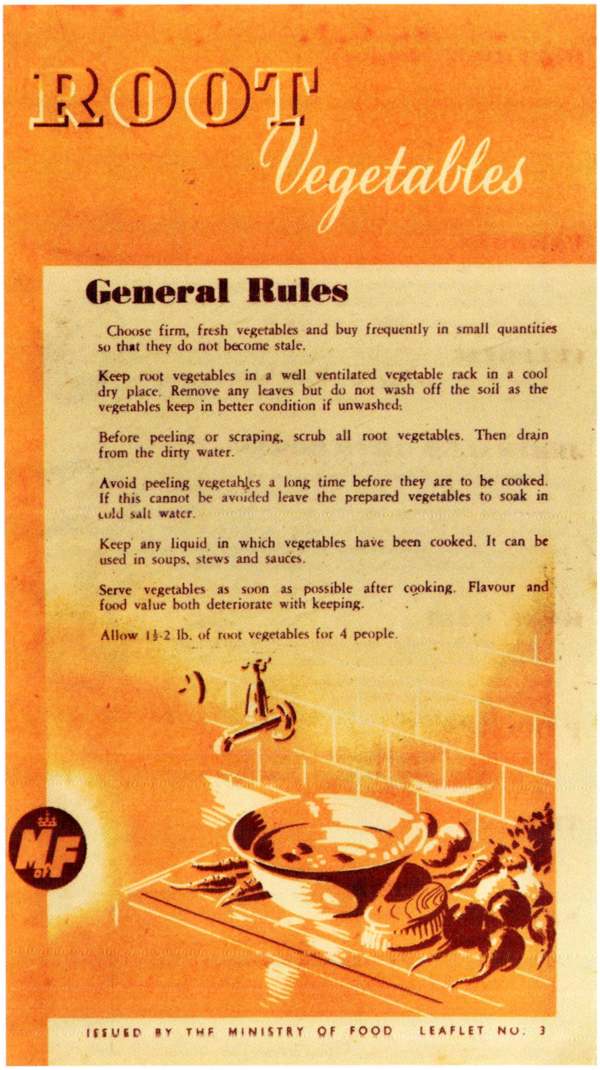

***126** Ministry of Food leaflet regarding root vegetables, 1939-1945.*

A girl said to me recently *Mother always seems to wear shapeless clothes. She likes the sort of things I wouldn't be seen dead in - good tweeds, cut straight all the way down. Daddy is the same. He won't have the least suggestion of a waist in his coats. David* (her 20-year-old brother) *likes his clothes to follow his shape and so do I. It's the same with shoes. I hate good shoes. I like cheap, jolly sort of shoes which you wear for a season and then throw away.*

I agree with the mother about shoes. I much prefer *good* shoes.

As regards make-up, I use it myself sometimes with secrecy and cunning - never blatantly for artistic effect, though I can appreciate the effect when this is done cleverly by the right people. I have absolutely no prejudice against it except when used by school-girls. I was recently urged to use it by two girls in their twenties. *Why are you afraid of lipstick?* asked one. *You'd improve yourself enormously if you used it* said the other. My father was horrified recently when my fifty-year-old sister had a permanent wave. Anything *artificial* upsets him. Nearly all my middle-aged neighbours disapprove of make-up. *I suppose I'll have to put up with it when Joan's 21,* said a clergyman to me the other day, *but how I shall hate it*! *I can't stand lipstick* a bank manager remarked to me the other day. The three daughters of an influential lady who lives here have been forbidden by her even to use powder.

I have noticed that the girls of about 20 whom I know are slack about their under-clothes. They don't ever seem to bother to mend them, and a few months ago, when staying with a young friend, I was interested to discover that a rag I thought was a floor wiper was her *other vest*. Externally this girl was always perfectly and fashionably dressed.

My idea of having *a good time* is certainly altering. A few days ago a girl burst out to me on the subject. *Mummie and Daddy always accuse me of being restless. Why do you want to be eternally running about and wanting to go to the pictures? Their idea of pleasure is to sit still in a room in dead silence with a book*.'

She also thought the young needed to earn their own livelihood:

'I think everyone should be trained to earn their own living. All the young people I know take it for granted that they must *do something* though many have no ideas about what they want to do, though they know what they do not want to do.

I have a neighbour with a young daughter who was educated solely by her mother. She has not yet done any work and is quite obviously in the marriage market. The brother has had a public-school education and is to go into the army. My doctor has two sons who are being trained for careers. The daughter left school without even attempting to get her school certificate and is at home doing nothing and learning nothing. However, the mother still talks about deciding on a career.

On the other hand I know several people who have taken up work which would've been considered *infra dig* when I was young. Unable to pass exams, one of my cousins joined the army as a private. Another (son of a canon) is a policeman. A girl I know has become a mannequin, another became a children's nurse. All these people felt that they must do something, even if their parents couldn't afford to train them for jobs. Among my generation, I notice a sneaking desire to keep a daughter at home. One friend swore she would never keep her daughter at home but though that daughter worked for a year as a cook in a school, she has now been at home attending tennis parties for three years.'

Some of her opinions on race were sharp including on the French ('emotional, excitable and judging by the humorous papers they only have one joke'.), the Jews ('treacherous, mercenary and ungrateful') as well as the Germans ('I cannot be reasonable about Germans. I have only known one German man and the only thing I remember about him is his revolting way of eating lightly-boiled eggs. I have known a few German girls and women - frowsty, well-meaning and unattractive. I think that almost without realising it, I still regard them primarily as the people who killed my brothers. I cannot understand a people who behave as if they had one mind and that not their own. In my better moments, I am sorry for them.'). Those on Black people partly reflected her experiences in the British Empire when she lived in Nigeria. She wrote:

'I feel a faint revulsion towards educated Negroes. This prejudice was much stronger before I lived in Africa where I grew to like and admire them when, in their own environment, and to a large extent, overcame my

127 Wartime poster, drawn by a Nigerian artist, showing local products including milk, hides and skins.

> feeling of physical repulsion. In spite of a very warm feeling of affection for certain Negroes, I invariably washed after touching their bodies. I regard them as a race of clever and teachable children. Their memories are remarkable and I think that makes them seem more intelligent than they really are. I admire them very much for their goodness and generosity to each other, their good manners, their gaiety and the irrepressible smutty humour.'

Evacuees

In September 1940 Mrs Pickwoad described the evacuees in Crediton ('As far as I can see, our area is being inundated with evacuees, both private and those evacuees under the government scheme. This flood of people seems to have been renewed since the attack on London started.') and in greater detail:

> 'Crediton is full of evacuees. Very often they get so bored or find their billets so uncomfortable that they return home after a few weeks. I have noticed that the local people are inclined to be very critical and lodge many complaints against them. My char woman had a little boy billeted on her, but he ran away twice to join his mother and was eventually allowed to stay. She said he was rude and unmanageable and complained continually about his food. Others complain of dirtiness. A friend of mine is a billeting officer. Recently a woman told her that she had complained to the woman who was with her that her child had made a

128 Poster in the series 'Empire War Workers in Britain', featuring Jack Smith, a tank worker from Nigeria.

mess on the carpet. *There*! replied the evacuee mother, *and I told her always to go on the linoleum*. My maid's mother had a woman and baby sent to her, though she had no beds available – only an unfurnished room not used because it is damp. She complained but was told she must *make the best of it*. She very much resented this.

I meet a great many evacuated mothers and babies at the local welfare centre and find them very much more attractive and human than the local woman.

I also see a certain amount of difficult children who are billeted at the Liberal Club here, in the care of an excellent matron. They sometimes come up here to play and I like them all very much and so do my children. They are all very happy and jolly and have adapted themselves remarkably well.

A few days ago an expectant mother, with a child of two, arrived there having nowhere else to go. She had lost all her possessions. I took some things for the new baby and for herself, but she turned away from me and wouldn't speak. She is slightly mentally defective. She had to sleep in the dormitory with all the children. She was sent to Newton Abbot, but they were unable to have her, apparently, as she was sent back and she utterly refuses to go to a poor law institution. Now she is to return to London!

On the whole, people here are anxious to do all they can to help, but they often find their visitors a great trial. Bed-wetting seems to be the commonest trouble and a reluctance to do any work in the house to help.

The clerical staff of the Gaumont British film company is established here. A good deal of building has been done for them and their presence has also been good for trade. They were at first regarded with great suspicion (I heard them described as a fast-looking lot) but they have now been more or less accepted. Pastry cooks and sweet shops do a roaring trade and usually seem to be sold out, but then we have troops here as well.'

***129** British (and American) shoppers were asked to walk rather than consume petrol in their cars.*

25 February 1942

Life in 1942 appears to have been more uncertain. Her movements were recorded on Wednesday, 25 February:

'9.00 June brought husband and self breakfast in bed (fishcakes toast and marge and coffee) because we've both had flu and I only started getting up again yesterday afternoon.

9.45 Got up but didn't wash because all the pipes are frozen and the nearest water was in the pump in the garden. Made my bed and swept and cleared up the room a bit. Made children's beds and washed the linoleum in their room and tidied up generally. Did Flying Officer Ball's room (F. O. Ball has been billeted on us for the last 16 months or so). He makes his own bed and always leaves things nice and clear.

Went down to drawing room and had tea with husband and June and Tuppy who is home from school with tummy trouble. Wrote three letters and did some mending till 1pm. Listened to news.

1.05 Had prepared by char (Mrs M) stewed rabbit with vegetables grown by self (leeks, parsnips, carrots, sweets and home-bottled tomatoes) and pancakes served with lemon squash. After lunch knitted and at about 2.30 went into garden. Cleaned out the dogs' house and gave them fresh straw and brought in a truss of oat straw for the goats and cow to eat. Unfroze pipe with boiling water and got pump going. Cleared out three rabbit hutches and shed, and dug parsnips for them and fed them all. Discovered a litter June had overlooked. Inspected damage done to kitchen garden by goats while I was ill. Laid table for tea.

4.30 June got tea - bread and marge and honey.

5.00 Helped June wash up and laid table for supper. Made some soup out of remnants of stew and boiled carrots and potatoes for a *Dr Carrot* dish to serve with sausage.

7.00 June came in to say cow had vanished from field. I wasn't allowed out but June and husband went out to search. Both very wild and despairing. Husband fruitlessly ringing up farmers etc., and saying *he has a feeling* cow will never be seen again. F.O. Ball discreetly silent and me suggesting things and getting snubbed for undo optimism. Put T. & S. to bed.

After the soup and sausages husband went out in car but returned still more despairing. June silently vanished. I sewed.

At about 9.05 June returned having found cow (caught and put in shed by farmer) and led it home on its halter while riding her bike. In the meantime we had listened to 9.00 news. After Mr Ball had gone to bed and June to her bath (the first for days). I sat and talked to husband till 10.45 (about branding and insuring cows, about Tuppy and about Russia). Had bath and, after husband had listened to news again, got to sleep after a lot of coughing. Woken by telephone at 12.15. Husband had made mistake and should have been in Exeter on observer duty at midnight. Got up and made him coffee and sandwiches while he dressed. A lot more coughing and eventually sleep.'

130 *Ovaltine advertisement, late 1930s.*

Life remained busy a year later, on 10 February 1943:

'Got up at 7.30 and got tea. Dressed and got children's breakfast (sausages, Bournvita and toast) by 8.10. Milked the cow and goat. Got breakfast for self and husband by 9.00. After breakfast took cow out to pasture, tethered goats, moved the utility rabbits onto fresh grass and also moved daughter's guinea pigs. Mixed up the hens' mash. Washed and scalded dairy utensils, put milk on to scald. Tidied up a bit indoors and had cup of tea with husband at about 1.30.

Did a little digging and planted two rows shallots. Went to town on bicycle to hunt for rice and collect sack of scraps (peelings) for animals.

Lunch 1.00 Liver and leaks and potatoes, prunes and custard. Immediately after lunch planted another row of shallots and one of broad beans.

2.30 man arrived with large load of barley straw. He dumped it in a field and I spent next two hours carrying it, one bundle at a time, to the three different sheds which it filled. It rained and blew and the cow and pony both tried to escape through the gate every time I opened it. (my husband went to his observer post after lunch)

At 5.00 my youngest daughter (who had a half holiday) got her foot stepped on by pony and I had to apply iodine and a bandage. Milked cow while Tuppy (aged 11) got tea ready. Hurried over tea, washed up, collected rabbit food and fed my 10 Angoras. Took some milk to a neighbour and some to my mother. Did the blackout, shut up the goats, shut up nest boxes, saw to utility rabbits and fed and shut up dogs. Did some ironing and then sat down and read to children for ½ hour.

Cooked supper (chopped up remains of sausage, liver and bacon fried with rice and then simmered together in gravy till mushy) and junket. Gave children supper (liver mixture and Ovaltine to drink) and sent them up to bathe. Had supper with husband on his return from post at 8.30.

Listened to news for a few minutes before washing up. Scalded dairy things, made porridge ready for breakfast and laid table.

10.00 – 10.30 Knitted a sock

10.30 Soaked in a very hot bath to deal with rheumatic aches, then read *Marie Curie* until husband came to bed.

NB from 9.30 – 2.30 I have a char 5 days a week which includes Wednesdays.'

Her hopes for 1943 were limited:

'Resigned to the idea of increasing difficulties at home and terribly apprehensive over the three boys who spend their leaves with us and almost belong to the family. I expect frightful casualties and I cannot hope that I am going to continue much longer without suffering. I think this year will see Germany crack but I think the cost is going to be appalling. As a matter of fact, I try not to look ahead but to cope with each day as it comes and to enjoy people while I have them, shutting my mind against the future. The only fears I have concern people, and 1943 is so packed with those fears that I rarely dare face them.'

In 1942 she had had war weariness:

'My personal desires are at present just the outcome of war weariness. I want to escape from hens and goats and potatoes and as many household cares as possible. I should like a paid job with some leisure and regular working hours. I'm sick of a fourteen-hour day but I don't expect any changes of that sort. What I hope for most is simply the feeling of security which makes raising a family worthwhile. I want to be able to stop wondering if my daughters will raise sons to be butchered in the next war. My plans and desires are all the outcome of present conditions.'

Even so, there were aspects of British life she felt important to maintain such as the rhythm of Sundays ('I like the traditional English Sunday just as it is, complete with church bells, best clothes, roast beef and general British hypocrisy. I do nothing to contribute to all this except to cook the usual Sunday dinner but I like to see other people doing it all. I would hate it to be changed. I can't explain why I feel like this, but Sunday seems to give value to all the other days of the week, I appreciate them more because of it.'). Mrs Pickwoad also managed to retain a sense of humour. The only comment she had heard regarding catching venereal disease concerned the church: 'I have been told that only bishops get it off lavatories.'

After the war Mrs Pickwoad continued to live in Crediton and died in 1989.

DARTINGTON (& EXETER, BUCKFAST ABBEY & DARTMOOR)

Before the war Dartington was mainly a rural parish, situated on the River Dart some two miles from Totnes. In 1939 it was known for the Hall, with its estate of some 3,000 acres, which had been purchased by Leonard and Dorothy Elmhirst in 1925. By 1937 it was attracting exiles and refugees from Germany and Spain. Amongst them were Gustavo Durand (1906-1969), a noted Spanish composer and Republican commander who married a wealthy American heiress at the Hall in 1939. Two years later much of its community had been hollowed out by the war but it retained a string quartet, a choir and the Jooss Ballet, a repertory company founded by German-refugees Kurt Jooss (1901-1939) and Sigurd Leeder (1902-1981). In 1941 the Hall also housed twenty babies from bombed-out homes in Plymouth and by 1942 there were also 250 London children. Many of these evacuees came from Clapham and were offered a few hours work in local farming. Some reached school-leaving age and found agricultural jobs. One boy said 'I don't expect I'll go back to London when this lot's over. It's the

131-2 Exterior and interior views of the Globe Hotel in Exeter which was destroyed by an incendiary bomb in 1942.

countryside for me now'. The parish population in 1931 was 692.[135]

14. Leslie Hughes, Lecturer, 1937

Thirty-three-year-old Leslie Ernest Charles Hughes (1904-61), the son of a London butler, recorded his 'motoring holiday' when he travelled from London to Dartington. Mr Hughes wrote a day-survey in 1937 which entailed a visit through Devon.[136]

12 August 1937

'Globe Hotel, Exeter, looking onto Cathedral Close. Tea brought about 8.30, get ready for joining lady friend at breakfast, get newspapers, complain that noise of rats behind the panelling was disturbing and room changed for next night. Read *Baedeker* aloud at breakfast.

10.15. Enter cathedral for look around before the service at 10.30. Note red cassocks of large number of choir boys and the man who is ringing the bells, and depart to get car from garage five minutes away. Return for coats and decide to go as far as Plymouth via Torquay.

Pass Newton Abbot to Torquay and note palms and red cliffs, place is probably over-rated but crowded with holiday makers. Drive round front and off to Totnes for Dartington Hall but realise too early for calling on such a place. Notice however Buckfast Abbey on the map a few miles further and go there. Find huge car park and wooden shops just before the gas works, which is about 200 yards south of abbey. Buy refreshment and ices and sample of Buckfast china from the local pottery to give

133 A view of High Street in Exeter, 1865, from Fore Street. Most of these buildings were still standing in 1937 and escaped the bombing in the war.

to friends in London who appreciate delicate colouring and design.

At Buckfast Abbey (Cistercian) the edifice is nearly complete and fashioned from two colours of stone. Enter and note candles and confessional boxes and large pipes of organ and the console. Exit to attached

134 'Dartington Manor House, Devon' by John Edmund Buckley, 1800s.

shop which is crowded with holiday visitors buying curios and photographs, an apparently lucrative business. Outside as part of the Abbey is car park and flower beds. One fancies there will be soon sideshows as well as refreshment huts. Hear organ from outside and return to watch monk playing some doleful voluntary.

Return to car through diminutive village and return along the road to Totnes and note entrance to cultivated garden belonging to Dartington Hall. Inside open gate is a map of the estate and indicates the way to entrance, which is easily found after passing through a farmyard stretching across minor road. On alighting see party being shown round in the distance and catch these up at open-air theatre which was tilting yard centuries ago but now consists of terraces and a rake down to a grass stage for open-air work of the ballet school. We have missed the description of the old hall but this is a little importance since it is not mentioned in *Baedeker*. The estate comprises 3,000 acres employing 1,000 people in local industries such as wood, agriculture, pottery weaving, etc., the school (co-ed) having grown up as an experiment with employees' children but now attracts wide clientele totalling 130 (ages 2 to 18).

Move off in car, giving two girls a lift to sawmill which is comparatively extensive and deals with the wood from the estate. We cannot then go to see the cider made because it is being made wasp-proof and these are very troublesome at the moment. We then go back in the cars to the weaving mill where all the work is done by hand. There is a showroom with exquisite materials but it is difficult to see how machine articles can be competed with except for the luxury market. Pass along the road to the studio or display room where all the products of the estate wood work, pottery, etc. is displayed. Take Devonshire tea in apple garden attached.

About 4pm return to car and drive to Plymouth via Kingsbridge. Plymouth naturally [an] old town and we drive round the front under the Hoe. Leave Plymouth by the residential part and decide to go over Dartmoor via Yelverton which is due north about 6

135 *Mr Leslie Hughes came to see Dartmoor's striking landscape as depicted in John White Abbot's watercolour entitled 'Leigh Tor Rocks at Poundsgate, near New Bridge on the Dart, Devon', 1800.*

miles. North East for 20 miles to Moretonhampstead with Princetown with prison about halfway. Very few cars, cyclists or pedestrians since the hills are steep, views are very fine. Off the moor we traverse more winding hills and valleys back to Exeter. Decide not to have supper at the hotel but visit cinema to see Tauber in *Pagliacci*, not [a] very good film (know the opera well) but excellent recording of Tauber's voice and is valuable on that account.

On previous evening after supper we had also been to cinema to see the last half of Astaire film, mainly to notice that provinces have cinemas which are technically superior to many West End leading cinemas. After cinema, had coffee and sandwiches at café in High Street. Bed about 11.30, start for London about 11am, arriving about 8pm. So far kept to schedule which means seeing maximum in minimum time. Have no use for just wandering on from one place to another.'

He added 'my lady friend is beginning to read maps and sign posts intelligently, since these activities are inhibited for the driver when there are so many fast cars and lorries on the road. We go slightly wrong sometimes but it does not matter, there is no hurry and plenty of time allowed'.

By the following year Mr Hughes was employed as a lecturer in electrical engineering and was involved in an accident which caused the death of a fifty-eight-year-old man in London. He testified to the coroner that he had passed his driving test in 1937 and since then had driven some eight thousand miles. Mr Hughes died in 1961.[137]

EXETER

By 1939 the city had been the regional capital for many hundreds of years. Woollen cloth had brought prosperity in the seventeenth and eighteenth centuries but that industry collapsed by 1800. Exeter was unable to identify another manufacture of that magnitude and instead the city had a range of small firms. It also became attractive to retirees. In the 1800s it was known for being the seat of local government, a cathedral city and a centre of education.

Some of Exeter's experiences in the Second World War were largely unanticipated. The population in 1931 was recorded at 66,039 and by 1939 it had increased to 73,030.[138] The city hosted foreign servicemen, particularly Americans, from 1942 to 1944, in preparation for the invasion of France. Initially it had attracted Westminster civil servants but they fled following the French capitulation. They were replaced by evacuees with a general consensus that Exeter was a safe city. Gerald Richards, an eighteen-year-old at St Luke's College who was normally resident in Falmouth, wrote for MO in November 1939:

> 'Many evacuees are placed in houses whose inhabitants are either far above their social positions or far below. The changes from town to country life is normally disliked by most adult evacuees. For example, young unmarried women and children from London billeted near Exeter [are] perfectly comfortable but want to go back because life there is too monotonous and too quiet.'[139]

Bombing in April and May 1942 caused extensive damage and the exodus of many children. In 1942 an MO Writer at Bristol recorded a conversation about Exeter:

> 'Alex F. returned from his holiday and gave us an account of the damage at Exeter. He told us that after the first raid some mention was made in the press

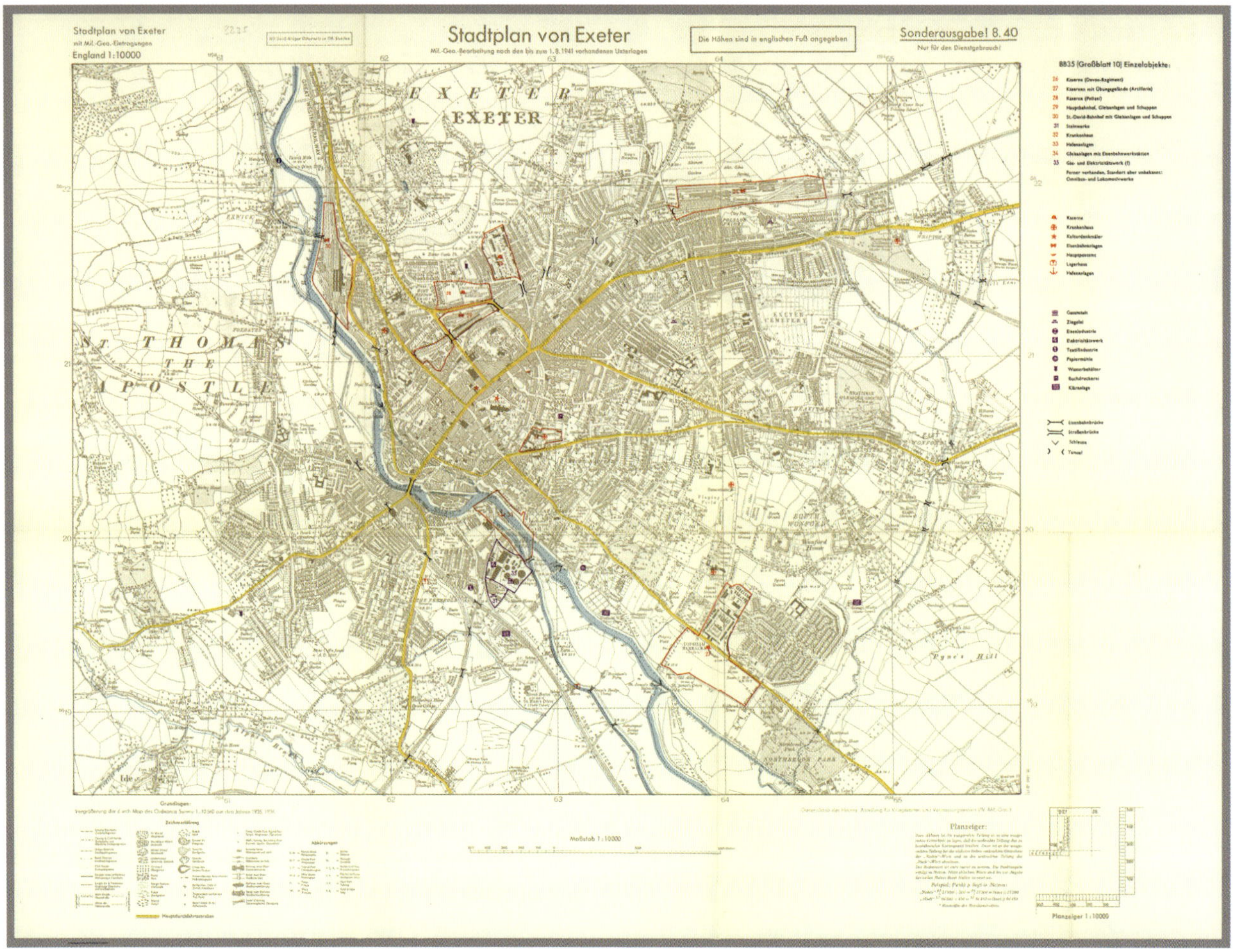

136 German street plan (Stadtplan) of Exeter which was prepared for the bombing of the city. This was based on the Ordnance Survey map, with purple symbols for industrial sites, red for strategic sites and principal roads in yellow, 1940.

GB 13 105 b c
N. f. D.

Exeter
Kasernen

Karte 1 : 100 000
Engl. Bl. 36b

Bild Nr. 278 Z 40 **Geogr. Lage** 3°31'30" W, 50°43'30" N, **Höhe ü. d. M.** 40 m **Stand** XI. 40.

500 0 500 1000
Maßstab etwa 1: 13 500 (1 cm = 135 m)
Lfl. Kdo. 3

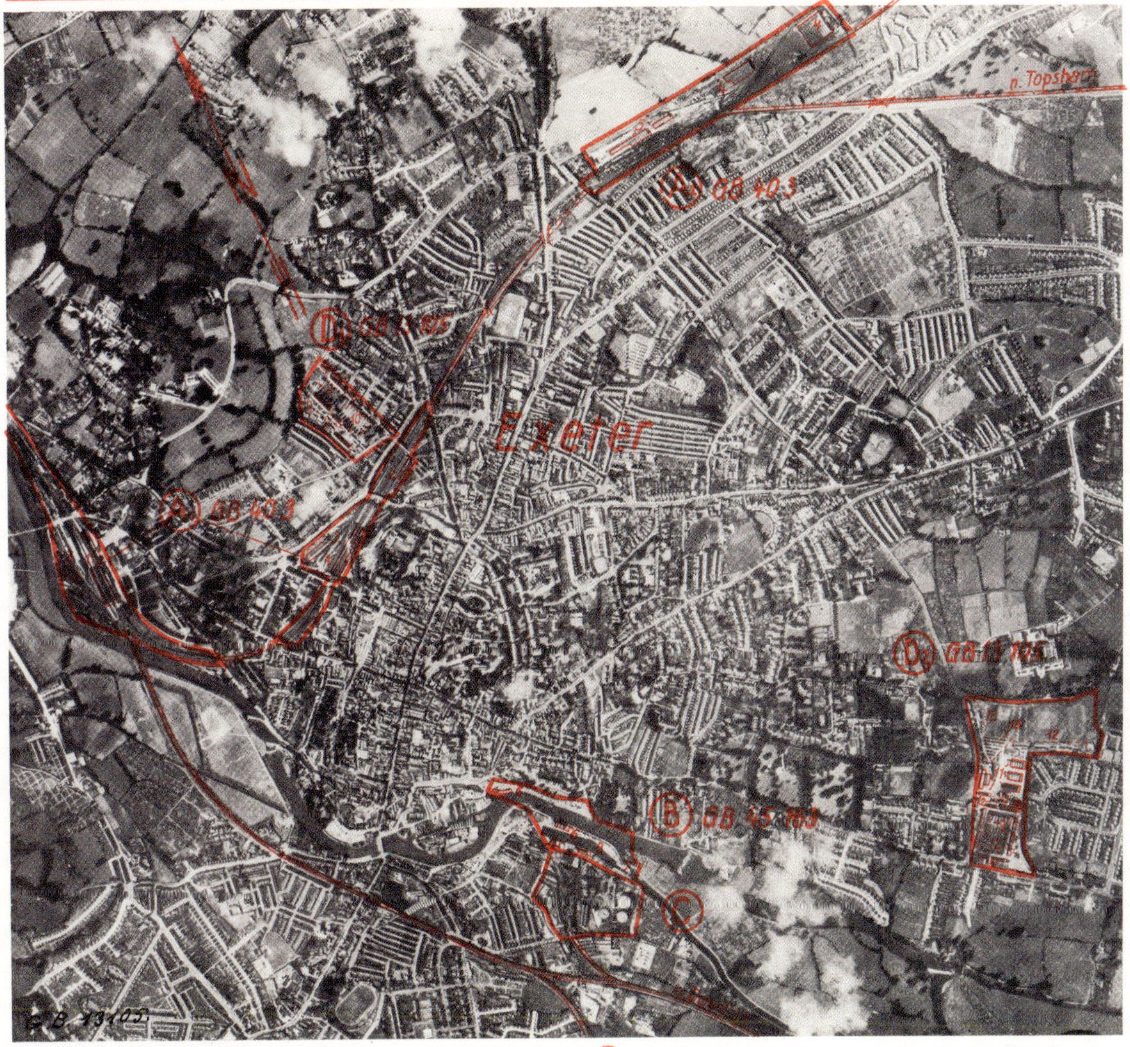

(A1) GB 40 3 Bahnhof

1) Bahnhofsgebäude und Bahnsteigüberdachungen	etwa	7 000 qm
2) Güterhallen	etwa	3 000 qm
3) Lokschuppen	etwa	700 qm
bebaute Fläche	etwa	10 700 qm
Gesamtfläche	etwa	150 000 qm

(A2)

4) Werkstatthallen	etwa	13 000 qm
5) Lagergebäude	etwa	3 500 qm
bebaute Fläche	etwa	16 500 qm
Gesamtfläche	etwa	160 000 qm

(B) GB 45 163 Hafen

6) Lagergebäude	etwa	2 200 qm
7) 2 Schleusen		
8) Hafenbecken		
Kailänge etwa 1 100 m		

(C) Gaswerk

(D1) GB 13 105 Kasernen

9) 7 Kasernengebäude	etwa	5 000 qm
10) 15 Unterkunftsbaracken	etwa	1 000 qm
bebaute Fläche	etwa	6 000 qm
Gesamtfläche	etwa	46 000 qm

(D2)

11) 6 Lagerhallen	etwa	4 000 qm
12) 15 Kasernengebäude	etwa	4 500 qm
13) 30 Unterkunftsbaracken	etwa	7 000 qm
bebaute Fläche	etwa	15 500 qm
Gesamtfläche	etwa	130 000 qm

137 *Aerial view included in the Luftwaffe target dossier for Exeter, 1940.*

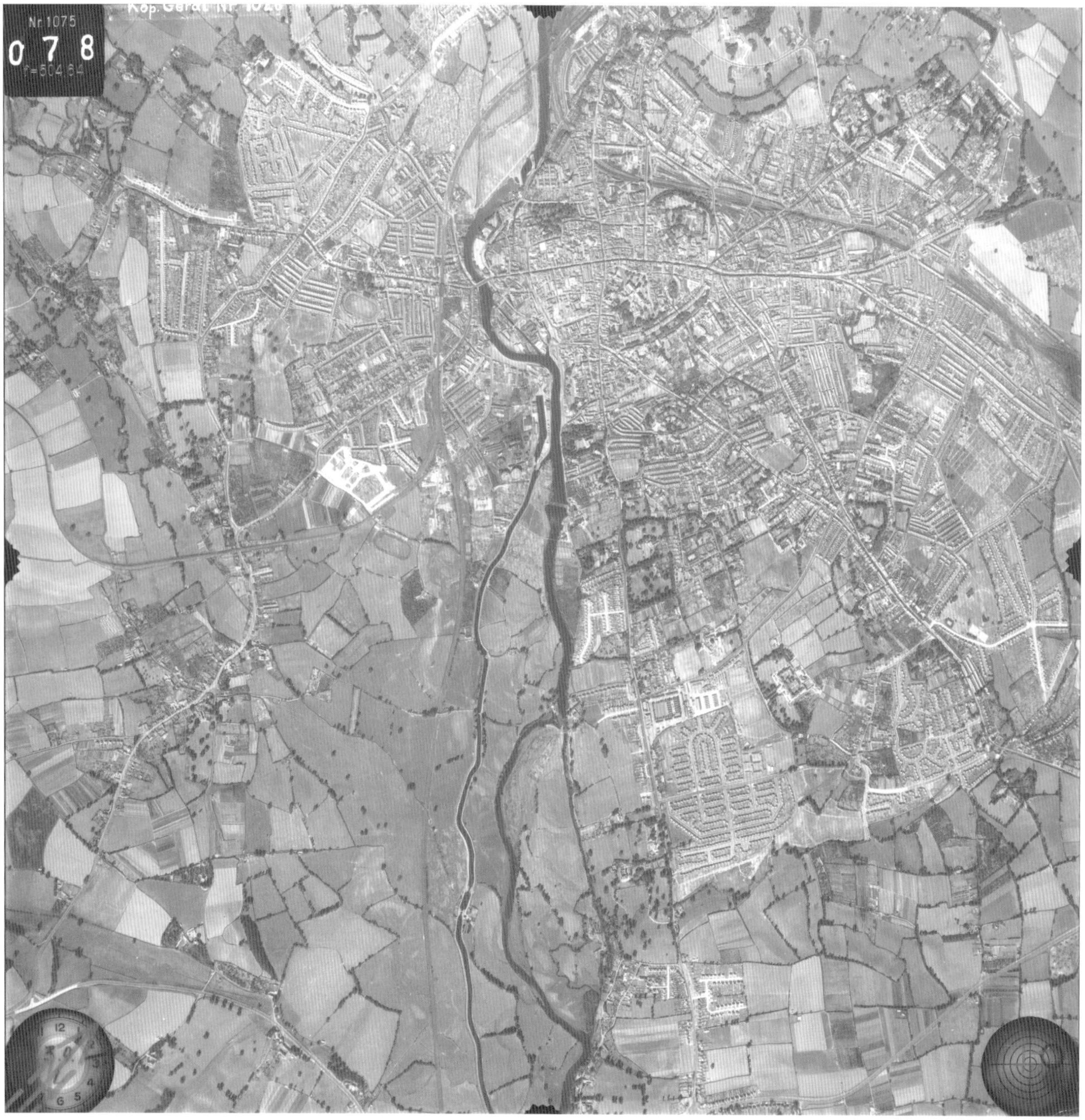

138 The Luftwaffe's aerial photograph of Exeter, 3 September 1940.

that the cathedral had not been hit. This caused a considerable amount of ill feeling amongst the townspeople for they considered that their homes and lives were of more importance than the cathedral. Further raids did damage the cathedral and because of the press comments little regret came from the townspeople.'[140]

MO Writers in other parts of the country occasionally mentioned Exeter including Noel Willmett, a thirty-four-year-old radio operator living in Wales. He adopted a baby girl:

'Her mother was a Northern Irish girl, aged 23, who was working in England for one of the ministries at Exeter. I think her father was an American soldier with a wife in America. He is now in France. It was quite an accident that the mother came to Newport to have the baby. She is an intelligent, educated girl and was very sorry to lose her baby but felt it was for the best. She cried the day we took it away and almost marred our pleasure in having her. She told us she had concealed the matter from her parents in Ireland.'[141]

Some Exeter references were short such as one written in 1942 from Dorset ('The night watchman, who is an ex-naval man, told me that it was only just by luck he had not sent his best false leg off to be done up. He had a bit of digging he had not got done or it would have been bombed in Exeter.')[142] and another was written that year in Sheffield ('Met a woman in a shop today who told me her mother, father, sister, brother-in-law and two children were all killed in Exeter, direct hit on their house. I could see she didn't comprehend it and had to tell folk to try and convince herself. She phoned her brother at Plymouth to ask should she go to Exeter but he said he had been and there was no trace of any of them or any of their possessions, that he felt done in after his visit, so she had better just stay in Sheffield.')[143]

Not every comment was positive such as one written in Yorkshire in 1942 ('Mr Brown - the gas man - has a business in Exeter and he thinks the workers there are awful due to the big difference between the proletariat and the professional classes. They are ignorant - almost illiterate according to him - and make rotten workmen. No interest or pride in their jobs. I didn't feel in the mood for an argument and anyway he knows business acquaintances of Frank and it wouldn't do for Frank to get the reputation of having a Red wife.')[144] while others are distressing ('Had a very moving description of a young teacher's experiences in Exeter's last raid sent to me by her mother. She says *One speaks quite lightly of blitzes, destruction and death without really feeling how dreadful it is, because the experience which carries it all home has not been gone through. I have gone through it now, stood outside a blazing, crumbling house, beside people that you do not know whether they are dead or alive, waiting, waiting for a doctor, for a squad and fire engine to rescue others trapped inside, calling for help. They were burnt alive.* The girl says that though the raid was hell, it's the days afterwards, especially the dead body of a little girl who had been in her class, that she will remember.')[145]

The Ministry of Information reported public opinion and rumours in Exeter as elsewhere. This included in May 1940 'cinema managers in the Exeter district have been told by some of their regular patrons that the showing of the film *Hitler, Beast of Berlin* should be abandoned next week as Haw Haw has threatened that Exeter will be bombed if it is shown. This story is apparently widely believed.'. The following month it recorded 'Exeter is anxious about its anti-aircraft defences as there is said to be no barrage or searchlights. Strong criticism is made of inadequate defence arrangements.' In July the ministry noted 'A false alarm of parachutists at Exeter demonstrated a prompt and efficient reaction by the LDV, and has increased local confidence.' and 'Exeter citizens are demanding the camouflage of petrol storage tanks following a reported German claim that these had been damaged.'

A number of observations continued to be made through that summer such as 'Exeter and Swindon reacted excellently to their first daylight raid, and streets were quickly cleared', 'Exeter is stated to be very far from dismayed that it was raided two nights ago. This undercurrent of satisfaction is said to be associated with a feeling that the city has *grown up*.', 'In Exeter the view is held that bombs were dropped recently through bedroom lights being switched on as soon as householders were awakened by sirens.', 'Rumour in Exeter that the local squadron secured most victories in last Sunday's air battle makes many think that the proximity of a champion squadron adds to Exeter's vulnerability' and that there was 'Dissatisfaction in Exeter because there are apparently no protective fighters or anti-aircraft guns, and the siren policy is a chief topic of conversation'. The following month, in September, the ministry reported 'some dissatisfaction reported from Exeter and Penzance that bombs were dropped without the sirens being sounded'.[146] Seven MO Writers commented at length on Exeter during the war.

15. Sidney Turner, Clerk, 1939

Sidney John Turner (1893-1960) was a married forty-six-year-old builder's clerk who lived at 1 Alma Cottages in Parr Street in 1939. He was a directive respondent on several occasions.[147]

Directive: the generations

In 1939 Mr Turner answered questions about generational differences ('the clothing of the younger generation is definitely healthier and more becoming, more sensible although the tight collars and superfluous clothing with which we were loaded was considered sensible 40 years ago.') and ('we find ourselves at variance with the younger element, who appear to us to be bent on having a good time at no-matter-whose-expense. Money is made to be spent without thought for tomorrow. Family life is a back number to young people who regard their homes as mainly sleeping and eating places.').

Exeter
from the Canal

Exeter.

Exeter

Exeter

He was ambivalent that the younger generation's morals were better ('The modern youthful attitude towards sex questions generally seems to me to be all to the good. Our ideas, based on ignorance were often prurient and our ways of obtaining information were furtive, but which of the two generations was the more moral {moral in the sense of real clean living and thinking} is I think extremely debatable.').

He had given careful thought to his retirement:

'Up to the present, saving has been impossible. At my age, 46, insurance (endowment) would be a burden without being of much benefit. The total income for a year which enters our household from all sources is never more than £236. Out of this, we pay mortgage interest on a cottage (which is equivalent to rent), take a holiday abroad nearly every year, pay for that portion of secondary school education not covered by my daughter's scholarship, buy books and subscribe to Boots and *Times* book club and live fairly comfortably. Needless to say, this would be impossible without a careful wife (who is not looking over my shoulder as I write). She saves many pounds by making clothes for herself and daughter. In addition 10% is set aside for charities, not necessarily organised charities.

My income is not likely to be increased, but if it were, we should probably save most of an increase towards repayment of a mortgage and to form the nucleus of a retiring fund. Any substantial increase would mean that retiring age would come nearer. At present it seems hopeless to think of this for another 20 years (66) but I can't believe that the years after 60 can be as full of enjoyment as those before.

There are so many places to see and things to do when I retire. I want to live in France for a year. I want to read all the books I haven't time for at present. So my form of saving would be present self-denial in the hope of future enjoyment.'

Mr Turner was mindful his circumstances resulted from his family's earlier poverty:

'This is a legacy from a poverty-stricken youth. My father was the eldest of 12. His father was a farm labourer on 13 shillings per week. By comparison, my father with a family of 2 and 27 shillings per week in 1914 was well-off, but by comparison with my daughter's school days, mine was poor.'

Three years later No. 1 Alma Cottage was destroyed in the Blitz but Mr Turner survived losing his home and died in Exeter in 1960.[148]

16. Gwen Holmes, Librarian, 1939-40

Exeter-born Gwendolyne M. Holmes (1916-2010) was a twenty-three-year-old assistant librarian when she began writing for MO in 1939. She then lived with her aunt and uncle at No. 52 St Anne's Road in Polsloe Park. Miss Holmes contributed responses to five questionnaires in 1939 and 1940. She explained her reason for writing for MO as 'it's the only chance I have of being able to say exactly what I think without someone contradicting me or saying I'm being silly'.[149] Her contributions included her views of William Joyce: 'I have not yet met anyone who takes Lord Haw Haw seriously. Most people seem to tune in to his broadcasts for amusement. Personally, his whining voice annoys me intensely and I have not listened in to him for some time.'

Miss Holmes' wartime inconveniences were the effects of petrol rationing on local bus services, the increased cost

145 *52, St Anne's Road, Exeter, the home of Miss Gwendoline Holmes while she was writing for Mass Observation.*

OPPOSITE: 139-44 *Views of parts of Exeter which, with the exception of the cathedral, did not suffer bomb damage.*

of living including of silk stockings and the limited opening hours of shops and cinemas. She also wrote:

> 'I overhear a number of wartime grouses from subscribers to the library where I work. These are mostly middle-aged, well-to-do women and their grumbles are usually about petrol-rationing (four fifths of our total number of subscribers live in the country and have to cut down their shopping expeditions to the town), the blacking-out of their houses and the problems of evacuees.
>
> The chief difficulty here in Exeter seems to be with mothers and children. Numbers of these have returned to their homes. Some of the school-children were rather difficult at first – especially in the matter of food. They refused cooked dinners and asked for cake and demanded fish & chips & beer for supper. One country housewife with two young schoolgirl evacuees found that they would not eat meat and vegetables for their dinner if they knew there was a pudding to follow – such things as apple tart and Devonshire cream needed all their appetite! She solved the problem by the threat *No dinner, No pudding*.
>
> Another difficulty is the problem of clothes. Many of the children came wearing thin summer clothes and appeals to their parents have failed to bring winter coats and shoes, and in some cases the hosts have had to buy the necessary clothes. On the whole the children are settling down very well now.'

St Anne's Road was bombed on 4 May 1942 but No. 52 appears to have escaped damage. Miss Holmes died in Tiverton in 2010.

17. Reginald Harpur, Retired Engineer, 1940

Sixty-eight-year-old Reginald Charles Harpur (1872-1959) recorded travelling from his home in London to Penzance in 1940. He does not appear to have been accompanied by his wife Rosa whom he had married in 1899. Mr Harpur was a retired electrical engineer and lived at 25 Kirkdale with housekeeper Dorothy Woods (1888-) and widowed Winifred Edith Gunton (1888-1965), a commercial traveller. Mr Harpur contributed diaries for every war year except 1943.[150]

1940

On 21 December he wrote:

> 'We arrived about 4.15pm and put up at the Acland Hotel in Sidwell Street. The name of the street for a moment reminded me of the modern poets of Sitwells, although I have never done more than glance at a few of their verses but seeing a large church in the street dedicated to St Sidwell I realised my mistake as not even Edith Sitwell can qualify for saint-ship…
>
> As the staff of the Acland is very much reduced, they were not able to give us an evening meal at the time we wanted it, so we went out and fed at the Bude Restaurant in Sidwell Street and listened to their band, which played music and gave me a pain as I listened.
>
> Afterwards we visited the Odeon Cinema and saw a very amusing picture called *Old Mrs Riley in Business*. I laughed more than I have done so for a long time and everyone seemed to enjoy the picture immensely. During the show, an Alert was sounded and a good many people left the cinema but we remained in our seats. Nothing happened and the All Clear went about 9.15pm. After we headed back to the hotel, where D[orothy] went to bed and W[inifred] & I had a cider in the bar, learning that no bombs had been dropped near here for a long time.
>
> In the middle of the night there was another Alert and some people in the hotel got up and went downstairs. I heard a plane in the distance a couple of times but there was no gun fire so I went to sleep until the All Clear woke me up again for a few minutes.
>
> I had a touch of indigestion during the night and had to sit up in bed for a time until my stomach recovered its normal condition. Before breakfast W. and I sent to fetch the car, which had been left in a garage up the road instead of in the little yard adjoining the hotel. The garage was locked up and we had considerable difficulty in finding our way in from the back.
>
> No one was in attendance and the place was full of army lorries and cars, some of which completely blocked our car from coming out. At 9 o'clock a number of soldiers came into the place and helped us to clear a way and start the car, and eventually with their help we managed to get out of the place before any of the attendants turned up. We left the Acland Hotel about 9.30am…'

A few days later, on the 26th, they stopped in Exeter on their return to London:

> 'We arrived soon after 4pm and found that we had

***146** Sidwell Street before the destruction of the war.*

forgotten to put our gas masks in the car this morning. We posted a card to H asking him to forward the gas masks as soon as possible just in case Hitler should find out that we have left them behind and gives orders for a prompt gas attack on London.

We stopped at the Acland Hotel again. Tried to find another garage but had to go to the same place again, which was nearly full. It was very foggy in Exeter when we arrived but maybe that is an advantage we did not properly appreciate.

Food in the Acland Hotel was a little severe and we could get only eggs on toast for our meal. After that we went to the Odeon Cinema outside [of] which there was a long queue of people waiting for the cheaper seats, so we had to pay more to get in.

The first picture was *Its in the Air* with George Formby in the principal part. I have not laughed so much for a long time and my stomach was quite sore before the end of the picture… It was as dark as a bag when

***147** The site of the Acland Hotel, Sidwell Street, 2025. The building was destroyed by German bombs in 1942.*

we left the cinema, the street was so crowded that I collided with a few people as we walked the short distance to the hotel.

We left Exeter about 9 o'clock (am) and just as we started The Alert sounded but I heard no planes or guns and we proceeded towards Honiton.'

Mr Harpur continued to write for MO until 1951. He died in London eight years later. His administrator was Winifred Gunton.[151]

18. Doreen Reilly, Teacher, 1940 & 1942

In the spring of 1940 Miss Doreen Constance May Reilly (1914-1994) stopped at Exeter on her rail journey from Bodmin to Sussex. She was twenty-six-years-old, stood at five feet six inches and had fair hair and hazel eyes. Since mid-September 1939 Miss Reilly had been employed as Assistant Mistress at Roedean School in Brighton.

The war had overshadowed her Cornish holiday (`Sister of woman I lodge with and her two daughters came to lunch. The eldest is 19, a waitress at Plymouth. She has been engaged twice. One man went down with the *Thetis*, another, a petty officer, was run over by a lorry full of drunken soldiers.'). Earlier that year she had expressed her views about war ('I was brought up to believe that the Great War was a war to end war, and for a long time could not realise how statesmen could be such fools as to allow war to develop. Apart from the sentimental reasons such as hatred of death and injury, it is the absolute waste and misdirection of energies that sickens me. To think what constructive work could be done for man's benefit with the money and manpower now being thrown away. It is sheer stupidity.')

1940

Reilly wrote a diary in 1940 and was a directive respondent from 1939 to 1942.[152] Her account of 10 May 1940 was brief:

'I came down to breakfast at 9am in the Great Western Hotel at Exeter where I had spent the night. There were several men in the dining room engrossed in their papers. The waiter asked me if I had heard the news that Holland and Belgium were invaded. I had not. Nor could I stay to hear the special news at 10.30.

I left the hotel and went to look round Exeter. I walked round the cathedral and sat for a few minutes looking upward at the fan vaulting. A business man (by looks) came and knelt in prayer at a side altar. Then I bought a *Daily Sketch* and read it sitting in the Close. I walked round and saw one or two men sitting in their parked cars listening to the 10.30 news. About 12 o'clock I bought a local paper, *The Echo*, giving the latest news.

I had lunch in a café. The waiter was a Belgian. He told me that his parents were trying to sell their house in Belgium but now the Germans would put a bomb on it. He was very cheery. He and another waiter were laughing and saying they would probably not be there next week. I went back to St David's and caught my train to London which was running in two parts.'

148 The Great Western Hotel where Miss Doreen Reilly stayed in 1940 while writing for Mass Observation, 2025.

In 1921 Miss Reilly, who had been born in Cornwall, lived with her parents at Plymstock in Devon. Her Irish-born father served in the Royal Army Medical Corps. She returned to Exeter in the summer of 1940 (two months after her first visit) and obtained a position at Bishop Blackall School. She wrote:

'Coming here (Exeter) from Brighton in July last, my object was to look for rooms for myself and my mother. I had made arrangements to stay in digs while I looked round and then I was going to spend the rest of my eleven weeks' holiday with the Land Army. I spent a most depressing week of wet weather looking for rooms but could not find nothing. Refugees from the Channel Islands were pouring in and everywhere was full up. The answer at every door was the same. I could not room-hunt all the time and it was difficult to know how to fill the days as I did not know anyone at all in the city. I began to make arrangements about the Land Army but I was told there was no one needed at all. I was willing to go anywhere and had had farming experience but the good weather had benefited the farmers. I tried the WVS and found my services at canteen or driving unneeded. I went to help sort waste paper for an hour or two but this was a dusty job indoors and for the sake of my job, I did not think eleven weeks of this would be good. I gave up hope of finding rooms and persuaded my landlady, where I was to take my mother, as she really only wanted students who were out every day.

Meanwhile, I met a man who ran a taxi business. He

said I might come and amuse myself in the garage and do some odd driving just to keep myself occupied. I enjoyed this very much and was interested to learn about the business from the inside. I used to wash and polish cars and drive them to the workshop for repair etc. I had just sold my car before leaving Brighton (at a great loss for £5 but no one was buying them there then) and the garage owner lent us a car once or twice to take mother out, who had now come from Cornwall. My holiday was then cut short by three weeks as the school here opened sooner than was expected.

***149** Miss Doreen Reilly, April 1944.*

Since the school opened girls have been pouring in from evacuation areas. There have been nearly 200 new this term. The forms are huge and of course this means extra work but I personally don't mind until it comes to the making of books.

We have had little of the blitz, some bombs have fallen in the district and a few of the girls have had their houses damaged. There is not enough room for the whole school to shelter in the building so on hearing a siren the girls (except juniors) scatter into neighbouring houses.

So far, the war has made the following differences to my life. I go out very little. I miss my car and coming to a city & knowing no one owing to war there is little opportunity to meet people, all the activities of clubs, societies being limited, neither am I fond of going out in the blackout. In peace time, I should have joined a night school or the art school & sports clubs. But my work keeps me busy, and in my spare time I go for country walks and now and then to the pictures. Most Sunday mornings I ride a horse.

When a siren goes at night, I take no notice, as we have no shelter. I object to sitting on the stairs for endless hours but if things began dropping close, I should go down I expect.

I miss London and being able to visit friends, although I may go to Derbyshire at the end of this month. I am grateful to be well-housed, in a job and that my life has had no major upsets as yet, but most of my great interests, such as archaeology and the circus have to be shelved for now.

In regards helping the war, I knit comforts, collect wool from hedges and collected pounds of acorns, etc.

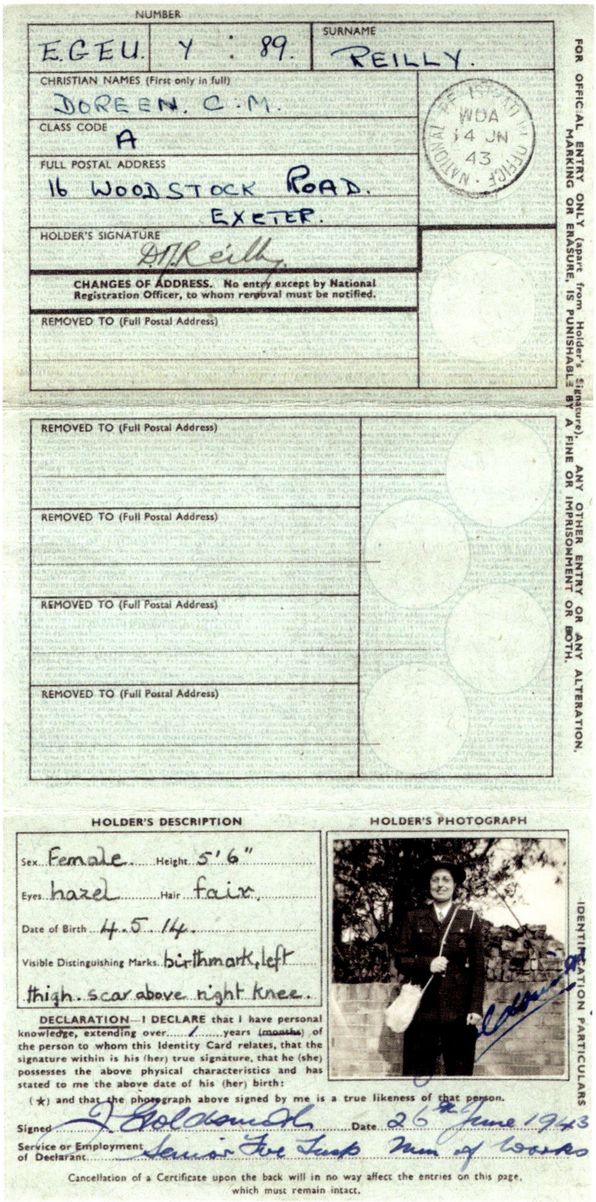

NUMBER E.G.E.U. Y : 89. SURNAME REILLY.

CHRISTIAN NAMES (First only in full) DOREEN. C.M.

CLASS CODE A

FULL POSTAL ADDRESS 16 WOODSTOCK ROAD. EXETER.

HOLDER'S SIGNATURE

NATIONAL REGISTRATION OFFICE WDA 14 JN 43

CHANGES OF ADDRESS. No entry except by National Registration Officer, to whom removal must be notified.

REMOVED TO (Full Postal Address)

REMOVED TO (Full Postal Address)

REMOVED TO (Full Postal Address)

REMOVED TO (Full Postal Address)

REMOVED TO (Full Postal Address)

FOR OFFICIAL ENTRY ONLY (apart from Holder's signature). ANY OTHER ENTRY OR ANY ALTERATION, MARKING OR ERASURE, IS PUNISHABLE BY A FINE OR IMPRISONMENT OR BOTH.

HOLDER'S DESCRIPTION

Sex Female Height 5'6"

Eyes hazel Hair fair

Date of Birth 4.5.14.

Visible Distinguishing Marks birthmark, left thigh. scar above right knee.

DECLARATION—I DECLARE that I have personal knowledge, extending over 1 years (months) of the person to whom this Identity Card relates, that the signature within is his (her) true signature, that he (she) possesses the above physical characteristics and has stated to me the above date of his (her) birth:

(★) and that the photograph above signed by me is a true likeness of that person.

Signed [illegible] Date 26th June 1943

Service or Employment of Declarant Senior [illegible] Min of Works

Cancellation of a Certificate upon the back will in no way affect the entries on this page, which must remain intact.

HOLDER'S PHOTOGRAPH

IDENTIFICATION PARTICULARS

***150** Miss Reilly's ARP card, 1943.*

> Apart from fits of loneliness and feeling the horrible sameness of life here at the moment, things peaceful on the whole.'[153]

25 February 1942

Miss Reilly continued to live in Exeter and recorded her life:

> 'Alarm clock rings at 7am. I have just had the Monday and Tuesday off for our half-term holiday but this is also a half-day so don't mind going back. Hear landlady's husband going downstairs to make their early morning tea (I don't have it), light fire in dining room and heat water for washing.
>
> 7.20am. He knocks at my door with hot water. I get up and go to bathroom to wash. Come back and get into bed again as I need not start dressing until 7.50, but have to wash earlier as the man wants to shave. He takes a long time. I am late if I wait until he has finished.
>
> 7.50 Dress, turn on wireless in bedroom softly so as not to disturb next-door man who works late at night. Just hear news summary, then go down to breakfast.
>
> 8.05 Breakfast – porridge, three pieces of toast, butter and homemade apricot jam.
>
> 8.25 Leave house. Walk 3 miles to bus stop. Catch bus to city. Walk across city and take another bus to the school.
>
> 9 o'clock Arrive in school. Start the day with 80 minutes art lesson in my own form. Always look forward to it this as the children do excellent work and we all enjoy it. Get materials ready.
>
> 9.30 Prayers. Art lesson. Children work on big sheets of sugar paper with charcoal and powder paint.
>
> 10.20 Geography lesson with 8 to 9-year-olds. Subject, the Nile.
>
> 10.55 – 11.15 Break. Sell chocolate (½d bars) to children.
>
> 11.15 Free period. Collect up children's paintings drying in the kitchen as there is no room for them in form room. Read *Picture Post* by staff room fire.
>
> 11.45 – 12.15 Give demonstration nature lesson in my form to university students. Subject, hazel flower and wind pollination.

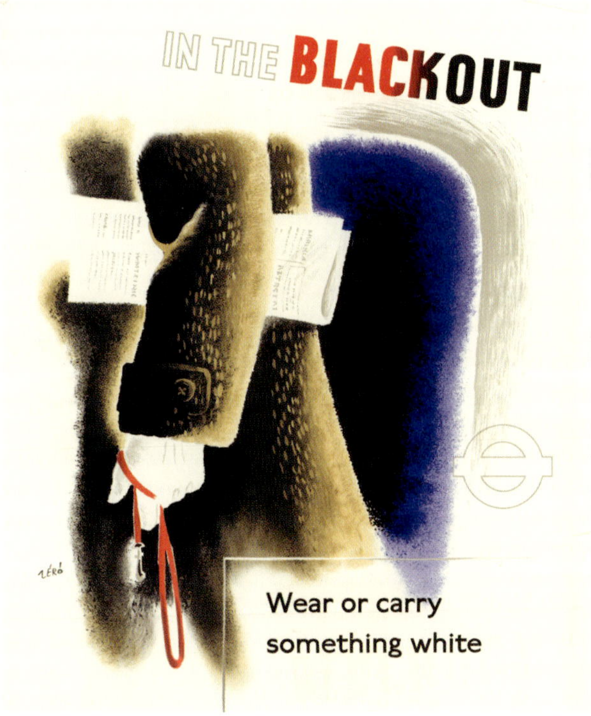

***151** Poster for blackout by 'Zero', otherwise Hans Schleger, 1943.*

> 1215 See children off premises. Catch bus into city. Go to eating house where they know me well. Many business people feed here every day. No menu, you have a large (1/4) or small (1/1) of whatever is going, sweet (4d) or cup of tea and cakes, etc. I always have a large - today Toad in the Hole, turnips, cabbage and boiled potatoes. Buy two penny cakes and 2d apple turnover and pay at the desk. No bill.
>
> 1 o'clock Walk through city to where my mother lives. She is an invalid and I am bringing her a book I've just finished reading from Boots - *American Hazard* which I enjoyed very much. Sit and eat my cakes. Then rush back to my lodgings. Change into cycling clothes – Navy slacks, woollen hood zip jacket, skiing gloves.
>
> 2 o'clock Set off for Woodbury Common where friends of mine have a farm. Lovely sunny day but bitter wind. Lots of blackbirds and thrushes flitting low in the hedges and several chaffinches.
>
> 2.50 Have cycled 6 miles. Arrive at the farm. Help break sticks as trees have just been cut down and the mother (wife of retired public school master) with eldest son and youngest married daughter are tidying up. They are elm trees and on the small twigs the pink

flower buds are swelling. Gerald, the white goat, follows me about nibbling the buds. It is like a dog and jumps up unless dealt with firmly. The mother goes in to crush some china to give hens who are pecking their eggs. I move my bike nearer the house and find some papers I was bringing out to show the daughter I'm missing. I was telling them last time I was out about the holidays I used to have excavating and about the morgue of 10 skeletons we dug up on Maiden Castle. I am worried at the loss of photos as they are treasured souvenirs.

I say goodbye as I must cycle back to look for them. They may have dropped out my lower bag anywhere on the way. Just before I leave the lady knocks on the study window and asks husband if he saw them as he had just returned from village and post office. He says they are on the kitchen table, he was reading paper (*Picture Post*) on the way and kicked them. I am relieved. We go in and have a cup of tea and ginger cake. We talk about the good news that a cousin of mine, well-known to them, has just reached England on leave after 3 years in the Gold Coast.

5.30 Leave. Still very cold. Cycle back, fast as downhill nearly all the way. Get back 6.10.

6.10 Wash and change under-clothes as I'm going to a dance.

6.30 Supper. Plate of rabbit stew, bread, margarine and jam. Dress. Put on blue white-spotted changeling-dress with blue silk jacket over. Sitting reading [while] waiting for girlfriend to call for me. The dance is one the local Channel Islanders Society is getting up at one of the big hotels to raise funds. We have no partners and are rather shy of going.

8pm Friend comes. Take bus to city reach hotel 8.30pm. Put cloaks in cloak room and luckily see [a] man we know well on the door. He takes us to join his wife and their party. These people are Islanders. We don't see many others. We dance with each other, mostly women together. I dance with a man I know by sight in the *Paul Jones*. In a lady's *Excuse Me* I go and ask a blind man I often meet at whist drives. He dances wonderfully well but another girl cuts in so I go and cut in and dance with the man who met us at the door. The dining room is cold and we keep going back to sit near the radiator. The man stands a round of drinks. He has beer, his wife port, my friend is teetotal and will have coffee later. I don't want anything but say I will have a shandy. I can hardly finish it. We are amused watching the other people. People seem to dance in such strange attitudes these days.

The time passes quickly. At 12.10 the man and his wife think they must leave as a friend is in their house to keep an eye on their two children. They offer us a lift home which we readily accept although we would like to stay for the end. But it is a cold night and we must have quite a long walk.

I am the last to be dropped. I creep about the house filling my hot water bottle and am in bed by 1am. My feet are tired as I don't often dance and I can't get back to sleep easily as I keep getting cramp in my toes.'

Two months later Mrs Alice Gertrude Reilly was living at 5 Lower Summerlands when Exeter suffered its most extensive bombing. Her home was destroyed. She survived the bombing on 4 May but died the following month possibly of shock. Miss Reilly searched through the rubble at her mother's former home and, with the aid of a wire coat hanger, retrieved a hand mirror and photo frame. By 1943 she was living at 16 Woodstock Road in the St Loyes district of Exeter and served as an air raid warden. Later that year she sailed to South Africa to take up a teaching post in Natal and in 1945 Miss Reilly married John Barfield near Pietermaritzburg. She remained in South Africa and died there in 1994.[154]

19. Donald Middleton, Student, 1941-2

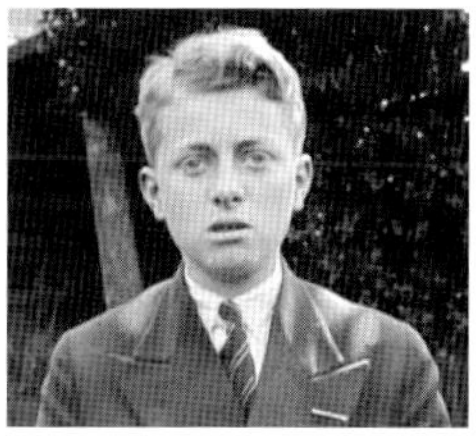
152 Mr Donald Middleton before the war.

Donald King Middleton (1922-2015) normally lived at 34 Sherwood Road in Birmingham but in 1941, aged nineteen, he was enrolled at St Luke's College in Exeter. Less than eighteen months later the college buildings were destroyed by German bombs. Two years before Middleton came to Exeter, the college was mentioned by a letter-writer to *Picture Post*. A fifteen-year-old criticised the editor for including photographs of 'nearly-nude women' at a Hollywood night-club and writing 'piffle' about corsets and strip-tease. His, or her, preference would be photographs of St Luke's College. Students may have been aware of the letter. His diary covered 1941 to 1942 and he also responded to directives in 1942 and 1943.[155]

1941

'September 16th 1941 Travelled to Exeter by train to begin my autumn term in residence at college. The journey was accomplished from Birmingham in fair time, though the number of people travelling far exceeded the number the train could comfortably carry. One seemed to see as many women members of the forces travelling as men and some of these, standing in corridors, complained of great fatigue. Conversation between those in the same compartment was surprisingly scarce. Rarely did anyone address a fellow passenger who was a stranger to say more than a few polite platitudes. Very few people read or occupy their time in other ways – they just sit staring at the wall before them or vacantly out of the window. Is this a sign of intense thought? I very much doubt it!

September 17th Life in a residential college, partially financed by the Board of Education, can be particularly boring. This one, St Luke's, Exeter, has the advantage of very congenial surroundings but even so the rules and regulations which exist for the express purpose of *spending public money well* are without number.

The Board is terrified lest there should be a failure amongst the students in their finals. In such an event, they would consider not the future of the student but the waste of the money expended on his training instead. Instead, they insist on compulsory hours of study so that the worst student should do enough work to scrape through his exam and become a qualified school master even if his intellect is seriously poor. The Board, being a financial rather than an educative institution, leaves no responsibility with the student but employs every means within its power to enforce paying results.

September 19th The way in which the typical English woman spends her afternoon is perhaps remarkable in the present circumstances. I was free from lectures and wandered round the city of Exeter. The streets were filled with shoppers whom we will presume were lawfully occupied. But the gardens of the city were filled too – women (mothers mainly) respectfully dressed in *afternoon* clothing, sitting or lying with their children in the sun. On the whole the groups are separate: one mother is not in the least interested in what the others are doing. Reading or occupation with other work seldom takes place. Sometimes the mother will play with the child but she soon becomes bored and continues idly to sit and watch the child amuse itself. At about 4.30 one by one these groups disappear and out of the gardens streams a continuous flow of slowly-moving perambulators.

September 20th In conversation with an owner of a clothing factory in Exeter. He referred to the coupon rationing system as *red tape and silly regulations which will wear itself to a standstill in the near future.* He went on *The system is based upon the integrity of the retailer to a large extent. He has to fill an envelope with 500 coupons and can get a 500 voucher for it. There is no check upon whether or not the envelope contains the requisite amount of coupons but the ordinary retailer is honest enough. However, the idea is so polluted by Jews, with no reputation to lose even if they were caught, that*

153 St Luke's College facing Heavitree Road, 2025.

154 Northernhay Park where mothers of evacuee children visited during the war.

it will break down. This may be only one point of view but it does indicate that there is some annoyance at the abuse to which the system is liable in the clothing trade.

September 21st My comments on September 19th referring to the women of Exeter are borne out by conversations with the inhabitants of the town. They complain bitterly of the hundreds of evacuees (mothers and children) in the city and of the fact that the women who are most unoccupied in the day go from shop to shop buying the articles which are most scarce while the inhabitants have no chance to do likewise!

September 22nd I am a non-conformist myself but I attended the Evensong service in the cathedral today. It was interesting and beautiful but if typical of the sincerity which lies behind Church of England services, then I am not impressed. The endless repetition of words chanted meaningless by small boys with beautiful voices, but who obviously await the opportunity to get out of the cathedral, annoy me, and I say with T. S. Elliot *Oh Lord, deliver me from the man of excellent intention and impure heart.*[156]

September 23rd In conversation with a local Grammar School master on the subject of the determinist theory of history. Said he *Have you ever read* Britain *by Mass Observation*?"

I replied in the affirmative.

That system, based though it is upon a pseudo-psychology, did prove helpful in realising how easily swayed public opinion really is. In fact, it showed what public opinion is, rather than the newspaper reports of so little value to which we've been used.

I enquired why *pseudo-psychology*.

Because the facts they gain are generally fairly objective. But the flavour they are given by those who are responsible for interpreting them is liable to unbalance the results.

I tried to disillusion him...

September 24th In the local bookshop a woman (middle-class, educated, rather an extrovert – possibly) picked up and read T. S. Eliot's *Dry Salvages*. After a time she said to her companion with obvious sincerity and appreciation *God! How this man can use words*!

Is the general public interested in poetry? I tend to think there is a definite increase in the public's appreciation of poetry and in the number of people reading it, especially of contemporary verse. This is probably borne out by the rapid sale of *Penguin New Writings*.

September 25th Why is art taken as a means to fill the pockets of capitalists? At the local theatre the lowest price is normally one shilling but when a Shakespeare company arrives to produce *The Merchant of Venice*, *Hamlet* and *Richard III* in one week's stay, all prices automatically increase so that the lowest is 2/6!

And too in the Exeter local library there is a notice offering two extra tickets (in addition to the normal General & Non-Fiction) to those who want them. I asked for these tickets. Reply – *No, sorry! We don't let students have them*!' Why on earth not? Who but students are likely to require and need four books out at once?

September 27th Went [on] a long cycle ride through Devon mainly along coast near estuary of river Exe. As a town dweller I was suitably impressed by the first sight of the sea which I had for over two years. The enormous defences which dominate the promenade at seaside resorts such as Teignmouth give what normally is so pleasant a very ominous bearing. Noticed thousands of soldiers about in seaside towns, all very obviously doing nothing – taking women to the pictures, aimlessly strolling about the streets in groups, eating enormous meals alone in restaurants - as though on a Saturday afternoon they choose to make up for the deficiencies of army food in the week.

October 2nd Went to see Donald Wolfit in *Hamlet* at the local theatre. His acting as Hamlet was really great but so much so that he almost overshadowed the weaker brethren in the cast. Two points missing from the performance: 1, Why must the audience clap individual characters as they perform a particular part well? Why can't the value of the interpretation as a whole be applauded because surely this is a vital matter? 2, Why do so many comparatively uneducated people go to see Shakespeare now? Is it merely a cloak of *intellectuality* or have they a genuine delight in Shakespearian plot?

October 4th Returned to Birmingham in afternoon by train. The compartment was filled from Cheltenham

to Birmingham with a family of lower class (for identification – not snobbery!) people who insisted on maintaining a running commentary on the journey in a tone loud enough for the whole carriage to hear…'

Mr Middleton travelled to Birmingham to attend a Conscientious Objectors Tribunal hearing on 7 October. The members were told his objections to fight were based on a desire to follow the teachings of Christ and they required him to work fulltime in land work or civil defence. He then returned to Exeter:

'October 11th Went to recital of modern English church music in Exeter Cathedral. The quality of the playing (organ, cello and piano) and singing was superb. The cathedral nave was filled with people from all classes of society and I wondered whether they were all here out of pure interest in music especially modern church music. The majority of the audience was very attentive but some insisted on going out during the performances and creating a disturbance. The use of the cathedral for purposes other than religious is a point of note: their original intention was not for use as concert halls. The actual pros and cons of the matter I have not decided in my own mind though I am distracted from the music by the beauty of the architecture!

October 13th How remarkable that some older people still possess a horror of *the doctor*. An old lady who cleans my rooms has been unwell for some weeks and today has stayed away. Her deputy in describing, in most vivid terms, her illness says *Of course, she would be better, I expect, if only she would see a doctor. But she refuses and if I sent one to her, she would not see him, because I've tried it on other occasions.*

October 18th Visited an exhibition of modern British Art in Exeter. This small exhibition aroused much interest amongst the inhabitants of the city – mainly because it had been widely advertised and many people have been to see it. It is, however, noticeable that the modern artist, though expressing the spirit of the age in which he is living, is not expressing himself in a way in which contemporary people comprehend. This is obvious through the amazed expressions on persons' faces as they look at some pictures.

October 21st Woman (possible 60+) cleaner: *No, I don't dance – of course I couldn't now but I have never done so. Well, you see, I was brought up religious-like, and not going to dances I began to think, and decided, that they did you no good (not that they do harm, mind you), so I never went. And I don't like the pictures either – give me the theatre, its more like real life.*

October 22nd Hairdresser in Exeter (45): *I don't like large towns and cities. Admittedly they have advantages but after experience in both the large and the small, I've decided always to live in the smaller towns. It seems that in a big city everyone becomes so much engrossed in the size of the place and loses one's own self.*

October 24th Young woman, in conversation with man in RAF on a train: *I've got to register on Saturday next. What form of national service will you do? I've not thought about it yet, shall I have to do something? Of course, but take my advice, and don't join the Forces.*

4th November Was suddenly called to the local hospital (with two other fellow students) for a blood transfusion. Apparently, they wanted three pints of blood immediately, but they had only two pints in stock, so they used those two and one more directly from us, putting the other two back into stock. The effect of the transfusion on us was scarcely noticeable, although they took a pint from each of us. The system in the hospital which, nowadays, permits such a lack of blood to be in storage, is rather deplorable, I thought.

19th November Met a housewife (23, husband away) who works at a large food retailer. On the topic of rationing, she admitted that she did not even know the amounts of rationed food allotted to each person. *I never bother*, she said, *I always get as much as I want*! Also, a retired gentleman and his wife, inviting me to lunch: *Our rations are alright, we get far more than we really need for the two of us.*

20th November Noticed several placards in the main street today: *British troops smash through Libya, Russians repel all German attacks, Frantic German retreat in Libya, Heavy British raid on Germany.* Who is winning this war, anyway?

***OPPOSITE:* 155-64** *Scenes of wartime destruction in Exeter.*

25th November Great excitement has been caused in Exeter by the second air raid warning in a week being sounded, after a lull of over a fortnight. Certain strange noises (possibly AA fire) was heard during the warnings and there is a general fear that bombing on large scale is beginning again. This city, which has never been badly raided, is far more fearful than Birmingham which has been blitzed well…

February 16th [1942] Travelling from Birmingham to Exeter by train I was impressed with the extreme melancholy of everyone who I could see. There was not one conversation being held in the whole saloon (central corridor, tables, compartment) of about 60 people. Very few were reading and those, only popular newspapers and magazines (*Daily Mirror* and *Illustrated* in great vogue), some were contemplating smoking but the majority were asleep. It was 3.00pm… It is well acknowledged that English people are not good mixers but is this solemnity remarkable? (Singapore fell yesterday)

February 17th A schoolmaster at Exeter Public School, in conversation with me, noted how general school-boy opinion (so often are reflections of their parent's thoughts) is distinctly swinging against Mr Churchill. He, the Prime Minister, is often referred to as a stooge. This is only remarkable as compared with his overwhelming support a year ago.

February 18th I and my fellow students are doing teaching practice in schools of Exeter and Devon County. Before evacuation we had worked in Birmingham schools and the differences in atmosphere is noteworthy. Especially in the county the conditions under which the school exists – buildings and equipment, are extremely bad. There is no cooperation between different departments (if the school happens to be reorganised which is rare). The teaching is very inefficient and half-hearted and there is a very frequent use of corporal punishment. On enquiring into this state of affairs from an official of the local education authority, we find that the suggested explanation is that the scale of pay for teachers is so low that only the poorest type even teach in this district *and the school is made by the teacher* he added!…'

In February 1942 Mr Middleton answered an MO question on the British Empire ('I fear that I rarely think about the British Empire. It seems to be rather an encumbrance and responsibility which we hang onto for the sake of prestige. Economically at present we are dependent upon the empire, I suppose.') and on his diet ('I live at a residential college and the food we eat is really good. The only shortage seems to be of meat but we get our rationed quantity. Meals are perhaps a little unvaried but on the whole nutritious. I hear no grumbling by housewives but this is probably because of lack of contact with them in their affairs.').

25 February 1942

He also recorded his activities on Wednesday, 25 February:

'7.15 Rise, wash, make bed and clean shoes

7.45 Breakfast

8.15 Tidy bedroom and read

8.45 Morning chapel

9.00 Prepare black-board maps for a history lesson at school (I am at present teaching in the school attached to the college at which I am studying.)

9.30 Scripture lesson – *The Temptations*

10.15 Arithmetic lesson

11.00 English dictation

11.45 Reading *Wind in Willows*

12.30 Out of school, continued letter to girlfriend

1.00 Dinner

1.30 Read and marked English exercises

2.00 PT lesson

2.45 Singing lesson

3.30 Changed to suit of white flannels. Opened parcel from home. Continued letter to girlfriend. Drank tea and ate biscuits.

5.30 Tea

6.00 Talked with fellow student – day's experiences

6.30 Worked on next day's lessons

8.00 To near-by restaurant for something to eat

9.00 Worked on lessons

10.00 Went to library to fetch books

10.30 Worked on lessons

OPPOSITE: 165-8 *The British public was reminded through posters of the importance of the colonies in the war effort.*

THE EMPIRE'S STRENGTH
HERRICK
DO YOU KNOW THAT THE
COLONIES
produce over half the world's rubber and a third of the tin: that they are rich in sugar, tea, coffee, cocoa and fruits: that Colonial copper, gold and oil are increasingly important.
THESE ARE THE SINEWS OF WAR

YOUR GROUNDNUTS HELP TO FEED
THE EMPIRE'S FIGHTING MEN
DIG FOR
VICTORY

EMPIRE WAR WORKERS IN BRITAIN
A VOLUNTEER FROM
BRITISH GUIANA
FOR VICTORY
Many girls from the West Indies have volunteered for service with the Auxiliary Territorial Service. Some, volunteering for service abroad, have come to Britain; more are on their way. Every girl in the A.T.S. has an equal chance of promotion or of taking a commission. Above is Private Diana Williams, a recruit from British Guiana. Part of Diana's work consists of helping with the maintenance of army vehicles. Here she is seen beginning on the job of retreading a tyre in the corner of a repair depot in the Midlands.
GPD. 365/97

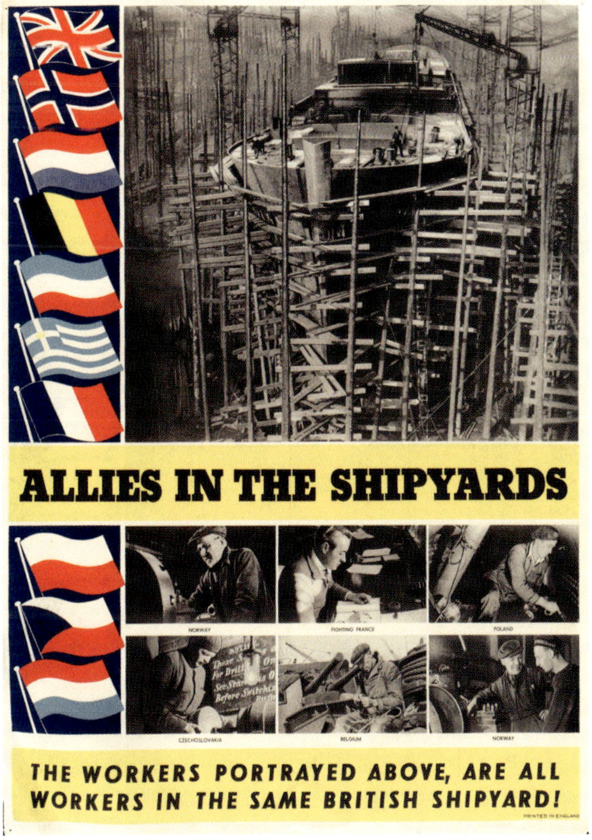
ALLIES IN THE SHIPYARDS
NORWAY
FIGHTING FRANCE
POLAND
CZECHOSLOVAKIA
BELGIUM
NORWAY
THE WORKERS PORTRAYED ABOVE, ARE ALL
WORKERS IN THE SAME BRITISH SHIPYARD!
PRINTED IN ENGLAND

12.00 Wrote to girlfriend, finished the letter!

12.45 Wash and to bed.'

Two months later the Luftwaffe attacked Exeter over four nights as part of the Baedeker Raids. St Luke's College was heavily damaged but by that date Mr Middleton had returned to Birmingham. He continued to write for MO through 1943. Mr Middleton had a distinguished career in the diplomatic service and died in 2015.[157]

20. Thomas Brody, 1942

Thomas A. Brody lived at Exeter Hall on Pennsylvania Road when he answered a directive on 5 April 1942. This college residence for men had been renamed in 1940: it was previously known as Kilmorie. It is more likely that Brody was a student than a member of staff. He had lived in Britain for the previous five years but no biographical details have been found for him other than he had formerly lived on the Continent. He referred to himself as a foreigner.[158] In only a few weeks' time the city would suffer four Baedeker attacks.

Mr Brody wrote about the prospect of a German invasion of Britain:

'It seems to me that too many people are actually looking forward to invasion in a way, hoping for a relief from routine for something that will pull the nation together or some such aim. Personally, I am more scared than anything else of the prospect. Having been in Nazi-occupied countries, I can well imagine what it will be like. I have a friend, a refugee, who intends to poison himself the moment the Nazis come into the neighbourhood. I am very tempted to follow his example.'

He also recorded his views on sport:

'I have never been in the habit of going to horse races and boxing fights, hence possibly my prejudice against them, and have not done so since the beginning of the war either. On the whole I have been given far more to intellectual hobbies and have done only very little in the way of sport. I take part in games of hockey with great pleasure and during the summer I swim a lot. In past years I have done a good bit of training on foot and with a bicycle and still feel just the same about these sports as before the war, in that I want to take part rather than watch, but the time I have been able to spend on them has been considerably reduced by other activities due to the war.

169 Kilmorie Hall, later Exeter Hall, Pennsylvania Road, home to Mr Thomas Brody when he wrote for MO.

Tours are out of the question, too, because of the complicated police procedure which would be required for me as a foreigner. In the past I used regularly to play two games of hockey a week and spend some time in practice, during the winter but now I hardly play one game in two weeks. In the summer I swam according to the weather, sometimes for hours every day but in the last summer I was not once in the water. I hope to go training again, however, this summer.'[159]

No details of Mr Brody's subsequent life have been found.

21. Jenifer Elliott, Demonstrator, 1943

Lewisham-born Jenifer Caroline Elliott (1909-1976) of 10 Haldon Road answered a directive in 1943. Two years earlier she had married her husband Robert in Cornwall. Her responses were mostly about clothing of which she preferred utility items except for stockings which she considered to be poor value. She also knitted her own gloves from odd balls of wool.[160] Mrs Elliott wrote in more detail:

'The main changes in my clothing habits since rationing began are as regards wearing old clothes. Clothes and shoes, which I should normally have thrown away, are mended and renovated and made to last much longer. Even then they are usually not

170 *10 Haldon Road, the home of Mrs Jenifer Elliott in 1943.*

thrown away. For instance, a petticoat too worn to be wearable, provides enough stuff for a baby's dress and a much-mended coat made a skirt and jacket for a small girl. On the whole, I dress in a very similar manner and in similar colours as before and change clothes as usual. I have given up wearing hats except on formal occasions. In my work (cookery demonstrator) I used to wear white overalls for morning preparation as well as for demonstrations. Now I reserve the white overalls for demonstrations and wear coloured aprons in the morning. I have also given up on wearing white shoes and stockings for demonstrations.'

Mrs Elliott died in 1976.[161]

TOP RIGHT: 171 *Humorous card of a woman wearing only a helmet and apron because of clothes rationing, by Laurie Tayler, 1939-45.*

RIGHT: 172 *Humorous card of three women in uniform ogling the evening dress of a mannequin, by Bert Thomas, 1939-45.*

EXMINSTER

Exminster, situated on the western bank of the River Exe and increasingly on the outskirts of Exeter, was a large village in the late 1930s. In 1931 the population stood at 2,807. The parish was dominated by the Devon Mental Hospital which had opened in 1845. Part of it was temporarily converted, nearly a century later, for the medical treatment of German interns. The Luftwaffe attacked Exminster on two occasions. On 23 April 1942 bombs fell on the hospital and parts of the complex, including two Emergency Medical Service wards, were destroyed. Eight individuals were reported as being killed (fifty-four-year-old William Goss, sixty-year-old Frederick James Land, seventy-two-year-old Septimus Norman, fifty-eight-year-old Charles Henry Crowdera, thirty-six-year-old W. L. Flood, twenty-five-year-old A. Yarow, eighty-year-old John Albert Moore and eighty-nine-year-old Arthur Russell) and three dozen more men and women were injured. In the autumn of 1940 evacuees had been housed in the hospital for a short period.[162]

173 Photograph of the hospital in Exminster taken by the Luftwaffe, 30 August 1940.

22. Gustav Jahoda, Soldier, 1942

Twenty-one-year-old Vienna-born Gustav Leopold Jahoda (1920-2016) was at Exminster Emergency Service Hospital when he answered an MO directive.[163]

1 March 1942

Private Jahoda outlined his daily activities two months previous to the bombing of the hospital. His days had little variation:

> '5.00am Reveille
>
> 07.00 Up patients, get up, wash, dress.
>
> 08.00 Breakfast
>
> 09.00 A bus took us to a centre of Occupational Therapy for the re-education of injured limbs, these are all sorts of handicrafts, basket-making, woodwork, weaving, etc.
>
> 12.00pm Return to the hospital, pay parade for up-patients
>
> 12.30 Dinner
>
> During the afternoon we had a session of the hospital Brain Trust consisting of doctors, nurses and patients. A sergeant of the Army Education Corps is the question master. Every ward sends a number of questions in and the slogan to encourage them is *Can you beat the Brains Trust?*
>
> 16.00 Tea, there were heated arguments about the subjects discussed in the Brains Trust.
>
> 18.00 Supper
>
> I read a book and wrote a few letters until
>
> 20.00 Bedtime
>
> 21.00 Lights out. The wireless is left on until the end of the 9 o'clock news.'

Directives: prejudice and the Empire

He also commented on prejudice:

> 'Many people belonging to the wealthier classes are prejudiced because they attribute every evil to the lower classes. At the same time, the opposite is equally true. In conversation with some of the so-called *better-class* people, I found they put the whole blame for our unpreparedness at the beginning of the war on the socialist and communist workers *who wanted disarmament*. Workers again usually mention the *vested interests* without however in most cases being able to give any specific reasons.'

174 The former Devon County Lunatic Asylum at Exminster, 2025.

Jahoda also gave his views on imperialism:

> 'Like probably many people from other countries, I did not before the war understand the essence of the British Empire. I thought of it in terms of the French Colonial Empire. It seems to me now that the *Commonwealth* should be extended to as many nations as possible to avoid the formation of *opposing groups of powers*. The ideal being a world federation.'

While at Exminster Mr Jahoda interviewed some sixty individuals regarding the reporting of German atrocities. He concluded that men and women living in bombed areas or who had previous contact with Germans were more likely to believe press stories. Mr Jahoda also believed women were more radical in their views. On 18 August 1941 a member of the MO staff attached a memo to this report:

> 'Jahoda is a new observer with some relevant university training. He is, I think, French. Have warned him MO cannot be responsible for the questions he asks in doing these surveys, which seem of considerable value.'[164]

Mr Jahoda was in Liverpool by April. After the war he was naturalised, graduated from Birkbeck College and in 1964 was the founding professor of the Department of Psychology at the University of Strathclyde. He died in 2016.[165]

ILFRACOMBE (& CLOVELLY)

Ilfracombe has been the largest seaside resort in North Devon since the early 1800s. Its population increased in the first year of the war from nearly nine thousand residents to some twenty thousand. The increase included evacuees and servicemen. The population of Ilfracombe Urban District grew by 14.6%.[166] Rumours were current across the country in July 1942 that various towns on the South coast were to be cleared of its population; 'Ilfracombe, it is said, is to be partially evacuated'.[167]

In 1938 'W. G. S.', a thirty-four-year-old married Clerk in Charge at Midland Bank who was born in Ilfracombe, sent his views on the Czech crisis to MO: 'It was a nation worth preserving. After all was said and done, if one had a diseased appendix, one had it taken out'.[168]

175 German aerial photograph of Ilfracombe, 31 August 1940.

23. Agnes Norman, Housewife, 1940

Mrs Emily Agnes Norman (1886-1948) was a married fifty-four-year-old from London, and then Hertfordshire, when she went on holiday. Her diary often reflected her dismay with the war including passages such as 'Mrs J. here this afternoon. She said half-in-fun and half-seriously that she would like to wring my neck when I suggested that the British and French were largely to blame for the war…' and 'My domestic Mrs S said that Hitler was very clever in taking Norway and was *making history*. Many of the remarks she makes are obviously what she has heard made in the various flats in which she works. As I feel sure she repeats what I say, I do a little peace propaganda.'

> 'March 20th Left for a week's holiday in North Devon. Travelled down part way with three soldiers in our carriage. They had hardly a word to say to each other or to anyone, and hardly looked at the newspapers we offered them. One slept, one had a most distressing cough and the other just sat. Anything less like *brave boys* or *heroes* I could hardly imagine. No doubt they were conscripts wishing they were anywhere but bound for another camp.
>
> March 21st Went to Ilfracombe in morning. Thought the town looked deserted. A few people were in the shops but little business was being done. Very few people on the front although it was holiday time. Certainly the weather was rather chilly, but indoors the municipal band played to only two persons.
>
> Easter Monday, 1940 Went to Woolacombe. Very dead-and-alive. The shop people spoke well of the soldiers who had been billeted there and were sorry they were gone.
>
> March 25th The people in our hotel told us that they did a good trade with the officers who were billeted in Ilfracombe while they were there. We were told that they were mostly a gently-reared lot and were all right so long as they were comfortably housed. But for no reason which appeared, they were moved somewhere near Nottingham and were put under canvas in the bitter winter. Sixty of them died, we were told. I asked whether anyone was held accountable for this tragedy and was told not as far as was known. Most of the soldiers appeared to have been bank clerks and men of that kind.

***176** Mrs Agnes Norman.*

> March 27th Returned home. More soldiers in our carriage…'

Mrs Norman was born on Merseyside and raised in New Jersey and then in London where her family became members of the Purleigh Brotherhood Colony, the self-sufficiency initiative which was influenced by the writing of Tolstoy. Her subsequent years would also be influenced by independent thinking. In 1905 she worked for the Food and Betterment Association in Liverpool and fourteen years later she married Clarence Norman, a well-known Conscientious Objector, in London where she died in 1948.[169]

24. Ellen Ausden, Teacher, 1940

Miss Ellen Joyce Ausden (1896-1974), a forty-six-year-old teacher from Watford, had a wartime holiday in North Devon. In 1938 she first wrote for MO and described herself as an elementary teacher who had been born on Boxing Day in 1896 and was the seventh child in a family of nine:

> 'From 2 years to 7 years of age had ringworm and attendance at school was perfunctory until 7 years old.
>
> 1909 Won a county scholarship and attended Watford Girls' Grammar School for next 5 years.

1914 (Sept.) Became Monitor-in-Training at a girls' junior school.

1915 (Sept.) Appointed Uncertificated Mistress at a girls' junior school.

1918 – 1920 In training at Hockerill College, Bishop's Stortford (Church of England).

1920 (Sept.) to 1921 (Dec.) Teaching in Croydon in girls', infants' and senior mixed schools.

Easter 1921 Was concerned in the Croydon Teachers' *Strike* on account of salary troubles.

1922 (Jan.) Appointed to junior mixed school in Watford, by Herts County Council.

1934 (Sept.) Transferred to newly re-organised junior boys' school. Am still working there.

Physique: Height 5 feet 4 inches. Weight above average owing to large bones. Constitution good, though liable to chills and prone to rheumatism and indigestion. The latter followed semi-starvation and unsuitable food of war-years and culminated in an appendix operation in 1925.

Religious Views: Brought up in nonconformist ideas though without any compulsion. Chose Church of England when 8 years of age. Confirmed in 1913. Worked in Sunday Schools, at Missionary activities and in choirs, and general church work until 1933. Since then have not attended church services or meetings.

Political Views: Labour Party views, not necessarily socialistic ideas, approaching from trade union angle. Believer in Consumers Co-operation. Anti-war.'

Miss Ausden's leisure time was spent enjoying music, reading, foreign travel and walks in the countryside as well as knitting, mounting pictures and tackling crosswords and other puzzles.

She wrote diaries from 1939 to 1954 and in 1957 and also responded to directives from 1939 to 1955.[170] She occasionally displayed feminist sentiments ('I am getting tired of women, young enough to study for themselves, just agreeing with their husbands' ideas, and repeating their statements parrot-fashion'). She also commented on freedom ('Notice on a milk-man's *pram* ORDER NOW FOR PASSOVER and thought how glad I am that there is such freedom for Jews in England').[171]

1940

Miss Ausden travelled by train to Ilfracombe and had day trips to Clovelly and Buck's Mill.

'July 27th At the last moment the coach tour I had planned was cancelled owing to many people cancelling their bookings. So a week at Ilfracombe was booked for me. I was disappointed as I had looked forward to the road journey to the west through Savernake Forest and Dorsetshire with the comparative freedom from other traffic on the roads. However, I had not been to Ilfracombe, so I was seeing a fresh place.

The railway stations to Euston seemed quite deserted and were abnormally quiet for an end-of-July Saturday. One station, Queen's Park, I think, had a bicycle rack (such as should be provided by the way outside shops and at bus stops, to avoid the latest nuisance.).

Reaching Waterloo with 35 minutes to spare, I decided to go straight on to the train. I realised afterwards that I should not have got a seat had I left it later. The refreshment *prams* on the platforms, seldom seen before the war, were well-used.

The train was filled with many, obviously motorists, to whom train travel was unaccustomed. Picnic meals were well to the fore, an outcome of rationing, no doubt. After enquiry, I found that a proper lunch was served on the train (but not tea). As I was coming so far, I was booked for the 4th service at 2pm. People came into the dining car, but every seat was booked, and they could not be served. The food was good but lukewarm, the coffee watery and nearly cold.

July 28th On an excursion, we passed through a little village where outside a cottage the notice *Sunday papers sold here*. There was no sign of placard or newspaper racks. It seemed almost furtive.

It is very strange to go through villages and towns, as well as stations on the railway, and to see all names covered. I had not studied maps beforehand, as I might have done had I known, it gives one an uncanny feeling not to know.

We had just left Barnstaple when a loud bang announced a burst tyre – the very first in my experience in spite of all the hundreds of miles I have travelled in cars and coaches. The tyre was very worn.

Later on, I saw the first piece of war damage that I have seen (other than news reels). It was a broken hedge where an enemy bomber had crashed through when brought down damaged. Last week's party had made a detour to see the wrecked plane, which of course, is now cleared away.

A new contingent of soldiers came in and I was struck with the number among them wearing glasses. They seemed to be of the student type, clerical and office workers, which probably explains it. In any group of 3, 4, 5 or 6, only one is without spectacles.

July 29th At a hotel for lunch, we heard the 1pm news, the first we had had a chance to hear, without definitely asking. Once again there was a spontaneous chorus of *Good* when the number of enemy planes brought down was given.

A solider home on leave, thinks the war will be over by Christmas; at least, he *hopes* so!

A woman with a schoolboy son said as she passed me *There's one thing. If they invade England we shall stay here. We shan't go back. I'd rather be here than in London.*

The evening's entertainment in the hotel (provided on Sundays and wet nights by the WYA leader) was a well-known London music-hall artist from Maskeleynes. He is only too glad to have bookings in hotels and certainly he was well-appreciated by the amount of talk in the coach today. (I did not hear him myself. I felt like walking and enjoying the sunset, rather than sitting indoors.).

July 30th On our coach trips we had the unusual experience of going along lanes so narrow that the hedges brushed both sides of the vehicle. There was practically no private car traffic and only twice was any backing [reversing] done, once by our coach.

One thing reminded of the days of the first *charabanc* rides, the stares of the people, not the children but more the adults and those who looked as though they once had cars of their own. Perhaps it was the unexpected movement in empty roads.

***177** The dramatic coastline, and its isolation, drew visitors to Lynton during the war. They were attracted to features such as the Valley of Stones (or Rocks) as depicted by Francis Oliver Finch (1802-1862).*

At Clovelly, where we took our packed lunches to a pub, so that we could get drink, I heard the words *Time, ladies and gentlemen, please* for the first time. I had tea before I started eating, so I did not hurry to finish my sherry before 2pm.

Afterwards, some of us decided to go by boat to Bucks Mill rather than climb the cobbles. Our boat was taken by a fisherman who was most interesting when the conversation turned to the war.

1, No night fishing, so often the catches were very small.

2, Mackerel in summer, herring in winter.

3, No shortage of food felt during the winter, with stored food from gardens and orchards.

4, The evacuees from Deptford and Lambeth had settled down comfortably. Three children (1 girl, 2 boys), the eldest ten, had started to walk home, with gas masks and about two shillings six pence, and had walked about six miles when they were seen by an AA scout, who 'phoned to the village and kept them till someone fetched them. The other children sometimes teased the three about their attempt to go home.

5, A farmer who came out one night, with a lantern and leaving his door open, when he heard a probable enemy plane, had two bombs drop on his farm. He admitted all this quite openly, so could not grumble at the result – every window broken, two craters in a field and a pasture, and various damage to walls, etc.

The boatman said that up to now, no man from the village had died.

The talk roamed over the subject of raids, the character of Germans, Italians, Belgians and French, and the effect of mines, bombs and wrecks in fishing waters.

In the last war the English Channel was disastrous to the trawl nets of the fishermen, now it would be the North Sea. We wondered whether any wrecks might be cleared away.

A plane was practising bombing a smoke-marked target out at sea and in the following talk I learned that, during the night when my bedroom window had rattled, there had been an explosion to cause it.

I got very tired during the week of hearing that every plane we heard was a *Jerry* and every noise, *Jerry's come*. People didn't like to be reminded that Sir Philip Joubet had said that it was practically impossible to tell a British from an enemy plane. All the week, I was not convinced that enemy planes were seen every night. In any case, their noise was not sufficient to get out of bed for.

July 31st Saw a postman on horseback for the first time; also coloured beehives (as in Switzerland) and a hunt – hounds, redcoat huntsmen, etc.

Two men were making screens for covering church windows and spaces in screens of which quite a lot had already been done.

An old chap in a tall, grey hat had a Mickey Mouse Circus. He was very entertaining, a real showman and he answered any questions about the training of the mice, of which he had about 15. He had named them all – Greta Garbo, Ginger Rogers (whom he sent through a match-box for slimming exercise) and Cobber Kain (through the rings). *One of them's only got three legs. He was born like it. Don't think he lost it in an air-raid 'cause he didn't.*

At the end he banged on his little truck and said *All take cover – air raid!* And the mice crowded over the end, into the little box in which they stayed between *performances*.

Later, the talk veered round to the war again. Someone had heard a fortune teller (who was seldom wrong) say that the war would last 100 days from the capitulation of France, when Hitler would give in.

August 2nd I went to Exeter by train and at Barnstaple three London children were put into my compartment, evacuees going home. A London woman (from the same district it transpired later) was going home after visiting her children. The eldest boy, about 10 or 11 years, wanted to go home. I heard him say *The house was very nice. The boy in the family wanted to have all his own way. There was a girl too. She was all right.* The younger boy, about seven years and six-year-old girl, did not want to go home. The woman promised to wait at Waterloo until their father met them.

Later she had the little girl on her knee so that she could see more of the country through the window space made smaller by the blackout edging. The little boy opened a packet of sweets and handed them round the compartment. The rest he put loose into a pocket. A young soldier, going home on leave, found a badge and gave it to the elder boy who was delighted with it.'

In 1943 Miss Ausden spent Easter in Sidmouth. **(56)**

LYNMOUTH (& DREWSTEIGNTON)

The North Devon resort of Lynmouth and the Dartmoor parish of Drewsteignton were not untouched by the war but neither suffered aerial bombardment or were filled with military personnel. A London MO diarist left the capital on 31 August 1941, at the start of the heavy bombardment of London, for a holiday in Lynton, the town perched above Lynmouth. The two places had a combined population of some 1,800 people and attracted those who sought safety from German bombing. While at Lynton, this Writer learned of the capital's air raids through newspapers, letters, telephone calls and from two parties of relatives who joined them. He added:

> 'During our stay, we also met various evacuees who had mostly come away after the start of the raids; they had stories of land mines and all manner of disheartening tales. The whole town, residents and all, seemed to be buzzing with air-raid gossip, and the general impression we got was of ear-splitting noise all night, bombs falling right and left, and London well on the way to being a heap of smouldering ruins.'

He returned to London and concluded the damage was not as severe as he was told and decided 'at Lynton everyone thought that if they had the choice between Hell and London, it might be wisest to choose the former'.[172]

***178** View near Watersmeet, early 1800s, by James Bulwer (1794-1879).*

25. Naomi Mitchison, Writer, 1941-5

Naomi Mary Margaret Mitchison, later Baroness Mitchison CBE (1897-1999), was the best-known MO Writer who commented upon Devon. She was an established novelist and poet when she visited North Devon during the war. A committed socialist and anti-fascist, she stood unsuccessfully as a Labour candidate in Scotland where during the war the family home was located. Her biographer has described Mrs Mitchison as 'imperious, sensitive, wholehearted about issues that fired her imagination, fond of real-life dramas, often yielding to an urge to outrage, yet easily hurt and desperately in need of love and reassurance.'[173] Her diaries are littered with the war's impact but she was also able to spend time travelling between her homes in London and Scotland and visiting friends across the country. She was also a friend of Tom Harrisson, one of the founders of Mass Observation.[174]

Her MO diaries include visits to teenage daughters Lois and Val who were enrolled at Badminton School which had

***179** Lynton in 1906.*

***180** Mrs Naomi Mitchison probably in the 1940s.*

***181** Miss Lois Mitchison as a teenager.*

been evacuated from Bristol in 1940. The Boarding School was housed in the Tors Hotel and the Manor House in Lynmouth.[175] Miss Margaret Miles (1911-1994), one of the staff mentioned in the diary and who later remembered Mrs Mitchison's visits to the school, recalled:

> 'The initial numbers were small but as the war intensified more and more girls came and we spread over the whole village. One of our more nerve-wracking duties was the *bus*, when we had to collect and count the girls after supper, arrange them in a tightish crocodile, conduct them through the blackout down uneven zigzag paths and drop them off at their various houses.'[176]

Her obituarist defined Miss Miles as 'stout of shoe, bobbed of hair, square of face and sensibly suited at all times'. She taught history in a number of private and grammar schools before becoming headmistress of two schools.[177]

1941

In October Mrs Mitchison wrote of her first visit:

> '10th, Train from Waterloo to Barnstaple, only fairly crowded, then bus on to Lynmouth. I feel fantastically tired, and woozy and almost fail to recognise Miss [Beatrice May] Baker, Lois' headmistress, who promptly asks me to lecture to the literary society. When I see Lois, she adds that she will be there and I mustn't make a fool of myself! A nice, rather old-fashioned hotel, full of large pictures of stags at bay and plush. Lois in very good form, working hard for Certificate; says she is thinking she'll get through her Matric. next summer, but at girls' school one always says one is sure one is going to fail. In the meantime, the Certificate year feel awfully superior to the Juniors!
>
> She is still violently feminist and feeling this is a man's muddle. We listened to the news and she hated the idea of reprisals for Crete. I said that was how one would feel immediately, but probably after the war everyone would feel differently, but anyhow, it was probably just as well that as many as possible of the Hitler *Jugend* [Hitler Youth] should get killed. They were spoilt as people and would never be happy or anything but misfits in a decent world. She says that most of the girls have parents and brothers in it; often mothers as well as fathers…
>
> 11th, went up to the [Tors] Hotel where the school is and saw Miss Baker, discussed Lois' future, what school she should take at Oxford, etc. Miss B. very keen she should go straight on, not be deflected by war-work. Says that a lot of her girls are marrying very young, at nineteen or twenty, to equally young husbands. She is bothered about it. Saying when are we going to send an Expeditionary Force to the continent to help the USSR and is it true that there are those in high places who don't want to help? Said also how much she missed the

school expeditions to Geneva. School catering not too difficult, they have made a lot of jam.

Then pick up Lois, went over the school, saw her dorm in the lower building and ate mulberries from the school tree. Wandered about Lynton which seems quite a shopping centre, bought a comb, a toothbrush and a farmer's diary, also some apples, enquired the price of some brass things to hang on horses, but didn't like the looks of the man in the curiosity shop, so didn't buy any. Came back to lunch which Lois enjoyed a great deal! She got a few sweets, too. Felt very tired and lay down for an hour after lunch but had a nasty dream, as I usually do when I sleep in the day-time. Then went for a walk up to Watersmeet, talking about life, poetry, etc. She says everyone at school hates the Americans for being superior and hypocritical and not coming in! I tried to put the American point of view. I wonder how usual that is? She definitely wants to be a journalist and writer, to travel and write as she goes. I say that writing is a bit like transport, a sort of between thing, not direct production. I also say that I think there will be few obstacles in the way of women doing any kind of job after the war.

We had tea at a cottage, very good, with blueberries, some cream that tasted suspiciously real, hot scones and jam. I bought some honey and chocolate stuff to give the rest of the family. In the fruit shop I noticed a crate of oranges, but gathered, from what the shop-woman was saying to another woman, that she was keeping them for people with young children.

Four girls came in to dinner, a very pretty blonde, a small intelligent one and a large less intelligent one. The blonde was intelligent too, at least on the surface, she behaved very easily and gaily, but so pretty one didn't notice. Also a Czech girl, very silent, bad at English, to whom they were all very intelligent and helpful. Half the time they gossiped about other girls and mistresses, also about what they were going to do. They all wanted definitely to do jobs, I thought. They also talked a lot about food! I think the school food is pretty good but they long for more sweets. I'm not sure that they wouldn't be just the same in peace-time but perhaps it's accentuated. One had been out with her mother and talked about the food she had there. But they all looked very well and obviously realised they aren't starving!

182 Seven members of the Mitchison family from left to right Lois, Denny, Naomi, Val, Dick, Av and Murdoch.

After dinner, I went over and had coffee with the staff, then talked about writing and historical novels to them and to the girls of the Literary Club, a lot of very intelligent-looking and also good-looking upper-middle-class girls in their becoming uniform (which nevertheless they loathe!). The only one who asked a question was a Jewess (also several of the staff) but they seemed to be interested and to be following keenly. I talked to them about the mechanics of the thing, the difficulties of writing, how it was a real, skilled job and got harder with each successive book. And I talked to them about the special problems of historical novels. Afterwards, the staff asked me some more questions, and gave me lemon barley water, which was delicious. A lovely, star-lit night.

12th Lois came over for breakfast, then we walked by the Valley of Rocks and round, eating blackberries, of which there are quantities everywhere, even close to the houses. I suppose there were so many to start with that everyone is tired of them. The school picked over 200 lbs for jam.

A lot of soldiers about – so the girls are supposed only to go out in fours. We met a lot of girls on their way to

183 Lynmouth with the Tors Hotel perched above left.

church, which they seem to go to, I asked Lois what was thought of her for not going, she said, oh, she supposed people thought she was a Jew! She says she and her gang keep up a great fight to stop girls just thinking they are going to be wives and mothers. But a lot of them leave after Certificate, some to go home, others to nurse or do other war work. She of course, will stay on; is very keen about going to Oxford and getting at least an Exhibition.

In the afternoon we went for a longer walk, round over Countisbury Hill and down into the West Lynn valley. I thought I saw two ravens. Had tea at Watersmeet and back at blackout. Lois talking about *after the war*. If only one had the least idea what it would be. That doesn't worry her though. She doesn't want security – or perhaps she has it of some kind. Showed me quite a competent short story she had written, which she wants to try on a paper; I told her one or two things she must do to it and suggested she should try another one too. Also, one quite good poem, a romantically gloomy nature one. She is beginning to be able to write and longs to be published, to be able to drop the paper casually in the room as she goes through! She is passionate about Spain, against Halifax and Chamberlain and respectable Americans and English, rather un-instructed. I tell her she is like a gun without ammunition, she must be sure of her facts.

It was quite cold by the end of the day, *seasonable* everyone said. Anne's mother, who is doing food office, identity cards and all that here, came in to ask if Lois could stay with them at half term. Says Anne can come up to us at Christmas as far as she is concerned, she doesn't want to be the grabbing kind of mother. She seemed nice and intelligent and unlike the school mothers whom Lois described…

Talked to the host of the hotel, who is nice, a nature lover. He says that after a spate the river drops suddenly and the temptation to get the salmon with a gaff or a spinner on a line is too much! We agree that poachers are mostly nice. He says with great approval that all this land is under National Trust and carefully planned for.

13th Rather an uncomfortable journey back, the bus late and very full…'

1942

A year later Mrs Mitchison returned to Devon:

'Nov. 2nd, spent the day with the girls and various friends, Val's San, Lois' Watty and Pam. Had a very good dinner at Myrtleberry [refreshment rooms], tea with cakes and supper here. The woman at Myrtleberry wonderfully servile, hoping we had all we wanted, apologising for shortcomings! And here lovely sweet, saffron-coloured, cream-filled cakes and macaroons! Gee. We talked mostly about school, quite intelligently, about history, people, etc, not much about current events. Got and roasted lots of chestnuts. Then was roped in by some of the senior girls to whom I'd talked the night before to play charades; found myself organising that, and then a parents' charades at which I acted Miss Baker! It was all very funny and well-taken. I provided most of the clothes. Then talked history with [Margaret] Miles, one of the staff, and about the difficulties of teaching here. They speak on the whole well of the staff but critical of some, value good teaching.

'3rd, Another day with the girls. We went up the very fine East Lynn valley, up to the town where we bought six cream or very near cream buns, got the rest of the sweet rations, the girls are rather dissuaded from getting them but mostly try to. The place is full of food and fruit drinks and oranges which I'm sure don't all go to the children.

I saw Miss Baker who was very nice, as usual, thought very well of Val, hoped she wouldn't become completely part of the machine; apparently the school have the impression that she has completely adapted. Miss B not very keen on Lois going into the ATS, says they waste their good people so badly…

The parents talk a lot of rot, about hair styles and clothes and such, and about what a wonderful job for a girl it is to be secretary to a great politician, never to be the great politician themselves! Very little talk about the war, except, after the girls left, some parents talking about all the many brass ornaments in the hotel, wondering whether there weren't rather fewer and asking if the old cannon had been taken away from the walk above the beach (they are there still!).'[178]

She had another visit on 6 November. There was an additional reason to visit Devon: she spent time with Rudi Messel (1904-1958), a longstanding friend. She mentioned Messel in her autobiography ('Once he asked me to tie and beat him, which I did, making fierce faces and quite enjoying it.').[179] Messel was a British filmmaker, author and Labour party activist. He stood for the South Molton constituency before the war and settled at Ford House in Drewsteignton. He appeared in local theatrical presentations and was described as 'a strikingly handsome figure'.[180]
Mrs Mitchinson wrote:

'Travelled down to Lynmouth, writing all the way, except that I met Anne and then Commander Young. Everything much as ever, nice to see the young, Lois in rather a flap about being a House Captain and exams and so on. Everyone finishing off things for the bazaar. Various mothers who all know me, but whom I simply can't remember the names of. Good dinner! The weather down here was awful and half the potatoes rotted.

Played around with Lois, Val and, on and off, Anne and others. Lynton still the home of the black market though no more cream buns. Lois had saved three of her beautiful school oranges for my birthday. In the afternoon a junior school play and then the sale and side show at which they made £117 for the hospital, etc. But I got involved in a fine row with Mrs Firth who tried to make me promise not to see Anne etc, constantly changing her ground, saying I gave Anne ideas, Anne wasn't strong (just as Mrs E said about Joan once), Anne had met Jimmy Maxton in London! And so on. I told her she was going the way to make Anne hate her, and in time I shook her. Poor Anne came in in the middle.

Then we had dinner and after dinner had a long talk to Miles, the nice Marxist history mistress, who said how difficult it was to get books, so far from a library etc. Dick decided to give the school £80 to buy books, some from Miles, the rest chosen by VI. Lois awfully bucked.

7th to 8th An awfully nice weekend, only I kept on writing my book which is at the most exciting stage where it is like reading something only very slowly, because I don't know what is going to happen till I have written it. I only know just before I write it what it will be. Meanwhile we went for walks, masses of girls came to tea, we played games, I doing a lot of organising, talked to parents, ate apples and sweets and orangeade and so on. On Monday, in a fit of enthusiasm, a lot of us danced reels and things in the road – and Lois took a collection for the cottage hospital just to be on the safe side!...

9th to 11th

Three good days with Rudi, no longer at Ford [House] but at a smaller farmhouse, gaily painted, with a lot of his old furniture, and books and some nice modern pictures, masses of dogs including a very decayed old sheep dog and Terence who lives completely in the past. Lovely farm buildings, not very elaborate but what's needed on a farm. Red Devon cattle, sheep, mangolds all in, potatoes being dug. He was as sweet as ever, rather grey-haired but no less good-looking and his hair still crisp and wavy and using the same scent. It was all rather nostalgic but I wrote my book hard, only being lured into potato gathering one day – a poor crop in numbers but a sufficient number of huge ones. Also, herding the sheep which was rather fun, they are much tamer than ours. I think he is succeeding in producing a community and a form of good life. They were all acting *Hamlet*. Farm meal times and so on and the house definitely a farm. The men all call him Sir and me Naomi. I wrote two chapters of my book and slept well, wish I could have stayed a week...'[181]

1944

On 17 November she again visited North Devon:

'Met Lois at Paddington. She had seen Miss Grier at LMH who encouraged her to volunteer for foreign service and not to turn up next year, as they would be frightfully crowded owing to the govt having suddenly extended the length of course allowed. We had rather a crowded journey to start with, and very wet, and we went to a frightful hotel in Lynton as the Lyndale was shut. It is incredibly Victorian and gloomy and full of decaying elderly people and the food not much either and no cider. I could really have done with some alcohol. I went on writing my book, though with considerable difficulty and no nice run of inspiration or whatever it is, and I don't know what it will be like. Ruth was better when we rang up last night.

***184** Ford House in Drewsteignton, the principal home in Devon of Mr Rudi Messel.*

Unfortunately, they didn't let Val or Watto come to dinner, so I haven't seen them yet.

18th to 19th It was quite fun on Saturday, apart from the awful weather, running round Lynton and Lynmouth, shopping – I got a baby's bottle for Ruth to replace the one I cracked and went to the nice book shop and got some children's books for the tree etc., also lots of apples at various places, buns and so on. Val and later Watto were up most of the time. We went down after supper and had coffee with Miss Baker. She was rather anti-ATS and Lois sat on the edge of the sofa blushing and rather furious. We discussed the Labour Party, Cripps, etc.

A wild gale in the night rattling the windows so I slept badly and have been tired all day. Val and Watto turned up, later Seed and another girl. We played snooker very badly, ping pong and adjectives & adverbs.

There is something rather sinister about this hotel with the howling wind and old ladies and plush sofas and lavatories out of order. I seem to get nightmares and have a continuous headache. My foot still aches a lot where Jo trod on it and altogether feel miserable. Lois thinks of spending a night with Lou, wonders if Dick will mind if she only has a night in London. I say go and stay with Lou. It used to be such fun staying with other girls of one's age and one never gets that again. Margaret Miles came over in the evening and we all, including Lois, drank rum and peppermint, a filthy

185 View from the Lyndale Hotel.

drink I thought, but nice talking to Miles, who is going to Bristol to do teachers' training under the MacNair scheme. She'll be good.

20th Left after paying a rather extortionate bill – especially for the t[letters obscured]e taken by Val and Watto, five shillings for almost un-eatable dinner, two shillings for tea mostly provided by us, etc. The bus to Barnstaple, the small train, Rudi at the station. We went in and had a drink of cider at the pub and drove back through the rain making silly jokes. When I got to the house and stepped over the threshold of the room, I suddenly burst out crying because it was like coming home. Then we had dinner with Leslie and sat talking away about ourselves and our friends and books and politics and farming and then we put the cows in the lovely shippen and we put the bull in. It was so nice carrying hay and bruised oats, I was hardly envious of the great barns and all the stirks [young bulls or cows] and the Christmas geese, only pleased they were doing so well. And we went on talking and I had a lovely bath and there was a fire in my room and we had tea in the kitchen with Edith and the children and it was chicken for tea, and Rudi went off to rehearse *Macbeth* and I am sitting by the fire, feeling happy and released, not even worried that it is only for twenty-four hours, feeling out of time, releases and my headache gone, and I think in a minute or two I will be writing my book again. I suppose Rudi and I love one another without either of us wanting anything from the other – anything other than trust and amity and kindness. And the whole house seems full of that.

21st to 24th I came back regretfully next day – we'd had a violent argument about nationalism last thing at night in the course of which I lost my temper with the boy, this peculiar insolence of the sassenach, taking his own point of view for granted, treating Scotland as a county. But he was rather drunk. It was lovely to have breakfast in bed the next morning and lie in bed afterwards for an hour writing. Walked across the fields to the bus. R. talking of a possible marriage. I don't know what to think.'

A few days later Mrs Mitchison added:

'Nature note I forgot from Lynton - Val's group have a peculiar gesture which is their signature tune or secret sign, that of hitching up a belt on which they are wearing a notional s. t.! In my time we found the onset of puberty something disturbing and rather shameful, whereas these are as pleased as savages. I think a good thing though rather disconcerting.'

1945

She was back three months later, on 4 February:

'Talked to people in the train. Val met me at the Lyndale [Hotel] looking marvellous, this wild rose colour and her hair new washed and softly dusky. We had a damn good dinner too and cider. There are lambs in the fields already.

4th This break and stolen day with Val, as with a lover, the sheer delight in her beauty and keen, sensitive mind. We walked up the West Lynn, the dung and cream-coloured spate water thundering down, the rhythmic throb like a musical pattern, the snow-bruised ferns and laurels. Talked about what she was going to do and what sort of people one should try to be, about what might be done for the world and with one's talents. Seed came to tea and supper. Good meals again… I do wish this wasn't the last time I'll be coming down here where I like it so much and find I can work. But they seem to be moving the school back to Bristol next term.

5th To Yeoford, talking to Mrs Wood, a rather nice school mother I've been meeting, like so many unhappily married, trying to keep a job and a child, rather vaguely *of good will*, very friendly.

Then I dropped into the life here, into my own place, cider at the pub, boiled potatoes and farm butter for dinner. I helped a little snedding [pruning] turnips, easy for someone else! Saw the rick of rye that is about to be thatched, the cows, the lovely clean shippen. Meanwhile, was writing, got on well and fairly steadily. R went off to rehearse *MacBeth* in the evening, came back cross, but easily soothed, and read me some of his play on Arthur. As usual, a bad choice of words but full of ideas and a kind of springing goodness. We talked till late about everything under the sun.

6th Again, the rhythm of life here, as though one were long married. He brought me up breakfast in bed before going off to the beasts at the other farm. I had slept with bad dreams, through too much thinking about my book. I got up leisurely, writing and sometimes reading Koestler's *Darkness at Noon*, gloomy enough in all conscience and good. Nice Leslie coming in like a cheerful shorthorn bull. The drink at the pub at Gosseyford [Gooseford, Whiddon Down], Rudi without class feeling, half getting it across to the others…

7th Edith brought me breakfast, tea, fried egg, toast and bread and their own butter at a quarter to nine… I stayed in bed till a quarter to ten, reading R's reminiscences, or rather brushing through them, and writing bits of my book. Then I got up, thinking it was a bit windy for threshing but possible. I took down a telegram as I was the only person in the house. Then Edith came back; I asked her about the threshing and she said the tractor had broken down and they were waiting for a neighbour's.

… I heard the other tractor, so I got some more coal from the yard and at about 11.30 went out to the stack. I took out my notebook and went on writing while they were mucking round with the thresher getting it set up. Then R came and they got the tractor in place. He went on the rick and I on the platform where I passed the sheaves to George who fed them in. It was very prickly stuff and a high wind. I was afraid R would be blown off the ridge of the stack. We went on till 1 but got little down as things kept on going wrong.

We came back at 1 for dinner which we had in the sitting room by the arm[?chair] fire, with Leslie. We had boiled potatoes and farm-butter and ham sandwiches and Leslie had pasties. They had tea and I had milk. We talked a little about the news and whether the French should be represented at the conference but mostly about the farm work and people.

Leslie went off at 2 and we followed later, but found the tractor wouldn't start. I am used to that and went and sat under the stack and wrote my book and talked to the dogs. It wasn't my responsibility so I didn't worry. Finally, it started and we worked on and off till about 4.30. I was raking the chaff, what they call the dowse here, from under the thresher with a long-handled grip, what they call an evil here. The chain kept on slipping and sometimes the knotter thread broke. We only got a cartload which will scarcely do them for bedding over the weekend. A couple of good sacks and some poor stuff, but I didn't think much of the quality. However, I know nothing about rye. Mr Endicott, who used to farm here but has retired and is now on the County Ag. Committee came and looked on but he didn't hold with it, I don't think, as he never grew rye himself.

Meanwhile, a car had gone for Charles and the bass drum which he had got for the play they are producing. I had never met him before but he turned up while R was having his bath, about 5 o'clock and we talked a bit. A nice, rather ugly Jew. Obviously an extremely good musician. Here they work seven to one at most farms and about a quarter to eight to one here, with a break at eleven, and then from two to five. Much shorter hours than Kintyre.

Then I had a bath and came down, having changed into my semi-new dress and silk stockings and got rid of the rye prickles, and we listened to the 6 o'clock news but the Russian advance isn't going so fast, I suppose the thaw. My eyes were and are still sore from the rye, and my job, though light, meant having my face in it a lot.

We had tea in the kitchen at 6.30, soup and oxtail stewed with potatoes and cabbage and cheese toast. Edith and husband and children there too. I had milk, the rest tea. I rather miss never having fruit or pudding or jam here. I was still thinking of my book but it seemed to stick so when they went to the rehearsals of *Macbeth* at the pub, I finished reading Koestler's *Darkness at Noon* and then wrote this. It is now nine o'clock and I am going to go on with my book if I can get it unstuck. They will come back about 10.30, talk about rehearsals and then C will play *Tannhäuser* and *Parsifal* and we shall go to bed about midnight.'

The following morning Mrs Mitchison caught a bus to Exeter and then travelled by rail to Wales. No subsequent visits to Devon have been found but Mr Messel married Judith Birdwood two years after the end of the war. The two acted together as Algernon Moncrief and Lady Bracknell in the Turnpike Players of Whiddon Down's production of *The Importance of Being Earnest* in 1948. Mrs Michison and Mr Messel appear to have remained friendly: in 1950 she wrote the libretto for a 'ritual opera', entitled *The Corn King*, which was based on her novel. Eight years later Mr Messel died suddenly aged 52 in Spain.[182]

Mrs Mitchison's remarkable output continued after the war and it is notable for its variety including science fiction, fantasy and children's books. She was well-travelled and known for her advocacy for such issues as feminism, socialism, Africa and Scottish nationalism. In 1964 Mrs Mitchison became Lady Mitchison when her husband was made a life peer. Her daughter Lois served in the ATS until she contracted tuberculosis in 1944. She became a journalist in the Far East and fulfilled her ambition of being a published author when *Gillian Lo* was published in 1964. Her friend Anne Firth (1926-2013) also served in the ATS before becoming a model and actress but her main employment was in script-writing, including for *Tenko* and *Ladies in Charge*.

MORETONHAMPSTEAD (& TORQUAY)

Before the war this small market town on the edge of Dartmoor had some 1,587 residents. In 1940, three years after the Moretonhampstead account, a London MO Writer recorded a conversation he had concerning the village:

'A naval officer at work has been away for 2 weeks at Moretonhampstead in Devon. His story: There was a terrible spy mania. We (2 of them) used to go fishing at the Torquay reservoir on Haytor. The story got round that two mysterious strangers, who had bought a map in the village, had been seen visiting the reservoir and we were interviewed by the police.

The Local Defence Volunteers there are taking anyone they have a grudge against into custody for a night or two for being a Fifth Columnist. Some of the LDV themselves are being roped in. The Colonel-in-Charge of the LDV has recruited the youth and beauty of the village into a special corps to get off with any visitors to find out if they act suspiciously in any way. These girls have a very secret password – *Charles Korers* which is what they call themselves. The password is very secret so don't tell Hitler!'[183]

26. Colin Neck, Teacher, 1937

Twenty-five-year-old unmarried Colin Glover Neck (1912-1944) wrote two itineraries in 1937 while on holiday from his job as a geography teacher at Queen Elizabeth's Grammar School in Tamworth. He was known for his prowess in cricket. His holidays were spent at Tor View, his family home at Moretonhampstead, with his older brother Harold Raymond (1909-77). The siblings had been born in Moreton as had been their father Samuel Harold (1873-1949).[184]

29 August 1937

'11.15am Quayside, Torquay. I am sitting in a car outside a solicitor's office. I hear a voice say, *How much longer are you likely to be here, do you know?* I turn my head and see a young police constable. I tell him that I can't say with certainty but that I am waiting for my brother who is inside the solicitor's office and has promised to be *only a minute*. Then policeman says, *Yes, well of course you don't know how long he may be. Can you drive? Yes.* Policeman points out that the streets can't be used as parking places and that there is a parking place around the corner and another free place some way further on.

I get him to repeat his directions and he finishes on an apologetic sort of tone explaining again that *You can't park in the streets.* (He is being as *nice* about it as he can.) I agree with him and drive off. I drive to the parking place and tell the attendant that I only want to stay a couple of minutes because the policeman has shifted me on. He says that it isn't worth parking for a couple of minutes. I ask him where the free car park is. He says round the corner, etc. etc., and then *How long do you think you'll be?* I repeat that I shall only be here for a minute or two and explain that I am waiting for someone. He tells me *You'll be alright here for ten minutes.* I say *Thank you very much* and get out of the car to see if my brother is coming.

11.00am [sic] Smith's Bookshop, Torquay. I am looking at some Penguin Books when an assistant (young, male) says (I think rather aggressively) *What can I get you sir?* It seems to me obvious enough that I don't want to buy anything yet. I feel faintly annoyed and say *Nothing for the moment, thank you. I'm just having a look.* I buy an Ordnance survey map. The assistant (female) irritates me slightly by looking around and talking to another assistant whilst giving me my change. My pride is injured.

I am waiting to bet on a cricket match in Exeter. An elderly man watching asks me who the teams are. When he hears that our team is Chagford he asks me if I know a Mr Selwey. I don't. (I don't live at Chagford). We discuss the merits of the two sides. He is surprised that a small village can field such a side, says *I regard Cricket as one of the finest past-times.* Tells me the score in the match between Surrey and Middlesex which he has heard on the wireless. Subsequent conversation leads me to believe that he has little practical experience of cricket but he obviously idealises it as *a pastime*.'

Mr Neck also wrote an itinerary for 12 September when he was still at Tor View. He noted it as a typical holiday Sunday spent at home. He remembered it was an 'Observance day'

***186** View of Court Street, Moretonhampstead, taken nearly from the home of the Neck family.*

***187** Tor View, the family home of Mr Colin Neck in 1937.*

and because of this was able to recall two dreams: in one he had been climbing the Alps and in another he was given wings by a Bird Man.

'Before I got up it was obvious that the weather was perfect, a bright sun shining in a clear sky and a very light North East breeze blowing. I assumed that it would last and spend some time in the early part of the morning wondering how to make the best of it. By half past twelve, however, practically the whole sky was obscured by clouds that had crept up un-noticed…

Rose 9 to 9.15. Drawn into garden before breakfast to enjoy the sun.

188 *View of the source of the rivers Tamar and Torridge on Dartmoor by J. W. Turner (1775-1851), c1813.*

Breakfast.

Sit on the veranda in front of the house and wonder how to spend the day. Very pleased with the sunshine. Write short note for this report and then read a canto of the *Faerie Queene*.

11am Go indoors and fetch the *Sunday Times* which I read for twenty minutes or so.

11.20 Shave and change into light alpaca coat and cleaner pair of grey flannels. Ask Ray (my brother) whether he proposes to stay in bed all day. (I feel rather resentful at his being in bed because I want to get out into the country somewhere). Tell him I am going to fetch the car and go out to North Bovey, by the river. Get car and find Ray nearly dressed. We both go down by the river at North Bovey and look for trout. See numbers of small trout, a water net and what Ray claims to be a wild duck. (I don't think so). Ray sees a kingfisher by this stretch of water for the first time. I notice the sky is clouded over.

Return to the village and have a drink in the village pub. *Locals* are asked by a stranger about Widdicombe Fair which takes place shortly. One of them asks me about the prospects of Moreton Football team in the coming winter.

During lunch I suggest to my brother that we walk to Cranmere Pool. There is no sun now but it is good weather for walking. After some discussion, it is agreed that we go to Castor Rock in the car, so that Father can have the afternoon on the Moors as well, whilst Ray and I walk towards Cranmere. Mother goes as well, to look after Dad who has suffered from arthritis this last eighteen months.

We reach Batsworthy (near Castor Rock) about 3pm. At the point on the North Teign where we leave Mother and Dad there is a large granite block with a hole, diameter about a yard, worn away by swirling stones. Mother says it is *lucky* to crawl through it. I go to investigate it and do crawl through the hole. Does this symbolise a re-birth I wonder?

Ray and I decide to walk up toward the houses of the North Teign. After twenty minutes or so, there are signs of drizzle. Twenty minutes later it is raining fine rain. The country is desolate – we are about two miles away from Cranmere Pool, the heart of Dartmoor. Eventually we decide to turn our faces homewards (5pm) and go as shortly as possible over the Moor and across bogs. When we reach the car our socks, trousers and sports coats are thoroughly wet but sitting in the car isn't as uncomfortable as I had imagined.

6.30pm. Home. Change (for the third time today). Pleased to see a fire burning and have tea beside it in the armchair. Settle down to read but to my surprise find that I don't enjoy any of the authors I try. I reject in turn, Mouro, Yeats, *Chapman's Odyssey*, Shakespeare (*Troilus and Cressida*) and Pope. Pope pleases me the best and I read a hundred lines or so but, in the end, decide that I am in a restless, change-of-season mood and can't read anything. I am quite happy doing nothing.

Just after 8 o'clock Ray and I go out to the Warren House Inn – 6½ miles away on the *roof* of Dartmoor where we used to have a bungalow and where we are well-known. On the way out I recall that although I can't read any author with enjoyment, I have the taste of several in my mind. I think that in a week or two I shall be reading Grey and Johnson and others.

At the inn conversation is more desultory and less lively than usual but everyone seems fairly happy. Stay until closing time (10 o'clock).

Supper. Bed (about 11). Write short notes for report in bed. Read Robert Graves and Ronald Bottrell for a quarter of an hour in a detached, inconsequential, retrospective mood – just to see how they seem after 12 months or so of neglect. A sort of poetic post-mortem. A good day. Sleep.'

Seven years later Pilot Officer Colin Neck died, at the age of thirty-two, on 23 December 1944 at Antwerp. He had joined the RAF and served with the British Liberation Army. His death was caused by enemy action.[185]

NEWTON ABBOT

The town lies at the head of the Teign estuary and became an important railway junction following the arrival of the South Devon Railway in 1846. It greatly increased in size and its Victorian prosperity can be seen in a number of substantial public and private buildings. The town had 14,809 residents in 1939, an increase of some 1.6% from the previous year.[186] It has been estimated that the town had sixty-five air raids in which some fifty high explosive and eight thousand incendiaries were dropped. Twenty-two people lost their lives in two attacks on 20 August 1940 and 25 April 1942.[187]

27. Edgar Wiggins, Pathologist, 1942-5

Edgar Dunstan Wiggins, a plant pathologist from London (1911-1993), worked at Seale-Hayne Agricultural College and lodged nearby with his wife Marjorie. The college, situated some three miles from Newton Abbot, had opened in 1920. He was thirty-years-old when he first wrote for MO.

Mr Wiggins' job precluded him from wartime service ('As a conscientious objector I am not interested in the war effort which I regard as misguided and ante-biological. I am fortunate in having as an occupation something that continues to be humanity's prime need in peace and war. I am concerned with the pests and diseases of agricultural plants and my conscience is satisfied that I am serving the community to the best of my ability.').

Directives: prejudice, race and sex

He wrote for MO from 1942 until 1945 and contributed five particularly unusual passages.[188] One concerned his personal prejudices including one regarding Rab Butler:

'Being naturally suspicious of everyone, I find it almost impossible to compile a list of personal prejudices. Here are a few that come forward.

Men: tooth-brush moustaches, striped trousers and black jacket, Homburg hat, RABly handshakes, a passion of orderliness and tidiness.

Women: coloured finger nails, long finger nails, make up (other than the irreducible minimum of face powder), *Edwardian* coiffures, permanent waving, slacks (breeches or shorts are alright)'.

He expressed an unusual view on race:

'I have always been open-hearted to coloured people, perhaps patronisingly, perhaps chivalrously. In later years respect has come. But a good test is to ask yourself, how would you like to be bettered by a coloured man? Would I take kindly to having a coloured man as my superior? I don't know. The fact probably is that a coloured man who could rise to such a position in the world as it is today would be such a superman that he would command my respect irrespective of colour.

I have known only a few coloured people, but I have been impressed by their quiet dignity and humility. I don't mean obsequiousness but humility in thought about life and the universe for example. How I would welcome these traits in Western Europe. I feel sure I should get on well with the coloured person as [a] colleague. I don't think the war has changed my feelings towards coloured people. The Japanese I regard as having usurped their culture in craving to become bastard Europeans.'

His third passage was on sexual decadence:

'The so-called moral standards of sexual behaviour have undoubtedly lowered in recent years. This was only to be expected from the impossibly repressed state to which sex was relegated. When sex was synonymous with sin and both shunned accordingly, the view of sexual morality as seen through complacent rose-tinted Victorian spectacles was an utterly unreal one. Sooner or later the myth that man nominally lives as a sexless creature was bound to be exploded. It has taken two wars to do it. In the first war sexual laxity took place but was kept out of sight and hearing. In this it has been recognised by nearly everyone including officialdom. We now see venereal disease advertised in the papers, that is a good indication. Sex education is being boosted in schools, that is another. Conclusion, the so-called sexual morality decline is really sexual behaviour getting to normal.'

189 The seduction of an American airman, 1940s.

Evacuees

He also wrote an unusual text on local evacuees:

'The evacuee problem in this district was complicated by the fact this was one of the banned coastal areas prior to the invasion of June 6th. Evacuees filtered into the area in spite of the ban and it would appear that providing they had friends or relatives to go to, the police did not turn them back. When the ban was lifted and evacuation was officially directed to this area, holidaymakers also flocked to the district. The view expressed by hoteliers and lodging-house keepers was that the accommodation of visitors was their normal livelihood and that having been deprived of it for a good portion of the season, they were entitled to try to recoup their losses and did not see why they should be compelled to take evacuees at a few shillings a week. Much bad feeling was aroused in Torquay (South Devon) but how it was finally settled by the authorities I do not know.

Three series of summonses for refusal to take evacuees have been heard in surrounding districts. None of these appeared to be lodging-house keepers and the excuses given were all domestic reasons of health etc. The chief complaint about evacuees is of their ingratitude and fickleness. They demand refuge and attention as a right yet flit back to London at the first sign of slackening of the attacks, often leaving unpleasant memories behind them. The whole reception of evacuees was very different from what it was earlier in the war'.[189]

Directive: the atomic bomb

His final unusual passage reflected his work as a scientist. In August 1945 he wrote of the Atomic bomb:

> 'As a scientist this issue touches me very nearly. It is one of those happenings which is so staggering that one only feels the stun of it sometime after the realisation has sunk in. Let me say quite frankly and without fear that subsequent centuries will [not] prove me wrong that this is the third of the greatest discoveries of man. The first and second being respectively the discovery of fire and the discovery of agriculture. It is impossible to exaggerate its significance. We have used our superlatives so lavishly in this age of wonders that now we have no terms in which to express our feelings about this. Perhaps silence is the only thing that can express it. Every person, every group, every community will sooner or later have to re-orientate their ideas.
>
> This, paraphrased in various ways, is all I have been able to say to people who have discussed it with me. Laymen, that is, who are all really mystified why so much fuss has been created by what is to them one of a number of miraculous developments. But even to the ignorant, something of the order of the new departure has penetrated. Perhaps it is the magnitude of its effects which startles them. I am certain that only a few are aware that something <u>fundamental</u> has been brought about. I have often wondered what it was like to live at one of the turning points of man's evolution. Now I have experienced it.'

Mr Wiggins had moved to Lustleigh by 1945 and commented on it in 1947 ('In this country village of 300 inhabitants people are known to one another as personalities. We know the family circumstances (and in many cases the history of) the parson, the postmaster, the schoolmaster, the milkman, etc. Speaking generally, there is friendliness and co-operation all round… I should explain that I am only at home at weekends and that if I were here all the time, I should probably know everyone and all about everyone'). He left Seale Hayne shortly after the war ended and died in 1993.[190]

NEWTON FERRERS

This parish, situated on the Yealm Estuary some nine miles from Plymouth, had a population in 1931 of 884 residents.[191] In the summer of 1940 *Illustrated Sporting & Dramatic News* recommended the village for a holiday:

> 'Rivers or estuaries seem to be popular parking places for guest houses of the right kind. The Sheiling at Newton Ferrers is a case in point. It is a small house, run in the homely manner, the right manner for sensible people. Perched on a hillside and facing the sun, the Sheiling has that indescribable atmosphere of calm that enables you to shrug your shoulders at Hitler and all his works. Definitely a good place for a holiday at this time. Bathing may be forbidden on some of our coastlines, but not on the banks of the Yealm, but five minutes' walk away, while boating, fishing or yachting can be enjoyed from the same nearby source'.[192]

The following spring, during the height of the bombing of Plymouth, the Cliffside Hotel advertised special rates for those whose homes had been destroyed by air raids.[193]

This would suggest the village was a quiet escape from war but, to support the defence of Plymouth, it hosted an anti-aircraft battery at Netton and a searchlight at Preston as well as an RAF station (Number 13 Balloon Centre) at Collaton.[194] There was also some bombing (see Yealmpton) including in November 1940 when a number of high explosives and incendiaries fell. Seventeen air raids were recorded for Newton Ferrers and the surrounding villages.[195]

An MO Writer from London, who had a holiday in Newton Ferrers in June 1942, wrote:

> 'In Newton Ferrers there was little sign of war; they tell me 225 bombs have been dropped on the place, that no one has been hurt and one garage is the only building damaged. They are suffering from the naval casualties however, seven men, all reservists with families, having been lost in one ship recently.
>
> On the way home, while waiting for a taxi, two soldiers with a lorry came to me to claim acquaintance. Their homes were in Peckham and one of them had been an inmate in the institution for unemployed there and the other a bus driver with children at *my* school.

190 General view of Hiroshima, Japan as seen from vicinity of 'zero', shows complete devastation as a result of atomic bombing, 1945.

We groaned together & felt a common delight in the Londoner and then were swept apart by the stream of life.'[196]

28. Tom Edridge, Writer, 1939-42

Tom Guy Edridge (1901-1982) was born in Luton, married Vera Williams in 1928 and they moved to Devon in about 1936. They lived at Windrush in Court Road, Newton Ferrers. By 1938 Mr Edridge was treasurer of the River Yealm Regatta.[197] He was a directive respondent from 1939 to 1940 and in 1942.[198] For MO he described himself as 'late business, at present unsuccessful writer' and 'late business, trying to write'.

Mr Edridge explained his relocation:

'For the first 35 years of my life I lived in a manufacturing town and grew to hate it, and during the last 10 years or so I knew quite definitely what I wanted. It was to live in a Cornish or Devon village, on

191 'Noss, South Devon' by Walter Stuart Lloyd (1845-1959).

***192** Mr Tom Edridge did not specify which traditional cure-all tablets his father used.*

an estuary which had plenty of trees nearby. I longed for the sea, for the quietness of a village, to get away from towns. The opportunity came, I had to make a change and I selected this village, which provides in full measure the things I desire most. I am, in the Wordsworthian manner, a lover of nature. I hate the noise and bustle of modern life and perhaps, like the alleged ostrich, I can see here less vividly the ominous signs of trouble ahead. A cowardly action but I have no faith in a future life and this village existence I embrace almost passionately. I still get an emotional thrill from the fact of being here and not in a town.'

He perceived considerable differences between him and his father, also called Tom, who was a plait merchant in Luton:

'I don't feel particularly representative of my generation but here goes. My tendency during my twenties was to mortify the flesh - eat very simply, take no alcohol, no smokes, wear as little clothes as possible, take long walks, keep out of crowds, bedroom windows wide open - the usual combination. My parents I think would not have liked to be unconventional, they did what others did without attempting to question or analyse. My father had a cure-all in some famous pills used in the family for a generation. A bath per day was considered a necessity by my father and he was fastidious over cleanliness.

Chief difference I think lies in the importance of fruit and uncooked food in my diet. For 12 years or so I was vegetarian, but even now I very rarely *go out to dinner* neither should I if I could afford it. Rice puddings and others of that species have diminished in importance. I doubt if my wife produces half a dozen puddings a year. Fruit in some form is the usual sweet. My parents would probably have had the fruit in a pie. Coffee has I think become much more widely drunk and tea is not often taken in my house. Alcohol we never take; my wife dislikes it and on scientific, as well as social lines, I have prejudices against alcohol. I can realise it's importance in drab lives, but I never see a crowd of young people drinking beer etc. without feeling an antipathy towards the process. My parents approved of moderate drinking and were sure it *did them good*. My father insists on the health value of a glass of stout. One of the things that stirs anger in his son is the sight of *beer does you good* sort of advertisement. If money was of no consideration I doubt if I should take anything. My parents did not consider themselves hospitable without offering a guest a whiskey. My guest get coffee. Cold meat I imagine to be less popular in tin stuff widely used by most folk now.

I have never had the concern for clothes that my father had. Hats I have not worn since I lived in a village and could please myself. I imagine this disregard for appearances to be general. I wear an absolute minimum, shorts in summer and by the time I have finished with clothes a tramp would reject them. I never remember seeing my father in a suit even slightly *shabby*. He thinks a gentleman should look smart. If I go shopping in the nearest town I generally change into a less forlorn pair of bags and a coat instead of the usual pull-over. Evening dress I hate.

I am 38, so the frivolities of youth tend to be disillusionment now; not that my ideas of a good time were very different then. My ideas now of a good time in order of choice, a, a good argument with one who can make an art of it and who, like me, is not worried about converting the other talker, b, listening to really good music, c, walking among trees and near water without noisy people to spoil it, d, sailing a boat.

My father at 77 thoroughly enjoys going to Newmarket or watching any sport - golf and cricket and football. He used to be keen on a dinner and theatre; something to laugh at. Masonic dinners he revels in. He likes the conventional seaside holiday, staying at a decent hotel - my idea of hell. In short, he likes a crowd, I do not.

There is very little friction in my married life. What there is may perhaps be termed psychological, a rarely-mentioned but slight resentment that my wife lacks the real maternal instinct (resentment on my part.) Occasionally it is hinted that I am overfond of getting my own way. In this I feel convinced that she is of the type who rarely takes the initiative. She never suggests a song to sing, I have to make the suggestion or the direction for a walk, etc. Any interest taken in me by other females would tend to produce mock serious back-chat. Rows scarcely ever happen - neither of us have *tempers*.

Before marriage there was often heated discussions with my father, an old-fashioned no-thinking conservative, about my *strong opinions*. My mother used to resent strongly the time and money which my father put into Masonry. Because of the ostentation and ceremony, I despised this movement. My father's chronic vice of being late for meals, taking one and a half hours to get up in the morning (mostly in the bathroom) used to upset my mother a good deal. On the whole my *strong opinions* were the chief bone of contention and my associations with men whose opinions were decidedly not conservative. As it generally takes two to make a real row, and I don't go in for tempers, real rows were uncommon.'

Directives: race, language and attitude towards Germans

Mr Edridge also answered MO questions on race:

> 'Negroes I take to be, on the whole, less developed mentally than Europeans or Asiatics, simple and unsophisticated in a way I should not imagine Indians to be. I think of them as 100,000 years behind in mental evolution but I often doubt if they are much worse off for it. What is a Negro? Is a primitive bushman one? Is a Zulu one? I have read American literature – *Porgy*, *Emperor Jones*, etc. but don't know enough to judge of the colour problem. At school we used to get coloured boys, though more often from India, and they appeared to be accepted by us without much question'.

He also commented upon the use of slang:

> 'I may occasionally use the following – *Cheerioh*, *bye-bye*, *ta*. I resent strongly *Okay* and many Americanisms and have always been conscious of an anti-film feeling.

Newton Ferrers (links) — Noss Mayo (rechts), von Westen.

193 Photograph of Newton and Noss included in the printed materials for the German invasion of England, 1940.

Have never heard *Okidoke*. I never use *Old Boy* or the others on your list but then I am of the type who would rarely get as far as *darling* or *my dear* with a woman and don't quite like to hear others use such familiarities in public. With men I might occasionally address them as *Guv'nor*. I like to call people I know well by their Christian names but take some time to reach that stage. Yet I make friends fairly quickly. I have no antipathy to *Mate*, like *Pal* less but these are terms I do not often hear. *Old Boy* suggests insincerity, it is used with discrimination. Everybody is *Old boy* hence it has no value. *When everyone is sombodee, then noone's anybody*, see W. S. Gilbert.'

By November 1942 Mr Edridge was serving in the RAF and was posted to Cribb's Causeway near Bristol. He admitted what had changed his attitude towards Germans:

'I was a strong supporter of the League of Nations and bordering upon a pacifist. I have been cautious of my feelings towards the enemy, conscious of propaganda; trying to hold on to my old ideals of the essential brotherliness of men, but my present mood is one of bitterness and hatred for the German race. (I try foolishly to exclude the women and children from my conception of this race.) I feel that they do constitute a menace towards civilisation and that ruthless liquidation of millions may be in the long run the wisest way. I believe their instinctive attitude to the social problems approximate more nearly to the wolf pack than our own. I want to see them completely disarmed and controlled internationally, and punished by real suffering for what they have brought upon mankind. I have doubts at present if this instinctive attitude can be educated out of the Germans, in short, I who once professed myself incapable of killing any man, would relish the idea of the German leaders suffering prolonged physical tortures as being the only way of teaching them. The rational side of my nature is uneasy about these feelings of revenge and cruel retribution, but my uppermost attitude is - get the wind down and kick them hard. (shades of Montague's *Disenchantment*) This is a considerable change since the early months of the war, a hardening and stiffening. I do not forget Brahms, Goethe and the delightful aspects of German culture and national habits but the evil aspects appear to outweigh. The treatment may have to be like a surgical operation for cancer.'

Mr Edridge continued to write after the war: in 1947 he read two of his short stories to members of the Newton and Noss Women's Institute but came to specialise in horticultural features. As late as 1982 he wrote for the *Western Morning News*. He died while living at Newton Ferrers in 1982.[199]

NORTH MOLTON

This remote Exmoor parish had some 938 residents in the 1930s. An aircraft reportedly crashed here during the war.[200]

194 West Yarde Farm near North Molton, the former youth hostel at which Joseph and Nina Gregory honeymooned in 1941.

29. Joseph Gregory, Postal Sorter, 1941

Twenty-six-year-old London postal sorter Joseph Benjamin Gregory (1915-) recorded his wartime honeymoon with Nina (1911-1999), his thirty-year-old bride. They had recently met and subsequently had a holiday together in Cornwall in the spring of 1940 but he had forgotten what she looked like ('She seemed shorter than I had imagined her since last we met and a little different in facial features but her heart and spirit were the same as ever'.). Within a few days he was smitten ('that youthful adventurous spirit which is so irresistible and yet so delicately feminine that it needs support and encouragement.').

Ten months later, on 7th February 1941, Mr Gregory successfully faced a Conscientious Objectors' Tribunal in London and five days later travelled on the *Torbay Express* to Paignton. On his arrival he obtained temporary ration cards for the honeymoon, ate fried sole and chips at Rockies and celebrated his impending marriage at the Gerston Hotel. This took place the following day in the parish church and the reception was held at Evans Café. That day the couple left for a week at a youth hostel outside North Molton. The former farmhouse at West Yarde operated between 1932 and 1946. In 1935 it was described as 'A redbrick, blue-slate-roofed house, not beautiful...The common room and men's dorm were in one of the outbuildings grouped around the farmyard with its dung-heap... [The outlook was a] slate-roofed barn opposite and a green tree rising above it. The hostel itself was all new wood inside; it was very bare and crude, with a thoroughly dangerous staircase or ladder up to a sleeping place. The stoves were almost hopeless and the lighting, a single hurricane lantern, very poor... You go through one of the outhouses to a lane for the lavatory.'[201]

Honeymoon

The couple may have needed to be economical in costs:

> 'We caught the 12.31 train from Paignton to Exeter. Quite a gathering to see us off and much hand-waving and cheering. Fortunately we had the compartment to ourselves all the way to Exeter. It was a grand feeling to lay back in each other's arms and feel that now we could enjoy peace together. The mist had cleared and the sun shone out from big patches of blue in a sky of broken cloud.
>
> We changed at Exeter, getting into a little push-and-pull train which took us to Dulverton where we changed again for South Molton. On the Dulverton train was a beaming-faced guard who was very attentive to us and looked after us and our luggage. From Dulverton to South Molton our only fellow passenger was an old lady who had travelled alone from Carshalton (Surrey) to join her son in North Devon. The scenery around here was simply grand with quite a residue of autumn colours which seemed to defy the winter bareness.
>
> We were met at the station by Mr Huxtable who took us in [his] car to West Yarde. We found our hostess very kind and extremely obliging. The food is good and there is plenty of it.
>
> Nin and I spent the evening after tea in front of the fire talking – then supper and then bed. We spent a perfectly happy night but were rather tired in the morning.
>
> Friday, February 14th Arose about 7.30 and breakfasted at 9. Mr Huxtable took us down to Brayford in his car where we caught bus into Barnstaple. Weather cold and inclined to rain. Arrived in Barnstaple about 11am. Walked around the shops and bought Ruby a present of a pair of stockings and a birthday card. We then lunched at Bromleys' Café, then to the Regal Cinema and saw the *Ghost Breakers*. This quite entertaining. Caught the 5pm bus back to North Molton via South Molton. Commenced walking back to West Yarde but, after losing our way at first, finally got a lift for some

distance. Had a late meal of hot meat pasties and then spent the evening on the settee in front of the log fire. Writing up my diary with Nin's assistance, we read *Adelphi* magazine. Went to bed at 10pm and slept at intervals. These of longer duration than on the previous night.

Saturday 15th February. Arose at 8.30. After a darn good breakfast of *bubble and squeak*, bacon, eggs and marmalade etc. (we are well-looked-after here), we walked down into North Molton where we arrived just after mid-day. We took some snaps on the way as weather looked promising. Changed my wages postal draft at the Post Office and sent off card to Ron W.

Nin and I also visited the Poltimore Arms and drank each other's health with a glass of port. Having missed the noon bus into South Molton, we commenced to walk. This morning we seemed incapable to taking anything at all seriously, and dithered and dallied, cutting sticks and generally mucking about. Hence, we did not reach South Molton by 2pm. Feeling pretty hungry, we decided that the Romansleigh visit would have to be postponed. We got a bus back to North Molton and then walked back to West Yarde where we had a good dinner and tea. We spent the evening in much the same way as yesterday. These evenings are truly delightful, our mutual interests seem to provide us with a wealth of enjoyment and happiness.

Went to bed at 10.30 happy and contented but too much in love to sleep well, as was indicated by our rather sheepish looks in the morning.

Sunday 16th February Arose at about 9am. After a very good breakfast of fried bacon, eggs, bubble and squeak for both of us, we sat in front of the fire and read and talked, it being a very windy and wet morning. We had run out of cigarettes and could not buy any within a radius of three miles.

Sitting together we got rather emotional and found it necessary to go upstairs to the bedroom to appease our desire – which we accomplished with the greatest mutual satisfaction just before dinner.

After dinner we set off in spite of the wind and rain to Brayford, where we intended both to go to church and also to get some cigarettes. Although we arrived in time for church, we were both so wet through that we decided it would be unwise to sit about, so walked on to Brayford, where we managed to get two packs of 20 Players at a bungalow on the road side.

We returned over a little bridle path which took us over some muddy country across the hills. On our return we spent the evening the usual way. Bed at 10.

Monday 17th February Got up about usual time (about 8.30). We walked into South Molton where we had two ports each in the Poltimore Arms. We then bought some delicious cheese (officially unattainable) and biscuits in a village shop. This we ate on the bus while journeying to Barnstaple. When we arrived, we had a light meal in a café and then went to the Regal Cinema and saw *Pride and Prejudice* starring Greer Garson. This really a good film which both of us thoroughly enjoyed. Caught 5pm bus back. Walking in from South Molton and arriving at West Yarde at 7.30. After a delicious meal of hot meat and veg pie, we spent the remainder of the evening reading together on settee in front of the fire. Retired about 10.30. Not such a restful night but nevertheless strictly enjoyable.

Tuesday 18th Feb. Arose about 8.45. Rather a misty morning. Walked into North Molton, getting a lift in a Great Western Railway lorry for a mile or so. Each of us had a Guiness at the Poltimore Arms and a pleasant little discourse with the landlord. We poured over maps together and discussed the best way of reaching our intended destination, which was Odam Hill, Romansleigh, to call upon Dick Richards. Also, we wanted to see Yarde Farm, Roseash, which was once Nin's mother's home. Before leaving the pub we had a game of rings. I was top scorer. Nin however excelled on the Bagatelle.

We caught the noon bus into South Molton and thence started to walk in the direction of Romansleigh. A kindly policeman succumbed to Nin's charming smile – result being a lift as far at the Butcher's Arms. Here we attempted to get lunch but the landlady could only provide beer and a piece of cake, the latter which she gave us. After a little chat with her, on the war and how it affected food supplies, and on vastly exaggerated tales of raids, we marched on towards Romansleigh and after a little difficulty in finding Dick's whereabouts, we finally discovered him engaged on constructing a duck house.

He seemed pleased and certainly surprised to see us. After introducing him to my wife, we chatted for a while on position of COs in regards to possibilities of employment in agriculture. The position seemed that there was plenty of work but most farmers refused to employ COs. The *Western Mail* had, he said, refused to put in the words CO in his advertisement for work. We exchanged accounts of our respective experiences before the appellate tribunal and they seemed very familiar. Dick then gave us a brief account of his present occupation which he seemed to regard as very unsatisfactory, he had in fact already given notice to leave.

We felt the visit worth-while. Next, we attempted to find Yarde Farm. Our search, however, was not wholly fruitful, for our intense hunger together with the difficulty of finding the place, made it necessary for us to discontinue the search, get a meal and commence our return. I was nearly despairing when Nin, with latent intentions, disappeared into a farm yard, where a thresher was making a *dickens* of a row, and returned with the good news that a farmer's wife would provide us with tea. The meal was delicious and appetising and well-fortified us for our walk back to South Molton.

On the way back we visited a village school which possessed the advantage of having lavatories without slot machines. We completed the final stages of our journey to South Molton by bus arriving there at 7. Three quarters of an hour elapsed before the arrival of the North Molton bus. After phoning our hostess and notifying her of our late return, we spent the time in the bar of the George Hotel, where in front of a blazing fire we talked and drank whisky and port and spent a few coppers on slot machines. The latter entertainment cost me a pack of 10 cigarettes to Nin.

We caught the North Molton bus and then walked to West Yarde with wind, rain and snow blowing in our faces – arriving at the farm just after 9. A delicious meal awaited us – rabbit pie and veg and sweet of apple pie, cream and tea. Feeling very tired we went to bed almost immediately.

Spot of love – plenty of sleep <u>tonight</u> – spot of love.

Feel on top of the world.

Wednesday Feb. 19th Arose at usual time. A light covering of snow on the ground when we looked out. Some sun at first, so went out and took some snaps of the house. Later the snow began to fall heavily again. We went up to the Inn at Yarde Down and had a drink or two each. The fascination of this place is the big open old-fashioned fire which is in the bar. Returned for dinner. The snow continued to fall heavily all the afternoon. We sat together in front of the fire. Nin read aloud to me and then I dozed. We found it necessary to go up upstairs together to the bedroom, for a well spot of love before tea.

After tea we packed most of our things ready for departure in the morning. The snow had ceased and the sky was starless but the wind was very strong. Tonight for the first time we could hear a constant drone of enemy planes, apparently making their way to South Wales (Swansea).

At the inn, where we spent the evening, we played darts and sat in front of the big open fire, talking with the landlord and another visitor, a farm hand. We stood them a drink and asked the chances of me getting a job down here on the land. The chances seemed quite promising until I revealed I was a CO and then it fizzled out.

We got back to West Yarde just after 10. After a light supper of cocoa and bread, butter and biscuits and cream cheese, we went to bed and after a little love-making slept very well until about 6.'

The couple left West Yarde the following morning and took the train at South Molton. They parted at Dulverton, she travelled back to Paignton and he returned to London. Mr Gregory's mother had not attended the wedding and was, along with other family members, unhappy with the marriage ('Mother still a bit cold towards me, she seems she hasn't got over it yet').

In early April Mr Gregory relocated to West Looe in Cornwall where he and his future wife had holidayed in 1940. He worked as an agricultural labourer and was joined by Nina. The port was bombed their first night. On 10 April they travelled to Paignton through Plymouth ('a pretty bad mess – damage concentrated in a small area of the town but this part almost completely demolished.'). The following day they visited the Pavillion and there was an air raid ('a beautiful moonlit night but *Jerry* was present later and dropped a few hundred incendiaries along the front – one warden reported killed. Much excitement in the town over this, as apparently the worst raid of the war for Paignton but to me it appeared rather insignificant'.) On 24 April he noticed while working in West Looe that there was smoke at Plymouth ('Saw while cycling to the farm what at first thought to be huge black clouds but afterwards I realised that this was smoke from bombed oil tanks at Plymouth, one of the results of last night's raid. My suspicions were confirmed later when, from a better vantage point, I would see the thick pall of smoke, rolling and curling skywards from two distinct points. The easterly wind then caught it and blew it along the Cornish coast. At times while working in the field it hid the sun just like a cloud. It continued all day and was still pouring forth on Friday morning.').

Shortly afterwards the couple moved to Gloucestershire and in 1955 relocated to Cambridgeshire.[202]

***195-7** Three views of Paignton, 1905.*

PAIGNTON

This seaside town, located in Torbay between Torquay and Brixham, is known for its climate and long stretches of sandy beaches. It developed in the late eighteenth century into becoming one of Devon's premier resorts. Its pier opened in 1879. The town had 25,227 residents in 1939, an increase of 15.1% since 1938.[203] Air raids were recorded as taking place on 3 August, 4 September and 30 December 1942.[204] One list of air attacks taken at the time noted eight bombings; these occurred on 12 September 1940, 13 March 1941, 11th to 12th April 1941, 10 May 1941, 4 September 1942, 30 December 1942, 21 January 1943 and 13 February 1943. Thirty-four deaths were recorded.[205]

A fifty-nine-year-old MO Diarist, living in St Ives in 1940, reported the resort had been bombed earlier that year ('I get reports from a married daughter living near Paignton, South Devon, where they have suffered pretty badly from bombardment. They have become *Peace Friends*, she says, in the district.').[206]

30. Jack Lindsay, Writer, 1937-9

Australian-born Jack Lindsay AM, FRSL (1900-1990), was the son of Norman Lindsay (1879-1969), author of *Creative Effort* (1920), and the brother of the writer Philip Lindsay. Lindsay himself wrote some 200 books. He was married, a vegetarian, became a member of the Communist Party in 1941 and gave his 'recreation' for *Who's Who In Australia* as sunbathing. He was described as having blue eyes, a medium build and standing five feet eight inches with 'dark hair turning grey, face and chest pitted with pock marks, partial denture in upper jaw'.[207]

In November 1937 Mr Lindsay used his bank for his postal address ('As for several reasons, my stay in the cottage is shaky. I give the bank as settled address'). He led a peripatetic lifestyle having previously lived in Cornwall and for a short while at Blackmore Gate outside Barnstaple. He appears to have resided from 1933 at Seaways in Cliff Park Lane at Goodrington, from 1936 to 1938 at Whitstone in Preston Down Road at Paignton and from 25 August 1938 to 7 January 1939 at High Ridge in Long Lane at Shaldon. The Devon Constabulary investigated Mr Lindsay during the war and noted that he had left one address 'in the early hours of the morning owing rent and a number of debts in the district'. His residence in Devon may have been a consequence of his relationship with Elza de Locre, a poet who had family in Combe Martin. On 7 January 1939 Mr Lindsay moved to 1 Broadpark Road in Livermead in Torquay and, by 22 September, to Dorset.[208]

Directives: personal appearance and anti-Semitism

A biographer later commented that Mr Lindsay was known for a 'Bohemian carelessness about his clothes and grooming' whereas the police summarised him as 'of eccentric habits and untidy appearance'.[209] This was confirmed by Mr Lindsay himself in one of his directive responses.[210] In 1939 he described his wardrobe ('I don't wear a suit and don't possess one. The last I bought was in 1933. The previous one, 1929.') and gave his thoughts on men's fashion:

***198** Preston Down Road, the home of Mr Jack Lindsay in 1937 and during part of 1938.*

'I have fads or I would have if I had any money. I should prefer to wear only cotton, no animal matter and for boots good vegetable products. However, this kind of thing needs a lot of cash. My reasons are partly emotional. I can't bear any form of parasitism and man's dependence on animals I consider loathsome (am vegetarian in diet, no animal products, again very hard for a person without much money), partly for health considerations, since I don't see how anyone can be healthy while wearing or eating animal stuff. Also, since unearthing the various womb-fantasies in myself, I dislike animal clothes further. [Gustav] Jäger, the man who started one branch of woollens, by the way was a paranoic with fantasies about the necessity for animal stinks to protect one. That's enough about fads.

I dislike fashions in either men's or women's clothes. Style is a matter of personal taste and non-distortion of the body is another matter. About 99% of fashion however consists of distortion and is thus lunatic in various ways and so I dislike it, as I imagine any same person would.'

In March 1939 Lindsay commented upon a baker's wife's appraisal of Adolf Hitler: '*He's a demon that Hitler... What do I think he'll do? God knows, I don't. But he's a demon.* I reply to further question about possibility of holding him up. *I don't know. He's got a lot behind him he has.* Impossible to find out what the something is. *But he's a demon.*'

His notes in February 1939 on eight conversations regarding Jews were more substantial:

1. 'Woman, middle aged, manageress of Kingswear railway hotel (don't give this locality if you quote the remarks since it might injure her). Met in a railway carriage. She was rather drunk: gin. And, between working her skirt up over her knees,

informed me that all the troubles of the world were caused by Jews. As a rattle-pated woman, she was apparently expressing what she heard discussed in her hotel.

2. Same day, in a stationer's shop in Paignton, a large pompous elderly man, middle-class, turned from remarks about local municipal affairs to say that the Jews were running the world and something ought to be done about it. The stationer agreed emphatically.

3. Business man of Exeter, met on Starcross railway station where we had a long wait, started off a conversation which went on for twenty minutes as one long diatribe against the Jews. Had a queer, fanatic jerky way of talking. Conversation began something like this, *All the world is off its head nowadays… speed nothing but rush… nothing orderly or contented. What we need is more of a prim-i-tive outlook, prim-i-tive. And then of course there's the Jews… It's a common error that they are God's chosen people. No, No. They were cursed of God,* then a long babble about financial control of the world being in the hands of International Jews, interlarded with continual biblical quotations to prove that the Jews were accursed. Looking at me with quick side long glances, stopping jerkily, talking about something else and then starting on the Jews again.

4. Middle-class dealer in antiques at Teignmouth. *Mind you, I don't agree with all Hitler does, but you can't blame him about the Jews.*

5. Middle-class woman, *The Jews deserve far more than Hitler had done to them. They're the vilest people on earth. Look how they treat their women. I've known something about their family ways from the inside. They're brutes.* etc.

6. Shopkeeper (ironmonger) at Teignmouth. *It isn't only what the Jews have now. Hitler wants to stop them from going on to get more and more. They have to be stopped.*

7. Woman (landlady) at Falmouth. *Of course, I know its dreadful about war… but I must say I admire Hitler, the way he's put life back into the German people.*

***199** 'Maneater' poster depicting Adolf Hitler as a wild beast, devouring human remains with skulls from countries invaded by Germany, 1941.*

Daughter, *He's given them self-respect and saved them from chaos.*
Mother, *And, it's not his fault the Jews had to have something done to them. You can't trust a Jew.*

8. Woman. *The Jews are sweaters. They'll do anything for money.*
These are the most salient episodes that come to my mind. Of the many middle-class people, only one, a young fellow of the bank class type (had the *Daily Telegraph*) said that Hitler was merely using the anti-Semitic stuff to cover up the internal problems of his regime.
So my general impression is that anti-Semitism is very strong indeed among the Middle Classes and that it only wants a proper lead to become highly inflammable and dangerous.'

11 November 1937

Perhaps Mr Lindsay's most distinctive account is of a morning when he lived in Preston Down Road at Paignton:

> '8 o'clock, I write the answers to some debt demands. Then (for company and escape), go and see what bird friends of mine are about. A young blackbird is very tamely asking me for food. I feel sure he is one with which I was friendly some months ago, when he was very young; has the same look about the eyes. Birds have quite a lot of distinctive touches when one gets to know them well. He is certainly too tame for a stranger; the first real winter frosts are making the birds anxious.
>
> My neighbours are as follows, 1, on right a largish house, well-kept, 2, on left, a spinster with caravan, etc. At back, 3, a retired clerk or something of the kind (retired to the ease of perpetual plus-fours on his lean shanks and perpetual quarrels with his wife). He is somewhat deaf, so speaks with a raucous voice and his wife and daughter have got into the habit of shouting at him in same tone till they are (it seems) unaware of the harsh carrying power of their voices. Also, 4, at back a lower middle-class family, the old man pottering about in his vegetable garden most of the time.

Main characteristics

> 1, highly respectable, think themselves high-class pillars of society, and are trying to sell their house because the council is going to widen the road (now only a lane) and they will lose 14 feet of their garden. Usual damned insolence of such people. A strict (ever-so-kind on the surface) mother, she lets her boy cry for hours sometimes, she won't have any *nonsense* and would of course be horrified if she saw a pestered working-class mother slap her child.
>
> 2, a bit loony. I mentioned last month how she was painting her sheds. Not painting today, but she has been at it again during the month. Though she has only a tiny plot, she has had a gardener working on it, first crazy pavement, then digging up again, new trees, then grass lawn and what not. She is a *lover of nature* so she says. Which is her way of excusing herself for living in a caravan. She spends the worst winter months with a sister at Brixham and tries to let the caravan during the summer.
>
> 3, ultra-respectable, being clearly on a low level of pension or annuity or some such thing. Live chiefly for their cheap motor car, which however in the summer they hire out (I heard a discussion about it). They would have horrors if they knew this was known.
>
> 4, the only decent people. The old man isn't bad. Since I have been here, he has plucked up courage to work in his garden in any old costume. At first, he kept carefully to a white coat, to placate the people of 1.
>
> 9 o'clock I go upstairs and look at my novel where I had left off. It seems rotten. I don't dare to read the part I have already written or I'd be too depressed to go on. I now work straight onto the typewriter without revision or rewriting; otherwise I get lost in wandering. (Previously I used to write a first version in tiny script about 1,500 to 2,000 words to a quarto page writing without break, doing a 120,000 novel in about 18 to 20 days, then copying out and amplifying a very little. Now I haven't the patience or interest to do a first draft). I dislike writing, having so many resistances to wear down before I commence. If I had no responsibilities, I should give myself up to political work, the only kind that seems to me to be worthwhile now.
>
> 10 o'clock Without having written anything, I get ready to go out. Go out and walk along the seafront. The day is bitterly frosty, but the sea is mostly clear. A fair amount of seaweed has been thrown up on beach. Three men are collecting it. I talk with the man who has come up on the asphalt front and is loading sacks full of the seaweed onto the back of his bicycle. He is a would-be gentleman farmer, probably doing badly. His manner is rather timid, defensive and placatory. Seems to think I'm criticising his right to take the seaweed. He says that there have been few of the eastern winds that bring the weed up this year. *I've seen it that thick the council had to send men with carts and spend £100 a day to get the beach cleared for the visitors*. An obvious exaggeration. He wants to impress me with the fact he is doing a social service and taking the seaweed for manure. His face is thin but purplish, his eyes bloodshot. We discussed the kind of weather needed to bring up the weed.
>
> At the other end of the beach I pass two small-allotment men who are also collecting the seaweed, putting it into barrows. I have a few words with a tubby fellow

and ask him how far he has to take the stuff. Only over the ridge, but he doesn't seem enthusiastic. His friend down on the beach, I know. A burly retired policeman with a small strip of ground where he grows vegetables. He's a fine chap, rather typical of the politics of the men roundabouts.

(A summary of his opinions: *I vote Liberal or I used to. I've no use for any of the parties now. Liberals dead. Conservatives would shoot us down if it meant a penny more on their incomes. Labour, a lot of skunks that think only of feathering their own nests. No brotherhood anywhere. It doesn't take me in.* With some such remarks as *Police officers have had their wages raised, not the rankers. I know the old trick, Bribe the men in charge, split the men. It's done everywhere.* A queer mixture of political knowledge and ignorance. Keen on *brotherhood* but can't find it anywhere.)

10.30 In Paignton I go to the bank to draw a pound and see if any letters. (As for several reasons, my stay in the cottage is shaky. I give the bank as settled address.) A photo that I wanted for the Moscow articles I am sending off. I slip that into the Moscow letter. Also, a letter from John Allen asking me to make alterations in the declamation I wrote on China. It is to be done by some Chinese amateurs for the big performance; the alterations relate to bringing the work into line with this fact. (It was written as for non-Chinese).

The clerk in the bank says very amiably *It's cold today*. The first time he has ever spoken personally to me. I am quite astonished. Go to Post Office and post my letters and buy stamps.

10.45 I go to lavatory at top of square (working class end). It is one of the places in which I have scribbled political slogans. This one is *Support the people of China and Spain against Fascism*. It is usually rubbed out but this time it has been heavily scored out and someone has written *Go Back to Russia*. This depresses me because it makes me realise once again how powerfully Beaverbrookism is embedded even in the working classes, especially in an unorganised area such as this.

Nobody worries to rub or cross out the many obscene comments scrawled all over the lavatory. For instance, there is one in large block letters next to my political one, *My sister can take six inches easily.* But my anti-Fascist slogan at once attracts hatred.

I look at the book-trays in the second-hand furniture shops. Then go to have a cup of coffee. (My one form of debauchery. There is a wireless in the café and it is run by some not bad-looking middle-class girls. A bit of nostalgia on my part.) A clergyman and his wife come in. Perfect types, on the caricature level. He is short, handsome, reddish beefy. She is thin, big-nosed with all the lines of her face going downward. They start reading the newspapers, full of interest in the Cenotaph ceremony and very fussed about the episode of the man breaking through and running at the King.

Her main comment: *How silly*. They look through for all the photos of royalty, charmed every time most by Queen Mary, *Isn't she sweet? Look there kissing…*

The girl is trying to get some breakfast behind the curtain near me. *No rest for the wicked* she says to me as customers come in to buy cakes.

(Everyone is very patriotic in this neighbourhood. They were all, working and upper-class, solid against Edward. Many women, so a stationer in the working-class part told me, were so frantic they would have liked to murder Mrs Simpson.)

I buy some envelopes from Smith's, speak to the library girl about new books. Go to the Health Food store, and buy some things from the flat-chested, anaemic-looking girl there. Although an absolute believer in nature methods of diet and curing, I must confess that only the most awful abortions of humanity seem attracted by such things, mostly horrible-looking women with bad constipation. This is not a generalisation made on insufficient evidence; for it was made even more luridly to me by a friend, also a naturist, who for years was an employee of one of the largest London health food stores and manufacturers.

I go to the greengrocers. Asking among other things about tomatoes. I am shown some for four pence (the local ones eight pence). I ask where they come from.

Girl: *Canary Islands, I think.*
I: *Franco holds those islands, doesn't he?*
Girl: *Yes, I think so.*
I: *Well, I object to General Franco.*
Girl: (instantly and fiercely) *So do I.*

This was the first sincere remark she has ever made to me. The two girls in the shop treat me with amiable contempt since they think it queer for a man to be buying food regularly - at least after the summer months when he might have been camping somewhere.

I come round by the harbour, but none of my fisher friends are there. I buy the *Tribune* in the shop there. An old woman is complaining loudly because her *Church Standard* hasn't come in.

11.45 Reaching home, after some chats with the birds, I again look at my novel and depress myself about it. Then I start typing out the Chinese poem from the new angle. I enjoy that. I feel alive.

12.10 I go and get the *Daily Worker* which has now arrived by second post.

12.15 I get myself my lunch. Lettuce and tomatoes, and some potatoes fried in nut fat. Being more than usually hard-up, I can't afford olive oil. For salt I have some spinach salt. I haven't eaten mineral salt for seven years. Which is the chief reason for my good health despite all my worries etc. Mineral salt is sheer poison for the blood-organs and stomach. But people who live on eating corpses can't do without it.

I have no washing up. About one minute per week suffices, as it is only animal products that produce filthy plates, pans, etc.'

After moving to Bournemouth Mr Lindsay relocated to London where, in 1941, he was conscripted into the British Army. By the time of his death in 1990 he had published more than 160 books.[211]

31. William Lindop, Clerk, 1939

William John Lindop (1922-1988) was a sixteen-year-old clerk living with his parents at 53 Merritt Road when he began writing for MO in 1939. He answered five directives and described himself for the project.

'Present occupation: accountant's clerk.

***200** Mr William Lindop.*

***201** Merritt Road, Mr Lindop's home in 1939.*

Life story: uneventful, father died when I was 10, I won scholarship to Grammar School at 12, passed Oxford School Certificate at 16, and entered present employment about a month ago.

Physique: height 5 feet 10 inches, weight about 10 stone, health good. Sorry, but cannot enclose photograph.

Religious views: belief in a God and in the teachings of Christ, disgust with all churches.

Politics: leftish, no allegiance to a particular party but believer in a People's Front.

Special interests: books, mainly political and the Co-Operative Youth Movement, also any discussion.

Home: in fairly small seaside town, on the outskirts, overlooking the main road to Plymouth. My home itself is in a block of flats, with low rent and a few facilities (ie gas cookers and electric light, but small gardens and no bathrooms).

I work at a rather larger seaside town – Torquay – on the main street and in a roomy, well-lit office, with another clerk. The firm is fairly small, occupying two floors. I work on the second.'

Directives: public attitudes and anti-Semitism

Mr Lindop relayed the conditions under which four men and women felt war with Germany would be justified:

'Housewife, 35, If Hitler starts anything in Europe.

Electrician, 30, If Hitler attempts to pinch another country.

Postman, 40, If anyone attacks our Empire.

Bus driver, 35, To honour our pacts and promises.'

He also described his personal feelings about Jews ('I think that the Jewish race is much the same as any other race except that it has no settled country. Organised anti-Semitism in any country is a sign of its decadence.') as well as of society in general ('Mainly tolerant although some people still believe that all Jews are rich people who live by sweating their employees. No organisation has yet been to collect for Lord Baldwin's appeal, but I suppose it would get a good response.'). Lindop did not personally know a Jewish person but wrote he was familiar with one by sight. He also felt there were few fascists in Torquay ('We have a very small number of fascists, but unfortunately, an even smaller number of Jews.').[212]

Mr Lindop was called up three years later and was posted to India. He married in 1946, had two children and was a lifelong socialist.[213]

32. George Shipway, Retired Draughtsman, 1943-4

George Walter Shipway (1876-1961), worked as a railway draughtsman in Cheshire. He married Gertrude Prosser in 1910 and lived in China in the 1910s and 1920s. Their three children were born in that country. Following his wife's death in 1943, he married Muriel Chipper (1904-1968). Mr Shipway revealed in his diaries that he was brought up as a Baptist and later attended both Unitarian and Quaker meetings. In the 1940s he began an interest in Spiritualism. Mr Shipway joined the Vegetarian Society in 1897 and his diet was clearly of great importance to him. Something of his character comes across in his discussion of personal prejudices ('I am prejudiced against smokers, non-teetotallers, meat-eaters, those who arise late, those who read yellow press, against people who take up room on pavement, against people who swear.') and his thoughts on women ('I note with amusement the increase of babies to obviate being appointed to munitions. I regret illicit sexual intercourse. Apart from the war, I disapprove of so many women remaining unmarried or being married and not having children. I am now a widower but if I can find a suitable woman - vegetarian etc., I shall hope to remarry and have children!').

In March 1943 he bought No. 6 Cockington Lane in Paignton and moved in shortly afterwards. He was then sixty-seven-years-old. Mr Shipway wrote diaries from 1939 to 1945 and was a directive respondent in 1939 and 1940.[214]

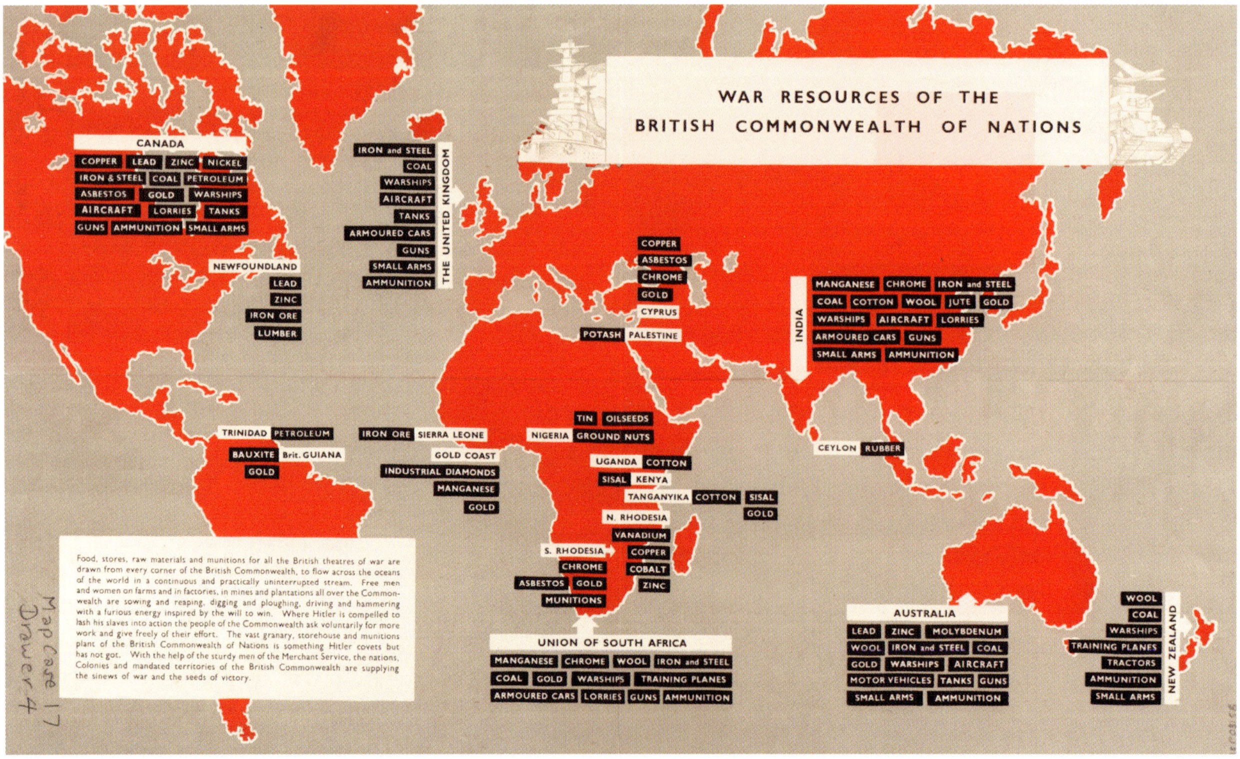

***202** The resources of the empire, c1939-45.*

1943

'10 September
… An auction was held during the week and my wife and I attended. There seemed no shortage of money. Apart from useful and necessary articles, objects of mere interest fetch good prices: a Chinese junk (nothing wonderful about it) fetched 35 shillings. A case of miscellaneous Chinese figures fetched 42 shillings 6 pence. I was told the next day that the amount obtained (for the whole) was 50% higher than had been expected.

We often have *Alerts* but they rarely last long. Often there are bangs but we assume it is our own people practising! We are not prone to seek shelter but, as it happens, there is no shelter near us to seek! Some folk have Morrison shelters but we have not (we merely *carry on*).

10 November

I am generally up about 6… I nearly always listen to 7 o'clock news. My early mornings are unsettled by the rapid *late-ning* of the raising of the blackout. I prepare my own and my wife's breakfasts: quite different. My wife has tea, warmed stewed fruit, thin bread and marg. with crust off (I eat the crusts always and enjoy being able to enjoy them!), honey, crushed cashew nuts. My breakfast is THICK bread with edging of peanut butter with inside part jam (a device to avoid sticky fingers); often a little rice pudding and stewed fruit. NO drink (I drink a lot between meals, vegetable water from dinner. I scrub potatoes (steamed in their skins); gather vegetables from garden and cut it up (coarse leaves boiled in lowest part of steamer and softer parts steamed in top part, with potatoes in middle portion). We had lots of runner beans from garden, and now have Brussel sprouts, spinach, cabbage and Savoys: ample.

If weather is fine, I often wheel my wife out in invalid chair.

Domestic help comes Tuesday morning and Thursday afternoon: a great help. I try to be out while she is here. Often I go hawking vegetarian literature: very few people buy and then I hand them a leaflet. Quite a few will buy a 6d or 2d leaflet. Rarely men, women mostly busy but rarely rudely abrupt. I combine this hawking with exploring in unknown parts of Paignton and inspecting bungalows and gardens.

Very little gardening these days. Terrible *counter-attack* by weeds will require resolute efforts later. Am gathering dead leaves.

Have attended a few meetings. Yesterday afternoon to hear a woman missionary from China; three Saturday afternoons to Workers Educational Association lectures, also a Saturday afternoon meeting of Co-Operative Party. This was about equal sexually, but others [sic] far more women than men. Had attended Quaker meeting in Torquay until blackout interfered. There is a Quaker meeting first Sunday in month at home of *elder* near us: I attend regularly, and my wife sometimes: attendance 5 to 10.

Have applied to Employment Exchange, have advertised in two papers but am without *gainful occupation*. (Really, I wonder how I should find time for it, even if it came! I can only give part-time because of my wife requiring me at home sometimes.) After all the talk about shortage of man-power, it is surprising that I cannot find a job.

Always lots of young airmen in town: several hotels taken over for them. They walk in a different way from soldiers: more nervy, swing arms much more vigorously. Football on the greens; running about the town with nothing on but shorts. Also, numerous Americans.

We have much more sunshine than near Manchester but also dull, chilly days and rains. Some days are Perfect, sunny and warm.

8 December 1943

My wife is ill, so I am not so free. We live a very quiet life, rarely meeting anybody or having anybody call. A week's visit from daughter-in-law was pleasant. She is at a hostel for unwell children run by Quakers near Newmarket. Her husband, our son, is in Italy.

Very uneventful life. Nothing much to expect except that we ardently wish for the war to end. Very few Air Raid Warnings, none on Saturday evenings (my fire-watching night). A rally of firewatchers was supposed to be held a few nights ago but few had come when I left. As my wife is ill, I only remained a few minutes.

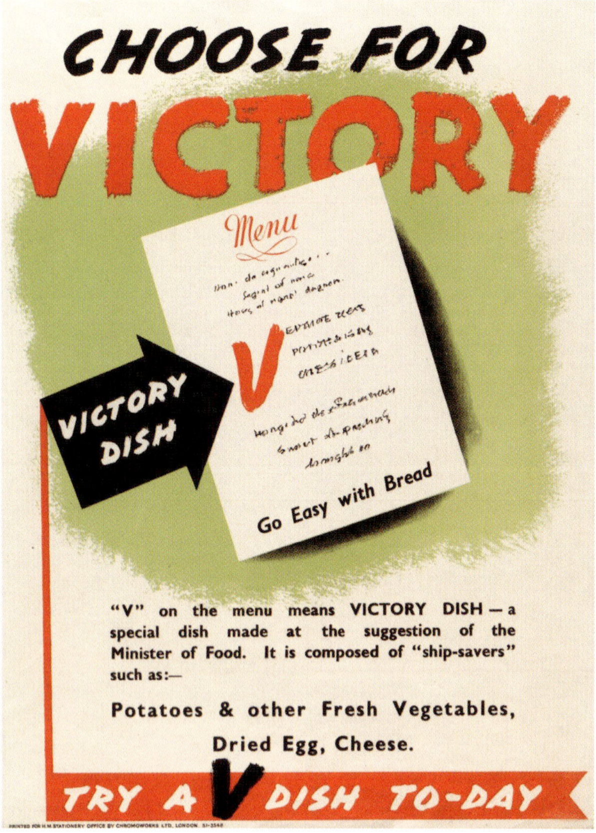
CHOOSE FOR
VICTORY
Menu
VICTORY DISH
V
Go Easy with Bread
"V" on the menu means VICTORY DISH — a special dish made at the suggestion of the Minister of Food. It is composed of "ship-savers" such as:—
Potatoes & other Fresh Vegetables,
Dried Egg, Cheese.
TRY A V DISH TO-DAY
PRINTED FOR H.M. STATIONERY OFFICE BY CHROMOWORKS LTD. LONDON

DIG FOR
VICTORY

DIG FOR VICTORY
For their sake-
GROW YOUR OWN
VEGETABLES

Your own vegetables
all the year round . . .
if you
PRINTED IN
GREAT BRITAIN
PRINTED FOR H.M. STATIONERY OFFICE
DIG FOR
VICTORY NOW

We get our stores from our local branch of the Co-operative Society with no trouble. I went today to hand in our order and could hardly get in because of the long queue. I merely handed in my order book and left at once; never stand in queues! Coal we have obtained is quite good, larger than earlier delivery. Also had a load of logs.

No cycle rides lately. I only go Sunday mornings because of traffic and the Sundays seem wet.

9th [December]

Serious development. My wife is now in a nursing home as she has partial paralysis, very quick decision. It is strange to be typing this alone in the house, and I fear I am unable to supply any more interesting matter. It will be wiser if I pack up what I have already typed and get it off, in case it gets mislaid during drastic interruptions.'

1944

In 1944 Mr Shipway engaged more with the outside world as Torquay became involved in the invasion of France which took place on 6 June.

'13 April 1944. I am very unsettled indeed: have no idea what may be in store. A few days ago I offered my services to the Friends Service Council (Quaker foreign mission) for China. I did this as exchange fluctuations make it impossible for the average Englishman to be able to subsist in China whereas I can live entirely on Chinese food and in Chinese conditions. They declined. I have since applied to the Foreign Office but have received no reply. I may merely mention these to show that anything may happen. On the other hand, I am content to remain here. I like the district and the house is convenient, with a fine rural outlook. I have let some rooms furnished. I stipulated for a vegetarian and have had four – three generations! Two children, mother and grandma. The grandma has now returned to her home in Cheshire. The husband is here over the holiday. I get on remarkably well with the tenant, try to suit her convenience in the kitchen. (I cook alternate days enough for 2 days and warm up half for breakfast the second day so as to be free from kitchen.) I have my breakfast before tenant is up. I like having the children about so this is quite satisfactory and profitable!

I still miss my wife very much and life is really somewhat miserable. I loathe just cooking for myself only. My two rooms are choked up with accumulations. I have sold lots, but lots more must go. I ought to be spending much more time in garden than I do. I set myself various tasks, go from door-to-door hawking: cruel sports, proportional representation, Socialist Christian.

A few weeks ago I visited Sidmouth and addressed the local vegetarians on A Vegetarian In China. They seemed pleased. I stayed two nights and it was a pleasant change. A few weeks before I stayed a few days with friends from Lancashire near Tiverton.

What I do with my time is a mystery! I seem always busy and yet there is little to show. Occasionally I clean my two rooms (I have done the bedroom today) but not often. The rooms are too littered up to attend to them properly. I am still selling things but it is unsatisfactory and I do not enjoy it.

I paid £750 for the house and have now instructed an estate agent that he can sell it for £1,200 of which I will donate £400 to the National Trust. I really do not want to leave the house until something makes me leave. Some folk blame me for restricting the purchaser to rich people, but that is how I feel. I attended the auction of a bungalow which fetched £1,320 and so I decided this house is worth £1,200 and I do not want to sell it to a person who does not appreciate the rural view.

Lots of Americans all around; processions of cars and lorries of all sorts.

I attend Quaker meetings, often Unitarian services occasionally and Spiritualist meetings sometimes. Before my wife's death I had become friendly with a vegetarian and then discovered him to be a Spiritualist. Since my wife's death I have been making *scientific investigations* but so far I am unconvinced either way. The mediums seem genuine folk, and yet it all seems weird. The messages reporting to come through from

***203-6** Wartime posters encouraging kitchen economy and domestic vegetable gardens.*

207 *Poster acknowledging the financial support of Ascension Island in the work of the Red Cross, c1939-45.*

208 *Black American musicians of the Special United States Naval Construction Battalion, noted as 'somewhere in England', 14 Dec. 1944.*

my wife and my mother are that I should not make hurried decisions but await something later (really what I am doing).

It is beautiful to live here; I enjoy the sea and views. I enjoy occasional cycle rides.

12 May 1944

There seems a great scarcity of workmen for anything essential and yet non-essential work can be seen in progress. Near here a long boundary wall has taken the place of a fence which was by no means in poor condition. A bricklayer has been working on this for several weeks. A bungalow visible from our back windows is having extensive alterations and men have been working there for several days. A large bay window is being put in and alterations made to the roof.

Vast numbers of American troops are all around here, always busy with works of various kinds. From my windows I can see prominent red crosses on large tents, evidently intended as field hospitals. There are a lot more about 2 miles away. Vehicles of all kinds, very light to very heavy, are constantly hurrying in both directions, sometimes long processions. One wonders what it is all about, after many weeks of it the consumption of petrol must be enormous. A surprisingly large proportion of the Americans are coloured.

Since the loss of my wife in December, I have been feeling very unsettled… I had a tenant for three rooms until last Monday. We got along very well on the whole, but I felt compelled to suggest that she might possibly be more comfortable elsewhere, as she had very modern ideas about not checking children, and it became intolerable. I found the two-year-old son hammering with a bottle on the wardrobe mirror! So now I am alone and have started spring cleaning.

Almost every afternoon I sally forth to hawk literature. I have different districts for different *causes:* cruel sports, proportional representation, Socialist Christian. I have leaflets to hand to non-purchasers who are numerous but on the whole people are quite friendly. It gives me an opportunity of seeing some beautiful gardens. There seem to be no lack of gardeners.

We have had lots of wonderfully warm weather with

209 *American servicemen in an English pub, as depicted by Herman B. Vestal, 1945.*

vivid sunshine. The trees and hedges are well advanced, more like the end of May. Some early mornings have been cold.

13th

What else shall I type to fill up with? Yesterday evening I went to call on an elderly friend (age 77) who has recently moved from a large house to a somewhat smaller one. The new house has a very wonderful view of part of Torbay and of Torquay in the distance, while nearby are beautiful gardens and - what appealed to me most of all - houses designed by architects and of dignity and beauty. Especially, that they had steep roofs. Nothing detracts from the appearance of a district than houses with roofs other than steep. Of course if people insist on flat ceilings it is expensive to put steep roofs but it is quite possible to use a steep roof with no extra expense, if the roof is allowed to shear off part of the room next ceiling. The houses all around where I live, including my own, are ugly because the roofs are not steep. Letchworth Garden City is wonderful because of this. There is a regulation that the roofs at the ridge must not exceed a right angle. (I lived at Letchworth many years ago, about 20 years).

15 June 1944

There were evidences of preparation for the Second Front several days earlier. The bay was unusually full of ships of many kinds. I have a note for Friday 19th May particularly. On Sunday night 28th there was a severe air raid. No bombs were dropped quite near me and no windows were broken nearby. But several bombs were dropped in scattered districts, mostly Torquay, where there was quite a bit of damage done and several people killed. People generally seem to have remained calm but a friend told me of [a] young woman who was entirely unnerved and hysterical. The first definite sign of [the] Second Front was on Thursday, June 1. I happened to have gone down to the main road about 8.30am and found children excited because the buses, which usually take them to school, had stopped running. Rumour said trains also had stopped. During the day traffic was diverted from the main road so as to give any army lorries a clear run. For some time cyclists were allowed, but for a time they were made to walk and not ride. (What earthly difference could this make? Absolute tyranny!) The bay continued full of ships of all kinds until Sunday 4th but on Monday 5th the bay was empty and on Tuesday we heard the attack had begun. What a relief! I felt so exasperated and contemptuous, for years back I had written to Churchill suggesting that a forlorn hope attempt by elderly volunteers should be made, and I volunteered. This was when Russia was being driven back.

We are wanting rain very badly indeed. We are asked not to *waste water*. All water from washing, washing-up etc. I store for watering the garden and also use some from the tap but not much. I have not used a single clothing coupon! I think I ought to be awarded the Order of Merit or something like that! Also, I have depended upon the garden for all vegetables since January except that I spent eight pence for lettuce and cress when my daughter-in-law visited. This is excepting potatoes which we were advised <u>not</u> to grow. This means I abstain from what I have not in the garden, and of course the diet is more monotonous than most people would like. I gathered stinging nettles as a vegetable for weeks to give variety! I have not tasted rhubarb. But I keep very well. A touch of lumbago made me creep about bent like an old man, but it soon went.

Where'er I go,
Folk shout *Hullo*

How's the lumbaGO?

While I have forgotten all about it!

I still go around hawking. The majority decline and a very few even decline a free leaflet. Some purchase readily, while others ponder and hesitate. I never return home with none sold. It is very humble work but it must have its small influence and no opportunities of exerting greater influence come my way. I always seem busy, have no *leisure*. I have patching jobs to do while listening to talks on the wireless. I mark the items on the *Radio Times* which I wish to listen to and arrange my gardening etc. accordingly. It is now six months since my wife died and I still feel her loss very much. I had instructed estate agents to offer my house for sale at £1,200 of which I would give £400 to the National Trust, as I did not feel justified in pocketing it myself. This was a *challenge to fate* but now I have withdrawn the offer and decided to remain here. This has made me feel far more settled.

210 *Paper bag encouraging food economy.*

21 July 1944

Last month I mentioned absence of rain but now this has been amply rectified. The hill opposite me was turning red but now it is green again. Garden produce is coming on well. I buy no vegetables except potatoes. Lots of wee raspberries in the ground and I invite folk to come and help themselves.

The barbed wire is being removed from the [sea]front and it makes it very much nicer. With evacuees and removal of ban, the population is increasing.

I always keep busy: am finding time for Mass Observation stuff because heavy rain prevents my intended expedition. In addition to my hawking of literature, I have been asked by Women for Westminster to tackle jobs and also have been collecting Commonwealth subscriptions and selling *Commonwealth Review*. I was also invited by Sidmouth Vegetarians to give them another visit and address.

No bomb attack of any sort since I sent last diary. The place seems strange without the throngs of Americans all around. There are still a few about, sometimes more than a few, sometimes rather hilarious, inclined to maul young women about - some of whom object, but some not. There are numerous Military Police about but I have never seen these interfere with their nationals: I have never happened to see them when their nationals in the vicinity are hilarious [boisterously merry].

I am now alone in the house not having secured another tenant (who must be strictly vegetarian).

I am a amateur printer and occasionally am *moved* to print slips. One I printed some weeks ago on the Responsibility of Women led to the Women for Westminster movement being mentioned to me. Now I have set up type for a slip Pacifists Should Repent. I sent this to the Ministry of Information to be censored and the approval came very quickly and I shall now go ahead and print a few on second-hand paper (postal rappers, etc).

22 July

I find it difficult to think of matter to complete this page as my life is very uneventful. I am generally up very early, sometimes 5.30, and find jobs in the garden until I can see properly in the house. I still have some spring-cleaning to do but it is mostly over.

Now that evacuees and visitors are arriving, there is trouble over the buses being filled up so quickly. The services are excellent and the woman conductors of

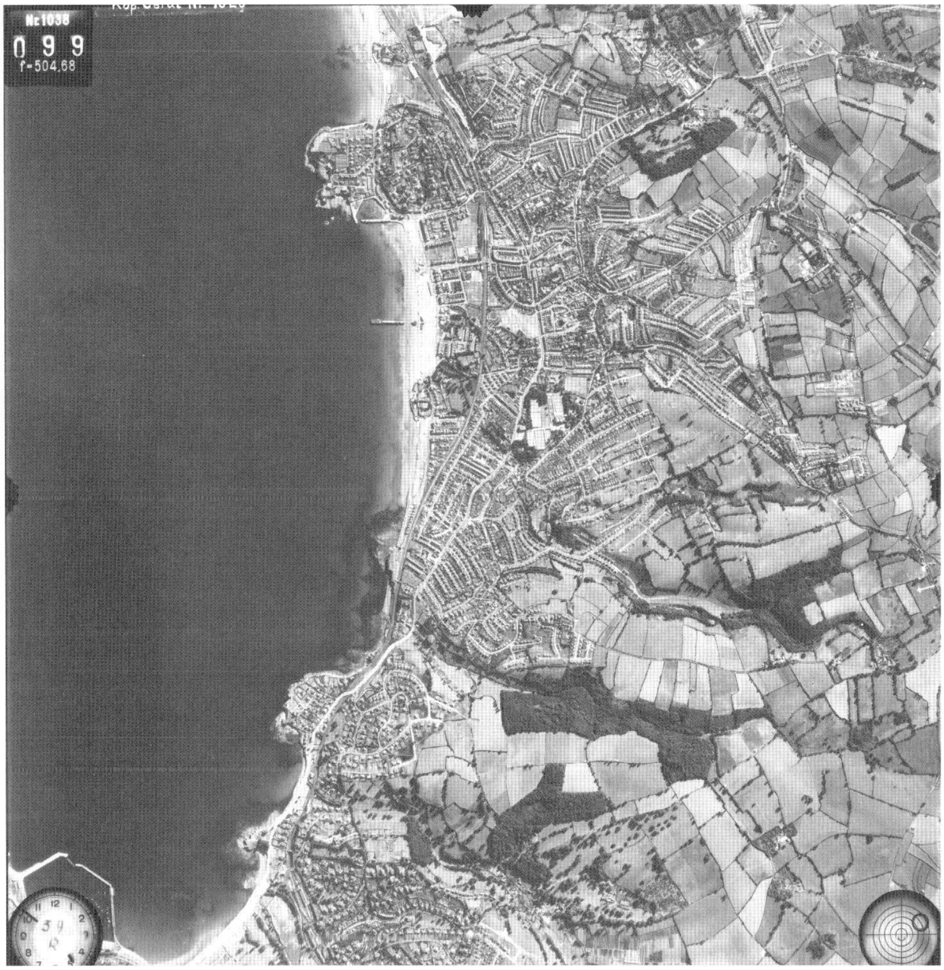

211 Luftwaffe photograph of Paignton, 3 September 1940.

a high grade. It is suggested they turn to this work in preference to munitions. They are dressed with khaki overalls with scarlet trimming and lettering, which is very effective; very different from slouchy uniforms in some other parts. The evening run from Torquay is beautiful, with the sun on Brixham and the hills above. Torbay impresses me as being very beautiful.

Gun practice takes place frequently and at the outset it is startling. I was at a meeting when a gun started near at hand and I felt sorry for one woman who started very noticeably.

What else? I am keen on finishing this because I want to type an important letter and here I am sitting awaiting *inspiration*.

I have been in touch with Spiritualists, hoping that I might be put through to my wife who died last December. I regret no success but I shall continue. I am really perplexed. A friend finds it easy to scoff at the whole business as a fraud; but to me it is not so easy, as some of the folk seem quite the reverse of rogues and humbugs. The congregations are predominantly women.

21 August 1944

I sent a letter to the Friends Relief Service asking if they had any vegetarian evacuees who could occupy my house and as an afterthought, I said that, as I had nobody dependent upon me and was not unduly perturbed at the thought of death, I would take the place of anybody in the office who is unduly distressed by the flying bombs. Not wanted at office, but they would be grateful if I would act as domestic colleague at a hostel in Hampstead for four weeks…

I have married again! Very soon after my first wife died, last December, I concluded I should marry again. I had been in the habit of reading to my wife and wheeling her out in invalid chair. Unsuccessful in finding some elderly man or woman for this, I reckoned I should have to find some elderly woman as wife. Then cooking for myself alone revolted me, then the question of house and house-full of accumulations, perplexed me, especially as it was so difficult to fix reasonable prices for selling towels, curtains etc. and I realised much would never sell but cost good money if on remarriage I wished to restock a home. Then I wished for children to prevent the Shipway clan from extinction. Much puzzled as to how to find a suitable wife; vegetarian, tolerant of my economy and other fanaticisms. A niece (wife's sister's daughter), who was known to me well for many years, came for a short holiday having been working vigorously at nursing. She naturally found me somewhat desolate and took pity on my lone condition and suggested coming as housekeeper but this would be awkward when I found my second wife. However, as she is quite willing to be vegetarian, and knows my *little ways*, we concluded it would be better for her to have the superior status of wife and were married on August 10th. She could not leave her nursing without notice, and I wished to keep my promise as domestic colleague, so we separated three days after marriage and met and returned together to Paignton on September 14th.

Yesterday 21st we attended a discussion group of Women for Westminster and I was asked to take the chair (the only man). Fair discussion on housing. Rather sad tendency for three groups to be talking together at same time! Wife became member (I joined weeks ago).

14 October 1944

Occasionally see Americans about, zips, lorries. At Churston between here and Brixham, I noticed a vast store of barrels in a field and possibly this may be a petrol store. This surmise may be supported by the fact that I noticed a large pipeline running for a long distance, over a mile probably. Several airmen about, sometimes drilling, often a few in mufti among the uniforms. Also bands of sailors drilling. Last Tuesday I saw them with gas masks! Running about, one on cycle. Of course, no bombs here. Last night several steamers in Torbay, but generally very little…

3 December 1944

Barbed wire defences along the seafront have now almost disappeared. Men have been working with pneumatic drills removing concrete pill-boxes and forts, and are still working at removing a rough stone and concrete wall all along the front. Seeing what shortage of men there is for repairing houses damaged in raids, all this work seems to be quite wrong. It should be postponed till the houses are again in order. However, it is very nice having the seafront nice again. How very much I enjoy walking by the seafront.

Often there seems to be lots of soldiers about, of different kinds, including lots of Americans. Still, there are army lorries and zips and dispatch riders at much too great speeds.

Absolute freedom from anything like air raids. Most people regard the war is over, as far as we are concerned. Blackout regulations have not been rescinded here but the rigid observance is not continued…'

Mr Shipway continued to live in Paignton until his death in 1961.[215]

33. Robert Wright, Driver, 1943-4

Robert Leslie Wright (1899-1983), a married forty-five-year-old delivery driver who lived at 65 St Mary's Park in Collaton, was a directive respondent from 1942 through to 1950. In October 1943 he wrote about his personal prejudices:

'With regard to prejudices against habits, I cannot think of any that do not come more properly under the heading of *manners and behaviour* such as spitting indoors, which I definitely dislike. Another aversion is that man who digs you in the ribs or slaps you on the back. With regard to looks, I admit to a preference for smart good-looking women rather than ugly, untidy ones, but who wouldn't? I dislike the habit of whistling and object to the person who pushes in out of turn in a queue.'

Evacuees

Mr Wright composed two particularly vivid accounts of Paignton in 1944. In one he described the sudden movement of people:

'*Fly bomb* evacuees started coming here even before the lifting of the travel ban on this area (South Devon coast). When the ban was lifted there was a great deal of criticism locally because holiday-makers as well as evacuees were permitted to travel. Naturally, the hotel and boarding-house keepers wanted the holiday people. Recognised business houses were excused from the billeting which the private householder thought unfair, because he had to take evacuees when he wanted to make a bit of extra money taking visitors. Private residents, who did not want either the evacuee or the visitor, were annoyed because as one woman said *They'll come here and take all our food again*. A workman said *the trains and buses are bad enough now. The queues will be worse than ever*. On the other hand a boarding housekeeper remarked *Thank goodness, I don't know what we should've done if they kept the ban on all summer* and a hotel keeper *A lot of people would have been unable to pay their rates and many would have had to close down altogether.*

So we got a flood of mixed evacuees and visitors. This has certainly put a most severe strain on local transport. Workers going from one town to the next are crowded off buses by holiday-makers. This is a very sore point, particularly at midday and the evening, as there are long queues all day after the early morning. The food situation seems to have been fairly well taken care of, although there is a serious shortage of café accommodation, largely due to lack of staff, and there were long queues two or three times daily at all eating places. In the private houses the evacuees seem to have been fairly well-received. A welfare worker remarked that they seemed *a cleaner a lot than last time*. A number of hostels have been opened by the local council (more than in 1940 to 1941) for children and mother. A beach-chair ticket-collector remarked *I have never seen so many pregnant women in my life, like a lot of b.... prize marrows*.'

A few weeks later he described the mood in Paignton as being 'impatient':

'I meet a lot of people here in the course of my work (delivering laundry) and the spirit prevailing at the moment, and for some time now, is one of impatience.

My boss is impatient because he is short of labour and cannot maintain his turnover although there is an abundance of work to be done.

The work girls are impatient because they cannot keep pace with the work which comes pouring in, because of shopping difficulties and in many cases because their men folk are away. Also, because they are not afraid of losing their jobs, they do not hide their impatience.

My customers - housewives and/or boarding-house keepers - are impatient because they are kept waiting longer than ever before for clean linen, because of high costs and shortages, and because they have many bookings but little or no staff to cope with same. One gets the impression that they worry more about the day the laundry is coming home than about the day the war will be over. Or rather that they are only anxious for the war to hurry up and finish so that they can get on with a job of making money and look forward to getting more staff, more supplies, more visitors and more money. They have not the same sympathy without those suffering in other countries that they had at the time when occasional raids brought the war nearer home to them.'

Directive: the end of the war

There was an unexpected end to the war in the town:

'VJ Day was celebrated quietly here in Paignton (small seaside town). Some excitement previous night when Canadian airmen made a bonfire, breaking down council signs, fencing, flagpoles, etc. but some of these were rescued by local residents.'

Weeks later Mr Wright presented his thoughts about the future including regarding the atom bomb ('Wonder and admiration at skill and knowledge of scientific workers. For the future I consider the implications, on balance, good. Have always held that the worse and more widespread the effects of war, the sooner it would be abandoned as a means of attempting to gain ends.'). He had expressed his feelings about the end of the war ('Chief feeling one of great relief that the slaughter in Europe is ended. Particular relief for the people of London where I have relatives and friends. Next thoughts go to returned prisoners and liberated peoples.'). In 1945 he leaned politically to the left: he commented that his 'present attitudes' were towards the Conservative Party (suspicious), Labour Party (sympathetic), Liberal Party (tolerant), Communist Party (sympathetic) and Commonwealth Party (admiring).

Mr Wright was listed in the 1921 census as working as a journalist's assistant in Yorkshire. His life after writing for MO was not apparently recorded: little has been gathered other than that he died in Devon in 1983, ten years after his wife Doris had passed on.[216]

212 The seventeenth-century establishment of the naval dockyard remains at the heart of Plymouth's identity. Thomas Rowlandson captured its busy nature in 1817.

PLYMOUTH

The union in 1914 of Plymouth, Stonehouse and Devonport created Devon's largest city but by then the port had been greater in all but name for more than a century. Its traditional mercantile role was supplemented in 1691 by the establishment of a royal dockyard and by 1931 the city had a population of 208,182. In 1945 Lord Astor commented upon the sense of self-identify in Plymouth:

> 'What is the spirit of Drake which still persists in Plymouth and the spirit of the Navy? It is a strange thing, invisible, intangible, imponderable, and we know now, of an audacity well-nigh incredible.'

Tom Harrisson, one of the founders of MO, later cited Plymothians' belief in themselves when assessing the war's effect on them. The organisation conducted a series of investigations into Plymouth, its greatest effort in the county.[217]

Plymouth's large and impressive collection of war memorials on the Hoe kept war a constant presence in the city's daily life through the 1930s. This was more so than in any other part of Devon. Plymothians were already more security-conscious and better-defended but the prospect of war in the 1930s ensured Plymouth was Devon's most protected community.

It had been largely anticipated that the port would be a strategic target for the Luftwaffe. The first air raid alert sounded on 30 June 1940 and the first air raid took place shortly afterwards, on 6 July. The last attack occurred on 30 April 1944. During those four years there were 602 alerts and 59 attacks. According to official calculations, this caused the deaths of 1,172 people and there were 3,269 injuries. Seven individuals were declared 'missing'. The number of damaged buildings which had to be demolished was 3,754. Despite the danger, local children were not evacuated until 1941.[218] In June 1941 an MO Writer in the South East related what he described as a piece of typical English understatement. His mother on holiday in Devon had informed him 'we met several people removed from Plymouth, that is not a very desirable place to live in, from all accounts'.[219]

Plymouth's MO diarists commented on air raids as did others living across Britain. One from Hampshire visited in June 1942 and was critical:

> 'Plymouth has been convalescent after the raids, while remembering that they had been badly served by their own representatives. No water, no adequate fire service, no alternative accommodation for the homeless and so on. When other fire services came to help the hoses didn't fit, no nozzles and so on, same old story, but all the people to whom I spoke were grateful for the

help given (especially to the WVS for their service) by the ARP services from other areas not blitzed and safe. Shops have reopened away from the centre of the town, there were many luxuries available for those who knew the way and people were delighted to share their luxuries with us. This was refreshing to us after 2 years of Hampshire temperament.'[220]

On 9 July 1941 a sailor at Torpoint recorded rumours he had heard about the opposite side of the Tamar River:

> 'During the morning, and throughout the day, hear a number of rumours about last night's raid from people coming into the sick quarters from the camp proper. One is that the naval dockyard at Devonport was severely damaged, another that a bomb landed on our own establishment over the way and a third that the victualling yard (whatever that may be) at Devonport was destroyed. I believe that the story about victualling yard is largely correct: various sources confirm that it has suffered extensive damage.'[221]

Other MO Writers also remarked upon wartime Plymouth including from London in 1939 ('I am in Plymouth at time of writing and here the war seems very remote, apart from an abundance of uniforms. The local inhabitants have only heard of air-raid warnings as *something which has happened in Edinburgh*.'), from Buckinghamshire in 1941 ('I was out to tea and someone said that a wounded Nazi airman was in hospital in Plymouth. He wept and said that he had intended to drop his bombs into the sea and was horrified at the damage to the town.'), from Kent in 1941 ('I hear that Plymouth has been bombed to bits and is in a far worse state than Southampton or Coventry or London. Thousands go every night and sleep on the hills outside the town, often with little or no covering. The place is in a terrible condition.'), from Edinburgh in 1942 ('Plymouth letter – M & her friend – teachers - have at last got a house – one of twins – the other half blown off by blast - land mine. Rent reduced from £96 to £86 owing to damage. Much too expensive for them but they are glad to get their furniture together and have a home. Poor souls, they have had a hard time after their blitzing.'), from Cardiff in 1942 (railway stop at 'Plymouth where I had an hour to wait. Terrible damage at Plymouth, whole streets of houses roofless, but saw none at Exeter - though it has suffered greatly.'), from Hampshire in 1943 ('my mate tells me his Plymouth sister is in trouble again. Another house busted over her head. This is the third or fourth time but she still sticks to her hubby and Plymouth.'), from London in 1944 ('Aunt Win is in Plymouth now, she has moved from Sherborne and is in charge of the officers' block there. She seems to be pleasantly impressed by everything at Plymouth, apparently there is much more luxury than there was at Sherborne.') and from Hertfordshire in 1944 ('George Hesketh, Flying Officer RAF, a gynaecologist and surgeon by profession, came for the weekend. Faith lives with him in a flat in Exeter when they can, with a view to matrimony when he gets a divorce. This is kept a secret from part of her, and our, family and makes life very complicated for her. In Exeter they are regarded by their neighbours as an ideal, happily-married couple. George went into the RAF in 1940, was out for part of 1942 and 43, and then was called back in. But from the Service point of view it's his legal wife who counts. He is also involved in a bankruptcy, so all is not well.').[222]

In the summer of 1942 a former Plymothian lamented:

> 'From Mrs Voke and from Mr Bruce I have heard of the damage at Plymouth but never a word about the spots that I treasure. Mr Bruce could not fasten on the Technical College at all (my old school, though called Devonport Second School by day). I think that must be gone for how could he fail to see it if it were standing. Nor could he figure Stoke Damerel church. How dear is that memory! And there in the *Observer* today was my article on the way Plymouth has tackled the problems caused by the blitz and a paragraph reads that many of the parish churches in Devonport are unusable and their function has been taken over *by the ancient mother church of Stoke Damerel*. Stoke Damerel is safe. That is good news.'[223]

On 2 August special correspondent Edith Oakley described the Stout Heart of Plymouth in *The Observer*; she felt that what forcibly struck visitors after three years of war was 'the resilient, irrepressible spirit' of Plymouth. She conceded that it had lost much of its most familiar and characteristic aspects and that a great part had been reduced to ruins. Miss Oakley highlighted that at Devonport the destruction had left 'an island of working-class houses and tenements almost untouched'.[224]

Early in 1941 the Ministry of Information established an Intelligence office in Plymouth and compiled weekly reports of public opinion, reactions, morale and rumours. Intelligence had been gathered in a less organised mode in 1940 including in July ('Anxiety at Plymouth inasmuch as people state that a German raider was able to dodge in and out the clouds for over an hour eluding AA fire without a single British plane appearing.', 'Complaints again from Plymouth of lack of co-ordination of sirens.', 'Plymouth,

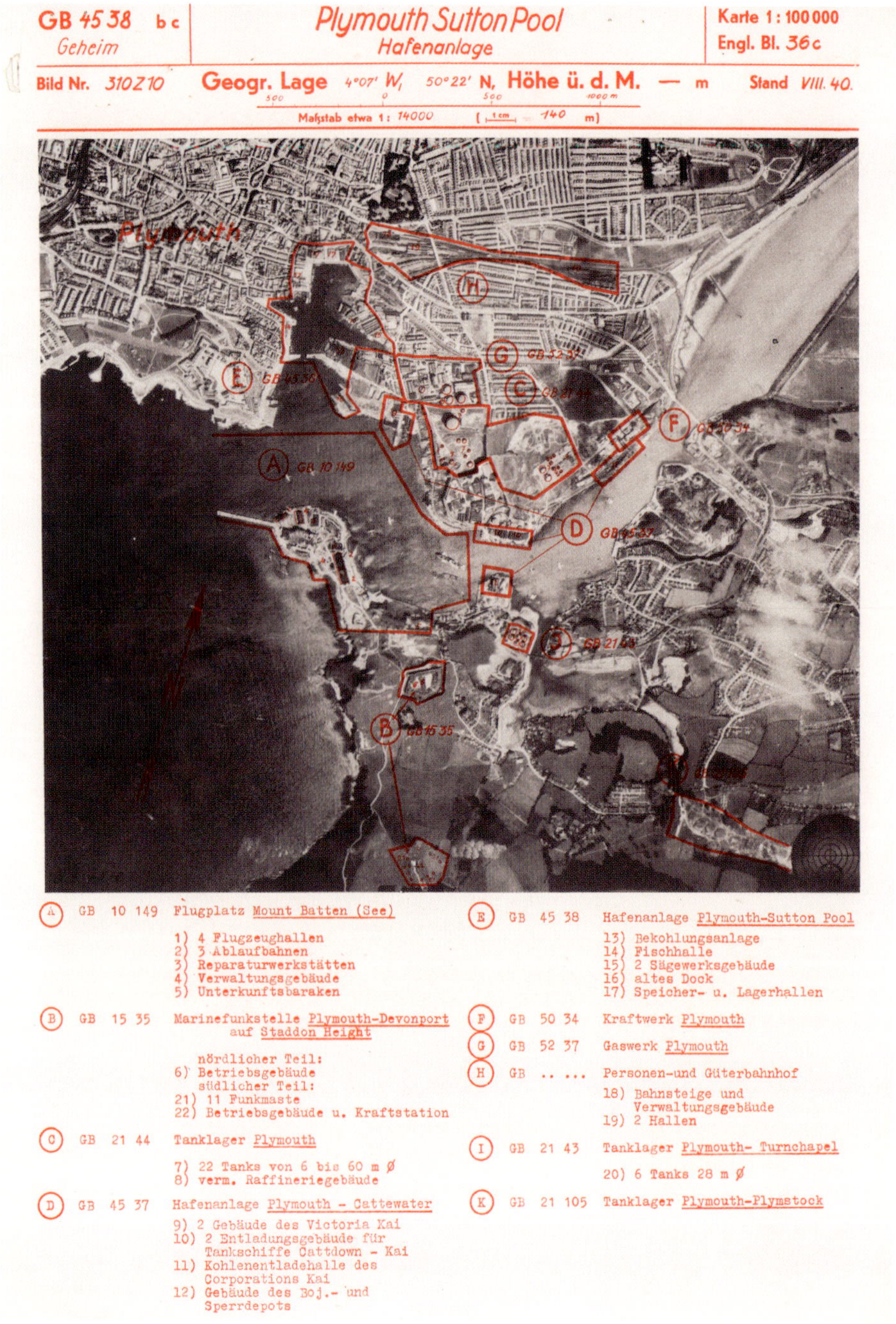

213 German aerial photograph of Sutton Harbour, Plymouth, 1940.

which has suffered heavily, is standing up to the raids philosophically. There is, however, a good deal of anxiety at the absence of detailed casualty figures.', 'Morale still high in Bristol and Plymouth, particularly among working-class. Increased strengthening of defences having good effect on morale. Return of children to evacuated areas causing some concern. Suggested that gossip about dates of invasion has had an adverse effect.').

Reports continued in August ('Some concern in Plymouth that an enemy plane was able to circle for several hours without a fighter appearing. People consider that the prospects of invasion are receding. There are rumours of supposed air raid damage') and September ('After several days of comparative peace people of Plymouth are expecting a big attack, but except for a feeling that deep shelters should be provided, there is little concern and no alarm').

The Ministry compiled an extensive report on Plymouth in March 1941:

> 'In Plymouth the people stood up to the blitz "exceptionally well". For the first few nights afterwards, many went out to the country in cars and slept in them.3. There is some criticism of the civic organisation at Plymouth on the ground that it has not stood up to the blitz too well; this is attributed to the concentration of local power in "a few elderly hands".4. The first raid opened within half an hour of the departure of the King and Queen who had been touring the city. During the day, the rediffusion relay system (which serves about 10,000 homes) broadcast details of the Royal tour. The public linked the raid and the Royal visit together, attributing the one to the other, and suggesting that the local rediffusion of the details of the tour was unwise. The rumour that the blitz was due to the Royal visit has been reported from other regions, and is similar to the recent rumours that other blitzes followed visits from prominent people. It is reported that as an aftermath of the Portsmouth raids, there is an undercurrent of uneasiness among civilians as it is believed that certain naval and military establishments in the neighbourhood are being evacuated. Civilian workers, both in the dockyards and the civil defence services, claim that they should not be treated with less consideration than the fighting services. The facts are that one Naval unit only has been evacuated; this was because its accommodation had been destroyed.'[225]

At this time four other reports were written by MO (**40-43**).

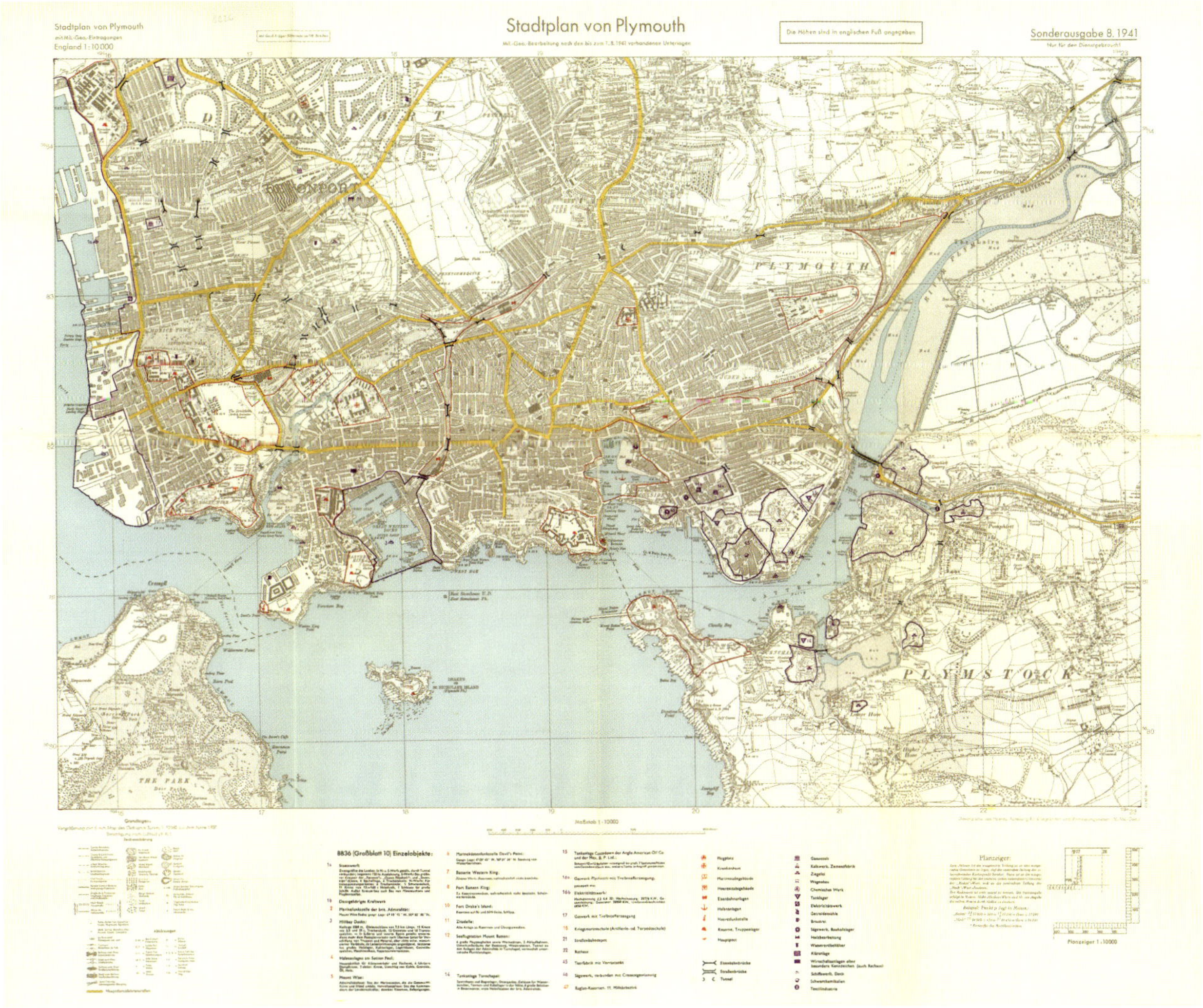

***214** German street plan (Stadtplan) of Plymouth, with purple symbols for industrial sites, red for strategic sites and principal roads in yellow, 1941. (David Rumsey Collection).*

***215** Luffwaffe photograph of the Barbican, 30 August 1940.*

34. Edward Glanfield, Student, 1937

In 1937 Edward Dalzell Glanfield (1916-1997) was an undergraduate at Exeter College, Oxford, and during the summer break resided with his parents at 4 Lockyer Road. That year he wrote four day-surveys for Mass Observation; three concerned Devon on 12 July, 12 September and 13 December.[226]

12 July 1937

The first day-survey detailed life in Plymouth:

***216** 4 Lockyer Road, Plymouth, the home of Mr Edward Glanfield in 1937.*

'Occupation: normally this day would have been an ordinary one in the life of an Oxford undergraduate second year on long vacation, i.e. a certain amount of reading for one School (Honour School of Jurisprudence in my case) mixed with a certain amount of dissipation.

***217** In the late seventeenth century the Royal Navy began extending its operations to sites around the ancient town of Plymouth. Hendrik Danckerts depicted the port in 1673.*

As it happened, I had only returned from five days in London the previous Saturday and from the moment of my arrival I had to spend almost all my time in entertaining a Fellow of my college who invited himself for the weekend. He left on the morning of July 12th. I generally have to write several letters on reaching home once more. This occasion was no exception. Thus July 12 was abnormal in so far it was largely devoted to correspondence. (Perhaps I should add that I enjoy writing letters and take some time over them. I hardly know anyone else who does so.)

Health: unnoticeable, therefore good for me.

Weather: grey skies and intermittent drizzle the whole day, with a temperature warm enough to make the atmosphere very clammy.

Description of surroundings: My home lies between the beginning of the residential district of Plymouth and the beginning of the city itself. It is near the main road running from the city centre to Tavistock in northern Devon, also near a large and hideous council school and the modern showrooms of the Barton Motor Company. The house is un-detached, forming part of a row of almost exactly similar houses. Inside they are large and roomy (three storeys), outside they are examples of late nineteenth-century architecture of a better sort (which is not saying much). Their gardens, though well-kept, are of an apologetic size, front and back. The value of the property has much depreciated since my family first came here in 1925 and two or three houses for sale or to let have been empty for some time.

My work, reading law, is done either at home or at Oxford. I can think of nothing interesting to say under this head.

As for Plymouth itself, Devon in the main is not an industrial county, and Plymouth depends most for its wealth upon the Royal Naval Dockyards. There is a small RAF sea-plane base by the Cattewater and Army and Marine barracks. Recent manoeuvres, however, suggest that while Plymouth is well-fortified against sea attack, it is extremely vulnerable from the air. It is also a port of call for various lines. The accumulating silt in the Hamoaze (estuary of the Tamar) makes a tender necessary but the Great West Railway boat train often reaches London in under four hours. There is a fair-sized fishing fleet harboured up the Plym estuary, but it seems to have fallen on evil days.

With regard to industries, Plymouth has bacon and baby-food factories, the famous Coates Gin Distillery and a brewery (Dartmoor water is exceptionally soft), dyeing and cleaning works, and printing presses employed by some of the best London publishers e.g. William Brand. Outside the city is a large receiving station of the Rediffusion Company (which relays wireless programs to subscribers' houses by wire). Car-selling flourishes. One firm alone has sold well over

1,000 cars since last September.

For the rest, Plymouth depends on entertainment and tourists. It has now only one theatre (purely variety and reviews) but there are at least a dozen large cinemas and more are being built. There is no foreshore and bathing is indifferent. Plymouth will never be a seaside resort despite all efforts to make it one. The town is badly built and contains little of interest but there is a reasonably good centre for attacking Dartmoor and other parts of Devonshire worth seeing.

Report on July 12th

7am Roused by daylight; went to sleep again, trying to make up for several late nights.

8.15am roused again by early morning tea. Thoroughly awake this time. Continued reading Sayer's *Busman's Honeymoon*, though I don't usually read in bed before getting up.

9am Breakfast gong. Got up reluctantly.

9.30am Down to breakfast. Unable to read *Western Morning News* as usual out of politeness to my guest – a Fellow of my college. As a result, I finished by the time everyone else had done so.

10am Taxi arrived for my guest 10 minutes too soon. This garage is always over-punctual. They never come less than 5 minutes before they are expected.

10.10am Antiquated platform-ticket machine refused to work. I asked for a ticket at the booking office. The clerk (wearing a felt hat) politely insisted that the machine would work. I tried again; no result. Clerk wound up machine with a huge crank; still no result, whereupon he inserted a penny from his own pocket, which did do the trick. Told me I must have put my penny in *wrong side up*.

10.15am On platform with my guest. Large crowd, mostly families with small children, probably returning from early holiday. Also, soldiers and a few naval officers.

10.25am Enter that abominable train, the West to North of England (so-called) Express. It stops at every station it possibly can. Great West Railway loco, 4.6.0 *Broome Hall*, badly needing a clean, and a train almost entirely composed of L.M.S. stock, looking filthy and decrepit. Already fairly full of passengers from Cornwall and a now-seething mob expecting to find room on it but only a restaurant car is added. At the rear, indeed, it seemed that a coach was being taken off. While trying to settle my guest comfortably in his compartment, I noticed that manners went by the board in the attempt to grab a seat. I imagine that most of these passengers were North Country. Devonshire people are generally far more solid and easy-going. However, there is rarely enough room on this train, the best of a poor service to the North. I have noticed an atmosphere of shoddiness and inefficiency over the Great West Railway of late, most unusual for this company. And why so many railway accidents this year?

10.35am On return home, saw that Great West Railway have started enlarging North Road Station. They haven't much room to do it.

10.45 – 1.15pm Rest of morning spent in attending to arrears of correspondence and to seeing a garage-owner about a second-hand car. He told me this is an awkward time for buying them.

1.15pm Lunch, a fairly substantial meal for the sake of my small sister who does not stay up for dinner. I am eating much more for lunch at home than I do at Oxford but, so far this vacation, it has not made me feel like a boiled owl as it usually does, so have withheld the change in diet I meant to make for myself on returning home. Just as well perhaps, my Oxford lunch Ryvita, butter and a glass of Rioja might offend the cook.

2pm – 3pm Reading Dorothy Sayers and digesting.

3.15pm Went for usual afternoon *constitutional*. Air still clammy and oppressive. Pavements wet with drizzle and a few leaves blown down by a slight gale the night before made my progress slippery. Little to be observed: one or two old ladies probably paying afternoon calls, tradesmen's vans and errand boys, a number of large cars passing on the Tavistock Road mostly containing only the driver, a bicycle with a small Union Jack fixed to the front mudguard and several nursemaids with their charges, all of the former being unprepossessing and some downright ugly. However, the servant problem in Plymouth is acute. There would almost be murder done if one of our own two maids thought that the other was getting more time off than herself. I noticed that some prams were fitted with a kind of stream-line mudguard. This is probably meant to pander to the nurses' desire for smart equipment quite as much as to amuse the child.

4pm Noticed a small crowd of mothers waiting for their children outside a council school – only one man amongst them. Such scraps of talk as I heard seemed to refer to the progress of said children.

4.20pm (after children had been let out of council school). Watched two little boys from top window. They were grubbing about in a gutter-puddle for what looked like match-sticks. One pushed the other over; the latter didn't seem to mind. Then they flung wet leaves at each other. No particular game seemed to be on at the moment; there are, or at least there used to be, seasonal bouts of whipping-tops, marbles, etc. played along the street on the way home.

I passed the rest of the day in reading, writing and eating. The weather was so unpleasant that I did not go out more than I had to. Thus, it gave little scope for Mass Observation. Nothing else happened that is worthy of report.'

Mr Glanfield later wrote about Belstone. (7) Until 1942 he served in the Royal Army Service Corps and subsequently worked as a school teacher including at Brambletye School which was normally at East Grinstead in West Sussex but was evacuated to Lynton during the war. A former student has recalled him as 'a wonderful man, a fierce disciplinarian but very fair'. Mr Glanfield died in Hertfordshire on 21 October 1997.[227]

35. Thomas Colston, Clerk, 1938

On 1 August two teenage boys from Ely in Cardiff had a one-day adventure in Plymouth. Thomas J. Colston (1921-1969) and his brother George (1923-) may have been on a lark. Equally, they may have simply gone to Plymouth in order to fill out the day-survey.[228] Thomas listed his age as 17½.

31 July 1938

'At 12.00 midnight on Sunday July 31st, I was standing with my brother, who is younger than myself, on the Cardiff General Station, awaiting the arrival of the 12.30am train to Plymouth.

The train set out punctually at 12.30 and for the next 5 hours we thundered through the countryside towards Plymouth, our destination. Dawn began to break at about 4.30am and we could dimly see that we were travelling with only a wall between us and the sea. I was awake throughout the whole of the journey, but my brother slept a good bit.

It was quite light when we arrived in Plymouth Station (North Road) and, after vainly trying to get some food at the station restaurant, we set off into the town to find some café that might cater for night and early morning visitors. Strangely enough, we were unable to find one, although we searched all over Plymouth and it was not until 9.00am that we were able to find anything to eat.

We stopped at a small café cum sweet-shop and ordered cold, cooked ham, bread and butter and tea, the whole of which cost us 1/6 per head. There was little tea and its quality was not good. The ham was salty but plentiful and, though, perhaps, on any ordinary occasion I would not have stomached it, we were by this time so utterly weary with hunger that we would have eaten much worse than salty ham.

After our meal we set off, refreshed, into the heart of the town. After looking around for a few minutes, we set off towards the Hoe. Here we bought tickets for a deck chair and sat down to rest, for, as can be imagined, after walking all over Plymouth for the last 3 hours we were fairly done-in.

The sun was now blazing away in a sky of such brilliant blue that it was painful to see. My brother went to sleep almost immediately, but as I rarely sleep except in bed, just sat watching the people bathing and [listening] to the band playing on the promenade. This place was the most wonderful sight I've ever seen. There was a destroyer lying just out in front of us, as we looked towards the sea, six sea-planes, with their wings glinting in the sun, lay motionless in the harbour on our left, the sea was as blue as the sky, only the sky looked like a sheet of metal, while the sea looked like crinkly, blue glass.

We sat there for about an hour and a half. Then we decided to go up into the town and have a wash and something to eat before going to Devonport to see the navy display.

We did this but while we were having dinner, consisting

***218** Cardiff in 1789 by Julius Caesar Ibbetson, before its great Victorian expansion.*

of egg and chips, bread and butter, and tea, the sky became cloudy. It was now about mid-day and the heat was indescribable.

We caught a bus stating as its destination the RN Barracks.

Arriving at the barracks we got out of the bus and were waiting in a queue at the gate of the dockyard when it suddenly became dark, so dark in fact that the cars had to put their lights on. The whole queue suddenly made a dash for shelter under the sun-shades of the shops. In a few seconds the storm was upon us. The wind was blowing at a tremendous pace and it rained in sheets. Every now and then vivid flashes of lightning lit up the darkness and were followed shortly afterwards by terrific claps of thunder.

Then the shop-keepers came out and put up their shades, for the wind and the rain was tearing them to shreds. In a few minutes we were both soaked and, seeing a bus coming around the corner, I made a dash for it.

We asked the conductor if he would put us down near a cinema. This he did and then for 2½ hours we stood in a queue under a shelter erected outside the cinema, the rain pouting down in torrents most of the time.

At about 3.30pm three of my Cardiff friends, all of them Jewish, came into the queue to shelter. They told me they were on a hiking tour with Plymouth as their base. They had apparently been walking all over the West Country, sleeping at hostels in various towns. They left us after a few moments.

At about 5.00pm we went into the cinema. There was a good show on but I've forgotten the title of the films. There was a very good organist too. Half way through the performance we had ice-cream, of which we were very glad, being very thirsty.

At 8.00pm we came out of the cinema and after some difficulty we found our way to the station and, after having some lemonade at a small shop and buying some chocolate, we arrived there at about 9.00pm.

The train was due out of Plymouth at 9.20pm and while we were waiting for the train my brother sat down on a bench, while I went to the end of the platform where a crowd of my fellow-Welshmen, most of them drunk, were singing. I sang with them. We sang *Hen Wlad Fy Nhadau, Bread of Heaven* to the tune *Cwm Rhondda*, *Genevieve* and all the other songs that Welshmen sing on holiday.

The train was fairly punctual and I slept most of the journey. I can't remember much about the journey for when I was not asleep, I was too tired to take much notice of anything.

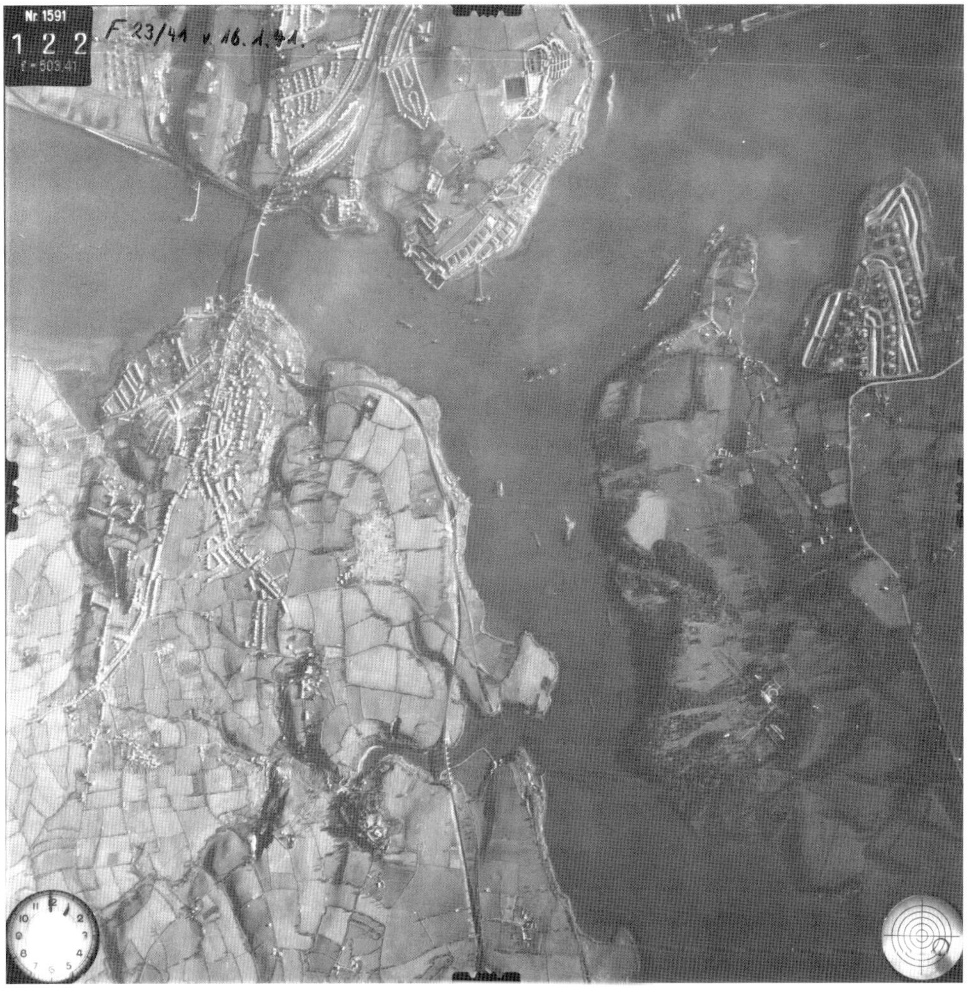

***219** Saltash photographed by the Luftwaffe on 16 January 1941.*

Thus, because of the rain we had travelled round about 200 miles to see a cinema show, but I think, on the whole, I rather enjoyed the whole affair, even the thunder-storm.'

36. Margaret Kornitzer, Journalist, 1939-40

Miss Margaret Hester Kornitzer (1905-96) was a journalist and author resident in Cornwall in 1939 but moved to Sydenham outside London within a year. She described herself for MO:

'Child of a Jewish (Austrian, British Naturalised) father, English (English & Scots, Tyneside school teacher) mother. Moved to London at age of 1. Father in Hatton Garden, pearl expert. Lived Epping Forest & Ilford area until 1915, went to private and then council school. 1915 – 1920 travelling with parents (New York, 3 public schools; Canada, Japan, to Manilla where three years private, central and convent schools, home via Singapore February 1920). Public school until 1924. Secretarial training, free-lance writing. Jobs in publishing, engineering, advertising, etc. Author of *Modern Woman and Herself* (Cape). Could not make free-lancing pay, so am in a staff job at the moment.

Physique: stock size 5 feet 5 inches. No physical deformities, no particular looks. Reasonably healthy. Church of England. Was brought up *to believe in God* without bias to adult decision. After many years [of] thought was confirmed St Martin-in-Fields, 1935. Don't fit in politically to any party, say a sort of Liberal Socialist.

Interests: chiefly literary and social. Run a society of about 100 for taking interest in South Wales unemployed, have adopted a village; member of VAD since 1935.

Work in Cliffords Inn, Fleet Street. A modern office building, central-heated. Live in five-bedroomed house in suburban (Beckenham) road. One maid, when we can get a maid.

Note: my mixed parentage, above, gives me a certain interest, perhaps. Also the fact of extensive travelling and adolescence in the tropics. These things have certainly affected me a great deal in all directions. The Jewish-English strains give rise to a good deal of internal stress.'

Miss Kornitzer wrote two passages about Plymouth in her diaries. The first was written on a train journey from Cornwall to London on 7 October 1939:

'At Plymouth a lot of naval men on leave from the Far East came on – a young marine in our compartment had been away 3 years. He said he had 58 days' leave but didn't expect to get more than 3 weeks but seemed quite cheerful about it. He left the East before war broke out and his troopship had been dodging about in convoy quite a bit. In my compartment also were a cheerful widow and her daughter, the latter expectant coming back from a few days' looking about in South Cornwall for a house to evacuate to. They had been staying in a very badly lit and badly blacked-out hotel and had combed a certain district for accommodation but without much success.'

She made the same journey ten months later:

'The other side of Saltash we stopped in an exposed position for 5 hours, as Plymouth was getting a *straff*. It was impossible for me to sleep as I was in the middle, but an RAF man did. We had a good view of the raid, and also participated, as bombs were pretty near, including my first screamer, rather less terrifying, even in those circumstances, than I had expected. I had the wind up, but I don't think I have any signs of this. The palms of my hands sweated. Soldiers stood at the windows the whole time and gave an amusing running commentary. So far as I can see the Jerries did not try to push home any attack but bombed about dropping bombs as and when. All fires lighted were soon dowsed, apparently. Rather wonderful. I heard later this was the town's worst raid.'[229]

That day, 26 August 1940, was noted differently by the ambulance service in Plymouth:

'Widespread damage. During this longest raid to date on the district, many High Explosives and Incendiary bombs were dropped. Fires on the Cornish Heights near Downderry, house-boat at Hooe Lake, Torpoint, etc. HE bombs on Ford House (several inmates killed in a corridor), also bombs at Stoke, Hartley Vale, etc. (the latter did not explode and evacuation of danger area effected). Surrounding district also suffered. During the height of raid a rather serious accident at Manadon Hill – collision in which a military vehicle was involved. Casualties conveyed away safely.')[230]

37. Edward Billington, Clerk, 1939

In 1939 nineteen-year-old Edward Roy Billington (1919-1991), who lived with his parents at 4 Kinterbury Terrace on Bull Point in St Budeaux, answered three directives. He was employed as a clerk in the city's treasurer's office. Mr Billington described himself to MO:

'Present occupation: student.

Life history quite uneventful at least so far.

My special interests are music & general reading of anything scientific. My hobbies consist of listening to good music and collecting gramophone records of same. I am Socialist in my political views and never stop to think too much about religion.'

Directives: jazz & anti-Semitism

Billington answered questions on jazz:

'I listen to jazz music only when better programmes are not available. It's a form of entertainment that requires no concentration. I have a few dance records but have now given up buying them as they are only popular for a few weeks and then become obsolete. The elder members of the family do not care much for jazz especially *swing*. The quieter type of music is preferred.

I know of a working girl of about 20 who on arriving home from work finds there is dance music on, immediately commences to glide around the room with an imaginary partner oblivious of the fact that she is still wearing outdoor clothes. (overcoat etc.)

I have just taken up dancing and go on the average once a fortnight. At times it strikes me as a most queer past time, but certainly forms a good method of recreation. At present a dance is something of an ordeal to me, but I generally enjoy them once I have started to dance.

The tune is more easily remembered than the words. These words are often so foolish that they are not worth remembering. I never bother to learn the words at all. The words of the songs mentioned are pure rubbish, although the tunes are not bad. Several persons seem to like the words of *Music, Maestro, Please*, but agree with me as to the other tunes. Many people I have asked say they remember the words only because they've heard them so many times.'

In June 1939 he wrote about Jewish people:

'The general feeling in my district is that the Jews should have a home in Palestine, and this feeling has been strengthened considerably since the recent outrages committed by the Arabs. I have neither seen or heard of any signs of anger against the Jews. In fact I have got the impression that the people of Plymouth do not take as much interest in politics or questions of importance as they should. This especially applies to the average man.

I am certainly in favour of the Jews having a national home in Palestine. Those there already have done much to benefit the land and have cleared much land that had hitherto been useless. I know several Jews but must confess that their appearance and demeanour have by no means impressed me. I am afraid that *funny stories* concerning Jews are out of my category.'

Mr Billington married two years later.[231]

38. Eleanor Humphries, Housewife/ Part Time Social Worker, 1940

Thirty-seven-year-old married Eleanor Humphries, of Blackheath in London, was born in America and married an Australian in 1921. She only mentioned Devon in passing but described herself at greater length than any Devon Writer. Amongst the many details she disclosed was that she stood at five feet two inches, had brunette hair, weighed eight stone and three pounds, was a non-church going Anglican, was an inactive member of the Conservative Association and had previously been drawn to Socialism, was 'childless by accident and not by design', disliked musical films, was assisted in her home by Kathleen, a daily maid, had a cocker spaniel named Wags and had a fear or Alsatian dogs and spiders.

Mrs Humphries worked at the Citizens Advice Bureau with refugees and it was there that she met a thirty-eight-year-

***220** Mrs Eleanor Humphries in 1940.*

old British chemist, his wife and their two children along with two French children. Plymouth played a part in their escape from the Nazis. Mrs Humphries wrote on 22 July 1940:

'The family lived outside of Paris, had a country house at Sarthe. When it looked like Paris [was] falling and the raids were bad, they packed up and went to Sarthe, about 300 miles away. The day after they arrived the village was told they must evacuate. Some great friends lived there asked the Bs to take their two children... When they got to Paris [the] raids were worse than ever – it was just before the capitulation. On the way to Paris, they had been repeatedly machine-gunned by German planes and had had many miraculous escapes from bombs.

Now they must try to reach England. Loaded up the car and made all haste for Brittany. When they arrived at Brest there were no more boats for civilians and the army were busy trying to get their personnel off. B. finally found a fishing boat, the captain said he would try to get them to England. He had never been more than 30 miles away from the French coast and had no charts but they set off. More bombings but it was alright after they had been about 10 hours out. They got to Plymouth 48 hours later.'[232]

These refugees then travelled to London.

39. Hugh Dent, Teacher, 1940

Leeds-born George Hugh Rains Dent (1912-1966) was an English master at Plymouth College. In 1939 he lived at 111 Chapel Road with his wife Lorna (1910-1993) and the following year they moved to East View in Fernleigh Road. Mr Dent was a Conscientious Objector. He kept a diary from 1939 to 1940 and contributed replies to three directives[233] including a relevant passage early in the war in September 1940:

221 Eastview in Fernleigh Road, Plymouth, the home of Mr Hugh Dent in 1940.

> 'Air Raids have changed life very little: a welcome break in afternoon school, a nuisance at other times. Make up bed in shelter at night: argue with wife as to whether it's better to be safe or cold (comparatively safe or certainly cold). Policy 50/50. Raids all night a damned nuisance as I'm a warden.
>
> Air warfare has made us group more, e.g. play bridge many nights instead of staying at home reading or listening in. Do far less preparation for next day's (next week's) work. This partly because I'm awaiting call-up. Practically no effect on general mental attitude. Have made a will.
>
> Meal times unaltered; scepticism either advanced or retarded as the raids seem to repeat for about 4 days. Keep bed, cards, light and clothes in shelter basement. If we go, we rush down at last moments in pyjamas, dress there and go to sleep sometimes. Few raids last more than an hour. Then come up.
>
> Test gas mask weekly at ARP meeting. Always carry it and tin hat. Find tin hat keeps off rain but alarms people when worn only for that reason.
>
> Many people left Plymouth in June when raids started, especially from wealthy area. Several trickling back.'

1940

Mr Dent's diaries began just as the situation in France deteriorated. That summer the first bombs fell in Plymouth.

> 'May 7th 1940, D. H. (schoolmaster, 29), his wife is worried to hear that teachers from 25 to 30 won't be reserved after summer. He's a Conscientious Objector and she's troubled that even if the Tribunal leaves him at his job, the governors may sack him and he won't get it back after the Armistice. I was certain she would have no grounds to think that, feeling that a non-council school will show a lead in tolerance that places like Torquay won't have the courage to. However, she won't know till after the tribunal in August. The head won't know whether he's got to replace DH on the staff and they will all be a bit on edge about it…
>
> Saturday 11th Entertained a not-too-easy boy of 11 for the day. Chance as the war gave us the show of a lifetime to take him to. A barrage balloon lost some of its content and embraced a chimney on the Lord Mayor's house. We got a front stand, great excitement as firemen and RAF gradually released it and it stopped in a wide street. I see it's replaced already 9 hours later. He enjoyed it no end and talked with great pride of

222 'Two RAF pilots from the Bay of Biscay Patrol and their WAAF companions tour historic Plymouth, walking past barrage balloon', 1943.

our balloon. Balloon-men at Ford Park giving bits of balloon cloth as souvenirs to schoolboys. The photo that the press ought to have got was of the gardener still watering Drake's bowling green while the whole of the rest of the Hoe watches the wrecked balloon: *The Armada Can Wait* for a heading. [A member of Plymouth's Ambulance Service noted that at 6.57pm the balloon 'broke away or partially deflated and fell on the roof at Elliot Street. Subsequently got down to the street and was emptied and folded.'[234]]

Sunday 12 May Too soft for this generation. Two retired naval commanders on the committee of the private subscription library, when Miss G. suggested that of course they couldn't possibly consider a CO for library, [responded] *Will that make him any less efficient at his duties, Miss G?*

Sunday 26 Big round up of aliens in Plymouth, including Hans M., nice boy, but far too clever to be about. The 16-year age limit seems to me rather high. I know plenty of 14-year-olds who'd be magnificent spies. Still, the tribunal that Hans went before seems to have been rather a mockery. It would be better surely to take all aliens into internment camps for protective custody, for their own sake if they are reliable, since the Local Defence Volunteers will not be taking any chances with people who don't speak perfect English.

May 31 [1940] I know quite a few men who were in the local territorials and who went to France some weeks ago. Gradually I am getting to know that first one and then another has managed to get home again and this gives rise to the hope that the withdrawal will be almost completely successful. By the way, I knew that two of these fellows were back in England before ever it was admitted on the radio that men were being got across. The scenes at Boulogne must beggar description and the thought of all that our men are having to put up with, makes one feel exasperated. If only one could release some super-human force which would blow Jerry to smithereens! One feels so helpless over here, knowing what is going on over there and also knowing that the bombing and blasting will continue for some time yet.

Friday June 7th Took ARP practical test, putting out incendiary bomb and its attendant fires. Glad to have done it, as it only signifies one experience to see that it's only a job like all others. RL is joining the Artillery. I thought A would be very upset but she feels so sure that the war will end one way or the other by September 1940 that she isn't much worried. He came to make certain that we'll have an occasional bath ready for him if he's in barracks locally.

223 British prisoners at Dunkirk, 1940.

Saturday June 8th, Tennis and bridge. Nothing much on the news but a fine bandwagon at night. Then went to the Hoe where there was lots of shipping looking magnificent, both picturesque and powerful.

Sunday June 9th Across by motorboat, very funny to see all those whom a year ago would have scorned us as trippers queueing up to to pay their sixpences, since practically all other coast excursions are out-of-bounds. Onto the moor in the evening with the Es in their car. He full of fury at the enormous wastage of petrol in the RAF. Another bathe, and the evening on the moor one of the loveliest ever. The platitude *Isn't it absurd there's a war on in this weather*? really meant something.

Monday June 10th ARP gas lectures 140 minutes – good going!

Tuesday June 11th R. L. (30) came in for a final supper before joining the Artillery. They had given him a list, the size of two new stamps, of articles to bring with him. He wondered if a tooth brush and a little reading matter would be *de prop*, and was glad to find a thigh-pocket that would hold a Penguin book. But I can't see him without his dressing-gown and bedroom slippers and all the luxuries of the world. There's something to be said for making officers of the class that aren't tough enough to stand life in the ranks.

Met Peter E. (23), back from Dunkirk. He said he was frightened to death for the first five hours under aircraft bombing, then felt alright. He was always an independent lad, scholar of New College, and its queer to see him as a cog in a machine, taking his job utterly for granted…

Monday June 17 Blackest day so far. A scarcely smiled all day and was longing for me to say something cheerful and when I did, she simply argues it out. ARP lecture No. 3 in evening, pretty good. Trying on gas masks, difficult owing to spectacles.

Tuesday 18 June Just about as black. Expected air raid at night and were back at the old September state, when we said on going to bed *See you when the sirens go* and were relieved *another night over* when we woke up without a raid.

Wednesday 19th June Bridge in the evening cheered A up a bit, though she kept saying that she couldn't see any reason to be cheerful, though however much she argues she can't convince herself, let alone me, of how we're going to be beaten, but I can't convince her how we can beat them.

H.G. (male 35) simply says *The side with sea power always wins* and that even if we're confined to one corner of the British Isles by invasion, he can't see how we can lose.

Saturday, Sunday, Monday 24 June ARP lecture. Sergeant E. lectured magnificently for 145 minutes! My own feeling with the anti-gas clothing on was that I was so much cumbered & short-sighted by it that I should be useless in any job of work.

Tuesday 25 Long discussions at the ARP post as to the extent that wardens should be out in raids, the most interesting feature of which was the obvious preference we all shared for being told what to do, rather than being left to use our judgment. Rumours of which the raided towns were, and nightly we expect it to be

224 A British searchlight at work, undated.

Plymouth, over which planes certainly passed last night. A still quite hopeless about the outcome of the war.

Friday 28 Our first raid alarm. Put all our clothes, etc. ready at night. We're had our windows gummed-papered for these days. At 12.48 A said *Look at the searchlights, ought we to get our things in? The sirens will go any moment. I do hope we haven't had a yellow warning or you'll have to go down to the port*. We each had ¼ second's peep from near the window and the lights were marvellous, all over. Sound of a few planes, buzz, less, buzz, less, not rising and falling but on and off. I don't think either of us felt scared. We blacked out so we could put the light on, and then the sirens went, and we were quickly downstairs to the basement. As one fussed, how old L (the landlord, ?68) was magnificent. He only kept on saying *All this modern civilisation, we did very well without aeroplanes*. We could hear a slight noise of planes, and very distant firing, not much of it.

Everyone was quite genuinely cheerful and not rattled. I knew it was sense to keep my tin hat on, but I didn't partly because I was the only one who had one and partly because I didn't want to seem fussy. We hadn't a light as the skylight wasn't blacked. I didn't think we should hear the All Clear but it went about 2.15 and I went out to see if there was any damage, knowing that the absence of noise that it was very unlikely. Called Thomas, my ARP mate, who said he'd heard a biggish bang (which we hadn't) and seen something drop over the Sound (a flare?).

Did our beat, signed up at the post and then home

and rather jokily. It was a lovely night. I liked the head warden's greeting *Hello Mrs Dent, Lovely night, isn't it? Is your husband up?* Then upstairs to drink tea and the landlord's daughter came up and we discussed additional comforts for the cellar.

Sunday July 7 The motorboat boat trip across the Sound is cancelled as they don't want small ferries holding 100 in the water while we're having planes perpetually hovering about. So we went to the beach below the Hoe and were drinking tea when the alarm went again. Sirens inaudible but the café man blew a whistle. Plenty of the soldiers who'd been bathing there were *tough* and stayed out of cover but the rest of us went into the café which has a good stone roof. Didn't see anything.

The afternoon raid, 6.15 to 7.15, was a bit more lively. I heard a plane race across East to West, then the sirens went and L & I went to the basement. Things quiet and boring for an hour, though I had a little fracas with L as to whether I should, as a warden, go out to see everything was ok. Then we went up to the sitting room window to see what was doing; the buses were still stationary outside the shelters in Alexandra Road but there were quite a number of people out in the streets.

Suddenly there was a burst of AA above one's heads, quite close and we rattled down again. Later, we heard a man shouting something like All Clear or Fire. Never discovered what. There certainly wasn't a fire. CP and N had seen it all from a nearby hill where they were walking: CP (almost triumphing in misfortunes) said that the raider *Did just what he liked*. Actually, he was chased all round though he did get one big one in 500 yards from the gas works, which killed 4 people. We both half-wanted to see the crater of the other bomb. We'd seen smoke directly above the Hoe, but partly we reckoned we'd see lots of fresh craters with less effort in the future and partly we didn't want to get stuck down there if there were another raid.

Tuesday July 9 No raid all day! Coming in damp, a good deal of mist. A few suggestions that Hitler is now being supplied with the right weather for his invasion. Very heavy gunfire out in the Channel: big naval battle? ARP meeting at the post pm: telling us of details of the late raids on Plymouth. We (my wife) especially very glad to learn that six bombs have fallen within 1½ miles of our flat and an AA gun fired within ¼ mile yet the noise hadn't been at all terrific. Alarming perhaps, but certainly nothing like deafening.

Wednesday July 10th Woken up at 6 by a big bomb explosion; our 14th raid in 12 days. Quite three minutes late the Devonport sirens went, and then the Plymouth one. Raids 15, 16, 17 at 7.15, noon & 11.30pm. The first two not notable but at the night one we heard six bangs which turned out all to be bombs, before the AA firing started. [A member of the city's Ambulance Service recorded 'sirens sounded at 6am. Bombs dropped Exeter Street and St Jude's area. Demolishing several houses including a public house (rear). Also, more bombs in Leigham Street and Hoe District. Dead and many injured.'[235]

Friday 12 July Little raid at 6, just the wrong time to get up, since it's not worth going to bed again and for the second time in my life I was so tired that I sat down to shave. However, a raid at 9.20 saves me from having to teach first period. The six bombs last night had been dropped in a line near Milehouse; at least half a dozen of the boys were missed by less than 150 yards but none of them seemed scared. By a miracle there were no casualties at all. In the evening Plugge and his wife came over to sleep in the bottom flat; last night they counted six explosions getting nearer and did not know how many more there might be. They seemed pretty rattled. Argument over the truth of our air success bulletins. SRL quotes an RAF man as saying *Divide by three*, but I think I trust them.

Saturday July 13 Wrote to YTSH (old friend) and MH (who taught me from 1920 to 1930) to see if they'll give me a testimonial of sincerity to use before the Tribunal. Relieved when I emerged from dentist chair without an alarm: to have to suspend in the middle of a filling might be agony.

Sunday July 14 Another night without a raid. Went up to the park. Am thinking that its thoroughly stupid now for people to go on to the Hoe, crowded, exposed and shelterless. Our Sunday morning trip is getting more and more curtailed. SRL & his wife (both about 26) in a flap about whether to move their furniture out of Plymouth. The tobacconist has been telling them that half the parents will be taking their sons into the country and they're both very het up at the possibilities

225-234 *Ten views of Plymouth, early 1900s.*

of staff being cut, etc. Since we've nowhere to move out stuff to if we wanted, the problem's easier for us! I contradicted the tobacconist's prophecy: I've only heard of three of these moves so far, though obviously there'll be some more.

When the raid came, two of the women remarked that it was a relief, they had feared that since we'd been raid-less for 50 hours, some new devilment was being hatched. It was a very short one and we heard possibly one bomb. Then RL (gunner 31) took us on to the moor in the car, a great treat for him to get out of uniform and into riding kit. He knows an Official Secret that he's very pleased about and is one of the few I've met who doesn't divulge anything even to his nearest & dearest. Had to sleep at the RAF post in case anything happened to the full-time warden. We'd had long and rather acid discussion over whether one man should sleep in the presence of one woman; result, of the two sectors sharing the post we single-man it, they double-man it. Had a bad night in a squeaky camp bed but the morning was lovely at six: no raids.

[15 July] Successfully got through the first morning of the exams without a warning, which came at 1.35. Half an hour standing in the passage, NL (28) and I wanting the party to keep quiet so we could hear what was going on aloft, the women wanting a merry party so they couldn't. [A member of the Plymouth Ambulance service recorded '1.35 air raid warning. Sirens sounded All Clear at 2.01pm. No injuries in Plymouth City but machine-gunning etc, including Embankment and Plymstock first aid post. Bombed cook-house, RAF station, Mount Batten but only one injured.'[236]]

Lettuces coming up well but I didn't know what a menace slugs were till I became a 16 Square Fort gardener. So we got through the afternoon exams successfully.

18 July Raid again (23.00) half after midnight, when we'd both just gone to sleep and were feeling bloody awful. Two rounds of cigarettes. All Clear after half an hour. A German flew high over a few times, then our fighter lower.... We were quite surprised we didn't get another in the night.

It came at 11.30 and slightly cut into the exams. Boys no end cheered. I had to entertain 11-year-olds with games. They & I forgot all about raids. A still alarmed about impending invasion, possibility of being stuck apart when I'm at camp next week, etc. Had a colossal row with YL (married to another CO) who entirely lost her temper with A because she said we were notably inconsistent & A complained that she was & they couldn't agree to differ. YL poured all her wrath on my head too, but her husband tried to make it up without being disloyal to her. It's queer that the only people we've had unpleasantness with because we're COs are COs themselves.'

Mr Dent also summarised the effect of the war on Plymouth College in 27 points.

1, All carry gasmasks at all times.

2, Afternoon periods cut short during winter months.

3, Five members of staff already serving.

4, Two out of three servants serving: prefects take over some of their easier work.

235 Advice for shelter hygiene, early 1940s.

5, ARP arrangements: all small boys in reinforced basement, seniors in lower corridor, glass protected by *Blast-proof* paste. Staff when possible continue teaching. Fire and sand buckets in porch.

6, 1/3 of sports field occupied by barrage balloon encampment.

7, Big increase in OTC, whose seniors are automatically in LDV and guard BBC at night.

8, Scouts engaged largely in collecting waste paper, increase in first-aid work.

9, 4 out of 15 staff ARP wardens, one boy a shelter guard.

10, Go slow on stationery.

11, Not much obvious change in amount of work done. Some seniors badly at a loose-end with no prospects before them. LDV guards often practically asleep next day.

12, Boys living far out often very late.

13, Parents may send boys late after a disturbed night, at their discretion.

14, Games supervision handicapped by absence in service of younger members of staff.

15, Head dishes out National Savings Certificates. Staff make collections of Savings by forms. A typical weekly sum £2 10s. Record of £135 in National Savings Week for whole school.

16, Relations of staff and boys more chatty than in peace.

17, Marking and preparation by staff less thoroughly done relaxation of the *vital-to-push-on* attitude.

18, Headmaster and governors disagree on whether to sack two COs on staff. Judgment deferred till after tribunal. Afraid of complaints by parents, but a number feel that what matters is efficiency, not private views.

19, Subjects of English essays, Latin sentences to naturally tend to the war.

20, Speculation on the effect of an air raid during the Certificate exams.

21, Four boys lost their fathers on *Courageous*.

22, Several parents worried by cost of school *extras*, e.g., scout camp.

23, Vague evacuation plans in air: parents and staff alike very much against having boys billeted out.

24, 15-year-old German Jewish refugee free at the school. Immensely popular; higher than halfway up his class in all subjects.

25, Lady substitutes tried in first term; replaced by men, slightly less efficient on the whole.

26, The school a wonderful centre for rumours and reports.

27, School evening activities (plays, societies, etc.) stopped for duration.'[237]

Mr Dent continued to live in Plymouth after the war: he gave public lectures, including at Swarthmore in Mutley Plain, and served on the committee of the Plymouth Proprietary Library.[238]

40. First File Report, 1941

MO made four file reports on Plymouth in respect to aerial bombardment and morale. The first, of 29 January 1941, also examined Portsmouth. It concluded that in Plymouth 'damage was relatively slight and morale excellent. The dislocation of gas supply was the only major blitz feature. Considerable underlying anxiety is probably present though local leadership appears extremely confident of the town's abilities'. Moreover, it was noted morale was 'exceptionally good though there was considerable underlying tension about bigger attacks expected in the future'.

In particular the report outlined the effect of recent experiences:

'Coming from Portsmouth to Plymouth was rather like going from Manchester to Liverpool. In Plymouth there was cheerfulness everywhere and a real *carrying on*.

Not that it is fair to compare Portsmouth and Plymouth directly. For in Plymouth, the damage has been much less severe. Indeed, Plymouth can hardly be described as a blitzed town. This does not prevent Plymouth from describing itself as *having been blitzed*. You have definitely to look for damage in Plymouth and there is no visible damage whatsoever to the town centre,

236a-b *Two views of Plymouth Sound by Charles Baskerville entitled 'Plymouth Harbor Barrage Balloons', 1 June 1944, and 'Plymouth, England', 2 June 1944.*

a crucial point as regards morale we believe. Large parts of Plymouth are practically untouched by air-raids. Transport and others apparently unaffected but light and fuel. There were considerable inadequacies in the bus services causing some irritation. This does not appear to be wholly associated with recent developments however.

Nor has water been cut off, but electricity was interfered with for a short time and gas seriously affected. It was the cutting off of gas all over Plymouth which registered most of all on the inhabitants. Everywhere there were comments on this subject, notices about it in shops and restaurants, several big laughs about it at the Music Hall. There was some grumbling about the delay in getting it back but most people seemed to regard it as rather a joke – the undertone of picnic atmosphere, noted at Southampton, here in Plymouth not overlaid by more serious disturbance or destruction.'

The Writers made nine points in relation to morale:

'1, Morale in Plymouth was good. In fact, judging by the criteria we have adopted in other towns, it was exceptionally good. People here seem to be well aware of the war – they had enough raids over a long period, without being even secretly weary or deeply worried about it.

2, But a considerable part of the population are nervous about bigger attacks to come. Some people are going to cellars and shelters immediately there is a warning, and were observed spending the whole night under most uncomfortable circumstances, without a single gun being fired or bomb dropped.

3, There were also signs of weakness among some women, especially middle-class women. Several of these had greatly exaggerated versions of damage in other parts of the town.

4, The by-now familiar pride in their damage was present in Plymouth. Several people actually said that *it was as bad as Coventry*. We have already discussed this in detail above, but we may add that in the case of Plymouth this disproportionate idea is likely to lead, unless attended to, to a severe reaction if a much more destructive raid took place.

5, Quite a common idea in Plymouth is that blitzes come at the weekend. This may make some people who should be getting rest and relief at the weekend experience anxiety of a rather useless type.

6, There was very little conversation among random *verbatims* and *overheards*, that dealt with raids. Less than one conversation in a hundred was on this subject, during the period from four days after the raid to seven days after the raid. The parallel figure for Portsmouth would be about fifty out of a hundred.

7, Gas mask carrying was low – lower than London.

8, Night life can best be described by the single word *terrific*. This is mainly due to the navy who swarmed through the city at night, often shouting and singing, often well-encouraged by drink. The pubs were open and crowded in the last hour. There were very few women in them. There was a great deal of singing, *Bless em all* being the dominant song as in Liverpool. The main popular dance hall was crowded, with the navy predominant. Several shooting and slot machine arcades were moderately patronized, again mainly by the forces. The Palace Theatre, Plymouth's Variety place, was well-filled. On Saturday night every stall was occupied, mainly by civilians, a large proportion of whom occupied the same seats every Saturday and who had not failed to turn up because of any blitzes. Cinemas were crowded and queuing after dark.

9, This Music Hall show was called *Go To It*. Most of it did not refer in any way to the war, but the three best received songs were *If I only had wings* (an RAF song), *Keep smiling through* (civilian morale song) and *There'll always be an England*. The audience were noticeably responsive and taking up songs from the stage, especially *Tipperary* and *Pack up Your Troubles*. The most applauded turn was a group of extremely energetic acrobats, the Four Bobrics.

The main turn was Stainless Steven and he used many war jokes, starting on the local gas situation, and *I've only had one hot meal since Sunday - horseradish and a rissole*. He made a whole series of jokes on local transport facilities and got the biggest laugh of the whole evening when he referred to the trams as *those instruments of death that flash past*. He made a number of jokingly cynical references to civilian morale, *Even Sir Francis Drake and Britannia are sticking it up on the Hoe*.

He describes the morale of Plymouth schoolchildren as 100%. For instance, their knowledge of money: twelve pennies make one shilling, twenty shillings make one pound, five thousand pounds make one Spitfire, one Spitfire makes thirty *Messerschmitts*.

This joke was second biggest laugh of the evening, while the third came when he described how he went to Devonport and found all the flags out and drums beating. He asked a sailor if there had been a big victory. The sailor replied *No, two packets of twenty Players arrived in the town*.

Well-received were his references to Bristol, where he was the previous week. He said that during a warning the orchestra could only play *tremulo*, milk bars could only make milk shakes. Other big laughs came from jokes about rations, blackout, Mussolini, American destroyers (derisive jeers from some sailors), General Soddu (play on his name) and more stuff about traffic congestion, eg *What does it matter if Germany does invade us? They won't get across Union Street*.'

The Writers also discussed the effectiveness of local political leadership, street shelters and communal feeding in a city which had yet to be tested.[239]

41. Second File Report, 1941

Circumstances had changed in Plymouth when the second MO report, of 1 April 1941, was written. Four investigators were involved; three of them had written the First File Report. Their investigation followed a period from a heavy attack on the evening of 20 March through to another ten days later.

These air raids came in the wake of a visit by the King and Queen. The report highlighted public concern that three days before the BBC had broadcast news of the visit and that this was the cause of the bombardment. The Writers quoted 'a working-class woman… in violent mood' saying '*they should never have broadcast it.. they tell us to keep our mouths shut!*'

The Writers concluded that morale ranked with Liverpool ('when allowance is made for the very serious damage done to Plymouth') but warned 'there is an appreciably large and qualitatively important group with very bad morale'. It was judged that those with the best morale were male and those who had remained in badly hit areas. 'Moderate' morale was found with the middle classes and among the elderly. The worst morale lay with evacuees and among women who had stayed in Plymouth.

The report noted that in late 1940 and early 1941 there had been a lull in bombing and that many had subsequently reflected upon this and concluded that they had become complacent. Comments were recorded from a working-class

***237** ARP themed cigarette cards, 1940s.*

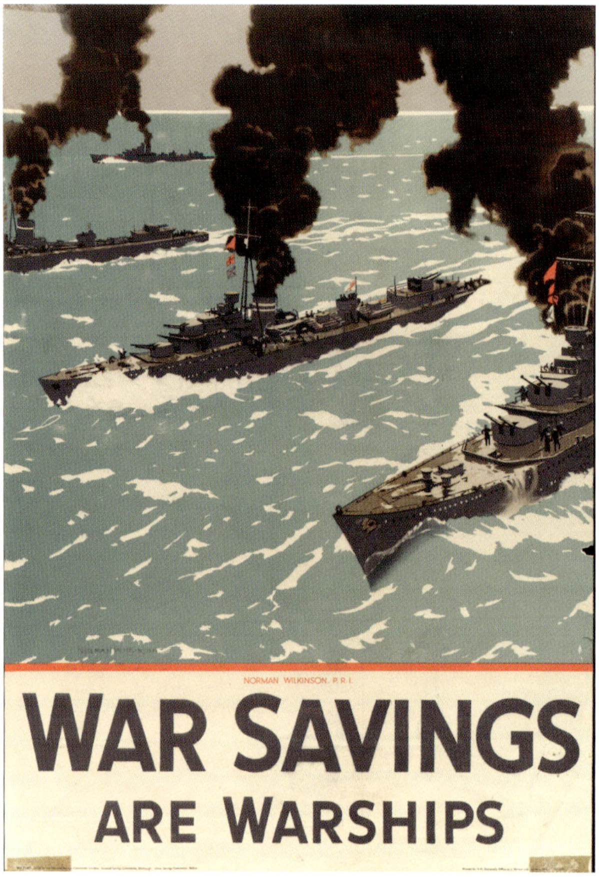

238-9 *Two posters advocating savings bonds, early 1940s.*

man (*'We never kept up our fire precautions as we ought to have. That was the trouble.'*) and from three working-class women (*'It serves us right in a way for getting so behind.'*; *We here were getting too, what do they call it? Com-plass-ent. We'd got so that none of us expected any raids. Then we had a rude awakening.'*; *'Well, what can you expect? It's our own fault for being slack'*).

Some 700 people died in the attacks but MO suggested that the public suspected the actual figure was higher. Comments were recorded (*'I reckon deaths approach a thousand. It's downright wicked.'*, *'Thousands. It's so depressing to think of it.'*, *'There were hundreds dead. Still digging them up. There was one shelter underneath a building where a 150 people were buried and they've given up digging for them now because it's hopeless.'*)

Air raids dominated general conversation; MO estimated it comprised some eighty per cent of all the talk overheard:

> *'There were six of us down at the club. Got in just in time.'*
>
> *'Ah, the old guildhall. I haven't been down to see what it's like.'*
>
> *'You can't transact anything like that by phone.'*
>
> *'I can hardly recognise anything. Lots of things you can hardly recognise.'*
>
> *'Remarkable number of escapes.'*
>
> *'I have seen them all laid out in the mortuary.'*
>
> *'And what has he gained from it? Nothing. Nothing at all.'*
>
> *'A dear little kiddie murdered.'*
>
> *'You never know where you are these days.'*
>
> *'They were wanting a small house or a few rooms somewhere in the country.'*
>
> *'Bombs, all over the Palladium.'*
>
> *'Makes you think they were after the King and Queen, don't it?'*
>
> *'They're burying hundreds every day, I'm sure.'*

'The whole place was aglow. You could see to read a newspaper. I sent the wife and kiddies over to the shelter. I was in the house myself. You never saw anything like it.'

'I wasn't in a shelter either. Never been in a shelter. Don't fancy your shelters. I don't mean I was outside all the time, mind. I was in a house near the park a bit of the time. And I had a drink, a couple of Guinness, when it was all over.'

The Writers also investigated sightseeing:

'There was very extensive damage tourism on Sunday March 23 when people came into town from miles around. Here are two comments, one from a tourist, the other from a resident

'I went in on Sunday to see what damage had been done. I took the wife and kids. We all went round and had a look.'

'The heartlessness of some people – them which came around here to see the sights as though it was Guy Fawkes night. It was bonfire night alright. All day long after the raids they come and had a look and enjoyed it.'

But compared with some other places, sight-seeing soon fell away and did not persist as a sort of obsession for the most part. On a conspicuous corner a house, which had received a direct hit, had just one wall left standing, and in it a fireplace, with a mantelpiece, and on the mantelpiece a clock still apparently going. This clock aroused comment from practically every passer-by on several different days of observation, and over and over again was the subject of delightful comment. It seemed to act as a kind of relief. It suggested almost the basis of this sort of post-blitz morale campaign which is really necessary and completely un-attempted: THE CLOCK GOES ON TICKING.

Another form of relief was provided by the RAF, in the form of a Junkers 88 dive-bomber brought in on two lorries and placed in a square in the destroyed part of the town on March 27. Crowds of passers-by examined this from 2 to 20 minutes each. The overwhelming effect was one of pleasure, interest and, again, relief. This bomber was a kind of explanation, a context figure, something to touch, something which could be understood, which made the vast chaos all around somehow more real, intelligible and concrete to the still-amazed inhabitants of Plymouth. Thus, many people would put out their hand and touch the fuselage, sometimes holding it there for quite a long time. Others, and not only the young, scratched their names on the paint, which was covered with hundreds of names. People talked with unusual readiness to strangers standing by them, discussing the plane.

The men were largely interested in the material, the engine and the craftmanship, which were repeatedly praised. By far the commonest comment of women was on the size. Many seemed amazed at the size of the plane, the length of it, the weight of it. Some seem to have a mental idea of an enemy bomber as a tiny, remote thing. In hundreds of overheards collected, none were hostile and none inferred reprisals. There was much questioning as to where the plane was brought down, and in this as on all other subjects, no information was provided. Current gossip was that it came from Portsmouth, and this was the source of some disappointment. People would have preferred a Plymouth plane. A good many also thought it had crashed, as there was no very apparent damage from gunfire. Some people said that such a big plane ought to be easy to hit and went on to voice feelings about the inadequacy of the anti-aircraft.

The general effect of this plane was unmistakeaby to give people pleasure and relief, in rather a friendly and benign way. The idea of showing the plane - the Ministry of Information seemed to know nothing about it - was definitely an excellent one, just the sort of propaganda which is needed under such circumstances. But the full effect was reduced by merely showing the plane. A pilot speaking about it and conducting people round it could have vastly increased the interest, and could have put across indirect propaganda points of view, e.g. stressing the superior workmanship of our own engines. As it is, the plane was very much an anti-ersatz and pro-German-workmanship piece of propaganda. It would also have been useful to have one or two labels or notices giving elementary facts about the plane and its parts. The thing that interested people most was the bombing apparatus; but many people miss this and did not realise its existence.'

Shelters were investigated and the Writers concluded that Plymothians avoided surface shelters, that a considerable number of people were leaving the city at night in order to sleep on the moors and two underground shelters had provoked comment. Reaction to one was positive but the other had been pierced by a direct hit and 'by the side of this shelter an old man was seen to stand most of the afternoon, accosting passers-by and telling them that down there his sister and her husband had been killed'. They added 'his voice and his face trembled and shook and he was near collapse.'

Other comments were made on the disruption to public utilities, the availability of canteens and communal feeding, and the carrying of gas masks. Signs at bombed shops were

240 Poster praising the pilots of the Royal Air Force, 1939.

also noted (including 'BOMBED, BLASTED, BURNED. But Still Beating the Blitz' and 'CHEER UP, BLITZNESS AS USUAL'). Public entertainment was also commented upon:

> 'There was nothing to do in the evening in Plymouth except drink. The younger people, especially girls between 16 and 21, therefore wandered loose with nothing to do in the evenings in a general breakdown-of-habit atmosphere. Investigators got the impression that they were much more ready to be picked up even than in January. The absences of night life cast an expectant gloom over the whole city. In Devonport normal night life continued and observations of a music hall show, etc. were made there and are available in our files.'

The clientele at pubs was analysed and it was found that only 9% were female and that two thirds of the men were in the armed services.[240]

42. Third File Report, 1941

The third report, of 4 May 1941, covered the period from the last heavy raid (30 April) to the 3rd of May. Two of the investigators had compiled the two earlier reports.

It noted that the Writers had not seen such devastation in any other part of the country; this was recorded in both the centre and in the loss of domestic buildings in the outlying areas. They thought 'the dislocation of everyday life also exceeds anything we have seen elsewhere and an enormous burden is being placed upon the determined spirits of the people'. The Writer also highlighted 'the disastrous chaos' which prevailed in the evacuation of the city.

Plymouth had endured unparalleled levels of random death and destruction from the new German tactic of intensive bombing night after night. The Writers suggested the people of Plymouth:

> 'are not defeatist, far from it. But they are defeated. Their town has suffered a major military defeat and they, the untrained and undisciplined soldiers of the Home Front, can (at present) do nothing much about it'.

They concluded that Plymothians were 'putting up an impressive show of courage and cheerfulness under the most trying circumstances which any town has as yet experienced.' Moreover, they felt the strong local pride of local people, together with a toughness of spirit, made them determined to show they could take it as well, if not better, than other British cities. There were five groups in respect to morale.

1, A stay-put population ('staying voluntarily and refusing to budge from Plymouth whatever happens. This is the most conspicuous group within Plymouth, because it carries on its activities as normally as possible and makes up practically all the people who now walk the town at night for pleasure or duty. A large part of the gayest and bravest of these are young people and we especially noticed the high spirt of young girls aged 14 to 22.').

2, A resident population unable to leave (they 'would like to get out but can find nowhere to go, cannot afford [to] or has to stay for other reasons. Here morale is not always so good and might rapidly deteriorate in the case of further raids'.).

3, Nightly trekkers with affected housing ('whose homes are more or less damaged and unsuitable for sleeping in, i.e. compulsory trekkers.').

241 Barrage Balloons over Plymouth, 1944, by Tracy Sugarman.

4, Nightly trekkers with unaffected housing ('whose homes are undamaged and who go out because they are afraid to stay at night.').

5, Residents who have left the city ('Many of these have their homes not seriously damaged and they include appreciable proportions of air raid wardens, fire-watchers and others with responsibilities, though on the whole these people with jobs to do in a blitz have the best morale of all, precisely because they have got something to do and do not wait passively for possible death.').

An independent investigation by the Ministry of Information at this time confirmed the File Report and added:

> 'For the present, Plymouth as a business and commercial centre of a prosperous countryside has ceased to exist. The children from two-thirds of it, the aged, the infirm, and the great army of pensioners who

always live in dockyard towns and naval ports, will, for the time being, dwell in the countryside around. Given a few weeks, however, all will, no doubt, recover their poise, and the absence of further continuous raids will enable the city to improvise arrangements and resume its shaken life. It would be wrong to assume that the people are broken. But equally it would be suicidal to ignore the implications and symptoms of the actual state of affairs, and to avoid probing the disturbing causes of the aftermath of some of the fiercest raids yet made upon a provincial centre.'[241]

The Ministry of Information conducted a second report a month later, from 5 to 7 May. It concluded that morale remained good, cited estimates of 15,000 houses having been damaged and questioned the official figure of 1,200 casualties. The report also outlined the number of trekkers who left the city each night and pointed to the lack of preparation by the council leaders ('a vivid impression of lack of directive in the blitzed areas').[242]

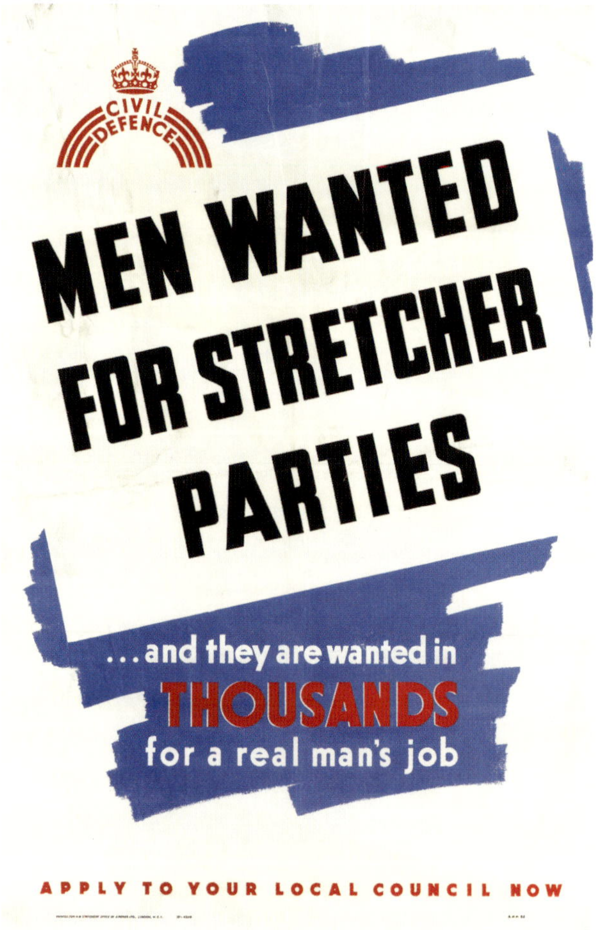

242 Poster calling for men to help in stretcher parties, by 1942.

43. Fourth File Report, 1941

The final report, of 6 October 1941, was written to learn organisational lessons from air attacks up to that date. An exercise had been conducted involving all parties concerned with another evacuation of Plymouth. The report recognised the severity of confusion which had prevailed and the disastrous effects which had arisen from the lack of coordination in the city' welfare provision.[243]

44. Douglas Darknell, Poultry Farmer, 1941

Douglas John Darknell (1895-1957), a poultry farmer living near Wells in Somerset, received a visit from his sister who lived in Devonport at 10 Second Avenue.

'Received a call from my eldest sister and her husband from Plymouth. They were having a few days' holiday and, happening to be staying close at hand, they came over for a few hours. I was interested to hear from them of the air raids last spring. They told us that the last raid was the worst of the lot. Previously, they had many raids of a few planes and people said that if they were the Hun's worse effort, they could manage alright. However, when they started in earnest a different story had to be told.

G[ladys Andrews] lives close to one of the dockyards at Devonport, and when the raids started, she opened all windows in the house and then went to their Anderson shelter taking their two dogs with them. Asked how the dogs behaved, they said that one of them slept through it while the other gave start occasionally when the bombs dropped near.

243 10 Second Avenue, Devonport, the home of Mrs Gladys Andrews in 1941.

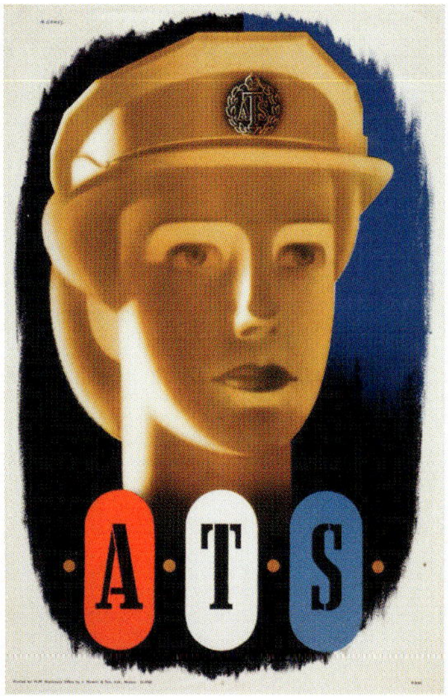

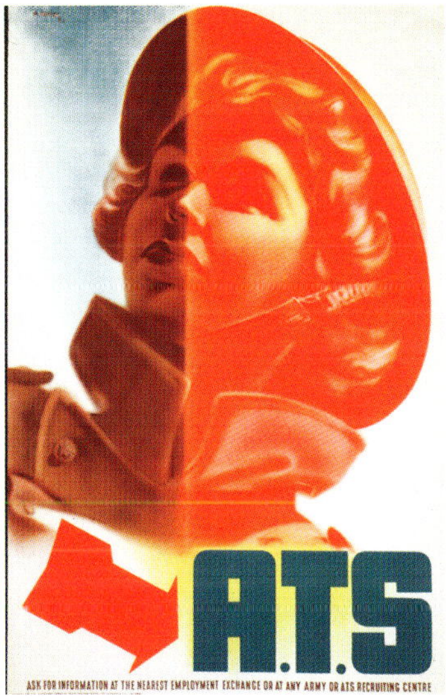

244-7 Recruiting posters for the Auxiliary Territorial Service.

During the last raid they said there was such a cloud of dust that they thought the house was gone. However, the only damage done was the loss of the windows and some of the ceilings cracked. Their chief fear was that as so many of the people around them had left their houses unattended, a fire might be started and their own house would be burnt to the ground. They intended to stay where they were until the position became impossible. The food position was good after the raids and they were able to get more than their rations. They thought this was because so many people had left the place. The windows were soon replaced with some frames made from felt which G bought.'[244]

45. Veronica Jenkin, Librarian, 1942

Amy H. Veronica Jenkin (1921-2002) relocated from Cambridge to Plymouth following the blitz in 1941. Twenty-one years old, she was employed by the council to help resurrect the city's library service. She may have been in Devon through her father: Harry Jenkin (1889-1947) was a Methodist minister who had been born in Devonport. In 1919 he was in India where he married and where two years later his daughter may have been born. In August 1942 Miss Jenkin wrote:

'I think I am doing a good and necessary job at this moment. I have a temporary job at the Plymouth Public Library. They lost all their books in the blitz and have received thousands of donations besides terrific compensation from the government. The task of checking, stocking and cataloguing these is Herculean and the staff inadequate.

But within the next fortnight I shall be absorbed into the ATS. I am frankly sceptical about my contribution to the war effort as an Auxiliary Territorial. I am forced into the ATS since I could not be a schoolteacher, and cannot afford to take a Social Science Certificate and would like to do.'

Shortly afterwards she had moved to London and her experiences confirmed her hesitations: 'since I have joined the army, I have seen that muddle and compromise and blind idiotic rules are everywhere'. It appears that she had not yet fully embraced army life in the following year: 'I have been in uniform for the past six months, on leave I delight in getting into civilian clothes, especially frocks.'[245]

46. Nigel Bartlett, Sailor, 1942-3

Twenty-year-old Fleet Navigating Officer Francis Nigel Oldfield Bartlett (1922-2011) was born in Stroud and enrolled on a course on marine and aeronautical engineering at the Royal Naval Engineering College. He may have lived in Devonport when he responded to fifteen directives in 1942 and 1943.[246] Not surprisingly, the navy dominated his activities:

25 February 1942

'7.45am I got up, quick wash and over to breakfast of porridge, bread, marmalade and coffee.

9am till 1pm, instruction in a lecture room. Watched a lot of naval ratings digging paths, and had a discussion on whether the work was necessary.

Lunch Irish stew – suet pudding.

Read *News Chronicle* for 20 minutes.

1.45pm till 4.15pm, instruction in lecture room.

Tea. Shave and wash. Decided to get outside for fresh air and change of scenery. Walked to central police station to have firearm's certificate amended. Nothing much on at cinema, so returned for supper at 7.00pm, consisting of soup and bully beef, having unsuccessfully looked for a girlfriend who I had met a week ago.

After supper discussed various explosives which might be home-made. Started discussing Russian music with someone I did not know well and it turns out that he is like myself interested in politics and holds Socialist views. I began to think that the Left covers a much larger number of people than is generally supposed.'

Directives: food availability, women, language and public houses

At that time he described the local availability of food:

'The food situation here in Plymouth is good compared with the surrounding rural areas. This is probably due to easier transport facilities. Bakers and cake makers are noticeably well and lavishly stocked, well up to peace-time standard. Any shortage would seem to be more in the vegetable line. Grocers are well-stocked and I have seen very little queueing. Chocolate and cigarettes short. Biscuits easier to get than most places. Most of the restaurants and eating resorts deal almost exclusively with fried bacon, sausages and/or chips and offer little else. Women seem reasonably satisfied with the situation and deliveries - a good deal of scavenging for the scarcer things goes on.'

Perhaps this was not a surprising account but his thoughts on women were:

'I think the women are standing up wonderfully to war inconveniences. The members of the women's services are consistently cheerful in spite of the fact that many are doing dull, commonplace drudgery. The fact that all the younger women are in uniform has made a huge difference. That uniforms are all attractive and thus the fact that all come up to a high standard of charm in the dress line makes the plainer ones look prettier. Also the fact that a woman's dress now tells one nothing of her circumstances or *class* means that men and women, who would not usually make friendships, all mix up well. The older women have an unenviable lot, yet carry on quietly and cheerfully while their world crumbles away.

On the whole, the older women seem more adaptable

***248-251** Photographs of destruction in Plymouth, before D-Day, probably taken by Pete F. Ferguson.*

and willing to accept change in customs and ideas than the older men. The younger women seem to stand up better to drudgery than men and do not complain about having to do cooking or being stewards etc. They seem less concerned about what will happen after the war than men.'

Fleet Navigating Officer Bartlett was also candid about language:

'I am not affected by obscenity or swearing. We are human and need to let ourselves go sometimes. Swearing is only a safety valve. Deliberate and calculated cursing or damning of someone else is not good and happily rare. As for obscenity, I don't see how anything can be obscene in itself and I enjoy seeing some people shocked out of their ruts by occasional bouts of licentiousness.'

In particular, he pointed out:

'I use any words I consider expressive amongst men of my own age. When I talk to my parents, women in general, children and older men, I do not use certain words, the probable reason being that they would be offended. Words I do not use to these people – swear words: shit, bugger, f*ck, balls, turd, shite, bloody. Other words: spew, pissed, spunk, arse, crap, blast.'

Fleet Navigating Officer Bartlett added:

'One or two Polish and Norwegian swear words of the *obscene* type have become universally adopted in my unit (navy) where we are mixed up with Poles and Norwegians. A typical new Norwegian word is *fahn*, corresponding to *bugger* [sic]. I do not care, or get offended, if I hear other people using any language.'

In May 1943 he appraised pubs in Plymouth:

'Most of the pubs are too big and too swamped out by sailors. With these big pubs I miss the personal patronage of the landlord and the homely companionship of the small pub where the customers are regulars. Many of the pubs around here are changing into road-houses. This road-house type of pub is the type I dislike. The customers are migratory; the bar is large and overcrowded. There is a high percentage of women in uniform and as many drink spirts as beer. I also dislike the large, dark and dingy town pub – the *Tottenham Court Road* type, with frosted glass windows and marble-topped bar. I like the small country inn with its darts and shove-ha'penny, and the secluded small-town pub down a side street.'[247]

Mr Bartlett married Gladys Winnington-Ingram in 1952 and died in 2011.[248]

47. Elizabeth Wardale, Teacher, 1943-4

Sixty-two-year-old widowed, and German-born, Elizabeth Wardale (1881-1957) was a languages teacher at St Dunstan's Abbey in North Road West when she recorded her day's itinerary in 1944. The day and boarding school for girls was under the auspices of the Community of St Mary the Virgin in Wantage.

12 February 1944

'Get up at 7.10 without much enthusiasm, another day of the war. No bath in the school hostel and, in the morning, no hot water. Wash in the cold. Put on clothes which had been laid out methodically *ready to be picked up in case of emergency*. Take my torch and walk over to the abbey for breakfast, in the dark, over the road, through the quad and the cloisters, down the stairs which are still blacked-out. Breakfast: cereals, cold milk, bread and dripping, and tea. Return to the hotel, my bed in my still blacked-out room. Go to School. It is a cold and palely sunny morning with the balloons very high in a colour-less sky. Gunfire in the distance, practice? Lunch at 1, then school, tea, preparation and correction of school exercise books. Supper at 7.30, preceded by long walk in the dark. Bed.'

The war had clearly impacted upon Mrs Wardale's mental health and she admitted 'the war had got me down, I cannot always control waves of depression and irritability.' Four months earlier she had explained that books were an emotional connection to other people:

'Perhaps my repressed maternal instincts have found this channel. I certainly feel the urge to suckle others with my books, there is always someone lying, restlessly, at times, on my intellectual breasts. But perhaps I am less maternal, than bent on sharing the ideas and pleasures which have meant much to me; what I really want perhaps is to be at one with my fellow human beings.'[249]

Mrs Wardale explained that the books she reread were E. M. Foster's *Howard's End*, *A Passage to India*, *Where Angels Fear to Tread*, Dorothy Richardson's *The Tunnel* and other

252 St Dunstan's Abbey, North Road, Plymouth, the home of Mrs Elizabeth Wardale in 1944.

novels by Henry James and Marcel Proust as well as Charles Dickens' *David Copperfield*. She added:

'Dickens belongs to another category and what I am going to say does not apply to him. E. M. Foster, Dorothy Richardson and Marcel Proust have made it possible for me to go on living. They unravel what to

253 Mrs Wardale in a collection of family photographs.

me seems hopelessly tangled and give value to what at times would seem completely valueless. They open out vistas and reconcile me to life, in different ways. These great authors succeed in breaking down the conventional barriers between man and man, and in their vision a world in fragments becomes whole.'

Mrs Wardale also addressed the mental effects of war and her general outlook on life. She replied:

'The manners of my surroundings often go against my own particular grain (looks and habits, expect very noisy habits, do not seem to affect me). When I was young, and younger, up to the age of about 45, the English *could do no wrong* and I am all the more surprised and saddened to find that now I am living with the members of the English School staff, I allow myself to be irritated by their attitude to life, as expressed by their manners.

First, table manners. But here, from the outset, it is necessary to distinguish between the older and the younger members of the staff. The older members put the quick handing of dishes and cruets first and go about this business with a grim determination which chokes all talk. Any little hitch, caused by absent-mindedness or slowness in the uptake or interest in what is being said, is treated as a crime.

The younger members of the staff seem to be less perturbed about the speed or lack of speed with which mustard is handed to X, before the idea of mustard has formed in X's brain. Their idea of a meal seems to be more Continental. They just eat and talk and laugh, fend for themselves and casually see that other people have something to eat: they are not obsessed by the same rigid ideal of table manners.

Then there is this *sense of humour* which you *must* have. To be without a sense of humour is as bad as being unwashed and the most appalling thing is that anybody may suddenly make the discovery and declare that you have no sense of humour and if this happens, well, then you are in the soup once and for all.

The quality of this sense of humour is never questioned, it being taken for granted by the happy owners that every brand is the right brand. Can you burst into a loud laugh at a moment's notice just because you want something to be funny? If you can, you have a sense of humour and you are saved.

A strange thing too (considering the fact that this sense of humour is more than beauty and riches and intelligence and good health) is that you can pat yourself on the back and say *my sense of humour*, without being thought conceited. X, Y and Z talk daily about their sense of humour and remain un-snubbed. Why?'

In 1929 Elizabeth Freundlich, when aged forty-seven, had married seventy-two-year-old Francis James Wardale (1856-1942), a civil servant who was a fellow of the Royal Astronomical Society. She died in 1957 in Leicestershire.[250]

48. I. Shorland, 1945

This directive response of May appears to be the only contribution to MO made by I. Shorland of whom nothing more has been discovered.[251] His account of VE Day and other public events around that date appears to have been derived from local newspapers, notably the 22 May edition of the *Western Morning News*. Of much more interest is his 'A cross-section of Plymouth's public opinion'. He canvassed 110 men and 60 women regarding their plans for VE Day:

254 Fundraising badge for Salute the Soldier Week, 1944.

'Twenty men from the dockyard, approximate age 28, said they would get drunk.
Twenty men from the dockyard, approximate age 50, said they would get drunk.
Twenty demolition [men], approximate age 30, get drunk.
Twenty railway men, approximate age 28, get drunk.
Twenty transport men, approximate age 30, get drunk.
Ten army get drunk, ten navy get drunk, ten air force get drunk, all approximately 28.

Twenty women, housewives, approximate age 30, give a party.
Twenty factory women, approximate age 28, go to the local.
Twenty shop women, approximate age 20, go to a dance.'

Directive: the end of the war

Of Plymouth's VE Day celebrations he wrote:

'We went to bed glad on Monday night and woke up on Tuesday full of joyous expectation. I was out very early. The streets looked very bare but by 8.30 small knots had formed at good shops. By 10 o'clock the spirit of the day asserted itself, flags and buntings appeared, bells were rung, guns fired and thousands paraded the streets. Celebrations were aided by brilliant sunshine with flags and other emblems making splashes of colour on the bomb-scarred buildings. The Hoe seemed the focal point for celebrations. Large numbers danced until midnight. Loudspeakers had been erected on both sides of the Drake statue; at one time there were about 900 dancers.

During a display of high spirits, about 30 deck chairs were burned on a bonfire. The police handled the crowd with great tact and gradually dispersed it.

Lady Astor set the ball rolling when she organised community singing on the Hoe, earlier in the afternoon she attended a big tea party for children. Thousands of citizens assembled in the vicinity of the ruins of the ancient mother church Saint Andrews to hear the prime minister. It seemed fitting that this setting should be the heart of Plymouth's honouring the end of hostilities in Europe with tears, gratitude and prayers. From the sturdy tower came the peals which have for centuries marked great occasions.

Plymouth paid a high price for her share in the glory of victory, it was a sacrifice which history will record as an inspiration to future generations. Our Lord Mayor [Henry George Mason] issued the following message: *All have borne sacrifice, hardship and loss with great understanding, fortitude and courage and now has come the reward, a total victory.*

Plymouth's great Thanksgiving parade took 50 minutes to pass the stand where the Lord Mayor took the salute. On the platform were Admiral Sir Ralph Leatham [Commander-in-Chief, Plymouth], Lady [Enid] Leatham, [Hugh, Fifth] Earl Fortescue, Lady Astor and others. Brilliant sunshine brought crowds of people out. As the parade passed the base, six Sunderland flying boats came flying over in salute.

On Monday 21st Lady Leatham accompanied by the Lord Mayor and the Lady Mayoress opened the RNAF [Navies] Week, fortnight. One of the most striking features is the half-size replica of the *Golden Hind* which sailed in the Sound, huge crowds lined the Hoe and Barbican to watch the little ship make its maiden voyage. This was under the command of Lieut. Cam Perkins, on board was Lord and Lady Mayoress, Air Vice Marshall Maynard. The little craft left the West Hoe Pier driven by its s.h.p. engine, once in the Sound the sails were unfurled and she entered the Barbican under full sail, firing a four-gun salute. The party stepped ashore at the historic Mayflower steps.

Another exhibition was opened at the Barbican this afternoon by Air Marshall Maynard, was an air-sea rescue launch.

At the Royal Citadel Tattoo. The Tattoo was very colourful and inspiring. The finale was a picture; against a background of soft religious music the choir with their red cassocks and white surplices walked to the front, across the parade ground came the sound of the vesper bell, followed by the massed choirs [of the Royal Marine Church and the Dockyard Church] singing the *Nunc Dimittis*.

On Wednesday 23rd Plymouth Social Club, Chapel Street, held a victory party for children. The Lord Mayor said he was glad to see the people of Plymouth were entertaining their children.

May 25th the Lord and Lady Mayoress arrived in Plymouth this afternoon to meet Lord and Lady Alexander.

May 26th this morning the Lord and Lady Mayoress of London, and Plymouth, met the executive committee of the week. Sir Frank and Lady Alexander enjoyed a short sail in the model *Golden Hind*, later they were guest at luncheon of the Lord Mayor of Plymouth. The mayor of Plymouth performed the opening ceremony at Abbey Garage of W. Mumford Ltd, test-house, a landing craft engine [exhibition].

Sir Frank and Lady Alexander are the guests of Sir Ralph and Lady Leatham [at the Grand Hotel]. The Lord Mayor of Plymouth invited Sir Frank Alexander to declare the week open, masses of pink and blue hydrangeas and geraniums decorated the platform. In the evening the Lord Mayor of London took the salute at the Royal Citadel Tattoo.

Hundreds of people queued today to see the German U-boat. The U1023 had been brought to Plymouth specially as a result of Admiral Sir Ralph Leatham. U1023 is equipped with the Schnorchel apparatus.

The Lord Mayor and Lady Mayoress of London accompanied by the Lord Mayor of Plymouth visited the prisoners-of-war guild party [at the Public Junior School in North Road] for tea. Alderman Mason welcomed the men home and said he hoped that they would soon be able to forget the past and settle down to a very much happier future.

Sunday 27th. The Lord Mayor attended [a service of thanksgiving for prisoners-of-war at] St Catherine's Church this afternoon.

May 28th. The Lord Mayor and Lady Mayoress with Sir William Mounstephen attended Devonport Central Hall.

May 30 The Lady Mayoress opened the Salvation Army garden party. The Lord Mayor visited Plymouth's Junior Technical School Sports.'

PLYMPTON ST MARY

This large ancient parish has been largely subsumed within Plymouth. During the 1930s it had some 5,077 residents. During the war the parish was a popular destination and throughfare for Plymothians who at night trekked to escape the bombings. On one night in April 1941 it was estimated that seven thousand people stayed overnight in Plympton. The most destructive attack took place on 13 June 1943 when there were five fatalities. In 1944 and 1945 the parish hosted a large number of Italian and German prisoners of war.[252]

49. Frank Way, Teacher, 1943

Thirty-five-year-old Frank Samuel Way (1907-1994) was visiting his parents at Tor Cottage in George Lane when in July he attended an agricultural show outside Plymouth. This was probably the Grand Show and Gymkhana held at Roborough.[253] Way was employed as a schoolmaster at the Blue Coat School in Reading.

July 1943

'Got up about 9am, the weather being finally decided as being just bearable for me to go to a horse and cattle show at a village some distance away, on the road to Tavistock. Not knowing buses, I took a chance and went in good time, and had to wait nearly half an hour before a bus came which fetched up at the rural station where I could get a train nearer to my destination.

There was quite a little crowd gathered waiting for the train and many were bound for the show. I fell in with the local ironmonger and an old man that was retired and had lived in those parts when he was a boy. We went past a large ordnance factory that used to be manned by British troops and now by US, as I heard someone, possibly maliciously, say, so that our chaps would go and do the fighting. The ironmonger volunteered that he did not like them, but said perhaps I was partly right in thinking that they were less noisy and aggressive than in the last war.

When we got out of the train, after some ten minutes run, I fell in with a man from Lancashire who is down here with a firm that is doing demolition or building in Plymouth or some such…

The rest of the time I seemed to spend near the bar, with occasional excursions to see items of special interest. My friend and his wife left the rest of the party about 5.30 and we debated how to get back, while having some beer in the pub opposite the ground. We eventually decided to walk, about 5 miles, and set off to the next pub, just for one for the road. We had done the easy part, all down-hill, and got a lift. The pub at home where we finished up sold out after two rounds and we went up the road, and they found some folks were going to a place a bit farther, where friend's mother-in-law and party were staying, and we went on there, arriving about 9 and thence got another lift back at closing time. It's a good thing to know farmers and live in such a district at such times.

When I got in my father was gone to bed and I had some discussion of him and his fatal illness with my mother, some light being shed on the family and its failings in general. After having several cups of tea and helping wash up, I read some more of Margaret Kennedy's *The Midas Touch*, while on the throne, and noted some passages which I hope soon to transfer to my scrap book and which also seemed pertinent to a discussion I had with an AT one glamorous afternoon on the river at Pangbourne recently, when I thought she was interested in me, mistakenly, as it turned out. And so, about 1am, to bed.'

Mr Way's father died three months later. He had written about this in May that year: ('Father a weak and obstinate character, addict of whiskey, mean when in drink and surreptitious about it. Mother having the usual life of a drunkard's wife.'). Mr Way had left home in 1925 and did not return until the year his father died.[254]

PLYMSTOCK

Plymstock is a large parish on the edge of Plymouth Sound and the Cattewater and had a population of some seven thousand people before the Second World War.

50. Peter Hore, Clerk, 1942

Peter Hore (1924-), a seventeen-year-old clerk who lived at Elston in Dunstone Road at Plymstock, worked in Plymouth. He answered thirteen directives in 1942 and 1943.

Directive: reflections on war

In his first response, written in January 1942, he reflected that the war had made him mature for his years:

'I think the war has made me grow up mentally far quicker than I should otherwise have done. When war broke out, I was fourteen and at school. But for the war I should still be at school, whereas I am now at work and am Home Guard and I suppose I've learnt more about the world in general in the last six months than ever before.'

He also gave his views on four races. Mr Hore regarded the Japanese to be 'an extraordinary race – clever, conceited, unscrupulous, ruthless and fanatical.', the Chinese were 'a great nation which is as far behind western civilisation today as it was ahead of it two thousand years ago.', of the Russians he wrote 'I think of them as a rather inhuman nation but I don't quite know why, unless its from books about the revolution.' and he thought they were 'Not unlike ourselves, but take themselves more seriously.' Finally, in respect to the French his view was 'I cannot believe that the majority of the French people were in favour of the capitulation.'

25 February 1942

He did not describe his daily itinerary on one day in February 1942 as being exciting:

'8.00am Get up, have breakfast.
8.30 Go to work in father's car.
8.45 Arrive at office, carry typewriters from air raid shelter.
9.00 – 1.30 Write receipts for cash received in post.
1.30 – 2.30 Walk to Communal Feeding Centre and have dinner. Walk back.
2.30 – 2.45 Drink tea in office
2.45 - 3.15 Enter cash items on sheets
3.15 Drink more tea
3.30 – 4.15 Balance cash-sheets with cash, endorse cheques, fill in paying-in book.
4.15 Carry typewriters downstairs again.
4.45 Go home in car.
5.00 Have dinner.
5.30 – 8.30 Listen to wireless and read.
8.30 Go to bed early owing to bad cold.'

Directives: post-war education, Sunday observance and the supernatural

Two months later Mr Hore was more responsive in respect to three questions. He wrote:

'I feel that it is a great pity that I was never taught the history of the town I live in. I was not aware that Plymouth had many historical connections apart from Drake and his bowls and I certainly never knew that it was besieged in the Civil War until I read a book on the subject from the public library. A term could very profitably be spent on local history with a visit to the local museum and would undoubtedly prove interesting to pupils.'

He also explained his views on how Sunday was observed:

'I have two objections to the traditional English Sunday. One is that is an unhappy day for children, who are made to wear their best clothes and keep quiet, and the other is that although nominally religious, its significance has become chiefly social and conventional.'

Mr Hore also wrote about the occult:

'I think that of all supernatural occurrences that are reported perhaps 50% have some perfectly natural explanation. Another 10% are due to hallucinations or mental strain but the other 40% are due to some supernatural cause. In illustration of the first category, I would like to relate the story of my uncle who lives in the Cornish village of Landulph. On one occasion he was returning home at night from the neighbouring village of Cargreen and had to pass a chapel which was reputed to be haunted. As he approached it, he heard a most bloodcurdling sound, something between a snore and a bubble. He is a most determined man and although not exactly encouraged, he resolved to find out what it was. It turned out to be due to a man who was returning home in a very inebriated condition and had gone to sleep at the side of the road. While moving about in his sleep his head had fallen back over the edge of a ditch, with the result that he was partly choked and was emitting this horrible noise. Had anyone of less determined will come upon him, me for instance, I should have returned home by a circuitous route at extreme speed with a tale that would have increased the reputation of the spot tenfold.

Unfortunately the only two real ghost stories that I know to be true were told me by a friend who is himself an Observer so I will leave it to him to recount them.'

Directive: holiday arrangements

That summer Mr Hore commented on local swimming:

'I don't know whether any special arrangements have been made but the usual bathing facilities on the Hoe are still available and to judge by the hordes of people coming away from the Hoe when I leave work at 6pm, a lot of people are taking advantage of them and spending their holidays at home.'[255]

Mr Hore's subsequent history has not been uncovered.

***255-6** Two views of Postbridge in the early 1900s.*

POSTBRIDGE

Postbridge was one of the county's most remote locations during the war, situated in the centre of Devon on the road from Moretonhampsead to Two Bridges.

51. Gwendolyn Dunlop, Housewife, 1941

In 1941 Mrs Gwendolyn Elizabeth Dunlop (1901-1985) was a forty-year-old mother of two sons when she visited Dartmoor. That year Robert F. Dunlop (1929-1970) had been evacuated with the rest of Pinewood School, an establishment founded in 1875 in Berkshire and moved shortly afterwards to Farnborough. Some 41 boys were enrolled but had been relocated several times before being sent to Devon. One of them later recalled the school comprised 'two small hotels' and another boy remembered the accommodation as 'two main buildings, one was really the village pub and it was like an old stone cottage. The other was a small hotel called Dartfordleigh. Lessons were all in the building on the road, East Dart. It was a hundred yards away along a track. On the right was bumpy grass sloping up to our playing fields, on the left the ground had been made into a big vegetable patch where all the boys helped grow things such as potatoes and beans.'[256]

Mrs Dunlop left from her home in Swindon:

'November 8th, F[ergus] got his 48 hours leave and we set off immediately after breakfast by car to visit R[obert] at his Prep. School on the top of Dartmoor. F had put in an application for petrol for the trip on the grounds that we would anyhow have to hire a car at Exeter to take us the 20 miles onto the moor and to fetch us again, which would also be very expensive. It was, however, a very pleasant surprise that they actually gave us coupons for the holiday. Marvelous sunshine and autumn scenery put us both in a holiday mood.

Gave several lifts, the most interesting being to a Naval officer on leave making his way to Dartmouth to visit boys who had been at the Prep School near Windsor where he was a master before the war. He seemed to be doing instructional duty on shore and happy and interested in his work, having wanted to go into the navy as a boy.

Reached the school about 2.00 and given late lunch. Watched a game and then had tea with R and strolled about. Saw the chickens R and other boys are looking after. They feed and clean the houses and even pluck the cockerels which are killed for the table.

Had supper with the staff, and two or three other visiting parents followed by interesting exchange of views about education (boarding schools versus day schools, the value of university life in a post-war world, etc.) and comparison of different voluntary war work being undertaken by various mothers. General agreement that it was difficult to get anything that did not mean hours of boring waiting about, which also left a mother free to be with her children in the holidays. One said she was driving a rescue car in London and would not go to the country for fear of having nothing to do, but her children spent the holidays with a granny in a safe area and she then took more time off and visited them several days a week but this meant she was unable to qualify for admission to classes that were arranged in languages and other subjects to relieve the monotony of waiting and to enable people to train for post-war jobs.

257 *The East Dart Inn, requisitioned by Pinewood School during the Second World War, 2025.*

November 9th, Left F to have a long sleep in bed and went myself to the school service held by the headmaster in the tiny village church three quarters of an hour before the public service. A few hymns, prayers and a psalm, and a reading by the master.

Rain kept us indoors all morning but after lunch we motored over to Tavistock with Robert and a friend of his to visit F's brother who is on the HQ of the SW Command near there. Returned at 6.00 when F gave the boys an informal song recital which seemed to go down well.

Spent the evening in Matron's room. All agreed that both the boys and staff were happier at Postbridge than they had been in the more perfect and luxurious surroundings from which they had been ousted by the government a year ago. Being in the centre of a small village community, instead of isolated in the middle of a large park, was the chief asset. They had little difficulty with the domestic staff, as the servants' hall was allowed to keep open house every evening to the men from a lonely AA battery on the moor and even got up whist drives, etc. for them every now and then. Matron was amazed how fit the boys were up there and free from colds and petty illness. She thought they had all grown much hardier.

November 10th Had an early breakfast with the school and set out for home in pouring rain. Long dull drive except for giving a short lift to a Polish airman, who told us how he had escaped from Poland through Hungary and Yugoslavia and fought three months in France. Then to England on the *Andorra Star*, a week before she was sunk…'[257]

The following year Robert Dunlop wrote about the holiday given to mark 29 June (St Peter's Day) in *The Blue and Grey*, the school's magazine.

'Monday morning dawned with a clear sky; in fact thoroughly promising. After our breakfast we were told that we were walking to Dartmeet, about five miles down the river, and that our lunch and tea were being taken in Mr Wakeham's car together with a few of the smaller boys, who were unable to walk the distance.

We set off eagerly quite soon after breakfast and only stopped after climbing the slopes of Bellever Tor. At the top we rested for a short time, while we surveyed the surrounding country from the massive granite rocks that have made this tor renowned.

Resuming our way, we soon came to Dartmeet after traversing Laughter Tor. On arriving we found Mr Wakeham with the lunch awaiting us. After a good bathe in a large-sized pool not far up the West Dart, we came back for our meal, for which, I consider, the catering staff deserve the highest praise. After this we were left to our own resources.

Numerous species of *lepidoptera* were found in the vicinity, and some of us spent the afternoon catching specimens for our collections, while others tried to catch the various kinds of dragon-fly which fluttered over the water, but this was rather difficult owing to

258 Polish troops marching in Great Britain, undated.

their speed. The remainder of us either *explored* or played on the many boulders in the middle of the river.

A second bathe then followed: this time longer than before, as the water was much warmer. We returned for tea, and when we had finished, gathered our belongings together for our journey homeward. And so we got into bed, tired but thankful for such a fine day.'[258]

The school continued at Postbridge until 1946 when it relocated to Bourton in Berkshire.[259]

RINGMORE (& PLYMOUTH)

In this coastal South Hams parish, some fifteen miles from Plymouth, lies the Pickwick Inn at St Ann's Chapel, a hamlet only a mile from the village. In 1931 there were only 252 parishioners. In 1941 the rector decided resident evacuees were to be charged ten pounds for their burials in the parish churchyard instead of the standard five-shilling rate for local people. His innovation may have been the consequence of his rectory having been requisitioned the previous year. Air raid precautions included the installation of a searchlight at Marwell.[260]

52. Mariella Vaughan, Actress, 1940-1

In 1939 Mariella Vaughan (1911-1962) was a twenty-eight-year-old actress from London who, alongside Donald Pleasance, was a member of the Plymouth Repertory Club. Previously she had been in the Canterbury Repertory Players.

During these years she bore three different names. As Jean Marie Vaughan she was the daughter of South African-born Frederick Theodore Vaughan (1888-1960), a car salesman, and his wife Isabel (1889-1962) of 53 Upper Park Road in West Hampstead. In 1934 she married Reginald Maynard Bennett (1904-1988) and became Jean Marie Bennett. Her stage name at this time was Jean Marie Vaughan until 1936 when she changed it to Mariel Vaughan. It was at this time that the couple separated and on 7 September 1940 she changed her name by deed poll from Jean Marie Bennett to Mariella Vaughan. Two days earlier she explained in her diary that she intended to change her married name to her stage name but needed the permission of her husband with whom she had not lived for five years nor seen for six months.[261]

Mrs Vaughan wrote five diaries from 1939 to 1947, a day-survey in 1938 and was a directive respondent in 1939, 1940 and 1942.[262] In 1938 she was a pacifist (as was her husband).[263]

In 1940 she left Devon to live with her parents in Hampstead but the bombing in September of a neighbouring house convinced her to return to Devon. In December 1940 Mrs Vaughan recounted the effect of the war on her.

***259** Miss Jean Marie Vaughan and her fiancé Mr Reginald Bennett, 1934.*

***260** The Pickwick Inn, Miss Vaughan's home for several years during the war, 2025.*

1940

'My life has changed so completely in the past year that I find it very difficult to answer this question. Last year I was working in the theatre in Plymouth and was hopeful of carrying on my career in spite of the war. This year I have left my home and my parents in London and I am always rather worried about them particularly since I am so very fond of them and they are sending me an allowance to enable me to live in a safe area. I am living with friends whom I hardly knew a year ago.

My life has no settled future. The plans I had of taking up another career if the stage proved a failure are now very uncertain and in 1941 I shall do no more than live from day-to-day. I used to have many ideals and beliefs in the ultimate betterment of social conditions and of man becoming far happier owing to the help of psychological treatment and of the decline of crime and mental derangement. Now I have very few such hopes. Perhaps the change in my mental outlook is due to the fact that in a bar of this kind one meets very unintellectual types and sees them so often in the state of intoxication, then you cannot help realising that the only thing a great majority of humanity responds to is the power of money and sexual excitement and revenge.

At one time I either lived at home, where I did not come into contact with many people, or worked in the theatre which I suppose is a little world of its own. Life seems more sordid to me now. And I either stand a little aloof from it or in despair have drinks myself and try to enjoy the moment. Then it all becomes unreal and the disappointment becomes less intense.

A year ago I had not seen the terrible site of ruins and devastation nor heard people talk of the death of hundreds as though it is of little importance. I find I think less perhaps because I cannot face it. 1941 seems to me to hold very little future for my own part. All I can do is live in the moment and if I have my friends and a certain amount of pleasure and love and affection, I shall have to be content. I cannot feel very optimistic about the outcome of the war. I think nothing can be worth all the suffering and agony of

***261** German aerial photograph of the coast at Ringmore, 30 November 1940.*

the peoples of all countries. Nothing perhaps except a universal socialism and a chance of peace for many generations to come, but I do not think this war will lead to anything so idealistic, but just another repetition of itself. I feel completely disillusioned about 1941 both internationally and personally.

My Christmas will be rather different this year. I shall work here and help in the bar. I shall send hardly any presents or cards. I no longer feel any interest in them. I shall only send to a few relatives and old friends. I shall not have any different food as I have become a vegetarian.

I seem to have very little opinion nowadays. I do not read the paper very much nor do I listen to the wireless. The whole thing depresses me horribly. I am afraid I am going through a period of extreme escapism. If I did want to inform an opinion I should talk to all types of people and try and find out the trend of thought. I do not believe half the newspapers or the wireless say. I always feel they try to be over optimistic to keep up the peoples morale, so the more optimistic they get the worse I think the situation really is. I'm afraid this is a very little help to you.'[264]

1941

By April 1941 Mrs Vaughan attempted to evade the bombing by sleeping outside London and returning home each morning. She then decided to return to Devon:

'Thursday May 8th I caught a train from Paddington to [South] Brent. The train was fairly full. I read most of the time *Time, Sex and Pain* by Gerald Heard, except for an interesting conversation with some RAF officers. Had lunch on the train. Arrived about an hour or less late at Brent and changed into a local train to Kingsbridge. My friend was waiting for me there and we taxied to her pub about 12 miles away. We stopped on the way at a little pub and had two drinks. I discovered there were practically no cigarettes in Devon. This worried me as I could have brought a few packets from London had my friend warned me. We got 10 each from the pub. She had no stock at all at their inn.

We arrived at her place. It is now packed out with government surveyors come to assess war damage at Plymouth. They said that the damage at Plymouth is far more concentrated and therefore worse than any of the other towns they have worked at (Sheffield, Liverpool, Birmingham etc.) Had supper and several drinks and went to bed early.

May 9th Got up fairly early. One of my friends went off with several of the government men who drove her up to London for a weekend. I stayed to look after the pub with the younger of my two friends. Spent a fairly busy day at the inn, saw lots of my friends who came over for a drink. The locals were full of talk about the 11 bombs which dropped in fields near them during one of the blitz at Plymouth. They seemed very nervous and although they have suffered no casualties, had less courage than the towns people I have talked to. One of them, a farm labourer, goes off to work with a gas mask in a tin hat etc. They were rather put out by the altered time and some of them were still working by the old time. They were also very worried about the *crops* and lack of rain.

***262-5** Four views of Plymouth before the war.*

I met some friends from Plymouth. One is an officer in the Home Guard. He was blown up and his friend killed during one raid and has a stiff leg now with three shrapnel marks in it. Another was a girl who worked in Paignton but was too frightened by the thought of incendiary bombs to stay there! Went to the bluebell wood in the afternoon. Served drink all the evening. Did a good trade.

May 10th Very much the same as May 9th. Except in the evening when we had a rather nasty experience. Three evacuee women came in and had a few milk stouts and were enjoying themselves in a harmless way when one of the local women came in to buy cigarettes for her husband. The others knew her. She looked a poor pathetic thing almost half-witted, dressed in rags, so one of them asked her to have a drink but she was terrified and refused, saying her husband would *beat her up*. However, chaffed her out of the [blank] and bought her a beer. Later I bought her another. I felt very sorry for her. She was so harmless and hardly spoke a word. Then in came her husband (I did not see this) and she scuttled out like a frightened rabbit. He cursed and swore and tore after her saying he'd *rip her up*. Neither my friend nor I heard this, till they were both gone. Then the evacuee women told us and we did not know what to do, whether to ring up the police or what. It appeared that she had been removed from him twice and gone back again. We did nothing but worry but he could not have done much because there were no rumours the next day, but we did not see either of them again.

May 11th A nice and restful day as the bar hours were less. We spent a long afternoon walking and had tea in a neighbouring village. It rained a little but I enjoyed myself. This particular woman and myself have so much in common.

In the evening a very drunk man came into the bar and wanted to buy me round after round of drink, but I refused all but the first. He afterwards went and smashed his wife's nose and blacked both her eyes, because he had let her come to Devon as an evacuee and had heard she was sleeping with soldiers. And so he came down and *beat her up* and took her mother, who had caused the mischief, back to London. The evacuees certainly have a name for *carrying on* in the village.

May 12th. Same kind of day, except that we had lots of trouble over lack of spirits to drink and cider running out etc. I got a little drunk myself on cider and rum but only happily so.

May 13th Much the same. I cannot remember which day that the Hess news started but I do know people were talking of it incessantly when it did.

May 14th The older of my friends returned from London, having spent £15 in her weekend. She had a hectic night during the Saturday blitz but looked much better.

May 15th Nothing sensational. All the men were back and we played darts a lot. I have improved immensely but my side lost heavily in a game of cricket we had.

May 16th Plymouth My friend and I took the morning bus into Plymouth. It puts you down on the outskirts now near Mutley Plain. T got her haircut and then we walked into Plymouth itself.

I could not believe the utter devastation there. All the centre of the town, the place where our theatre club was, and all the restaurants and shops I used to know so well and gave me such a happy time, existed no longer, only piles of ruins. My friends had of course described the scene to me but until I saw it myself (and I have seen quite an amount of the London damage) I did not imagine that anything could be so devastated. It really was amazing and I felt almost like crying; to stand in the middle of George Street and instead of seeing shops on either side, my hairdresser which I used to patronise once a week, Boots where we used to have tea when meeting friends in order to listen to the small orchestra and see many of the local people, Goodbody's where I have so often had coffee between rehearsals or to discuss business with various people, there was nothing to see except piles of stone and dust and steel girders broken and twisted, so that we had to consider a moment before we said *That must have been just where Boots used to be*. Dingles where I used to have romantic teas and really exciting tete-a-tete luncheons - all gone. Our favourite *after the show* supper place for a final drink and a sandwich. Instead is an empty shell. My solicitors in Prince's Square burnt out and finished and all the small local shops which were near to my old *digs* are no more, although I can remember so well all the people I used to have a gossip with on my way to the theatre club. How kind they were and how they used to patronise us once a week. Hardly anything but memories remain for me of the Plymouth which gave me so much happiness. The pier burnt out, all the places and people I like so much a heap of rubble. I think it affected me much worse than London because although I have lived there for the majority of my life, it is so large and impersonal. I love parts of London and have been happy in some places but some of those places still stand and most of my friends exist but Plymouth is finished and it welcomed me, a year and a half ago, a perfect stranger and made me very happy and it did make me feel very lonely that it is no more existing except in my memory.

My friend and I walked over the ruins. The sun was burning down and we felt hot and disheartened. We found one public house still open, only one in the centre of the town. We know the head bar-maid quite well and went in to see her. She only had one junior bar-maid left. The place looked much as it used to except that it was roped off outside and pieces of masonry seemed in danger of falling on our heads at any minute. We had several drinks and heard the news. She had had to fight the fire with a stirrup pump from late at night till early morning during one raid and was very proud that they had managed to save so much. We met another woman who used to work in another public house which had been destroyed. She told us that the owners of that one had evacuated to Cornwall but were coming back to Plymouth if they could find suitable premises. No more big raids are expected in Plymouth, but only on Mutley and everyone living in Mutley is apprehensive.

After that conversation in which we learned that typhoid is thought quite a likely result of the destruction and that mothers have been told to remove children immediately. The sewers were hit I believe, and people put on their gas masks thinking it was a gas raid.

We heard too that the fires were not efficiently tackled. In fact, that hoses and apparatus were sent from a neighbouring town but when the new fires broke out the apparatus did not fit and were quite useless. Also, that the equipment of the Home Guard is wholly inadequate there. All this being very depressing, we went in search of another friend of mine but she had moved to Devonport and no one knows what happened to her.

We bought some second-hand books and then walked

266 *Mutley Plain, a favoured shopping destination after the bombing.*

back to Mutley where my woman friend met an admirer of hers for tea and went to Goodbody's and I met a man friend of mine and went to another restaurant. We then motored to Modbury with T's friend and he left us as he had to get back to Cornwall and could not take us any further owing to petrol shortage. We had a game of darts and a beer in a Modbury hotel and then walked four miles to our own home. Finished a very tiring day working in the bar.

May 17th Nothing very much.

May 18th Apart from bar work, spent the day walking and sunbathing in the woods. Lovely.

May 19th Caught the early bus to Plymouth, met a friend with whom I spent an hour before catching a train to Bath. Had a crowded journey with a lot of mothers who had been visiting evacuated children.'

In 1946 Mrs Vaughan joined a theatrical company near Birmingham ('which was pretty terrible and I did not enjoy much') and afterwards volunteered at a Steiner School at Clent but resumed acting the following year. She died in 1962.[265]

ROBOROUGH (SOUTH DEVON)

This small village in Bickleigh outside Plymouth had less than two hundred residents in 1931 but during the war it not only had an aerodrome but a decoy airfield on Roborough Down.[266] An MO report, written on 1 April 1941, described the use of the village hall following the heavy bombardment of Plymouth:

'This is being used as a rest centre. Outside the hall stood a large van of the Queen's Messengers. Nearby stood seven males (40 to 50) and female 25 Class C [artisans and skilled workers] and 14 children were playing around. Female 25 was drinking soup supplied by the Queen's Messengers and three of the men were having tea and potted meat sandwiches. Inside the hall, the hall is about 40 feet by 25 feet and it was pretty full with 34 females, 4 males and about 50 children, most of them sprawling about the floor. No age group appeared to predominate among the children but the people were almost entirely of Class D [unskilled workers]. There were no beds, no bunks. Most people had brought some sort of covering – travelling rugs, blankets, a few sheets and much non-descript stuff were strewn about the floor and everyone seemed to stick to his or her particular piece of floor, sitting or lying on the covering. At 7.35, Male 45 Class C entered the hall and announced: *Will you all keep quiet, please, and settle down. Until we settle down, we can't give out blankets*. There had been a good deal of noise – general conversation but not actual remarks audible, and the request was met. The noise died down. I reflected as he left the place that this was poor accommodation, anyway, no beds, no bunks, no mattresses, no palliasses, just a hard floor and some blankets and other comparatively thin material.'[267]

***267** Roborough's village hall, 2025.*

***268** Cartoon spoofing American servicemen by George 'Stil' Stillings of Exeter, 1944.*

53. Arthur Hopkins, Clergyman, 1943

Unmarried Reverend Arthur Leslie Hopkins (1900-73), who lived in Lincolnshire, visited his brother at Roborough outside Plymouth in 1943. He wrote:

'Tuesday, 6th July, 1943. A long, tiring, crowded, uninteresting journey from London to Plymouth. It was too crowded to do or to read anything, the only bright spot was that everyone seemed to be in a good humour. Reached Plymouth on the minute and was met by my eldest brother whom I had not seen for 7 years. He is Agent of the Bank of England. The centre of Plymouth is worse than I have seen anywhere.

As I stepped from the train, an alert was going and shortly after the guns started. It was a lone raider and all was over in 7 minutes, without any bombs dropped, or as far as I was concerned a plane seen, most likely dropping mines just out at sea. Tea in the Bank of

England and then bus out to Roborough, where my brother has lived since his house by the bank was destroyed in the April blitz. Roborough a fine spot 6 miles out and 600 feet up. Talked of family affairs and so to bed.

Wednesday, 7th July. Very cold and very bright, went for a short walk in the morning, was struck how different farming is here from Boston. Very untidy and much waste land. Hedges uncut and ditches filled. Lunch in Plymouth with Noël Coward, whom I hadn't seen for years but he hasn't changed a bit. Went to see him in *Present Laughter* in the afternoon, and laughed more than I have done for years.

Met Colonel R. this evening who spoke very bitterly of the high pay the American troops get. Here I quote his own words. *The girls in my village were a nice crowd until the Yanks came – now they say* Why Should we work much, when we can earn £20 to £25 a week by being prostitutes to the American forces? *And there is now hardly a woman – married or single – who is not a prostitute.*

I heard this about a young woman in the WAAF. Her mother died just before the war and left her a good income in gilt-edged holdings. Her father died in the summer of 1940 and his money was in property in London, all of which was destroyed in the raids late in 1940. There is now no income from the father's estate and will not be until after the war. It was valued for death duties before it was destroyed and, therefore, she has to pay at that valuation. So, she has had to sell out a large proportion of her gilt-edged securities to pay the estate duties on property which is now a ruin through no fault of her own. This seems to me to be very hard. The local MP, through my brother, has taken the whole thing up but with no result. She has to pay as the property was valued before the raids.

Thursday, 8th July 1943

Have been walking alone all day on the moors and covered just over 25 miles. I came back more convinced than ever that more might be made of the farm lands. They are full of weeds and many want to be drained. I saw very few people and masses of wonderful wild flowers, many of which were quite new to me.

Friday, 9th July 1943

Went into Plymouth to have a good look around. There is most certainly more damage here than I have seen anywhere else and I have seen Coventry. I came across a meanness here today that I hadn't known for many years. Twice by trams I bought newspapers today only to find when I opened them that they were old papers. The food shops seem very full of stuff except for green veges. It started to rain about 4.30 so I caught the 5.00 bus back and had to stand all the way…

Sunday 11th July 1943

Yesterday it rained all day without a stop, besides which this place was in the clouds… I was going to turn on the news at one, not having heard it earlier, when my sister-in-law said it was out of fuel (as they are nearly out of their dry battery). But I persisted to hear about the [Sicily] invasion. Excitement. Today has been just as wet. I was making up my mind to walk 2¾ miles to church when I got a message from a hotel some ½ mile away to say several people would like a service but they were even further from a church, did I feel like doing anything? I was rather surprised but went down with some of the household here. There were just over 30 people present. We said Mattins and sung 2 hymns, *There is a green hill far away* and *Eternal Father*. I did not give a sermon, but in 2 minutes reminded them it was Sailors Sunday. I was not going to have a collection but someone after service suggested a plate should be put at the door for the Sailors' Society. The result was £7 4s 6d. The rest of the day I have been reading.

Monday, 12th July 1943

A fine day at last. Started out just after breakfast and got back just in time for evening meal, having walked something over 25 miles. I was quite surprised at the amount of fine timber to be found near the sides of most of the rivers and it seems to have been carefully looked after which is strange in Great Britain.

I went into the pub at Buckland Monachorum for half a pint at lunch time and found 2 interesting notices. The first begging people not to steal glasses, it read thus:

Black is the raven,
Black is the rook,
Black is old Hitler,

The world-famous crook.
But blacker the person,
The ill-mannered louse,
Who takes the glasses,
From this public house.

I have written it from memory but I think that I've got it right. The other notice read:

To members of the American Forces, your paymasters make ample chances for you to change your money. We greatly regret that we cannot accept dollar currency.

The corn is turning quickly despite the cold weather.

Tuesday 13th July 1943

A wet and fine day. I went by train to Princetown and walked back part of the way in the clouds. I was horror-struck with the awful grimness of the prison. It is one of the few big prisons in England that I had never seen, and it is by far the worse of any of them. Of what I saw going over and the conference I had I cannot unfortunately write. I can think of no place more likely to cause moral and mental deterioration than Dartmoor for a long term. Those who built the place, as well as those who have administered it until quite recently, could have known nothing or cared less about the real welfare of the prisoners. I found all the officials most kind and helpful in letting me know anything I wanted.

The walk home is about 12 miles of which 11½ are downhill, by the time I got back the tops of my toes were most uncomfortable. I was interested to see the large amount of the moors above Yelverton which has recently been planted with soft wood. In a few years' time the whole aspect of the countryside will be changed. Spent the evening writing my prison report and trying to keep warm.

Wednesday 14th July

We actually saw the sun for ten minutes, but while I was getting up. Then, again, the clouds came down followed by the rain. I have spent nearly all day reading and writing confirmation addresses. In the evening some people came in to see my brother and sister-in-law.

They talked of the Southern Europe fighting and all seemed pleased at the way things were going. There seemed to be a sober optimism amongst them. The chief topic was about the orders given the previous night to the Roborough Home Guard. It seems that they were told that they were no longer to have ordinary parades, but that they were to take it in turns to go one night in five and man the coast defence guns. Going on duty from dark to dawn. Now this doesn't sound too bad, until you look more into it. The guns are about 10 miles from here. There is no direct transport. The buses which run within 2½ miles from the guns via Plymouth stop at 8.00pm and do not start again until 7.45am. Most of the Roborough Home Guard are farm workers and the point is how are they to get to and from the guns and at the same time do their extra harvest farm work?

When they raised this point the dug-out Staff Colonel, who came to tell them of their new orders, took up the attitude that orders were orders and that was that and there was nothing more to be said. It is all very well for those in authority to take this attitude, but what about the small one-man dairy farmer, and there are many in Roborough, with half a dozen cows and a few acres of ploughed land? If he is on the guns all night, 10 miles away from home, no transport provided. If he cycles, he must walk more than half of the way because of the nature of the country. How is he to get his cows milked for the morning collection? It is hard enough now, but what about later in the year during the dark mornings when he can't leave the guns until 8.30 or 9.00, then what about the 6.00am collection of milk? *Orders are orders*. Such a foolish, unsympathetic remark and such gross misunderstanding of the lives of men under them cause great dissatisfaction. Colonel Blimp seems far from dead.

15th July, Thursday

Another awful day…

Sunday, 18 July 1943

I cannot think why people talk of *Sunny Devon*. For the last three days it has been a steady downfall of rain and I have hardly been out of the house. But at last I am feeling really rested. Went to church this morning and was struck how dreadfully mournful a service can be. Really, I cannot wonder at so few people being there with a morning like it was and a service like, I am told, it always is...

Monday, 19 July

Rain again, but not quite so much as usual. Had to keep to the roads as the moors were too wet. Saw a lot of American soldiers. I wonder why so many of them wear silver rings on their first finger.

Tuesday, 20th July

Left Roborough in heavy rain. Caught the Southern Railway train from Friary Station, as I wanted to go to Woking and not to London. As far as Okehampton 6 people in the compartment...'

Reverend Hopkins died thirty years later.[268]

SEATON

This coastal resort, situated in the south-east corner of Devon, had a pre-war population of 2,349 people. At the start of the war two defensive dams were built across the mouth of the River Axe. These were part of the 'Taunton Stop Line'. A holiday camp in the town was converted to house German and Italian subjects. It closed in the summer of 1940. Seaton was reportedly bombed on 18 August 1940, 12 August 1942 (causing the deaths of three adults and two evacuee children – six-year-old June Moore and her sister eleven-year-old Stella), 17 September 1942 and 26 October 1942 (in which another five people died).[269]

In addition to the following MO Writer, there was a second in Seaton who was also a headmistress. Mrs Hilda Peare, aged sixty, answered War-Time Directive No. 2 which was concerned with posters. Her responses were unusually brief. Her longest reply was 'I never bothered to read ARP instructions. In the country you don't ever carry your gasmask. I had to look for mine to come up to London today'.[270]

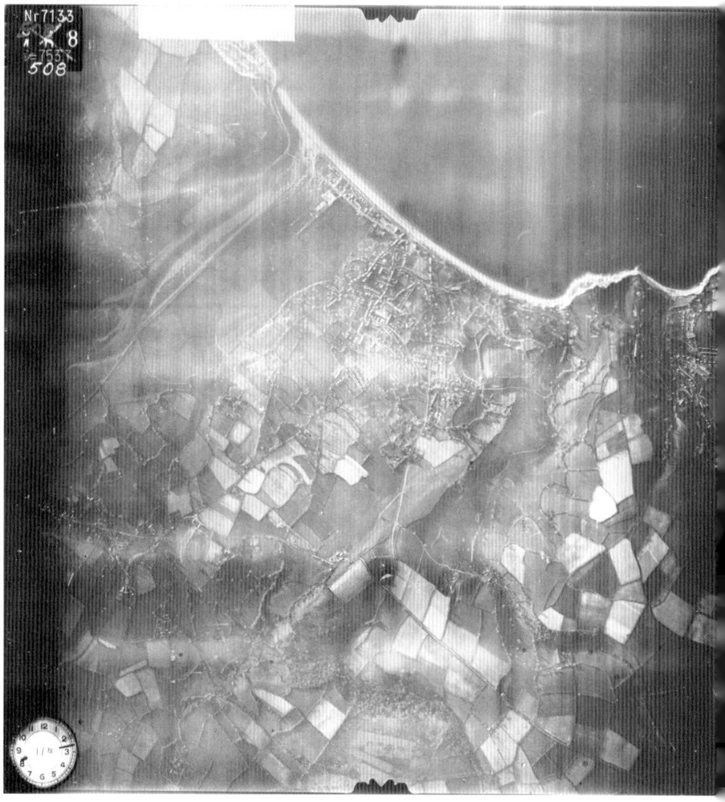

269 German aerial photograph of Seaton, 17 April 1943.

54. Miss Leigh, Teacher, 1940

Miss Leigh, the sixty-year-old headmistress of an unidentified mixed private school evacuated to Seaton, answered an MO directive on 26 April 1940.[271] Her school catered for girls aged five to sixteen and for boys aged up to eleven. She wrote:

'The boys are much more topical than the girls. They have the *Daily Telegraph* map and always follow the movements of the troops in Norway. They were thrilled of course about the *Altmark*, and the sinking of the destroyers, and everything like that. But the girls aren't very interested, they are absorbed in their own lives, which is now Seaton and everything to do with it.

One girl, aged 9, says she doesn't mind about the war if her father doesn't have to go and fight. She doesn't want him to do that. She also thinks that as there is no war in England there is no reason why she shouldn't go home (London). She is about the only one who talks much about the war. They all talk at once, you know, and it's really difficult to know much of what they are saying. The great thing is that they are so sure, they have such confidence in everybody. They're quite sure it is going to be all right now that the Navy is on the job, and are very disappointed now that it is not the Navy. They liked it much better when there were the ships going down. One boy said, *This bombing of the aerodromes. What's the good of bombing the aerodromes? Where are they going to put their aerodromes when they go there? Would they have to rebuild them to land their planes or what?* They are quite certain that we are going to be in occupation.

They are quite serious about it, but they think it is a magnificent thing. They talk about their own people a great deal. You see this Robert -- his father is a doctor out there. He's glad his father isn't in Norway, he's in France. None of them have fathers actually in danger. But the boys definitely, two or three of them, would love to be out there helping. They would love it. One boy, aged 8, whose parents are in Brazil, hoped that they would be able to see the *Graf Spee* going down.'

She also asked seven pupils six questions. The first was which side do they think will win and why. They all answered England and added:

'1, Because they are sensible and we keep our plans quiet.

2, Because we are strong and we have a lot of soldiers.

3, Because we have a strong navy even if they have got better soldiers.

4, I think they will win because they have got more people on their side.

5, Because they have more countries to help them and their navy is strong.

6, Because we have a bigger navy.

7, Because it is stronger.

If you were not British, to what country would you like to belong?

1, Swiss

2, American

3, Holland. I would like to be a little Dutch girl.

4, Swiss.

5, American or Austrian (not when belonging to Germany).

6, A native in India.

7, American.

If you were a grown-up man would you fight in the Army. Give the reasons for your answer.

1, No, because I would like to live and not be killed.

2, No, don't know.

3, Yes, if I could be in charge of the trenches.

4, Yes.

5, Yes, because we are fighting against Germany and it is a cruel country.

6, No, because all my relations are in the Navy.

7, No, because it is dangerous.

What do you think of the blackout?

1, It is beastly.

2, Very nasty indeed.

3, Quite a good thing but with the boards up in the bedroom it is too hot.

4, It is a bother.

5, Horrible, but useful to the country.

6, It is troublesome.

7, It is quite fun.

Has the war made any difference to your life?

1, Yes, I don't get so much to eat.

2, Yes, I would not have come to school.

3, Yes, because we had to go away at Christmas and it is partly why I am here.

4, Yes, because we would still be living in Chiswick.

5, Yes, food and petrol rationing.

6, Yes, otherwise I would not be here.

7, Yes, because I would not have come to school.

How do you know what is happening in the war?'

'1, I do not know much.

2, I have no idea.

3, I don't know unless I see a part of the newspaper on the notice-board.

4, I hear people talking about it and Miss Leigh (head mistress) tells us.

5, By the newspaper, wireless and Mummy's letters.

6, I do not know very much.

7, Miss Leigh tells us.'

On 6 July she wrote further:

'We are having the time of our lives here; the good people round, including Leslie, declare that enemy planes fly over every night and during the day too. They are all so clever that they know them by the sound of their engines. Personally, I never listen and I don't quite see how these people, so stupid about most things, should suddenly develop all this intelligence. They hate me because I never believe anything. However, it is quite certain that we've had no raid or warning. Really and truly I don't believe there ever will be a warning here, if we get a raid, it will be here before anybody knows.

All the Germans have gone from the camp and some I think are now at the bottom of the deep blue sea, once again the know-alls here say they were in the boat that was torpedoed. The beach is better protected, they've dug an enormous trench, 15 feet wide, and are fixing barbed wire and iron stakes in huge cement blocks [which] are being placed all along the front and at the entrance off all roads leading from the front, cars can dodge in and out, but no tank could get through.

So far, the parents have been fairly sensible and I hope they will leave the kids here… If things get serious and the coast places are evacuated, goodness knows what will happen, but I refuse to think about it till it comes.'[272]

No details of Miss Leigh's subsequent life have been found.

SIDFORD

This hamlet between the village of Sidbury and the town of Sidmouth had a population of a few hundred residents at the start of the war. Cheshire-born Miles Rathmell, a thirty-one-year-old gunner in the Royal Artillery and former town planner, came to Sidford in 1942 in order to visit his widowed mother who lived at 2 Fire Beacon Lane ('In the hamlet in South Devon, where I spend my leave, church-going seems to be the same now as it was before the war, from superficial observation'.).[273]

270 Vale Cottage, Sidford, home of the Hill family in 1939.

55. Diana Murray Hill, Artist, 1939

Diana Marian Murray Hill (1910-1994), was born in Hertfordshire but moved with her parents in 1938 to Vale Cottage in Church Street in the hamlet of Sidford. She was then twenty-eight, unmarried and listed as an artist and mural painter in 1939's national register. In 1941 her father, a solicitor, died in Exeter but his widow continued to live in Sidford.[274]

During these initial months of the war Miss Hill recorded Sidford with a flair she later demonstrated to the reading public in *Ladies May Now Leave Their Machines*, a semi-autobiographical account published in 1944 of munitions' work in the Second World War, and in *Wanton in the South* in 1946. The narrator of her first work was Di, a young woman from a South Devon village, and she once again demonstrated her skill at literary caricature. One reviewer called it gay, bitter, rebellious and highly amusing. Another noted this was in semi-fictional and semi-autobiographical form and added it would be depressing were it not for the author's 'bright and friendly way of writing that makes her book entirely engaging'. The book was a commercial success: it went into several editions. Perhaps her style, first demonstrated in Sidford, is rightly termed 'direct good-humoured realism'.[275] During the war Miss Hill had been employed for two years in a machine shop of Rotol Ltd in Gloucestershire. The name of the firm was a portmanteau of ROlls-Royce and BrisTOL.[276] Like Sidford, she wrote about those she personally knew.

Miss Hill wrote about evacuees and a village dance in 1939.

Sidford

Miss Hill agreed with John Betjeman's view of the village ('It is very over-developed, anyway on the Sidmouth road beyond the cross-road, which is ugly, also villas are beginning to spring up along the start of the Byes – and will probably continue to spring up as [Walter John] Drake, the builder, is said to own every field in the Byes but two between Sidford and Sidmouth, although he claims to be *as fond of the Byes as anyone'*). Even so, she praised the scenery ('there is such variety of scenery surround it in every direction that you can never exhaust it. Hills, apple orchards, river, streams, woods, fields, sea, red cliffs, all beautiful enough to take your breath away and I mean it. In fact, the country is so gorgeous and the air so like wine, that living there is like being in a rarified existence.')

Miss Hill noted agriculture as the chief industry and described the farms as thick as mushrooms:

> 'The whole life of the village is permeated by the sights and sounds of farming and by the remindings of routine jobs that go on every day of the year at the same moment of the day. Dyer's 2 dirty old sheep dogs, with curling tails lying about at the corner of the Byes, ready to spring into life when the cows crowd out of the mucky yard and emerge contemptuously into the main road to hold up coast road traffic. You can't go for a walk without seeing some plough at work over red earth or meeting some old labourer with a sack over his back in the half light of a narrow lane and as you sit at meals you see the tops of the broad chestnut backs of horses over the macrocarpus hedge and the red-conditioned faces and oatmeal heads and shoulders of the men in the wains they are drawing. Notices of fresh Devonshire cream are up in all windows, in a place so luscious and plentiful with drenching rains, warm sun, green grass, it's not surprising that the people are contented and unmoved.'

Miss Hill's account of Sidford is similar to Margaret Halsey's *With Malice Towards Some*, a 'witty and wicked commentary' published in 1938 of Exeter and 'Yeobridge', a satellite village. One reviewer noted 'as a description of purely surface life in the English provinces, there is scarcely an untrue or even exaggerated word in the book'.[277] However, unlike Halsey, Miss Hill also reported on weighty wartime topics, notably evacuees. With eyes equally sharp to those of Halsey, she observed 'heaven's inhabitants':

> 'These fall into two sections, the villagers, or those who live here by nature, and the immigrants, or those who have come here by choice, a peaceful resting-place after the turmoils or disappointments of life, although some of these last have always lived in the neighbourhood (it is Sidmouth that goes in for most retired immigrants).
>
> Getting the last lot over first, as they rule the roost, or think they do, and die so strangely out of harmony with their surroundings. The usual (or unusual) feudal mass, taking their cardboard anachronisms without a smile.
>
> The Dowager Lady [Beatrice] Cave of Paccombe [1892-1951], widow of former GOM of district, chief presence at all gatherings and meetings, giver-away of prizes and chief oracle. Above all, anyone who has anything to do with organising functions, collecting money for presentations, etc. must be a *lady*. Apart from slight naughtiness, Lady Cave is a homely old girl at heart and the inside of her house (beautiful outside) is hideous.
>
> Her son, Victor [1897-1960], aged about 39, is a little loopy, also lame. He excels at croquet which he takes seriously, and also at games of skill like darts and shove-halfpenny. He is a big figure at local fetes. But he has no luck with his Aberdeens (1 shaken to death by mastiff on first entering manor grounds, 2 committed suicide, 3 escaped and returned to vet's daughter, 4 is still in possession but looks a bit craven).
>
> Lady Barnes of Knowle, very *haute monde* wife of Sir Reginald Barnes, brother of the Vanburgh sisters. Keeps herself very much to herself at palatial manor among Harcombe hills. Shooting-parties, week-enders, Conservative members for tea, etc. but all very remote and apart from the lower world. Occasionally gives an unwilling bow for form when met shopping in Sidmouth. Youngest son at Eton.
>
> Dowager Lady Cave's daughter-in-law, Lady Cave, lives at Sidbury Manor which owns cottages round, etc. Nothing much is seen of her (husband retired drunkard).
>
> Mrs Sheldon, also living at Sidbury, is a giver-away of prizes, etc. and one of the best people. She was known to say *My dear, the woman come to live in the house opposite is a FILM-FAN!! She wears trousers! I believe her mother is a lady, but I haven't called on her, one has to draw the line somewhere.*

***271** Applegarth, home to the Brown family in 1939, now known as the Salty Monk.*

At the bottom of Sidford's Church Street live the Browns of Applegarth. Mrs [Dorothy] Brown, a widow having lived at Plymouth, attends high church at Salcombe Regis (vicar is friend), paints rapturous Sunday School saints and Greek drapery, has a Siamese cat and a spaniel. Art Student and devoted daughter.

High Street	Mr & Mrs [Edward] Green, retired banker and wife
	Dr Wikes, retired doctor, wife and daughter
	Mr & Mrs Vair, retired clergyman
	Mr [Herbert] Mole, retired banker
Down Sidmouth Road	
	Dr [Eric] Lightwood, practising doctor, 2 daughters
	Miss Vincent, from Leicestershire
	Miss Wright, retired schoolmistress
	Reeds, retired banker, dominating wife, mental son
	[William] Aireys, schoolmaster, retired clergyman and wife

Other Sidbury figures appearing at Sidford are Mr Gill Crichton (conventional and Scotch), Thornton sisters (Conservative workers), Mr [James] Prendergast, the vicar and his wife.

The more hide-bound of these figures exert an influence of rules and standards which has its effect on the *behaviour* of even those who might once have been disreputable. They come to Sidford casual, but they very soon start putting on their hats and gloves to go up the high street and go calling and tea-drinking with fervour.

At local gatherings and fetes these higher figures maintain an aloofness and graciousness, and remain a consciously different faction from the rurals.

The Villagers

Whether these resent the rule and aloofness of the gentry is difficult to know. They appear to take it as their due, and certainly are very friendly to anyone who approaches them or talks with them. They all have natural good manners, children included, and giggling is more or less unknown. They are talkative and plausible and above all never hurry themselves. Very straight-forward in all their doings, so that religion, politics etc. they take as it comes. Living in such beautiful and peaceful surroundings, they are easy-going and unsharpened by having been brought into contact with poverty, bad health or materialism. Imagination is not their strong suit, in a land flowing with milk and honey, they don't seem to need it.

Coming up the main street (Church Street) from the popular Blue Ball, over the post bridge (one of Sidford's historical monuments, the other is 1573 porch house further up the street on the other side, said to have been used as a shelter by Charles II), past the hideous red church on the right, you come to the Byes, leading off down a lane to the left through a field-path to Sidmouth.

A little higher come the shops – [James] Vinnicombe, the baker, with 2 sons [Frederick, Phillip] and cow-like film-going daughter [Betty], Anstis, the butcher (name Fairchild, but having married Sidbury's butcher's daughter, carries on under the same name), owns a car which carries him to and from his farm, plays the organ at church. Clifford Toose, the chemist, choirman and star of the local dramatic society; Luke Seward, chapel-going grocer; Fisher's dairy with 2 daughters attending refined school in Sidmouth, Dimond the barber with hairdresser wife, and Thomas, owner of sweet-and-cigarette shop, local drunk (Welsh), with wife and mother-in-law.

At the top the Post Office, where you sometimes have to get 7 shilling postal-orders and a 6d one to make up 7/6, and if they're out of change-of-address forms you're unlucky.

Also, in main street live old [Henry] Westcott, the cobbler, who waylays you in his den and talks for hours; Gaut, the electrician, who is out all day and after eighteen months has not been able to supply us with an inverted lamp-shade. The workshop of the brothers Northcott (who married sisters), working like the dwarfs in *Snow White* through the open half-door full of wheels, planks and hen-houses. They can make you anything most beautiful, and cheaply. There are other cottages, where bearded old boys sit by the gate on a wooden-chair watching what goes on in the street and couples who have been born in the parts come back to die. Also a crescent known as *the alley* of handsome white council houses with gardens, [Pterocarpus] macrocarpus hedges and arches; and the laundry.

In the middle of the street, on one corner of the Byes, at her brother's farm, reigns Miss [Emily or Annie] Dyer, and all day from early till late continual court is held at the front-door porch between her and the villagers who come with their jugs to fetch milk.

From early morning Miss Dyer's shrill sing-song Devon voice rings out, greeting her clients, rating the children, passing the time of day. Much of it is lost by my ears, that I can only hear by straining at the windows, and much of it is of absolutely no importance whatever which is the best part of it, in fact many curse the shrill of her piercing remarks, but I wouldn't be without it or miss seeing children standing on the bench to seize her knocker and waiting cringing for her appearance to ask for a ball they have sent into her garden. An awful pause, *she'm coming* and a flood of rhetoric.

Harold Willy's impatient, but fairly curbed, shouts of *Miss Doiyrr*? as he waits outside with his jug, and finally with a grunt of exasperated patience, climbs on to the seat and takes a swing through the air like the man on the flying-trapeze, snatching the knocker as he comes.

Miss never hurries herself. But, *Mornin, Mrs Lane, you'm looking up well, You caant beat a Blenheim, can 'e*?, *Some of uns for ut and some of uns agin ut, an un*?, all carry the same indisputable weight, the same infallibility as her manner when clipping the hedge.

The Children of Sidford hunt in different groups.

First and foremost Harold Willy, six-ish, the limb of the village, violet-eyes and hoarse-voiced with patched knickers too large for him anchored by colossal braces. Lives with brother Morris (8), father and sister working at the laundry. Mother is dead, other sister lives up High Street with her grandmother and elder brother with Mr & Mrs Lane at bungalow by the Post Bridge. Mickey Lane and brother from this bungalow pushing sister recklessly about in pram, stopping with precision.

Arnold, cherubic-faced smaller boy, sitting on door-step up village.

Jimmy Thomas from *the alley* where the father lives with a girl, his wife having left him and small sister Nina, very beautiful with fair-hair and brown eyes, about whom a lurid future is painted by better-class mothers.

Quite a lot of these sing in the choir (not Harold) and used to amuse themselves playing on logs in fields but now in newly installed recreation-grounds along the Byes. These sometimes ring at your door either saying they have *come ter see yer* or to ask if you have any old balls, jug-cards, watches, flags, Christmas cards.

There is also Stanley Maer (8), in and out of Torrington Tubercular home and pests of the village, Ronny and Gordon Reeves who seems mental.'

Miss Hill was certain of the principal activities in the village. For the 'immigrants' it was tea-drinking, social calling, shopping, bridge parties, otter hunts and beagling. Villagers were different in that they indulged in beer-drinking, sport, local fetes, flower shows and events at the Institute and Workmen's Club. However, she thought their chief activity was talking ('the women at each other's gates and the men at their beer in the Blue Ball or the Rising, the first of these is the most popular, especially on Saturday nights.'). She had further thoughts:

> 'With everything goes sing-song gossip. Gossip reigns, in a different grade with Sidford's gentry, over the tea-cups, and over the coffee cups at the Sidmouth gossip shops, the Mocha and the Willow Tree, some of this only a passing the-time-of-day, some more active.'

She felt that religion was not of great interest in the village ('either because there is no need for dope or consolation, or because the kind of service that goes on at the parish church is extinct and they know better than to be done by it'). Miss Hill estimated that a quarter of the villagers attended the Anglican church and added 'non-young members when asked why they don't go, either make excuses or laugh it off'. Reverend Annesley Prendergast had been vicar for 38 years and was described by Miss Hill as an:

> 'old school type of country parson like good-looking sheep (wife organist and general energetic organiser and gossip-spreader), reputed to be snob but very kind and charming. Has curious impediment in speech, sounding accent on last syllable of words, minis ter, Jes us, God Almight teh. Usual type of sermon *No woun dah the sons of Thun dah* but has a poetic and scholarly

strain, avoiding platitudes and the usual obvious remarks on political situation. Occasionally lets himself go with a thundering and rousing sermon comparing Revelation with present day materialism.'

She also noted of him:

'Airey, very dreary dry-as-dust schoolmaster. Sermons almost always on standing at edge of grave, but has been known to preach on silver lining. NB there are fruity bits of gossip in circulation in the village concerning the scandalous private life of Airey.'

In 1939 Miss Hill recorded conversations she overheard during the March crisis when on the 15th Germany occupied the remaining parts of Czechoslovakia. It prompted Prime Minister Chamberlain to guarantee, on the last day of the month, that Britain would defend Poland.[278]

'April 7th, gardener, 23, married with small child, *Them two be one* (Hitler & Mussolini), very worried about situation, he would have to join up. Considers situation much graver than in September because so many more countries involved.

April 9th, vicar, 60, *You should hear my wife on Mussolini. She wants to get at him and fight him single-handed.*

April 9th, vicar's wife, 53, *I'm not down on the government on anything but I do think Chamberlain let the smaller countries down* (Czechoslovakia, etc.). *He says first of all if Cz. is attacked and France goes to help, he will stand by France, then slide out of it. Doesn't keep his word. If I were one of the smaller countries I wouldn't put my faith in England for a minute – a country that wasn't going to keep her word. Although I do think Chamberlain is very sincere and conscientious.*

April 10th, retired bank manager, 51, *Things look bad, worse than they have been before. It seems silly to me the premier having to go all the way to Scotland for a holiday. Why couldn't he choose somewhere nearer? He must have known really. What I can't understand is that the government must know about these things before they materialise. The intelligence service must be informed or they must be a pretty poor intelligence service…*

April 13th, barber's wife, 30, *What do you think of the situation? I'm afraid I don't really understand it. I don't follow it you know, except by following the papers. It doesn't really mean much to us down here. In September it was nasty, but you get used to it when it keeps on happening.*

Old nurse (60), *That poor old queen and that dear baby, I am surprised they are alive.*'

First Day of War

Miss Hill wrote about her experiences of Friday, 1 September, the first day of the war, and mentioned Theo Brown (1914-1993), then an art student living at Applegarth in Sidford and later Devon's leading folklorist and lecturer at the University of Exeter:[279]

'At 10.30am as Ma and I were waiting for bus to beach at Sidford Post Office (after day in which optimistic opinions of *no war* were at their height), Theo Brown, looking very untidy in a striped jumper and dirty pair of grey slacks, emerged from the telephone box and said had we heard Germany was already at war with the Poles & had taken Danzig and Krakow? We thought this was a rumour but was confirmed by several people in Sidmouth. One felt a little like cotton-wool, or waking out of a sleep of nasty dreams to find they were life itself. Entered the bank, sat on umbrella stand instead of chair and was politely given chair instead. Last bathe on crowded beach. Kicking waves vigorously and shouting farewell to cliffs. Head cleared, shakiness gone. Had also realised now that morning incoming evacuation of mothers and children would be on 3rd. Asked trains in Sidmouth – only 10.00 and 1.20.

Evacuation day, Sunday 3rd

Sitting in arm-chair reading, suddenly received carmine telegram *priority* stamped. Evacuation pushed ahead one day – report for duty 9am Saturday. Dropped telegram, asked for phone to get someone to drive to Exeter – upstairs to pack rucksack. Helped by Jean Lightwood who turned up fresh & eager & stayed to tea. Went off directly afterwards, in taxi to catch 5.20 which was running after all, after swiping table clear of chocolate biscuits, currant cake, some bananas.

***OPPOSITE:* 272** *Poster advocating the safety of children in the countryside, 1941.*

CHILDREN
are safer in the country
. . . leave them there

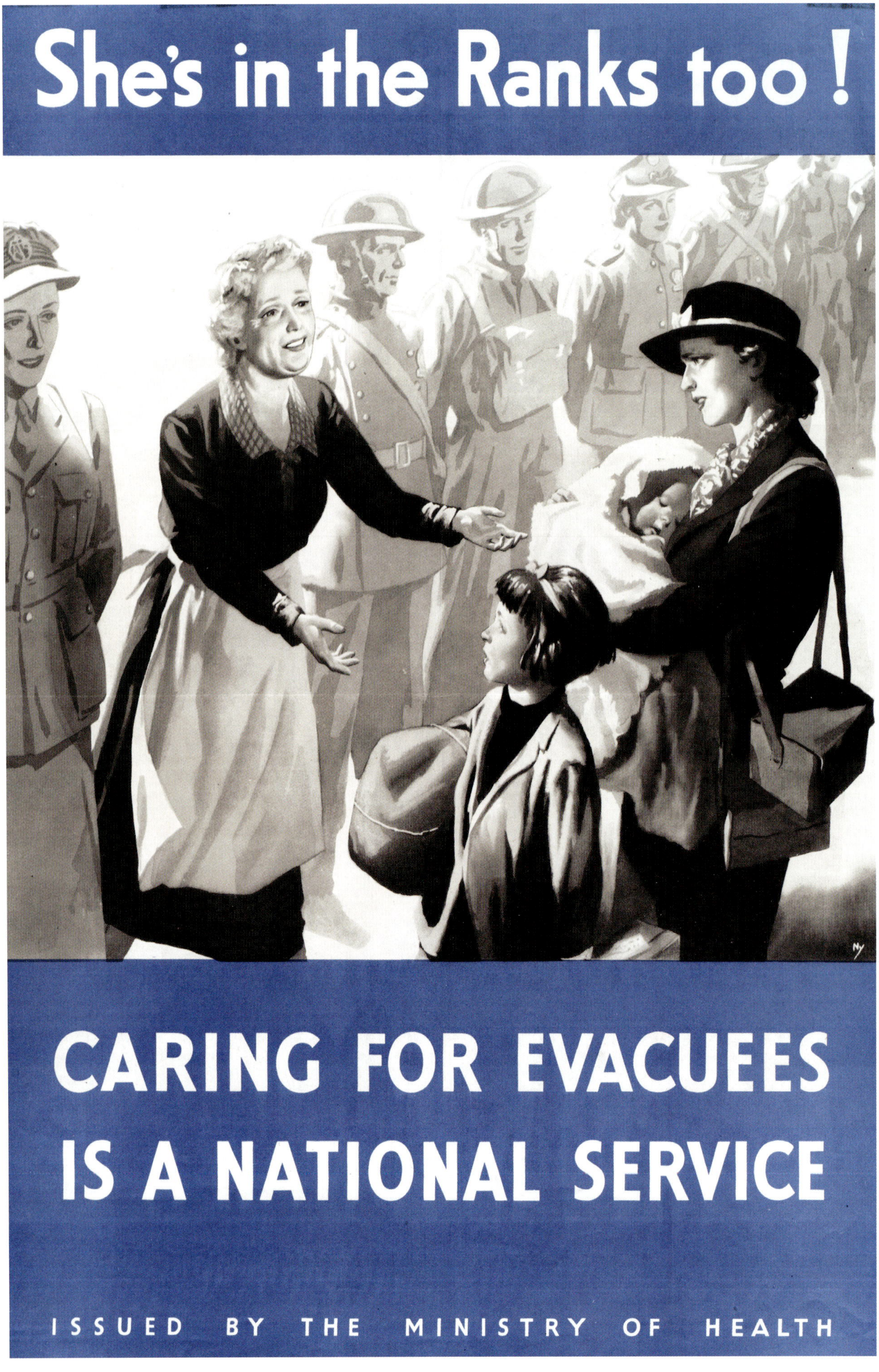
She's in the Ranks too!
CARING FOR EVACUEES IS A NATIONAL SERVICE
ISSUED BY THE MINISTRY OF HEALTH

Sidmouth station fairly deserted, one or two forlorn groups standing about with cases. Found empty carriage to sit in and have chat with Ma who sat opposite to have a smoke of Woodbines. Both every cool, detached, discussed uncertainty of future (awful poster outside of Worthington's, colonel in buff dressing gown with toys, grinning father -Christmassy). I spoke of horrors in detached way, thinking them all out coldly. Ma said her duty to stay and look after Father, I told her she mustn't go potty. She said she didn't mind this as much as seeing me off to school and went off down platform to exit, turning to wave at intervals.

Quartet in carriage to Sidmouth Junction, youngish couple, toothless fair naval man and swarthy woman, young boy opposite and sister in my corner. Young boy produced crab and made it walk on seat. Football pools. Discussed Hitler, *he would have a lot to account for*, cracks about ditto, very smart. Wounded works at Roehampton, shouldn't be seen, no sort of life. Girl said *Hitler should have one arm blown off, one leg off, part of face shot off and live till 100 in agony*. Boy said *no more football pools* and was annoyed he had just sent in his sixpence.

Very smart, jaunty, labourer-looking man, brown, cap set on one eye, well-set-up, holding forth smartly to adulatory audience of men and women relatives. How it was with him in last war etc, something about passing police station and *Come in, see me sometime*.

After ages train came in, packed from Exeter. Boarded train and rushed up corridor, found seat in 3rd class by woman who had evacuated her children to Exeter and was going back to her husband opposite Woolwich Arsenal. He belonged to Decontamination Squad. Everybody discussing evacuation at Exeter – lots of children, lots of helpers. Paper boys outside at Yeovil. Bought paper. No one wanted to see paper (*Express & Echo*). Threw it out of window…'[280]

Miss Hill wrote at length about evacuees in the village:[281]

'With regard to the impact of evacuation on village life, it is rather hard to find out anything, as Sidford itself did not have many billets and the few evacuees it did have, with very few exceptions, have returned.

I tried to find out, at Salcombe House, what reasons the evacuees had for returning, but it was very difficult to extract anything from either the organiser or the mothers, as although the former had a list of which mother went and when, she couldn't give me (or remember) the different reasons & I didn't happen to be there when most of them were going back & would only find out the instances I gave.

Sidford is definitely changing from other impacts, chiefly circumstantial, ie, pervading influence of manors etc. is rather fading out owing to Dowager Lady Cave having retired to Sidmouth (as Paccombe House was too remote to keep maids), Lady Cave also, possibly temporarily, from Sidmouth Manor. Rumours of impending divorce from husband.

Also, another very important change that has just occurred, is advent of new vicar for Sidford and Sidbury (taking place of old man who had never moved out of the place for 38 years) who is young and progressive and has come with his wife straight from Finland, having been about in various places such as Paris and Canada.

Impact of war is also hard to judge, beyond seeing children playing in the street with mothers chatting about their sons training in vicinity (return of these in khaki for weekends) and some talk about *blood-shed* etc., also funeral at Sidbury of Gaut, mother of Sidford electrician, who was one of the RAF men over Kiel Canal and was later killed in a war accident.

I will try to glean other news at Sidford house-to-house collection I have let myself in for on purpose, also at *Guest Night* at Woolbrook church hall.

I think about the only difference in attitude of villagers to townsfolk brought about by evacuation is that before it Londoners were an unknown quantity and this has accustomed them to the kind of conditions they live in. Otherwise, they have reacted by resentment, sympathy and tolerance according to their natures, and the ones that have gone back have been wiped off their slate.'[282]

***OPPOSITE:* 273** *British poster praising women for hosting evacuees, April 1941.)*

274 In 1939 Sidmouth retained its reputation as a genteel resort, depicted in its early days by James Bourne in 1805. Miss Diana Murray Hill wrote that the evacuees challenged its decorum.

Evacuees

Evacuees were a matter of particular interest to Miss Hill and they were her principal reason for writing the report. She noted some of the substantial buildings in the area, notably Paccombe and Salcombe House, which were initially used for evacuees before given over to other wartime uses. Her account differs in tone from the positive public pronouncements published in newspapers. These stressed the hearty welcome given by local people to grateful evacuees.

Miss Hill made detailed notes on 2 November 1939:

'Here in East Devon, as elsewhere, shake-up of classes and change of surroundings not always happy. East Enders bored to death in some cases with country, miss matey company and fish & chips of town life, must crowd altogether.

People in reception areas in most cases unaware of East Enders existence, or anyway their way of living, in most cases uneasy or angry to be brought close up against it or attitude of make the best of it. Those in charge of evacuee parties sometimes treat [them] as strange species.

In extreme cases, evacuees with sores, impetigo, contagious diseases take umbrage at being isolated, or make no effort to accommodate selves to country life and different conditions of living. And receptionists outraged, resent this close sight of evil conditions having been thrust upon them, for which they take no responsibility and wish to shut out of lives.

Treat to see Sidmouth's selectness leavened with bits of life – little boys swimming like frogs, fishing from quay, families on beach instead of spinsters (also litter in fields and streets treated as public lavatories – *not much room now in sea* according to Mr Green). Select Sidmouth turned into Blackpool overnight.

Children enjoy themselves, if not parents, and quick change of health astonishing. As girl of 18 (doctor's daughter) remarked *It is a pity it needed a war to make classes aware of each other's existence.*

Total number of evacuees to East Devon District 2,634.

Sidmouth 673, Ottery St Mary 388, Honiton Borough 408, Honiton Rural District 1,165 (Awliscombe 70, Branscombe 28, Broadhembury 92, Buckerell 54, Combe Ralegh 22, Cotleigh 30, Dunkeswell 62, Farway 48, Feniton 32, Gittisham 77, Luppitt 91, Monkton 57, Northleigh 32?, Offwell 35, Payhembury 79, Plymtree 56, Sheldon 32, Talaton 96, Upottery 114, Widworthy 21, Yarcombe 37).

A further 107 Sidmouth evacuees were housed in 2 empty houses in the district; 56 at Salcombe House, Sidmouth, 50 at Paccombe House, Harcombe. (These last were sent on to Tiverton less than a week after their arrival.)

Paccombe House

This is a roomy farmhouse type of house, low-built with a veranda, tucked away at the end of a valley beyond Harcombe, standing up on a little plateau of its own, remote, with gorgeous views down on to wooded slopes, half a mile down a lane from Sidford. Formerly dwelling of Dowager Lady Cave and son and vacated by her about a month ago for Sidmouth.

On Tuesday morning, Sept. 5th, hearing they wanted some helpers and sleep-at-nighters, I walked up.

Found crowd of mothers, with children playing about, sitting about on lawn in canvas chairs (having passed 1 mother and grandmother on way sitting on seat down lane, with 2 children squatting on grass). Seemed fairly aimless and resigned.

In charge were 2 Conservative workers from Sidbury, Miss Thorntons, & one 28-year-old lecturer from LSW, Miss Le Mesurier, who had brought them down. They had arrived on Sunday at midnight in a thunderstorm, were destined for some other part of Devon, but train had got bored & dumped at Sidmouth. They came from Camberwell.

Mattresses had been raised from Messrs Field of Sidmouth and mothers (20 mothers, 30 children) parked out on floor in different rooms.

Shortly afterwards, clothes lines were erected, ARP blinds, a wireless provided and a rota drawn up for daily duties (ie getting breakfast in morning, washing up, etc.). Cooking was being carried out under British Legion woman. Later found that 2 women voluntarily took over breakfast getting, [?Mrs] Heard & Sparks, continued throughout. One of these suffered after-effects of rheumatic fever.

All mothers did own rooms.

First aid inspection took place daily under a Miss Thornton.

I took small children of mothers each morning in summer house and a friend played games with bigger ones on lawn till they went to school.

Mothers lived on hopes of letters from husbands. One morning, having made noises with children on Woolworth musical instruments – saxophone, whistle, drum, concertina – marched them out playing on to lawn and asked mothers to sing a tune, expecting old-world melody. Broke with one accord, led by Granny,

275 *An early view of the River Sid, c1852, capturing the rural character appreciated by Miss Hill but not by all of the evacuees.*

into *Lambeth Walk*, fullest vocal.

Occasional visit from Pritchard (evacuation officer), Blanchard (surveyor carting wireless, etc.), vicar's wife saying *We must keep happy*, etc.

Miss Thornton very capable, attitude towards mothers a trifle too organizatory and from different level. She was surprised at mother's treatment of children, *No discipline whatever, if the mothers want the children to behave, they hit them. We must give the children training*.

Le Mesurier much more used to them but apt to treat rather like cases, with detachment. Complained of being sent away.

The children seemed happy, one older one, James, spoke with rapture of having 4 plates of porridge. Miss Thornton said good food made all the difference to the mothers' states of mind, and that if they were left alone, they fought.

The whole party was moved suddenly on to Tiverton by bus on Saturday morning. Some said *it was a pity just as they had settled down*. Others *They wished it was home they were going to* and others, *that as long as they were all together, they didn't mind.*

Specifications made by Le Mesurier for their future accommodation was that Sparks and Heard deserved special mention and that Freddie Beall (one of 8) must go on a farm. One woman, found to be m[entally] d[efficient], with baby with whooping cough, was taken separately to relations.

On Saturday afternoon, a party of their husbands arrived at Paccombe, in high spirits, having got hold of a lorry and driven from London. They thanked the kind ladies for looking after their wives and set off for Tiverton. (A week later their place had been taken by Cudham Hall Children's School. Also Westcliff Girls' School at Sidbury Manor.)

Salcombe House

These were accommodated as the Paccombe evacuees (56). Many mothers were pregnant and had been intended for other parts better equipped. Salcombe House, large vacant house at Sidmouth end of Sid Road. These mothers and children were mostly tougher than Paccombe, several cases of impetigo (2) and vermin, mothers quite often leaving children for pubs and coming back drunk.

Party at first in charge of eccentric VAD, Sabrietta Lamb, who insisted on no work being done by the mothers because some were pregnant. All sat about doing nothing. After Paccombe exodus, Pritchard cunningly supplemented her by Miss Thorntons, saying VADs should not be burdened with such work.

Things were then better organised. Shifts of local nurses, cooks, helpers. Gifts advertised for in papers and pulpits. Mothers had work allocated. Bad cases of impetigo etc. shifted on. Sand pit given for children. There was a lot of shifting, also of evacuees returning from different reasons, others coming on from private billets, etc.

Apart from this, fairly contented atmosphere. The first baby was born on October 11th, the second a few days later, where the mother had been shifted for it to Exmouth, but returned. By October 25th the number was 10 mothers, 14 children.

There were also small quarrels and tensions. One of these because a prominent helper had taken it upon herself to have a child's hair cut. This was Johnnie Birch (1½ years). His mother had had a nervous breakdown before coming, partly owing to bad health of small baby, Teddy. Became moody at Salcombe, effect of war strain and had to be sent on to Axminster where she developed Bronchial pneumonia and did not recognise her husband when he came down to see her. Johnny (and baby) were left behind at Salcombe House, both made rapid recovery in health, Johnny unrecognizable and looked after by mothers in turn and helpers.

This hair-cutting caused rift between two parties, including autocratic district nurse, further rift caused by Thornton putting bully-beef in shepherd's pit and another helper, in charge of feeding, agreeing with mother that she would not give it to her children.

On Oct. 25th each mother was being called in to Miss Thornton's office in turn *to be read riot act for neglecting duties.* Many jokes cracked while waiting, and one remark *This is more like prison than a home.* But on same day mother upstairs with new baby said she had refused to go anywhere else to have it, she was happy here and knew she would not get such good care anywhere else. Staff have own room to sit in and get own meals. Two always on night-duty.

<u>Husbands</u>, various husbands came down to see wives.

1, Mrs – with 2 children, husband's London fruit shop had gone shut at outbreak of war, he had opened another near Bedford. Came down to see wife September and told her to stay. She said *Just as well he wasn't staying longer*, she didn't want to be an expectant mother too. But soon after he went, she got bored and returned to London, although at time of his visit she said she was getting used to the country.

2, Mr Birch came down October 7th (?) to visit his wife at Axminster and see children at Salcombe House. Seemed grateful.

3, Mr Emery (soldier) and grown-up son shortly to be shipped east, came down for weekend October 20th. Told Miss Thornton it had taken 5 years off his life to see his wife in such good surroundings.

4, Mr Hayward, came down for weekend October 28th

for christening of child. Said he was glad she was *down here out of the fogs*.

5, Mr Robertson, early middle September, sent wire to his wife, tough, 2 children and expecting another in a month, *if you don't come back tomorrow, I shall leave you*. She went the next day.

Helpers at Salcombe House began with too many, including several societies, and had to be thinned down. It was funny to see one woman come in to give Teddy his feed, dressed in a marocain dress, with reversible satin facings, sitting crooning away to him, as though he were her own best-loved child instead of a half-starved creature, a cross between a gooseberry and a weasel.

One child of 4, who had never been known to utter, spoke at last to say *Shut that bloody door*.

All seemed to know every word of tunes like *Lambeth Walk*, *Chestnut Tree*, etc. before able to speak. Even Johnny able vaguely to croon *Boomps a Daisy*.

On September [blank] Mr Pritchard took me round with him to visit evacuees at Sidbury. Questions to be asked from householder were:

1, if comfortable.

2, a, meals in with family, b, buying own food and cooking themselves.
If a, how much is paid (suggest extra to billeting 10s if mother only, 14s mother and one child, 17/6 mother and two children.
If b, pay cost of gas, question of coal.
Pritchard had come down from London where he was member of LCC and lecturer in geography at technical institute. Later, his wife and 3 children came to Sidmouth and he returned to London to continue boys' clubs which he thought would be needed more than ever in blackouts.

Sidbury

These were nearly all billeted out on the villagers and in council houses. The first lot had gone on to be nearer friends in another area.

1, cottage on Vicarage Hill

Old couple around 80, evacuee mother, child of 1½ and baby (later moved to Salcombe House). All merry and bright. Dear old couple, *they knew what it was to have children, Everyone had to do their best these days.* etc. Meals in together.

2, Chapel Street cottage

Women of 50 with married daughter living elsewhere. One evacuee mother with two children. All have food together. 7/6 paid for all 3 (being slightly done by evacuee according to Pritchard). *Doesn't want to make*.

Hillside Council houses

A, married woman of 55, had been ill. Not down on register to take people but said *If needed, doors will be open*. Husband said *We'll be British and sit up*. Mother of 28 and 2 babies arrived 11.30pm Sunday September 10th. Babies cried all day, mother very good mother, but also cried because she was cut off from 2 little girls stuck with their aunt in Birmingham, having gone there after holiday in Belfast. (these came down later and all turned up at Salcombe House September 25th.) She pays for food [which] householder orders. Householder takes no money for electricity or vegetables, as woman is so poor. No clothes, etc. They take turn and turn about with babies and housework.

B, Evacuee daughter of house, out of work, office-cleaner from Wandsworth (2 girls 8 & 10). Wants to find job in Sidmouth.

C, Householder postman's wife with working daughter. Two tough evacuee mothers 32 & 36 with 2 boys & 2 babies. (wireless on full pitch, mothers knitting). Both going back to husbands. Also, expense to have 2 places going. Pay 15s each (including kids), persuaded to stay [on for] another fortnight.

D, Going back tomorrow, sent for by husband.

E, Very satisfactory. Married woman householder 42, healthy-looking evacuee of 30 with boy of 4 and baby. Boy playing with others outside, tadpole in jar etc. Baby enjoyed by householder. All happy. But evacuee's husband sent telegram for her and she said *What do the children matter – it's the husbands we care about!* with broad smile. So has sent telegram back to say *Coming*, forgot to say time so excited. But she would like to stay if it weren't for him. Householder wants to keep children but mother says *They will play up*. Both best of friends.

F, Young woman householder. Dreary widow evacuee with small boy. Pays for what she eats. Ok but would like someone younger for company.

Other Cases

Sidford

1, Four women evacuees with children, came down Sunday 10th Sept., after the 2 hours' air-raid warning. Impossible to stay on after that in such state of tension, were beginning to faint and drop teapots. Also, had heard rumours of air-raid at Chatham.

2, At well-to-do house in Sidford. Widow and art student daughter. One woman with little girl and baby. All [blank]. Got comfort and good meals but very depressed (would never sit in garden) & left them after a week to live in small working-class house opposite where 3 other evacuee friends were already billeted. Whole lot soon returned to London (end of September).

3, Mr Green, retired banker and wife. 2 little girls 8 & 10 (brother next door). At first cried all time. Mrs Green gave pennies every day. They didn't [blank] Soon stopped and settled down cheerfully. Enjoyed baths. Were given dressing gowns and new coats. Mrs Green taught [them] to say *please* and *thank you*, and *if you don't call people Sir & Madam no one will like you*. Soon became pride of village and Mr & Mrs G. Accompanied for walks and to church, were given clothes by neighbours. Went and enjoyed school at Sidbury till diphtheria kept them away. Given money boxes and saved up for presents for parents. Promised stockings at Christmas, etc.

Encouraging behaviour of householders at Manston (council houses near Sidford)

A, very pleased with evacuee who was retired trained nurse and looked after her own children when she went out.

B, Cheerfully took on, and managed better than mother, 3 obstreperous boys of about 5 – 8 and coped with their heads which were dirty.

***276** A poster encouraging the public not to gossip, c1939-45.*

Sidmouth

2 wives in billet together. 2 husbands said they must not return home on any account and they had kept old home and were both being looked after by mother-in-law.

(also at Sidford)

Wife of evangelical parson said with shocked complacency she was glad her evacuees had gone home they were so dirty. Pritchard said if she had any idea how many people had to use the lavatory she wouldn't be surprised.

Spinster in bus talked in shocked loud voice in front of other evacuees saying she had heard some were dirty and some went to bed in their boots.

Camberwellians complained that people in Sidmouth were not nice. They were stand-offish in buses and shops.

But pub-owners in Sidmouth said clients from Salcombe House *were very nice women*.

Villager (farmer's sister in Sidford) to returning evacuee *It's all very well getting out of the way of the war, but there a'nt naw plaice like whoame*.

Mr Green (bank manager, 60) said he thought evacuation was good on whole but some misfits. Good shake-up for everyone. He thought the difficulties were coming when husbands stopped sending money and went off, and parents moved from home and left children to mercies of the receptionists.

Miss LeMesurier (LSE lecturer, 28) wondered what would happen when the illegitimate children started at Crediton etc.

Woman at Broadhembury (56, with 16 cats, 13 cows, sheep, donkeys, ducks, 2 peacocks and 2 dogs) said most of the evacuees round her way had gone back. Some had said they would get free passage by shutting themselves up in train lavatory.

She had refused to house any, although before petrol rationing started, six coster donkeys and 2 dogs were to have been sent down to her.

Vicar of St Francis Woolbrook

Evacuees 1 boy of 10 and mother. All happy. But boy said *No fish and chips* and missed *liquid*. When asked what liquid said *You know, liquid*! *What kind of liquid*? *Green liquid, when you have 2d worth fish and chips, they give you half a pint. When you have more, they give you a pin*t. Liquid from eels.

Rumours of *n*gger* and *Limehouse* evacuees at Exmouth. Also story from Sidmouth doctor of Chinese boy (presumably at Exmouth) who passed blood but householders didn't do anything about it as they thought perhaps the Chinese were like that.

Letter in Medical Journal from doctor complaining of outrage of objectionable scum being poured into clean homes.'

Another report was sent from Miss Hill in December 1939:

'Sidford Evacuees[283]

1, Mrs [Dorothy] Brown, Applegarth. One youngish woman, small child and baby. Good food, comfortable billet, 2 bedrooms. Nice garden. Miserable all time, never went in garden, always in street. Left about 2nd week in September to join friend at:

2, Mrs [Blanche] Reeves, in cramped conditions in working-class villa opposite. She already had 1 woman with girl and baby. Both left about mid-September. Mrs Reeves said they couldn't settle and didn't try to. They were miserable. Husbands fetched back mid-September.

3, Nice old woman in Porch House (villager), had one mother and child. Very nice, accommodating. All got on well together. But her sons had been evacuated to other part of county. She eventually went back (end September) because her husband was out of work and she didn't like him sending her money.

4, Mrs [Emily] Marchant, wife of gardener, Orchard Close. Had 3 women down after 1st fortnight of war, unable to stand strain of air-raid alarms. Appeared quite happy. As far as I could discover, they were all gone by middle of November, but whether they had returned or been moved to another billet, I couldn't find out. (Mrs Marchant had gone off somewhere to have a baby.)

5, Dreary old spinster, respectable working-class, with pet, from villa off High Street. Had had boy of 9 and girl of 17, found boy a trial & both too much trouble (her health was bad) although they had liked it alright. Both left end of September. (Visiting evacuation officer had found her very trying when he called at beginning of Sept.; wanting to charge 30s each per week, and wouldn't listen to anything he said.)

6, Mrs Dalling along Sidmouth Road, wife of Free Evangelical minister. Very unpleasant and complacent. Her evacuees had left early in September and she was glad to get rid of the dirty creatures.

7, Mr & Mrs Green, retired banker and wife at High Street. Undertook to have 2 girls for 3 months. They were aged about 8 & 10. After preliminary day or two's howling, both settled down well, all village and especially Mr & Mrs Green, took great interest. Took out for walks, gave clothes, etc. Enjoyment all round, very affectionate, received money from mother, went to Sidbury School. Then suddenly (Nov. 21st) along with talk of Christmas stockings, etc. received a letter from mother enclosing fare, saying come home at once. The youngest girl had been writing home saying the smaller brother was being ill-treated at school and they had all been sent for.

Two sides to this question

Mrs Green said it was made up. The boy had had one rap over knuckles. The people he had been billeted with had written to headmaster and it was practically all exaggeration and she thought partly because the girls didn't want to take an exam.

Muriel Maaer, villager's daughter, who was in the boy's class, said that the mistress had continually made him cry and that the girls hadn't been used to the kind of work they did and so were not taken as much notice of as they might be.

Anyway, Mrs Green had received letter from girls' mother after their return, thanking her from the bottom of her heart. She had never seen them looking so clean, neat, etc. (the eldest girl, night before she went, had thrown her arms round Mrs Green and said *Mrs Green, I do love you and I don't want to go*.)

Yes, she was proud of them, they didn't tell lies or break anything, the only thing they did was scratch the enamel of the stairs with their boots. She would have been heartbroken if they hadn't been grateful. But it made a lot of work, she got up at 7 each morning, packed their food for school, gave them breakfast and extra meal in evening etc. The maid was a bit tired of them. No, she couldn't say she'd enjoyed having them. You couldn't get fond of Cockney children like children of your own class. Why? They used to say people and houses were lousy and that grated.

Villagers (Mrs Northcott & woman in Orchard Close) said they thought evacuation was a good thing for the children's health.

An old labourer, watching boys playing noisily in stream at Manstone stood surveying benevolently, said to younger labourer, *They'm doant get noa chance of country life, you naow, they'm making most of it.*

From Salcombe House

November 13th Mrs Higgins and 2 kids (having been since war began) left for visit in London (with borrowed suitcases etc.) & did not return.

November 20th Mrs Cotton returned from 2nd visit to London (3 children). He was going to be called up in January (husband) and said *You needn't think you're staying here, because you're not* and wouldn't live in flat alone. She liked it although sometimes dull *but we must put up with that.*

November 23rd Mrs Emery stand-by of Salcombe House, having been since beginning, went back with one child and expecting another. Her husband had got more leave and she didn't like boy of 16 hanging about with nothing to do. Otherwise she wouldn't have gone (child put on pounds).'

A Sidford Dance

On 20 August 1939 Miss Hill described a village dance:

'Dances at Sidford every Saturday, at Sidford Institute Hall, situated about 200 yards down *The Byes* from main street of Sidford. (The Byes – a narrow lane or by-path leading from Sidford to Sidmouth, through lane and meadows via the river Sid).

Time from about 9 or 9.30 onwards till slightly after one o'clock. Announced on board propped on ground at corner of Sidford end of Byes. Sidford Institute is fair-sized hall (Edwardian) with pillared, slated veranda standing back in clearing down this lane (also used for Women's Institute, political meetings, etc.). Cards and motor-cycles of dancers are parked in this clearing.

Arrived about 10pm, enter at side-door 1s tickets bought from woman with printed roll at table just inside, in passage. Coats hanging on legs either side. Printed notices *Ladies*, *Gents* beyond. Door to hall on left of passage. At 10 only about 20 people all told, mostly sitting round, fairly glum, bunch of girls together, bunch of men together, some mixed sitting, one or two couples dancing. Band *Blue Ramblers* on dais on far end. One smart girl in printed *crepe de chine* at piano, with moustached stripe-blazoned man at elbow; piano didn't sound much, seemed like dumb

277 *British poster recognising the work of women in munitions, 1940s. During the war Miss Hill spent two years working in a factory outside Bristol.*

keys. Three others on dais with blue placards of *Blue Ramblers* in front – one trombone, one trumpet, one drum plus jazz, etc. Trombone and trumpet dreary with spectacles, drum more spry, jumping about on seat.

Goodish floor, wooden chairs all round walls, bright unshaded bulbs, door at far end (leading into another room) with table in front with table cloth on it. Two guardians of the hall, middle-aged, female, sitting near it.

Dancers dressed very neatly, girls in *crepe de chine* short dresses, or linen, one or two suits, some bare legs – hair neat. Men in grey flannels and odd coat, shirt open at neck, one or two – but not many - without coats – aertex or ordinary shirts – and exceptions in complete suits, collar and tie.

Fairly glum look at 10, not much life, lights shining strongly on faces of sitters out. Two very pale girls at door end, with pasty faces, spectacles (one in jersey and shirt), youth between, all inactive (thought *those girls won't get anyone to dance with for a dead cert*). Other small group huddled together at end by band, looking unrestrained but fairly listless. Anticipation quiet. String of about five men, all fairly good-looking, sitting by door into passage. These remained like this till the *Paul Jones* and some returned after.

Warm night, lots of windows round hall, blue cotton curtains, mostly open including 2 at far end looking onto Byes, long window at one side. Strings of flags, mostly small Union Jack across ceiling. Two pictures on walls, one of Edward VII in naval uniform, other small plumed hat, little India official-looking man. Didn't recognise anyone except one youth I had seen about village.

Sat opposite string of youths. I wanted to see if any of these could dance with me, but boy with one who had expressed intention beforehand of dancing with village girls changed his mind and stuck to me. Only one girl he liked look of, in green suit, but didn't know what he'd do if she said she didn't dance.

Things began to get easier.

Anticipatory girls got a few partners (string of youths still unbroken), one man in particular seemed going round dancing every dance and earnestly, different girl almost every time. Intense opaque brown eyes, fairly he-man looking, but with hunched shoulders, sweaty face, gave impression of aggressive studiousness. Danced well, as did practically everyone, especially men. By this time about 15 women to 18 men. Things warming up slightly, but no rowdyism, company taking amusement naturally and congenially. All hair brushed, fairly open faces, mostly healthy-looks.

Cries from 3 men for *Boomps a Daisy*. No response from Ramblers whose tunes were for the most part about 10 years old. *Louisville*, *That Grand and Glorious Feeling*, etc. No *Chestnut Tree* or *Lambeth Walk*. At intervals trumpet or saxophone would stand up and announce *The next dance*... This last part inaudible, so took it to mean simply that the last dance was over.

At about 11.00, *Paul Jones*.

By this time the majority were dancing fairly often, even including – I noted with glad surprise – the spectacled pasty-faces. Quite a lot of good-looking men with plain girls, all enjoying themselves. No pinching, kissing or giggling.

For the *Paul Jones* the girls were fairly slow in getting up – men waited till girls' ring was got going – one or two then half a dozen more etc., till all were in rings or very nearly all.

I danced with

1, Blond youth of about 23, tweed top coat, grey flannel trousers (very good dancer, swung around easily and with verve).

2, Visitor to Sidmouth, this was first time he had been. Came up by bus, walking home.

3, Slightly older man, shop assistant from Newton Poppleford. More sophisticated. Didn't talk much except to comment on age and familiarity of tunes which were then *Whispering* and *Go to Sleep my Baby*, slight laughter.

4, Sweaty earnest he-man, turned out to be not student but farm-hand from Woolbrook Farm. Talked easily, danced very well, holding slightly away, hand clamped on side of ribs, Waltz, very prim. *No, he didn't get up at 5, got up 6.30. Weren't it hot*? Hair dark, eyes brilliant, but no abatement in thoroughness of dancing.

5, good-looking, fair-haired youth, nice expression – one of the unbroken string.

Self *Do you live at Sidford*?
a. Naw.
Self *Do you live at Sidmouth*?
a. Naw.
Self *Do you live at Sidbury*?
a. Yes.
Self *Do you like it as much in winter as summer*?
a. Yes.
Self *Have you ever walked up Roncombe Hill?*
a. Yes.
Self *What's your job*?
a. Brr.r.r
Self *Lorry what*?
a. Lorry Brr.r.r.r
Self *Do you drive lorry about*?
a. Naw.
(something about hanging on back?)

After *Paul Jones* several, including this youth and No. 1, returned to original seats and remained throughout evening.

Things now definitely warmer in all respects. About 35 women to 40 men. Refreshments served on table by door, queued up for in one interval only. Lemonade, thick sandwiches, sausage rolls. New arrivals included girl from Sidmouth hairdresser's (who beamed on me) plus boyfriend, 2 sheepish youths with scarves round necks who looked like lords of the manor from somewhere, one (the only) middle-aged woman and a crowd of about 5 of more sophisticated-looking men and girls, probably from Sidmouth. One girl very saucy, dark blue bow in waved hair, vivacious eyes. Back chat near table (man – *Have a sausage roll in its skin*. She – *Thanks*. Man – *Do you like them curled or straight*?

278 Artwork which appeared in Miss Hill's book on munitions work, 1944.

She – *I don't mind either way*). These appear to be only smarter there – probably shop-assistants.

About now a spectacular entrance was made by two men direct from the Blue Ball (Saturday night) who came staggering gallantly into the hall and through the crowd up to our end of the hall (the Byes end), faces suffused with utter happiness and threw themselves upon two pals sitting there. If they could have crowed, they would have. The two entrants were older than the other men present, who on the average were about 25. Both looked slightly like returned sailors. One about 53, shortish, fattish, with cap on the back of head, blue suit, toothless. The other about 40, lean, bronzed, rakish, with brown suit hung on him and white shirt open at throat, hair careless, cigarette stuck behind ear. Two friends well set-up young men, sitting without girls, one dark, the other ruddy with carnation in buttonhole. These two didn't seem to mind the onset, bore it with equanimity and seemed rather pleased at visit than [blank], in fact reception throughout hall seemed tolerant, no freezing up, but smiled upon as pleasant diversion. No throwing-out or cold looks.

Party sat down on 4 chairs, visitors produced beer bottles hitherto bulging from pockets, set on floor between feet, made free play to pals. Rakish one insisted on tipping bottle too frequently to ruddy young man's mouth, impasse ensued, coughed up onto floor. Slight coldness of ruddy young man but quick recovery. Both drunks sudden inclusive leering glance round hall, focussing evilly. Music started up. Rakish drunk stands up, arms sinuously above head, does voluptuous harem-sway. Then falls upon ruddy friend. Toothless drunk follows suit, they both sway back-to-back. Then Toothless makes feint on dark pal, who giggles. Sailor then appears, walks up and takes one bottle, no offence taken. All sit down for another all-round swig. Rakish drunk seeing self grinning, holds up bottle and offers swig. Self answers *Not thirsty thanks*, and dark young pal grins back widely, till his mouth nearly splits.

Much dumb-cat-calling and side-play now going on from male onlookers through windows behind them, motioning to various friends to come out. Dancing at height, amusement warm but straightforward. Two drunks stop bullying friends and dance together through room, continuing thus for some time. Wonderful care-free ambulation, beautiful attitudes, tango-like flamingo stretches, cigarette still behind ear. Dark young pal comes and sits one chair off me till fallen upon and carried off by Toothless.

More dancing, he-man still going strong among girls, mopping brow. Sit-out youths still sitting out, some together, some solitary. *Yes* and *Naw* man shifted and came and sat one chair away from self with empty chair in between. For one dizzy moment I thought he was going to ask me, or sign me, to dance but was he? *Naw*.

Some people now standing in door watching. Drunken couple still gyrating, at close of mutual dance doing graceful exaggerated sweeping-cap-off bow to each other.

12 o'clock left.

Fair collection of cars, motor-bikes, etc. outside hall. These make foul noise going past houses up Sidford Street, turning out of Byes engine noises, cat-calls, songs.

On this occasion we heard that shortly before we left there had been collision at mouth of Byes between car and motor-bike, and shortly afterwards difference of opinion between driver of Baby Austin and gentry's car whose lights had failed. Owner of Baby Austin loud in anger, a bit bibulous, *He was driver of Devon General for 20 years, he knew what he was doing; always type of people in failing-lights car that gave the trouble. He wasn't drunk, he wasn't. He was driver of Devon General, etc. They might be out of gear, but they couldn't meet him out of gear.*

This went on with no reserve on Devon General's part, although slight hushing on other, for some time beyond angry heads had been put out of bedroom windows with voices attached.'

In 1941 Miss Hill's family was increased when Phyllis Calvert, the film actress, married Miss Hill's brother Peter Murray Hill (1908-1957), a former actor. Miss Hill was employed as a housekeeper near Bristol in 1951 but returned to Devon in about 1966. She lived at Sandy Knapp, a bungalow she had built between Tipton St John and Venn Ottery outside Sidmouth. In 1972 she recalled:

'I first made the acquaintance of Tipton St John's station in the spring of 1938 when my parents came to live in Devon. There was a through coach to Sidmouth on the 11am train from Waterloo. If we had not booked this, we emerged at Sidmouth Junction [now known as Feniton Station] from the powerful steam monster that was the Plymouth train to find a toylike vehicle resting quietly on the other side of the station platform. Into it we got while a varied crowd of people fussed about till they were disposed in the right first or third-class compartment. We arranged our luggage so that no one should trip over it on the way to the lavatory which opened off the compartment, and we sat for quite a time admiring the reproductions of East Devon landscapes which adorned the walls. Our feelings of expectancy were whetted by this lack of action.

At last, with a toot, we jerked off and settled into a fast-rocking motion, the smoke from the engine flying like a feather to cast its shadow on the green pastures on the way to Ottery St Mary. In the fields on our right a board on struts announced the existence of King's School, of ancient foundation, then came the rosy brick of the eighteenth-century mill, unencumbered by the extension added later by The Switchgear.

The next station was a small one. It bore the name Tipton St John in white lettering on a green enamel board. Here there was quite a commotion; a railwayman walking down the train to throw open every door and enquire *All passengers for Sidmouth*? For Tipton was a junction and Exmouth-bound passengers must alight and wait for another train to swoop them off through the fields by the Otter to Newton Poppleford, East Budleigh and Budleigh Salterton to Exmouth. We smug Sidmouthians stuck our heads out of the carriage windows to watch the ejected ones gathering to brood over their cases in the little green painted shelter before we took the steep ascent, plunged headlong through the banks of Harpford Woods, emerged under the shadow of Fire Beacon and steamed through Woolbrook into the haven of Sidmouth Station: the journey's end.'

Miss Hill died in 1994.[284]

SIDMOUTH (& EXETER)

In the 1930s this seaside resort was not only fashionable but celebrated for its genteel charm. There were 11,249 residents in 1939 and Sidmouth's economy was dominated by tourism and supplemented by fishing and lace-making.[285] A number of buildings were requisitioned or adapted for war use including the Knowle as a convalescence home and later as an officers' training quarters while the Drill Hall became a temporary shelter following the evacuation at Dunkirk. Various hotels were taken by the RAF for accommodation of its servicemen. In 1940 the RAF established a station in the town which began as a radio direction finding unit.[286]

In 1942 a Sussex MO Writer recorded:

> 'My sister, who was two months in the London bombing in 1940, says she does not undress now at night. They have many Alerts, as all the planes which go to Exeter and elsewhere in the South go over them (Sidmouth).'[287]

Air raids were recorded in and around Sidmouth including on 3 September 1940, 15 April 1941, 28 November 1941, 2 July 1942, 30 November 1942 and in early December 1942 the Luftwaffe attacked Sidmouth with machine-gun fire.[288] Four months later Miss Ausden noted a bomb had fallen in Sidmouth.

Sidmouth had a second MO Writer in addition to Miss Ausden: in November 1939 Dr Jessie Blundun, a fifty-two-year-old doctor from Sussex, wrote from the Hotel Riviera. He commented upon the war's inconveniences ('1, constant feeling of tension with regard to possible air raids; 2, disruption of home life, owing to members of family on war service or leaving home for safer areas; 3, curtailment of travelling facilities; 4, blackout; 5, rising prices; 6, lack of news'). What little *grousing* he heard came 'chiefly from middle-aged and elderly people who have left their homes in or near London who say *I do miss my home*.' He also explained his current experiences of blackout ('There are two sets of curtains, one light and the other thick dark-lined velvet, quite efficient. But it is a nuisance having to sleep with curtains drawn or else use a torch if one wakes in the night… The blackout does not seem to be complete in this place. I have seen cars with brilliant lights going down the Esplanade at night. I should suggest greater stringency in keeping the regulations.'). He returned in 1943 and later recalled it as his last 'real' holiday, 'I remember best the freedom from bomb damage and risk of air-raids, and the peace and serenity of the countryside.'[289]

***279** The Riviera Hotel, Sidmouth, at which Dr Jessie Blundun stayed in 1939, 2025.*

Another MO Writer, from Sussex, thought in 1942 that the war had improved the health of her sister who had moved to Sidmouth:

> 'My sister, who is older than I am, seems to have improved in health since the war. She had been a semi-invalid for years – acted so – but slept in a cellar in a deck chair for two months during the worst of the bombing in London. Then was bombed out, and went to Sidmouth where she is with nice people. I visited her this year and she, who couldn't walk five minutes without stopping to rest, now walked me off my feet, three or four miles in the morning and vexed with me because I wouldn't go out again in the evening. I wrote her once that two planes (Jerries) had been brought down, not so far from here (last spring), that most of the neighbours were out and saw them, but I, thank goodness, slept through it all. She wrote, if it had been her, she would have been cross if it happened there and she had slept through it. I think she really enjoys the thrill of it all and doesn't really care. Probably it has sent her blood-pressure up, but it makes her feel full of pep, some excitement in a rather dull life.'[290]

56. Ellen Ausden, Teacher, 1943

Miss Ellen Joyce Ausden (1896-1974), a forty-six-year-old teacher from Watford, spent her Easter holiday in Sidmouth having previously vacationed in North Devon.[291] **(19)**

> 'Thursday April 22nd, at 8.30am I started off for a holiday at Sidmouth, my sister coming as far as Waterloo to carry my bag. There was no crush anywhere. There were no platform tickets and my

280 Undated pencil drawing by F. M. Hayman of High Street, Exeter, including the Church of St Lawrence. Miss Ellen Ausden later saw stone from this church salvaged for use as a garden wall in Pinhoe.

281 Pinhoe in the early 1900s.

sister was not allowed to come onto the train. The tea wagons were a great boon and it was easier to get a cup of tea than in 1940. The travellers were much more interesting than pre-war ones probably because they were car-users. Most in our compartment discussed choral music. It was a revelation to me to see the preparations that had been made in 1940 and since against enemy invasion.

Friday, April 23rd On a board *Danger: path to cliff closed* and written in pencil *Effect of seagull bombing.* At night the siren went and a few minutes later the house was shaken by a bomb falling. I was on the fourth floor and for the first time realised why people came downstairs during raids. There was a strange sound later like a mighty crack, but nothing was heard falling. It was probably a gun fired without the sound echoing amongst the hills. A neat remark from one of the other guests My *trouble is the dancing years.*

Saturday, April 24th One has to be very early for buses here. I reached a queue at 1.40pm for a 2 o'clock bus to Exeter. When the coach came in it filled up at once. A Canadian Air Force officer got out rather than stand. The load changed during the journey but the bus was full all the time and at three places little groups were left behind.

Coming home after visiting a friend at Pinhoe, I got to the bus station at 5.45 for the 6.10 bus there were already more than enough for one load. However, a second bus was filled, as soon as it came in, from a special journey to Plymouth as the girl conductor told me later.

The centre of Exeter was a mess with more bomb damage than I saw in the centre of Manchester. My friend at Pinhoe had made a new garden banked up with large red stones from the bombed Saint Lawrence's church.

Easter Sunday I was on a hilltop and a boy about 10, with a younger sister, suddenly he said *Bells, Jill, Bells*! The church bells from the valley sounded very lovely and must have been an experience for those two.

At lunchtime the two children of the proprietor's family (girl 14, boy 13) were talking about searchlights and how they could be used after the war. The girl's idea was to have one at each end of the seafront to shine a floodlight with a band stand in the middle.

Easter Monday was fine and warm during the afternoon. Many people were out but there were no crowds. People had brought their own meals and flasks were in evidence.

Tuesday, April 27 In a café for *elevenses* the conversation at a big table next mine got onto war conditions. The man of the party (he might have been an army officer on holiday) said that of all the places he had been to since the war Sidmouth showed least change. Yet he had heard more grumbling there than anywhere else.

Wednesday, April 28th A wonderfully interesting evening; a clergyman, who said he ought to have been a sailor, had some entrancing tales to tell of ships and seamen, convoys, submarines and wartime journeys. Early in 1940 he had taken a party of children to New Zealand. He described a sub attack at night on another ship in the convoy and how next day their own ship was quite alone and never again saw sign of the convoy. When the ship entered the Panama Canal and US soldiers boarded it, the children were frightened at first, thinking the soldiers were pirates who had captured the ship. However, by the end of the canal trip no soldier had any button or badge left on his clothing or any piece of equipment that the children could take as a souvenir.'

In 1938 Miss Ausden had noted in her self-report that Watford was a dormitory town for London workers and that 'it is healthy with very pretty surroundings and there are some lovely spots to see at any time of the year.' She appears to have spent the remainder of her life in the town and died there in 1974.[292]

SOUTH HAMS (& BUCKFAST ABBEY & WIDECOMBE-ON-THE MOOR)

This diarist stayed at an unspecified location in the South Hams, the collection of parishes in South Devon which lie to the east of Plymouth and west of Totnes, running between Dartmoor and the English Channel.

In 1939 an MO Writer (a nineteen-year-old assistant librarian in Bristol) recorded an incident which had recently occurred somewhere in the South Hams:

'Mr AHC, a lame solicitor, exempted during last war, was belligerent. Said he *This country is damned slack. It wanted tightening up*. As part of the tightening process, he had taken part in a childish spy-hunt. He told us about it proudly. His hotel on the South coast harboured an Austrian Jew, a refugee. He had been there several months and was quite liked. On occasion he went into Dartmouth where AHC observed him asking people questions. He admitted that he overheard some of them and they were quite innocent. But he *spoke* to the local police. He *got in touch* with CID. He *protested* to the hotel manager. Without avail, fortunately. He spoke darkly of the Secret Service. He did get the manager to search his room and, so keen was he on his nonsense, that he considered the absence of any incriminating documents to be itself incriminating. No doubt, there was a short-wave transmitter embedded in the mattress, and, no doubt, carrier pigeons were released every night in hundreds. Anyway, Mr C was in his element. He told us all about it. He lurked. He followed, tracked, traced and ambushed the poor man like a silly boy-scout, carefully *covering his traces* and making himself a public nuisance all over the South Coast. Tightening up the country.'[293]

That year another MO Writer who was a part-time resident of Dartmouth observed the port 'appears to have almost no Jews'.[294]

282 The Butterwalk in Dartmouth, c1900.

57. Judith Hall, Land Girl, 1944-5

Nancy Judith Hall (1921-2017) was twenty-two-years-old when she travelled from Somerset to visit her boyfriend Dennis Puckett (1921-1993) somewhere in the South Hams. She was serving in the Land Army and wrote diaries for MO from 1939 to 1945 as well as answered directives. Her diaries for 1944 and 1945 include time spent in South Devon.[295]

283 Widecombe as depicted in 1922 by Sir Walter Westley Russell.

1944

'Wednesday, March 22nd It is my weekend and I have arranged to stay at D[ennis]'s new place in South Devon. I am looking forward to it immensely.

Friday, March 25th B[etty] went off in the first train home for her week's leave. Another of the staff travelled with her and two of the residents. I managed to get off an hour earlier from work & caught the 4pm train down to Devon. I arrived 7pm and dear D met me at the station & escorted me back to the family where he is living. We had dinner & a pleasant evening round the fire. A nice household with several visitors this weekend as they take in paying guests.

Saturday, March 26th A glorious day and all seemed right with our world (unfortunately the thought of the rest of the world being right too was out of the question and seemed to hang in the background however happy we feel in one another's company). We took a picnic and walked across the moors to Widecombe. It is a quaint little village & though obviously had received hundreds of tourists in pre-war day, was quite deserted. Of course it made it much nicer for us to wander around, in a tea place & in the church with only the villagers about. It seemed a long way back but we enjoyed the quiet beauty of the hills, moors & villages. It was 6.30 when we got back to the house & we had dinner & another evening round the fire.

Sunday, March 26th A perfect day. Warm & sunny as May. After breakfast we went for a walk in the woods by the River Dart. It looked more lovely than I have ever seen any river look. The daffodils, violets & primroses are a sight & the birds were singing & love-making too. After lunch we walked to Buckfast Abbey & sat inside & heard part of a service. It seemed weird to think about the lives of the monks. It seems so unnatural to sequester oneself entirely as they do, living a life of worship.

We had tea at a delightful wayside café & walked back for dinner at 7pm. We also went to look at the land D & his partner (with whom he lives) is working. After helping with the washing-up D & I escaped to my bedroom & spent the evening talking & making love. He is a dear & I don't think I shall ever want to give him up. He is very much in love with me and looks upon me as his future wife. I am sure I might do far worse. I am sure he will make a good husband and I know he is very true. I asked him why he was first attracted to me and he said it definitely wasn't my looks, because after our first meeting when he was rather struck by me, he could not remember one bit what I looked like! I had to laugh at him, but I thought that was encouraging, as my looks will probably alter more in the course of years than my personality. I find D has not had a series of love affairs like I had in the years between 15 and 21 but appears to have waited until he hit upon the right *cup of tea*. He says he was too much occupied with other matters until a year ago and the girls he met either ignored him or he disliked them. Am I as unique as all that, as he has not led a secluded life? We seem very suited to one another & I think I can make him happy.'

1945

Hall continued with Dennis and on 28 July 1945 wrote in her diary:

'Travelled in a packed train to Devonshire arriving 1pm. It was clearly a case of survival of the fittest on the railway with standing in the carriages as well as the corridors. D & I passed the day pleasantly together in walking, walking, eating, love-making & attending the village flower show which was fun.

Sunday, July 29th. We went to Plymouth today. We went to visit my late working companion still in hospital after a spinal graft (TB). It is amazing how cheerful and happy she seems and is a lesson to all of us. I am not madly in love with D these days, but exceedingly fond of him. We are always happy together but when I get away from him, I forget him. He, poor lamb, is ever faithful to me.'

There had been another visit in November, 1944:

'Friday day off & went by train to Exeter to meet D. We had a pleasant day in spite of the rain which came down gently all day. Had nice lunch & tea, explored the town, cathedral, etc. and went to the pictures. We saw film *Double Indemnity* which is exciting pre-war kind of story of a planned murder.'

Five months later Miss Hall continued to have doubts over marriage ('He cannot afford to marry me unless I work as well. The thought of this frightens me because I don't think there would be much security in that. We might have a child which would put us in financial straits and as the war appears to be nearly over, married women in jobs won't be welcome. I love him and would marry him if he could keep me, which is what I want. I would rather remain as I am if I am to go on working… Marriage is a state which I am more cautious to enter than many, because I don't want to think afterwards, I didn't know when I was well off… I am not one to think there is only one man to make me happy.' However, in 1947 she married Dennis Puckett. Mrs Puckett died in 2017.[296]

SOUTH MOLTON

This North Devon market town had some 2,832 residents during the 1930s.[297]

58. John Hobbs, Teacher, 1937

284 Mr John Hobbs in the 1930s.

Twenty-three-year-old John Sanders Hobbs (1913-2002) was born in North Molton where his father was a butcher. By 1921 the family had moved to South Molton. Mr Hobbs subsequently achieved first class honours at Cambridge and became a geography teacher in Cheshire. In 1937 he returned to South Molton for a holiday with his wife Kathleen who had been born in Shanghai but whose family hailed from South Molton. Mr Hobbs described himself as having socialistic politics and as modernistic in his religion. In his itinerary of 12 April he mentioned the imprisonment of William Southcombe, aged 53, on charges of fraudulent conversion of public funds. Mr Hobbs' did not comment upon pre-war preparations but did refer to the war in Spain.[298]

'No interesting local events. Film at local cinema *Life Versus Secretary*. I did not want to see it.

Awakened 8.30 am. Breakfast in dressing gown, as is often my custom on holiday! Lingered over breakfast and London papers (the local paper is weekly & appears towards the end of the week. Includes separately in brief report of items relevant to Monday 12th) and was not washed or shaved until 10.30.

10.30 – 12.30 devoted to private work. 12.30 – 1 lunch. Table talk mainly on dentists and teeth. I had a dental appointment for the following day.

1 – 2 wrote letters to friends.

2 – 4.30 a walk with [Fred Howe] my closest friend and student at University College of the South West, Exeter, now on vacation. Nothing exceptional on the walk. As usual, we put the world right between us, discussing

especially the Spanish Civil War and the Marriage Bill (with special reference to the reactionary attitude of the Church on all matters of social reform).

4.30 - 5 Read *Punch*.

5 – 5.30 Tea, discussion on an event that has been exciting local interest – the jailing of the former Borough Treasurer for misappropriation of borough money. He was sent to prison (18 months) a few weeks ago but the matter is still one for talk, because his wife has been in a mental home for some years and does not know her husband's position, although for the last few months she has become much better and able to leave the home. The position is a, if she is told, she may have a mental relapse and b, if she is not told, it really means keeping her in the Home when she is fit to leave.

5.30 – 6.20 Visited my tobacconist and a friend who keeps a music shop. Discussed the coming Max Baer and Tommy Farr fight in both cases and generally agreed that Baer would win.

6.30 – 8.20 Visited my wife's grandmother and talked of family affairs for an hour and was then forced to play some hands of whist with her and two of her grandchildren.

8.30 – 9 Evening meal at home. Conversation on family affairs.

9 – 11 Read a detective novel.

11 Bed.'

Mr Hobbs stayed at Marley House, the family home which has since been demolished to make way for a health centre. In 1941 was commissioned in the Royal Artillery and was later transferred to the Army Education Corps. He died in 2002.[299]

STOKE FLEMING

This coastal village immediately to the west of Dartmouth had 630 residents in 1931. At the start of the war Dartmouth had a population of 5,831 and experienced a 2.2% decrease that year.[300] During the war a training camp was built to the southeast of Blackpool Bridge. Mrs Friend, the village's MO diarist, recorded Stoke Fleming's air raid of 17 December 1942 which was also noted in the *Western Morning News*:

'Shortly after noon yesterday four enemy planes came in from the sea and dropped bombs and machine-gunned a South-West village. All fell on loose earth. One was on a farm where three pigs were killed. Two of the bombs did no damage. Another fell on garden land at the rear of a street, where considerable material damage was done. The bomb made a crater 40 feet across and the blast wrecked houses in that street.

Several families have been rendered homeless, but a considerable portion of their furniture may be salvaged. The bakery was damaged, also a boot shop.

The villagers congratulated themselves on their miraculous escape. There was only one serious casualty - Mrs Harriett Bowden, aged 76. She was sitting in her room when a bomb fell and her window was blown inwards, the glass cutting her head and arm. She was conveyed to hospital, and is in a serious condition.

Police and civil defence services visited the village, and many willing helpers came in from the countryside. The villagers made light of their material damage and discomfort, and were thankful that their casualty list only numbered one. The church lost some slates off the roof and portions of three stained-glass windows were blown out. The parish hall was badly damaged and books belonging to the County Library were removed to a new home.

An Air Ministry and Ministry of Home Security communique last night stated: *Shortly after noon today bombs were dropped in a village near the South-West Coast of England. One person was injured and little damage was done.*'[301]

A manuscript book of bombing casualties in Devon noted that three individuals were lightly wounded. They were seventy-year-old Mrs Henriette Bowden of Bailey House, fifteen-year-old Reginald William Charles Dubell of 2 Bailey Cottages and thirteen-year-old Florence Elizabeth Eileen Burdett of Tremlett House.[302]

In respect to this attack, Mrs Friend wrote of the assistance rendered by her and other villagers. Otherwise, she comments, in passing, on servicemen in the village but made no mention of the Americans training nearby in preparation for the invasion of France.

Parts of the parishes of Blackawton, East Allington, Sherford, Slapton, Stoke Fleming, Stokenham and Strete were evacuated in December 1943 in order to be used for battle-training. A month after D-Day building repairs began in order to allow the return of villagers. That July one journalist waxed lyrical ('No smoke curls from the chimneys. No cat washes itself on the cottage doorstep. No hen clucks in the backyard and no sleek cattle graze in the over-grown fields. Not a sound disturbs the unnatural silence of the South Devon evacuation area which a couple of months ago was the scene of mock battles by means of which our American allies prepared themselves for the invasion of Normandy.')[303]

285 A photograph of Mrs Muriel Friend, taken in about 1937, which she sent to Mass Observation.

59. Muriel Friend, Domestic Worker, 1940-5

At the start of the war Mrs Muriel Irene Friend (1905-1977) moved from Norbury in London, where she lived with her husband Robert (1897-1960), a school enquiry officer, to Hassocks near Brighton. They had met in 1925. On 31 August 1940 she took a holiday in South Devon. Mrs Friend wrote diaries, day-surveys and directives from 1937 to 1950.[304]

In 1938 she had lived with her husband in a recently-built estate in suburban Norbury. She described the district as lower-middle-class and as 'ordinary suburban life'. Her subsequent embracement of life in Stoke Fleming may have been a reaction to her existence as a South London housewife. In 1938 the couple discussed a trial separation.

In 1940 Mrs Friend initially spent a fortnight in the Socialist Seaside Camp at Rockvale Cove in Stoke Fleming where she had previously holidayed. After a fortnight her husband suggested that she remained there. The camp had been established by Rowland Barrett (1877-1950), Socialist and Devon Secretary of the National Union of Agricultural Workers,[305] and his wife Marion (1879-). In 1924 one of the campers described it as hanging 'on the side of a cliff on the wildest coast of Devon' where 'the seagulls circle and shriek over the white-foamed sea, which thunders against the rugged rocks and roars its way into the deep caves'.[306]

After a short period Mrs Friend came to work at the camp and moved from a tent to a hut. Later she lived in the Barrett's bungalow where she nursed Mrs Barrett. She spent much of her time tending to the campers, working in the vegetable garden and administering the use of the cove. Her leisure time was spent swimming, sunbathing and playing games such as Mahjong and chess. Her husband was absent from her life but other family members appeared such as her sister Grace (1903-1974), nephew John and niece Faith. She attended a high-profile lecture given in Torquay by her brother William John Brown (1894-1960), General Secretary of the Civil

286 Tents perched along the cliff edge at the camp.

Service Clerical Association from 1919 to 1942. He was elected as a Labour MP for Wolverhampton West in 1931 but resigned the whip and for one day joined Mosley's New Party.[307] She kept a diary throughout the war years and nearly

***LEFT:* 287** *Rockvale Cove.*

***ABOVE:* 288** *The cove and some of the holiday camp accommodation.*

always referred to individuals by the use of an initial. Among the topics she recorded was meeting two young servicemen who referred to themselves as being part of the 'Suicide Squad'. They may have been serving with Special Operations Executive which had been formed in 1940.

1940

'6th Sept. 1940, Had a farewell social in the evening to which all 8 campers came. Had cocoa with the Rs in their hut about 10. At 11, while we were talking, the alarm sounded and *All Clear* sounded about 11.30. Previous to alarm we heard an explosion which Mrs R. thought was a convoy being bombed at sea. He said we could only move our ships at night now.

Saturday, 7th Sept, Heard an explosion about 8.30. Saw smoke a good way out from land and a ship making towards it. Saw off the Rs from Stoke Fleming, feeling very sad as I am now the only person left in camp. Rested in bed in afternoon. In evening 4-6 went on to beach and sunbathed. Then played chess with R & afterwards Mahjong with him & his wife. They live in a bungalow. Had to sleep alone in a hut in camp but soon slept & had a good night.

Sunday, 8th Sept. 7-10, had breakfast and wrote 2 letters. 10-11, chatted to R who came to see if I had a good night. He is lame & I appreciated the effort he made to get from his bungalow to the camp, hilly ground. 11.30, I had hot milk & finished letter-writing. Wrote up diary. Rested in afternoon & played Mahjong in evening with R & M…

Tuesday, 10th Sept. Went into Dartmouth to cash a money order for R. Registered at employment exchange. May stay here for winter if any quieter here. Went to the pictures in Dartmouth and saw *French Without Tears*. Usual evening programme – Mahjong…

Saturday, 14th Sept. Had a letter from my husband R[obert] saying he thinks it a good idea for me to stay here and that he will send my money on every month. He enclosed £5. I sent £2 to my landlady at Hassock to cover my room till end of month in case there is an invasion & I want to go back. Shall stay another fortnight perhaps indefinitely.

Had lunch at the S's shop in the village. Picked a lot of blackberries by the waterfall here, & near R's garden & M boiled them & squeezed the stones through muslin to make blackberry jelly. I then played a game of chess with R. Played Mahjong in evening, with R, M, and Mr L who does odd jobs about the place weekends.

Sunday 15th Sept. Sat on a seat overlooking the sea

289 *Drawing by Charles Baskerville, 2 June 1944, entitled 'Invasion Craft: D-Day minus two, Dartmouth Harbour'.*

& wrote 2 letters. On Saturday night, just after I had come up to bed, my brother [William] spoke on the wireless giving incidents from his life, with the comment *I should not have been allowed to do that in Nazi Germany!* R told me he considered it the best piece of propaganda he had heard, so I wrote a note of appreciation to my brother W. R & I were disappointed I did not hear him.

Afternoon Went on the beach with Mr L. We swam & sunbathed & he talked about the 10 years he spent in Australia. Feel safer swimming when there is someone on the beach with me. Evening played Mahjong & Can you Go?, finishing by singing some hymns played by M. We sang my brother's favourite hymn tune *Rest* at my request. Went to bed about 9.30. Mr L escorted me up the slope to my hut in bright moonlight.

Monday, 16th Sept. Morning. Went to the village shopping. Mr L went back to his work. News of 153 German planes brought down Sunday, & coast to London littered with them. We lost 25 planes.

Afternoon. Went to the beach and splashed about in the surfy waves as tide was coming in. Was sunbathing on top of a rock when a [RAF] plane rounded the rock which bounds this cove. It was about level with height of rock & seemed coming straight for the cove as if to land, flying very low. I crouched down behind a rock, dreading machine gun fire. When I looked out again

290 *Luftwaffe photograph of Stoke Fleming (at the bottom) and Redlap Cove (at the top), 21 October 1942.*

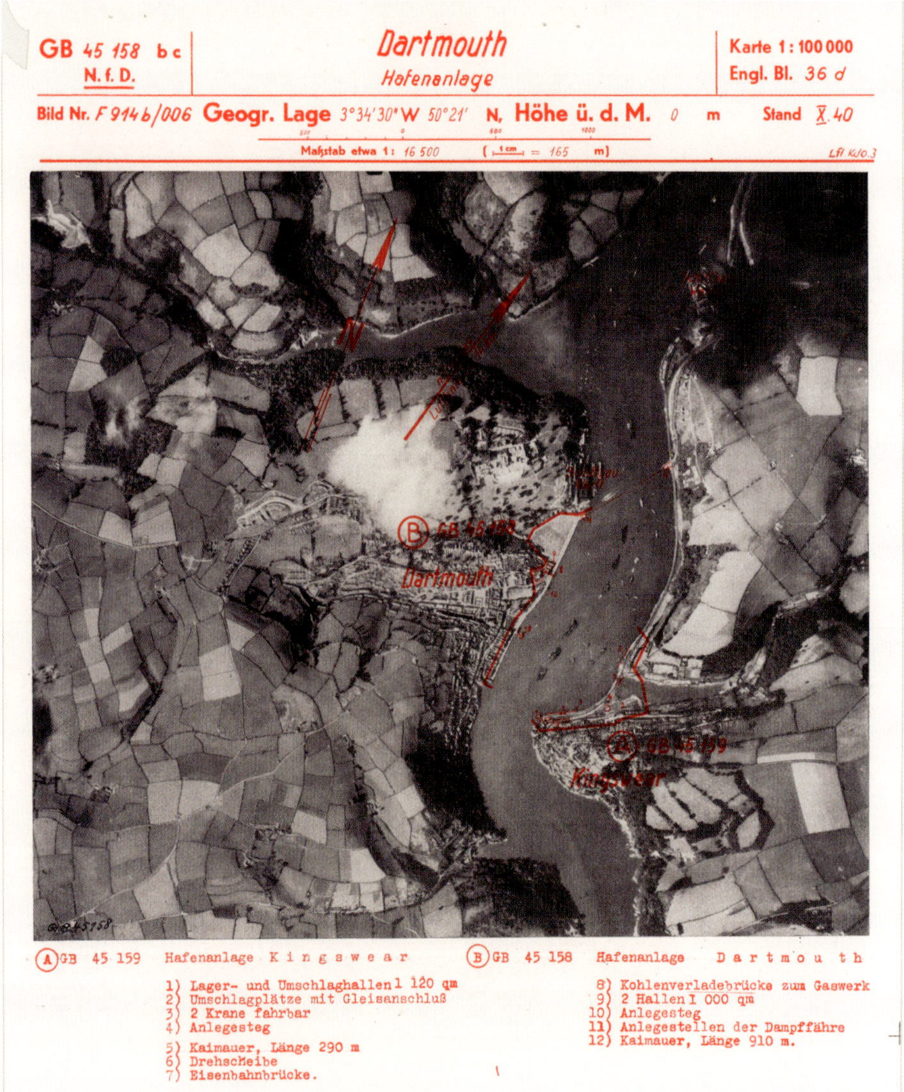

291 *German aerial photograph of Dartmouth and Kingswear, 1940, highlighting strategic sites in red.*

the plane was gone – it must have turned & ascended over the top of cliffs. It had yellow on the wings & I did not know what nationality it belonged to. M said she thought it was Italian. She had seen it from the bungalow…

Tuesday, 17th Sept. Went with R to Brixham where he was interviewing the *hard core* of the unemployed for the Ministry of Labour. We had lunch at Deller's in Paignton. Then I went to Torquay shopping. I bought a warm dress for evenings and a hot water bottle etc. We had tea at Brixham. Our train was an hour late, there was no bus & we had to phone for a car from Stoke Fleming at Dartmouth, getting back about 9. Glad to get out of Dartmouth. Explosions in the direction of Totnes.

Wednesday, 18th Sept. Playing chess with R when a telegram came from A, a man who was here last year in the autumn. R sent a reply that he should come now (he asked if he could come soon). It will be pleasant to have another camper here. Afternoon, rested and went to village. Evening, Mahjong.

Thursday, 19th Sept. Had a letter from sister G, asking for more details about this camp. She sounds quite phlegmatic about the air raids, says they sleep on a mattress inside shelter at night. No signs of panic from her and she is highly strung too. Wrote to R, thanking him for money…

Monday, 23rd Sept. …Caught the 1.15 bus to Dartmouth & had dinner in a café there. Two men were

292-5 *Four photographs of USS LST-289 entering Dartmouth after being torpedoed by German MTBs off Slapton Sands on 28 April 1944. Mrs Friend largely refrained from commenting on naval matters.*

seated at the various tables & we chatted a bit. One was a Londoner. He was on holiday near his evacuated children. He was getting a job down here. He was awaiting his wife's arrival. His home had been bombed. His wife had written saying she could not tell all. He thought I would be wise to stay here. The other man had a brother in the RAF who had just finished his 48th flight over Germany. He said there was not a wall 3 feet high standing at Bremen. We had bombed them so badly. He said he expected Italian airmen over here soon – no one had told him so, but he had this idea. Went to the pictures till 5. Had to walk home as no bus till 8…

Wednesday, 25th Sept. My sister G[race] arrived with her 2 children, worn out with weeks of sleeping in shelters. They stayed in this camp till Saturday 5th Oct. when they got rooms in Stoke Fleming…

Wednesday, 9th October Had breakfast, made shopping list, wrote a.p.c. and got diary ready to send to Mass Observation. Last evening R was impressed with Mr Churchill's speech, said it was hopeful & that there was some fine language in it. Is going to dictate it to me for shorthand practice when the paper comes through. We haven't had yesterday's paper yet!...

Thursday, 10th Oct… G shares a sitting room with her landlady. There was a coal fire and the table laid neatly for tea with a vase of flowers in centre and paper serviettes. I sat in the drawing room in front before tea; it looks out to the sea. Mrs B, the landlady, does her sewing in this room and her machine is in front of the window. G & I sat talking and G read me a letter from her husband J in London. He had put a PS that he had just had to rush out to deal with a Molotov Bread Basket which landed in this street in Streatham Vale. Clad in trousers and tin hat the men rushed out and put out the bombs which landed mostly in front gardens luckily. I cannot help admiring J, who writes six-page letters to his wife after coming home from work and cooking a meal and before going into dugout for the night…

I wish all evacuees were as lucky as G who has the use of a lovely light sitting room and kitchen on ground floor and rents two bedrooms above, for 10 shillings a week.

Friday, 11th October, 6am, Woke up in darkness & heard the sound of aeroplane, followed by a bomb near. Wondered if bungalow had caught it & walked down to see. Building looked alright… I have heard two aeroplanes buzzing about the last few minutes. The moonlight sets up fresh air activity. Have just heard another bomb & seen an airplane going off across the sea… Found out the early morning bomb was on Kingswear, Dartmouth…

Sunday, 13th Oct., R had made an arrangement with Mr H, the local tailor, who is on lookout duty on the next cliff, Redlap, that we should walk over there & that R should entertain him and his mate with solos on his ocarina, so the three of us walked up from bungalow. The wind was whistling round, so we all had cocoa in my hut before we went, that is, all save M, who could not come as the walk would have been too much for her. We took sticks to help us over uneven ground. The moon was covered with clouds but there was a subdued light which helped us to find the way. We went down this cove & across the cliff & finally approached their tiny hut when R started playing his signature tune *God Save the King* which was agreed on as the signal of our approach. Mr H came to meet us, looking very pleased to see us & guided us in. The two windows faced on to the cliff. There was no lighting but an unlit stove in the corner could be used. A bench ran down two side of hut & Mr H brought out a deck chair for me, the first woman, he said, who had visited them there. There was just the two of them on guard. Mr H & a younger man who is the gardener for our next-door neighbour. R played *Whisper & I shall hear*, a tune which he says sounded through every ballroom about 1898 & which Mr H, who is about his age, appreciated. I only know it through coming across it in a song book of well-known tunes…

Monday, 21st October Afternoon, did some errands in Dartmouth for R, returning just after 5. It was a beautiful sunny day. All I wore to go in was a cotton frock. Coming back I put on a costume coat. I sat in some gardens near the quay before the bus went and wound wool which I had just bought to make some gloves. It seemed very quiet there & happy. There were a good many women sitting on the seats, probably some of them evacuees. There were also a lot of sailors strolling about or on the seats, French or Polish by their talk…

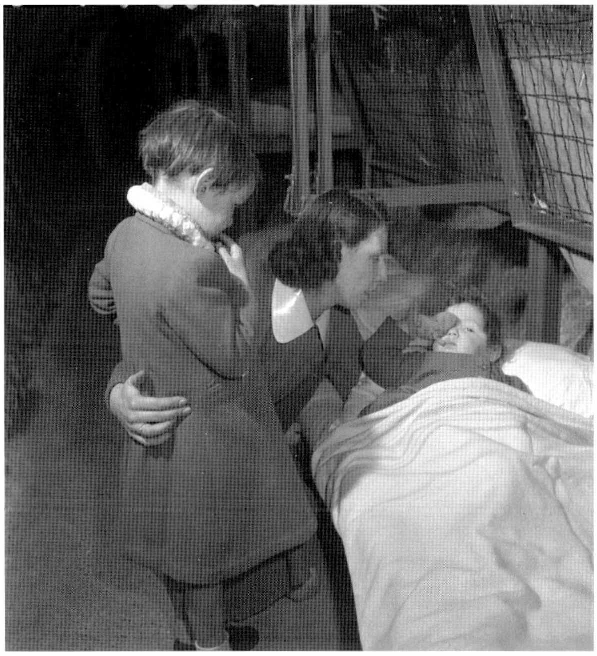

***296** Mrs Friend recorded hearing about sheltering during bombing in wartime London.*

***297** A woman with two children in an underground shelter during the bombing of London.*

We both thought it a splendid speech. R thought Churchill was the right man in the right place. The last sentence was worthy of a Socialist orator & is obviously insincere on the lips of Churchill who is not of the class which cares a button about the aims or rights of working people…

Tuesday, 22nd October… G came just after dinner and read me a letter from J, her husband. What a bit of propaganda for the peace movement it would make – written in the midst of a raid. Every time a bomb dropped, he wrote an X. First, he rushed out to find a house in his street razed to the ground, luckily it was empty. Then more bombs, which hit the row of shops at the end of his road in Streatham Vale. He said the shops were gone, with a crater beneath them big enough to take the shops. With tin hat on, he went over the ruins, helped out an old couple on the ground floor. One woman was having hysterics because her husband could not be found. He said if G could see that corner now, she would be sick. He finished by declaring against the slaughter of innocents involved by war. This letter deserves publication. J seems touched to the heart by what goes on around him, yet finds time to keep in touch with wife and family. Last week she received a trunkful of clothes packed by him, including two picture books for the children and a bar of chocolate which we cannot get here…

Tuesday, 29th Oct …We went to see Mr S., the editor of a Dartmouth paper & R tried to interest him in the subject of sawdust, which is being burned and so wasted in the big sawmills and yet scientists have proved it can be used for many things including the manufacturing of sugar! Mr S. clasped his hands to his head in astonishment when he heard the latter. But he was off to the police courts and could not listen very long. He was scathing on the subject of evacuees saying that if all the women and children had left London when the government told them to, they would be comfortably settled by now. We had a glass of milk and an Eccles cake in Daries & then went into the gardens. Walking along the quayside we noticed the trees which were growing, not having been planted more than a year or two, they were some of them acacias. We could not make out the others as they were bare of leaves. In the gardens there is a monument to the man who invented the first steam engine. R showed me a tiny pool I have never seen before, with a lot of very bright and flourishing goldfish in it. Roses were still in bloom.

***298** Cautionary American poster by Ben Shahn warning of the conditions in occupied France, 1942.*

There are cactus trees and palms in these gardens.

We got to Paignton just before 1, and had lunch. We went round Woolworths before lunch and bought a small lamp complete except for glass which we got at Timothy Whites. After lunch went on to the front and sat in a shelter, eating fruit tarts bought at Woolworths. Then I walked with R to the Employment Exchange and he went in to his meeting. I went into a number of greengrocers' shops trying to buy dates and they had none. Finally bought 2 packets, which R said was not the best way of buying them as they were more economical bought by the pound. Still, I thought myself lucky to get any at all.

Went into a number of shops trying to get a woollen petticoat for M. Three did not stock any. Finally, got one for 6 shillings 11 pence, which seemed fairly reasonable…

Friday, 1 Nov. …We called on my sister G on the way to ask if she knew of a room going for A. He can't stay in a tent indefinitely. Her husband had written that he had three days' leave due and would try to get down soon to see her. He reported the time bombs had been removed from W. H. Smiths in Kingsway by Capt. Davis who removed the one from St Paul's. He said it was because it was opposite Air Ministry that bombs were removed…

Friday, 8th Nov. …Found A was back from Dartmouth, having obtained a medical certificate again from his doctor. He reported a dog fight between planes over Dartmouth and one English plane down in the sea…

Tuesday, 12th Nov. …Went to see G, her landlady came back from Plymouth Sunday. The same day she accepted two soldiers to live in the house. They are aged 23 and 25. G said they had all stayed up till 12 the previous night talking. She said she liked one of them called Roy. She has been curling her hair at the sides lately and said her husband would think it was because of the soldiers. Mrs B asked me into her sitting room to see the soldiers and they seemed very nice boys. Her husband J is coming on Friday. His letter said the shelter is now too damp and he wears his tin hat indoors on account of the huge lump of shrapnel that fell. He gave a picture of himself doing his chores in tin hat and frilly apron, singing aloud to keep cheerful, that made me laugh…

Sunday, 11th Nov. … J had arrived at 8 the previous night and was staying till Thursday and looked a bit tired but not nervy like A was when he came. Paddington had been bombed the night before he came and one train came to Dartmouth on Saturday instead of two. J had come all the way in the lavatory, with six other people. The people he was with had spent six weeks living in the Tube, they were women. They seem to have enjoyed the sociability there. There were always some forms of entertainment going and people played musical instruments, etc. But they have fights too, now and then, when someone takes over someone else's pitch. They were working class people. J said people would meet to keep this communal life up after the war, especially women, evacuees, etc.

We had roast beef for dinner and milk pudding afterwards. I have been having vegetarian meals lately except for a rabbit once or twice. After dinner, while G and Mrs B washed up, J and I had a talk, and to my amazement J was boosting Hitler all the time, saying he was a Socialist, who had taken the only means he could of improving the Germans' standard of living. He said it would not affect him (J) if Hitler won and came here. I pointed out ways in which it would. J said his wife's brother would almost certainly be executed and his wife put into a concentration camp. He said he would rather a minority be disposed of than war go on. When I pointed out how Hitler had enslaved the Poles and other nations, J said I was going by papers and what I had heard, which was probably not true…

The two soldier boys were moved on Thursday and no one knows where they have gone. They called themselves the *Suicide Squad*. G said she had heard they are landed off boats on the coast of France to get information.

After tea, at which Mrs B joined us, we sat and talked round the fire. I left about 8.15. J walked with me to the village and then I came down the lane alone. J said his wife and family had been absent 2 months but it seemed more like 6…

Wednesday, 20th Nov. …afternoon, watched 4 battleships from balcony of bungalow with M, they came in quickly from near to the horizon, each only showing a pointed stern, then two went round towards Dartmouth and the other two remained. Two airplanes were circling round. One battleship was signalling to an airplane. Finally, the planes went off towards Start Point…

Wednesday, 2th Nov. … I went on to G's with currants and sultanas I had ordered from Co-op for her (two pounds). Found her doing her washing. She had got home late previous morning after gossiping with some women and landlady had reprimanded her for washing up being left, so today she was trying to fall in with landlady's plans, doing washing in morning and cooking in afternoon, to leave kitchen free for landlady Thursday. I didn't stay long. Called for bread and came home. The baker's wife had been up all night baking as her husband is not well and extra baking of bread to be done, as village full…

Afternoon, sat on Seagull Seat for an hour with R. It was a glorious afternoon, clear and sunny, warm in the sun where we sat. A bomb fell with a terrific crash as we sat there. It sounded as if it would be Dartmouth. Then the Air Raid alarm went, followed by a little gunfire and the All Clear about ¼ hour afterwards… About 7 there was another really loud explosion, then till about 9, gunfire, which shook the bungalow. We had heard a plane over, before the explosion. We had supper together in M's bedroom as she was upset by the raid and did not want to be left…

Sunday, 8 December …had a nap, I slept till about 4, could hear the drone of a plane & felt sure it was a German. Then the alarm went from Dartmouth. There were 3 or 4 dull crashes which sounded like small incendiary bombs. Then the All Clear went. I was afraid to go out of hut till the plane had gone, it and the bomb sounded so near. When I looked at the sky I saw puffs of white smoke, as if there had been firing. R said he thought what I thought were bombs, were firing. He

299 *'The Rhino's Fleet' by Dwight C. Shepler illustrating the propellers in the Dart estuary, 1944.*

only reckoned there was one bomb dropped…

Wednesday, 11th Dec. …waiting for doctor's arrival. He and R came in about 12.30. He examined M and I made tea for them. R had come in his car (the doctor's) to show him this out-of-the-way place and had had to make his round of visits with him. They had a cup of tea and then went to fetch car from a neighbour's drive where it had been left. The doctor, who was 75, was acting as locum for the Dartmouth doctor. He was not used to car, which was a large one. He had come from North London and said he would rather be there, plus bombs, than trying to negotiate the narrow streets and hills of Devon.

Afternoon. Got dinner & went to Miss B.'s house to help R repair the gate which the doctor had crashed his car into while trying to get out of drive! R filled in cracks in paint with putty & banged two panels back in position, afterwards painting damaged part over. Miss B. very amiable and gave us a bunch of violets just picked from garden for M…

Thursday, 12th Dec… At 9am got up and went to village for M's medicine, & also arranged to fetch some oil. Mrs J, where we buy it, asked me if R was throwing the oil over the cliff, if not what on earth was he doing with it? I told her his wife was confined to bed. This is the third lot of oil we have had within a week, but R wants 2 or 3 gallons in reserve as if the supply runs out, we have no coal or grates to burn it in in the bungalow… Got 5 gallons oil and ½lb biscuits as I saw some tins of biscuits came while I was waiting outside the shop. Biscuits are practically unobtainable at times…

Monday, 16th Dec. …When we were talking in the hut, R asked me if I would come with them if they gave up this place and went into a cottage and I said I would. He wants me as a companion to him and M…

Tuesday, 24th Dec. …The librarian said to somebody who was in there that she had not heard anybody say *A happy Xmas* and, but for her two small children, would not celebrate it…

Tuesday, 31st Dec. …G told us she had got to move from Mrs B's. Mrs B. spent Christmas at Plymouth at her sister's house. In a raid last Saturday half the house was blown down. They all came out safe from an underground cellar. One old lady had been too stout to get down there & they had pushed her into a cupboard under the stairs with a candle. When they let her out, she was safe & the candle still alight. Mrs B. said the worst part was when they came out of cellar into the open air & the shrapnel was falling around them. They buried their faces in shrubs but she said they would have got the shrapnel in their behinds if they had stayed long. Her sister called out *Won't anyone take us into their shelter*? & a boy came up & helped them into a neighbour's! There were no wardens about. The bombs were dropped in rows; they heard one very near & then their own house was hit. The house was set on fire, what was left of it. Mrs B.'s sister has lost her house, which was her means of livelihood by summer letting, & all her possessions. Her niece married in October, has lost her trousseau & Mrs B. has lost all her nice clothes which she took for Christmas. She is having her sister & her daughter into her house & G has got to move, through no fault of her own. G does not want to go into S. House where the life is communal.'

***300** Russian poster depicting Hitler as part-wolf having his back broken by the United States, Great Britain and the Soviet Union, 1940s.*

1941

In 1941 Mrs Barrett's health deteriorated and Mrs Friend moved into the bungalow to help care for her. Much of her life continued as before including tending to the vegetable plots, volunteering at the library and collecting two pence from visitors wanting access to the cove. Her sister Grace found lodgings in Dartmouth. Mrs Friend attended the meetings of the Dartmouth Group of Anglo-Soviet Public Relations Association (later the Dartmouth Anglo-Russian Society) which were held at the headmaster's room in the naval college. On 23 June Mrs Friend wrote with some excitement:

> 'On Sunday morning news that Germany had marched on Russia was taken up to the camp by R who was wildly delighted. In the evening Churchill's speech was listened to by all after the concert. Two girls who are Communists tittered at his high-flown speeches about humanity & another woman too took his words derisively – as if this government cares anything about humanity!').

War news regularly featured including oddments ('February 26th Walked to village to post letters in morning. Soldiers were shooting on opposite cliff & shouted at me when I wanted to take the camp path, so I went up the steps instead.'), the landing of Rudolph Hess ('it seems to be a matter of class, the well-to-do have a fellow feeling for him') and on one occasion ('shocking raid on Plymouth Tuesday kept us awake for hours').

A range of visitors came to the camp including Jack H. ('whose work is at a first aid post in West Ham'), Bill P. ('civil servant, his work to do with engineering examining interchangeable parts for airplanes'), a young Norwegian ('secretary to the Norwegian Ministry of Finance'), Mr W. ('friend of Mr R.'s who came down Friday for a short holiday. He lives at Teignmouth where raids have been bad. Three people killed next house to his & a hospital opposite bombed. He is suffering from shock & needs rest.'), two women with the London Auxiliary Fire Service and two actors from the Unity Theatre in London.

1942

In 1942 Mrs Friend wrote nine unusual passages.

'Sunday, 5th April, at 8 R banged on door and said *Christ is Risen*. I said *I hadn't yet*.'

'28 May, L. had painted a round metal buoy salvaged from beach with Hitler's face, done in tar on a background of cream paint & we fixed it up as a target on a tree branch & R & L & M had a few shots at it with an airgun.'

'29 May, collected another buoy given us for a Mussolini target. L at once gave it a coat of mixed cream and green paint. He wants it to have a sickly hue.'

'3rd June, earned the nickname of One Dart Dinah through my prowess with a single dart'.

'7 June, at camp concert J gave an account of fighting in Spain. He was a member of International Brigade there.'

'24 August, two planes came in from sea & two bombs were dropped near, at Tor Cross as we afterwards found out'.

'6 September, went with R on his *dawn patrol* as coastguard. Miss RD came too. Started out at 7. Went to various points from here to Blackpool Sands where coast visible, to see all clear of enemy craft, etc. Most points on cliffs we approached through people's gardens... to Captain W's house for particulars for article R writing up about their tame hen blackbird. Saw this bird, it comes on to the finger of Miss N., Captain W's niece. The Captain showed R and the rest of over his house. We saw 10 Rhode Island chicks, with their mother, in his yard. They call them *the boys*.'

'17 Dec., at 12.05 noon, three bombs dropped on Stoke Fleming, hardly a window left intact, slates off a lot of roofs. Parish hall, scene of last night's concert, desolate with all windows out, doors off, roof damaged, library ditto. R came in at 12.45, had taken shelter just out of village and turned back to give aid. He went on duty and I took his dinner to hut, then went to village & called on the Gs, helped make up bed in another room for old couple, their own room open to sky, only wisps of thatching across. Got back 4.45, had tea and read till R returned 9.30. He said the Gs were nearly straight, MO District Organiser for WWU, who had come for an evening meeting, having spent the time putting doors on. One person slightly injured by raid.'

***301** The inspiration for Rockvale's two painted buoys: Benito Mussolini and Adolf Hitler photographed in Munich, 1940.*

'18 December, 2 to 6.30 in village helping R put up doors for people. We put up 5 doors, finishing with Capt. W's house where they gave us some tea. Brought back some grocery and tools on barrow.'

1943

Mrs Friend's entries for 1943 mostly consisted of notes of her everyday life; she worked part time at the library, looked after the small holding and in the summer collected money from swimmers. Her leisure time was spent playing chess and Mahjong in the evenings and swimming during the summer.

Some entries related to wartime event such as that of

25 January ('20 enemy planes came over village at 4pm, dropped bombs somewhere within 5 miles of it'), 27 January ('R said yesterday's raid was 15 miles off. The 20 planes we saw were English but they coincided with the sound of bombing.'), 13 February ('At about 12 loud bangs nearby. R went to village to see if bombs landed there. Was told Dartmouth hit.'), 18 February ('Went with R to take sack of books to soldiers operating a gun on cliff near. Had left some books and were standing talking to soldiers when a bomb dropped

302 Local girl by a sign announcing the evacuation of local residents in the area around Slapton, 29 December 1943. Mrs Friend must have been aware of the movement of local people and the military exercises but refrained from recording any mention in her diaries.

303 Village scene prior to the evacuation, 29 December 1943

304 The evacuation of local residents just a few miles from where Mrs Friend was living, 22 April 1944.

somewhere, there was a cry of *Action* and soldiers go to guns and fired. It was a bad spot to be, the noise was terrible, we dropped flat on ground near. Raid said to be at Kingswear, in our village, nobody knows for certain.') and 31 August ('Went to beach with R to get hold of sailor reported to be down there, bathing nude, found he had gone, broken through hedge into meadow.').

1944

In 1944 Mrs Friend would have been aware of the large number of Americans stationed in and around Dartmouth in the months preceding D-Day but her references to them are disappointingly scarce:

'R was sent home early from Auxiliary Coastguard Drill and brought the news of the start of Second Front. It turned my stomach over to hear it and I told him so. About 10.30 last night I heard rumbles and concussion at sea and wondered if it were the Second Front. Both M and R had heard it, they said this morning and had thought the same. R & I listened to 12 mid-day announcement about it and she said it was a relief to her to know the Second Front had started. R said that his friend Mr H. had said the same thing this morning. Capt. W., who came to tea, said he knew the invasion had started because of the continuous firing for 3 hours in the morning. A soldier from an evacuated area near had no idea the invasion had started, in the afternoon, as there was no wireless in his camp. The Post Office girl was jubilant about it.'

1945

Mrs Friend's references to the end of the war in 1945 were minimal. Her answers on MO questionnaires provide incidental insights into her life and character such as those on clothing in 1942:

'I wear a woollen vest 2 or 3 weeks, for instance, as they don't get very dirty. I leave off my silk knickers in the summer, wearing a long silk vest under a cotton frock, or I have done without even that. It saves wear and tear on clothes and I am always in and out of a bathing costume in the afternoons. I could not wear so little in more *civilised* conditions.'

That year she explained her everyday fears in five categories:

'Being left entirely alone. I must have a communal life to fit into. No good as an individual. No initiative. Need protective influence.

Being killed, or worse still maimed, in an air raid.

Being a slave as a result of Germany winning or being shot off. I don't often fear this as I don't think Germany will win.

Being stuck into a factory with a routine job and a lot of noise.

Town life, which I hate.'

Her first reason is significant. Perhaps her most revealing passage was one that year in which she explained what home meant to her:

'A place where I relax. Where I can carry on my interests, and keep my few belongings. Where there are other people to talk to and have meals with and play games with. I am at home at my present residence, where I have a room to myself and a communal life at meals and during evenings'.

Mrs Friend continued to write for MO until January 1950. She was presumably living at Rockvale Cove when Rowland Barrett died on 26 September that year. His obituarist described him as 'one of the pioneers of the Labour movement'. His ashes were scattered amongst the pine trees at the cove. Mrs Friend died twenty-seven years later.[308]

***305** American infantrymen disembarking at Slapton, in preparation for the invasion of France, 1944.*

306 *Aerial view of practice landings at Slapton Sands, 17 March 1944.*

307 *Rehearsal operation at the north end of Slapton Sands, 1944.*

308 *Watercolour by Dwight C. Shepler, 1944, of the American exercise at Slapton.*

309 *Medical attention during the Slapton exercise, 1944.*

310 *Amphibious landing operations at Slapton, 1944, with Rockvale Cove a few miles up the coast.*

311 A view of pre-war Fore Street in Tiverton.

TIVERTON

Tiverton was one of Devon's leading manufacturing centres of woollen cloth despite being destroyed by a series of fires from 1598 into the early 1700s. The collapse of cloth-making in about 1800 was quickly followed by the arrival in 1816 of John Heathcoat and his lace factory. The town has since been dominated by it. In 1939 Tiverton had 10,641 residents and experienced an influx of 771 people that year, an increase of 7.8% in the population. The rural district had grown by 5.9% in that first year.[309]

By the autumn of 1940 some 800 mothers and children were billeted in Tiverton. During the war a camp was built for prisoners-of-war. It is now the site of Petroc College. Devonport Girls' High School, Plympton Grammar School and Pembroke House Prep School relocated to Tiverton during the war while Collipriest acted as the headquarters of the American 4th Infantry Division's signals and cavalry reconnaissance troops.[310] An air raid took place on 31 July 1940. About this time five people in Tiverton were reported to be wounded by bombs: sixty-year-old Thomas Hill and sixty-five-year-old Agnes Hill of Belmont Dairy and seventy-one-year-old Elizabeth Tucker Denner, fifty-one-year-old Clarice Pretoria Padden Skinner and fifty-two-year-old William Henry Willis, each at the Public Assistance Institution, were reported as being 'lightly' injured.[311]

There was a second MO Writer in Tiverton: Diarist Alice Mercer was unmarried and lived at 4 Highland Terrace. Only her responses to a questionnaire of May 1942 survives. She then wrote of her taste in literature and thoughts on death including of her own ('Think about it very little. The war has made a little difference to this. Not especially afraid of it but have never faced it.'), her fiancé ('I am conscious of pushing away the thought of death for my fiancé. Consequently, I rarely consciously consider it but it is probably often in my unconscious thoughts. This is only since the war.'), her parents ('Have lately come to realise that someday parents die, even my own. No connection with the war.') and friends ('a schoolgirl whom I taught died recently. This is the first person I have really known well who has died and I was much affected. Main feeling: that anyone with such a good life obviously before her should miss it is very sad.').[312]

60. Anonymous, Serviceman, 1942

On 14 March 1942 an anonymous serviceman writing from Hayne Court in Bolham outside Tiverton submitted a report on the popularity of radio programmes amongst the army. The most popular was BBC Dancing Club followed by Hi Gang, Old Town Hall, Yours Vera Lynn and ITMA:

> 'Reliable reports of the British Army's reaction to radio programmes any use to you? It's an eye-opener that all troops listen to without dissent is BBC Dancing Club. Then of course comes the various variety features and near the top is Vera Lynn. Know her? Treacly-voiced female who sobs nostalgic matter in the microphone until the [for]lorn troops literally weep with frustrated longing and the barrack blankets get stiff with starchy products. This is no exaggeration of her effect. I loathe her, and it is significant that all the anti-Vera reports come from *responsible* groups – professional NCOs, groups of soldierly spirit, pre-war volunteer ATS and the like. It seems that the ordinary-run ATS dote on Vera too, though I've never been able to observe their bedroom habits.
>
> I want to get her stopped. I expect you know that the only *crime* so extensive as to impair seriously our military efficiency is that of chaps *chucking absent* in order to go home to the wife or girlfriend. Most of our chaps are civilians in all but the uniform; their only fixed idea is how to get out of the army, their gnawing worry is that some damned wealthy war-worker is prodding their fancy-piece. These sentimental broadcasts were put on for the French troops too and had great effect. Then when the invasion came, a large number of units were rendered ineffective because so many sentiment-saturated soldiers *chucked absent* in order to go to their women-folk in the threatened districts, or in the opposite direction to *protect* their loved ones. Others had their women close by and dodged the column in order to stay with them. And the general feeling, among the troops, radio-nurtured, condoned all these things.'

Hayne may have been used to house convalescing servicemen: in 1939 the national register recorded Michael Snowdon, an incapacitated military man.[313]

61. John Duffin, Student, 1942-3

In 1942 nineteen-year-old Dewsbury-born John Michael Duffin (1923-2000) lived with his parents at The Haven in Barrington Street. He was a former pupil at Blundell's School and Balliol College, Oxford. His father, Joseph, was headmaster of a local secondary school. Mr Duffin responded to two directives in 1942 and 1943.[314] He explained his view of corporal punishment:

> 'Physical punishment for children should be as infrequent as possible. I know that a *heavy hand* will usually quieten a child, but too much of it may lead later to unpleasant results. In schools I think only headmasters should have the right of caning; the system in public schools for monitors to cane smaller boys is damaging and degrading both to themselves and their victims. I think physical punishment for adult men should only be for serious sex offences.'

10 February 1943

A month later he recorded his movements with the caveat that 'This cannot be taken as a normal wartime day: I am waiting for call-up and have no regular job except that of a temporary unpaid assistant at the local library':

> '8.15 Got up. Shaved, dressed, had breakfast and read the *Daily Telegraph* thoroughly.
>
> 9.40 Fetched some potatoes for the dinner.
>
> 10.00 – 12.20 Worked at the library.
>
> 12.25 Laid the table, did odd jobs.
>
> 12.40 Lunch.
>
> 1.05 Went down to the Great Western Railway station (Tiverton).
>
> 1.13 – 1.50 Travelled to Exeter.
>
> 1.50 – 2.30 Went up to the city, caught a bus out to the Devon County Library.
>
> 2.30 – 2.50 Searched in vain for two books, but managed to get a third I wanted to read.
>
> 2.50 – 3.35 Caught a bus back to the city, rooted around in the SPCK bookshop and in Wheaton's bookshop. Bought *Screwtape Letters* and *Christianity, Politics and Power*?

3.35 – 3.40 Caught a bus to station and waited in train.

4.45 Arrived back in Tiverton.

4.45 - 5.25 Dried wet clothes, did odd jobs, rested in front of fire.

5.30 – 6.00 Had tea and helped to dry dishes, etc.

6.00 – 6.40 Did the Blackout in all the house.

6.40 – 9.45 Read book and listened in to wireless for Tchaikovsky's violin concerto.

9.45 – 10.25 Talked and had a little supper.

10.45 Bed.'

Mr Duffin also recorded how attitudes had changed regarding money, clothes, security, class, sex, politics and conscientious objectors:

> 'I have, I confess, always taken money for granted. Now, after an expensive year at a university, I begin to see how valuable a thing it is, how hard to earn, how easy to spend.
>
> Till a short while ago I took a little notice of clothes. Now I find that dress is important and that clothes give a rough indicator of social class, perhaps even of character at times.
>
> I was brought up in a secure atmosphere, with little to fear. War did not affect this very much, as we live in a small country town. When I consider what the post-war situation will be like, I hope for, and shall work for, as great a degree of security as possible.
>
> Intellectually, I have been influenced by Marxism; having therefore theoretical hatred of the rich and respect for the poor. My views have changed through experience. I admire many working men, but many wish to see a higher standard of living coupled with equality of opportunity. Brought up in a middle-class household myself, I always distrust the rich, especially the remnants of the old aristocracy and am wishing to see them taxed out of existence.
>
> I had very little to do with girls when I was at school but now I am increasingly attracted by them.
>
> In late 1939 I wanted some sort of *aristocracy of intellect*. In mid 1940 I was strongly Marxist which gradually faded from red to a mild pink. Recently I've become most antagonistic to Marxism but nowhere near so hostile to communism as a programme of political action. In April 1942 I studied the Labour party's programme with which I now find myself in general agreement.
>
> When war began. I absorbed current cliches and thought we should carry on the war to its finish with the invasion of Norway, Holland, Belgium, France. My attitude became strongly pacifist. I thought I should become a conscientious objector to myself when the time came, in contrast to my father and my school teachers except one and everyone else who were strongly in favour of resistance. Then I came to realise that my attitude was based on selfish grounds and gradually I came round to support the war.
>
> I am now quite prepared to go on military service (and am as a material fact awaiting my papers daily). But my attitude towards objectors is this: some object on sincere, idealistic grounds, some because they have a love of quiet and comfort. The first I admire. The second I do not. But the laws with regard to objection are very considerate. One of the things by which British democracy is distinguished from dictatorship and one of the things we fight to preserve.'

Mr Duffin married in 1952 and died in 2000.[315]

TORQUAY

This seaside resort had grown in the late eighteenth century to become Devon' largest seaside resort by the late 1800s. It was known not only for its picturesque coastline but for its impressive villas set amongst the 'seven hills'. In 1939 there were 52,227 residents. The town experienced an increase that year of 7,787 people, a 17.5% growth in population in one year. Included in that number were probably pupils from six London schools which relocated to the resort.[316]

Various MO Writers mentioned Torquay such as one in 1939 (a London woman of 27) 'was evacuated with her firm to Torquay and wrote to a friend today *We don't mix very well with the natives. They're a queer lot and open their mouths at us. The digs are alright. Not much food but I'm not a big eater. Poor Podgy! She goes about with her tongue hanging out, she gets so hungry*', another in 1942 ('one of my aunts writes that some of the canteens in Torquay had to be closed because the RAF were getting physically unfit through over and unwise eating'.), and one in 1944 from Sussex ('one of our girls is going with a sister who is taking her baby to a cousin at Torquay. The tale is that this holiday was partly fixed up before the doodle-bugs began. Then, when the government scheme appeared, Mrs X pushed the baby to the doctor and said he screamed for every doodle - to the neighbours' surprise - so now she will go at the government expense').

One Writer referred to a German radio programme featuring William Joyce and Torquay ('instead of dialogues between Smith and Schmidt you have previously heard, through the good offices of Lord Haw Haw, a dialogue between Smith and his wife in a hotel at Torquay and what a dialogue! *Oh, I say, old thing* Smith explained to his wife and there are frequent *Dammits* and *old Joseph Murgatroyd at FO*; and it was all so perfectly Whitehall-old-school-tie that it might almost have been in a sketch at Unity Theatre').[317]

In March 1940 one of Mass Observation's Writers outside Devon heard from friends 'they want to come back, are tired of Torquay and do not think it will be dangerous to return, *We have been gone six months and no raids*!'[318] Later that year a London evacuee commented that in Torquay 'they get odd bombs off and on, and the sirens usually go off afterwards, but compared to London it's very quiet'.[319] Two years later another in Bedford heard from her brother in the RAF in Torquay that 'they had a five-minute blitz at Torquay and one plane came down on the beach and burnt itself out.'[320] In 1944 a London teenager returned home after having been evacuated to Torquay since the summer of 1939. An MO Writer noted 'three weeks ago came home having left school. He started to work at Erith Oil Works and after being there for ten days was involved in the rocket incident there last week and has had both legs amputated. This is a dreadful affair and proves really that no amount of dodging bombs is really fool-proof.'[321]

312 Photograph entitled 'Office Girls Leave London: two of 800 girls employed by a London insurance society leaving for Torquay whence the staff was transferred when the war situation became ominous', 20 September 1939.

Torquay had as many as nineteen German air attacks which caused, according to reports made at the time the deaths of 173 men, women and children. The most harrowing attack was that of 30 May 1943 when 21 children died in the Anglican church at St Marychurch which had a direct hit. The following day an MO diarist living in Bristol commented 'Talk is spreading about the size of German bombs. Apparently, a complete church was blown up by one bomb at Torquay yesterday'.[322] The last air raid took place on 29 May 1944.

313 Pre-war Babbacombe.

There were also deaths from 'friendly fire'. British landmines accidently exploded at Anstey's Cove on 8 October 1940 and 3 July 1944. Three people died. There was another death on 17 February 1942 when a cannon shell exploded in a private house.[323]

The German attacks were not intended merely to intimidate residents; there were a number of targets in Torquay including American servicemen. An MO Writer in Bristol reported in January 1944 that 'a middle-aged wife of a schoolmaster told me that the US troops were quite well-behaved in the Torquay district.'[324]

The Ministry of Information reported public feeling including in July 1940 ('Torquay complains that some people appear to be taking no part in war effort and ask for compulsory service. Also complaints of the inefficiency of the warning system.'), in November 1942 criticisms were made that there were too many women in 'funk-holes like Torquay and Harrogate who are still having a good time', local concerns regarding inadequate defences were repeated in June 1943 and indignation was expressed over press coverage highlighting the number of tourists in August 1943.[325]

In the spring of 1941 a national newspaper labelled Torquay a 'funk hole', a place to bolt to for safety, following remarks made by a local councillor ('many evacuee adults are standing at street corners and staying in hotels doing nothing for the town they are using as a funk-hole').[326] By the autumn it was reported from Torquay that there was a national campaign against the town only because 'a few dear old ladies were to be seen in fur coats on the front'. John Daw, the chairman of Devon County Council added to the controversy by claiming Torquay's 'wandering Jews' were not sufficiently patriotic. This racial association was picked upon by Writers, including No. **64**. In 1941 another in Kent commented:

> 'Professional woman, 45, said how she was sickened during a convalescence at Torquay. She said it was full of Jews, thriving, money about and Jewesses in the most brief bathing dresses, sunbathing, & drinking cocktails, & fat mammas in satin looking like fat seals with their undulating behinds. Mentioned it to other people who all said they had heard how Jews had migrated to Torquay and EVERYONE said in a matter-of-fact voice *Wish a few bombs would fall at Torquay*'. The following year another MO Writer, in Kent, heard a man comment on Torquay having been bombed 'Serve all the Jew-Boys right, trying to run away, its full of Jews'.[327]

62. Boris Ford, Student, 1937

In 1937 India-born Richard Boris Ford (1917-1998) was a twenty-year-old Cambridge undergraduate student when he recorded his life over two days in July and September. He was temporarily living in St Marychurch. These were Mr Ford's only contributions to MO.[328]

Mr Ford provided useful background details relative to his routine ('During the day, as for the whole of this month, I was doing academic work, by which I mean that I read novels – my subject being English literature – and play the piano – which I learn. Thus the day was quite normal, considered as one of those which fall into the two months or so in the year when I work in the vacation.') and answered a question about his health ('no better or worse than usual. By which is meant that one does not tend to take much account of one's health unless it is either damned bad or damned good. That I was suffering from a cold does not alter my verdict, as I nearly always have a cold, and this has long ceased to be considered as part of my health. The weather was cloudy throughout the day and very close. In the morning it drizzled in a bored way, giving this up after lunch. For an hour or so around about 5 o'clock the sun appeared. I had, as far as I can remember, no striking dreams. I have an idea that I had a dream which was an emasculated version of the one I dreamt the previous night, but since I have forgotten the dream I dreamt then, it is not much help.').

He also explained his personal circumstances at Summerlands in Trumlands Road:[329]

> 'I am for the present living in a semi-detached house in St Marychurch. The house I know to be semi-detached; a stray visitor would not, as the entrance is through what is really the side of the whole building. Thus the side of the whole is the front of our house, and it would not occur to anyone that there might be another house running out at the back of ours. The neighbourhood is *good*; the inhabitants go to church and the trades-people are *very decent people*. St Marychurch is a suburb of Torquay, the suburb in which the aged come to die and don't. The houses are large and uninteresting, and in this area of a uniform pattern with their owners. No-one does anything very much; some, it seems play golf, the remainder bridge. And, during such of the day as remains, they gather together in committees, tending the Poor and Needy, or praying for the Heathen. And they show their true Christian contempt for Things of the Flesh by a seemly parsimony.
>
> Excluding a few small-shop-assistants, it is hard to find anyone in this suburb under the age of 45. A few there are, one or two maids, some babies opposite, and indeed three youths and five girls. But these latter give the impression not so much of being young as of being in vigorous training for old age. To them this is no tragedy, for they know not themselves nor their neighbours, and consequently live in a state of blissful ignorance.
>
> Over this flock of sheep moves the eye of a celibate vicar. Everything about him, from his reproductive organs (with which the Lord was tactless enough to provide him) to his domestic staff is rigidly male. It even seems probable that he eats no meat without having determined the sex of the animal from which it is carved. He preaches, as a result, a sermon of over-powering stupidity, often weeping and always moaning. Nervousness has resulted in him always ending <u>every</u> remark with *ye know*, the first word said very short. His latest remark to me was *Oh, how-d'you-do, ye know*. He is often in the thoughts, if seldom in the company, of his parishioners. Which is indeed better than the converse.
>
> In conclusion, one has only to add that the air is excellent and that there is no public clock, library or convenience in St Marychurch for its full charm to be apparent to all.'

Mr Ford provided an outline of his life on 14 July but preceded it with a note that 'I should say that, apart from one servant, the only other occupant of the house besides myself is an elderly spinster aunt, recently retired from being a housemistress at Roedean.' His aunt Mary Marjorie Ford (1877-1948) would become a Senior Warden for the ARP in 1939.[330]

14 July 1937

> '8.10 Got up. Went down to see if there were any letters for me. There were none, which was singularly annoying as I had counted on three, all from females. I went back upstairs, and had a bath. My enlightened plan – this plan is reformulated every morning – that I would have a bath of sufficient brevity to enable me also to shave before breakfast was, as usual, not carried into effect. I arrived down five minutes late.
>
> 9.05 Ate breakfast. The conversation was as meagre as I could make it, it still being too early for any kind

of briskness. Such conversation as took place was on the weather, on the permanence of my cold and the remedies that had failed to remove it, and on the complications involved in removing my 14-year-old sister [Mary Irina] from Roedean at the end of her school term – whether she should be fetched by car or should travel by train. It was decided that as the tutorial staff at Roedean do not permit girls over 14 to say to the booking office clerk that they are under 14, that she would have to be fetched by car.

9.30 Breakfast ended, and cleared away by ourselves in order to preserve the energies of the one domestic. I read the *Times*. I do not do the crossword.

10.10 Retired to the lavatory-bathroom to shave, etc. etc.

10.35 Played the piano, Bach's Preludes and Fuges.

11.15 Turned on the wireless, in order to hear a gramophone recital of Bach's Three-Piano Concerto in C played by a posse of French ladies, Handel's *Queen of Sheba* overture, and Beethoven's Eighth Symphony. But was greeted only by those damned bells they play for want of anything better to do. At last, seven minutes late, the recital began. The Bach was indifferently played – and the announcer was patently new to the job of putting on records; the break in between was deplorable and he must have lost the next record each time or been smitten with the vapours it was so bad. Lack of time forced him to omit the Handel, which was a pity, as it is a singularly fine recording, by Tommy Beecham. The Beethoven is a very good Symphony, coming with the Fourth after the Sixth. (How many people, out of a hundred or even a thousand, like the even numbers best? Perhaps two!) But the wretch turned the thing off before the end, as there was no more time. Which quite spoilt the whole Symphony. During the last movement, which I know well, I spent the time evolving for it the choreography for a ballet. It really would do excellently.

12. Finished Peacock's *Nightmare Abbey*. My aunt entered at one point, and, having said I really ought to be working, remarked that I must read Mariah Edgeworth, whom she claims to be far-and-away the most famous of the early nineteenth century writers. I did not reply.

1. Dinner not being ready, I played some Bach.

1.10 Ate lunch, as the meal turned out to be. Talked first about the Chinese situation, but, as both of us knew no more about it than we had read in the *Times*, we soon left this topic. Went on to discuss who my aunt should invite to her next Bridge party, and whether she could fit in three tables. And we ended by agreeing that the BBC is going to seed, and that the various and multifarious shortcomings of that Institution need public advertisement. But neither of us offered to write to the *Times* about it.

1.30 Played a Mozart Sonata on the piano.

1.45 Read George Eliot's *Adam Bede*.

4.30 [sic] Went into the village to buy a *News Chronicle*, as the *Times* had not told me sufficient about the Labour Spain demonstration in Trafalgar Square. The *News Chronicle* did not tell me any more. Also waited while some stitches were sewn into my sandals.

4.30 Ate tea alone, my aunt having gone out to a tea for the Friends of Melanesia.

5.5 Played some more Mozart.

5.35 Wrote a letter to my sister, in answer to one of hers.

6.10 Read *Adam Bede*.

7.35 Ate dinner. Conversation started on the remarkable dullness of the Friends of Melanesia; and went on to a comparison of the Staffs at boys' and girls' schools, in particular the great differences in the number of teaching staff at each.

8.10 Listened in to some twaddling play by [Noel] Coward with Marie Tempest.[331]

8.15 Drove my aunt to a Bridge party, to which I had been invited, but from which my cold had saved me.

8.40 Read *Adam Bede*.

9. Listened to the News.

9.20 Read *Adam Bede*.

9.40 Listened to a concert, of Correlli, and Gordon Jacob. How remarkably strong, for a second-rate composer, is the influence of Delius today?

10.40 Read till about 11 o'clock and then went to bed.'

Mr Ford revealed he had no religious beliefs but had joined a political party:

'I don't suppose I can possibly give any meaning of freedom in the space at my disposal, any meaning that would be worth giving. Suffice it to say that I am a Communist, and that Marx, Engels, Lenin and Stalin seem to me to have said a great deal to which I am in agreement. But to this I would add that everything in the Soviet garden does not seem to me

***314** A poster issued by the Army Bureau of Current Affairs of which Mr Ford would later become part.*

What are YOU
doing about
EDUCATION?

to be blooming. And – need I say? – I am not thinking of the Trials, which give me no qualms; but rather of the cultural situation, and the dictatorship of taste and feeling. If you want a one-sentence definition, I would say that freedom for me means the right and opportunity for a person with a social conscience to be happy in the way which seems to him or her most satisfying. And the *with the social conscience* clause seems to me of great importance.'

Mr Ford was born in Bombay (Mumbai) and described his father Geoffrey (1883-1964) as 'a Brigadier (General) in the Indian Army; but, in spite of this, is most enlightened; Cole-lite politically' and summarised both parents in some detail:

> 'Towards my parents my feelings are not very strong, having lived apart from them a great deal; they in India, I in England. But I get on very well with my father, easily and without forcing the relationship. With my [Russian-born] mother [Ekaterina Gorkhover] I have never got on very well; we have almost no interests in common at all, and are temperamentally not suited. Of late, however, the energy demanded in fighting has been too great, and easier terms have resulted. I have not had a home in the usual sense of the word. In India we travelled about a great deal, and in England I have stayed in many homes, mainly those of close relations. I thus have no feelings for any home or home-life.'

13 September 1937

A month later Mr Ford once again recorded the day's events. He preceded it with a note that:

> 'It was a typical Sunday, by which I mean that the customary visit to church in the morning was postponed till the evening, as the weather suggested that tennis might prove a more congenial occupation than devotion, and that the evening visit was then conveniently forgotten. During the summer this arrangement is quite normal. A very little experience has shown that it is much easier to promise to do something and then to *forget* it than to refuse to do it at once. With us, there is actually no compulsion to go to church; it is merely felt that my aunt, a devout Christian, likes us to go; and as the house in which we are staying belongs to this lady, that may be a good reason for doing so. On the other hand, it is one more good reason for not having anything to do with relations.'

His itinerary was:

'8.30 Rose, dressed slowly and washed – but did not shave. We eat breakfast at the same time on Sundays as on weekdays, not because any of us much want to, but because the aunt goes to an early service which ends at about 8.50, and does not therefore feel any need for breakfast at any but the ordinary hour of nine.

9.00 Breakfast. Sunday breakfast is a weary meal, there being no mail and no newspaper. It thus has an air of pointlessness about it, and one is forced to make conversation, which is very trying so soon in the day. On this Sunday, however, matters were somewhat less dismal by the welcome return to porridge; during the summer we eat those Post Toasties things.[332]

9.30 Retired from the dining room to an empty drawing room, and played the piano. Was twice interrupted, which always greatly annoys me. (Why do people never seem to mind interrupting a person playing the piano, but never dream of intervening in the middle of a game of tennis? Yet the latter is much more easily interrupted, and need not cause much inconvenience.) The first interruption was caused by my father, who suggested we should postpone our visit to church and play tennis instead. The second was caused by the aunt, who decided she had some letters to type. As a typewriter is not the most pleasing accompaniment to Mozart, I left her to it.

10.35 Started shaving.

11.00 Changed for tennis.

11.10 Went to play tennis. It proved not to be the tennis it might have been, and, on the whole, we did little but pick the balls out of the bottom of the net. Still, even this, spread over an hour, can be quite a manly-enough exercise.

12.30 Returned for lunch. On Sunday lunch is taken a quarter of an hour earlier than on weekdays, so that the elderly domestic may catch her bus, Sunday being her half-day out.

12.45 Lunch. Conversation was abundant, but of no lasting significance, being mainly concerned with the faults of deportment and manners discernible in my sister, aged 14. As she was present at this castigation, and is an indefatigable wager of verbal guerrilla warfare, this meal proved somewhat difficile and disturbing for the digestive tracts. It was eventually decided to go up onto the Moors for a picnic.

1.30 Sought recuperation in more playing of the piano.

2.5 Left in the car for the Moors.

3.10 Reached the place at which we intended to picnic. But it had now unfortunately become rather cold, and so, while the others went for a walk – I don't think they wanted to, but felt that there is some fundamental law which demands that one shall not visit the Moors without walking over them, a law which no man shall question (this walking fetish would bear study) I sat in the car and read *Money* by Emile Burns.

3.40 Others returned, looking very cold and miserable. As it was by this time raining slightly, it was decided to drive on.

4.20 Stopped under some trees for tea, which proved to be a wet and soggy meal. Devonshire cream is nice enough, but is not an adequate or even suitable antidote to rain.

4.40 Returned home.

5.45 Reached home. Listened to the wireless, to a talk on the cinema (I often wonder what is considered to be the necessary education or qualification for the aspiring film critic; perhaps that he should have once been an unsuccessful book-reviewer. At any rate, this one said nothing of any subtlety, but merely outlines the plots of half-a-dozen films he had just seen, occasionally giving us the benefit of his technical erudition, by calling, for instance, a *short* a *short*, or by referring to *O'Flaherty's superb camera sense*, etc.) and later to Solomon, who played the Waldstein and a hocus on Chopin. It is remarkable how few of the pianists can resist the temptation to indulge themselves with Chopin. I do not think it is any coincidence that all but a few of the greatest pianists are also unmarried. Chopin's appeal is largely erotic, though, if such a thing is possible, his is rather a Platonic eroticism.

6.45 Read *Money*. (by now church is successfully missed)

7.00 Supper. Roused by *Money*, discussed American crash of 1929 and its causes.

7.35 Played the piano.

8.10 Enter family; stopped playing, and finished *Money*. Discussed Douglas Credit, a pet theory of the aunt, though she knows next to nothing about it. With no difficulty defeated her in straight sets, and proved, in the same mouthful, the inevitability of Marxism. A little jiggery-pokery with *booms* and *slumps* and *planned production* and this is very simple, too simple, even, for the suspiciously-minded.

8.50 Listened to the News.

9.5 Read Eliot's *Selected Essays*. I had not before realised how witty Eliot can be, for instance in *Thoughts after Lambeth* and in *Arnold and Pater*. And what a remarkably lucid and expressive prose style he has! This reading was much interrupted by discussions on the Far East, Italy, piracy.

10.50 Rest go to bed. Found a copy of Fallada's *Little Man – What Now?* in the room, and decided to read it, having heard it so much discussed.

11.45 Having read about half the novel – it is wonderful how quickly one can read a modern novel, a bit suspect too! - went to bed.

12.10 In bed. Finished *Little Man*, which I decided did not merit any closer reading. It is one of those well-intentioned novels – Storm Jameson and Compton Mackenzie also wrote *well-intentioned novels*– but with no evidence of an acute sensibility directing the issues. And novels which remember to get in their quota of *he felt her breast under the smooth silk* and *the wonderful curve of her thighs* are hardly original, in fact are merely flank-rubbing with the now Great Lawrence, and also making sure of their sales.

1.05 Go to sleep. An Ordinary Sunday, and a day hardly any different from any other.'

Two years later, while still an undergraduate, his essay on *Wuthering Heights* was published and Ford subsequently became Professor of Education at the Universities of Sheffield, Sussex and Bristol. An obituarist noted his 'ability to combine very many of those talents, interests and activities within the confines of his own and, it must be said, unique personality that marked him out as an exceptional and highly influential figure. He was a kind of walking, talking and teaching intellectual collective in his own right'.

315 Photograph of Canadian servicemen entitled 'Beside red Devon cliffs, with the luxury resort of Torquay in the background, these three British Columbian airmen at the RCAF Reparation Depot seem to think that an English cigarette is a poor substitute for a Canadian one', 26 August 1945.

Mr Ford's political interests continued during the war: he was a leading figure in the left-oriented Army Bureau of Current Affairs (ABCA) from 1941 to 1945 and was editor-in-chief of the Bureau of Current Affairs from 1946 to 1951. Fortnightly pamphlets focused upon 'attention on various problems without being dogmatic about their solutions'. In 1956 he was appointed 'TV's first head master' in delivering television's first lessons for British schools. Prof. Ford died on 19 May 1998.[333]

63. William Welsman, Typist, 1938

William Abraham Hyman Welsman (1917-1987) was a twenty-one-year-old shorthand typist living with his mother in London when he visited Torquay. He wrote for MO about the 'Czechoslovakia Crisis', the events of autumn 1938 during which Adolf Hitler annexed the Sudetenland, the region of Czechoslovakia which had a large German population. Mr Welsman's uncle persuaded his mother to drive her family to Devon to escape imminent war. They stayed in Daddyhole at the Dorchester Hotel (which was destroyed by fire in 2009). Mr Welsman cautioned that his quotations were not 'exactly verbatim but fairly accurate':

> 'The first morning I was at the Torquay hotel, the 29th of September 1938, a middle-aged lady asked my mother where she could get her gas-mask, as she had previously been fitted and had heard such awful stories

of how some gasses burn one alive that she was anxious to get it. I don't know how much help a gas mask would be to her in this respect, but she seemed to imagine it would give complete protection. Anyway, I was sent off to find out the answer to her query and ascertained that Torquay's supply had not been sent down from London up till then. For quite a while, I could not persuade her to believe it. As far as I can gather, she is an artist – a painter of miniatures...

My first impression on arriving at the Torquay Hotel was that almost complete disinterestedness reigned. In London, people spoke and thought of nothing but the next war. In Torquay, everyone felt fairly safe, one imagined, and the crisis was just very important news of no immediate personal significance. It seemed a different world altogether.

During a few brief minutes in the evening, I heard two or three old ladies and gentlemen asking each other casually when definite news could be expected. One man said he considered nothing much would be known for quite a day or two, and it seemed generally imagined that Mr Chamberlain's third German trip would be protracted.

When, late in the day on Friday the 30th of September, I managed to get free of family affairs and my own, and go to the Information Bureau for a few leaflets, I said to the man in charge that the war danger seemed to have passed. He concurred, adding *For a while at any rate.* I continued, *I don't think the Czechs were worth fighting for, were they? No*, he said, *it wasn't worth a great war just over that.* I mentioned that neither side would have won if we had fought it out; we should all have gone down together. He seemed to agree, but of course this may have been out of politeness, he was a very courteous public official. Of his own accord, he said *No, I don't think there will be war in my time now.* (I suppose he was 40 or 50 years old). *It was much better to settle things by agreement*, I went on. He answered with a most original remark (for a member of the British public) *Yes, and after all, the country (*Czechoslovakia*) didn't exist before the last war. No, you are right*, I answered, *The Czechs have been lucky to have had those German-peopled lands so long.* We closed the little conversation on this note – that the Czechs had no right to Sudetenland and that they ought not reasonably to expect to hold it...

A note about the road journey from London to Torquay on the 29th of September. We were on the Salisbury route – I believe not the chief one to Exeter – and the whole time (about 8 hours), we noticed probably no more than 20 or 30 cars with luggage going away from London. There were <u>certainly no signs</u> of <u>any great exodus</u> as <u>far as we could see</u> – just a mere trickle westwards...

4 October 1938, In the train today between Torquay and Churston, I had a brief conversation with a grizzled old builder, complete with bag of cement. He agreed with my statements, without comment, that we had had a very remarkable escape from war, that there was nothing really worth making a war about and that even if permanent peace had not been assured, the world was lucky for a few years' respite from one.

He made only two original remarks himself on the subject. Both were sudden and disconnected. The first was *I suppose they're filling in the trenches in the London parks now. Did they make some in Regent's Park?* He was interested to have the one or two particulars I could give him as he knew Central London a little. The second abrupt query, a few minutes later, was *Chamberlain's getting a good bit of criticism now, isn't he?*'

Mr Welsman pondered whether his acquaintance was merely repeating media reports and concluded it was impossible to know whether any shared comments were honest.[334]

64. Reginald Gorrill, Student, 1939

Reginald Gorrill (1921-1970) was an eighteen-year-old medical student who wrote one diary during the early days of the war.[335] He also answered questionnaires that year and these help to build a picture of him.

Directives: personal appearances, generational differences and dance halls

In April Mr Gorrill described his appearance:

'I like personally to be quietly dressed, grey being my usual colour, hands clean, nails short, black shoes and tidy hair. In others I like a little more colour, tidy hair, no showing very obvious signs of hair cream, decent shoes and well-kept hands.

I nearly always do my hair, my hair being very unruly. I

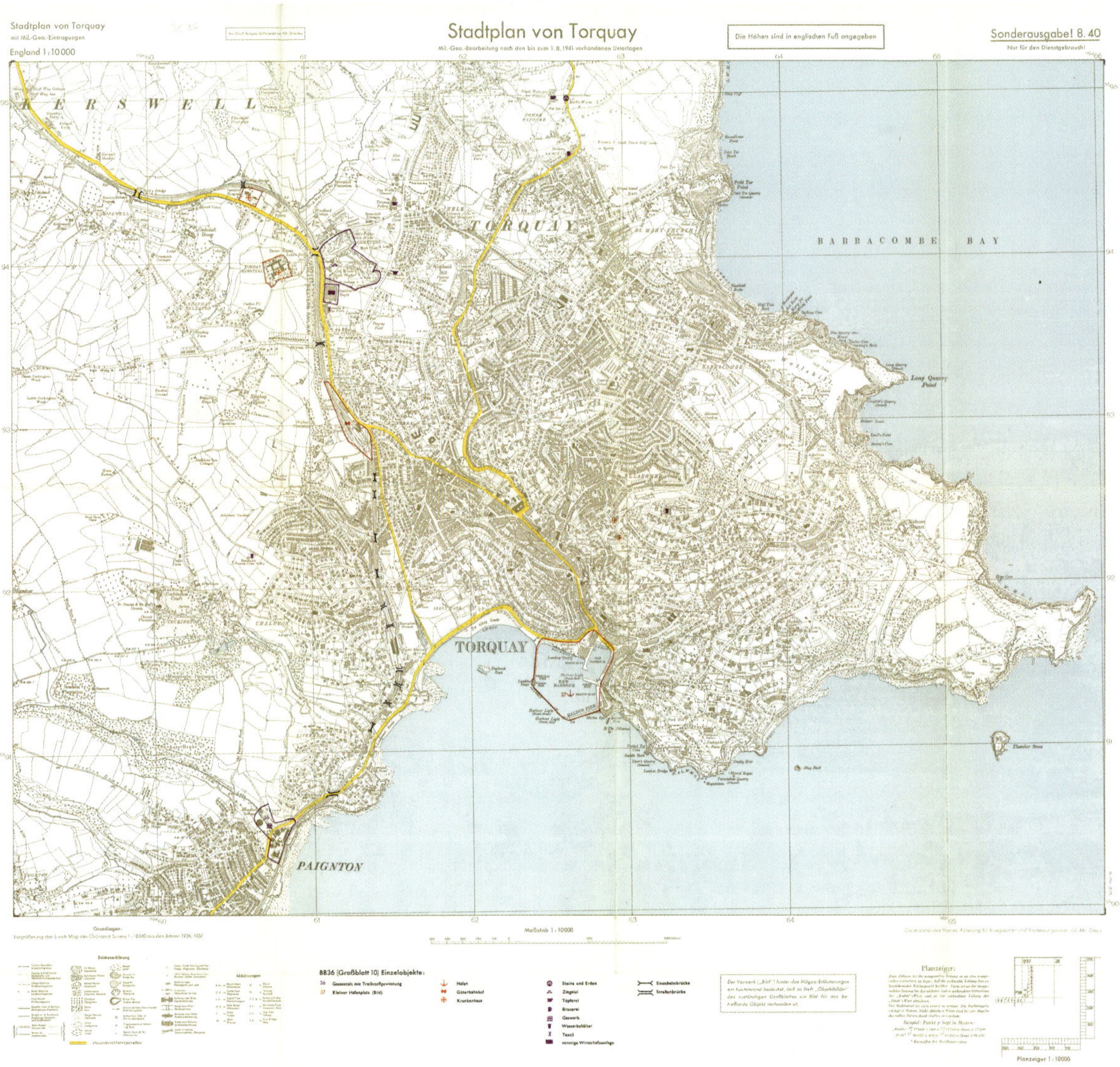

***316** Torquay's Stadtplan (street plan) provided in the German target dossier, August, 1940. Main roads are highlighted in yellow and strategic sites are in red.*

try to keep it just quiet and no more. I wash my hands carefully and keep my nails short and clean. I chiefly do these things because I like to look presentable. I keep my hands clean also because in chemistry if you don't, you aren't due in this world long.'

Mr Gorrill lived at 4 St Marychurch Road with his parents and recorded generational differences:

'They believe in washing before meals, cleaning one's teeth at least once a day, in the morning always. They believe in a bath once or twice a week, supplemented if need be, while I like one every day. My parents believe in plain food with very little variation. I like a plain breakfast and dinner but a varied light lunch and tea. On diet, my parents have a fixed belief in boiled vegetables which I refuse to share. On clothes, my parents like the old-fashioned vests while I like the newer lighter kind. Also, they have a different taste in cut and colour, liking navy, blue and brown while I stick to grey. Liking me to wear a raincoat, while I like a light summer coat. In shoes we like the same type but go to different shops. They use True Form while I like Russell & Bromleys.'

Other differences concerned leisure ('They really don't seem to have very interesting views of having a good time and they never seem to want to go out and get one. They have a great dislike of *horseplay*.') and himself ('Personally I like to walk or skate or do something to have a good time. I would rather go cliff-climbing with a friend than drink at all seriously in a pub.'). In regards romantic relationships there were also differences ('My parents seem to have the idea of the male putting the girlfriend on a pedestal. They don't believe in any physical violence between husband and wife.') whereas he had different thoughts ('The girlfriend should be a friend with an intelligent outlook on life. Sex problems etc. should be discussed long before marriage. Also, if a wife does something really silly, I don't see why the husband should not tan her.').

He was single and had attended one dance where he does not appear to have danced himself. He described dance halls as:

> 'centres for many of the poorer people where they may, for a small sum, hear music they can understand, dance and gain the acquaintance of the opposite sex in a manner not applicable elsewhere. Many fellows get their girlfriend at a dance where they could speak to her without preliminary introductions often difficult to arrange.'

It was his opinion that professional dance partners were:

> 'in many ways a boon to a young man who, with a spare evening in a big city and knowing no one, is able to get company. However, it is the source of considerable vice and, on the whole, I think should be done away with or else the morals tightened up.'

1939

His diary was written at the start of the war in September 1939.

> 'Note owing to lack of matter, the diary is rather sketchy. It is compiled from my own diary (personal) and notes I have made and kept but not included in my own diary.
>
> Sept. 2, 1939, Saturday. I spent the morning blacking out windows, small ones were painted out, rest had paper strips around edges. Electric bulbs were taken down, replaced by new ones of much smaller wattage. Went out in blackout, found hundreds out doing the same. Everybody seemed calm, almost like blind man's bluff at a Christmas party. Joyous shouts from groups who became broken up as they then tried to get in touch. Remarks were heard were *Where are you? Is this a game or something? Look at those lights, somebody will cop it*!
>
> Sunday. Declaration of war. One household nearby gathered around wireless set, sang national anthem. This was the only demonstration I saw. There were crowds around Territorial. I asked two people why. General guess was waiting for something to happen, what they didn't know. During the afternoon people kept off the streets except the sea front. Beaches were nearly deserted except those filling sandbags. In the evening I counted the gas masks in two hours.
>
> Monday 4th Sept. Shops looked as usual, only some had paper stuck around edges. Everybody I spoke to expected air raids on London hourly. Very little war talk, mostly about private matters, neighbours, etc. I got the feeling that war hadn't broken out for Torquay. Crowd around Territorial Drill Hall. Counted 36 gas masks during afternoon (note all counts exclude members of armed forces etc.) and 25 in the evening before it got too dark. The loss of the *Athenia* struck Torquay, with the fact that war had broken out, some Torquay people were on her. Dropped into a pub with some friends in the evening. Nothing different except harder to find one's way in.
>
> Tuesday. Had a coffee in most popular café, no change except old wartime tunes were being played and a few of the people joined in. Counted 65 gas masks in morning, 19 being carried by children. Found children and many employees had to carry them. In bus I heard an old man say to a young soldier *They supply you with such good clothes made of such good cloth*! Also, *It will end in a B[loody] revolution* (in Germany). Some annoyance at closure of cinemas. Bulk of people surprised England hasn't been raided yet. Feeling about sinking of liner has died away already. Shops like Woolworths are building light strips around the doors.
>
> Wednesday. Except for reported attempted air raid on London, nothing was heard. Many people shook their heads and said *Now you watch*.
>
> Thursday. Met two men from Lancashire and Kent. Both said that in Torquay nothing might have happened as far as they could see.

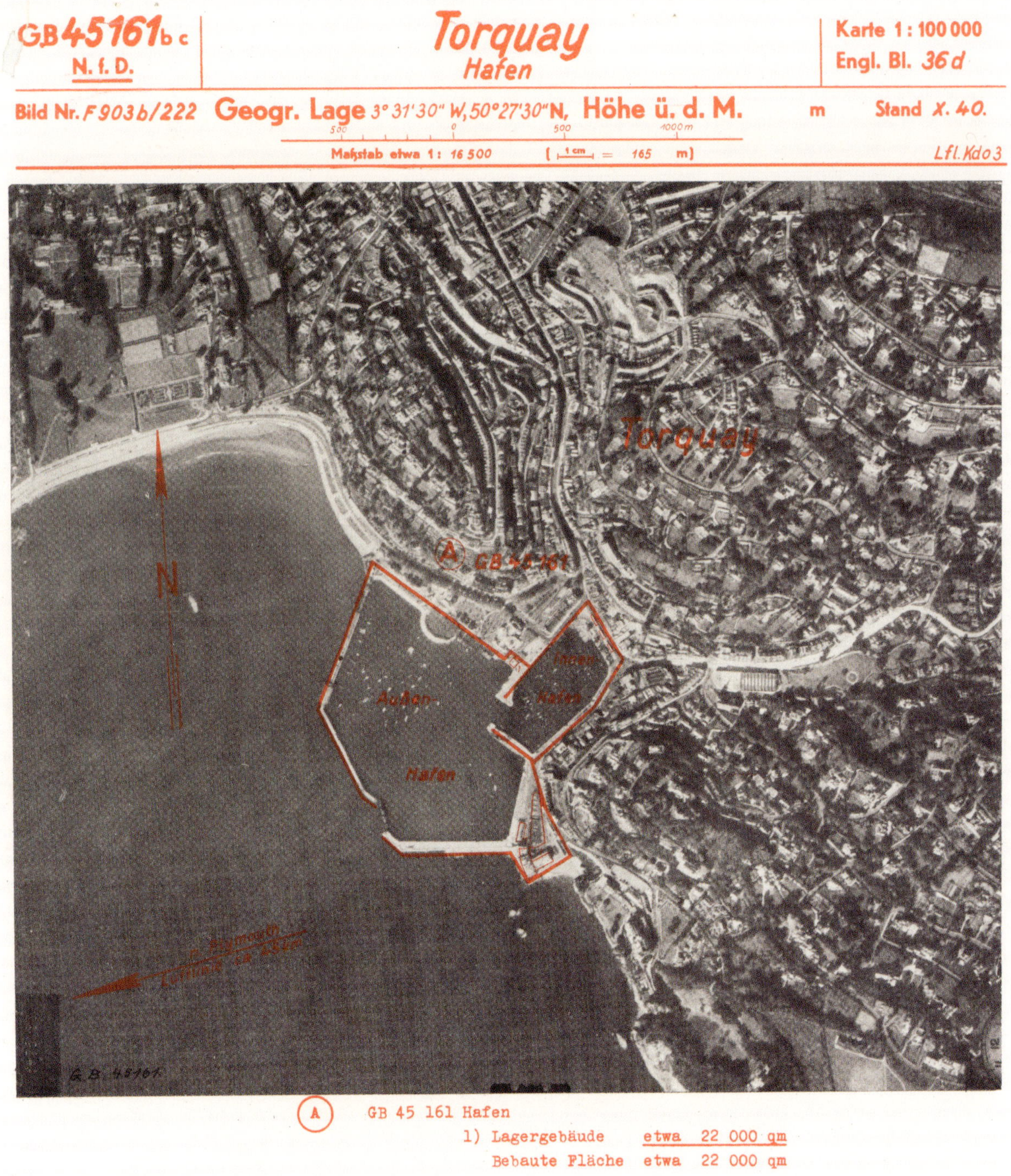

317 German aerial photograph of Torquay Hafen (harbour) with strategic sites identified in red, 1940.

Saturday 10th. Had tea with friends on beach near the people filling sandbags, literally thousands have been filled chiefly for police station, fire station and hospital I hear. The fact that England hasn't been bombed & France hasn't had a major engagement on the western front seems to surprise them beyond expression. Hitler's lightning war certainly has some believers in England.

318 *Russian poster, 1943.*

From now until the 18th nothing happened. Less people were in the streets in the evening and was talked about a bit. The general attitude is, this is different from what I expected, the army will get me when they want me, I am going to carry on and carry on they did. People talked of films, babies and gossip, but very little about the war.

Monday, 18. HMS *Courageous* was torpedoed. This hit Torquay, as within 100 yards of where I live two separate homes lost the father. Heard words were said about the ship since she was a reserve boat. Many seemed to think that she was unsafe. Why I don't know except that she sank quickly. Everyone I asked (19 in all) had only admiration for the U boat commander, there were no hard words about him, only respect for such nerve.

Thursday 21. One of the largest local shops caught fire and as the AFS were there, I kept a close eye on them. Their little engines did amazingly well and I came away with the feeling that if my house were struck, one of those engines wouldn't take long to put it out. Later, I asked my friends (about 7 or 8 of them) and they all said that the pumps did better than they expected.

From now on the conversations heard in the street are more and more on the subject of Russia. The fact that she invaded Poland wasn't well-received and as she marches on the people I overhear talking seem very puzzled. They don't call Russia the Red Menace as the politicians seem to, they just wonder and hope Russia doesn't come in against us. Nothing but admiration seems to be felt for the Poles. On all sides I hear *Plucky devils. They would have given Germany hell if Russia hadn't attacked as well. Poor devils. If we could only help, can't we do anything?*

25th Monday. After this date cars became scarcer on the roads. I saw only 5 one evening when I cycled along what was once the busiest road around here. And at night I only saw 8 on the same road.

29th Friday. It looked as if Russia and Germany were in together. Of all the statements I heard I think this is typical, it is by a widow of 50. She said *I don't understand politics but we musn't give in after what they did to the Poles.*

30th Saturday. I went in the evening to see *Confessions of a Nazi Spy*. The audience was quiet throughout the whole show and only clapped at the end. I hear that in some towns the film was the cause of much more lively behaviour.

Nothing much doing now, so I will close this diary. I hope to send in a fuller diary every week now.'

Four weeks previous to the diary Mr Gorrill had won the Macloghlin Scholarship for Medicine and entered the University of London.[336] His change of circumstances may have prevented his continuing to write for MO. Mr Gorrill died in 1970 at the age of forty-eight.[337]

65. Kathleen Tipper, Typist, 1941-2

319 Miss Kathleen Tipper in the 1930s.

Shorthand typist Kathleen Tipper (1919-2017), lived with her family in a council house in Eltham outside London. She was twenty-two years old when she wrote of her younger brother Philip (1925-2012) who was evacuated to Torquay with St Olave's Grammar School. She wrote on 11 September 1941:

'We are astir very early, I went with Mother to see Phillip off. Mother is exceedingly glum, but is looking forward to Christmas time. I am afraid Philip still thinks Torquay *a dump and funk hole* and considers himself to be the equivalent of a convict in Dartmoor, furthermore he declares that after the war he will never go near the place again.'

She had three follow-up entries in 1942:

2 April 1942, 'Phil came home from Torquay today, he looks very well and says they had a raid there recently. A German fighter came down over the streets and let off his cannons quite happily. Phil says that all the locals stood and stared, only one man was slightly hurt. He says that the din was terrific and people were really frightened.' This was probably the attack of 27 March when two German planes dropped three high explosive bombs and machine gunned the harbour.[338]

29 April, 'Phil went back today – he didn't want to go but I am afraid he had no choice. I expect some of the parents kept their boys home, wondering no doubt if Torquay is a 2-star town!'

14 August, 'We had our first letter from Phil for over a fortnight and it contained a good deal of very interesting matter. At the ATC camp he had two flights and on the last day he went out in a submarine-chaser and they had machine-gun practice, shooting at moving targets, then they joined in a patrol. When he returned to Torquay, he found that his billet had been bombed. On Bank Holiday, apparently, 10 planes blitzed the town, dropped their bombs and machine-gunned the town. None of his things were seriously damaged but as a bomb landed in their back-garden, the house is in a real mess. The family were unhurt, this was fortunate, as there are three small children in the house. This was not all, early this week at an agricultural camp, he and some friends were picking broccoli on the side of a hill, two planes appeared overhead. These champion ATC boys identified them as friendly mustangs but a second or two later the so-called mustangs circled round and dived down on them, dropped six bombs and cannon-gunned the gallant harvesters who hastily dropped prone.

Phil says that the cannon-shells whistled past them and made a terrible din, the bombs fell about fifty yards off and sunk a launch in the bay. Mother became very indignant about all this, I think she imagines that Goering is after her ewe-lamb only. However, he must be quite alright because at the end of the letter he asks us to send him some eatables, preferably something sweet.'[339]

Torquay was attacked on 3 August; eight bombs caused the deaths of three men, three women and one child.

Kathleen Tipper never married and remained in London until her death in 2017. Her brother Philip joined the navy towards the end of the war and died in 2012.[340]

66. Phillip Daniell, Teacher, 1942-5

Leading Aircraftman Philip Allen Daniell (1921-1988) was born in Cornwall. He enrolled at the University College of the South West at the start of the war, left in June 1940 and begin lecturing at a technical college in Torquay that October. Five months later Mr Daniell enlisted in the Royal Air Force and in 1942 married Kathleen Tyler (1920-2013), a twenty-two-year-old widow. From 1942 to 1943 the couple lived with her parents at Sunny Ridge on Teignmouth Road in Torquay. He wrote for MO from 1942 to 1955.[341]

Directives: alcohol consumption and sex

Leading Aircraftman Daniell did not supply diaries but instead answered a variety of subjects in directives. Two responses on alcohol and sex stand out. In 1943 he wrote of his family's use of alcohol. His father normally only drank on holidays at home and had a single half pint of beer in the Conservative Club. He was frank about his mother's excessive drinking of stout ('A neurotic type, probably suffering from alcoholic and nicotine poisoning at times. Her indulgence in alcohol has had disastrous effects on our family life and we take what steps we can to prevent her drinking.') Leading Aircraftman Daniell himself first became drunk at the age of eighteen ('at a St John's Ambulance supper where I was performing with a n*gger minstrel troupe'). In 1943 he also described his drinking habits at considerable length including his current situation:

> 'I am a young person (22) and I drink mainly with my wife; less frequently with my wife and other men and women of our age. In a group we talk about our jobs, the unpleasantness of service life, dirty jokes, the failure of our families, past incidents and past drinking, the poor quality of English pubs. Behaviour of young people I see in pubs is invariably good. They appear rather shy and uncomfortable. This does not apply to Canadian soldiers.'

Daniell had two close friends while at college in Exeter:

> 'One of these was a woodwork student, a solid, hard-drinker with a good head. The other obtained an honours degree in history and first interested me in pubs as pubs. He compiled a list of the pubs in Exeter area (approximately 160) and the three of us set out to visit them. A book was kept recording our movements and the beer sold, accommodation and sanitary facilities of each pub visited. I never completed the survey owing to lack of funds and having a girlfriend. My two friends just got through their quota in a year, ending the hunt in a taxi.'

He commented that:

> 'This task involved walking miles in the blackout, drinking bad beer, drinking beer in filthy dingy pubs, forcing oneself to drink in order to get through the night's quota.'

Leading Aircraftman Daniell described public houses in Exeter:

320 *German map of Torquay Hafen (harbour) with strategic sites identified in red, 1940.*

> 'Out of 150 pubs, about 17 are worth a second visit. There are a particularly large number of small, cramped, dirty pubs; mainly converted private homes or specially constructed pubs which are still dark, cramped and unpleasant.'

As well as those in Dawlish:

> 'Of the 23 pubs in the town itself, not one is better than a low-class drinking shop. There is no pub – excluding hotel bars – which has any pretentions to comfort or luxury. There is no pub in town to which I can feel happy with my wife. Two miles on either side of the town are very comfortable country pubs with an excellent variety of drinks and fine views from outside terraces.'

He also wrote of Torquay:

321-2 Members of the 834th Engineer Aviation Battalion training aboard a landing craft at Torquay, 1944.

'The pubs are as good as one would expect in a high-class resort. In the town, and excluding hotel bars, there is only one (possibly two) First Class pubs (the Royal). As at Dawlish the three best pubs are two miles from the town… One very seldom sees young children in pubs. I practically never see young women without male escorts (except in the two pubs which are rendezvous for the local whores). Young people in pubs are mainly airmen. They are usually in parties of more than two. Often one sees two airmen with two girls. In the pub at Cockington (the Drum) one often sees young airmen alone with a girl. Young people seldom seem to drink much and almost never to get drunk.'

Leading Aircraftman Daniell's responses to questions on sex were more detailed than those of other Devon Writers. In January 1943 he explained whether his attitude towards sex has changed since the start of the war:

'Since adolescence I think I may say I have been broad and progressively-minded as regards sex. The restrictive attitude of the churches to sex was one of the chief factors leading me to abandon religion. I am interested in sex as a branch of human behaviour and sex occupies a large part of conversation and reading. During the last three years I have gradually lost all interest in the smutty aspect of sex. I am willing to exchange dirty jokes when required and I carry a stock of suitably dirty poems for social occasions. Since I have been married, I have become less willing to discuss my personal sex experiences with other people and never discuss my married life.

I am strongly in favour of improved sex education, freer sexual relations between unmarried persons, improved facilities for adult sex guidance. I am liberal in my attitude to the manifestations of sexual aberration and have upheld homosexual relations on several occasions though having so such tendencies myself.

That my views on sex are progressive was shown by the trouble in which both poetry and prose writing involved me at college.'

A month earlier, in December 1942, Leading Aircraftman Daniell supplied answers to 'sex life in wartime':

'Marriage & classes, there has been an astonishing number of marriages among by own friends during the last year. They are all people of 18 to 23, people who in peace time would not have married before say 28 to 30. I am struck by the rather unusual nature of these marriages, i.e. between students in very poor circumstances.

I myself have always said that I should not marry, and yet got married six months ago at the age of 21 though having no job to return to after the war and no private means.

323 'Four Coast Guardsman, serving as scouts and proceeding in a Landing Craft to the French invasion beach shortly before H Hour, get their heads together and display their full accord with General Sherman on the subject of war. They subjected their knobs to the shearing just to kill the time in the English Channel crossing', June 1944. General William Tecumseh Sherman was being remembered for having said War is Hell.

324 American servicemen aboard a Coast Guard manned assault transport in manoeuvres before D-Day.

I can think of six marriages among my friends which would not have taken place in peace time.

Sex in conversation, although sex forms one of the main topics of conversation among my friends and RAF companions, I have noticed a decrease in the intensity of interest in the subject, a decreased tendency to dwell on the smutty aspect of sex life, an increased tendency towards social disapproval of such matters. This may quite possibly be accounted for by the ordinary process of physical development and the movement from adolescence towards manhood.

On the other hand I have noticed since the war an increased willingness to discuss sex both in its serious and smutty aspects between the sexes and between young and old of the same sex. One aspect of this tendency is the increasing broadness of the humour sufficient to mixed audiences by stage comedians.

Extra-marital intercourse, although during the past year I have reached a stage of some familiarity with many men of various ages, backgrounds and types, I have not yet met a man who laid claim to having had intercourse with any woman other than his wife. The only exception to this is one Air Gunner with whom I shared a hospital ward at Christmas.

Blackout behaviour, etc., I have had little opportunity to study this. I myself have only found myself in a position to judge the behaviour of couples in the blackout on very few occasions. I have no evidence of the blackout, ARP shelters, etc. being used for immoral purposes to any great extent in any of the six towns I have lived in during the past two years i.e. Exeter, Dawlish, Torquay, Brighton, Filey St John's Wood. As a teacher concerned with girls and boys up to 19 years of age, I know of only two complaints regarding their sexual behaviour. In both these were simple cases of precocious youths and not connected with wartime factors.

Prostitution, I have never been accosted by a prostitute though I imagine I am not an unlikely-looking customer either as regards my personal appearance, apparent affluence or habits. None of my friends have told me of experiences with prostitutes although I have spent a fortnight billeted within a few yards of a noted area inhabited by prostitutes which is out-of-bounds to servicemen. I have never come in contact with its inhabitants and nor have my friends although we have previously spent considerable time wandering the

325 'French Coast Dead Ahead', American servicemen aboard a Coast Guard landing barge, 1944.

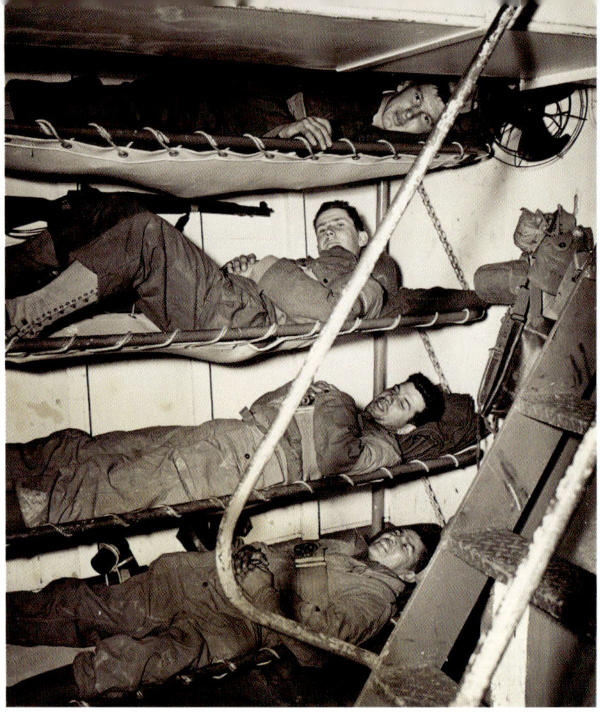

326 Four soldiers aboard a Coast Guard infantry landing craft crossing the Channel in the invasion of northern France, 1944.

streets and lounging in pubs and cafés. I know of no case in which a man or woman acquaintance of mine has entered into any financial transaction concerning sexual satisfaction.

One aspect of wartime sex life strikes me in my hometown [Falmouth]. There have been several cases of twenty-year-old girls, often staunch church workers, entering into relationships with middle-aged men. I do not know the nature of the relationships thus established. I have been struck too on returning to my hometown by the way in which girls who were scruffy children when I lived there, having changed into attractive and well-dressed women in the company of young service officers in pubs, etc.

Love-making techniques, I have been struck by the restrained nature of the love-making practised by young men of my acquaintance. This is based on their own admission, admittedly, but one would expect their own accounts of their activities to tend towards excess rather than restraint. At 18 I and my friends would frequently carry love-making even with comparatively strange women to the extent of nudity and mutual masturbation. It would almost seem as if such practice has been abandoned by the 18-year-olds of today.

Masturbation, among friends of my wife and myself we know of only one individual who practises masturbation. This is not to suggest that the remainder refrain from masturbation. It is simply a subject which is not discussed in its personal application. One friend of my wife's described it as *A disgusting habit in which I should never indulge.*

327 An American serviceman removes pieces of metal from the face of a fellow soldier on the beachhead in northern France, 1944.

General remarks, during the past three years I have been forced into intimacy with some 40 different men through either sharing a college hostel with them or sharing a service billet with them. These are seldom men whose acquaintance I have sought but have been forced on me by circumstances. They should thus be a fair sample of college and air-crew types. The general characteristics of these men as regards their sex life would appear to be as follows

328 American servicemen surround a farm house in northern France searching for a German sniper, 1944. The fate of individual overseas servicemen after D-Day remained largely unknown to their English friends.

329 Poster warning of the consequences of intimate relations, c.1939-45.

1, The girl at home aspect - most of the 18 to 21 have a girlfriend at home to whom they are engaged but with whom their relations have been strictly moral.

2, The girl or wife at home is not a bar to establishing relations with other women where one is stationed.

3, My own experience is that immoral or fast women are exceedingly difficult to find.

4, The behaviour of couples establishing temporary relationships is remarkably restrained.

5, The permanent staff get the best women is a common sentiment.

6, Young men are moral in practice but not in theory.'

In July 1943 Leading Aircraftman Daniell relayed conversations he had overheard amongst his fellow airmen. The first was on strip tease:

'A Only a pretty poor type of woman would do it.

B It's not such an objectionable thing as a woman cracking dirty jokes on the stage.

A It's married men who go to see those shows.

B At the Grand at Brighton the audience was mainly old women. I felt quite out of place there.

C That's true.'

Two other conversations concerned women in general:

'A *I wonder if women behave like men when they're on their own. Do they run round with nothing on and rub down in front of an open window?*

B *No.*

C *It would be a good thing if those conventions about nudity were got rid of, they're disappearing in the course of the war.*

A *For men at least clothes are needed to prevent the embarrassment of getting a stand in front of a bunch of women.*

B *Merely seeing a naked woman has no special erotic significance.*

C *I don't know the female figure is a very beautiful thing.*

A *But a woman wearing a pair of shorts is more beautiful than the same woman without.*

C *Women's behaviour is chiefly conditioned by what they think would be the opinion of other women rather than their own ideas of right and wrong.*

A *Yes, not many unmarried women would admit to their friends that they had had intercourse.*

B *I don't agree. At least ½ of my friends or my wife's have made that admission to us.*'

Near the end of the war, in 1944, Leading Aircraftman Daniell reassessed his attitude towards women:

'In 1939 I think I still had an idealist view of women. I sought to couple physical intimacy with mental and spiritual union and possession. I would be violently upset by the loss of a girlfriend. Now I have ceased to expect any great loyalty from a woman and have completely abandoned spiritual union as a practical goal while retaining it as an unreliable ideal. I have now separated the physical from the emotional more completely and can appreciate purely physical intercourse and association quite devoid of emotional significance'.

Leading Aircraftman Daniell served overseas in 1943 and 1944 and was posted to Cumberland by 1945. After the war he returned to Cleveland House on High Street in Dawlish where he had lived for a short while in 1941 and possibly 1942. Mr Daniell subsequently resumed his undergraduate studies at Exeter and was awarded an M.Sc. in Economics in 1948. He lived with his wife at the Manor House in the Strand in Shaldon. At some point in his military career Mr Daniell had lived in Toronto.[342]

67. Kathleen Daniell, Teacher, 1943

Kathleen Daniell (1920-2013), the wife of Philip Daniell, was employed as a geography lecturer at South Devon Technical College. Not only was this located in the same road where she shared her parents' home but her father was the principal. Mrs Daniell answered directives in 1943.[343]

Directives: sex, politics and nationalities

Like her husband she expressed her views about sex:

'My own sex life is much happier and freer. My attitude towards sex in other people has become much more tolerant. From taking a too morbid interest in other people's affairs in this respect, I feel more and more that is their business and no-one else's.'

She wrote about the availability of food:

'The food situation seems well-balanced in Torquay. There are few complaints and few shortages. Sometimes there is only one type of meat in the butchers throughout the town, i.e. either beef or mutton. There has been a shortage of sausages at times and fish can now hardly ever be bought. Most of the fish shops shut early in the day.

I said there are few complaints, but in women's attitudes, there is a growing weariness of calculating, adding up points, working out different menus, trying to disguise a potato.'

She had firm views on politics:

'I have taken a greater interest in them due to the fact that only since the war began have I realised that our *Glorious Empire* and famous democratic *Motherland* is in some respect not all it might be. I have taken a growing interest in Russia and therefore in communism and socialism and have naturally been forced to enquire in what respect they differed from capitalism etc.'

She described the Russians ('a wonderful people with high ideals, fighting like mad for their beliefs. Only a country with something worth fighting for would struggle on as they have done.') as well as the Japanese ('I have read stories of their terrible cruelty – probably newspaper propaganda – and on the other hand I have heard tales from more reliable sources of their courage and kindness.'), Chinese ('a peace-loving people until recently suppressed and brow-beaten by foreign interests in their country'), Americans ('I have heard only bad reports of their behaviour etc. in this country from those who have been in contact with them recently.'), French ('a growing dislike and distrust of the people as a whole') and the Jews ('pity and a desire to see a settlement of their problems after the war. I cannot really understand the anti-Semitic attitudes found in the forces and among many of my friends. In my own immediate circle, there is a growing indignation that many of the shops in the town are owned by Jews whose number here are increasing and is looked on with antagonism and dismay.').[344]

330 Aerial photograph by the Luftwaffe of Appledore, 31 August 1940.

WESTWARD HO! (& HONITON, BIDEFORD & NORTHAM)

The village of Westward Ho! was named in the late 1860s after Charles Kingsley's novel of 1855. Its situation, along Bideford Bay in the parish of Northam, leant itself to Victorian development. The larger parish had a population in 1931 of 5,563. The area around the village was used for a variety of war purposes including practice for the D-Day landings in 1944 and various military hardware experiments. Less well-known are military installations such as RAF Radar Station No. 19 which was built at Northam in 1941 and closed three years later. Temporary housing for Jewish refugees from Germany and Austria was also built and Seafield Holiday Camp was requisitioned. A range of defences were installed including anti-glider earthworks, anti-invasion barbed wire obstructions and anti-tank cubes. In the autumn of 1945 the military were engaged in continuous explosions in Westward Ho! and local residents speculated that servicemen were destroying the land mines buried in the beaches.[345]

At the same time evacuees were drawn to the village including in 1940 a London hairdresser, the first barber in Westward Ho! Part of Highgate School relocated to the village during the war and another with 50 children arrived in in 1940. They were joined shortly afterwards by 46 Bristol children.[346] Only hints of this can be found in the MO diary.

68. Reginald Harpur, Retired Engineer, 1941

Caldwell Harpur (1866-1945), who lived in Cornwall, received a series of writings from his younger London-based brother, Reginald (1872-1959), and presumably forwarded these to Mass Observation.[347] His first diary, written in 1941, contained opinions not commonly held, expressed or recorded such as those entitled 'homosexuality in women':

> 'I believe that the Roman Catholic Church does not allow two nuns to sleep in one bed because of the fear that their pent-up feelings might break out. I forget where I read about it, but it was in connection with a bombed nunnery where the nuns had to be herded together until quarters could be found for them. It seems to me that women are more prone to suffer from homo sex than men, as it is easier for a man to get a woman than for a woman to get a man, especially when she is getting on in years. Also, it is easier for a woman to attach a male member of rubber, which is quite effective, than for a man to attach an effective woman's member. Again, the soft body of a woman is more pleasant even for a woman to handle than the bony, muscular, hairy, skinny limbs of an average man.'

That year he had three holidays in Devon. Mr Harpur was estranged from his wife Rosa (who died on 1 October 1946) and was accompanied by 'W', most likely his housemate Winifred Gunton who had travelled with him in 1940. They drove from London in their car and stayed with his widowed sister Nora Moore (1877-1971) in her bungalow outside Bideford. There was also a visit to Mr Harpur's brother in either Penzance or Hayle. Their first trip took place in April.

1941

'10.4.41, Stopped at Honiton and had lunch at the Carlton Café [42 High Street] about 1pm. Day continued fine and it did not take long to reach Exeter, 16 miles away. As usual had a little difficulty in finding the way through to the Crediton Road but between Exeter and Crediton W was tired and had a few minutes doze in the car having driven 188 miles practically without a break, except for the half hour lunchtime.

On towards Barnstaple along the valley of the Taw, where the railway crosses and recrosses the river so many times that I lost count. The road, river and railway all twixt and turn in the valley, on one side or the other of the road, add interest to the journey when one tries to keep track of the railway and river. The fir-clad slopes of the hills are not yet at their best but later in the year this journey must be one of the good views in Devon.

We crossed the River Taw for the last time in Barnstaple and went onto Bideford where we crossed the River Torridge. Bideford was crowded with people who I felt sure were not natives of the place. We halted for a minute in front of the Kingsley Hotel [The Quay] which name made me think of the book *Westward Ho!* rather than of the man who wrote the book. The village of Westward Ho! was named after the book and I am wondering how many people there have a copy of the book.

We had a little difficulty in finding Nora's home, *Hartland*, but I eventually spotted it by seeing a hotel near the sea and remembering a particularly bit of very rough road which led up to it. Nora came to the door as I was opening her front gate to bring in the car. She, <u>Simba</u> and <u>Buchanan</u> are quite well but the scarcity of food is adding interest in the lives of the dog and cat and giving Nora something to think about.

We arrived at *Hartland* about 4.15pm after covering 236 miles since 6.15am this morning. Nora has had no news of [sister] Con[stance Harpur, 1875-1941] since the beginning of the month when Robin wrote her a long letter about Con's condition in the nursing home at Boscombe.

Simba the dog and Buchanan the cat are very important features in *Hartland* and Nora seems to spend much of her time in making sure that neither of the animals go astray. There is another cat, William, who goes out when he likes and returns when he likes but Buchanan has a wire netting run the length of the garden to march up and down in when he does require fresh air. He is a nice black-and-white cat, very solid and heavy with a white top on the end of his tail, somewhat lazy but inclined to be friendly when stroked.

Roma, a black-haired pretty young woman, Jack's particular friend, is staying with Nora but now she has got a job in an airplane firm at Bideford. Her particular job just now is testing American air pumps for the machines and finds the work very interesting and well-suited to her mechanical term of mind. At present she is on Night Shift and is away from the house from 7.30pm to 8.30am.

***OPPOSITE: 331** 'Maintenance - Instow', a watercolour by Dwight C. Shepler, 1944.*
***332** 'Appledore Ebb', a watercolour by Dwight C. Shepler, 1944.*

US 529
DWIGHT SHEPLER USNR

DWIGHT SHEPLER
133

333-4 A United States Air Force weather station in Devon, 4 December 1943.

She came in Friday morning with an account of a bomb being dropped on the airfield near Appledore only a few miles from here. Nora heard it coming down but was not sure about it being a bomb or a big gun until Roma confirmed her suspicions. Roma nearly lost one of her finger ends in a machine during the night as a piece of rag she was holding became entangled in the machine and nearly drew her hand in before she could release it.

Nora, W, and I sat and talked during the evening until bedtime about 10.30pm. I was so tired and sleepy that I have no distinct recollection of getting into bed, beyond the fact that I considered it a nuisance to have to take off my clothes and put on pyjamas for the first time since I was last in Cornwall.

11.4.41, Up about 7.30am and had bacon and egg for breakfast. Neither Nora nor Roma eat any breakfast. Left Westward Ho! about 8.30am and went via Northam to Bideford and along the road near the river Torridge as far as Landcross and then took the road to Monkleigh and along a very winding road through uninteresting country as far as Holsworthy. We had meant to go that way to Launceston but changed the route at Holsworthy and outside the church there asked the vicar, who was evidently on his way to conduct a service in the church at 10am, the way to Bude as my map of the district being of such a small scale it was difficult to be sure of the right turning across country to Stratton…'

A month later the couple were back in Devon:

'30.5.41, Down the steep road into Lynmouth carrying a letter which a soldier on guard at the top of the hill had asked us to post as soon as possible. That letter was finally posted in Westward Ho! We did not stop in Lynmouth but started up the winding hill on the road to Barnstaple. There is a very sudden turn in that road at Hillsford Bridge and we missed it, going straight on instead. This land is on the open moors and we did not find out the mistake for some time going as far as Brendon Common before a couple of girls told us that the only way was to go back by the way we came. I could not locate our exact position on the map so did as they suggested but now I wish that I had gone on until I could locate my position, as I'm sure that we should have arrived in Barnstaple an hour sooner.

Back we went to Hillsford Bridge and found the turning we had missed, which easily explained our mistake. Arrived at cross roads named Blackmoor Gate. I had a little argument with a man of whom I asked the way, as his direction did not seem to agree with my reading of the map. Instead of going straight on and turning left at the next cross roads, he told me to turn left and then right at the next cross roads which bore the name of *Cape of Good Hope*. However, he was so certain about the way that I followed his advice and thereby missed a very steep hill. Probably the steep hill is the reason that the buses go that way.

Arrived in Barnstaple and having crossed the River

Taw it did not take long to reach Bideford and then Northam at Westward Ho! where Nora was awaiting our arrival at 6.30pm more than 12 hours after we started out. A tiring journey, and we certainly shall not go back that way if we are at all in a hurry. Distance travelled today 246 miles.

31.5.41 At *Hartland*, Westward Ho!

It was 9.45am before we had finished breakfast. I say *we* but that does not include Nora as she does not seem to think that breakfast is necessary. Simba, the dog, woke me up this morning by touching my face with his cold nose. This morning we went to Hartland Quay. Hartland Point is occupied by troops so we could not go there.

After visiting Hartland Church, which is really in the hamlet of Stoke in the parish of Hartland, we picnicked on the high land overlooking the Quay. The church, dedicated to Saint Nectan, is a fine building and there is much inside to interest visitors... We had just finished our picnic inside a field when a man came along, the head gardener, and man of many parts as we found out by questions and the help of a cigarette which W gave to him. A mine exploded on the shore last November and damaged the hotel roof and windows on the quay but nothing happened to the rocks. It would take more than a German mine or even one of ours to disturb this coast. A wreck took place in December and the gardener was No. 1 of Rocket Apparatus and was proud of the fact that his first shot carried the rope over the wreck and the crew were rescued. The gardener is also sidesman at the church but was not there when Haile Selassie visited the place. The gardener looked after the electricity supplied to the hotel which was generated by a private plant and was proud of the fact that in spite of all his various jobs, and that he was ruptured and unfit for military service, he was never tired. We were very lucky in the weather this morning. The sun was hot, and the wind rather cool, blowing as it did from the north, but not cold enough to spoil the feast. I wish that you could have been there to enjoy the view if not the food which was beef steak etc.

1.6.41, The first of June and a fine day. Last evening we played Lexicon until after about 11 o'clock and I lost 4d. I heard the Alert somewhere about midnight but that did not keep me awake. A few planes passed over of which I was dimly conscious but they were carrying bombs to more important places than Westward Ho! While Nora was engaged on housework this morning, I and W walked up the Tors, high ground on the west of Westward Ho!, which is now the property of the National Trust. Steps in the winding pathways up the slopes are so high that a man of my weight and age had to hesitate at each step, both going up and coming down.

A young girl on the same seat told us that she was an evacuee from Bexhill, had come with her parents to Westward Ho! last April and preferred to sit alone reading a book rather than join with the children on the front. As she was only 13 years of age, I thought this rather strange but suggested that she should read *Westward Ho!*, which apparently she had not heard about.

On the way back, I purchased some bottles of beer at the Bay Hotel and got into trouble with W for carrying them in my jacket pockets (as the news this morning about rationing make it evident that clothes would be scarce in the future). This afternoon we went a short distance in the car and picnic in a wood near Yeo Vale, a large square house near the river a small stream which flows into the river Torridge about 2 miles south of Bideford... We have to curtail the mileage as much as possible as petrol is very scarce and we have a long return journey to cover before London sees us again.

2.6.41, I heard a siren more than once last night and planes were flying over most of the time while I was awake but nothing out of the ordinary occurred near here as far as I can find out. Roma, the young woman who stays here with Nora, must be a little mad I think. I talked to her on Saturday morning and she seemed alright but I have not seen her since. She and Nora have had a row and now she is sulking in her room which is in the roof of the bungalow and she has stayed there, as far as I know, all the time, though of course she may have gone out while we were picnicking on Sunday. Apparently, the row was due to the fact that Roma went out with Jack on his weekend visit and both of them got drunk. That is a normal thing for a young soldier to do if he can get a good supply of liquor but it is not normal for a young woman to do the same thing under any circumstances, hence the quarrel at the present moment. We are not sure whether she is up in her room or whether she has gone out and Nora is leaving her alone to get over her sulk in the usual way.

Nora, W and I had a couple of rounds on the putting green this evening and I did No. 18 hole in one.

As Roma had not appeared and as we were not sure that she was still sulking in her room in the roof of the bungalow, W went up the ladder to investigate and found that she was still there and had not apparently been out for a couple of days. This fact, more or less, convinced me that the young woman is a little mad. Nora would say *more than a little*.

3.6.41, Up about 8 o'clock. Learned that Roma had gone to work [having] slipped out of the house about 7.30am without a word to anyone although last Saturday morning, the only time I have seen her, she talked quite pleasantly to me and told me about her work and the interest she took in it. I wonder what is really the matter with her but whatever it is, it probably counts for her lack of friends.

After a good breakfast, W and I started off on our journey to London leaving Nora with regret as she had made us very comfortable under trying conditions. It was raining this morning when we started on our way and the sun has not appeared at all today. It was getting on for 10 o'clock when we left *Hartland* but as my watch had stopped at 9.20 and I did not notice this until I saw a public clock, I am a little doubtful about the time.

In Bideford W made a call on a firm on the chance of getting some extra business. Seed sown in the most unlikely places sometimes bear good fruit later on. It was raining fast when we reached Barnstaple but that did not prevent W getting some new bread rolls before we left that town. It was a pleasant drive through the Taw Valley in spite of the damp weather. There was a chance for a little mild excitement when we had the chance to race a train going towards Exeter and as the road, rail and river all run fairly close together along many miles of the valley there was something of interest to look at even when the train finally left us behind, though several times we caught it up while stopped at the railway stations.

It was about 12.45 when we reached Exeter having covered 55 miles, not very fast travelling but the time including W calling on a firm and a nap while in the Taw Valley. We did not stop at all in Exeter not even to ask anyone if bombs had been dropped there recently, as we had heard at Westward Ho! But went straight onto towards Honiton. We halted by the roadside in a wood halfway to Honiton and ate rolls and pork and cake and cheese, then onto the next public house for a drink. W chose cider, so I had the same. It was hours before we could forget that cider; my stomach was annoyed that I should put such sour stuff inside it and afterwards we both became very sleepy and almost torpid, so another nap was necessary before we reached Yarcombe, a few miles beyond Honiton.'

Their third visit took place in August:

'7.8.41, The weather was fine and warm and the car went well but petrol was getting very low when we arrived in Bideford so we had to make use of three precious tickets. We lunched in the car on the back of the river Torridge near Bideford, chicken and ham sandwiches with milk from a bottle brought from Truro.

We arrived in Westward Ho! about 2.20pm and found Nora at home, doing something in the garden with Simba, the dog, in attendance and Buchanan, the cat, not far away. Nora looking well, exactly the same as when I saw her last holiday. We had a couple of rounds of miniature golf during the afternoon and I lost 6d to Nora as I failed to do a single hole in one stroke. Roma is on night duty and left for work soon after 6pm.

8.30pm. We had fish for supper, followed by cherry tart. Broad beans were included and I have some doubts whether they will lie quietly in my stomach during the whole of the night. The seashore, which stretches away to the north across Bideford Bay, looks harmless enough but Nora says that a young couple were blown to kingdom come a month or so ago. The young man trod on a mine and vanished in this cloud of dust and the young woman running to look for him went up the same way. How thoughtless some folk are nowadays.

Westward Ho! is a quiet place to live in but no one can say that it will not be one of the spots on which Hitler will try to land an army, when an attempt is made to invade. We played Lexicon during the evening. I lost 2d, W lost 2d and Nora won 4d. We got too sleepy to continue the games after 10 o'clock and went to bed.

8.8.41, I had a few touches of sciatica during the night and half woke several times to turn and twist my left leg about to ease the pain. W too had sciatica rather badly and embrocated her leg during the night.

Nora got up about 6am and brought in some tea in a packet of Epsom salts which were extremely effective in my case. Roma had been at work all night and came in about 8 o'clock just after we finished breakfast and we're getting ready to start on a journey to London. It was raining when we left about 8.30am and Nora with Roma saw us off at the gate. She must have got very wet as it poured with rain then and at frequent intervals most of the day.

As far as Barnstaple it was a deluge and water found its way through the roof of the car. There was a thick mist and it was not possible to see enough to judge the direction, with the result that we missed a turning and went via Exeter instead of via Taunton as I meant to do. My available map was 8 miles to an inch and with this scale it is easy to go astray on a day like this. We reached Crediton before I really found out where we were, but it was fine Devon scenery through which we passed and going via Exeter had the advantage of familiar roads and good surfaces…'

The couple's next recorded visit through Devon was on 18th July 1945 ('Stopped at a garage for petrol between Honiton and Exeter. W. dropped her gloves and we had to go back to the garage to find them. The youth there had picked them up where the car stood. Exeter seems to have been knocked about a lot by bombs much worse than I had thought from accounts read. Between Exeter and Okchampton we stopped by the roadside for lunch, a couple of buns each with a hard-boiled egg, cheese and lettuce, with cider to drink. It was pleasant there with a good view of the moors to the south. 3.20 we felt like another rest near Lifton.').

WHITCHURCH (& TAVISTOCK)

This village, located on the edge of Dartmoor some two miles south of Tavistock, was formerly engaged in mining. In 1939 Tavistock had 5,691 residents and the population of Whitchurch stood at about 1,400. There was an increase of 10.4% in the population of Tavistock Rural District during the first year of the war. Diarist **68** came to Whitchurch after the war ended and thus did not experience wartime village life including any interaction with the nearby American field hospital at Plaster Down.[348] Five years earlier an MO diarist from Launceston in Cornwall visited Tavistock ('had a pasty for dinner at Tavistock on the way. Heard the woman's husband in a back room complaining that we'd been given his pasty.')[349]

69. Muriel Passingham, Retired Teacher, 1945

In the last days of the war Muriel Julia Passingham (1887-1969) relocated with her housemate Mabel Wiens (1889-1976) from Boscastle in Cornwall to Whitchurch near Tavistock. She was then a retired fifty-eight-year-old teacher of music. In 1910 Miss Passingham had advertised herself as an accompanist for concerts, 'at homes' and private practice. She also gave pianoforte lessons and then resided in

335 Higher Statsford in Whitchurch, the home of Miss Muriel Passingham in 1945.

Cricklewood in North London but moved to the continent shortly afterwards, returned to England during the Great War and was living in London by 1922.[350]

In 1921 the census enumerator recorded the Misses Passingham and Wiens were staying at a boarding house in Merionethshire and by 1930, until 1939, they were teachers sharing Greystead, a house in Amersham in Buckinghamshire. They moved to Cornwall at the start of the war but continued to own their Amersham home.[351] The two women lived together for some forty years and their relationship may have been more substantial than some would have questioned at the time. In her diaries Miss Passingham refers to Miss Wiens as 'a friend'. In January 1945 she noted she was 'now living with a friend very happily'.[352]

Miss Passingham was born in Bradford, where her father was a nature photographer, but the family moved shortly afterwards to Brighton. Wiens was born in Kent and her family often moved throughout the country. Her father was a German-born merchant. Neither of the two women married.

Miss Passingham wrote a diary which included August 1945 when the two women moved to Devon. Miss Wiens purchased Higher Statsford, a detached house in the small village of Whitchurch. Miss Passingham wrote:

> 'It would be difficult to imagine a more complete contrast than in the change in our circumstances since we moved from Boscastle to Tavistock! And as no doubt thousands of people have been experiencing similar changes in their lives in this transition period, I will try and record what have been the main features of contrast between the two periods.
>
> Firstly, we left Boscastle in a sort of *Blaze of Glory*, and so it seemed to us, not having expected the riotous send-off given to us by the students of the Ginner-Mawer School which included a presentation of a book token for £1 1s and a visit from the entire school singing *Auld Lang Syne* and *For They Are Jolly Good Fellows*. It was really most touching. We'd also been paying farewell visits and receiving them from all our friends in the village all the last fortnight. Everybody announced their intention of visiting us in our new home with their first basic petrol (those with cars).
>
> Arrived here, we spent the first two days in pouring rain expecting the furniture van and slept on the bare boards. We had ample opportunity to revise our first estimate of the condition of the house, which was by no means cheering as we came to the conclusion, like so many who have been forced into purchasing house property because there are more to be rented and so few in any case on the market, that the actual value is about 1/10 of the money given.
>
> In this case, not having a surveyor with us on our first visitation, we'd overlooked a large variety of dilapidations - skirting boards rotting, wide gaps in the floor, plaster peeling off - apart from the need of paint, distemper and stain all over the house. The garden too seemed to have increased 100 fold in weeds since we've seen it and we looked at each other in dismay and said *What have we bought*?
>
> When the furniture came the men proved highly unskilled and what hadn't already been damaged in storage, was chipped and grazed in bringing up the stairs. Nothing seemed to fit in anywhere and some of the really good old stuff looked out of place or unhappy in its new surroundings.
>
> However, we had ordered several pots of paint and distemper and after sorting out the furniture and rearranging it several times to our dissatisfaction, we set to work on the woodwork and some of the walls, turning the back room from dingy brown to white walls with a blue liquid lino floor. We got ourselves in a frightful mess but the result was a great improvement. I've never done such physical hard labour in my life, especially getting the glue-like substance from under the paper in one of the bedrooms. We also managed to get some plaster for the worst cracks in walls and even got a man for a day to do some odd carpentry and mend the bulges in ceiling.
>
> Gradually the house took on an entirely different aspect and the furniture seemed almost to suggest itself where it would be best at home. It now looks as if it had never been anywhere else, and a large rather derelict-looking room, which had been a children's playroom, is now what we call the *Studio* with divan bed covered with a paisley shawl and some of the *family* best pictures, a long low bookshelf and a guitar in a corner. We did the floor with permanganate and nearly killed ourselves polishing it. The garden is now full of vegetables and the promise of flowers next year and bears not the remotest resemblance to the wilderness we found when we came.
>
> We were so busy and so really interested in all this work, that it was several weeks before we realised that the life in Boscastle seemed already as if it belonged to the remote past. In fact I found it difficult sometimes to conjure up a picture of my bedroom at *The Haven*. We had only heard from two or three intimate friends and my favourite pupil (the little boy genius who had nearly

died of blood poisoning after I left). Surrounded as we now are with all our own belongings, I often found myself picturing rather my former homes than my more recent ones and even dreaded my notebooks once with my Brighton address (which I left when I was 18). For these short weeks it is very curious to realise that the war years seemed somehow to have been blotted out of our memory, including our new art, that of acting. It seemed as if we had dreamed that we had become quite successful actresses! We both found it very difficult to remember a single one of our old parts. I am recording this in detail in case other members of MO have had similar experiences.

Here, instead of knowing everybody in the district, we don't know a soul yet except our two old tenants in the lower floor and the former owner of the house and her three very unattractive daughters. So far, the future is not promising as regards work. We are told Tavistock is very *unmusical*. We asked several trades people if there were a dramatic society and were told there wasn't one. Though last week we saw posters of a performance of three players by the Tavonian Dramatic Society which we now hear has been functioning for years!

At first, we found the ride into Tavistock and back on our bikes and shopping, (especially on market days) very fatiguing, but are getting used to it and now rather enjoy it and have not so far missed contact with our fellows although it does seem very strange for all the people we meet in shops, the café and the streets to be strangers. But although we have not forgotten our good friends in Boscastle, we have felt the need here for a time to be alone in this magically peaceful spot. The war did not affect us physically and there were few outward and visible signs in Boscastle of the suffering of a world at war but when it was over, there was a feeling of vicarious relief and longing for silence, so strong it was almost as if we'd come from an area subject to air raids and gunfire! Although we'd had the wireless on to the last minute in Boscastle, we had no desire for it here for many weeks and were grateful we had no electricity for it at first. We had a writer friend to stay recently and he said he felt very much the same as we do.

With regard to the tradespeople here, we find them on the whole very much the same as in Cornwall - very friendly and obliging with the notable exception of the larger stores Woolworths, World Stores, International etc. where they have a different type of staff - for the most curt, impersonal and occasionally rude. The girls at Woolworths are almost like robots in their similarity - are about 15 or 16, all very made up, most of them appear to have adenoids with a vacant expression and they invariably put their hands out for the money or hand you the goods or change while looking either into vacancy or at each other or into the street. In the World's Stores I have twice had to interrupt a long conversation on their private concerns after waiting in vain to be served for about 10 minutes. We can get no repairs whatever done to bicycles not even a brake adjustment that would take only a few minutes. The man stands in doorway chatting with passers-by and whenever we ask him to do anything he always replies *Full up with repairs for the next three months*. Yet we have sometimes spent 2 or 3 hours in the town and have never seen this man anywhere else but lounging about. We can't make out in these cases whether it is because we are strangers, whether they have made so much money they won't bother with new customers or whether the man himself is incapable of doing repairs and can't get an assistant. Then we find strange anomalies, as, in searching for coffee in 5 or 6 shops in vain and being told there is a serious shortage, nobody can get any, to find a small shop a little further on that does its own roasting and grinding and seems to have an in-exhaustible stock of first-class coffee! Salad cream is unobtainable, then we find one shop with a window full. Yet customers complaining bitterly in the other shops that they can't get any. The queues are mostly on market days for fish and fruit and homemade cakes, but especially the latter. Women don't seem to mind standing in the rain for over an hour, even at the far end of a long queue, when it is quite obvious the cakes will be sold out long before their turn comes.

The bread is of very much better quality here than in Boscastle, and an enormous variety of it in several bakers. There is one first class restaurant with excellent service and good food. The cakes seem to be pre-war with a very high fat content. But how they achieve this when other shops sell cakes like sawdust is a mystery. We think they must have their own farm. The conversation of customers, where-ever we've been, always seems to be on demobbing of friends and relatives or clothing coupons.

VJ Day was quite uneventful as far as we were concerned. However much one told oneself that *Now both wars are well and truly over*, the shadow of the peace, which is no real peace, clouds any real feeling of relief and rejoicing such as one always imagined would come. But apart from that and before the announcement about the atomic bomb, I personally have had for some time, especially at night, a most oppressive feeling of foreboding which I put down to unremembered nightmares. I mean I used to awake feeling I had had some dreadful cataclysmic experience during sleep but without the least idea of the content of the dream.'

336 *Placing a caravan at Pathfinder Village, the 1950s.*

The two women subsequently joined the Plymouth & District Field Club ('very much in our line') and the Whitchurch branch of the Women's Institute ('the secretary and treasurer seem pretty deadly'). In 1946, after the members heard how to make shopping baskets from hedgerow plants, the 'entertainment was provided by Miss Wiens and Miss Passingham'. In 1950 the two women moved to a caravan at Winscombe in Somerset and shortly afterwards to No. 16 Six Acres at Pathfinder Village in Tedburn St Mary. For ten years they served as the community's librarians and were regular winners in the horticultural shows. Miss Passingham had joined the Society of Friends in 1942 and both women attended meetings in Exeter in the 1950s.[353]

WOODBURY

This large village and parish, situated near the Exe Estuary and off the main road from Exeter to Exmouth, had in 1931 some 1,637 residents. The MO diarist's account of Armistice Day in 1937 was corroborated by a journalist who noted it as a 'representative gathering' in which the headmaster marched the schoolchildren in procession headed by the girl guides and choir boys to the church where they had 'a simple but touching service'. The previous year the service had taken place in the evening.[354]

70. Charles Kinsman, Teacher, 1937

Charles Herbert Kinsman (1904-1980), the headmaster of the village school, was born in Totnes where his father was the licensee of the Bay Horse Inn. From at least 1935 he lived in Woodbury's schoolhouse with his wife Violet. They remained there throughout the war years.[355] Mr Kinsman wrote for MO in 1937 and described the events on Armistice Day.[356]

11 November 1937

'10.30 The school's children in procession led by Brownies, Guides, Wolf cubs and Scouts pass the village green.

337 *Woodbury School at which Mr Charles Kinsman worked and lived, 2025.*

10.31 Three women lean over the gates of their houses and remark *Morning, sir, and coldish this morning. The little dears* (referring to infants).

10.32 Two biggest boys without overcoats - one looks

338 Reaction to the news of the Armistice in London, drawn by F. Matania, 1919.

frozen. Leaves whirl along road in gusts of brown-yellow, crisp and dead.

10.34 Look behind and see my wife hurrying along with Baby John in pram. Miss N., one of my assistants, looks pinched with the cold and the teddy bear coat she wears is obviously a cheap one – nasty, coloured brown-yellow.

10.36 Miss F[ulford] marching ahead, a massive and patriotic figure in her Guide uniform, she must be to wear the stuff, halts the leaders and waddles back to ask me the right time. I take the church clock as my guide – we're ten minutes early! Why not march to the church and escort the vicar and choir to The Cross I suggest. She agrees. We right turn and walk up Church Lane.

10.40 Early for once. Last year it was wet and we arrived in church after the service had started.

10.42 Assistant Troop Leader arrives with the odd Guide. *Mr K*, she says, *you've spoilt the whole thing. Time's time and you left two minutes before 10.30am from the school.* I notice a poor little laurel wreath in her hand decorated with poppies. I apologise feebly because I was wrong but I felt like giving her a slap across the face. The dirty little snob and it makes it worse because she's such a pretty kid. She absolutely cut my wife and child standing beside me. I'll get even with her yet, if I don't no one takes a rise out of the pseudo-aristocrats.

10.48 I walk into church to find the vicar. Organist tells me he hasn't arrived yet. And I had to be at the church by 10.30 according to him!

10.49 The Reverend [R. H. Neely] and here boys dash in to robe for the choir. Pleasant-looking little fellows – almost cherubic in countenance.

10.50 Here comes the choir boys and girls and the aged vicar – gowned and mortar board on. He does look ill and smells faintly of raw mutton.

10.52 We move off the few yards to The Cross. I walk with the vicar. Only words he says – *Disgraceful they're running. I'm marching as in yours* and so he is!

10.53 A miserable semi-circle of uniformed children, my scholars. Many women and children, few old men with medals trying to look military. We sing through *Oh God Our Help in Ages Past*, one half being two bars behind the rest. The sun dazzles my eyes I close them and for a minute or so feel the warm rays pulsing through me - a glorious feeling. The prayers are over.

Silence – a child rakes her foot among the leaves. I

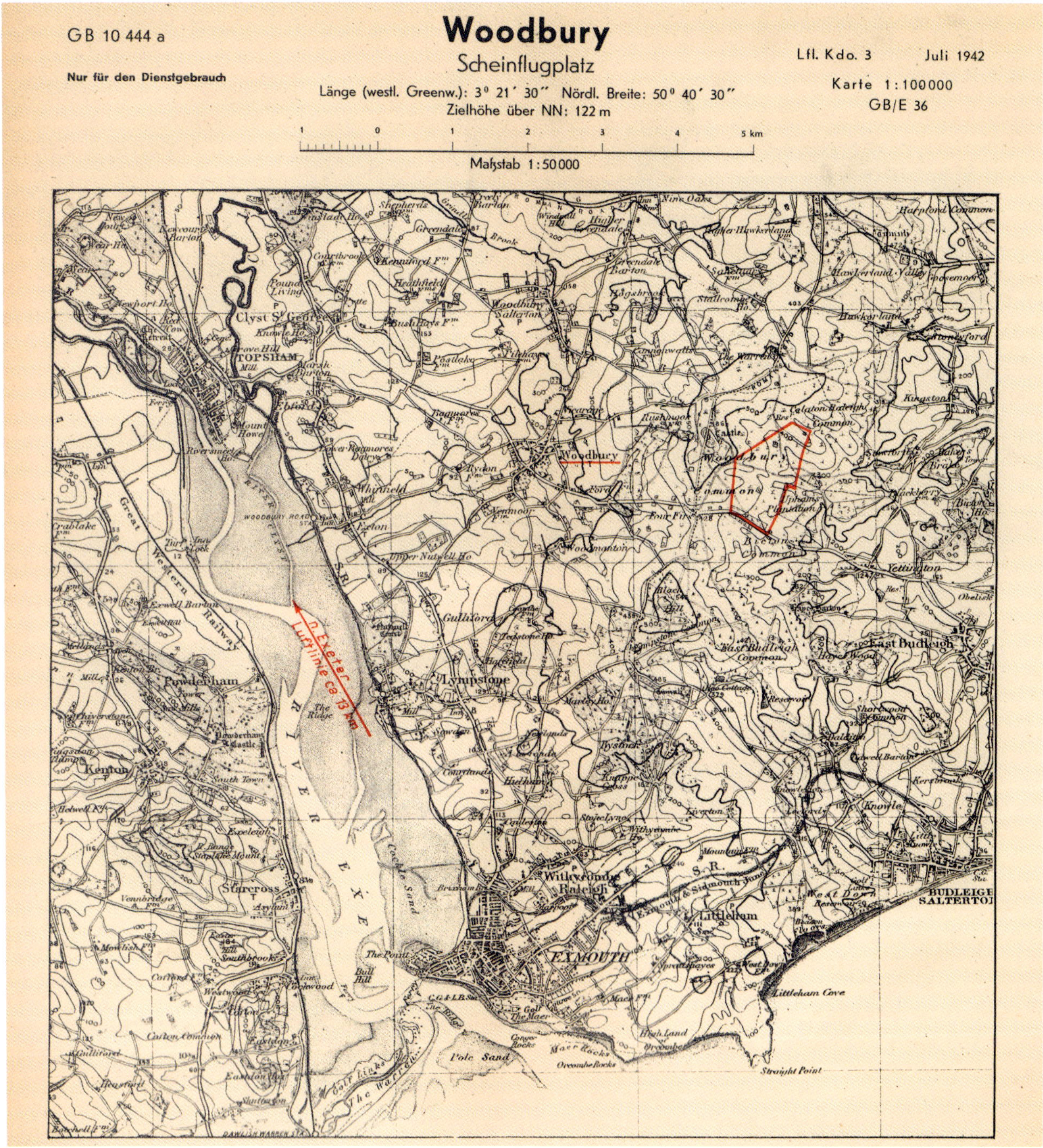

339 The Luftwaffe assessed Woodbury as it did the rest of the county, July 1942.

haven't heard a word of the service. A bugle sounds, is it the Reveille or Last Post? I don't know. How can I grieve for men I never knew and the ones I can hardly place - it's 20 years ago.

The king! The sudden stiffening by the older men.

It's all over. I walk back with the vicar to the church. He's frozen. *Everything went off splendidly*, he said, *but what a disgrace only one Armistice Day Service leaflet left in the church*!

11.00 The clock strikes 11am – we've finished our

service. Three minutes at least ahead of time!

I stroll back to the school with my boys feeling that the service needs changing somehow – for now it means but little to all.'

Eleven years later, in 1948, Mr Kinsman brought a legal action of slander, libel and conspiracy against nine villagers. He was supported by a petition signed by 158 people including the vicar but shortly afterwards left Woodbury. He died in 1980 in London.[357]

WOOLACOMBE

This North Devon seaside resort was anciently part of the parish of Mortehoe and increased in popularity and size in the early 1900s. It became distinguished as one of the centres of training by American troops for the invasion of France in 1944. An Assault Training Centre was established in 1943; over the following eight months thousands of servicemen are thought to have passed through the resort.[358]

71. Alice Raley, Secretary, 1945

Twenty-year-old Miss Alice Patricia Raley (1924-) was born in Lancashire and was working as a secretary in London when the Second World War ended. She observed:

'I'll record my impressions of VJ, as I saw it in a little holiday village on the north coast of Devon – Woolacombe.

I went on holiday in the midst of the excitement - on the Friday night. All day - or from lunchtime onwards, to be exact - there had been VJ crowds in the London streets; paper was showering down from office windows and other things too. There was cheering, shouting, singing all along Oxford Street, Regent Street and Piccadilly. In the evening people were prepared to have another VE night all over again, but no more news came through and somehow it seemed a little flat. When I drove through London to the station, at about 11 o'clock, crowds were little bigger than normal, and excitement had subsided, but the street gutters were choked with rather dirty paper.

That was all I saw of VJ in London. In Devon everyone was much more interested about their holiday - for many people the first seaside holiday for years - and apart from the paper queue in the morning (the only queue I saw during the week) there was little excitement. But on the Wednesday morning, as we walked down to breakfast, the sleepy little place was transformed. Every house had hung out a flag, or was busy doing so, and all down the road excited children

310 Mural entitled 'On the way to the assault boats', by Olin Dows, 1944.

were letting off penny squibs - which weren't dangerous but caused nasty shocks to our less robust nerves. We heard the news on the wireless that morning. The morning papers carried nothing and there were no evening papers. Nobody said very much; they were just sincerely thankful and then went off and really enjoyed themselves, getting quite a kick out of being the first people to be holidaying in peacetime.

That evening we all determined to celebrate. The children - there were hundreds of them - had a bonfire. Private parties sprang up all over the place and the few pubs and hotels were crammed. Everyone was friendly and jolly, as people are in small places. There was no unpleasantness, although most people had much more than their usual quota of drink and travelling went on far into the small hours. It was just grand fun - nobody had so far thought much about the peace. They were leaving that for men when they got home.

Next day we read the papers avidly, and were thankful that we hadn't been in the London crowds. There was more organised celebrating; sports were held in the afternoon and a dance in the evening. Again, everyone was out for a darn good time and they had it. By the next day most of the ardour had died down, which gave people time for recuperating and reflecting.

What reflections there were seemed to be just plain thankfulness; people who had friends and relations in the Far East of course felt it most. But it was grand, feeling that we weren't fighting anyone any longer. Mixed with this thankfulness, though, was the dread thought of the atom bomb and there was also on the part of most people determination to work hard and fight, if need be, for a decent Britain and a lasting peace.

In that little place, where I saw all kinds of ordinary people, young and old, just being joyful, I felt the deep and true humanity of the English race – and feeling that I could have little fear for their future.'

Miss Raley married in 1951.[359]

YEALMPTON

In 1931 this village, situated at the head of the Yealm estuary and some seven miles from Plymouth, had 1,114 residents. The RAF established a transit camp at Bedpark Plantation during the war. The parish did not escape bombing. Altogether, seventeen raids were recorded at Yealmpton and in the surrounding parishes; the first took place on 21 October 1940 and the last on 30 April 1943. The most destructive were in late 1940 when a journalist reported:

'Bombs which fell at Yealmpton killed five rabbits and injured two bullocks. Windows were blown out at Gnaton, the residence of Lieut. Colonel J. Craven Hoyle, and of some farmhouses and a cornfield was set alight. The tennis lawn in front of Alston Hall, Yealmpton, home of Major L. D. W. Sayers and Mrs Sayers, was damaged by a bomb and all the windows of the house were smashed. Two other bombs fell on land a quarter of a mile away and others were dropped in open country and the sea.'

It has been estimated that Yealmpton had seventeen air raids and that on 27/28 November 1940 more than 2,000 incendiaries and high explosive bombs fell in Yealmpton, Revelstoke and Newton Ferrers.[360]

72. John Landon, Engineer, 1942

John Charles Landon (1916-2010), a civil engineer, wrote for MO in 1942. He was born in Bedford and on the eve of the war lived at Sungarth, a detached house on the crest of Bowden Hill.[361]

25 February 1942

His daily routine was not obviously interesting:

'7.45 Rise and breakfast

8.30 Leave home for dockyard

9.00 Arrive dockyard and office work until 13.00

13.00 – 14.00 Lunch at canteen

14.00 Office work & visit to jobs outside

17.30 Leave dockyard and arrive home 18.00 for the *news*

***LEFT:* 341** *Aerial photograph of the Yealm estuary, 15 February 1943.*

18.30 Dinner

19.30 Bridge until 22.00

22.00 Supper & go to bed about 22.30'

342 Sungarth, Bowden Hill in Yealmpton, the home of Mr John Landon in 1942.

Directives: post-war society and death

Two of his answers to MO revealed thoughts on his future. In January 1942 he wrote:

> 'I feel that the war has given me a better sense of proportion and appreciation of true values. Things that seemed so important before the war were in actual fact very unimportant. Before the war I was very concerned about the future. Now the future is so problematical that I am content to *just wait and see*.'

He added in March:

> 'I hardly think about death now. Last year, after being in Plymouth through the heavy raids, I did often think about it and rather fatalistically did not expect to get through safely. Since then, I have met my fiancée and future wife, and the desire to live is such, that I hardly ever contemplate that the other thing could happen, in spite of the fact that I am a Home Guardsman and training to fight.'

A year later Mr Landon married Margaret Dennis, who lived at Valetta, in the parish church at Yealmpton. After the war he appears to have found employment in two colonies, Hong Kong and Singapore.[362]

***LEFT:* 343** *British anti-aircraft defences, undated.*

***ABOVE:* 344** *A Spotter, undated.*

CONCLUSION

Our Writers chronicled Britain during one of its most critical periods and in doing so they each preserved a version of their own lives. Many of them were vivid social commentators and their texts have a freshness which helps us in understanding the reshaping of society in the late 1940s when the war continued to overshadow Britain. Life became impacted by new political, economic and social forces including nuclear weapons, the Cold War, the dissolving of the British Empire, the creation of the United Nations, the election of a Socialist government, the establishment of the National Health Service and immigration from the Caribbean.

In 1945 blackout curtains were taken down, barbed wire was removed from beaches, public shelters were dismantled and the names of the fallen were added to Great War memorials. Some social activities had been maintained on a reduced scale: the middle classes in Budleigh Salterton continued to gossip over their games of bridge, the gentry hunted foxes in the countryside at Eggesford and anglers continued to fish in the River Dart. Tourism had been impacted but it quickly began to reach pre-war levels as holiday-makers eagerly escaped war-torn London and the cities of the Midlands and industrial North. They found that the war had dramatically altered the landscape of Plymouth and Exeter but the physical changes were relatively light in the resorts.

Since then life itself has, however, greatly changed: the county's population has become more diverse, world travel has become commonplace and technology links together, if not determines, the threads of our daily lives. Even as the landscape remains familiar, modern life has altered immeasurably.

Overriding change followed VJ Day when the bedrock of British society altered; since then we have lived within a very different social and political framework. A consensus grew out of the ashes of war that it was imperative that Western Europe must prevent further armed conflict and build a fairer, peaceful and safer society. The post-war social-democratic state was established amidst the yearning for greater egalitarianism.

It was at this point that Western Europe was faced with two separate and distinct developments regarding imperialism. In the late 1940s Europe began to agree that its colonies across Africa, the Americas and Asia should, and would, be replaced by self-determination: Britain saw

345 Visiting Kent's Cavern during wartime.

its empire comprising a quarter of the world dissolve in the 1950s and 1960s. Belgium, Denmark, France, Italy, the Netherlands, Portugal and Spain likewise gradually relinquished imperialism but there remain territorial outposts across the globe.

Even as the larger world became independent, Eastern Europe augmented the Soviet Empire. In 1949 Western Europe responded with an alliance with the United States and Canada through the establishment of the North Atlantic Treaty Organisation. Four decades later, the unexpected collapse of the Soviet Union brought in its wake unparalleled freedom for a generation of Europeans. Western Europe has largely been at peace since 1945, the longest period in its modern history.

The values that underpin our society were rethought following the struggles of the wartime generation. That post-war consensus was shattered firstly by Russia's attack on Ukraine in 2014 and most recently by the United States' open ambitions in Canada and Greenland. We have returned to the prospect of Might being unrestrained by Right; a state's power to seize control of another people through violence or deceit is no longer nominally tempered by the rule of law or moral legitimacy. The global systems which were established after 1945 appear to be crumbling. Moreover, human rights are valued less than before in the face of an advance of raw power and economic development. It is not just the West but the entire world which appears to be in a pivotal moment of change: the global order is being recast.

Perhaps this is a useful moment to examine the experiences of the thirties and forties when a generation faced a descent into chaos, anarchy and barbarism. Fear, hardship, privation, aerial bombardment, destruction and death became commonplace. So too did courage, stoicism and determination, let alone resilience.

There are valuable lessons to be learned from the late 1930s and early 1940s. One involves shared concerns about the movement of people. From the 1500s through to the 1930s England (and later Britain) experienced two great flows of migrants: from the late sixteenth century through to 1807 millions of Africans were taken to the slave islands while an even greater number of White British economic migrants settled in colonies across the Empire. This was suddenly interrupted in 1939 when several million children, women and men sought shelter in parts of the country considered safe. Many thousands of these refugees and evacuees arrived in Devon. Our Writers have shown that they were welcomed by some but were also disparaged, snubbed and resented

346 Jewish women and children liberated from a concentration camp in Austria.

by others. For the latter segment of society there were class and cultural differences which proved too overwhelming to overcome. In the following decades Devon did not experience massive immigration from the Caribbean nor did it receive many economic migrants from Asia. Instead, not until the opening decades of the twenty-first century did the first substantial wave of immigration since the war take place.

Once again, society is divided between those who feel a moral compulsion to offer asylum to fellow human beings in need and those others who resent migrants because of competition for services, housing and resources. However, it is the marked cultural differences which are equally problematic: most modern migrants are not White or Christian. It may help us to remember that the Second World War great migration involved people very much like those already resident in the county but even their differences were regarded as being too great to tolerate. Another important distinction between then and now is that from 1939 to 1945 evacuees and servicemen were compulsorily billeted in private homes whereas modern migrants and asylum seekers are housed in accommodation organised by the state.

The Writers raise another matter for consideration for the modern generation which, since Covid, has perceived levels of anxiety as being almost unique to the early twenty-first century. During the war all members of society had faced the possibility of invasion, some lived with the sound of air raid sirens and everyone heard daily news which included reports of the deaths of civilians as well as of servicemen. More than a hundred thousand Devonians suffered repeated days and nights of bombing. The dislocation of many in society, which produced refugees and evacuees, separated family and friends. Some children were placed in homes in which they suffered abuse of many different kinds and levels. In 1945, in contrast with today, any concerns about the impact of these experiences remained private rather than were publicly acknowledged or addressed.

The war's seminal moment may have been the appearance in 1945 of images of the concentration camps: the savage barbarity of the Nazis was confirmed amidst public feelings of anguish, repulsion and horror. During VE and VJ Days, and in the days and years that followed, Devonians reflected upon the cost of victory in terms of the loss of British life and the destruction of local buildings. In the early 1940s Devon had only experienced bombing from airplanes; it was spared the flying bombs, those early cruise missiles also known as the buzz bombs or the doodlebugs. Decades later, our modern missiles and drones are unthinkably more destructive. In 1937 Britain looked upon the bombing of the cities of Spain and realised that this level of destruction would follow from a British war with Germany. Today we see the annihilation of Syria, Gaza and Ukraine and understand how much more comprehensive the destruction of modern warfare has become. Portions of historic Plymouth and Exeter escaped bombardment in the 1940s; it is unlikely any remnants would survive today.

Just as in the late 1930s, we too are rearming and speculate openly about war in Europe. The continuity of the Western Liberal Democracies is once again threatened on their own soil. On 3 September 1939 Britain was in a state of disbelief when war finally came. Generations later, how soon will that day dawn for us?

Our MO Writers can teach us much about the nature of war but also draw attention to the expected and the unexpected, the avoidable and the unavoidable. Three years after the war ended Winston Churchill paraphrased Hegel when he said 'It has been well said that the only lesson we learn from history is that we do not learn from history'. Perhaps this collection of writings will help dispel that assertion.

347 Russian bombing of Lviv, 7 July 2023. In 2025 Britain learns about the nature of destruction in Ukraine from social media in a similar manner to how it watched news reels of the Nazi bombardment during Spain's civil war in the 1930s.

ILLUSTRATION SOURCES

Images appear through the courtesy of private individuals and trustees of forty-two organisations. Extensive efforts have been made to identify all copyright holders.

Yale University Library, **frontispiece**, Ms 671

Mitchell Library, State Library of New South Wales, **1**, 74VKm80aKA5A; **52**, 9WZW3gpY

David Rumsey Collection, **2**, **63**, **77**, **110**, **193**, **214**, **316**

University of Minnesota Libraries, Upper Midwest Literary Archives **3**, msp03681; **5**, msp03996; **6**, msp03723; **7**, msp03739; **12**, msp03662; **13**, msp04095; **14**, msp03666; **15**, msp03621; **18**, msp03393; **19**, msp03412; **20**, msp03422; **21**, msp03414; **28**, msp03269; **45**, msp03542; **59**, msp03125; **62**, msp03522; **64**, msp03522; **69**, msp03598; **70**, msp03563; **80**, msp03290; **83**, msp03532; **86**, msp03406; **91**, msp03489; **93**, msp03622; **95**, msp00355; **96**, msp03323; **97**, msp03315; **98**, msp03425; **116**, msp03359; **117**, msp03284; **127**, msp03649; **128**, msp0365; **165**, msp03560; **166**, msp03619; **167**, msp03661; **168**, msp03477; **199**, msp03151; **202**, msp03158b; **203**, msp03254; **204**, msp03466; **206**, mpw00088; **207**, msp03643; **224**, msp04037; **238**, msp03444; **239**, mpw00426; **240**, msp03114; **272**, msp03287; **277**, msp03733; **329**, msp03322; **343**, msp04040; **344**, msp04038

National Archives (USA), **4**, 44266314; **23**, 205583033; **28**, 12004000; **35**, 312320241; **50**, 1858202903; **53**, 261887052; **54**, 261887052; **60**, 515889; **65**, 44267185; **71**, 266694536; **73**, 234901730; **78**, 261887052; **79**, 261887052; **81**, 44267089; **82**, 4426726; **85**, 329591472; **90**, 513972; **92**, 7387441; **114**, 350881034; **129**, 44-PA-385; **136**, 261887242; **137**, 261887242; **138**, 261887242; **151**, 4426686; **173**, 220882273; **175**, 220898629; **190**, 148728174; **208**, 535858; **210**, 205575662; **211**, 220885898; **213**, 29066723; **215**, 220882; **219**, 286956404; **222**, 179036534; **223**, 540150; **236**, 6384967 & 6384966; **261**, 333363592; **269**, 313336143; **289**, 6384968; **290**, 313336823; **291**, 261887220; **298**, 513688; **301**, 540151; **305**, 12003993; **310**, 12003991; **317**, 261887991; **318**, 63797923; **320**, 261887991; **321**, 204886430; **322**, 204886442; **323**, 205578694; **324**, 205578410; **325**, 205578391; **326**, 205578691; **327**, 176887876; **328**, 176887822; **330**, 220898451; **333-4**, 80709AC; **338**, 329569596; **339**, 241202451; **340**, 6384977 **341**, 312320199; **346**, 531345

New York Public Libraries, **8**, 1213887; **29** & **237**, George Arents Collection

Private collections, **9**, **32-3**, **55**, **68**, **74-5**, **88**, **106**, **109**, **111-112**, **125-6**, **131-2**, **139-44**, **146**, **152**, **154**, **176**, **180-3**, **185**, **200**, **225-34**, **253**, **255-6**, **262-6**, **268**, **281**, **284**, **311**

Yale Center for British Art, **10**, B1975.4.1940; **31**, B1977.14.6093; **40**, B1977.14.354; **41**, B1975.4.740; **105**, B1977.14.6302; **177**, B1975.4.1513; **188**, B1977.14.4689; **212**, B1977.14.312; **217**, B1976.7.105; **218**, B1975.4.1929; **275**, B1981.25.173

Rijksmuseum, **11**, RP-T-1989-21; **34**, RP-F-T04655; **47**, NG-2006-52-7; **56**, RP-P-2018-801, *Weekly Illustrated Coronation souvenir and guide*, 24 March 1937; **76**, RP-F-F00681-AV; **94**, NG-2012-1-1

National Army Museum, **16**, 2000-05-1-11; **244-7**, 1993.11.1.97.1; 1993-11-1-96-1; 1993-11.1-104-1; 1993-11-1-117-1; **254**, 2019-02-17-1-1; **314**, 1999-01-36-1

Boston Public Library, **17**, 06 10 026065

University of North Texas, **22**, b2842869; **205**, ark:/67531/metadc540

Libraries & Archives Canada, **24**, R112-941-8-E, volume 36421; 315, box 36421, file UK-24108, item 6069420

University of California Berkeley, Bancroft Library, **84-5**, BANC PIC 2005.008:247-F; **87**, BANC PIC 2005.171:020—D; **118-119**, BANC PIC 2005.171:067-8—D

Library of Congress, **25**, D-009423 lot 3476; **26**, D-009999 lot 2252; **46**, BANC PIC 2005.171:048-D; **51**, LC-H22-D9159; **57**, Congress, LC-B2-3848-4; **99**, D-010011 LOT 2252; **100**, D-010009 LOT 2252; **101**, D-010008 LOT 2252; **107**, LOT 13415, no. 216; **195-7**, LOT 13415, nos 791, 793 & 790; **241**, PR 13 CN 2003:083, no. 8; **282**,

Lot 13415, no. 294; **296**, LC-F9-02-4501-028A, no. 3; **297**, LC-F9-02-4501-027A, no. 4; **313**, Lot 13415, no. 930

Hennepin County Library, **27**, MPWOO290; **122**, MPW00413; **273**, MPW00348; **300**, MPW00533

Wellcome Library, **30**, EPH651; **36**, 679461i; **121**, 202771; **123**, EPH/50/4; **189**, 97998i; **192**, 10932i; **210**, EPH/37/29; **235**, 24441i; **242**, y39awg6z

Victoria & Albert Museum, **37**, 21-1872

Metropolitan Museum of Art, **38**, 13.27.2; **108**, 1979.135.5

Boyden's Antiques & Interiors, **42-4**

Walters Art Museum, Baltimore, **66**, 37.943

Guy Peppiatt Fine Art, **71**

Museums Victoria, **58**, NU 41635; **72**, 42635

Milner Library, Illinois State University, **61**, ww2 uk-printed allies hitting back 037; **89**, ww2 uk-printed loose talk can cost lives 030

State Library New South Wales, **102-104**, ACP Magazines Ltd archive

National Library of Scotland, **120**, GFB.1

Unilever Archives & Records Management, **124**, 2001-80

Wander AG Archive, **130**

Getty Museum Collection, **133**, 84.XD.1157.2298

Chris Beetles Gallery, St James's, London, **134**

Cleveland Museum of Art, **135**, 2005.200

Express & Echo, **155-64**

TuckDB Ephemera, **171-2**

National Gallery of Art, **178**, 1951.16.195

Art Institute of Chicago, **179**, 1932.717; **186**, 1972.56

Mark Murray Fine Art, New York, **191**

Mclean County Museum of History, **248-51**, collection of Wilbur G. Ball

Pilsudski Institute of America, **258**

Pennsylvania State University, **276**

Mass Observation Archive, **220**, SR 233; **285**, SR 222.

Naval History and Heritage Command, **292-5**, 80-G-283500-1 & 80-G-K-2054-5; **299**, 88-199-EA; **302**, 80-G-252083; **303**, 80-G-252091; **304**, 80-G-253360; **306**, 80-G-251992; **307**, 80-G-K-1181; **308**, 88-199-DZ; **309**, 80-G-252091; **331-2**, 88-199-EF

London Record Society, **319**

Tedburn History & Information Society, **336**

University of North Carolina Greensboro Women Veterans Historical Project, **345**

Roman Baluk **347**, Lviv, 7 July 2023

The author **39**, **48**, **67**, **113**, **115**, **145**, **147**, **148**, **153**, **169-70**, **174**, **187**, **194**, **198**, **201**, **216**, **221**, **243**, **252**, **257**, **260**, **267**, **270-1**, **279**, **335**, **337**, **342**

Front cover illustrations taken from Fougasse's *Careless Talk Cost Life*. Back cover images courtesy (left and right) *Express & Echo* and centre, J. Paul Getty Museum, 85.XM.130.69.

REFERENCES

Diaries, day-surveys, file reports, topic collections and directive responses are located at the Mass Observation archive in the care of the University of Sussex and located at the Keep, Brighton.

1 *National Register United Kingdom and Isle of Man Statistics of Population on 29th September 1939* (London, 1939), p5.
2 The Keep, DS 676 (Aug. 1938).
3 The Keep, TC 25.
4 The Keep, D 5383. The fathers of Audrey and Colin Neck were brothers.
5 The Keep, DS 125 (Aug. 1938).
6 The Keep, DS 304 (July 1937).
7 Tom Jeffrey, 'Mass Observation A Short History' 10 (1999 edn).
8 The Keep, DS 909. A 'Miss Bere' wrote a day-survey in 1938 but this was not salvaged following a flood in the MO offices before the archive relocated; DR 3251 (July 1942).
9 The Keep, DR 1172 (Jan. 1939).
10 The Keep, D 5454 (May 1941 – June 1942).
11 The Keep, D 5427 (1941); D 5342 (1941).
12 The Keep, DR 1047 (June 1939).
13 The Keep, DR 2083 (June 1939).
14 The Keep, DR 1036 (Dec. 1940).
15 The Keep, D 5372 (1944).
16 *Daily Record*, 7 Jan. 1939; *Daily Mirror*, 31 July 1939; The Keep, TC 38 (music, dancing and jazz, 1939-41), box 2.
17 The Keep, TC 28 (dreams, 1937-48).
18 *Liverpool Evening Express*, 12 Feb. 1942.
19 The Keep, D 5349 (1944); DS 443 (July 1937); DR 2806 (Feb. 1942); DR 1099 (July 1939); D 5098 (1945).
20 The Keep, DR 2167 (June 1939).
21 The Keep, TC 65, record by D. H.
22 The Keep, DR 1086 (June 1939).
23 The Keep, DR 1085 (June 1939).
24 The Keep, DR 1528 (June 1939). The ten writers comprised F. R. Berkett Barker at Dawlish (DR 2693); Jessie Blundun at Sidmouth (DR 1577); Kenneth MacRae Burnett in Plymouth (DS 676); H. M. Butt in Plymouth (DR 3278); John Griffiths of Plymouth (DR 2372); Juliet L. Parker of Plymouth (DR 3251); Charles Phillips of Abbotskerswell (DR 1172); R. J. Powell of Plymouth (DR 1528. In his self-report Powell noted he was born in Bristol, was raised by his aunt and uncle and had worked in Yeovil, Southampton and throughout Devon and Cornwall.); Lewis Taylor of Exeter (D 2334); Minnie Watson of Monkokehampton (DR 3457).
25 The Keep, DR 3369 (March 1943).
26 The Keep, TC 62 (anti-Semitism, 1939-51).
27 The Keep, DR 1669 (April 1943).
28 The Keep, DR 2823 (July 1942).
29 The Keep, DR 1636 (April 1943).
30 The Keep, DR 2881 (April 1943).
31 The Keep, DR 3133 (July 1943).
32 The Keep, DR 2802 (Feb. 1942).
33 The Keep, TC 70 (transport, 1937-1943, 1963).
34 The Keep, DR 3278 (May 1943).
35 *Mass-Observation Report on Juvenile Drinking* (London, 1945), pp6, 9-11, 14.
36 *Oxford English Dictionary*.
37 The Keep, Directive Respondents 1029 & 2177 (June 1939).
38 The Keep, DR 1085 (June 1939).
39 The Keep, Directive Respondents 2177, 2165 & 2142 (June 1939).
40 The Keep, DR 2695 (July 1942).
41 The Keep, DR 1072 (July 1942) & TC 25.
42 The Keep, DR 1095 (June 1942).
43 The Keep, TC 29 (forces, men in the forces, 1939 – 1956), box 4; DR 3251 (July 1942).
44 The Keep, D 5383 (Sept. 1939 – June 1940).
45 *National Register United Kingdom and Isle of Man Statistics of Population on 29th September, 1939*, p5.
46 The Keep, D 5388 (Feb. – Dec. 1940). Mr and Mrs Norman were by this time living in Harpenden, Hertfordshire; *Selby Times*, 7 July 1916.
47 S. J. Hess, 'Civilian Evacuation to Devon in the Second World War', Univ. of Exeter PhD thesis (2006), pp262-3, 420-1.
48 The Keep, D 5039 (1940).
49 The Keep, D 5294 (1940).
50 The Keep, DS 153 (June 1937 – Sept. 1938).
51 The Keep, D 5390 (1940).
52 *Western Morning News*, 19 Aug. 1944.

53 The Keep, D 5127 (March – August 1942).

54 The Keep, D 5399 (1942).

55 The Keep, TC 35 (air raid shelter competition).

56 *Torbay Express*, 2 Sept. 1939.

57 British Online Archives, Military Intelligence Files: Land, Sea & Air, 1938-1974, MOI, Home Intelligence Weekly report, No. 218, 7 Dec. 1944.

58 The Keep, D 5039.1

59 Casualties Book. This volume was in private ownership in 2016 when I received a copy of it on a cd. Its current location is unknown. William Roper Harvey was injured in the bombing at the hotel.

60 The Keep, D 5390 (1941).

61 The Keep, D 5376 (1944).

62 The Keep, DR 2693 (June 1942).

63 The Keep, DR 1075 (April 1944).

64 The Keep, DR 2336 (July 1939; DS 346 (March 1937 – Sept. 1938); DR 2974 (Oct. 1943).

65 The Keep, DR 1094 (Dec. 1942); Critic, 'A London Diary', *The New Statesman and Nation* (12 Dec. 1942), p386. A year earlier Hugh Dalton had recorded this story in his own diary: John Wilmot, Labour MP for Kennington 'relates that a number of spinsters were sitting at long tables in a room in the Censorship Department going through intercepted correspondence. An old Blimp was in charge, on whom one spinster eagerly advanced and, holding up a letter, said *I am quite sure, sir, that this letter is by a Lesbian.* Whereupon Blimp, raising his eyebrows and his voice, cried *God, madam, I wonder if any of you girls can speak Lesbian*? Wilmot says this story was told to Miss Cracknell [private secretary to Sir Frederick Leith-Ross], who didn't see the point, and then to Miss Wood who did, and explained it to Miss Cracknell afterwards.': Ben Pimlott (ed.), *The Second World War Diaries of Hugh Dalton, 1940-45* (London, 1986), p334.

66 The Keep, DR 2165 (Dec., August & July 1942).

67 *Birmingham Daily Gazette*, 16 Oct. 1940; The Keep, DR 2844 (Feb. 1942).

68 Judith M. Bennett, 'Lesbian Like and the Social History of Lesbianisms', *Journal of the History of Sexuality* 9:1-2 (Jan./April 2000), pp11-12.

69 The Keep, TC 40 (post-war hopes, 1944); *Brixham Western Guardian*, 5 Dec. 1946; *Torbay Express*, 18 Sept. 1968. Edward Thomas Scott, a gunner, lived at 5 Salisbury Road.

70 The Keep, D 5118 (1943).

71 The Keep, TC 29 (forces, men in the forces, 1939-1956), box 2.

72 The Keep, DR 3576 (Aug. 1944).

73 The Keep, D 5283 (1943).

74 The Keep, DR 1264 (June 1944).

75 The Keep, TC 32 (women in warfare).

76 *Torbay Express*, 23 July 1940, 30 Aug. 1940.

77 The Keep, DS 452.

78 Ancestry, 1939 Register, Newton Abbot & Kingsbridge; *Exeter & Plymouth Gazette*, 6 April 1939; *Western Morning News*, 3 April 1940, 26 April 1944, 3 March 1961.

79 W. G. Hoskins, *Devon* (Newton Abbot, 1954), p523.

80 *Bromley & West Kent Mercury*, 21 Aug. 1942.

81 The Keep, DR 2796 (June 1942); Unidentified response (August 1942).

82 Hoskins, *Devon*, p523; *National Register*, p5; Hess, 'Civilian Evacuation', pp420-1, 449-50.

83 Wasley, *War*, p29; *North Devon Journal*, 7 Sept. 1939.

84 National Archives (USA), 12407455.

85 British Online Archives, Military Intelligence Files: Land, Sea & Air, 1938-1974, MOI, 88 89, points from regions; 17, No. 82, points from regions secret; 70, points from regions; 6 7 2 8 3 9 4, No. 2 New series, daily summary of information; 292 293 2 294 3 295, secret Ministry of Information weekly report by home intelligence, No. 13.

86 The Keep, TC 29 (forces, men in the forces, 1939-1956), box 2.

87 *Western Morning News*, 27 Nov. 1940.

88 Wasley, *War*, pp186-8.

89 *North Devon Journal*, 10 May 1945.

90 National Archives, AIR 22/75, RAF Weekly Intelligence, August 1941 – May 1942, Appendix A, p13; Walsey, *War*, p91.

91 Arthur Mee, *Devon* (London, 1953), p37.

92 *North Devon Journal*, 9 March 1939, 21 Dec. 1938.

93 The Keep, DS 008 & DR 1067 (Jan. & Feb. 1939).

94 Todd Gray, *Blackshirts in Devon* (Exeter, 2006), pp11, 18, 55, 64, 67, 75, 94, 100-105, 109-110, 127-30, 150, 160, 192-3, 279.

95 *North Devon Journal*, 29 June 1939, 22 Feb. 1940, 13 Nov. 1941, 4 May 1944. Their daughter Helen was born on 1 May 1944 in Middlesex.

96 The Keep, D 5091 & DR 2546 (Oct. 40 & Aug. 1942). Mr Gulliver also wrote (as EG) in 1942 & 1943 for MO following his return to Beckenham: The Keep TC 25.

97 Heritage Gateway, MDV50874.

98 The Keep, TC 5.

99 Philippa Bernard, *No End to Snowdrops* (2012), chapter 2.

100 The Keep, DS 461. He also answered a directive in November 1939: DR 2296 (Nov. 1939). Extracts from the account were published in Humphrey Jennings & Charles Madge (ed.), *May the Twelfth: Mass-Observation Day-Surveys 1937 by two hundred observers* (London, 1937), pp53, 225, 281, 299, 301. Kathleen Raine was one of the five junior editors.

101 *Kelly's Directory of Devonshire, 1939* (London, 1939), pp70-1; Hoskins, *Devon*, p523.

102 *Newcastle Journal*, 7 July 1952 & 25 April 1979; *Newcastle Evening Chronicle*, 14 July 1945; The Keep, D 5238 (1944).

103 *Newcastle Journal*, 25 April 1979.

104 The Keep, DS 304 (1937).

105 *Kelly's Directory of Devonshire, 1939*, pp78-9; *National Register*, p5; Hoskins, *Devon*, p524.

106 *National Register*, p5; Hess, 'Civilian Evacuation', pp420-1, 460; *North Devon Journal*, 19 July 1945.

107 *Western Times,* 22 Nov. 1940.

108 The Keep, DR 1980 (Sept. 1940).

109 The Keep, D 5377 (1940).

110 https://www.bidefordarchive.org.uk, 'Some memories of World War 2 in Bideford', 1/4/2013, accessed 18 April 2025.

111 *North Devon Journal*, 27 March & 3 April 1941, 6 Sept. 1945 & 3 Jan. 1946.

112 Heritage Gateway, MDV43276.

113 The Keep, TC 20 (reading habits, 1937-47), box 3.

114 *Exeter & Plymouth Gazette*, 10 Feb. 1930; The Keep, D 5263 & unidentified diarists (1939 entries); *North Devon Journal*, 3 July 1941.

115 The Keep, DR 1029 (June 1939).

116 The Keep, DR 1029 (June 1939).

117 Included as spare page with D 5250 (1939 entries).

118 The Keep, D 5398; DR 2493 (Aug.–Oct., Dec. 1940 and February 1942). Miss Pickwoad also wrote a three-page account of her first year in the Land Army: The Keep, TC 32 (women in warfare).

119 The Keep, TC 59 (children and education, 1937-52), box 1.

120 The Keep, D 5023; DR 5023 (Feb. 1949, Jan. 1951).

121 Ancestry, Bell family tree, accessed 1 Aug. 2025.

122 *Kelly's Directory of Devonshire, 1939*, pp162-3.

123 Harry Clement, *No Time to Kiss Goodbye* (no place of publication, 1995), iv-vi, 7-10. *Evening Dispatch*, 23 July 1942; *Shields Daily Gazette*, 4 Nov. 1944; *Western Morning News*, 7 & 8 Oct. 1941; hhtps://www.northdevoncoast-nl.org.uk.aircrash sites, accessed 23 May 2025.

124 *Western Daily Press*, 30 Dec. 1943.

125 The Keep, DS 293; DR 1241 (Jan. 1939, Jan. & Sept. 1940).

126 The Keep, DR 1241 (Jan. 1940); *Picture Post* 8:2, 13 July 1940; Ancestry, Clubley/Coy Tree, accessed 1 Aug. 2025.

127 *Torbay Express*, 23 May 1936; The Keep, DR 2874 (May 1943).

128 *National Register*, p5; Hess, 'Civilian Evacuation', p420.

129 Hess, 'Civilian Evacuation', pp89, 124, 216, 266.

130 The Keep, TC 5 (evacuation), Box 5.

131 *West London Observer*, 25 October 1940; Wasley, *War*, p186.

132 British Online Archives, Military Intelligence Files: Land, Sea & Air, 1938-1974, MOI, 40, No. 77, daily report on morale.

133 *Tiverton Gazette*, 31 Aug. 1920.

134 The Keep, DR 1558 (May-July 1939, Feb., June, Aug. & Sept.-Oct., Dec., 1940, April, Oct. Dec. 1942); DS 139 (1937).

135 Hoskins, *Devon*, p526; *Birmingham Daily Gazette*, 27 Nov. 1939; *Edinburgh Evening News*, 5 April 1941; *Western Morning News*, 1 April 1942; *South Western Star*, 10 April 1941.

136 The Keep, DS 349. He can be confused with J. Hughes, a moulder of Sheffield, who also wrote a day-survey in 1937.

137 *Middlesex County Times*, 21 May 1938; *Hampstead News*, 22 Sept. 1961; England & Wales Civil Registration Death Index, 1916-2007, p411.

138 *National Register*, p5.

139 The Keep, DR 2024 (Nov. 1939).

140 The Keep, D 5178 (1942).

141 The Keep, D 5233 (1945).

142 The Keep, D 5454 (May 1941 – June 1942).

143 The Keep, D 5447 (1942).

144 The Keep, D 5445 (1942).

145 The Keep, D 5402 (1942).

146 British Online Archives, Military Intelligence Files: Land, Sea & Air, 1938-1974, MOI, Rumours 25 May 1940; Action Points, 22 June 1940; Points from Regions, 22 June, 16 July 9, 11, 14, 19, 21 & 23 August & 18 Sept. 1940.

147 The Keep, DR 1629 (May, July & Oct. 1939).

148 Ancestry, Thomas/Setterfield/Lloyd/Raymond/Holman & Fulford family tree, accessed 1 Aug. 2025.

149 The Keep, DR 2269 (Oct. & Nov. 1939, Jan., Feb. & May 1940, March 1948). See also TC 20 (reading habits), box 3.

150 The Keep, D 5098 (1940-2, 1944-51). Mr Harpur's brother Caldwell was Diarist 1074.

151 Ancestry, Charlton/Squire/Carryer/Cokkinis family tree, accessed 1 Aug. 2025.

152 The Keep, D 5404 (1940) & DR 2047 (May – June, Sept. 1939, Feb. 1940, Feb.-March 1942, April 1947).

153 The Keep, TC 23 (air raids, 1938-45), box 9.

154 I am grateful to Stella Loterijman for information she has shared about her family; Ancestry, Guy Barker Jan 2010, accessed 5 Aug. 2025.

155 *Picture Post* 5:5 (4 Nov. 1939); The Keep, D 5149 (15 July 1941 – 26 Feb. 1942), DR 2961 (Feb., May, July, Sept., Nov., 1942, Jan., June, Dec. 1943).

156 O Lord, deliver me from the man of excellent intention and impure heart: for the heart is deceitful above all things, and desperately wicked.

157 *Daily Mail*, 22 March 1975.

158 The Keep, DR 3049 (March 1942); *E&E*, 28 Feb. 1940. There is no mention in the official university lists of staff or students: *Exeter University Register 1893 – 1962* (Exeter, 1970). He also submitted a report on Indian Independence Day on 30 January 1942 in Glasgow. He gave his address as the National Westminster Bank, Newtown, Mont[?gomeryshire]: The Keep, TC 25.

159 The Keep, DR 3049 (March 1942).

160 The Keep, DR 3398 (April 1943).

161 Ancestry, Masterson/Rees/Waterhouse/Payne family tree, accessed 1 Aug. 2025.

162 *Western Morning News*, 25 April 1942; *Torbay Express*, 15 Nov. 1944; Casualties Book; *E&E*, 21 Oct. 1940.

163 The Keep, DR 2928 (Feb., April – May, Aug., Oct. 1942, Jan., April, Dec. 1947, Sept. 1950 & Jan. 1951).

164 The Keep, TC 43 (propaganda and morale, 1939-44).

165 National Archives, HO334/190/32075; Ivana Markova & Andrew Jahoda, 'Gustav Jahoda', *Biographical Memoirs of Fellows of the British Academy*, XVIII, pp155-74.

166 Hess, 'Civilian Evacuation', pp228, 420.

167 British Online Archives, Military Intelligence Files: Land, Sea & Air, 1938-1974, MOI, 852, Secret, Ministry of Information Home Intelligence Weekly Report.

168 The Keep, DS 316 (July – Sept. 1938).

169 The Keep, D 5388 (1939-40); Ancestry, Steffi's Tree, accessed 13 Aug. 2025; https://nolessapersonage.uk.

170 The Keep, D 5240 (17 Jan. – 1 Dec. 1943) & DR 1048 (1939-55). The responses to the November, 1955, directive are too fragile for examination.

171 The Keep, D 5240 (1940).

172 The Keep, DR 2347 (Sept. 1940); *The Queen*, 13 April 1932.

173 Elizabeth Maslen, 'Mitchison [nee Haldane), Naomi Mary Margaret, Lady Mitchison', *Dictionary of National Biogrraphy*.

174 Judith M. Heimann, *The Most Offending Soul Alive* (Honolulu, 1997), pp25, 114.

175 *Western Daily Press*, 25 July 1940; *North Devon Journal*, 17 July 1941; *Cheltenham Chronicle*, 16 March 1946.

176 Jean Storry, *At Badminton with B. M. B. by those who were there* (Bristol, 1982), p25.

177 *Independent*, 29 April 1994.

178 The Keep, D 5378 (1942).

179 Imogen Woodberry, 'Varieties of Sexual Experience', in James Purdon (ed.), *Naomi Mitchison, A Writer in Time* (Edinburgh, 2023), p49.

180 *Torbay Express*, 9 Jan. 1939; *Western Times*, 22 & 29 Jan. 1943; *Western Morning News*, 25 Sept. 1940.

181 The Keep, D 5378 (1943).

182 The Keep, D 5378 (1945); *Western Times*, 9 April 1948; *Croydon Advertiser*, 9 May 1958; *Peterborough Evening Telegraph*, 30 Oct. 1950.

183 Hoskins, *Devon*, p529; The Keep, D 5039 (1940).

184 *Tamworth Herald*, 27 Jan. 1945; The Keep, DS 424.

185 *Western Times*, 12 Jan. 1945.

186 *National Register*, p5; Hess, 'Civilian Evacuation', p420.

187 Philip Carter, *Newton Abbot* (Exeter, 2001), p150. Those who died on 25 April 1942 comprised forty-nine-year-old Frederick George Pearse of 46 Keyberry Park, forty-two-year-old Thomas Wilfred Monagham of 4 Salisbury Road, seventy-year-old Robert Crute of the same address, sixty-eight-year-old Arthur William Whiteborn of 28 Torquay Road and sixty-three-year-old Samuel Fisher Chetham of 9 Courtenay Road: Casualties Book.

188 The Keep, DR 3090 (March-May, Aug.-Dec. 1942, Jan., March-Dec. 1943, Jan., March-May, June, Aug. – Sept., Nov., 1944, Jan. – Feb., May, Aug., Nov., Dec. 1945). There are also replies from 1946 to 1951.

189 The Keep, DR 3090 (Aug. 1944).

190 The Keep, DR 3090 (Aug. 1945); *Western Morning News*, 25 Feb. 1948; Ancestry, Whiting family tree, accessed 1 Aug. 2025. He lived at Thorn Laugh: The Keep, TC 84 (local council elections, 1937-51) & DR 3090 (Sept. 1947).

191 Hoskins, *Devon*, p530.

192 *Illustrated Sporting & Dramatic News*, 30 Aug. 1940.

193 *Western Morning News*, 21 May 1941.

194 HER, MDV51747.

195 Plymouth Archive, 2789.

196 The Keep, D 5433 (1942).

197 *Western Morning News*, 26 April 1938.

198 The Keep, DR 1460 (March–July 1939, Feb., Dec. 1940, Aug., Sept., Nov., Dec. 1942).

199 *Western Morning News*, 11 Oct. 1947, 4 Oct. 1980 & 10 April 1982; Ancestry, Pauls family tree, accessed 1 Aug. 2025.

200 Hoskins, *Devon*, p529; HER, 1097057.

201 HER for Exmoor National Park, MDE21374.

202 The Keep, D 5089 (1941). I am grateful to Howard Slater of the Trumpington Local History Group for details of the couple living in the parish in 1955.

203 *National Register*, p5; Hess, 'Civilian Evacuation', p421.

204 Wasley, *War*, p188.

205 Devon Heritage Centre, 6718a-O/A/7.

206 The Keep, DR 2041 (August 1940).

207 National Archives, KV 2/3252.

208 *Newquay Express*, 9 May 1935; *Western Morning News*, 24 Sept. 1936; *Reynold's Newspaper*, 4 April 1937; Anne Cranny-Francis (ed.), *The Fullness of Life* (2017), pp5-6; National Archives, KV 2/3252.

209 Paul Gillen, 'John (Jack) Lindsay (1900-1990)', *Australian*

Dictionary of Biography 18 (2012).

210 The Keep, DS 388 (1938) & DR 1368 (Feb. – March, May 1939, Jan. 1940).

211 Ancestry, 1939 Register, Bournemouth; Gillen, 'John (Jack) Lindsay (1900-1990)'.

212 The Keep, DR 1476 (Feb.-June 1939).

213 I am grateful to Janine Monaghan for these biographical details.

214 The Keep, D 5199 (1939-45) DR 1095 (Feb. – Sept., Nov., 1939, Jan. 1940).

215 Ancestry, Simpson family tree, accessed 1 Aug. 2025.

216 The Keep, DR 2852 (Jan.-May, Aug.–Dec. 1942, Jan., March-Aug., Oct.-Dec. 1943, Jan., March, May-June, Aug.-Sept., Nov. 1944, Jan.-Feb., May, Aug. 1945, May, July 1946, Jan., April, June, Sept.-Oct. 1947, March, Sept. 1948, Feb., May, July, Aug. 1949, July-Aug. 1950).

217 Tom Harrisson, *Living Through the Blitz* (London, 1976), p210.

218 Twyford, *It Came to Our Door*, pp11-15, 127-78.

219 The Keep, D 5010 (1941).

220 The Keep, D 5433 (1942).

221 The Keep, TC 29 (forces, men in the forces, 1939-1956), box 2.

222 The Keep, DR 2278 (Nov. 1939); D 5402 (1941); D 5325 (1941); D 5415 (1942), D 5030 (1942); D 5201 (1943); D 5443 (1944); D 5216 (1944).

223 The Keep, D 5390 (1942).

224 *The Observer*, 2 August 1942.

225 British Online Archives, Military Intelligence Files: Land, Sea & Air, 1938-1974, MOI, Points from Regions, 8, 9, 20, 22 July, 28 August & 20 Sept. 1940; Weekly Report, 26 March 1941.

226 The Keep, DS 304 (1937).

227 Personal communication from Guy Greaves, 3 July 2025; *Hemel Hempstead Gazette*, 30 Oct. 1997; *Supplement to the London Gazette*, 10 July 1942. I am grateful to Jenepher Allen for this reference.

228 The Keep, DS 611.

229 The Keep, D 5349 (1939 & 1940).

230 Plymouth Archive, 773/15, 26 Aug. 1940.

231 The Keep, DR 1280 (Jan., March & June 1939); *Western Morning News*, 8 Jan. 1941.

232 The Keep, D 5342 (1940) & SR 233.

233 *Yorkshire Post*, 1 Jan. 1937; The Keep, D 5057 (19 Aug. 1939 - 7 Aug 1940) & The Keep, DR 2532 (May, August, Sept. 1940).

234 Plymouth Archive, 773/15, 11 May 1940.

235 Plymouth Archive, 773/15, 10 July 1940.

236 Plymouth Archive, 773/15, 15 July 1940.

237 The Keep, TC 59 (children and education).

238 *Western Morning News*, 19 October, 5 May 1950; *Western Evening Herald*, 4 Sept. 1951.

239 The Keep, FR 0559.

240 The Keep, FR 0626.

241 British Online Archives, Military Intelligence Files: Land, Sea & Air, 1938-1974, MOI, 166 167 2, appendix, the Plymouth raids, April 1941.

242 The Keep, FR 0683, p152, Appendix 1, report on Conditions in Plymouth following the severe raids, secret.

243 The Keep, File Reports 0559, 0626, 0683 & 0903.

244 The Keep, D 5053 (1941).

245 The Keep, DR 3005 (April – June, Aug. & Oct. 1942, April 1943).

246 The Keep, DR 2695 (Jan.-Nov. 1942, April-May, July, Nov. 1943).

247 The Keep, DR 2695 (May 1943).

248 Ancestry, Pamela Ratliff-Stephens family tree, accessed 1 Aug. 2025.

249 The Keep, D 3553 (Feb. 1944 & Oct. 1943).

250 'Francis James Wardale', *Monthly Notices of the Royal Astronomical Society* 103: 102 (1943), p73. In 1929 Mr Wardale was living in Amesbury, Wiltshire, without his wife: 1939 register; Ancestry, Freundlich/Mill family tree, accessed 1 Aug. 2025.

251 The Keep, DR 3684 (May 1945).

252 Hoskins, *Devon*, p530; Wasly, *Devon At War*, pp87-8; Arthur L. Clamp, *Plympton During The Second World War* (Plympton, undated), pp22 & 38.

253 *Western Morning News*, 13 July 1943.

254 The Keep, DR 2844 (March 1942 & May, July, Dec. 1943).

255 The Keep, DR 2766 (Jan., Feb., April & July 1942).

256 Pinewood School, J. M. O. Snodgrass, 'Reminiscences', *The Blue & Grey* (1942), pp12-13. I am grateful to Emily Morley-Fisher for these details supplied from the school archive.

257 The Keep, D 5304 (1941-2).

258 Pinewood School, R. F. Dunlop, 'June 29th', *The Blue & Grey* (1942), pp11-12.

259 *Exeter & Plymouth Gazette*, 12 April 1946.

260 *Western Morning News*, 3 April 1941, 5 Jan. 1942; Heritage Gateway, MDV71960.

261 *Liverpool Evening Express*, 19 Oct. 1934; *London Gazette*, 10 Sept. 1940, p5465 & 31 Dec. 1940, p7320; *Kentish Express*, 4 Dec. 1936 & 29 Jan. 1937; *Western Morning News*, 13 Dec. & 28 Nov. 1939; *Halifax Evening Courier*, 15 Aug. 1950. The national register undertaken on 29 September 1939 initially recorded Jean M. Bennet as living at the Hampstead address but the entry was amended with the addition of Mariella Vaughan written in red ink.

262 The Keep, D 5250 (1939-41, 1946-7, 1953); DS 792 (Sept.-Oct. 1938); DR 1072 (Jan-Feb. 1939, Sept., Dec. 1940, July 1942). She continued to write from 1946 to 1951.
263 *Faversham Times*, 3 June 1939.
264 The Keep, DR 1072 (Dec. 1940).
265 The Keep, D 5250 (1941, 1946).
266 Heritage Gateway, Hob Uid 1024168 & MDV58008.
267 The Keep, FR 0683 (1941).
268 The Keep, D 5110 (1943); Patricia & Robert Malcolmson (eds), *A Parson in Wartime: The Boston Diary of the Reverend Arthur Hopkins, 1942-1945* (Lincoln, 2017).
269 Kelly, *Directory*, p690; HER, MDV7290; Walsey, *War*, pp32-3, 186, 188; https://www.bbc.co.uk/ww2peopleswar; *E&E*, 19 Aug. 1940; *Torbay Express*, 13 Aug. 1942; *Western Morning News*, 27 Oct. 1942; Casualties Book. The five who died in October 1942 were Mr and Mrs John and Isabella Cartwright, Miss Eleanor Ross and Miss Florence Sercombe, all of Seafield House, along with Dorothy Wilkin of Yarty House in Axminster; Hardy *et al*, *Sidmouth*, p16.
270 The Keep, TC 42 (posters, 1939-47), box 2.
271 The Keep, TC 59 (children and education), box 2.
272 The Keep, TC 66.
273 The Keep, DR 3096 (March 1942).
274 *Western Morning News*, 11 April 1942.
275 *Daily Dispatch*, 20 Jan. 1945; *Liverpool Daily Post*, 31 Jan. 1945; *Bookseller*, 18 April 1946. In 1933 Miss Hill had adapted a play (*The Wonderful Ingredient*) from a story of the same title by Stephen Southwold: *Dramas and Works Prepared for Oral Delivery* vol. 14, parts 3-4, no. 1 (Washington, 1960), p122.
276 *Gloucestershire Echo*, 25 April 1944; Bruce Stait, *Rotol the History of an Airscrew Company, 1937-1960* (Stroud, 1990), pp164-5.
277 *Bookseller*, 17 Nov. 1938; *Express & Echo*, 25 Feb. 1939; *Time & Tide*, 19 Nov. 1938.
278 The Keep, DR 1407 (March 1939).
279 1939 register, Sidford.
280 The Keep, TC 23 (air raids, 1938-45), box 1.
281 The Keep, TC 23 (air raids, 1938-45), box 1.
282 The Keep, TC 23 (air raids, 1938-45), box 1.
283 The Keep, TC 5 (evacuation, 1939-44).
284 *Somerset Guardian*, 19 Jan. 1951. I am grateful to Judith Taylor for details of Miss Hill's later life and for supplying her account of the railway station.
285 *National Register*, p5; Hoskins, *Devon*, p703.
286 Heritage Gateway, SDV364494 & 1414456; Hardy *et al*, *Sidmouth*, pp79, 169-80.
287 The Keep, D 5399 (1942).
288 National Archives, AIR 22/7, RAF Weekly Intelligence Summary 170, Sept. 1942 – March 1943; Wasley, *War*, pp186, 188; Hardy *et al*, *Sidmouth*, pp60, 65, 101-2, 152.
289 The Keep, DR 1577 (Nov. 1939).
290 The Keep, DR 1980 (Jan. 1942).
291 The Keep, D 5240 (1943).
292 Ancestry, Ausden family tree, accessed 1 Aug. 2025.
293 The Keep, D 5231 (1939).
294 The Keep, D 1409 (Feb. 1939).
295 The Keep, D 5324 (1939-45); DR 2038 (June, Oct., Nov. 1939, Jan., Feb., May, Oct., Dec. 1940, Jan., Feb. April, May, Oct.-Dec. 1942; Jan. 1943, May 1946).
296 *Bournemouth Times*, 11 July 1947; Sandra Koa Wing (ed.), *Our Longest Days* (London, 2008), pp242-3; Ancestry, Faupel family tree, accessed 1 Aug. 2025.
297 Hoskins, *Devon*, p529.
298 *North Devon Journal*, 18 Feb. 1937; The Keep, DS 342 (1937-8).
299 Ancestry, KJHMKH-2(2).
300 *National Register*, p5; Hess, 'Civilian Evacuation', p420; Hoskins, *Devon*, p532.
301 Heritage Gateway, MDV104553; *Western Morning News*, 18 Dec. 1942; Wasley, *War*, p188.
302 Casualties Book.
303 *Western Morning News*, 20 July 1944.
304 The Keep, D 5313 (1939-1950); DS 064 (June 1937 – Sept. 1938); DS 1642 (Sept, Nov. 1939, Jan., Feb. May, 1940, April, Aug.-Dec. 1942, Jan., April-Dec. 1943, Jan., April, June, Aug., Nov., 1944, Jan., May, Aug., Nov., Dec. 1945). There is also text too fragile for examination.
305 University of Warwick, Modern Records Unit, papers of Rowland Barret.
306 *Daily Herald*, 7 Aug. 1924 & 8 May 1925.
307 *Torquay Times*, 1 Aug. 1941.
308 *Exeter & Plymouth Gazette*, 6 Oct. 1950; Ancestry, Kendrick family tree, accessed 1 Aug. 2025.
309 Hess, 'Civilian Evacuation', pp420-1; *National Register*, p5; Hoskins, *Devon*, p533.
310 Heritage Gateway, MDV57281; Hess, 'Civilian Evacuation', pp440, 448, 458.
311 Casualties Book.
312 The Keep, DR 3146 (May 1942).
313 The Keep, TC 29 (forces, men in the forces, 1939-1956), box 2.
314 The Keep, DR 3331 (Dec. 1942, Jan. 1943).
315 Ancestry, Preston family tree, accessed 1 Aug. 2025.
316 *National Register*, p5; Hoskins, *Devon*, p533; Hess, 'Civilian Evacuation', pp420-1, 442.
317 The Keep, TC 5 (evacuation, 1939-44); D 5239 (1942); D 5376 (1944), D 5010 (1940).

318 The Keep, D 5342 (1940).
319 The Keep, D 5445 (1940).
320 The Keep, D 5335 (1942).
321 The Keep, D 5005 (1944).
322 Devon Heritage Centre, 6718A-O/A/7; The Keep, D 5128 (1943).
323 Devon Heritage Centre, 6718A-O/A/7.
324 The Keep, D 5128 (1944).
325 British Online Archives, Military Intelligence Files: Land, Sea & Air, 1938-1974, MOI, No. 47 Daily Report on Morale, 11 July 1940; Home Intelligence Special Report, No. 33; No. 140, Home Intelligence Weekly Report, 10 June 1943; Home Intelligence Weekly Report, No. 286.
326 *Torquay Times*, 19 Nov. 1937, 17 Jan. 1941; *Torbay Express*, 19 Oct. 1939; *Weekly Dispatch*, 2 March 1941; *Sunday Pictorial*, 23 March 1941. The term had been used in the resort as early as 1937 when it was suggested the Rock Walk could be burrowed into as a funk hole for local people.
327 *Torquay Times*, 26 Sept. 1941 & 17 Oct. 1941; The Keep, D 5412 (1941), DR 3253 (Oct. 1942).
328 The Keep, DS 287 (1937).
329 *Torbay Express*, 6 Sept. 1939.
330 *Torbay Express*, 6 Sept. 1939. She had been a pupil at Roedean and later taught there: *Torbay Express*, 12 Jan. 1948.
331 This was 'Hay Fever'.
332 Post Toasties, a version of corn flakes, were made by Post Cereals until 2006. They had been called Elijah's Manna until there were complaints by clerics: *New York Times*, 22 Feb. 2016.
333 *Independent*, 27 & 29 May 1998; *Manchester Evening News*, 9 Oct. 1947; *Bookseller*, 11 Aug. 1951; *Daily Express*, 28 Dec. 1956.
334 The Keep, DS 557 (Sept. – Oct. 1938).
335 The Keep, D 5084 (1939) & DR 1296 (Feb.-June, July 1939).
336 *Torbay Express*, 3 Aug. 1939.
337 Ancestry, Greenlyn, accessed 1 Aug. 2025.
338 Patricia & Robert Malcolmson (eds), *A Woman in Wartime London: The Diary of Kathleen Tipper* (London Record Society, 2006), p7; Devon Heritage Centre, 6718A.
339 The Keep, D 5443 (1941 & 1942).
340 Devon Heritage Centre, 6718A.
341 The Keep, DR 2979 (Feb, June, Oct.-Dec. 1942; Jan., March–July 1943, Sept. 1944, Jan., Dec. 1945, May, July, Sept., Nov. 1946, Jan., Sept, Oct., Dec. 1947, Jan., March, Sept., Oct. 1948, Feb., May, July 1949, Sept., Nov. 1950, Jan., March, 1951, Nov. 1955); The Keep, D 5051 (June 1943).
342 *Exeter University Register, 1893-1962* (Exeter, 1970), p68; the Keep, DR 2979 (July 1946).
343 The Keep, DR 3369 (Jan., March, April, June 1943).
344 Ancestry, Haydock family tree, accessed 1 Aug. 2025.
345 Heritage Gateway, MDV55665, MDV102172, MDV55667-8 & MDV102447; *Western Morning News*, 7 Sept. 1945.
346 *Evening News*, 2 Dec. 1940; The Keep, TC 59, letter, 13 Sept. 1940; Hess, 'Civilian Evacuation', 'Civilian Evacuation', p458; *Western Morning News*, 21 Feb. 1941; *Newquay Express*, 2 Jan. 1941.
347 The Keep, D 5098. See Mr Harpur's account of Exeter in 1940.
348 *National Register*, p5; Hoskins, *Devon*, p534; Hess, 'Civilian Evacuation', 'Civilian Evacuation', p421; The Keep, D 5393 (1944-6, 1953); DR 2895 (Feb., July, Aug., 1942; June, Oct., Dec., 1943, June, Aug., Nov. 1944, Jan., Feb., May, Nov., Dec. 1945, May, Sept., Nov. 1946; Feb., Oct., Dec. 1947; April, May, July, Aug. 1949; July, Aug., Nov. 1950; Jan., March 1951, Nov. 1955); Paul Rendell, 'Dartmoor Hospitals', *Dartmoor News*.
349 The Keep, D 5435 (1939-40).
350 *Hampstead News*, 13 Jan. 1910; *Kensington Post*, 29 Sept. 1922. In 1945 Miss Passingham referred to having lived in Austria for four years some thirty years previously: The Keep, DR 2895 (Nov. 1945).
351 *Newquay Express*, 8 Feb. 1945; The Keep, D 5393 (1945). Miss Passingham had lived in Amersham since at least 1930: *Buckinghamshire Examiner*, 16 May & 1 Aug. 1930. See also the issue for 4 April 1913. Miss Wiens appears to have resided in Amersham by 1922: *Bath Chronicle*, 1 April 1922. At Greystead she gave nature study lessons in 1924, taught German lessons in 1930 and had a preparatory class for children in 1935 and 1936: *Buckingham Examiner*, 24 Oct. 1924, 10 Jan. 1930, 27 Dec. 1935 & 10 Jan. 1936.
352 The Keep, DR 2895 (Jan. 1945).
353 *Western Morning News*, 8 Nov. 1946. The outline of the two women's lives is shown in Miss Passingham's diaries. Miss Wiens purchased Higher Statsford in July 1945: I am grateful to Andy Salmon for access to the house deeds; Pathfinder Village magazines, The Little Chapel, Tedburn St Mary.
354 *Exeter & Plymouth Gazette*, 19 Nov. 1937; *Western Times*, 13 Nov. 1936.
355 *Totnes Weekly Times*, 3 Oct. 1903.
356 The Keep, DS 377.
357 *Torbay Express*, 4 Sept. 1948; *Hull Daily Mail*, 1 July 1948; Ancestry, Kinsman family tree, accessed 1 Aug. 2025.
358 Wasley, *Devon At War*, pp122-32.
359 The Keep, DR 3119 (August 1945); Ancestry, Fowler-Dixon family tree, accessed 1 Aug. 2025.
360 Devon & Dartmoor HER, MDV55126; *Western Morning News*, 26 Nov. 1940; https://ryda.org.uk>The Spirit of the Yealm, accessed 1 May 2025; Plymouth Archive, 2789. An

earlier raid was recorded as taking place on 19 July 1940: Wasley, *War*, p186.

361 The Keep, DR 2778 (Jan.-March, May, June 1942).

362 *Western Morning News*, 3 March 1943; Ancestry, my family tree, accessed 1 Aug. 2025.

363 *National Register United Kingdom and Isle of Man Statistics of Population on 29th September 1939* (London, 1939), p5.

INDEX

Illustrations are indicated in bold

Also from **The Mint Press:**

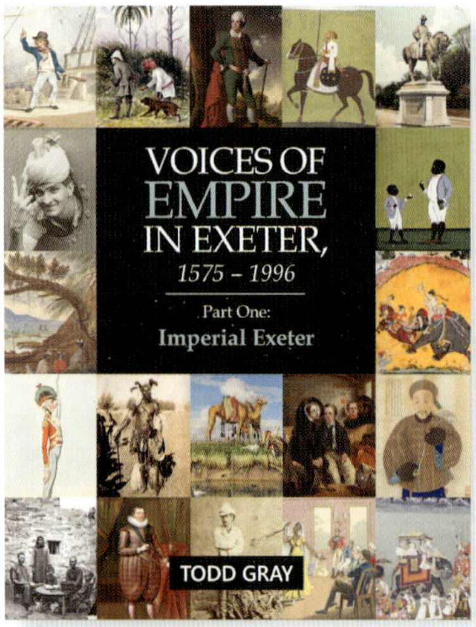

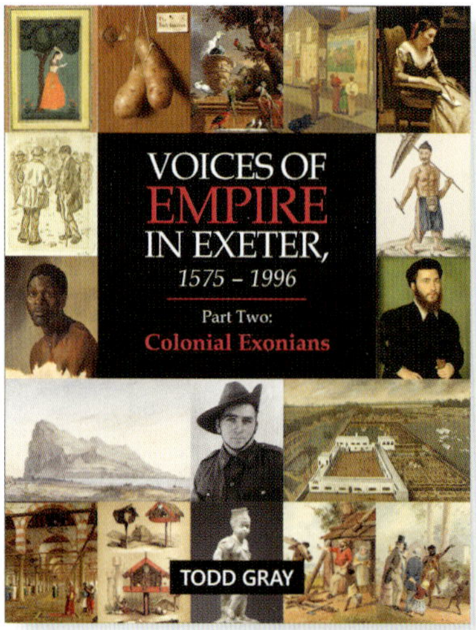

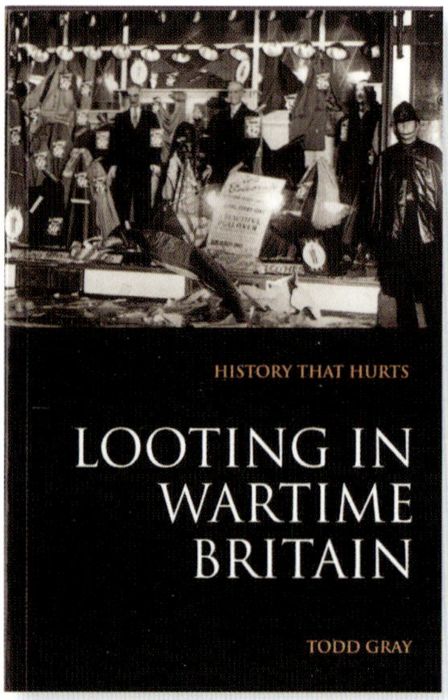

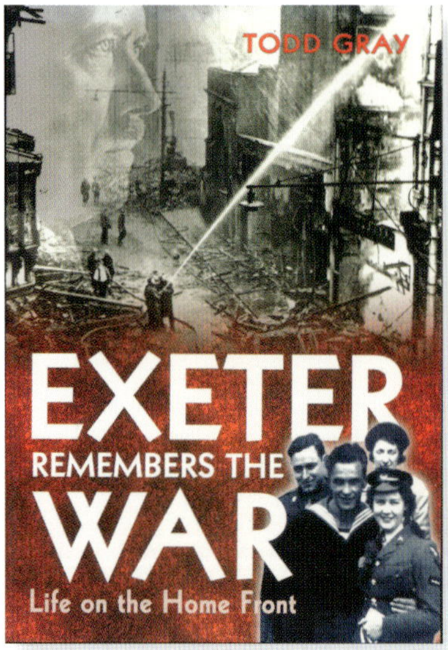